Clashing Views
on Controversial
Legal Issues

4th edition

Edited, Selected,
and with Introductions by

M. Ethan Katsh
University of Massachusetts at Amherst

The Dushkin Publishing Group, Inc.

The man who pleads his case first seems to be in the right, then his opponent comes and puts him to the test.

—Proverbs

Taking Sides ® is a registered trademark of The Dushkin Publishing Group, Inc.

Library of Congress Catalog Card Number: 90-81838

Manufactured in the United States of America

Fourth Edition, Second Printing
ISBN: 0-87967-927-1

 Printed on Recycled Paper

The Dushkin Publishing Group, Inc.
Sluice Dock, Guilford, CT 06437

PREFACE

> The study of law should be introduced as part of a liberal education, to train and enrich the mind. . . . I am convinced that, like history, economics, and metaphysics—and perhaps even to a greater degree than these—the law could be advantageously studied with a view to the general development of the mind.
>
> —Justice Louis D. Brandeis

The general study of law in colleges, universities, and even high schools has grown rapidly during the last ten years. Accompanying this development has been the publication of new curriculum materials that go beyond the analysis of legal cases and doctrines that make up much of professional law study in law schools. This book is part of the effort to view and study law as an institution that continuously interacts with other social institutions. Law should be examined from an interdisciplinary perspective and be accessible to all students.

This book focuses on a series of controversial issues involving law and the legal system. It is, I believe, an appropriate starting point for law study since controversy and conflict are inherent in law. Law is based on an adversary approach to conflict resolution, in which two advocates representing opposing sides are pitted against each other. Judicial decisions often contain both majority and dissenting opinions, which reveal some of the arguments that went on in the judges' chambers. Perhaps most relevant to a discussion of the place of controversy in the legal system is the First Amendment guarantee of freedom of speech and press, which presumes that we all benefit by a vigorous debate of important issues.

Since many of the issues in *Taking Sides* are often in the news, you probably already have opinions on them. What you should remember, however, is that there is usually more to learn about any given issue, and the topics discussed here are best approached with an open mind. You should not be surprised if your views change as you read the selections.

Changes to this edition This fourth edition represents a considerable revision. There are eight completely new issues: *Should Lawyers Be Prohibited from Presenting a False Case?* (Issue 1); *Is ADR (Alternative Dispute Resolution) Preferable to Litigation?* (Issue 4); *Should Student Newspapers Be Censored?* (Issue 6); *Religious Displays on Public Property: Do They Violate the Constitution?* (Issue 7); *Can States Restrict the Right to Die?* (Issue 11); *Should Drugs Be Legalized?* (Issue 14); *Should a National Gun Control Policy Be Established?* (Issue 15); and *DNA Profiling: Should It Be Used to Convict Criminals?* (Issue 16). For some issues, I have kept the issue but have replaced one or both of the selections in order to more sharply focus the debate or to bring the debate up to date: *Should Plea Bargaining Be Abolished?* (Issue 3); *Is Drug Use Testing Permitted Under the Fourth Amendment?* (Issue 5); *Is Abortion Protected by the Constitu-*

i

tion? (Issue 8); *Should Pornography Be Protected by the First Amendment?* (Issue 9); *Should the Death Penalty Be Abolished?* (Issue 12).

Supplements An *Instructor's Manual with Test Questions* (multiple-choice and essay) is available through the publisher for the instructor using *Taking Sides* in the classroom. And a general guidebook, which discusses methods and techniques for integrating the pro-contra approach into any classroom setting, is also available.

Acknowledgments I received helpful comments and suggestions from the many users of *Taking Sides* across the United States and Canada. Their suggestions have markedly enhanced the quality of this edition of the book and are reflected in the eight totally new issues and the updated selections.

Special thanks go to those who responded with specific suggestions for the fourth edition:

James Barr
Community College of
    Philadelphia

Mike Butera
University of Nebraska, Omaha

Phillip Finney
Southeast Missouri State
    University

David M. Horton
St. Edwards University

Maurice D. Lafferty
College of Marin

Rosemary O'Leary
Syracuse University

E. Peoples
Santa Rosa Junior College

Steven Matthew Sanders
Bridgewater State College

R. N. Singh
East Texas State University

David Warren
Duke University

Sharon Whitney
California State University, Chico

Kenneth P. Winter
Shippensburg University

Robert Yanal
Wayne State University

A note on case citations Throughout this book you will see references to judicial opinions. The judge's opinion or decision refers to the written statement of reasons the judge provides when making an interpretation of law or deciding a case. These opinions are printed and distributed in books called *reporters*, which can be found in law libraries and many university libraries. There are separate reporters for federal and state cases. When you see a reference to a case such as the following, *Brown v. Bd. of Educ.*, 347 U.S. 483 (1954), it means that the case with that name can be found in volume 347 of the United States Reports on page 483 and that the case was decided in 1954. When you see a legal citation with a series of numbers and words, the first number is always the volume number and the last number is the page number.

M. Ethan Katsh
University of Massachusetts, Amherst

CONTENTS IN BRIEF

CONTENTS

Professor Harry Subin examines the ethical responsibilities of criminal defense lawyers, describes a case he once handled, and argues that greater responsibility should be placed on lawyers not to pervert the truth to help their clients. Attorney John Mitchell disputes the contention that the goal of the criminal justice process is to seek the truth and argues that it is essential that there be independent defense attorneys who will provide protection against government oppression.

Former Stanford Law School dean Bayless Manning contends that our society and our legal system are suffering from too great a reliance on law to settle disputes. Law professor Marc Galanter contends that court statistics do not support complaints about excessive litigation and that litigation provides some benefits to society.

Professor of philosophy Kenneth Kipnis makes the case that justice cannot be traded on the open market and that plea bargaining often subverts the cause of justice. District Attorney Nick Schweitzer finds that plea bargaining is fair, useful, desirable, necessary, and practical.

Attorney Kenneth Feinberg describes the mediation process, including its informal, voluntary, and flexible nature, and argues that the process contains many advantages when compared to litigation. Professor Owen Fiss examines the nature and purpose of litigation and concludes that ADR should not be encouraged since litigation provides benefits for the public that are not obtainable through ADR.

Supreme Court justice Anthony Kennedy believes that drug tests of Customs Service officials are reasonable under the Fourth Amendment of the Constitution, even when there is no probable cause or individualized suspicion. Justice Antonin Scalia, in dissent, argues that the Customs Service rules were not justified, served no reasonable purpose, and are unnecessary invasions of privacy.

Supreme Court justice Byron White believes that school officials act under proper authority when they choose to censor school publications, or any other school-sponsored activities, because they, as well as parents and teachers, are responsible for safeguarding the values expressed by their schools. Stephen Arons, a professor of legal studies at the University of Massachusetts, argues that Justice White's decision in *Hazelwood v. Kuhlmeier* ignores the ways in which "majority-dominated schooling" can undermine education. To him, the policies of our schools and the opinions of our courts should teach us that "freedom of intellect and spirit" are necessary to a democracy.

Supreme Court justice Harry Blackmun argues that a crèche and a menorah on public property constitute a public endorsement of religion and violates the First Amendment. Justice Anthony Kennedy disagrees and argues that the First Amendment does not prohibit public celebration of events that have a secular and religious nature.

Supreme Court justice Harry Blackmun refers to historical attitudes, medical opinion, and legal precedent to defend the right of abortion. The solicitor general argues that *Roe v. Wade* should be overturned since Justice Blackmun's model is not warranted by the Constitution and too much discretion is removed from the states.

Judge Sarah Evans Barker outlines her opinion that the ordinances banning pornography as a violation of the civil rights of women are unconstitutional infringements on freedom of speech. Author Andrea Dworkin maintains that pornography should not be constitutionally protected because it is destructive, abusive, and detrimental to women, and violates their civil rights.

Supreme Court justice Thurgood Marshall points to past discrimination and argues that we must find a way to compensate for the years of disadvantage. Justice Potter Stewart contends that the law and the Constitution must not discriminate on the basis of race, for whatever reason.

Chief Justice William Rehnquist recognizes that a competent individual may refuse medical treatment but requires a showing of clear and convincing proof of the individual's wishes before allowing the termination of feeding to an incompetent person. Justice William Brennan argues that the Court is erecting too high a standard for allowing the individual's wishes to be followed and that Nancy Cruzen did indeed wish to have her feeding discontinued.

Michael Radelet, a professor of sociology at the University of Florida, is concerned about the growing acceptance of capital punishment in the United States and questions the state court's ability to correctly decide who should get the death penalty. The Judiciary Committee of the U.S. Senate reports on the need for capital punishment, both for its deterrent effect and as a means to protect society.

U.S. Court of Appeals judge Malcolm Wilkey raises objections to the exclusionary rule on the grounds that it may suppress evidence and allow the guilty to go free. Professor Yale Kamisar argues that the exclusionary rule is necessary to prevent abuses by police and to protect citizens' rights.

Professor Ethan Nadelmann claims that drug enforcement policies are not working and will never be effective and that legalizing drugs would eliminate many of the costs brought about by the war on drugs. Publisher and journalist Steven Brill maintains that government should not abdicate its responsibility, that legalization would make the drug problem worse, and that some segments of the population would be devastated if enforcement were stopped.

Mark Udulutch examines the gun control problem and asserts that gun control is necessary and that effective and enforceable federal regulations are feasible. Professor of sociology James Wright concludes, after examining how guns are used, that banning guns would not be beneficial.

Professor James Starrs claims that DNA tests are effective and reliable means for detecting perpetrators of violent crimes and should be available at trial. Attorney Janet Hoeffel denies that DNA tests are reliable and argues that admission at trial should be denied until standards are adopted and tests are conducted that show whether the test indeed is reliable.

Editor Jonathan Rowe examines the insanity defense as it is now administered and finds that it is most likely to be used by white middle- or upper-class defendants and that its application is unfair and leads to unjust results. Professor of law Richard Bonnie argues that the abolition of the insanity defense would be immoral and leaves no alternative for those who are not responsible for their actions.

INTRODUCTION

The Role of Law

M. Ethan Katsh

Two hundred years ago, Edmund Burke, the influential British statesman and orator, commented that "in no other country perhaps in the world, is the law so general a study as it is in the United States." Today, in this country, general knowledge about law is at a disappointing level. One study conducted several years ago concluded that "the general public's knowledge of and direct experience with courts is low."[1] Three out of four persons surveyed admitted that they knew either very little or nothing at all about state and local courts. More than half believed that the burden of proving innocence in a criminal trial is on the accused, and seventy-two percent thought that every decision made by a state could be reviewed by the Supreme Court. In a 1990 study, fifty-nine percent could not name at least one current justice of the Supreme Court.

One purpose of this volume is to provide information about some specific and important legal issues. In your local newspaper today, there is probably at least one story concerning an issue in this book. The quality of your life will be directly affected by how many of these issues are resolved. But gun control (Issue 15), the insanity defense (Issue 17), drug testing (Issue 5), abortion (Issue 8), legal ethics (Issue 1), and other issues in this book are often the subject of superficial, misleading, or inaccurate statements. *Taking Sides* is designed to encourage you to become involved in the public debate on these issues and to raise the level of the discussion on them.

The issues that are debated in this book represent some of the most important challenges our society faces. How they are dealt with will influence what kind of society we will have in the future. While it is important to look at and study them separately, it is equally necessary to think about their relationship to each other and about the fact that there is a tool called "law," which is being called upon to solve a series of difficult conflicts. The study of discrete legal issues should enable you to gain insight into some broad theoretical questions about law. This introduction, therefore, will focus on several basic characteristics of law and the legal process that you should keep in mind as you read this book.

THE NATURE OF LAW

The eminent legal anthropologist E. Adamson Hoebel once noted that the search for a definition of law is as difficult as the search for the Holy Grail.

Law is certainly complicated, and trying to define it precisely can be frustrating. What follows, therefore, is not a definition of law but a framework or perspective for looking at and understanding law.

Law as a Body of Rules

One of the common incorrect assumptions about law is that it is merely a body of rules, invoked by those who need them, and then applied by a judge. Under this view, the judge is essentially a machine whose task is simply to find and apply the right rule to the dispute in question. This perspective makes the mistake of equating law with the rules of law. It is sometimes even assumed that there exists somewhere in the libraries of lawyers and judges one book with all the rules or laws in it, which can be consulted to answer legal questions. As may already be apparent, such a book could not exist. Rules alone do not supply the solutions to many legal problems. The late Supreme Court justice William O. Douglas once wrote, "The law is not a series of calculating machines where definitions and answers come tumbling out when the right levers are pushed." As you read the debates about the issues in this book, you will see that much more goes into a legal argument than the recitation of rules.

Law as a Process

A more meaningful way of thinking about law is to look at it as a process or system, keeping in mind that legal rules are one of the elements in the process. This approach requires a considerably broader vision of law: to think not only of the written rules, but also of the judges, the lawyers, the police, and all the other people in the system. It requires an even further consideration of all the things that influence these people, such as their values and economic status.

"Law," one legal commentator has stated, "is very like an iceberg; only one-tenth of its substance appears above the social surface in the explicit form of documents, institutions, and professions, while the nine-tenths of its substance that supports its visible fragment leads a sub-aquatic existence, living in the habits, attitudes, emotions and aspirations of men."[2]

In reading the discussions of controversial issues in this book, try to identify what forces are influencing the content of the rules and the position of the writer. Three of the most important influences on the nature of law are economics, moral values, and public opinion.

Law and Economics

Laws that talk about equality, such as the Fourteenth Amendment, which guarantees that no state shall "deny to any person . . . equal protection of the laws," suggest that economic status is irrelevant in the making and application of the law. As Anatole France, the nineteenth century French satirist once wrote, however, "The law, in its majestic equality, forbids the rich as well as the poor to sleep under bridges, to beg in streets, and to steal bread." Sometimes the purpose and effect of the law cannot be determined merely from the words of the law.

Marxist critics of law in capitalistic societies assert that poverty results from the manipulation of the law by the wealthy and powerful. It is possible to look at several issues in this book and make some tentative judgments about the influence of economic power on law. For example, what role does economics play in the debate over drug use testing (Issue 5)? Is drug abuse a public health problem or an economic problem, in that it costs companies billions of dollars each year? In considering whether pornography should be prohibited (Issue 9), is the controversy purely over morality and values or is it related to the enormous growth of the pornographic videotape industry? Plea bargaining (Issue 3), which mostly affects poor persons who cannot afford bail, also involves the question of whether the law is responsible for or perpetuates poverty and economic classes.

Law and Values

The relationship between law and values has been a frequent theme of legal writers and a frequent source of debate. Clearly, there is in most societies some relationship between law and morality. One writer has summarized the relationship as follows:

1. *There is a moral order in society.* Out of the many different and often conflicting values of the individuals and institutions that make up society may emerge a dominant moral position, a "core" of the moral order. The position of this core is dynamic, and as it changes, the moral order of society moves in the direction of that change.

2. *There is a moral content to the law.* The moral content of law also changes over time, and as it changes, the law moves in the direction of that change.

3. *The moral content of the law and moral order in society are seldom identical.*

4. *A natural and necessary affinity exists between the two "bodies" of law and moral order.*

5. *When there is a gap between the moral order of society and the law, some movement to close the gap is likely.* The law will move closer to the moral order of society, or the moral order will move closer to the law, or each will move toward the other. The likelihood of the movement to close the gap between law and moral order depends upon the size of the gap between the two bodies and the perceived significance of the subject matter concerning which the gap exists.[3]

Law and morality will not be identical in a pluralistic society, but there will also be attempts by dominant groups to insert their view of what is right into the legal code. The First Amendment prohibition against establishment of religion and the guarantee of freedom of religion are designed to protect those whose beliefs are different. Yet there have also been many historical examples of legal restrictions or limitations being imposed on minorities or of laws being ineffective because of the resistance of powerful groups. Prayers in the public schools, for example, which have been forbidden since the early 1960s, are still said in a few local communities.

Of the topics in this book, the insertion of morality into legal discussions has occurred most frequently in the abortion, capital punishment, and drug legalization debates (Issues 8, 12, and 14). It is probably fair to say that these issues remain high on the agenda of public debate because they involve strongly-held values and beliefs. The nature of the debate is also colored by strong feelings that are held by the parties. Although empirical evidence about public health and abortion or about deterrence and capital punishment does exist, the debate is generally more emotional than objective.

Public Opinion and the Law

It is often claimed that the judicial process is insulated from public pressures. Judges are elected or appointed for long terms or for life, and the theory is that they will, therefore, be less subject to the force of public opinion. As a result, the law should be uniformly applied in different places, regardless of the nature of the community. It is fair to say the judicial process is less responsive to public sentiment than is the political process, but that is not really saying much. What is important is that the legal process is not totally immune from public pressure. The force of public opinion is not applied directly through lobbying, but it would be naive to think that the force of what large numbers of people believe and desire never gets reflected in what happens in court. The most obvious examples are trials in which individuals are tried as much for their dissident beliefs as for their actions. Less obvious is the fact that the outcomes of cases may be determined in some measure by popular will. Judicial complicity in slavery or the internment of Japanese Americans during World War II are blatant examples of this.

Many of the issues selected for this volume are controversial because a large group is opposed to some practice sanctioned by the courts. Does this mean that the judges have taken a courageous stand and ignored public opinion? Not necessarily. Only in a few of the issues have courts adopted an uncompromising position. In most of the other issues, the trend of court decisions reflects a middle-of-the-road approach that could be interpreted as trying to satisfy everyone but those at the extremes. For example, in capital punishment (Issue 12), the original decision declaring the death penalty statutes unconstitutional was followed by the passing of new state laws, which were then upheld and which have led to a growing number of executions. Similarly, in affirmative action (Issue 10), the *Bakke* decision, while generally approving of affirmative action, was actually won by Mr. Bakke and led to the abolition of all such programs that contained rigid quotas.

ASSESSING INFLUENCES ON THE LAW

This summary of what can influence legal decisions is not meant to suggest that judges consciously ask what the public desires when interpretations of law are made. Rather, as members of society and as individuals who read newspapers and magazines and form opinions on political issues, there are subtle forces at work on judges that may not be obvious in any particular opinion but that can be discerned in a line of cases over a period of time. This may be explicitly denied by judges, such as in the statement by Justice Blackmun in the abortion case that "Our task, of course, is to resolve the issue by constitutional measurement, free of emotion and predilection." When you read the opinion, however, you should ask yourself whether Blackmun succeeds in being totally objective in his interpretation of law and history.

Do these external and internal influences corrupt the system, create injustice, inject bias and discrimination, and pervert the law? Or, do these influences enable judges to be flexible, to treat individual circumstances, and to fulfill the spirit of the law? Both of these ends are possible and do occur. What is important to realize is that there are so many points in the legal system where discretion is employed that it is hopeless to think that we could be governed by rules alone. "A government of laws, not men," aside from the sexism of the language, is not a realistic possibility, and it is not an alternative that many would find satisfying either.

On the other hand, it is also fair to say that the law, in striving to get the public to trust in it, must persuade citizens that it is more than the whim of those who are in power. While it cannot be denied that the law may be used in self-serving ways, there are also mechanisms at work that are designed to limit abuses of discretionary power. One quality of law that is relevant to this problem is that the legal process is fundamentally a conservative institution, which is, by nature, resistant to radical change. Lawyers are trained to give primary consideration in legal arguments to precedent, previous cases involving similar facts. As attention is focused on how the present case is similar to or different from past cases, some pressure is exerted on new decisions to be consistent with old ones and on the law to be stable. Thus, the way in which a legal argument is constructed tends to reduce the influence of currently popular psychological, sociological, philosophical, or anthropological theories. Prior decisions will reflect ideologies, economic considerations, and ethical values that were influential when these decisions were made and, if no great change has occurred in the interim, the law will tend to preserve the status quo, both perpetuating old injustices and protecting traditional freedoms.

LEGAL PROCEDURE

The law's great concern with the procedure of decision-making is one of its more basic and important characteristics. Any discussion of the law that did not note the importance of procedure would be inadequate. Legal standards are often phrased not in terms of results but in terms of procedure. For example, it is not unlawful to convict the innocent if the right procedures are used (and it is unlawful to convict the guilty if the wrong procedures are followed). The law feels that it cannot guarantee that the right result will always be reached and that only the guilty will be caught, so it minimizes the risk of reaching the wrong result or convicting the innocent by specifying procedural steps to be followed. Lawyers, more than most people, are satisfied if the right procedures are followed even if there is something disturbing about the outcome. Law, therefore, has virtually eliminated the word *justice* from its vocabulary and has substituted the phrase *due process,* meaning that the proper procedures, such as right to counsel, right to a public trial, and right to cross-examine witnesses, have been followed. This concern with method is one of the pillars upon which law is based. It is one of the characteristics of law that distinguishes it from nonlegal methods of dispute resolution, where the atmosphere will be more informal and there may be no set procedures. It is a trait of the law that is illustrated in Issue 1 (Should Lawyers Be Prohibited from Presenting a False Case?).

CONCLUSION

There is an often-told anecdote about a client who walks into a lawyer's office and asks the receptionist if the firm has a one-armed lawyer. The receptionist asks why in the world anyone would have such a preference. The client responds that he has already visited several lawyers to discuss his problem but could not get a definite answer from any of them. Their stock reply to his question of whether he would win his case began "on the one hand this could happen and on the other hand . . ."

You may feel similarly frustrated as you examine the issues in this book. The subjects are not simple or amenable to simple solutions. The legal approach to problem solving is usually methodical and often slow. We frequently become frustrated with this process and, in fact, it may be an inappropriate way to deal with some problems. For the issues in this book, however, an approach that pays careful attention to the many different aspects of these topics will be the most rewarding. Many of the readings provide historical, economic, and sociological data as well as information about law. The issues examined in *Taking Sides* involve basic cultural institutions such as religion, schools, and the family as well as basic cultural values such as privacy, individualism, and equality. While the law takes a narrow approach to problems, reading these issues should broaden your outlook on the problems discussed and, perhaps, encourage you to do further reading on those topics that are of particular interest to you.

NOTES

1. Yankelovich, Skelly, and White, Inc., *The Public Image of Courts,* 1978.
2. Iredell Jenkins, *Social Order and the Limits of Law* (Princeton University Press, 1980), p. xi.
3. Wardle, "The Gap Between Law and Moral Order: An Examination of the Legitimacy of the Supreme Court Abortion Decisions," *Brigham Young University Law Review* (1980): 811–835.

PART 1

The Operation of Legal Institutions

According to much of what appears in the mass media, the public is increasingly disenchanted with many of the institutions that are part of the legal process. Critics complain about lawyers and their tactics, about courts that seem too lenient in their sentencing of serious criminals, and about the proliferation of needless lawsuits.

In this section we examine issues that involve our legal institutions, and the picture that emerges from these debates will reveal realities with which you may not be familiar.

Should Lawyers Be Prohibited from
  Presenting a False Case?

Is There a Litigation Crisis?

Should Plea Bargaining Be Abolished?

Is ADR (Alternative Dispute
  Resolution) Preferable to Litigation?

ISSUE 1

Should Lawyers Be Prohibited from Presenting a False Case?

YES: Harry I. Subin, from "The Criminal Lawyer's 'Different Mission,' " *Georgetown Journal of Legal Ethics* (vol. 1, 1987)

NO: John B. Mitchell, from "Reasonable Doubts Are Where You Find Them," *Georgetown Journal of Legal Ethics* (vol. 1, 1987)

ISSUE SUMMARY

NO: Professor Harry Subin examines the ethical responsibilities of criminal defense lawyers and argues that greater responsibility should be placed on lawyers not to pervert the truth to help their clients.

NO: Attorney John Mitchell disputes the contention that the goal of the criminal justice process is to seek the truth and argues that it is essential that there be independent defense attorneys to provide protection against government oppression.

In 1732, Georgia was founded as a colony that was to have no lawyers. This was done with the goal of having a "happy, flourishing colony . . . free from that pest and scourge of mankind called lawyers." While there are no serious efforts to abolish the legal profession today, public opinion surveys reveal that lawyers still are not held in the highest esteem. The public today may feel a little more positive about lawyers than did citizens of colonial America, and large numbers of students aspire to become lawyers, but hostility and criticism of what lawyers are and what they do are still common.

Part of the reason for the public's ambivalent attitude about lawyers concerns the adversary system and the lawyer's role in it. The adversary system requires that the lawyer's main responsibility be to the client. Except in rare instances, the lawyer is not to consider whether the client's cause is right or just and is not to allow societal or public needs to affect the manner in which the client is represented. The adversary system assumes that someone other than the client's lawyer is responsible for determining truth and guaranteeing justice.

The code of ethics of the legal profession instructs lawyers not to lie. However, it is permissible to mislead opponents—indeed, to do anything short of lying, if done to benefit the client. We have a system of "legal ethics" because some things lawyers are obligated to do for their clients would violate traditional standards of ethical behavior. As one legal scholar has written, "Where the attorney-client relationship exists, it is often appropriate and many times even obligatory for the attorney to do things that, all other things being equal, an ordinary person need not, and should not, do."[1]

In a highly publicized case that occurred a few years ago, two criminal defense lawyers learned from their client that, in addition to the crimes he was charged with, the client had murdered two girls who were missing. The lawyers discovered where the bodies were but refused to provide the parents of the missing children with any of this information. There was a public outcry when it was later discovered what the lawyers had done but their position was generally felt to be consistent with standards of legal ethics.

Why do we have a system that allows truth to be concealed? Is a diminished concern with truth necessary in order to preserve the status and security of the individual? What should be the limits as to how one-sided legal representation should be? Would it be desirable to require lawyers to be more concerned with truth, so that they would be prohibited from putting forward positions they know are false? In the following articles, law professor Harry Subin and attorney John Mitchell debate whether increasing the attorney's "truth" function would be both desirable and feasible. As you read the articles, determine whether Subin's suggestion is a dangerous first step toward a more powerful state and less protection for the individual, or whether it would increase public respect toward the legal system and the legal profession with little cost.

At the heart of the adversary system's attention to the relationship between client and counsel is the belief that there is something more important than discovering truth in every case. Finding the guilty and punishing them is not the sole goal of the criminal justice process. We rely on the criminal process, particularly trials, to remind us that our liberty depends on placing restrictions on the power of the state. The argument on behalf of the adversary model is that increasing the power of the state to find truth in one case may hurt all of us in the future. As you read the following articles, it will be difficult not to be troubled by the lawyer's dilemma; you may wonder whether there is any acceptable middle ground when state power and individual rights clash.

NOTES

1. Richard A. Wasserstrom, "Lawyers as Professionals: Some Moral Issues," 5 *Human Rights* 1 (1975).

YES

Harry I. Subin

THE CRIMINAL LAWYER'S "DIFFERENT MISSION": REFLECTIONS ON THE "RIGHT" TO PRESENT A FALSE CASE

I. THE INQUIRY

Should the criminal lawyer be permitted to represent a client by putting forward a defense the lawyer knows is false? . . .

Presenting a "false defense," as used here, means attempting to convince the judge or jury that facts established by the state and known to the attorney to be true are not true, or that facts known to the attorney to be false are true. While this can be done by criminal means—e.g., perjury, introduction of forged documents, and the like—I exclude these acts from the definition of false defense used here. I am not concerned with them because such blatant criminal acts are relatively uninteresting ethically, and both the courts and bar have rejected their use.[1]

My concern, instead, is with the presently legal means for the attorney to reach favorable verdict even if it is completely at odds with the facts. The permissible techniques include: (1) cross-examination of truthful government witnesses to undermine their testimony or their credibility; (2) direct presentation of testimony, not itself false, but used to discredit the truthful evidence adduced by the government, or to accredit a false theory; and (3) argument to the jury based on any of these acts. One looks in vain in ethical codes or case law for a definition of "perjury" or "false evidence" that includes these acts, although they are also inconsistent with the goal of assuring a truthful verdict.

To the extent that these techniques of legal truth-subversion have been addressed at all, most authorities have approved them. The American Bar Association's *Standards for Criminal Justice*,[2] for example, advises the criminal defense attorney that it is proper to destroy a truthful government witness when essential to provide the defendant with a defense, and that failure to

From Harry I. Subin, "The Criminal Lawyer's 'Different Mission,' " *Georgetown Journal of Legal Ethics*, vol. 1 (1987), pp. 125-138, 141-153. Copyright © 1987 by *Georgetown Journal of Legal Ethics*. Reprinted by permission. Some notes omitted.

do so would violate the lawyer's duty under the *Model Code of Professional Responsibility* to represent the client zealously.[3] The *Standards for Criminal Justice* cite as authority for this proposition an opinion by Justice White in *United States v. Wade*,[4] which, in the most emphatic form, is to the same effect. In *Wade*, the Court held that in order to assure the reliability of the pretrial line-up, the right to counsel must be extended to the defendant compelled to participate in one.[5] Justice White warned that the presence of counsel would not necessarily assure that the identification procedure would be more accurate than if the police were left to conduct it themselves. The passage dealing with this issue, which includes the phrase that inspired the title of this piece, is worth repeating at length:

> Law enforcement officers have the obligation to convict the guilty and to make sure they do not convict the innocent. They must be dedicated to making the criminal trial a procedure for the ascertainment of the true facts surrounding the commission of the crime. To this extent, our so-called adversary system is not adversary at all; nor should it be. But defense counsel has no comparable obligation to ascertain or present the truth. Our system assigns him a different mission. He must be and is interested in preventing the conviction of the innocent, but . . . we also insist that he defend his client whether he is innocent or guilty. The State has the obligation to present evidence. Defense counsel need present nothing, even if he knows what the truth is. He need not furnish any witnesses to the police, or reveal any confidences of his client, or furnish any other information to help the prosecution's case. If he can confuse a witness, even a truthful one,

or make him appear at a disadvantage, unsure or indecisive, that will be his normal course. Our interest in not convicting the innocent permits counsel to put the State to its proof, to put the State's case in the worst possible light, regardless of what he thinks or knows to be the truth. Undoubtedly there are some limits which defense counsel must observe but more often than not, defense counsel will cross-examine a prosecution witness, and impeach him if he can, even if he thinks the witness is telling the truth, just as he will attempt to destroy a witness who he thinks is lying. In this respect, as part of our modified adversary system and as part of the duty imposed on the most honorable defense counsel, we countenance or require conduct which in many instances has little if any, relation to the search for truth.[6]

. . . The article begins with a description of a case I handled some years ago, one that I believe is a good illustration of the false defense problem. I next address the threshold question of the attorney's knowledge. It has been argued that the attorney cannot "know" what the truth is, and therefore is free to present any available defense theory. I attempt to demonstrate that the attorney can, in fact, know the truth, and I propose a process to determine when the truth is known.

I then analyze the arguments that have been advanced in support of the "different mission" theory: that the defense attorney, even if he or she knows the truth, remains free to disregard it in presenting a defense. I argue that neither the right to a defense nor the needs of the adversary system justify the presentation of a false defense. Finally, I describe a new standard that explicitly prohibits the defense attorney from asserting a false defense. I conclude with some thoughts as to why this rule would produce a generally more just system.

II. TRUTH SUBVERSION IN ACTION: THE PROBLEM ILLUSTRATED

A. The Accusation

About fifteen years ago I represented a man charged with rape and robbery. The victim's account was as follows: Returning from work in the early morning hours, she was accosted by a man who pointed a gun at her and took a watch from her wrist. He told her to go with him to a nearby lot, where he ordered her to lie down on the ground and disrobe. When she complained that the ground was hurting her, he took her to his apartment, located across the street. During the next hour there, he had intercourse with her. Ultimately, he said that they had to leave to avoid being discovered by the woman with whom he lived.[7] The complainant responded that since he had gotten what he wanted, he should give her back her watch. He said that he would.

As the two left the apartment, he said he was going to get a car. Before leaving the building, however, he went to the apartment next door, leaving her to wait in the hallway. When asked why she waited, she said that she was still hoping for the return of her watch, which was a valued gift, apparently from her boyfriend.

She never did get the watch. When they left the building, the man told her to wait on the street while he got the car. At that point she went to a nearby police precinct and reported the incident. She gave a full description of the assailant that matched my client. She also accu-

rately described the inside of his apartment. Later, in response to a note left at his apartment by the police, my client came to the precinct, and the complainant identified him. My client was released at that time but was arrested soon thereafter at his apartment, where a gun was found.[8] No watch was recovered.

My client was formally charged, at which point I entered the case. At our initial interview and those that followed it, he insisted that he had nothing whatever to do with the crime and he had never seen the woman before.[9] He stated that he had been in several places during the night in question: visiting his aunt earlier in the evening, then traveling to a bar in New Jersey, where he was during the critical hours. He gave the name of a man there who would corroborate this. He said that he arrived home early the next morning and met a friend. He stated that he had no idea how this woman had come to know things about him such as what the apartment looked like, that he lived with a woman, and that he was a musician, or how she could identify him. He said that he had no reason to rape anyone, since he already had a woman, and that in any event he was recovering from surgery for an old gun shot wound and could not engage in intercourse. He said he would not be so stupid as to bring a woman he had robbed and was going to rape into his own apartment.

I felt that there was some strength to these arguments, and that there were questionable aspects to the complainant's story. In particular, it seemed strange that a man intending rape would be as solicitous of the victim's comfort as the woman said her assailant was at the playground. It also seemed that a person who had just been raped would flee when she had the chance to, and in any case would not be primarily concerned with the return of her watch. On balance, however, I suspected that my client was not telling me the truth. I thought the complaining witness could not possibly have known what she knew about him and his apartment, if she had not had any contact with him. True, someone else could have posed as him, and used his apartment. My client, however, could suggest no one who could have done so.[10] Moreover, that hypothesis did not explain the complainant's accurate description of him to the police. Although the identification procedure used by the police, a one person "show up," was suggestive,[11] the woman had ample opportunity to observe her assailant during the extended incident. I could not believe that the complainant had selected my client randomly to accuse falsely of rape. By both her and my client's admission, the two had not had any previous association.

That my client was probably lying to me had two possible explanations. First, he might have been lying because he was guilty and did not see any particular advantage to himself in admitting it to me. It is embarrassing to admit that one has committed a crime, particularly one of this nature. Moreover, my client might well have feared to tell me the truth. He might have believed that I would tell others what he said, or, at the very least, that I might not be enthusiastic about representing him.

He also might have lied not because he was guilty of the offense, but because he thought the concocted story was the best one under the circumstances. The sexual encounter may have taken place voluntarily, but the woman complained to the police because she was angry at my client for refusing to return the valued wrist watch, perhaps not stolen, but left, in my client's apartment. My client may not have been able to admit this, because he had other needs that took precedence over the particular legal one that brought him to me. For example, the client might have felt compelled to deny any involvement in the incident because to admit to having had a sexual encounter might have jeopardized his relationship with the woman with whom he lived. Likewise, he might have decided to "play lawyer," and put forward what he believed to be his best defense. Not understanding the heavy burden of proof on the state in criminal cases, he might have thought that any version of the facts that showed that he had contact with the woman would be fatal because it would simply be a case of her word against his.

I discussed all of these matters with the client on several occasions. Judging him a man of intelligence, with no signs of mental abnormality, I became convinced that he understood both the seriousness of his situation, and that his exculpation did not depend upon maintaining his initial story. In ensuring that he did understand that, in fact, I came close enough to suggesting the "right" answers to make me a little nervous about the line between subornation of perjury and careful witness preparation, known in the trade as "horseshedding."[12] In the end, however, he held to his original account.

B. The Investigation

At this point the case was in equipoise for me. I had my suspicions about both the complainant's and the client's version of what had occurred, and I supposed a jury would as well. That problem was theirs, however, not mine. All I had to do was present my client's version of what occurred in the best way that I could.

Or was that all that was required? Committed to the adversarial spirit reflected in Justice White's observations about my role, I decided that it was not. The "different mission" took me beyond the task of presenting my client's position in a legally correct and persuasive manner, to trying to untrack the state's case in any lawful way that occurred to me, regardless of the facts.

With that mission in mind, I concluded that it would be too risky to have the defendant simply take the stand and tell his story, even if it were true. Unless we could create an iron-clad alibi, which seemed unlikely given the strength of the complainant's identification, I thought it was much safer to attack the complainant's story, even if it were true. I felt, however, that since my client had persisted in his original story I was obligated to investigate the alibi defense, although I was fairly certain that I would not use it. My students and I therefore interviewed everyone he mentioned, traveled and timed the route he said he had followed, and attempted to find witnesses who may have seen someone else at the apartment. We discovered nothing helpful. The witness my client identified as being at the bar in New Jersey could not corroborate the client's presence there. The times the client gave were consistent with his presence at the place of the crime when the victim claimed it took place. The client's aunt verified that he had been with her, but much earlier in the evening.

Because the alibi defense was apparently hopeless, I returned to the original strategy of attempting to undermine the complainant's version of the facts. I demanded a preliminary hearing, in which the complainant would have to testify under oath to the events in question. Her version was precisely as I have described it, and she told it in an objective manner that, far from seeming contrived, convinced me that she was telling the truth. She seemed a person who, if not at home with the meanness of the streets, was resigned to it. To me that explained why she was able to react in what I perceived to be a nonstereotypical manner to the ugly events in which she had been involved.

I explained to my client that we had failed to corroborate his alibi, and that the complainant appeared to be a credible witness. I said that in my view the jury would not believe the alibi, and that if we could not obtain any other information, it might be appropriate to think about a guilty plea, which would at least limit his exposure to punishment. The case, then in the middle of the aimless drift towards resolution that typifies New York's criminal justice system, was left at that.

Some time later, however, my client called me and told me that he had new evidence; his aunt, he said, would testify that he had been with her at the time in question. I was incredulous. I reminded him that at no time during our earlier conversations had he indicated what was plainly a crucial piece of information, despite my not too subtle explanation of an alibi defense. I told him that when the aunt was initially interviewed with great care on this point, she stated that he was not with her at the time of the crime. Ultimately, I told him that I thought he was lying, and that in my view even if the jury heard the aunt's testimony, they would not believe it.

Whether it was during that session or later that the client admitted his guilt I do not recall. I do recall wondering whether, now that I knew the truth, that should make a difference in the way in which the case was handled. I certainly wished that I did not know it and began to understand, psychologically if not ethically, lawyers who do not want to know their clients' stories.[13]

I did not pause very long to ponder the problem, however, because I concluded that knowing the truth in fact did not make a difference to my defense strategy, other than to put me on notice as to when I might be suborning perjury. Because the mission of the defense attorney was to defeat the prosecution's case, what I knew actually happened was not important otherwise. What did matter was whether a version of the "facts" could be presented that would make a jury doubt the client's guilt.

Viewed in this way, my problem was not that my client's story was false, but that it was not credible, and could not be made to appear so by legal means. To win, we would therefore have to come up with a better theory than the alibi, avoiding perjury in the process. Thus, the defense would have to be made out without the client testifying, since it would be a crime for him to assert a fabricated exculpatory theory under oath.[14] This was not a serious problem, however, because it would not only be possible to prevail without the defendant's testimony, but it would probably be easier to do so. Not everyone is capable of lying successfully on the witness stand, and I did not have the sense that my client would be very good at it.

There were two possible defenses that could be fabricated. The first was mistaken identity. We could argue that the opportunity of the victim to observe the defendant at the time of the original encounter was limited, since it had occurred on a dark street. The woman could be made out to have been in great emotional distress during the incident.[15] Expert testimony would have to be adduced to show the hazards of eyewitness identification.[16] We could demonstrate that an unreliable identification procedure had been used at the precinct.[17] On the other hand, given that the complainant had spent considerable time with the assailant and had led the police back to the defendant's apartment, it seemed doubtful that the mistaken identification ploy would be successful.

The second alternative, consent, was clearly preferable. It would negate the charge of rape and undermine the robbery case.[18] To prevail, all we would have to do would be to raise a reasonable doubt as to whether he had compelled the woman to have sex with him. The doubt would be based on the scenario that the woman and the defendant met, and she voluntarily returned to his apartment. Her watch, the subject of the alleged robbery, was either left there by mistake or, perhaps better, was never there at all.

The consent defense could be made out entirely through cross-examination of the complainant, coupled with the argument to the jury about her lack of credibility on the issue of force. I could emphasize the parts of her story that sounded the most curious, such as the defendant's solicitude in taking his victim back to his apartment, and her waiting for her watch when she could have gone immediately to the nearby precinct that she went to later. I could point to her inability to identify the gun she claimed was used (although it was the one actually used), that the allegedly stolen watch was never found, there was no sign of physical violence, and no one heard screaming or any other signs of a struggle. I could also argue as my client had that even if he were reckless enough to rob and rape a woman across the street from his apartment, he would not be so foolish as to bring the victim there. I considered investigating the complainant's background, to take advantage of the right, unencumbered at the time, to impeach her on the basis of her prior unchastity.[19] I did not pursue this, however, because to me this device, although lawful, was fundamentally wrong. No doubt in that respect I lacked zeal, perhaps punishably so.

Even without assassinating this woman's character, however, I could argue that this was simply a case of a casual tryst that went awry. The defendant would not have to prove whether the complainant made the false charge to account for her whereabouts that evening, or to explain what happened to her missing watch. If the jury had reason to doubt the complainant's charges it would be bound to acquit the defendant.

How all of this would have played out at trial cannot be known. Predictably, the case dragged on so long that the prosecutor was forced to offer the unrefusable plea of possession of a gun.[20] As I look back, however, I wonder how I could justify doing what I was planning to do had the case been tried. I was prepared to stand before the jury posing as an officer of the court in search of the truth, while trying to fool the jurors into believing a wholly fabricated story, i.e., that the woman had consented, when in fact she had been forced at gunpoint to have sex with the defendant. I was also prepared to demand an acquittal because the state had not met its burden of proof when, if it had not, it would have been because I made the truth look like a lie. If there is any redeeming social value in permitting an attorney to do such things, I frankly cannot discern it. . . .

III. CAN LAWYERS "KNOW" THE TRUTH?

A. "The Adversary System" Excuse[21]
A principle argument in favor of the propriety of asserting a "false" defense is that there is, for the lawyer, no such thing. The "truth," insofar as it is relevant to the lawyer, is what the trier of the fact determines it to be.[22] The role of the lawyer in the adversary system is not to interpose his or her own belief about what the facts are.[23] Instead, the truth will emerge through a dialectical process, in which the vigorous advocacy of thesis and antithesis will equip the neutral arbiter to synthesize the data and reach a conclusion. . . .

. . . Suppose, for example, that I had interviewed the neighbor into whose apartment the defendant had gone following the rape—and who was unknown to the police. Suppose that he had told me that at the time of the incident he heard screams, and the sound of a struggle, and that my client had made incriminating remarks to him about what had occurred. It may be that there are reasons of policy that permit me to conceal these facts from the prosecution. It is ludicrous to assert, however, that because I can conceal them I do not know them. It is also ludicrous to suggest that if in addition I use my advocacy skills—and rights—to advance the thesis that there were no witnesses to the crime, I have engaged in a truth finding process.[24]

The argument that the attorney cannot know the truth until a court decides it fails. Either it is sophistry, designed to simplify the moral life of the attorney,[25] or it rests on a confusion between "factual truth" and "legal truth." The former relates to historical fact. The latter relates to the principle that a fact cannot be acted upon by the legal system until it is proven in accordance with legal rules. Plainly one can know the factual truth, for example, that one's client forced a woman to have sex with him, without or before knowing the legal truth that he is punishable for the crime of rape. The question is not whether an attorney can know the truth, but what standards should be applied in determining what the truth is . . .

IV. DOES THE TRUTH MATTER? APPRAISING THE DIFFERENT MISSION

We confront at last the "Different Mission" argument we set out initially to examine. It is that the defense attorney has a broader function than protecting the innocent against wrongful conviction. Equally important is the task of protecting the factually guilty individual against overreaching by the state. The defense attorney may well be able to know the truth, but can be indifferent to it because it is the state's case, not the client's with which he or she is concerned. Professor Freedman puts it this way:

> The point . . . is not that the lawyer cannot know the truth, or that the lawyer refuses to recognize the truth, but rather that the lawyer is told: "You, personally, may very well know the truth, but your personal knowledge is irrelevant. In your capacity as an advocate (and, if you will, as an officer of the court) you are forbidden to act upon your personal knowledge of the truth,

as you might want to do as a private person, because the adversary system could not function properly if lawyers did so."

The adversary system must function because it is our basic protection against governmental overreaching. The danger of such overreaching is so great, moreover, that we must allow the defense attorney broad latitude in disrupting that case, even by presenting a spurious defense.

Two principal arguments have been advanced to explain why the needs of the adversary system permit the attorney to assert a defense not founded upon the truth. The first is that a false defense may have to be asserted to protect the defendant's right in a particular case right to have a defense at all. The second argument is that it may be necessary to subvert the truth in a particular case as a way of demonstrating the supremacy of the autonomous individual in the face of the powerful forces of organized society.

A. Subverting the Truth to Protect the Defendant's Right to a Defense

The most commonly offered justification for a right to undermine a truthful case is that if there were no such right, the guilty defendant would effectively be deprived of a defense. All defendants, it is asserted, are entitled to have the state prove the case against them, whether they are factually innocent or guilty. If the spurious defense were not allowed it would be impossible to represent persons who had confessed their guilt to their lawyers, or who, in accordance with rules of the sort I advanced in the last section, were "found" guilty by them. The trial, if there were one at all, would not be an occasion to test the government's case, but a kind of elaborate plea of guilty. I believe that this argument fails for two reasons: first, because it proves too much, and second, because it is based on an erroneous assumption as to what the defendant's rights are.

If it were true that a false defense must be allowed to assure that the guilty defendant has a defense, it would seem to follow that presently established constraints on the defense attorney representing the guilty person, let alone an innocent person against whom the state had incriminating evidence, should be removed. An exception to the criminal laws prohibiting the deliberate introduction of false evidence would have to be adopted. Some have argued that a criminal defendant has a right to commit perjury, and that the defense attorney has a concomitant duty not to interfere with such testimony, or for that matter with even more extraordinary means of prevailing at trial.

The notion of a right to commit perjury, however, has been forcefully rejected by the courts[26] and by the organized bar, albeit less forcefully.[27] I suggest, however, that it cannot logically be rejected by those who espouse the Different Mission theory in defense of subverting the truth. If the right to mount a defense is paramount, and if the only conceivable defense which the guilty defendant can mount involves the defendant, or his or her witnesses committing perjury, and the defense attorney arguing that that perjury is true, then it follows that the restraints of the penal law should not be conceded to be applicable.[28] . . .

The extravagant notion of the right to put on a defense is the second fallacy in the argument supporting a right to assert a false defense. Again, a moment's reflection on prevailing penal law limitations on advocacy will demonstrate that the

defendant is not entitled to gain an acquittal by any available means.[29] Unless we abandon completely the notion that verdicts should be based upon the truth, we must accept the fact that there may simply be no version of the facts favorable to the defense worthy of assertion in a court. In such cases, the role of the defense attorney should be limited to assuring that the state adduces sufficient legally competent evidence to sustain its burden of proof. . . .

Subverting the Truth to Preserve Individual Autonomy Against Encroachment by the State

The second prong of the "different mission" theory is that the truth must be sacrificed in individual cases as a kind of symbolic act designed to reaffirm our belief in the supremacy of the individual. This theory in turn is argued in several different ways.

1. The false defense may be necessary to preserve the individual's access to the legal system.

This argument is based on the proposition that because the legal system is so complex, meaningful access requires representation by an attorney. An attorney cannot perform his or her function unless the client provides the facts. The client will not do that if the facts will be used against the client, as, in this context, by not providing an available false defense. Thus it is necessary to permit the attorney to conceal harmful information obtained from the client and to act as if it did not exist.

As I have argued elsewhere, the importance of confidentiality to the performance of the lawyer's role has been greatly overstated. Even conceding its value, it does not seem to me that permitting the attorney to achieve the client's ends by subverting the truth advances the cause of individual autonomy. The legitimate concern of those who advance the autonomy argument is that the government must be prevented from interfering wrongfully or unnecessarily with individual freedom, not that there should be no interference with individual liberty at all. Here we are positing that the government has behaved reasonably, and the lawyer knows it. In my view, permitting such a case to be undermined by false evidence glorifies winning, but has very little to do with assuring justice.[30]

2. A false defense may be necessary to preserve the rigorous process by which guilt is determined.

Those taking this view see the criminal process not as a truth-seeking one, but a "screening system" designed to assure the utmost certainty before the criminal sanction is imposed. Only by permitting the defense attorney to use all of the tools which we have described here can we be certain that the prosecution will be put to its proof in all cases. The argument seems to be that if the prosecutor knows that the defense attorney will attempt to demolish the government's case, the prosecutor will in a sense be kept on his or her toes, and will seek the strongest evidence possible.[31]

This position is difficult to understand. In the situation under discussion here the prosecution has presented the strongest case possible, i.e., the truthful testimony of the victim of a crime. In any case, it is one thing to attack a weak government case by pointing out its weakness. It is another to attack a strong government case by confusing the jury with falsehoods. Finally, as a proponent of this "screening theory" concedes, there may be a danger that if the prosecutor sees that the truth alone is inadequate, he or she may be inspired to embellish it. That, of course, is not likely to make the screening mechanism work better.

For others, the desirability of prevailing against the state seems to be seen not as a means to assure that the prosecution will strive for high standards of proof, but as a positive good in its own right. The goal, as Professor Schwartz has put it, is to prevent the "behemoth" state from becoming a "juggernaut."[32] Schwartz states that "[c]ross-examination to give the impression that [witnesses] are telling falsehoods may be justified as a way of keeping the state from overreaching,"[33] but we are not told what precise danger this will avert, or how it will do so. I cannot discern these, either, unless one takes the view that the exercise of a particular state power is inherently wrong, justifying resistance by any means. Otherwise, it would seem sufficient to insure that the defendant had a right to make a good faith challenge to the state's allegations.

V. ACCOMPLISHING THE DEFENSE ATTORNEY'S DIFFERENT MISSION—MORALLY

I propose a system in which the defense attorney would operate not with the right to assert defenses known to be untrue, but under the following rule:

It shall be improper for an attorney who knows beyond a reasonable doubt the truth of a fact established in the state's case to attempt to refute that fact through the introduction of evidence, impeachment of evidence, or argument.

In the face of this rule, the attorney who knew there were no facts to contest would be limited to the "monitoring" role. Assuming that a defendant in my client's situation wanted to assert his right to contest the evidence against him, the attorney would work to assure that all of the elements of the crime were proven beyond a reasonable doubt, on the basis of competent and admissible evidence. This would include enforcing the defendant's rights to have privileged or illegally obtained evidence excluded: The goal sought here is not the elimination of all rules that result in the suppression of truth, but only those not supported by sound policy. It would also be appropriate for the attorney to argue to the jury that the available evidence is not sufficient to sustain the burden of proof. It would not, however, be proper for the attorney to use any of the presently available devices to refute testimony known to be truthful. I wish to make clear, however, that this rule would not prevent the attorney from challenging *inaccurate* testimony, even though the attorney knew that the defendant was guilty. Again, the truth-seeking goal is not applicable when a valid policy reason exists for ignoring it. Forcing the state to prove its case is such a reason.[34]

Applying these principles to my rape case, I would engage fully in the process of testing the admissibility of the state's evidence, moving to suppress testimony concerning the suggestive "show-up" identification at the precinct, and the gun found in the defendant's apartment after a warrantless search, should the state attempt to offer either piece of evidence. At the trial, I would be present to assure that the complainant testified in accordance with the rules of evidence.

Assuming that she testified at trial as she had at the preliminary hearing, however, I would not cross-examine her, because I would have no good faith basis for impeaching either her testimony or her character, since I "knew" that she was providing an accurate account of what had occurred.[35] Nor would I put on a defense case. I would limit my representation at that stage to putting forth the strongest argument I could that the facts presented by the state did not sustain its burden. In these ways, the defendant would receive the services of an attorney in subjecting the state's case to the final stage of the screening process provided by the system to insure against unjust convictions. That, however, would be all that the defense attorney could do. . . .

VI. CONCLUSION

. . . If this proposal seems radical, consider that it is essentially an adaptation of what today is the principal function of the defense attorney in every criminal justice system of significance in this nation. That function is not to create defenses out of whole cloth to present to juries, but to guide the defendant through a process that will usually end in a guilty plea. It will so end, at least when competent counsel are involved, very frequently because the defense attorney has concluded after thorough analysis that there is no answer to the state's case. If that role can be played in out of court resolution of the matter there seems to be no reason why it cannot be played in court, when the defendant insists upon his right to a trial. The important point is that the right to a trial does not embody the right to present to the tribunal any evidence at all, no matter how fictitious it is. . . .

NOTES

1. *Nix v. Whiteside*, 106 S. Ct. 988 (1986) (criminal defendant not denied effective assistance of counsel when attorney refused to allow him to present perjured testimony); . . .

2. Standard 4-7.6 (2d ed. 1980 & Supp. 1986). The ABA apparently has had a complete reversal in its view of this matter. *See* ABA STANDARDS RELATING TO THE ADMINISTRATION OF CRIMINAL JUSTICE, Compilation, at 132 (1974). Standard 4-7.6 states that the lawyer "should not misuse the power of cross-examination or impeachment by employing it to discredit or undermine a witness if he knows the witness is testifying truthfully."

3. MODEL CODE DR 7-101(A)(1) and EC 7-1. DR 7-102 appears on its face to be to the contrary, prohibiting lawyers from, *inter alia*, conducting a defense merely to harass another (subd. (1)); knowingly using false evidence (subd. (3)); making a false statement of fact (subd. (5)); creating or preserving false evidence (subd. (6)); or assisting the client in fraudulent conduct (subd. (7)). None of the noncriminal acts with which this article is concerned, however, have, to the author's knowledge, been cited by the bar as coming within the proscription of DR 7-102.

A similar conclusion can be reached with respect to the *Model Rules*. Rule 3.3 is an adaptation of DR 7-102, *see* rule 3.3, model code comparison. Rule 3.1 suggests that the drafters approved of the precise conduct under discussion here, at least for criminal lawyers. The rule prohibits assertion or controversion of an issue at trial unless there is a reasonable basis for doing so, except in criminal cases. The criminal case exception is based upon the drafter's conclusion, mistaken in my view, that the constitutional requirement that the state shoulder the burden of proof requires that the defense attorney be permitted to "put the prosecution to its proof even if there is no 'reasonable basis' for the defense." MODEL RULES Rule 3.1 model code comparison.

4. 388 U.S. 218, 250 (1967) (White, J., joined by Harlan and Stewart, J.J., dissenting in part and concurring in part).

5. *Id.* at 236–37.

6. *Id.* at 256–58 (footnotes omitted).

7. She also said that he told her that he was a musician. The significance of this remark will appear shortly.

8. The woman was not able to make a positive identification of the gun as the weapon used in the incident.

9. A student working on the case with me photographed the complainant on the street. My client stated that he could not identify her.

10. The woman had indicated that her assailant opened the door with a key. There was no evidence of a forced entry.

11. *Cf. Stovall v. Denno*, 338 U.S. 293 (1967) (identification in which murder suspect shown alone to and positively identified by bedridden, hospitalized victim not unnecessarily suggestive and therefore did not deny defendant due process).

12. The dilemma faced by the lawyer is whether, in explaining to the client the legal implications of conduct, he or she is shaping the client's version of the facts. The issue was put dramatically in R. TRAVER, ANATOMY OF A MURDER (1958), in which the attorney explained the facts needed to establish an insanity defense to an apparently normal person accused of murder. *Id.* at 44–47. Whether I was quite as blatant I frankly cannot remember, but it is clear that I did more than simply listen to what the client said. I explained how one would make out an alibi defense, and I made sure that he understood both that consent was a defense to rape, and that corroboration was necessary to support a rape conviction.

13. *See* Mitchell, *The Ethics of the Criminal Defense Attorney—New Answers to Old Questions*, 32 STAN L. REV. 293 n. 12 (1980) (author properly analogizes lawyer's preference not to know of the client's guilt to the doctrine of "conscious avoidance," which constitutes "knowledge" under criminal law).

14. The notion that the defendant in a criminal case has a right to commit perjury was finally put to rest in *Nix v. Whiteside*, 106 S. Ct. 988 (1986) (criminal defendant not denied effective assistance of counsel when attorney refused to allow him to present perjured testimony).

15. This would be one of those safe areas in cross-examination, where the witness was damned no matter what she answered. If she testified that she was distressed, it would make my point that she was making an unreliable identification; if she testified that she was calm, no one would believe her. Perhaps this is why cross-examination has been touted as "beyond any doubt the greatest legal engine ever invented for the discovery of truth." 5 'J. WIGMORE, EVIDENCE §" 1367 (J. Chadbourn rev. ed. 1974). Another commentator makes similar claims for his art, and while he acknowledges in passing that witnesses might tell the truth, he at no point suggests what the cross-examiner should do when faced with such a situation. F. WELLMAN, THE ART OF CROSS-EXAMINATION 7 (4th ed. 1936). The cross-examiner's world, rather, seems to be divided into two types of witnesses: those whose testimony is harmless and those whose testimony must be destroyed on pain of abandoning "all hope for a jury verdict." *Id.* at 9.

16. On the dangers of misidentification, *see, e.g., United States v. Wade,* 388 U.S. 218 (1967). The use of experts to explain the misidentification problem to the jury is well established. *See generally* E. LOFTUS, EYEWITNESS TESTIMONY 191–203 (1979) (discussing ways expert testimony on eye witness testimony can be used and problems arising from its use).

17. *See Watkins v. Sowders,* 499 U.S. 341 (1981) (identification problems properly attacked during cross-examination at trial; no per se rule compelling judicial determination outside presence of jury concerning admissibility of identification evidence).

18. Consent is a defense to a charge of rape. *E.g.,* N.Y. PENAL LAW § 130.05 (McKinney 1975 & Supp. 1987). While consent is not a defense to a robbery charge, N.Y. PENAL LAW § § 160.00–15 (McKinney 1975 & Supp. 1987), if the complainant could be made out to be a liar about the rape, there was a good chance that the jury would not believe her about the stolen watch either.

19. When this case arose it was common practice to impeach the complainant in rape cases by eliciting details of her prior sexual activities. Subsequently the rules of evidence were amended to require a specific showing of relevance to the facts of the case. N.Y. CRIM. PROC. LAW § 60.42 (McKinney 1981 & Supp. 1987).

20. The client, who had spent time in jail awaiting trial, was not given an additional prison sentence.

21. The phrase is the title of David Luban's essay, *The Adversary System Excuse,* in THE GOOD LAWYER: LAWYERS' ROLES AND LAWYERS' ETHICS 83 (D. Luban ed. 1983).

22. *See* M. FRANKEL, PARTISAN JUSTICE, *supra* note 43, at 24. Judge Frankel, who is critical of this theory, quotes the famous answer of Samuel Johnson to the question how he can represent a bad cause: "Sir, you do not know it to be good or bad till the judge determines it." *Id.* (quoting J. BOSWELL, THE LIFE OF SAMUEL JOHNSON 366 (1925)).

23. MODEL CODE DR 7-106©(4) provides in part that a lawyer shall not "[a]ssert his personal opinion as to the justness of a cause, as to the credibility of a witness . . . or as to the guilt or innocence of an accused. . . ."

24. My "proof" that there were no witnesses to the crime would come in the form of an "accrediting" cross-examination of the complainant and/or a police officer who testified. I could inquire of both concerning whether they saw or otherwise became aware of the presence of any witnesses, and then argue to the jury that their negative answers established that there were none.

25. As all lawyers who are honest with themselves know, occasions arise when doubts about a client turn into suspicion and then moral certainty that a client is lying. Although his professional role may require a lawyer to take a detached attitude of unbelief, the law of lawyering does not permit a lawyer to escape all accountability by suspending his intelligence and common sense. A lawyer may try to persuade himself that he is not absolutely sure whether his client is committing perjury. . . . But all authorities agree . . . that there comes a point when only brute rationalization, moral irresponsibility, and pure sophistry can support the contention that the lawyer does not "know" what the situation is. G. HAZARD & W. HODES, THE LAW OF LAWYERING: A HANDBOOK ON THE MODEL RULES OF PROFESSIONAL CONDUCT 343 (1985) (citing M. FREEDMAN, *supra* note 6, at 52–55, 71–76 (1975)).

26. *Nix v. Whiteside,* 106 S. Ct. 988 (1986) (criminal defendant not denied effective assistance of counsel when attorney refused to permit him to present perjured testimony).

27. The *Model Code* prohibits the knowing introduction of perjured testimony or false evidence. MODEL CODE DR 7-102(A)(4). The *Model Code* essentially eliminates, however, the duty of the attorney to disclose the client's attempt to commit these crimes, by prohibiting such disclosure if it would reveal a protected privileged communication. MODEL CODE DR 7-102(B)(1). The *Model Rules,* however, prohibit the introduction of false testimony, and appear to modify the restriction on disclosure of client misconduct in this area. The *Model Rules* require the attorney to disclose to the court that false evidence has been introduced. MODEL RULES Rule 3.3. The disclosure requirement ends, however, if the criminal conduct of the client is not discovered until after the proceeding has ended.

28. For example, if in my rape case there were incontrovertible evidence that force had been used on the complainant, the consent defense would have been impossible. I would then have had to revert to the mistaken identification defense. Given the strength of the complainant's identification testimony, the defendant's or his aunt's perjurious testimony might have been necessary to provide a defense at all.

29. In addition to the laws against perjury, there are laws, for example, against tampering with witnesses, 18 U.S.C. § § 1512–14 (1982 & Supp. 1985) and bribery, 18 U.S.C. § 201 (1982).

30. It is ironic that some who have supported the right to put on a false defense do so as part of the argument that defending the guilty teaches a lesson to the defendant, especially the indigent defendant, that the system is fair. . . . Again, the problem is the failure to distinguish between the right to a defense and the right to a false defense.

Commenting on the criminal justice system in general, Jonathan Casper has observed that it "not only fails to teach [defendants] moral lessons, but reinforces the idea that the system has no moral content." Casper, *Did You Have A Lawyer When You Went to Court? No, I Had A Public Defender,* 1 YALE REV. L. & SOC. ACTION 4, 9 (1971). The same could very well be said of a method of representation in which the defendant sees the lawyer, an official of the system, attempting to win by engaging in conduct similar to that which may have brought the defendant to court.

31. The cross-examination of the "truthful" witness is justified . . . [because] [w]eaknesses in the witness' testimony brought out on cross-examination will make the prosecution understand the range in "quality" of evidence for subsequent cases so that in the future he or she will recognize and seek the best evidence possible. .

Mitchell, *supra* note 34, at 312 n.67.

32. Schwartz, *The Zeal of the Civil Advocate,* 1983 AM. B. FOUND. RES. J. 543, 554.

33. *Id.*

34. My colleague Stephen Gillers, for whose thoughtful criticism of my view I am indebted, called my attention to this illustrative case, ruled on by the Michigan State Bar Committee on Professional and Judicial Ethics:

A defendant is charged with armed robbery. The victim testifies that the defendant robbed him at 1:00 p.m. The defendant has confessed to his lawyer. In fact, the robbery took place at 1:30 p.m. The victim is in error about the time. The defendant has a solid and truthful alibi witness who will testify that the defendant was with the witness at 1:00 p.m.

The question presented was whether the defense could call the alibi witness. The Bar Committee answered affirmatively. Michigan State Bar Committee of Professional and Judicial Ethics Op. CI-1164, Jan. 23, 1987, *reported in* 3 LAWYER'S MANUAL ON PROFESSIONAL CONDUCT (ABA/BNA) No. 3, at 44 (March 4, 1987). I would agree. The state's proof of the time of the crime was incorrect, and therefore subject to impeachment. I would not, however, permit the defense to offer evidence that the crime occurred at 1:00 p.m. if the victim correctly testified that it occurred at 1:30 p.m.

35. I recently made an informal presentation of this position to a group of my colleagues, who beseiged me with hypotheticals, the most provocative of which were these: (A) A witness not wearing her glasses, identifies my client as having been at a certain place. If my client were in fact at that place, could I cross-examine the witness on the grounds that she was not wearing her glasses? The answer is yes: The witness' ability to perceive affects the quality of the state's proof, and the fact that she happened to be correct is irrelevant. (B) In the same situation, except here I knew that the witness was wearing her glasses. Could I cross-examine the witness in an effort to show that she was not? The answer is no: The state had adduced reliable evidence, and that is all that it was required to do.

I was also asked whether I would apply the same truth based rule and refuse, in the situation described in (B), to impeach the witness if I knew that my client were innocent. My first response was something of a dodge: If I knew that, it was difficult for me to see why I would have to impeach this witness. Ultimately (albeit tentatively) I would conclude that it was too dangerous to adopt the notion that even these ends justified subverting the truth, and I would not cross-examine on that point.

NO

John B. Mitchell

REASONABLE DOUBTS ARE WHERE YOU FIND THEM: A RESPONSE TO PROFESSOR SUBIN'S POSITION ON THE CRIMINAL LAWYER'S "DIFFERENT MISSION"

I. INTRODUCTION

In *A Criminal Lawyer's "Different Mission": Reflections on the "Right" to Present a False Case,*[1] Professor Harry L. Subin attempts to draw what he considers to be the line between attorney as advocate, and attorney as officer of the court. Specifically, he "attempts to define the limits on the methods a lawyer should be willing to use when his client's goals are inconsistent with truth."[2] This is no peripheral theme in professional responsibility. Quite the contrary, Professor Subin has chosen a difficult issue which touches upon the very nature of our criminal justice system, the role of the attorney in that system, the relationship of the individual to the state, and the Constitution. Further, Professor Subin takes a tough and controversial stand on this issue and, although I disagree with him, I respect his position. . . .

II. PROFESSOR SUBIN'S ASSUMPTIONS

Professor Subin rests his entire analysis on two basic premises: (1) the principle goal of the criminal justice system is "truth"; and (2) it is contrary to the goal of "truth" to permit a criminal defense attorney to put on a "false defense." In Subin's terms, a false defense is an attempt to "convince the judge or jury that facts established by the state and known to the attorney to be true are not true, or that the facts known to the attorney to be false are true." Such a defense is put on by: " . . . (1) cross-examination of truthful government witnesses to undermine their testimony or their credibility; (2) direct presentation of testimony, not in itself false, but used to discredit the

From John B. Mitchell, "Reasonable Doubts Are Where You Find Them," *Georgetown Journal of Legal Ethics*, vol. 1 (1987), pp. 339–361. Copyright © 1987 by John B. Mitchell. Reprinted by permission. Some notes omitted.

truthful evidence adduced by the government, or to accredit a false theory; and, (3) argument to the jury based on any of these acts." I take exception to both of these premises, as set out below.[3]

The Principal Concern of the Criminal Justice System Is Not "Truth"

The idea that the focus of the criminal justice system is not "truth" may initially sound shocking. I have valued truth throughout my life and do not condone lying in our legal system. But the job of our criminal justice system is simply other than determining "truth." . . .

A system focused on truth would first collect all information relevant to the inquiry. In our system, the defendant is generally the best source of information in the dispute, but he is not available unless he so chooses. The police may not question him. He may not be called to the stand with his own lawyer beside him and with a judge controlling questioning under the rules of evidence. The prosecutor may not even comment to the jury about the defendant's failure to testify, even though fair inferences may be drawn from the refusal to respond to serious accusations.

A system focused on truth would have the factfinder look at all the information and then decide what it believed had occurred. In our system, the inquiry is dramatically skewed against finding guilt. "Beyond a reasonable doubt" expresses the deep cultural value that "it is better to let ten guilty men go than convict one innocent man." It is a system where, after rendering a verdict of not guilty, jurors routinely approach defense counsel and say, "I thought your guy was guilty, but that prosecutor did not prove it to me beyond a reasonable

doubt." What I have just described is not a "truth system" in any sense in which one could reasonably understand that term.[4] Truth may play a role, but it is not a dominant role; there is something else afoot.[5] The criminal defense attorney does not have a "different mission";[6] the system itself has a "different mission." . . .

Put directly, the criminal justice system protects the individual from the police power of the executive branch of government. Between the individual citizen and the enormous governmental power residing in the executive stands a panel of that individual's peers—a jury. Through them, the executive must pass. Only if it proves its case "beyond a reasonable doubt," thereby establishing legal guilt, may the executive then legitimately intrude into the individual citizen's life. Thus, "factual" guilt or innocence, or what Professor Subin would call "truth," is not the principle issue in the system. Our concern is with the legitimate use of the prosecutor's power as embodied in the concept of "legal guilt." . . .

B. A Defense Attorney Acting in a Manner Meeting with Subin's Disapproval Is Not Putting on a "False Defense"

When placed in the "reasonable doubt" context, Professor Subin's implicit distinction between "true" and "false" defenses misportrays both how a defense attorney may actually function in a case, and the very nature of evidence in that case. His categories are too imprecise to capture the subtle middle ground of a pure reasonable doubt defense, in which counsel presents the jury with alternative possibilities that counsel knows are false, without asserting the truth of those alternatives.

For example, imagine I am defending a young woman accused of shoplifting a star one places on top of Christmas trees. I interview the store manager and find that he stopped my client when he saw her walk straight through the store, star in hand, and out the door. When he stopped her and asked why she had taken the star without paying, she made no reply and burst into tears. He was then about to take her inside to the security office when an employee called out, "There's a fire!" The manager rushed inside and dealt with a small blaze in the camera section. Five minutes later he came out to find my client sitting where he had left her. He then took her back to the security room and asked if she would be willing to empty her pockets so that he could see if she had taken anything else. Without a word, she complied. She had a few items not belonging to the store and a ten-dollar bill. The star was priced at $1.79.

In an interview with my client, she admitted trying to steal the star: "It was so pretty, and would have looked so nice on the tree. I would have bought it, but I also wanted to make a special Christmas dinner for Mama and didn't have enough money to do both. I've been saving for that dinner and I know it will make her so happy. But that star. . . . I could just see the look in Mama's eyes if she saw that lovely thing on our tree."

At trial, the manager tells the same story he told me, except he *leaves out* the part about her waiting during the fire and having a ten-dollar bill. If I bring out these two facts on cross-examination and argue for an acquittal based upon my client "accidentally" walking out of the store with the star, surely Professor Subin will accuse me of raising a "false defense." I have brought out testimony, not itself false, to accredit a false theory and have argued to the jury based on this act. But I am not really arguing a false theory in Professor Subin's sense.

My defense is not that the defendant accidentally walked out, but rather that the prosecution cannot prove the element of intent to permanently deprive beyond a reasonable doubt. Through this theory, I am raising "doubt" in the prosecution's case, and therefore questioning the legitimacy of the government's lawsuit for control over the defendant. In my effort to carry out this legal theory, I will *not assert* that facts known by me to be true are false or those known to be false are true. As a defense attorney, I do not have to prove what *in fact* happened. That is an advantage in the process I would not willingly give up. Under our constitutional system, I do not need to try to convince the factfinder about the truth of any factual propositions. I need only try to convince the factfinder that the prosecution has not met its burden. Again, I will not argue that particular facts are true or false. Thus, in this case I will not claim that my client walked out of the store with innocent intent (a fact which I know is false); rather, I will argue:

> The prosecution claims my client stole an ornament for a Christmas tree. The prosecution further claims that when my client walked out of that store she intended to keep it without paying. Now, maybe she did. None of us were there. On the other hand, she had $10.00 in her pocket, which was plenty of money with which to pay for the ornament without the risk of getting caught stealing. Also, she didn't try to conceal what she was doing. She walked right out of the store holding it in her hand. Most of us have come close to innocently doing the same thing. So,

maybe she didn't. But then she cried the minute she was stopped. She might have been feeling guilty. So, maybe she did. On the other hand, she might just have been scared when she realized what had happened. After all, she didn't run away when she was left alone even though she knew the manager was going to be occupied with the fire inside. So, maybe she didn't. The point is that, looking at all the evidence, you're left with "maybe she intended to steal, maybe she didn't." But, you knew that before the first witness was even sworn. The prosecution has the burden, and he simply can't carry any burden let alone "beyond a reasonable doubt" with a maybe she did, maybe she didn't case . . .

Is this a "false defense" for Professor Subin? Admittedly, I am trying to raise a doubt by persuading the jury to appreciate "possibilities" other than my client's guilt. Perhaps Professor Subin would say it is "false" because I know the possibilities are untrue. But if that is so, Professor Subin will have taken a leap from defining "false defense" as the assertion that true things are false and false things are true, for I am doing neither of those things here. The fact that one cannot know how Subin would reach this "pure" reasonable doubt case only reinforces my initial statement that Professor Subin's categories are imprecise.

Another perspective from which to look at the function of a defense attorney involves understanding that function in the context of the nature of evidence at trial. Professor Subin speaks of facts and the impropriety of trying to make "true facts" look false and "false facts" look true. But in a trial there are no such things as facts. There is only information, lack of information, and chains of inferences therefrom. In the courtroom there

will be no crime, no store, no young girl with a star in her hand. All there will be is a collection of witnesses who are strangers to the jury, giving information which may include physical evidence and documents. For example, most people would acknowledge the existence of eyewitness identifications; however, in an evidentiary sense they do not exist. Rather, a particular person with particular perceptual abilities and motives and biases will recount an observation made under particular circumstances and utter particular words on the witness stand (e.g., "That's the man"). From this mass of information, the prosecution will argue, in story form, in favor of the inference that the defendant is their man (e.g., "The victim was on her way home, when . . ."). The defense will not then argue that the defendant is the wrong man in a *factual sense*, but instead will attack the persuasiveness of the criminal inference and resulting story (e.g., "The sun was in the witness' eyes; she was on drugs").

In our shoplifting example, the prosecution will elicit that the defendant burst into tears when stopped by the manager. From this information will run a chain of inferences: defendant burst into tears, people without a guilty conscience would explain their innocence, not cry; defendant has a guilty conscience; her guilty conscience is likely motivated by having committed a theft. Conversely, if the defense brings out that the manager was shaking a lead pipe in his hand when he stopped the defendant, defense counsel is *not asserting* that defendant did not have a guilty conscience when stopped. Counsel is merely *weakening* the persuasiveness of the prosecution's inference by raising the "possibility" that she was crying not from guilt, but from fear. By raising such "possibilities," the defense is making arguments against the ability of the prosecution's inferences to meet their burden of "beyond a reasonable doubt." The defense is not arguing what are true or false facts (i.e., that the tears were from fear as opposed to guilt). Whatever Professor Subin cares to call it, this commentary on the prosecution's case, complete with raising possibilities which weaken the persuasiveness of central inferences in that case, is in no ethical sense a "false case." "False case" is plainly a misnomer. In a system where factual guilt is not at issue, Professor Subin's "falsehoods" are, in fact, "reasonable doubts."

C. Even If Criminal Defense Attorneys Do Raise a "False Defense," the Role of the Defense Attorney in the Criminal Justice System Permits Such a Defense

Professor Subin does not seek to eliminate all impediments to truth, just those based upon sound policy. In failing to appreciate fully the institutional role of the defense attorney, he glosses over a major countervailing policy: even if the attorney is putting forth what Subin would term "false defense," this defense is the side effect, not the goal or function of the defense attorney's role in the criminal justice system.

Subin apparently believes that the principal position he must overcome from his opponents who seek leeway with the "truth" is that such leeway is necessary to protect the adversary system, and the adversary system, in turn, is necessary to protect the factually guilty from "overreaching by the state."[7] My position, however, does not rest on these ideas. Though the adversary system serves to protect the factually guilty from state overreaching, my position is principally based upon the criminal justice system—a system with rationales different from the general adversary system, including the protection of the factually innocent.[8]

Our criminal justice system is more appropriately defined as a screening system than as a truth-seeking one.[9] The ultimate objective of this screening system is to determine who are the proper subjects of criminal sanction. The process goes on continually. Someone notices a window which looks pried open or a suspicious-looking stranger. Neighbor talks to neighbor, and information filters to the police. The police comb the streets gathering information, focusing upon those whose behavior warrants special attention Those selected by the police for special attention are then placed in the hands of prosecutors, courts, and juries who constantly sift through this "residue" to make final determinations about who is to be subjected to criminal sanction.

The criminal justice system is itself composed of a series of "screens," of which trial is but one. These screens help keep innocents out of the process and, at the same time, limit the intrusion of the state into people's lives. Each of these screens functions to protect the values of human dignity and autonomy, while enforcing our criminal laws. Further, to ensure that the intrusion of the state into the individual's life will be halted at the soonest possible juncture, our system provides a separate screen at each of the several stages of the criminal process. At any screen, the individual may be taken out of the criminal process and returned to society with as little disruption as possible.

By pushing hard in every case (whether the client is factually guilty or not) and thereby raising "reasonable doubts" in the prosecution's case whenever possible, the defense attorney helps "make the screens work" and thus protects the interests of the factually innocent.[10]. . .

III. PROFESSOR SUBIN'S APPROACH

. . . My analysis in this section will focus upon Professor Subin's basic approach to "defin[ing] the limits on the methods a lawyer should be willing to use when his or her client's goals are inconsistent with the truth"; i.e., distinguishing between the role of what Subin calls a "monitor" and the more familiar role of "advocate." . . .

To illustrate, imagine I am representing a defendant accused of robbery. I have seen the victim at a preliminary hearing, and based upon the circumstances of the identification and my overall impression of the witness, I am certain that he is truthful and accurate. My client has confessed his factual guilt. And therefore I "know" (in Professor Subin's sense) beyond a reasonable doubt that my client has been accurately identified.

In his direct examination, the victim states, "The defendant had this big, silvery automatic pistol right up near my face the whole time he was asking for money." In accordance with Professor Subin's view that defense counsel can "persuade the jury that there are legitimate reasons to doubt the state's evidence," may I raise the general vagaries of eyewitness identification?

All of us have had some stranger come up to us, call us by an unfamiliar name, and indicate they thought we were someone they knew. We have been with a friend who points to someone a few tables over exclaiming, "Isn't she an exact double of Sue Smith? Could be her twin," and we think to ourselves that other than the hair color, there is no resemblance at all.

Perhaps Subin would say I cannot make the misidentification argument. He might argue that the "legitimacy" of reasons to doubt the state's evidence is not to be judged from the perspective of a reasonable juror hearing the prosecution's evidence but from my subjective knowledge. Since I "know" that there was no difficulty with the identification, I cannot put forward a "legitimate" reason to doubt. If this is Professor Subin's meaning, I, as monitor, am left with the following closing argument: "Ladies and gentlemen, thank you for your attention to this case. Remember, the prosecution must prove each element beyond a reasonable doubt. Thank you." The Constitution aside, (and in my view this would be putting the Constitution aside), it is hard to imagine this is Subin's intended result.

"Legitimate reason" to doubt must refer to a reasonable juror's perception of the state's evidence, not to the defense attorney's private knowledge. Bringing out reasonable doubts in the state's evidence concerning the identification therefore must be legitimate, and yet this would seem to raise a "false defense" (i.e., mistaken identification). Presumably, Subin would permit this defense because of a greater policy than "truth," i.e., the right to have the state prove guilt beyond a reasonable doubt. If this is permissible in Subin's view, it is difficult to understand why it would not be permissible to call an expert on eyewitness identification to testify.

In the hypothetical case described above, I should also be permitted to bring specific evidence about the gun into my closing argument because it offers a "legitimate" reason to doubt the accuracy of the identification (e.g., "The eyewitness was not someone sitting calmly in a restaurant looking at someone else a few tables away. Here, the eyewitness had a gun in his face.") Of course, if I can bring the gun into my closing, I presumably can do it in a manner I believe most effective; for I don't believe Professor Subin's position is that you are permitted to do it, but not very well:

> And did he notice that gun? Was he staring at that big . . . silvery . . . automatic? Wouldn't you? Not knowing if this assailant was going to beat or kill you. Wouldn't your mind turn inward? Inward to that gun, to calming your fear of death, to not provoking this spectre who could end your life in a moment? Would you be thinking "Let me see. His eyes are hazel . . . I want to get a good look at him so I can identify him later"? Would you want to do anything to make that person with a big . . . silvery . . . automatic gun in your face think you could identify him? . . .

What then is Subin really saying? Subin could not mean by his reference to the "state's evidence" that I can use evidence of the gun to raise a reasonable doubt in aid of the "false defense" of misidentification if the information is elicited on *the state's direct examination*, but that I am not permitted to bring out the information through cross-examination or defense witnesses. He could not mean that information I thus actively elicit is not "legitimate" for raising doubts. Yet, the only mechanisms he lists for putting on a "false defense" are defense cross-examination, defense witnesses, and arguments therefrom. If this distinction between information elicited by the prosecution and that elicited by the defense is really what he intends to divine the legitimate from the illegitimate, it is a strange structure upon which to rest a principle of ethical guidance, especially given the nature of the trial process. As a practical matter, this structure would allow conviction or acquittal to rest on such fortuitous circumstances as whether, when asked on direct examination if he saw a weapon in the hands of the robber, the witness in our hypothetical answered:

> — "Yes."
> — "Yes. Pointing at me."
> — "Yes. Pointing at my face."
> — "Yes. A big, silvery, automatic pointing at my face."

Much of cross-examination emphasizes points elicited in the direct examination (e.g., "Now, this gun was pointing at you?") and expands upon helpful points made during the direct (e.g., "You said on direct the gun was pointing at you. Where exactly was it pointing?"). If Professor Subin would not let me aid the "false defense" of mistaken identification by this type of cross-examination, then my client's chances for acquittal will vary with which of these responses happens to flow from the witness' mouth during direct examination on the day of trial.

Statements, however, do not just, "flow from" witnesses' mouths on direct examination. Witnesses are often coached regarding their testimony. That reality is at the core of my next point. If the content of the prosecution's direct examination limits the range of my ethical behavior, then my adversary controls my client's fate by deciding what to ask in the direct examination (e.g., "When I ask you in your direct examination about the gun, be certain you *do not* mention that it was directly pointed at you, and especially *do not* say it was pointed at your face."). Is this prosecutorial manipulation, in conjunction with the serendipity of answers proffered on the prosecution's direct examination, the basis for Professor Subin's ethical standards for criminal defense? If not, and if I may fully cross-examine in support of my "false defense" of misidentification, then it is difficult to see Professor Subin's point.

It is possible Subin was thinking about a situation where a defense attorney argues that the crime did not occur at all. For example, assume that when asked by the prosecution where he was going with a wallet full of money, the robbery victim's testimony is that he was going to get his wife a gift because she was angry at him for wasting his paycheck gambling the previous week. In closing, the defense argues an alternative explanation for the information the prosecution has presented, one based on the possibility that the victim had created the entire robbery story to cover up further gambling losses. While this would be a "false defense," there appears no real difference between a "false defense" that seeks acquittal by raising doubts that the defendant committed the crime (questioning identification evidence), which Professor Subin would seem to sanction, and one which raises doubts, as in this example, that the crime occurred at all. The former more closely tracks the prosecution's theory that there *was* a robbery, but this is a distinction of no apparent significance. In both examples, the defense counsel takes information in the

case and arranges it differently than the prosecution to present alternative "possibilities" which resonate with reasonable doubts. Both are equally "false" in Subin's sense. Once Subin allows the defense attorney to argue reasonable doubts in support of a "false" defense, the line between the permissible and the impermissible is blurred and is definable only in terms of the false dichotomy between evidence brought in by the prosecution and evidence elicited by the defense.

Another indication that Subin would not adhere to the "stark" definition of lawyer as monitor is that he would allow the defense to demonstrate the inaccuracy of information that may be harmful to its case. Imagine that the robbery victim in my hypothetical testifies that Bloogan's Department Store, directly across the street from where the nighttime robbery occurred, had all of its lights on at the time of the robbery. In fact, I find out in investigation that Bloogan's was closed for remodeling that evening. Subin would undoubtedly allow me to bring this out. What, after all, would a "truth" theory be if I were not permitted to confront "lies" and "misperceptions." If Professor Subin permits me to bring out this "inaccuracy" on cross-examination and/or through other witnesses, he must also allow me to use it in closing or my initial access to this information would be meaningless. In closing, my only real use for this information would be in support of my "false defense" of mistaken identification. The line between advocate and monitor is again blurred.

Another example of the unworkability of his distinction between advocate and monitor is reflected in the defense lawyer's use of inaccurate information brought out in the prosecution's case that is helpful to the defense. The victim of the robbery now testifies that the robbery took place at 10 p.m. My client has a strong alibi for 10 p.m. I "know," however, that the robbery actually took place at 10:30 p.m. May I put on my alibi in support of my "false defense," raising doubts that my client was the robber? Subin would say yes. In a similar set of circumstances Subin stated: "The state's proof of the time of the crime was incorrect, and therefore subject to impeachment." This, however, is not "impeachment." The probative value of the information is not being questioned. Quite the contrary, the incorrect information is being embraced as true. A prosecution witness has simply made a "mistake" and Professor Subin allows the defense attorney to take advantage of it, furthering a "false defense." Without some analysis tied to the rationales for the advocate-monitor distinction in the first place, the distinction seems to depend on ad hoc judgments. . . .

A. A Reevaluation of a Monitor's Role in Subin's Rape Case

To summarize, our monitor may bring in information and draw inferences which support "false defense" if the information or inferences fall within any one of six categories: (1) quality, (2) reliability, (3) mistakes in the prosecution's case, (4) adequacy, (5) inaccuracy, or (6) legitimate reasons to doubt. These broad, imprecise categories are not very confining for a profession which makes its living developing plausible positions for filing things into categories. It is instructive focusing on Subin's principal example, the rape case in which he "knows" his client is factually guilty, with these categories in mind.

In that case, two principal pieces of information emerged which were potentially helpful for the defense: 1) the victim stated that the defendant took her to his apartment; and 2) the victim was left alone for a time in a hallway after the rape but did not try to flee. Professor Subin recognized the significance of these and other miscellaneous pieces of information for the defense:

> I could emphasize the parts of her story that sounded the most curious, such as the defendant's solicitude in taking his victim back to his apartment, and her waiting for her watch when she could have gone immediately to the nearby precinct that she went to later. I could point to her inability to identify the gun she claimed was used (although it was the one actually used), that the allegedly stolen watch was never found, that there was no sign of physical violence, and no one heard screaming or any other signs of a struggle. I could also argue as my client had that even if he were reckless enough to rob and rape a woman across the street from his apartment, he would not be so foolish as to bring the victim there.

However, Subin is unclear as to what he would have done with this information. He claims he would have had no right to raise the "false defense" of consent. He would not have cross-examined the victim or put on defense witnesses. Instead, Subin would "limit my representation at that stage to putting forth the strongest argument I could that the facts presented by the state did not sustain its burden." Assuming sufficient information was elicited on the victim's direct examination to make the two helpful points above, what "strong argument" would defense counsel Subin make? Without using any of the information helpful to the defense, his argument could not have been other than: "Thank you, the prosecution has the burden."

Imagine instead he had taken the information and argued as follows:

> This just doesn't make sense. If he took her to his apartment, he'd have to know he'd be identified within hours. There's no evidence he blindfolded her or in any other way made an effort to conceal the identity and location of the apartment. And here she'd just been raped at gunpoint by a man who, for all she knew, might now kill her, and she was alone in the hallway, neighbors around, a staircase 10 feet away leading to the outside and safety. Yet her testimony is she just sat there and waited for the defendant. None of this makes sense, and the prosecution cannot carry its burden if the story it is presenting does not make sense.

Would this have been a "false defense" for Professor Subin? The argument raises "legitimate" doubts. The fact that the prosecution's underlying story does not make sense goes to the quality, reliability, and adequacy of the prosecution's case. Maybe the line would have been crossed if as defense counsel he had added:

> Who knows from this evidence what really happened? Maybe she consented and then felt guilty—afraid to acknowledge the truth to herself and her boyfriend. Who knows? All we know is that the story does not make sense.

Does even mentioning the possibility of consent really cross Subin's line between the ethical and unethical? One major shortcoming in Subin's presentation is his failure to illustrate what a monitor in this rape case *may* do. He tells us what he would do, but does not show us what his "monitor's" closing argument would really look like.

Subin has left us in a quandary. The "stark" definition of monitor may have been at odds with the nature of the criminal justice system and the Constitution, but at least it was consistent with an unmitigated desire for truth. This current wavering line between advocates and monitors, based as it is on permissible versus impermissible information and inferences, is somewhat more in step with the Constitution and the justice system, but hopelessly vague and uncertain.

B. Bigger Problems: Constitutional Concerns and Jeopardizing an Independent Defense Bar

If Professor Subin's approach is more than a statement of his own private ethics, the vagueness and uncertainty of the line which divides the advocate from the monitor presents a serious problem. First, constitutional concerns additional to those already expressed may arise. Criminal defense representation touches significant interests: 1) protection of the individual from the state; 2) the freedom of the defendant in a nation which values liberty; and 3) significant constitutional rights (fourth, fifth, sixth, eighth, and fourteenth amendments). It is within these areas that the impreciseness in Professor Subin's categories comes to the fore. To the extent defense attorneys are guided by ethical rules which are vague about what conduct is proper, the representation of the clients is hampered. Counsel, uncertain as to appropriate behavior, may fall into a "conflict" between pushing the client's interests as far as is legitimate and protecting himself against charges of unethical conduct. Attorneys' decisions may then tend to fall on the self-protective side, raising constitutional concerns regarding zealous representation.

Second, if Subin's approach were enforced as a rule of professional conduct, the independent defense bar would be seriously jeopardized. Professor Subin may or may not be correct that the public and the bar have a low view of the criminal defense bar. Nonetheless, the independence of that bar has provided all citizens with significant protection against government oppression.[11] With Professor Subin's approach, however, if an acquittal were gained by a defense attorney who was a thorn in the government's side, the prosecutor's office might be tempted to file an ethical complaint stating that defense counsel should have known he put on a "false defense." Subin's position now becomes a weapon of repression in the hands of the government. Even if vindication follows upon a disciplinary hearing, time, expense, and public humiliation might ensue. This will deliver a powerful message to defense attorneys. Don't risk fighting, plead your clients guilty.

IV. CONCLUSION

Discussions of "monitors," "advocates," and "false defenses," while interesting, are premature. If the legal profession is ever to develop meaningful guidelines for criminal and civil attorneys, the focus must be on certain basic premises. Specifically, we must consider: What is the relationship between our criminal and civil systems, and what is the implication of that relationship for those practicing in the two systems? Is the criminal justice system primarily a truth system? Is it primarily a screening system intended as a check on governmental power? It seems to me that here is where we must begin.

NOTES

1. Subin, *The Criminal Lawyer's "Different Mission": Reflections on the "Right" to Present a False Case*, 1 GEO. J. LEGAL ETHICS 125 (1987).
2. Subin, *supra* note 1, at 125.
3. For a very well-thought out recent discussion which generally takes the position that the defense attorney's knowledge of the client's guilt should have no bearing upon that attorney's representation, *see* Kaplan, *Defending Guilty People*, 7 U. BRIDGEPORT L. REV. 223 (1986).
4. Mitchell, *supra* note 3, at 300–01.
5. For an interesting discussion of various justifications for the truth-dysfunctional nature of the criminal trial which implicitly leads one to conclude that Professor Subin's quest for factual truth is the least of what is going on, *see* Goodpaster, *On the Theory of American Adversary Criminal Trials*, 78 J. CRIM. L. & CRIMINOLOGY 118 (1987).
6. Subin, *supra* note 1, at 127–29, 143. As the title presages, Professor Subin makes this concept of a "different mission" the metaphorical focus of his article.
7. Subin, *supra* note 1, at 143.
8. For a defense of the lawyer's position as an "amoral" actor on behalf of a client which does not rely on the adversary system rationale, *see* Pepper, *The Lawyer's Amoral Ethical Role: A Defense, A Problem, and Some Possibilities*, A.B.A. RESEARCH J. 613 (1986).
9. Mitchell, *supra* note 3, at 299–302.
10. *Id.* at 302–21.
11. They did after all defend strikers in the early labor movement, were present during the McCarthy hearings and the Smith Act prosecutions and defended those voicing objections to the government's policies in Vietnam. Most of us take comfort in thinking they will be there in the future. *Cf.* Babcock, *Defending the Guilty*, 32 CLEV. ST. L. REV. 175 (1983–84) (discussing reasons to defend a person one knows is guilty).

POSTSCRIPT
Should Lawyers Be Prohibited from Presenting a False Case?

During the last thirty years, the legal profession has experienced unprecedented changes. The most frequently publicized development of this period has been the great increase in the size of the profession. The United States now has more than seven hundred and fifty thousand lawyers, more than double the number in 1970.

In addition to larger numbers of lawyers, recent years have seen the following significant changes take place: (1) A decline in the number of lawyers practicing independently or in firms and an increase in the number of lawyers employed by corporations and institutions. As a result, "a profession that was 85 percent self-employed in 1948 and about 60 percent self-employed in 1980 soon may be more than half employees." (2) Elimination of some anti-competitive practices previously enjoyed by the profession, such as minimum fee schedules and restrictions on advertising. (3) Increase in the size of law firms. The largest firms now have hundreds of lawyers with offices in many states. (4) Increasing heterogeneity of the legal profession. Due to the recent growth of the bar, the profession is younger, with more women and minorities. There are more fields of specialization and types of practice.

Clearly, the legal profession is not as stable as it once was. The work that lawyers do and where and how they are doing it is changing. This may have an impact on the ethical standards of lawyers. One of the characteristics of a "profession" is that it sets its own standards. But what happens when, because of changes in the makeup of the profession, it becomes harder to do this? What happens when there is less and less agreement in the profession about what the standards should be? What happens when there are increasing challenges from outside the profession to the traditional standards?

For further insight into the role and nature of the legal profession and of legal ethics, see Elliston and van Schaick, *Legal Ethics: An Annotated Bibliography and Research Guide* (Fred Rothman, 1984); Richard Abel, *American Lawyers* (Oxford University Press, 1989); Magali S. Larson, *The Rise of Professionalism: A Sociological Analysis* (University of California Press, 1977); Hazard and Rhode, eds., *The Legal Profession: Responsibility and Regulation*, 2d ed. (The Foundation Press, 1988); Babcock, "Defending the Guilty," 32 *Cleveland State Law Review* 175 (1983). *Bates v. State Bar of Arizona*, 97 S.Ct. 2691 (1977) permitted lawyers to advertise. Recent cases involving the ethical practices of lawyers are *Shapero v. Kentucky Bar Association*, 108 S.Ct. 1916 (1988), allowing lawyers to use mailing lists to advertise their services to potential clients, and *Nix v. Whiteside*, 106 S.Ct. 988 (1986), which held that it was not a violation of the right to counsel for an attorney to threaten to resign if the client insisted on lying while testifying.

ISSUE 2

Is There a Litigation Crisis?

YES: Bayless Manning, from "Hyperlexis: Our National Disease," *North-western Law Review* (vol. 71, 1977)

NO: Marc Galanter, from "The Day After the Litigation Explosion," *Maryland Law Review* (vol. 3, 1986)

ISSUE SUMMARY

YES: Former Stanford Law School dean Bayless Manning contends that our society and our legal system are suffering from too great a reliance on law to settle disputes.
NO: Law professor Marc Galanter contends that court statistics do not support complaints about excessive litigation and that litigation provides some benefits to society.

> Jarndyce and Jarndyce drones on. This scarecrow of a suit has, in the course of time, become so complicated that no man alive knows what it means—innumerable children have been born into the case, innumerable old people have died out of it; whole families have inherited legendary hatreds with the suit—there are not three Jarndyces left upon the earth, perhaps since old Tom Jarndyce in despair blew his brains out at a coffee house in Chancery, but Jarndyce and Jarndyce still drags its dreary length before the court.
> —Charles Dickens, *Bleak House*

In his report on his travels in America in the 1830s, Alexis de Toqueville wrote that "scarcely any political question arises in the United States that is not resolved, sooner or later, into a judicial question." In the 1920s, Harvard law professors Felix Frankfurter and James Landis wrote that "to an extraordinary degree legal thinking dominates the United States. Every act of government, every treaty ratified by the Senate, every executive order issued by the President is tested by legal considerations and may be subjected to the hazards of litigation. Other nations, too, have a written Constitution. But no other country in the world leaves to the judiciary the powers which it exercises over us." More recently and more cynically, historian Jerold Auerbach has commented, "In the future, each American will receive a law degree at birth, followed immediately by a court calendar date for his or her inevitable appearance as a litigant." Clearly, as these statements indicate, we are a legalistic society and have a long tradition of using law and courts to settle disputes. When social problems are identified, the typical response is and has been "there ought to be a law."

Compared to other countries, even highly industrialized ones, we are extremely legalistic. Japan, for example, has a population of approximately one hundred and fifteen million people but only ten thousand lawyers. The United States has more than double the population of Japan but over *forty* times as many lawyers. During the past twenty years, there has also been a marked increase in the number of lawyers in this country. Whether a litigation crisis has occurred may be debatable, but there is no doubt that we have had an explosion of lawyers.

In the following articles, Bayless Manning, former dean of Stanford Law School, asserts that there is a legal and societal state of emergency caused by too many lawsuits and too much reliance on law to resolve problems. In reply, Professor Marc Galanter argues that increases in lawsuits have not occurred at an alarming rate and that fear over a law explosion is exaggerated.

What could be bad about going to court to settle a dispute? Judge Learned Hand once wrote that "I must say that, as a litigant, I should dread a lawsuit beyond almost anything else short of sickness and death." Jerold Auerbach has stated that "root canal work seems mild by comparison." This suggests, quite accurately, that the process of suing, regardless of the outcome, involves some pain. Frequently, in a lawsuit, the only winners are the lawyers, since the process itself generally heightens tension, promotes hostility, and makes the parties more angry at each other than they were initially. Yet, more important than the consequences for individuals are the societal implications. Lawsuits should be a last resort, something done when all other attempts to settle the problem have failed. If there is a litigation explosion, it would suggest that other institutions that have been relied upon in the past are no longer working very well. Large numbers of lawsuits involving families may imply that the family as an institution is weaker than it once was. If one found large numbers of lawsuits involving schools or religious institutions, one could make a similar argument about the deterioration of those institutions. Conflict exists in all societies, but it is desirable to have many different mechanisms and devices for resolving the conflict. If there has been rapid growth in the use of law, therefore, it would suggest that these other institutions, which may be more desirable forums for resolving the conflict, and which may involve less cost, both economic and emotional, are no longer functioning efficiently.

YES

Bayless Manning

HYPERLEXIS: OUR NATIONAL DISEASE

"Hyperlexis" sounds like some sort of serious disabling illness. It is. Hyperlexis is America's national disease—the pathological condition caused by an over-active law-making gland.

Measured by any and every index, our law is exploding. New statutes, regulations, and ordinances are increasing at geometric rates at all levels of government. The same is true of reported decisions by courts and administrative agencies. Whole new legal fields spring into being overnight, such as environmental law; older fields like real property are experiencing infinite fission. Statutory codes, such as those in the fields of commercial law and taxation, are become ever more particularistic, longer, more complex, and less comprehensible. We are drowning in law.

Our situation is aggravated by the wind of legal commentary set off by the firestorm of law. Law has always been one of the garrulous professions, and modern communications gadetry makes it all too easy to record, reproduce, and distribute legal words. As in the wake of a great ship mewing seagulls follow, so legal commentators pursue the society's law-making machines, squabbling over the newly emitted material. Our law libraries are swamped, our citizenry is confounded by the legal blizzard, and our imperilled forest reserves are further depleted.

INCAPACITATIONS

Granted that we are awash with law, is it cause for any serious concern? Is hyperlexis a critically disabling disease or merely a nuisance? The answer is that it has already done a great deal of harm to the American body politic, and if it continues, it will incapacitate us in a number of different ways.

First, though not first in importance, is simple dollar cost. What does it cost to operate our elaborate institutional machinery of federal, state, and local courts, prosecutors, bailiffs, investigators, administrative agencies, police, examiners, lawyers, law schools, legal aid programs, law publishers, correctional facilities, etc.? We have no data on the amount of national

From Bayless Manning, "Hyperlexis: Our National Disease," *Northwestern Law Review,* vol. 71 (1977). Copyright © 1977. Reprinted by special permission of Northwestern University, School of Law.

resources that are devoted to operating our growing corpus of law. That, in itself, is a significant fact, reflecting the simple truth that we have never thought it important to ask the question. But the dollar figures are obviously measured in the tens of billions of dollars annually. Are we getting our money's worth as a matter of national priorities?

Second, on every hand we are presented with the visible fact that our legal system is clogging and choking into paralysis. Everyone knows that enforcement of the law has sunk to a new low for this country. Judicial and administrative backlogs make it impossible to dispose of disputes and charges expeditiously. The criminal process is in a state of epilepsy. This condition is caused in part by overcriminalization, by laws that declare behavior to be illegal but are either unenforcable or cannot be enforced with existing institutional means and resources. The flood of petitions to the Supreme Court is so great that numerous proposals are afoot to narrow the inflow if its work. The Chief Justice of the United States Supreme Court urges Congress once more to increase the number of federal judges to deal with the rising caseload. The same pressures are at work within the states. Insufficiency of resources produces the disgraceful, but necessary, practice of plea bargaining. The inability of traditional procedures to deal with the flood of automobile accident claims has led to experiments with no-fault administrative solutions. Probate procedure is a farce of delay and paper shuffling. Law suits are interminable, and it is no new discovery that justice delayed is often not justice at all. All legal circuits are overloaded and all warning lights are red.

Third, when the processes of the law coagulate, legislatures are deprived of the opportunity to make real public policy choices. It makes little actual difference what law is enacted if it will not, or cannot, be enforced.

Fourth, public respect for the law, and attitudes toward voluntary compliance with the law, are clearly declining. Voluntary compliance sags and a scofflaw attitude is bred when the law is not enforced, or when its enforcement is diluted or erratic. Those who might have been deterred from criminal behavior by the prospect of punishment are not deterred when they observe that the law is seldom enforced in fact. In such an environment, those who are apprehended and punished feel themselves merely the victims of bad luck or discrimination, and not the objects of evenhanded justice. Proliferation of judges, police, examiners, auditors, inspectors, and other officials inevitably increases the risk—nay, the certainty—that some will be corrupt or corrupted and thereby still further degrade the law in the public's eyes. A legal system that is not respected by its people cannot be made to operate at all.

Fifth, when burgeoning law and scant resources make it impossible to enforce all laws against all offenders at once, then discretionary choices must be made by police, by prosecutors, and by bureaucratic officials. Increasingly in the United States, the choice as to what to enforce and against whom to enforce it is made by those persons. The exercise of that discretion is an explosive matter of the utmost delicacy. It will inevitably become a focal point for improper pressures and corruption. Improperly applied, it will lead to petty tyranny and intolerable discrimination against some citizens.

Sixth, the purpose of a large part of modern law is the elimination of unfair or unequal disparities among citizens. But hyperlexis works squarely against that objective. In a highly regulated environment of intricate restrictions, those best able to survive are those who are able to hire the new class of form-filling consultants—experts (mainly, but not exclusively, lawyers) who can invoke rules on behalf of their clients and pick their way among the bramble bushes. Such trained talent is rare and expensive; inevitably it will largely be commanded by those persons and organized groups that are best able to pay. Though everyone suffers from hyperlexis, the small are injured more than the great.

Seventh, a point of special interest to lawyers, hyperlexis has undermined the function of precedent and *stare decisis* on which the continuity of the common law was based. The lower courts today still try to follow the mandate of the highest court in their jurisdiction. But in many fields of the law the sheer proliferation of legal variants in thousands of published judicial decisions makes it impossible in all but the most gargantuan litigation for the lawyers or the judges to review the relevant earlier cases. As a result, the lawyers and the court can only pick and choose from the relevant precedential material—a radical departure from the intellectual premises of classical Anglo-American jurisprudence. Foreseeability is a critical element in public confidence in the law. Hyperlexis is helping to undermine that foreseeability and that confidence.

Eighth, the key to the unparalleled success of the economic system of the United States lies in its flexibility, its ability to respond quickly. Increasingly heavy regulation of economic activities is load-ing increasingly heavy cost burdens on businesses and consumers. More serious than cost, the increased regulation and new requirements for prior clearances at all levels of government are hobbling the capacity of the economy to make necessary decisions rapidly. And it is not just private enterprise that finds itself regulated into slow motion. Governmental agencies also find themselves immobilized by their own regulations and stymied by those of other agencies.

Ninth, courts and legislatures have combined to produce a judicial process in which almost any proceeding will have some fatal technical defect, and almost any project undertaken can be blocked. Multiple appeals, collateral attack, procedural challenges, dilution of requirements of standing and the like are the hallmarks of our era. That every man should have his day in court is classical. But until now it has not been thought that every man should have 100 days in court, or that he should have a day in court on every social and political issue in the society. Proliferation of regulatory requirements and prerequisite clearances, dramatic increases in the circle of potential legal complainants and interminability of judicial proceedings are together making it increasingly difficult for the society to respond to the very social problems to which most of our regulation is addressed. The principle of "one person, one vote" threatens to become perverted to a principle of "one person, one veto." No society can operate on that basis.

* * *

Hyperlexis is not a nuisance. It is a heartworm that has a literally fatal potential for the body politic of this country.

DIAGNOSIS

If hyperlexis is such a pernicious thing, why do we not, in true-blue American style, get about the job of fixing it? One reason is that we are just now at the first stage of identifying the disease and of realizing that we have it. But the second and more important reason lies in Pogo's immortal words—"We have met the enemy and he is us."

A fair amount of talk is to be heard these days in many and diverse circles about the need to get rid of "overregulation." Most of this talk assumes, or implies, that "overregulation" is a unitary thing, that it is the nefarious product of ambitious bureaucrats or crypto-socialists, and that it can be cured by a few bold surgical strokes of deregulation. The facts are quite otherwise. Regrettably, hyperlexis is a subtle illness; its forms are many and its causes are multiple. Behind the superficial term "overregulation" a number of different phenomena and forces are at work, most of them deeply rooted in American society and American attitudes.

THE FEDERAL SYSTEM

Part of the hyperlexis problem arises out of our layered federal system, the most complex governmental operation in the world. We maintain thousands of law-making instrumentalities, each of which merrily generates law on its own with little or no regard to the others. The tiers of government have become far more than the traditional triad of federal-state-local, as counties, districts and varieties of regional authorities and functional commissions have emerged as law generators in recent years. Moreover, the interface between federal programs and the administrative structures of state and local governments is a jumble of non-connections and misconnections. Uncoordinated multi-layered regulations, licensing, and supervision have the capacity to bog down the workings of the entire society. . . .

USES OF THE LAW
AND
THE JUDICIARY

Critics of President Johnson's Great Society described its basic principle as follows: "Identify a problem, then throw money at it." But our true and peculiarly American governing principle, old enough and visible enough to have been noticed by de Tocqueville, is: "Identify a problem, then throw law at it." Despite repeated disappointments, it continues to be almost universally accepted by Americans that legal resort is the most effective way to solve any problem.

Similarly, it has always been a peculiarity of Americans to turn to their courts for resolution of difficult problems. The special role of the Supreme Court as ultimate arbiter of constitutionality enhances that impulse, but the people's faith and reliance in its judges runs both wider and deeper than that. Whether in matters of civil rights, town planning, the economics of the marketplace, or labor-management relations, to name but four, the judiciary will play a key, and often determining, role in the United States. The inevitable result is that we are the most litigious people in the world. We go to great lengths to find ways to cast any and every problem into the familiar pattern of a two-party adversary trial and take it to court.

INTEREST GROUP REPRESENTATION

Our political system for decision making is fundamentally built upon coalitions and trade-offs among elected representatives of interest groups. Though each of us may say that he wants less law and less regulation, that fact is that every economic, ethnic, religious, or ideological group in the society wants something supported, regulated, or banned by the law. Every interest group does its best to capture the legislative, administrative, and judicial system and harness it to its particular ideas of the good, the true and the profitable. Coalition voting patterns in our legislatures guarantee that those efforts will often succeed, and that every year there will be a bumper crop of new laws.

ELECTED OFFICIALS AND SCOREKEEPING

For elected officials, the most obvious route to reelection, and perhaps even to immortality, lies in new legislation. Who would recall Senator Sherman or Congressman Mann were it not for their Acts? As batting averages are to baseball players, stars to restaurants, ribbons to generals, and stock prices to corporate executives—so new statutes are at the heart of the scorekeeping system by which legislators are measured and measure themselves. No legislator gains recognition as a great nonlaw giver or as the Great Repealer.

PARTICULARIZATION

The national commitment to deal with the individual as an individual, to treat each case on its special merits, combines with our political system of interest group representation to produce law that is often highly particularistic. Every group and subgroup seeks to obtain, and often obtains, special statutory provisions expressly aimed at its own particular circumstances. The result is an impenetrable legal jungle of special provisions. A significant part of the hyperlexis problem arises from the effort to deal with problems with too great particularity. Contrary to surface impression, detailed specificity in a legal provision does not reduce disputes; particularization merely changes the vocabulary of the dispute. The most detailed statutes, like the Internal Revenue Code, are the ones that proliferate most rapidly and generate both the greatest need for administration and the most disputes.

TECHNOLOGICAL AND SOCIAL CHANGE

The rate of change in the modern world has no precedent. That fact, too, is a contributor to the law explosion. Technological change often demands new public agencies and programs. The birth of the Atomic Energy Commission and its recent transmutations toward a Department of Energy are illustrative. Major technological change also inevitably brings social dislocations in its aftermath. Increasingly, it is coming to be recognized that the losses from such dislocations should not all have to be absorbed by those industries, workers, communities and institutions that happened to be hit by the change. The implication of that statement is, once more, an expanded function for the legal administrative process in order to distribute the loss. Analogously, major social change such as black migration from the South, tends to lead to wider governmental activity, particularly at the federal level.

BUREAUCRACY

As spiders by their nature utter cobwebs and spawn more spiders, administrative agencies by their nature utter regulations and spawn more administrative agencies. Administrative agencies and programs are remarkably hardy, capable of surviving virtually any effort to uproot or cut them off. Growth in legal activity would not be so difficult to accommodate if old agencies died off as new ones appeared. Alas, the process does not work that way. Old laws and old agencies neither die nor fade away; being non-biodegradable they only accumulate.

NO BRAKES

Finally, a negative point is worth noting. As our legislative and administrative system operates, there are no internal forces at work that tend to counter the process of law generating, to act as inhibitors or governors. Externally the same is true since many interest groups work increasingly to add, amend or delete particular laws but there is no major interest group that focuses attention on the health of our legal order as a whole.

* * *

It is no wonder that the lawmaking engines of the United States grind out legal prescriptions like the fairy-tale salt mill at the bottom of the sea—unremittingly and in ever greater volume. Many powerful forces push in that direction, and no significant forces resist.

THERAPIES AND MITIGANTS

Can we do anything to check the advance of the nation's hyperlexis? A glance at the roster of root causes just listed will make it clear that most of them are congenital to our society and government. They arise straight out of the essence of the American experiment itself. They cannot, and should not, be made to go away. Our search therefore must be for helpful therapies and mitigants, not true remedies. In that direction, quite a lot can in fact be done if we will do it.

PUBLIC EDUCATION

Highest on the list of therapies is public education, with the term "public" referring not only to the populace at large but also to legislators, administrative officials and judges at every level of government. That educational effort should stress five propositions that are true of any legal system—five truths that today we either do not recognize or willfully brush aside.

Proposition 1: To declare a law is very cheap; to administer or enforce a law is very expensive.

As there is no such thing as a free lunch, so there is no such thing as a free law. To achieve even modest effects through law requires huge investments in institutional machinery. It is an ineluctable fact of life that every new chore we assign to our legal system must either be accompanied by a commensurate investment of additional resources into the legal institutional system, or the new legal initiative will merely dilute or displace institutional energies away from other tasks that have been assigned to the system.

We have finally begun to learn that the world's natural resources are finite and increasingly expensive. We will eventually have to learn that our legal system is also a limited resource. With a limited resource one must inevitably make choices and establish priorities among objectives.

Proposition 2: The secondary costs of a law are often greater than the direct costs.

Apart from the obvious direct costs for enforcement machinery, legal regulation often entails other hidden costs that are very large. It is not my point here, though it is true, that the substantive objective of a legal program often demands costly trade-offs as where, for example, pollution abatement may reduce productivity and increase unemployment and price levels. The costs to which I refer here are hidden, private administrative costs that are almost never recognized or considered.

How many millions of citizen-hours per year are poured into the preparation of federal, state and local income taxes—hours that could have gone into productive activity or into leisure time pursuits even more enjoyable than tax computation? What is the total national economic expenditure currently required of all employers and employing agencies to complete and file reports on securities issues, retirement plans, health conditions, taxes, safety, pollution, affirmative action programs and the like?

If we stay on our present course, a caricature of tomorrow's American society will be a six-person model—a regulator (and his lawyer), one who is regulated (and his lawyer) and an adjudicator (and his administrative assistant) which resolves disputes between regulator and regulatee. Without counting review mechanisms, that makes five persons engaged somewhere in the process of regulating the sixth, with four of them on the public payroll. Not even the bureaucracy of imperial China reached that height of civilization.

Ancient Mediterranean societies found it necessary to develop a paid professional class of temple votaries who assisted the citizenry in the complexities of their prayers and ritual sacrifices to keep on good terms with their deities. Modern America is generating a new class of form-filling specialists (many of them lawyers) to help the citizenry keep on good terms with their regulators. Every new statute or regulation adds to the number of the new class and increases the demand for their services. Members of the new class are intelligent and energetic, and their training represents a very large social investment. Are the costly skills of these professionals today being utilized to maximum constructive social advantage? What is the annual aggregate of their fees, and who really pays it?

The direct costs for legal administration and enforcement of our laws are only the tip of the iceberg of the true costs of a highly administered society.

Proposition 3: The capacity of law to change human behavior is limited.

To be effective, any law must rely upon a base of supporting public opinion and voluntary compliance. Even when those supports are assured as they are in the case of laws against violent crime, the actual effects of the law as written are always marginal. Where public opinion is indifferent and voluntary compliance spotty, the effects of law will be minimal, regardless of investment in enforcement. . . .

Proposition 4: Even where a law may effectively achieve its primary purpose, the side effects may be too great and too negative to warrant its adoption.

As in physics, Newton's third law of motion governs, so in a society every legal action produces its own reactions; those side effects are frequently both major and undesirable.

Tariffs and import prohibitions produce smugglers; harsh criminal laws generate plea bargaining; all-out enforcement campaigns threaten civil rights; extension of remedies and procedural nicety lead to judicial clog; protecting consumers by subjecting third-party financers to the seller's warranty constricts consumer credit and increases its cost; the most nobly inspired regulation breeds ignoble bureaucracy; minimum wage legislation contributes to unemployment; open-ended governmental medical assistance leads to inflation of medical costs and fraud; protective regulation for employees' retirement plans produces a decline in the number of such plans; high malpractice awards lead to soaring insurance rates, reductions in service, and increases in medical fees, etc., *ad infinitum.*

Law's benefits are not only limited; its by-products are often affirmatively damaging.

Proposition 5: Many problems are not amenable to legal solution at all.

Legal fiat cannot create resources; it cannot repeal economics; and it cannot supplant psychological causes of human behavior. Law is a useful tool; it is not an all-purpose tool.

We Americans act as though regulatory law were an all-purpose instrument,

free of negative side effects, and a free good. We must come to understand that regulatory law is in fact of limited utility, accompanied by significant and frequently harmful side effects, and expensive. A great deal of public education will be required to bring about that change. . . .

DECRIMINALIZATION

Virtually all students of the subject, and many criminal enforcement officials, now recognize that action should be taken to reduce the mass of criminal law now on the books. As the situation now stands, decriminalization takes place anyway, but it is done through police nonenforcement rather than by proper legislative act.

In a world of pure analytics and theory, the criminal law is recognized as overlapping with, but entirely separate from, moral prescriptions. There may be good reasons to make price fixing a criminal offense while the pulpits never mention it; religious leaders may inveigh against worshipping idols while the criminal law is silent on the subject. Ideally, too, since enforcement of the criminal law should be strict, certain and swift, in order to maximize its deterrent effect, the criminal law system should not be asked to do more than can be effectively and swiftly enforced.

In real life, however, the situation is very different. Most Americans do not distinguish between moral prescriptions and legal mandates. It is a striking characteristic of American history and attitudes that we have persisted in the idea that, though church and state are separate, the engines of the state should be invoked to punish all behavior that we find morally objectionable. As a result, our criminal codes are full of mandates about personal behavior that are unenforced but unrepealable; no legislator can safely vote to make activities legal that profoundly offend the moral and social sense of his constituents. As a result, decriminalization is very difficult.

Can nothing, then, be done? One thought would be for legislatures to embark upon a serious program of public hearings and review of local criminal laws specifically focused on three questions: Which criminal laws are not being enforced and why? What resources would be required to enforce them all? What priorities should be followed by enforcement officials if they are forced to give up enforcing some laws in order to apply resources to the enforcement of others?

The results of such an undertaking would be very constructive. The public, and the legislature, would have to confront the problem squarely and honestly. Pressures for still more criminal laws might be headed off. A few criminal statutes might actually be repealed. The public would learn something of the costs of increasing criminalization, and the low return. And out of the process, some sense of legislative priorities might emerge formally or informally, and thereby provide a more legitimate basis for selective nonenforcement than now exists. . . .

INSTITUTIONAL
CHANGE IN
THE LEGAL SYSTEM

Hyperlexis compounds, and is compounded by, other difficulties that beset our system of justice and dispute the resolution today. Those difficulties mainly arise from structural defects, from uninventiveness and inertia in the face of social change, from institutional anachronisms, from inattention to elementary principles of administration, and from the effort to misapply traditional processes to modern problems. We shall have to deal with those conditions as well as hyperlexis itself, and indications are that major changes are coming soon in our system of justice.

As the courts clog, mediation and arbitration are coming into their own as dispute-settling mechanisms. No-fault is nearly here in the automobile field. Simplified small claims court procedures available on a neighborhood basis are desperately needed and are coming. Paralegal personnel will become a useful resort to the average citizen. The docket of the Supreme Court will in some way be curtailed. Today's probate procedures will be superseded by simpler ones for most estates. The jury system will be made less expensive, in some circumstances through smaller juries, and we will eventually curtail its automatic availability. The extremes of proceduralism have been reached and the pendulum will swing toward limiting and eliminating appeals, speeding up the disposition of litigation by rigorous methods, narrowing the avenues for collateral attack, imposing order on class suits, and recognizing that issues of less moment do not demand the elaborate procedural safeguards that are appropriate for issues of greater moment.

More new ideas of this kind are needed to expedite the functioning of the system and increase its accessibility to the average citizen. Happily, most of the organized bar has come to see the desirability and inevitability of these developments and is today playing a responsible role in adapting traditional ways to new conditions.

THE LIMITS OF THE LEGAL SANCTION

Our legislatures, courts and agencies must eventually recognize, and the public must come to see, that the legal system simply cannot operate if it tries to provide for every citizen and institution a law suit against every other citizen and institution to resolve every difference of view or interest, to redress every perceived invasion of privilege, and to recompense every risk of living. The ultimate results of that approach will be to halt the legal process and simultaneously frustrate the society's capacity to make policy decisions. However unpalatable and unpopular it may be to say it in today's climate, the American legal system must continue to concentrate upon the rights of the individual, but it must now also turn its attention to the collective need of the community for a governmental and legal system that functions with reasonable effectiveness. The alternative will be a massive sociolegal traffic jam. In a legal system that tries to offer everybody a remedy for everything, no one will have a remedy for anything. . . .

CONCLUDING COMMENTS

The thesis of this article is easily susceptible to misunderstanding, not to say vulgarization. It should not be confused with standard conservative American political oratory decrying governmental programs and opposing social reform. The government will, and in my view must, often intervene in the social process through regulation and law. Many governmental programs in operation today are essential in a decent society, and more are imperative in the near future, particularly programs addressed to our cities and the problems impacted within them. The thesis argued here is a clinical one—a matter of cost/benefit analytics. As new programs are proposed, it must come to be recognized, as it is not today, that the cost of more regulation and law making are great and grow geometrically— and the payoffs decline correspondingly— as the nation's legal institutional circuitry becomes increasingly overloaded.

We all want our idea of the good to be done, and we all want everyone to receive justice. But law is not a free good. If we were willing to devote a large percentage of our GNP to an expanded system of dispute resolution, and another large percentage to enforcement of legal compliance, we probably could for a time make the present system work despite our overactive law-making gland. So far, however, we have not been willing to commit those resources. For the future, if we continue to generate new law at the rate we are going, no amount of resources will be sufficient to administer them effectively. Unless we change our ways along the lines indicated here, the inevitable result will be a gradual winding down of our legal system and a corresponding decline in the effectiveness of our law and of its standing in the public eye.

One should have no illusions that the democratic law-making process can be made, or should be made, a model of efficiency. Its democratic character is worth far more than cost/benefit elegance. It is inevitable that legislators and other public officials will sometimes use law making for moral posturing. If a bill is proposed to declare sin illegal, very few legislators can be expected to vote against it on the ground that it will not be effective, will be expensive to try to enforce, and will dilute the efficacy of the rest of the legal system—even though all that is true. Nonetheless, we can do quite a lot to build into the lawmaking machine a series of governors or brakes to inhibit our presently unrestrained law-generating process.

For the first time in the nation's history, today's public is politically receptive to understanding and responding to that need. We appear to have learned something from the inattention of Great Society programs to problems of implementation. Governmental effectiveness has, at last, begun to take hold as a political issue among the public at large.

Clearly audible in today's political sound backdrop is also a complaint by everybody—employer, worker, welfare recipient, real estate operator, government official, university administrator, policeman, doctor, lawyer—about the amount of legal paperwork they are required to do and the legal entanglements that encircle them. After a generation in which the most rapidly growing sector of the economy has been state and local government, all of a sudden a large segment of public opinion has begun to press for smaller government, not larger. The 1976 presidential candidates heard and reflected the same ground swell.

These public reactions are a direct product of hyperlexis—public reaction to a degree of legal pollution that is greater than the atmosphere can carry. We have now the political opportunity to get to work on the problem. If we let that opportunity slide by, hyperlexis will slowly but steadily drag our whole legal system to the ground and we shall have dissipated one of our most priceless national treasures: the confidence of the people in, and their voluntary compliance with, the law.

NO

Marc Galanter

THE DAY AFTER
THE LITIGATION EXPLOSION

Few Americans in the early months of 1986 could disagree with the observation of Senator McConnell that:

> Hardly a day goes by that we do not hear or read of the dramatic increase in the number of lawsuits filed, of the latest multimillion dollar verdict, or of another small business, child care center, or municipal corporation that has had its insurance cancelled out from under it.

The reason for higher insurance rates and crowded courthouses, he continued, is "quite simply, everyone is suing everyone, and most are getting big money." Americans have developed a "mad romance . . .with the civil litigation process." Two days later, introducing the Litigation Abuse Reform Act of 1986, he noted that "we are all suffering a progressively debilitating disease—the disease of hyperlexis, too much litigation."

This diagnosis is widely shared. Columnist Jack Anderson tells us that:

> Across the country, people are suing one another with abandon; courts are clogged with litigation; lawyers are burdening the populace with legal bills. . . .
> This massive, mushrooming litigation has caused horrendous ruptures and dislocations at a flabbergasting cost to the nation.

USA Today reports that:

> Everybody in the USA suddenly seems to want to sue anybody with liability insurance coverage. The explosion of litigation has choked court dockets. And too-few lawyers tell potential clients that some cases are a waste of time. . . .
> The greed has turned the temple of justice, long a hallowed place, into a pigsty. The time has come to clean it up.

The Aetna insurance company tells us that "America's civil liability system has gone berserk. . . . [It] is no longer fair. It's no longer efficient. And it's no longer predictable." The Chairman of the Board of the National Association of Manufacturers provides a vivid account of the crisis:

From Marc Galanter, "The Day After the Litigation Explosion," *Maryland Law Review,* vol. 46 (1986). Copyright © 1986. Reprinted by permission.

Like a plague of locusts, U.S. lawyers with their clients have descended upon America and are suing the country out of business. *Literally.* The number of product liability suits and the size of jury awards are soaring. Filings of personal injury cases in federal courts have jumped 600% in the past decade. Product liability suits filed in federal courts doubled from 1978 to 1985.

In 1974, the average product liability jury award was $345,000. Last year it averaged more than $1 million. . . .

Product liability suits have brought a blood bath for U.S. businesses and are distorting our traditional values. We're now the most litigious country on earth—one of every fifteen Americans filed a private civil suit last year. The judicial system is so clogged with cases, delays, continuances, appeals and legal shenanigans that it's slugging its way through a perpetual traffic jam.

These are only a few voices in a mounting chorus of condemnation and concern about litigious America. For almost a decade now, there has been increasing concern about the excessive legalization of American society. Many observers are convinced that America has suffered a hypertrophy of its legal institutions—manifested in the presence of too much law, too many lawyers, excessive expenditure on legal services, too much litigation, an obsessively contentious population enthralled with adversary combat, and an intrusive activist judiciary—and a concomitant erosion of community, decline of self-reliance, and atrophy of informal self-regulatory mechanisms. . . .

I would like to examine several aspects of the current discourse about litigation: the assumption that Americans are excessively litigious; the belief that this is displayed in skyrocketing court case-loads; and the tendency to see the costs but not the benefits of litigation.

I. THE MEANING OF HIGHER CASELOADS

The core observation that supports the "litigation explosion" or "hyperlexis" reading of contemporary American life is that there is more litigation—that is, that more cases are filed in American courts. Let me begin with some reflections on the meaning of this higher level of bringing cases.

Per capita rates of filing civil cases have risen in most localities during recent decades. Before these increases are taken as proof of runaway litigiousness, it should be noted that these rates are not historically unprecedented. Several studies document higher per capita rates of civil litigation in nineteenth and early twentieth century America, as well as in colonial times.

More than 98% of all civil cases are filed in the state courts. Hence, any major rise in the propensity to litigate should be detectable by inspecting case-load trends in the state courts. But until recently, comprehensive and reliable data on state court caseload trends have simply been unavailable. Through the efforts of the National Center for State Courts (NCSC), we have recently acquired the best data yet on state caseload trends, covering a number of states for the years 1978 to 1984. The litigation explosion view would lead us to expect this to be a period of steeply rising caseloads. But the NCSC data, . . . based on all courts that reported comparable data for the years 1978, 1981, and 1984, portrays nothing that resembles the assumed explosion. Filings of civil cases surged faster than population from 1978 to 1981, but from 1981 to 1984, when litigation explosion lore would lead us to expect an intensification of litigiousness, per capita rates of filing actually declined. During this period, filings in small claims courts—the courts most readily accessible to ordinary Americans—also fell. Tort filings rose steadily, but over the six-year period they grew by 9% while population grew by 8%. In the 1981-1984 period, in only five of seventeen courts for which there was tort data did filings increase significantly more than the population, while in eight of these courts, tort filings actually decreased.

This evidence of current American litigation rates does not suggest that rates of civil court filings are dramatically higher than in the recent past. Nor is it the case that American rates are unmatched in other industrial countries. Although many countries have much lower rates of litigation, per capita use of the courts appears to be in the same range as in America in Canada, Australia, New Zealand, England, Denmark, and Israel. . . .

The notion that Americans have an unappeasable appetite to pursue legal remedies runs counter to many stable features of our legal life. If there were a generalized litigation fever, loosening the restraints that inhibit the making of claims, we would expect to find that the increase was general—that the rate for all types of cases moved in the same direction. But as we see, some kinds of cases are increasing while others are decreasing. The world of litigation is composed of sub-populations of cases that seem to respond to specific conditions rather than to global changes in climate.

The rate of settlements remains high. The great majority of civil cases are settled. The portion of cases that run the whole course of possible contest has continued a long historical decline. In the federal courts, cases reaching trial have fallen from 15.2% of terminations in 1940 to 5.0% of terminations in 1985. In state courts, too, a smaller portion of cases is decided by full contest than in past.

Wary of risks, delays, and costs, litigants do not act as if propelled by an unappeasable appetite for contest or public vindication. For plaintiffs and defendants alike, litigation proves a miserable, disruptive, painful experience. Few litigants have a good time or bask in the esteem of their fellows[1]—indeed, they may be stigmatized.[2] Even those who prevail may find the process very costly.[3] (Which is not, of course, to say that litigants are necessarily worse off than if they hadn't litigated.[4])

A humble example will show the mythic character of the litigation mania. The greatest single source of the bulge in filings is the increase in divorce (and post-divorce) proceedings. "[D]omestic relations cases dominate state court dockets." All of us know many of the parties in these cases. Few of us, I suspect, know many people who filed for divorce because they were enamored of litigation or beguiled by lawyers. What attracts users is not, I think, the desire to use the legal system but the hope for a solution to what they consider an otherwise intractable problem.

For other groups of law users, too, using the courts appears the best of unpleasant alternatives. In a study of disputing in three neighborhoods of a New England city, Sally Merry and Susan Silbey conclude that their respondents:

seek to avoid court for a variety of reasons from fear of antagonizing the people they live with every day to the loss of control that court entails. When people do bring interpersonal disputes to court, they tend to be complex, intense, and involuted problems in which the moral values at stake appear sufficiently important to outweigh the condemnation of this behavior.

[F]or all respondents, turning to court and police with problems is a last resort to be used only if "the problems are very serious," "it can't be avoided," "it is absolutely necessary," and "you have tried everything else." . . .

II. THE CHANGING WORKLOAD OF THE FEDERAL COURTS

Although only a small fraction of all American litigation takes place in the federal courts, I would like to examine recent trends in the caseload and disposition patterns of the federal courts. The reason for focusing on the federal courts is fourfold. First, information about these courts is more comprehensive and continuous than for the state courts. Second, figures on federal courts are frequently cited as the proof of runaway litigiousness. Third, the recent elevation of filings in the federal courts has been more dramatic than in the state courts.[5] Thus, if there are portents of doom in the court statistics they ought to be discernible there. Finally, federal court litigation involves higher status actors and is more visible to and through the media. Hence, it occupies a portion of our public symbolic space far larger than its share of the caseload. . . .

[L]et us examine the available information on federal court caseloads for 1984, taking 1975 as a convenient baseline. Table 1[6] (see next page), which summarizes some of the data found in these reports, shows a striking 123% increase in filings over that nine-year span.

Do these figures manifest a generalized increase in the litigiousness of the American population, a lowering of public thresholds of legal irritability? Do they evidence the "increasing tendency of Americans to define all distresses, anxieties and wounds as legal problems. . . . [W]here Americans were once willing to withstand setbacks, they now turn to the courts for relief whenever things work out badly.

If we break down the overall increase we notice that the increase in filings over the nine years is heavily concentrated in a few areas. Indeed, five categories of cases—recovery of overpayments,[7] social security cases, prisoner petitions, torts, and civil rights cases—account for almost three-quarters of the entire increase in filings.

Half of the total increase is accounted for by two giant increases—recovery cases and social security cases. Each is the result of deliberate and calculated official policy—to recover overpayments of veterans' benefits by litigation and to curtail disability benefits by summarily removing beneficiaries from the rolls. Is the 413% increase in social security cases to be understood as an outbreak of litigiousness among social security claimants? Does it make sense to take the 6,683% increase in recovery cases as evidence of an outbreak of litigiousness among federal officials? Like social security recipients whose disability payments were terminated, federal officials were confronted with a problem and turned to the courts to solve it because nothing better was at hand.

But how about cases that reflect individual initiative rather than tracking the contours of changing executive policy—do these reflect an increase in litigiousness? Consider prisoner petitions: in our

Table 1

Filings In Selected Categories, 1975 and 1984

Category	1975	1984	% Change	Increase [Decrease]	Fraction of Absolute Increase '75–'84	Source: Annual Report at Page:
Total Filings	117,320	261,485	112.9%	144,165	100%	1984: 124
1. Prisoner Petitions	19,307	31,107	61.1%	11,800	8.2%	1984: 143
A. State	14,260	26,581	86.4%	12,321	8.5%	"
B. Federal	5,047	4,526	– 10.3%	[–521]		"
2. Recovery of Overpayment and Enforcement of Judgments	681	46,190	6682.7%	45,509	31.6%	1984: 135
3. Civil Rights	10,392	21,219	104.2%	10,827	7.5%	1984: 145
A. Public Accommodation	601	291	– 51.6%	[–310]		"
B. Employment Discrimination	3,931	9,748	148.0%	5,817	4.0%	"
4. Social Security	5,846	29,985	412.9%	24,139	16.7%	1984: 138 (1975: 226)
A. Black Lung	2,793	59	– 97.9%	[–2,734]		(1975: 228)
5. Torts	25,691	37,522	46.0%	11,831	8.2%	1984: 133 (1975: 194)
A. Products Liability	2,886*	10,745**	272.3%	7,859	5.4%	1984: 148 (1975: 218)
TOTAL OF FIVE "GAINERS" (1A, 2, 3, 4, 5)				104,627	72.5%	
SOME "LOSERS"						
6. Anti-Trust	1,467	1,201	– 18.3%	[–226]		1984: 151
7. Fraud, including truth-in-lending	2,237	1,842	– 17.6%	[–395]		1985: 280
8. Class Actions	3,061	988	– 67.7%	[–2073]		1984: 160

* includes 278 contracts cases
** includes 619 contracts cases

nine-year period, there was a 61% increase in prisoner petitions. During this period, the prison population of the United States grew by 74%. The number of petitions per 1,000 prisoners actually dropped from 73.4 per 1,000 in 1975 to 67.1 per 1,000 in 1984.[8] Whatever the explanation for these trends, it seems more likely to reflect responses to specific settings than the rise or fall of an appetite for litigious contest or a proclivity to define issues as legal wrongs.

The increase in civil rights cases displays a somewhat different pattern. If we can assume that the period from 1975 to 1984 is one in which discrimination was declining in many areas of American life, is not the increase in civil rights cases evidence of increasing litigiousness? Disputing about discrimination has a very distinct profile compared to disputing about other matters. The lowering of barriers multiplies potential instances of violation—for example, once members of a minority are hired, there is a vast increase in the opportunities for experiencing discrimination on the job. In discrimination grievances, there is a pronounced appetite for vindication of principle. One suggestive study reported that in contrast to other kinds of problems, in which most respondents sought "satisfactory adjustment," a strikingly high proportion of those experiencing discrimination problems sought "justice."[9] Yet those with discrimination grievances are inclined to "lump it." The Civil Litigation Research Project found that far fewer discrimination grievances were translated into claims than was the case with other kinds of grievances. In all types of middle range disputes combined, 1,000 grievances led to 718 claims, but in discrimination matters, 1,000 grievances produced only 294 claims.

Where discrimination claims were made, a high proportion ended up as disputes. But a relatively low proportion of these disputes was taken to a lawyer and a low proportion of these resulted in court filings. Overall 1,000 grievances led to 50 court filings, but in discrimination matters, 1,000 grievances led to only 8 court filings. Pursuing a discrimination complaint is an extremely painful process, exposing the claimant to social discreditation and self-doubt. Thus, discrimination is an area where a great appetite for vindication coexists with formidable obstacles to making and pursuing such claims, leaving a great pool of grievances that could become cases if those obstacles were dissipated. The increase in civil rights cases suggests that the pursuit of these claims is being successfully institutionalized.

This does not mean we should expect a continuous exponential growth of discrimination cases, for practices are changing, too, in the direction of the anti-discrimination norms embodied in the law. As nondiscrimination norms are institutionalized, disputing about discrimination may become more "normal," leading to levels of disputing similar to those in other areas.

In one kind of civil rights cases, we see a marked decrease in filings—public accommodations cases fell by 51% during our nine-year period. There were declines in other categories of cases, including several that represent major expenditures of resources for the courts. Antitrust cases declined by 16%. Fraud and truth-in-lending cases fell by 18%. Class actions, often viewed as an engine of legal aggression against business, fell by 68% from 3,061 in 1975 to 988 in 1984 (that is, from 2.6% of filings to 0.4%). And within the burgeoning social security areas, black lung cases fell by 98% from their 1975 level. A particular group of victims worked their way through the system—as asbestos victims are doing now.

Finally, we come to the area that has excited the most concern in recent debate about the litigation crisis—torts. Unlike these other categories, which have loomed large in federal courts only in recent years, torts have always rmade up a substantial portion of the cases entering federal courts. The influx of other business has in the past generation sharply reduced the percentage of tort cases. In 1960, 36.2% of all civil filings were tort cases. But due to increases in other categories, only 14.3% of federal court filings in 1984 were tort cases.

In our nine-year period, the number of tort filings increased from 25,691 in 1975 to 37,552 in 1984. Of this increase of 11,831, almost two-thirds (7,859) was contributed by an increase in products liability cases.[10] Products liability filings increased by 272% during this period, while the remainder of the tort category increased by a modest 17%. So it seems that within the tort category we have touched the fiery heart of the litigation explosion—a junction of rapidly mounting caseloads, expanding frontiers of liability and skyrocketing recoveries. To demonstrate "Burgeoning Tort Liability as a Major Cause of the Insurance Availability/Affordability Crisis," the Attorney General's Tort Policy Working Group cites as its first item of evidence:

The growth in the number of product liability suits has been astounding. For example, the number of product liability cases filed in federal district courts has increased from 1,579 in 1974 to 13,554 in 1985, a 758% increase. . . .

There is no reason to believe that the state courts have not witnessed a similar dramatic increase in the number of product liability claims.

We are advised to consider this increase as an "example," representative of some larger population of cases. What is in this "product liability" category? . . .

If we separate out the other tort claims from those labelled as products claims, we see that in the course of these twelve years they increased from 22,662 to 28,039—an increase of 23.7%. Products liability cases, on the other hand, increased 758% over this period—32 times as fast. The pattern of products liability claims in federal courts is distinctively different from, rather than typical of, other tort claims there—much less is it typical of tort claims elsewhere.

But what are these products liability cases? The six defined subcategories have been relatively stable. Filings in these subcategories increased from 1,278 in 1975 to 2,049 in 1985—a 60% increase. But they only make up a small portion of products liability category—44% in 1975, falling to just 15% in 1985. As the products liability category has grown over the years, an increasing portion is located in the "other" subcategory, which has grown far more rapidly than the specified categories. What are these "other" cases?

In good part the answer is that they are asbestos cases. During 1984, the form was changed to count asbestos cases separately. In that year, 2,788 of the 8,521 "other" products liability filings were asbestos cases. (Since the new forms were introduced about one-third of the way through the record keeping year, we may assume that the portion of filings that were asbestos cases was actually higher—

perhaps 4,000 or so if there was no seasonal variation.) In 1985, the first full year of counting asbestos cases, they made up 4,239 of the 11,505 "other" filings—31.1% of the whole products liability category.

It seems likely that asbestos cases have been a major factor during the whole period in which products liability cases have been counted. There is no direct count before 1984, but there seems to be a heavy concentration of "other" products liability cases in those districts that are the source of most asbestos claims. It is estimated that during this period there were more than 16,000 asbestos cases filed in the federal courts—that would be more than a quarter of the cumulative total of 60,508 products liability filings counted from 1974 to 1985.

In these asbestos cases, we again encounter litigation whose presence is not plausibly explained in terms of a change in the underlying proclivity to sue. By the early 1980s, broad dissemination of information about the injurious qualities of asbestos, the presence of an experienced asbestos bar, and concern about possible cut-offs of liability to future claimants, were mobilizing large numbers from the pool of asbestos victims—a pool that is destined to diminish over the coming decades.

If a single set of related products cases makes up one-quarter of the total, one wonders what other major clusterings are contained in this category. At least one other product—the Dalkon Shield—was the subject of thousands of cases during this period.[11] We might then expect that the major movements of the products liability category will reflect the flow and ebb of waves of litigation about specific products and will be affected by the devices for aggregating these populations of related cases.

The products liability category is often visualized as one that encompasses suits, involving "thousands of products," that have "jeopardized the health of many industries." Its growth then is presented as an index and portent of the general growth of litigation. But if it is a container populated largely by several epidemics of suits about specific products, it may have less generalizability. . . .

III. THE BENEFITS OF LITIGATION

What difference does it make? Why should we be concerned about the ebb and flow of different currents of litigation? We hear much of bizarre claims, immense jury verdicts, undeserved windfalls, the engorgement of contingency fee lawyers, financially devastated defendants, and other things that befall the specific participants in specific cases. Beyond this, we hear much about the deleterious effects of litigation in the large—that it dampens enterprise, distracts managers, makes doctors practice defensive medicine, increases the cost of products, keeps useful products off the market, etc. All of these attribute to litigation a powerful effect not only on the behavior of the immediate parties but on other actors who respond to the signals that courts broadcast by doing and avoiding and spending what they would otherwise not have done or avoided or spent. Are all of these ramifying effects on conduct undesirable, so that we should account them as costs? Or should some of them be accounted as benefits?

Current discussion of the litigation system displays sensitivity to the various kinds of costs, direct and indirect, that attend the system. But in considering benefits there is a tendency to focus only on the immediate distributive consequences for the parties. Thus, an insurance executive measures the efficiency of the tort system only in terms of compensation of claimants' economic losses, with no indication that this transfer might have any other effect. The same blindness to general and public effects is evident in a *Wall Street Journal* editorial questioning the need for public courts:

> If civil disputes can be satisfactorily resolved by arbitrators, why is there ever any need to settle them at public expense? Why should the taxpayers have to support a civil court system? More to the point, why should jurors have to pay in time and lost wages to enable a condo developer to extract a cash settlement from a builder? Private disputes, unlike criminal proceedings, often have no social consequences. The full costs should fall on the litigants themselves.

To balance the anecdotal stock, let me present a few recent items that caught my attention. I make no claim that they are representative of anything. But they do provide vivid illustrations of some of the beneficial effects of litigation. As an aid to memory, I give each of them a label:

1. *Cape Cod*—Consider the Cape Cod restaurant owner who "has begun giving classes to employees to help them recognize intoxicated customers who might later decide to sue him if their intoxication should lead to an automobile wreck. 'We've become our brother's keeper,' he says."[12]

2. *Madison Parks*—Or consider the changes in park design contemplated in Madison:

> The Madison Parks Commission, acting on advice from the city attorneys, has asked the City Council to remove asphalt under playground equipment in city parks.
>
> The asphalt, which was originally installed to eliminate mud and cut park mowing costs, would be replaced by softer materials, such as wood chips or pea gravel.
>
> "We want to put in something with a little give to it," said Mark Peterson, parks operations analyst. "It's a good idea, since (liability lawsuit) settlements are going through the roof."[13]

3. *Princeton Club*—Or consider the change in policy of a Princeton eating club:

> One of the three all-male eating clubs at Princeton University, the University Cottage Club, has voted to admit women.
>
> The decision, Wednesday night, by the 100-year-old club's graduate board for governors was made in the midst of a sex-discrimination suit filed against the clubs and university.
>
> "The suit encouraged us to look at the issue a lot more closely than we had in the past," the chairman of the board, James L. Crawford, said. "We feel it is the right decision for the long-term benefit of the club. Rather than being forced to admit women, it made sense." . . .
>
> Mr. Crawford said that the Cottage Club, a stately Georgian mansion where F. Scott Fitzgerald was a member, wanted to admit women voluntarily to avoid a possible court-imposed admissións process. . . .
>
> Mr. Crawford conceded high legal fees influenced the club's decision to admit women. He said the decision, which was not unanimous, reflected the results of a poll of club alumni. "The undergraduates would prefer to have kept it as it was."

According to the *New York Times*, the Cottage Club admitted its first women members in February, 1986.

4. *Georgia*—Or consider the impact of a recent wrongful discharge case at the University of Georgia:

> The Board of Regents of the University System of Georgia today [April 3, 1986] released a special audit report that showed a pattern of academic abuse in the admission and advancement of student-athletes at the University of Georgia for the last four years.
>
> The report concluded that the preferential academic treatment was given because of pressure from the athletic department. . . . The report also stated that the university offices who had admitted authorizing the academic exceptions said they acted with the knowledge of the university's president. . . .
>
> . . . Although such treatment for athletes has been rumored at many schools, many times, this is the first time it has been documented through an official investigation. . . .
>
> The investigation was ordered in the wake of a jury award of $2.57 million to Dr. Jan Kemp, a former English instructor in the Developmental Studies Program, who had sued the university, charging that she had been dismissed in 1983 for protesting favorable treatment given to student athletes. . . . The jury verdict stunned the university, the state government and legions of loyal followers of the athletic teams, and the affair has continued to unravel in ways harmful to the university's reputation. The state has appealed the case.

Each of these accounts reports changes as a result of litigation. In each case, the changes strike me as including at least some benefits. The flow of beneficial effects may be related to the litigation in different ways. In *Georgia*, the parties were still embroiled in onerous and expensive litigation when the above account was written, but they subsequently settled.[14] In *Princeton Club*, the litigation terminated early for the club that adjusted its behavior, but proceeded for the other defendants.[15] In *Cape Cod* and *Madison Parks*, behavior was adjusted with an eye to preventing harm and avoiding future litigation. This is the "[s]hadow of the [l]aw,"[16] and it may be a benign shadow.

To analyze this shadow, it is useful to distinguish between "special effects" and "general effects." Special effects are the effects produced by the impact of litigation (full-blown, attenuated, or threatened) on the parties immediately involved. General effects are (a) effects of the communication to others of information about litigation, including (b) effects of the response to that information.

Special effects are changes in the behavior of the specific actors involved in a particular lawsuit—like the Princeton Club or the University of Georgia or the plaintiffs who sued them. We can, in theory at least, isolate various kinds of effects on the subsequent activity of such actors. An actor may be deprived of resources for future violations. This is *incapacitation*. Or the result of litigation may be increased *surveillance* which renders future offending behavior less likely. The *Georgia* case dramatically illustrates this surveillance effect. Or the offending actor may be deterred by fear of being caught again. This is *special deterrence*. Or the experience of being exposed to the law may change the actor's view that it is right to exclude women or pass failing athletes or whatever. This is *reformation*.

In addition to these special effects on the parties before the court, there may be effects on wider audiences that we may call general effects. Litigation against one actor may lead others to reassess the risks and advantages of similar activity. We see this displayed in our *Cape Cod* and *Madison Parks* examples. This is *general deterrence*. It neither presumes nor requires any change in the moral evaluation of the acts in question, nor does it involve any change in opportunities to commit them. It stipulates that behavior will be affected by the acquisition of more information about the costs and benefits that are likely to attach to the act—information about the certainty, celerity, and severity of "punishment," for example. Thus, the actors can hold to what Hart called the "external point of view," treating law as a fact to be taken into account rather than a normative framework that they are committed to uphold or be guided by. The information that induces the changed estimate of costs and benefits need not be accurate. What a court has done may be inaccurately perceived; indeed, the court may have inaccurately depicted what it has done.

On the other hand, communication of the existence of law or its application by a court may change the moral evaluation by others of a specific item of conduct. To the extent that this involves not the calculation or the probability of being visited by certain costs and benefits, but a change in moral estimation, we may call this general effect *enculturation*. There is suggestive evidence to indicate that at least some segments of the population are subject to such effects. Less dramatically, perceiving the application of law may maintain or intensify existing evaluations of conduct, an effect that Gibbs calls *normative validation*.

In addition to these effects on the underlying behavior, litigation may produce effects on the level of disputing behavior. It may encourage or discourage the parties to a case from making (or resisting) other claims. And generally it may encourage claimants and lawyers to pursue claims of a given type. It may provide symbols for rallying a group, broadcasting awareness of grievances, and dramatizing challenges to the status quo. On the other hand, grievances may lose legitimacy, claims may be discouraged, and organizational capacity dissipated. These effects may be labeled *mobilization* and *demobilization*.[17] . . .

I am not claiming that these effects are optimal or that the benefits they produce outweigh all the costs or that existing litigation patterns represent the best way to achieve these benefits. But we should recognize that benefits are present and that any assessment of the social value of litigation must take account of them and must involve any attempt to estimate the *net* effects of present litigation patterns and the proposed or likely alternatives. These examples should also remind us that these effects are not ascertainable by supposition or deduction.

. . . Although reliable knowledge about litigation and its effects is thin and spotty, there is a flourishing folk sociology about the causes, dimensions, and consequences of the present "crises." Space permits only a few examples. One is the notion that there has been a runaway growth of tort litigation and an unparalleled enlargement of the tort system encouraged by the progressive loosening of liability standards. But as we have seen, tort filings have increased only modestly. While expenditures for the tort system have grown more rapidly than government as a whole or the Gross National Product, they have lagged behind other entitlement systems, such as public aid, government health care, and social insurance. Nor have tort costs outpaced those of Workers' Compensation.

Similarly, there are grounds for skepticism of the confident assertion that recent dramatic cost increases and restrictions on insurance coverage are closely linked to specified features of American tort litigation. A similar crisis in the mid-1970s proved short-lived and passed without any important changes in the tort system. Similar contractions of insurance availability seem to occur independently of the presence of these features. Ontario, which enjoys freedom from virtually all of the objectionable features of the United States tort system—jury trial, punative damages, contingent fees, open-ended awards for noneconomic damages—is experiencing a very similar insurance crisis.

IV. SURVIVING THE LITIGATION PANIC

I hope I have persuaded you that respect for the available evidence suggests a more benign reading of our current situation than is found in the discourse that depicts us in a lawsuit crisis, litigation explosion, etc.:

> —Higher caseloads do not reflect a heightened appetite for adversarial combat; they represent people trying to cope with problems in a given array of remedial alternatives.
> —We are not faced with an inexorable exponential explosion of cases, but rather with a series of local changes, some sudden but most incremental, as particular kinds of disputes move in and out of the ambit of the courts.
> —The effects of litigation include an admixture of benefits as well as costs— as do the alternative ways of handling such troubles; the net effects of each

type cannot be ascertained by deduction or supposition.

Why the consternation about litigation? Why is the bad face of law so evident and its good face hidden to so many? The answer is surely complex, but let me just mention a couple of things. First, litigation implies accountability to public standards. The heightening of public accountability is in many quarters an unwelcome counter to deregulation or self-regulation. The sense of being held to account has multiplied far more than cases or trials, for it depends, as we have seen, not on the direct imposition of court orders, but on the communication of messages about what courts might do. Law as a system of symbols has expanded; information about law and its workings is more widely and vividly circulated to more educated and receptive audiences. As a source of symbols and bargaining counters, litigation patterns have changed too. The predominance of cases enforcing market relations has given way to tort, civil rights, and public law cases "correcting" the market. It is such litigation "up"—by outsiders and clients and dependents against authorities and managers of established institutions—that excites most of the reproach of our litigious society.

The sense that America is uniquely cursed by rampant community-destroying legalism, unravelling the fabric of trust, distorting markets, and confounding authority, strikes me as yet another reincarnation of the worn cliché of America as a land of alienation and oppression. The American reality, in all of its puzzling complexity, is found wanting in comparison to an imagined harmonious and organic society. Instead of yielding to this cliché, we should take America's variform and changing patterns of litigation as a challenge to explore the central and distinctive features of this society.

NOTES

1. Few Americans engage in litigation as a sport, as do the Lipay described by Frake, *quoted in* Nader, *The Anthropological Study of Law,* 67(6) Am. Anthropologist, 1, 21 (1965). Nor is participation in litigation regarded as a mark of estimable personal skills—as it is among the Saga, *see* L. Fallers, Law Without Precedent: Legal Ideas in Action in the Courts of Colonial Busoga (1969); the Barotse, *see* M. Gluckman, The Judicial Process Among the Barotse of Northern Rhodesia (1955); the Arusha, *see* F. Dubow, Explaining Litigation Rates in Rural and Urban Tanzania (paper presented at the Annual Meeting of the Law and Society Association, June 2-5, 1983); and the Nandiwallas, *see* R. Hayden, "No One is Stronger than the Caste"— Arguing Dispute Cases in an Indian Caste Panchaya (Ph.D. dissertation, State University of New York at Buffalo, 1981).

2. The plaintiff in a plagiarism suit reports:
No sooner had the lawsuit been filed than stories appeared, little items in the trade press—"disgruntled author suing." And little jokes were heard about Levin and his lawsuits. . . . I was a troublemaker, always in the courts—"But I never before brought a lawsuit in my life! . . . " More jokes. And then there came a certain word. Levin was litigious. The word seemed to be echoing all around me. I was litigious by nature, a constant troublemaker.
M. Levin, The Obsession 145 (1973).

3. For example, the firefighter who quit her job after winning a discrimination complaint (she had been forbidden to breastfeed her infant during free time on duty) explained: "Ever since my suit I was fair game. . . . I was the brunt of all their hostilities." *Battle Won, War?* N.Y. Times, May 19, 1980, at E7, col. 3.
The victor in one of the classic church-state cases observed that:
Vindication by the highest court in the land did not make the McCollums heroes at home. It did not mean that we could quietly assume our former way of life and status in the community. We will never be forgiven nor accepted by those who fought and spoke against us; and many others are still fearful of appearing too friendly.
[My husband's] career suffered. True, he

could remain on the faculty; but his bargaining power for position, rank, and salary were gone. Institutions, we discovered, do not go out of their way to solicit for employment a professor whose name is associated so prominently with a religious issue. As dissenters, we were lucky to be able to stay where we were, let along expect to find advancement elsewhere.
V.C. McCollum, One Woman's Fight 195 (rev. ed. 1961).
A generation later, the black attorney who successfully challenged Alabama's law mandating a moment of silence in public schools reflected:
"Had I known what I was going to go through, I would not have filed the case solely because of the effects on my children. . . . They resent the fact that I brought the case. They received criticism at school. . . . My own children call it a stupid case.
In the black community, I'm sort of looked down upon. . . . That's the lasting effect. I've lost credibility in the black community."
Victor in Alabama Prayer Case Resented and Isolated, L.A. Times, June 5, 1985, at A12, col. 4 (quotation reordered).

4. In a follow up study of the litigants in the Buffalo Creek disaster,
Evidence . . . that the litigation was not prolonging their suffering, was obtained by a comparison of their responses . . . with those of a small group of nonlitigants. This comparison indicated that nonlitigants, if anything, were suffering more symptomatology than litigants. Certainly there was no evidence to suggest that the lawsuit was causing a prolongation of the psychic distress experienced by the survivors.
G. Gleser, B. Green & C. Winget, Prolonged Psychosocial Effects of Disaster: Study of Buffalo Creek 140 (1981).

5. During the six-year period 1978-84 in which civil filings increased 9% in state courts, *supra* p. 7, they increased 88% in federal courts, 1984 Annual Report.

6. Source of data: 1975 & 1984 Annual Reports, page numbers as noted in table.

7. The category "Recovery of Overpayments and Enforcement of Judgements" refers to civil suits, almost all of them filed by the United States, to recover overpayments of veterans' benefits (over 90%) and to recover defaulted student loans. 1984 Annual Report, at 132.

8. This is a composite of very different populations. As state prison populations grew from 242,750 in 1975 to 429,603 in 1984 and 463,378 in

1985, the rate of petitions rose from 58.7 per thousand in 1975 to 61.9 per thousand in 1984, falling back to 58.7 per thousand in 1985. But among federal prisoners (24,131 in 1975; 34,263 in 1984; 40,223 in 1985) the rate of petitions dropped sharply from 209.2 per thousand in 1975 to 132.1 per thousand in 1984, then jumped to 115.7 per thousand in 1985.

9. Mayhew, *Institutions of Representation: Civil Justice and the Public*, 9 LAW & SOC'Y REV. 401, 413 (1975). Mayhew reports, based on a study of Detroit metropolitan area residents, that of those respondents reporting serious problems, only a tiny proportion sought "justice" or legal vindication—except in discrimination. Only 4% of those with serious problems connected with expensive purchases sought "justice"; only 2% of those with neighborhood problems did so. But 31% of those reporting discrimination problems sought "justice."

10. In 1975 products liability filings were 2,886; in 1984 products liability filings were 10,745.

11. In October 1984, A.H. Robins moved to form a class of more than 3,500 pending cases with punitive damage claims. M. MINTZ, AT ANY COST: CORPORATE GREED, WOMEN AND THE DALKON SHIELD 240 (1985). According to the Legal Times Apr. 7, 1986, at 11, col. 2, the total number of Dalkon Shield suits by early 1985 was over 8,700. It is not known how many were in federal courts.

12. Lindsey, *Businesses Change Ways in Fear of Lawsuits*, N.Y. Times, Nov. 18, 1985, at 1, col. 3 (nat'l ed.). Consider also a report from Madison that "More and more people are being refused another drink or having their car keys taken away by bartenders wary of being found responsible for the damage drunkards can do when they hit the outside world." Stamler, *Bartenders Trade 'Set 'em Up Again' Image for None for the Road*, [Madison] Capital Times, Feb. 24, 1986, at 1, col. 1.

13. Waller, *Liability Fear Spurs Park Safety Steps*, Wis. State J., Aug. 28, 1985, at 4, col. 2. A year later, removal of the hard surfaces was completed and the process of replacement with wood chips was underway. Telephone interview with Dan Stapay, Superintendent of Parks, City of Madison (Aug. 11, 1986).

14. In post-trial proceedings, the jury award was reduced to $679,682.65 plus interest, costs, and attorney's fees by the trial judge. *Kemp v. Ervin*, Civil Action No. C83-330A, (N.D. Ga. Apr. 22, 1986) (order reducing jury award). A final settlement of $1,080,000 was reached in early May, 1986.

15. In June 1986, an administrative law judge found that the other two clubs had violated New Jersey's anti-discrimination law. *Judge Finds 2 Clubs at Princeton Guilty in Sex-Bias Lawsuit*, N.Y.

Times, Jun. 22, 1986, at 17, col. 5 (nat'l ed.). A month later, Princeton University, accused of "aiding and abetting" the club's discriminatory practices, settled with the complainant, paying $27,500 for her legal and other expenses. *Princeton Settles Suits on Bias*, N.Y. Times, July 23, 1986, at 12, col. 4 (nat'l ed.).

16. Since only a small fraction of behavior is regulated by full-blown adjudication, the influence of courts and rules on most behavior and on the resolution of most disputes is not direct, but through the anticipation of what courts might do.

17. Indeed, one of the most evident effects of recent litigation has been its profound mobilizational effect on various groups like doctors and insurers who are involved in political initiatives to change it.

POSTSCRIPT

Is There a Litigation Crisis?

In his best-selling book, *Megatrends* (1982), John Naisbitt argued that modern communications technologies make possible relationships and interactions between persons and institutions that could not exist in earlier times. He wrote that "an industrial society pits man against fabricated nature. In an information society—for the first time in civilization—the game is interacting with other people. This increases personal transactions geometrically; that is, all forms of interactive communication: telephone calls, checks written, memos, messages, letters, and more. This is one basic reason why we are bound to be a litigious-intensive society." The impressive capabilities of the electronic media undoubtedly do provide new opportunities for conflict to occur. Will we, however, also be likely to rely on litigation, rather than on some non-traditional technique, as the principal means for resolving these conflicts? Naisbitt's conclusion that our society will become "litigation-intensive" assumes that courts will be used the same way in the future as they are today, and it does not take into account changes that may occur in our attitudes toward law and in the manner in which law and courts are employed.

The news media have served to publicize claims of "hyperlexis" and of allegedly frivolous lawsuits. They may also be creating pressure for increased use of less formal, cheaper, and faster techniques of conflict resolution. As this occurs, hard choices will be made about which techniques are most appropriate for which kinds of problems and the benefits of litigation, which Galanter emphasizes, will be important to keep in mind.

Further reading on the litigation explosion may be found in Hurst, "The Functions of Courts in the United States, 1950–1980," 15 *Law and Society Review*, pp. 400–471 (1980); Friedman, "The Six Million Dollar Man: Litigation and Rights Consciousness in Modern America," 39 *Maryland Law Review*, pp. 661–667 (1980); Curran, *The Legal Needs of the Public* (American Bar Association, 1977); Clark, "Adjudication to Administration: A Statistical Analysis of Federal District Courts in the Twentieth Century," 55 *Southern California Law Review* 65 (1981); Saks, "In Search of the 'Lawsuit Crisis,' " 14 *Law, Medicine and Health Care* 77 (1987); Bunch and Hardy, "A Re-Examination of Litigation Trends in the United States," 1986 *Journal of Dispute Resolution* 87; and Catenacci, "Hyperlexis or Hyperbole: Subdividing the Landscape of Disputes and Defusing the Litigation Explosion," 8 *Review of Litigation* 297 (1989).

ISSUE 3

Should Plea Bargaining Be Abolished?

YES: Kenneth Kipnis, from "Criminal Justice and the Negotiated Plea," *Ethics* (vol. 86, 1976)

NO: Nick Schweitzer, from "Plea Bargaining: A Prosecutor's View," *Wisconsin Bar Bulletin* (vol. 61, 1988)

ISSUE SUMMARY

YES: Professor of philosophy Kenneth Kipnis makes the case that justice cannot be traded on the open market and that plea bargaining often subverts the cause of justice.

NO: District Attorney Nick Schweitzer finds that plea bargaining is fair, useful, desirable, necessary, and practical.

One of the most common myths fostered by television programs about lawyers concerns the place of the trial in our legal system. The television lawyer, who is invariably a criminal trial lawyer, defends an innocent individual and, at a particularly dramatic point in the trial, achieves vindication for the client. If you visit a courthouse, you may be able to find a trial being held that will resemble what you have seen on television. The lawyer may be less dramatic, the judge less dour, and the defendant less appealing, but the main elements of the television version of justice, such as cross-examination of witnesses, opening and closing arguments, and, perhaps, a jury verdict, will be present. What is important to understand, however, is that of the cases processed by the criminal justice system, only a handful are disposed of in this manner. Instead, as many as ninety percent of the cases are resolved through plea bargaining.

Plea bargaining is a method of avoiding trials by securing guilty pleas from defendants. It occurs primarily because trials are expensive and time consuming. In plea bargaining, the defendant agrees to plead guilty in exchange for an agreement by the prosecutor to reduce the charges or recommend a lenient sentence. The defendant essentially has a choice between going to trial and possibly being found guilty on a more serious charge, or pleading guilty now.

This is a difficult choice for any defendant, and at the center of the debate over the legitimacy of plea bargaining is the question of whether the defendant, in these circumstances, is making a voluntary choice. In the following article, Kenneth Kipnis argues that there is too much coercion involved for the choice to be considered voluntary, that the process is inherently unjust, and that innocent individuals may be coerced into pleading guilty. District attorney Nick Schweitzer believes that the system is not at fault and that if the standard legal procedures are followed, plea bargaining is not only indispensable but is also just and desirable.

Plea bargaining has been upheld by the Supreme Court, but only when the Court was persuaded that the plea was made voluntarily. Yet it is rare for a convicted defendant to make a successful challenge to the voluntariness of this guilty plea because the defendant must admit in open court, prior to making the plea, that it is being made voluntarily. What you will see in every courtroom in which plea bargaining occurs is a judge asking a defendant the following questions:

1. Do you understand the charges against you and the maximum penalties authorized by law?
2. Are you, in fact, guilty of the charge you are pleading guilty to?
3. Are you pleading guilty voluntarily?
4. Do you understand that you have the right to a trial by jury and that you are waiving that right?

Judges will not accept a plea unless the defendant answers yes to all of these questions. For a plea of guilty to be challenged later, therefore, the defendant must persuade a higher court that he was coerced into lying when he was asked these questions.

Another important issue in the controversy over plea bargaining is the fact that plea bargaining is mainly a poor person's problem. The reason for this is that the greatest incentive to plead guilty exists for those persons who are in jail awaiting trial and have not been able to afford bail. Their choice is to plead guilty now and get out of jail immediately or at some definite future date, or to insist on a trial, stay in jail until the trial occurs, and risk a long sentence if convicted. As you read the following articles, you should consider how important this factor is in making a decision about whether or not plea bargaining should be abolished.

YES

Kenneth Kipnis

CRIMINAL JUSTICE AND THE NEGOTIATED PLEA

In recent years it has become apparent to many that, in practice, the criminal justice system in the United States does not operate as we thought it did. The conviction secured through jury trial, so familiar in countless novels, films, and television programs, is beginning to be seen as the aberration it has become. What has replaced the jury's verdict is the negotiated plea. In these "plea bargains" the defendant agrees to plead guilty in exchange for discretionary consideration on the part of the state. Generally, this consideration amounts to some kind of assurance of a minimal sentence. The well-publicized convictions of Spiro Agnew and Clifford Irving were secured through such plea bargains. In 1974 in New York City, 80 percent of all felony cases were settled as misdemeanors through plea bargains.[1] Only 2 percent of all felony arrests resulted in a trial.[2] It is at present a commonplace that plea bargaining could not be eliminated without substantial alterations in our criminal justice system.

Plea bargaining involves negotiations between the defendant (through an attorney in the standard case) and the prosecutor as to the conditions under which the defendant will enter a guilty plea.[3] Both sides have bargaining power in these negotiations. The prosecutor is ordinarily burdened with cases and does not have the wherewithal to bring more than a fraction of them to trial. Often there is not sufficient evidence to ensure a jury's conviction. Most important, the prosecutor is typically under administrative and political pressure to dispose of cases and to secure convictions as efficiently as possible. If the defendant exercises the constitutional right to a jury trial, the prosecutor must decide whether to drop the charges entirely or to expend scare resources to bring the case to trial. Since neither prospect is attractive, prosecutors typically exercise their broad discretion to induce defendants to waive trial and to plead guilty.

From the defendant's point of view, such prosecutorial discretion has two aspects; it darkens the prospect of going to trial as it brightens the prospect of pleading guilty. Before negotiating, a prosecutor may improve his bargain-

From Kenneth Kipnis, "Criminal Justice and the Negotiated Plea," *Ethics*, vol. 86 (1976). Copyright © 1976 by the University of Chicago. Reprinted by permission of University of Chicago Press as publisher.

ing position by "overcharging" defendants[4] or by developing a reputation for severity in the sentences he recommends to judges. Such steps greatly increase the punishment that the defendant must expect if convicted at trial. On the other hand, the state may offer to reduce or to drop some charges, or to recommend leniency to the judge if the defendant agrees to plead guilty. These steps minimize the punishment that will result from a guilty plea. Though the exercise of prosecutorial discretion to secure pleas of guilty may differ somewhat in certain jurisdictions and in particular cases, the broad outlines are as described.

Of course a defendant can always reject any offer of concessions and challenge the state to prove its case. A skilled defense attorney can do much to force the prosecutor to expend resources in bringing a case to trial.[5] But the trial route is rarely taken by defendants. Apart from prosecutorial pressure, other factors may contribute to a defendant's willingness to plead guilty: feelings of guilt which may or may not be connected with the charged crime; the discomforts of the pretrial lockup as against the comparatively better facilities of a penitentiary; the costs of going to trial as against the often cheaper option of consenting to a plea; a willingness or unwillingness to lie; and the delays which are almost always present in awaiting trial, delays which the defendant may sit out in jail in a kind of preconviction imprisonment which may not be credited to a postconviction sentence. It is not surprising that the right to a trial by jury is rarely exercised.

If one examines the statistics published annually by the Administrative Office of the U.S. Courts,[6] one can appreciate both the size of the concessions gained by agreeing to plead guilty and (what is the same thing) the size of the additional burdens imposed upon those convicted without so agreeing. According to the 1970 report, among all convicted defendants, those pleading guilty at arraignment received average sentences of probation and/or under one year of imprisonment. Those going to a jury trial received average sentences of three to four years in prison.[7] If one looks just at those convicted of Marijuana Tax Act violations with no prior record, one finds that those pleading guilty at arraignment received average sentences of probation and/or six months or less of imprisonment while those going to trial received average sentences more than eight times as severe: four to five years in prison.[8] Among all Marijuana Tax Act convictions, defendants pleading guilty at the outset had a 76 percent chance of being let off without imprisonment, while those who had gone to trial had only an 11 percent chance.[9] These last two sets of figures do not reflect advantages gained by charge reduction, nor do they reflect advantages gained by electing a bench trial as opposed to a jury trial. What these figures do suggest is that the sentences given to convicted defendants who have exercised their constitutional right to trial are many times as severe as the sentences given to those who do not. In *United States v. Wiley*[10] Chief Judge Campbell laid to rest any tendency to conjecture that these discrepancies in sentences might have explanations not involving plea bargains.

. . . I believe, and it is generally accepted by trial judges throughout the United States, that it is entirely proper and logical to grant some defendants some degree of leniency in exchange for a plea of guilty. If then, a trial judge grants leniency in exchange for a plea of guilty, it follows, as the reverse side of the same coin, that he must necessarily forego leniency, generally speaking, where the defendant stands trial and is found guilty.

. . . I might make general reference to a "standing policy" not to consider probation where a defendant stands trial even though I do not in fact strictly adhere to such a policy.

No deliberative body ever decided that we would have a system in which the disposition of criminal cases is typically the result of negotiations between the prosecutor and the defendant's attorney on the conditions under which the defendant would waive trial and plead guilty to a mutually acceptable charge. No legislature ever voted to adopt a procedure in which defendants who are convicted after trial typically receive sentences far greater than those received by defendants charged with similar offenses but pleading guilty. The practice of plea bargaining has evolved in the unregulated interstices of our criminal justice system. Its development has not gone unnoticed. There is now a substantial literature on the legality and propriety of plea bargaining.[11] But though philosophers do not often treat issues arising in the area of criminal procedure, there are problems here that cry for our attention. In the preceding pages I have been concerned to sketch the institution of plea bargaining. In what follows I will raise some serious questions about it that should concern us. I will first discuss generally the intrinsic fairness of plea bargains and then, in the final section, I will examine critically the place of such bargains in the criminal justice system.

I

As one goes through the literature on plea bargaining one gets the impression that market forces are at work in this unlikely context. The terms "bargain" and "negotiation" suggest this. One can see the law of supply and demand operating in that, other things being equal, if there are too many defendants who want to go to trial, prosecutors will have to concede more in order to get the guilty pleas that they need to clear their case load. And if the number of prosecutors and courts goes up, prosecutors will be able to concede less. Against this background it is not surprising to find one commentator noting:[12] "In some places a 'going rate' is established under which a given charge will automatically be broken down to a given lesser offense with the recommendation of a given lesser sentence." Prosecutors, like retailers before them, have begun to appreciate the efficiency of the fixed-price approach.

The plea bargain in the economy of criminal justice has many of the important features of the contract in commercial transactions. In both institutions offers are made and accepted, entitlements are given up and obtained, and the notion of an exchange, ideally a fair one, is present to both parties. Indeed one detects something of the color of consumer protection law in a few of the decisions on plea bargaining. In *Baily v. MacDougal*[13] the court held that "a guilty plea cannot be accepted unless the defendant understands its consequences." And in *Santo Bello v. New York*[14] the court secured a defendant's entitlement to a prosecutorial concession when a second prosecutor replaced the one who had made the promise. Rule 11 of the Federal Rules of Criminal Procedure requires that "if a plea agreement has been reached by the parties which contemplates entry of a plea of guilty or nolo contendere in the expectation that a specific sentence will be imposed or that other charges before the court will be dismissed, the court shall require the disclosure of the agreement in open court at the time the plea is offered." These procedures all have analogues in contract law. Though plea bargains may not be seen as contracts by the parties, agreements like them are the stuff of contract case law. While I will not argue that plea bargains are contracts (or even that they should be treated as such), I do think it proper to look to contract law for help in evaluating the justice of such agreements.

The law of contracts serves to give legal effect to certain bargain-promises. In particular, it specifies conditions that must be satisfied by bargain-promises before the law will recognize and enforce them as contracts. As an example, we could look at that part of the law of contracts which treats duress. Where one party wrongfully compels another to consent to the terms of an agreement the resulting bargain has no legal effect. Dan B. Dobbs, a commentator on the law in this area, describes the elements of duress as follows: "The defendant's act must be wrongful in some attenuated sense; it must operate coercively upon the will of the plaintiff, judged subjectively, and the plaintiff must have no adequate remedy to avoid the coercion except to give in. . . . The earlier requirement that the coercion must have been the kind that would coerce a reasonable man, or even a brave one, is now generally dispensed with, and it is enough if it in fact coerced a spineless plaintiff."[15] Coercion is not the same as fraud, nor is it confined to cases in which a defendant is physically compelled to assent. In Dobb's words: "The victim of duress knows the facts but is forced by hard choices to act against his will." The paradigm case of duress is the agreement made at gunpoint. Facing a mortal threat, one readily agrees to hand over the cash. But despite such consent, the rules of duress work to void the effects of such agreements. There is no legal obligation to hand over the cash and, having given it over, entitlement to the money is not lost. The gunman has no legal right to retain possession even if he adheres to his end of the bargain and scraps his murderous plans.

Judges have long been required to see to it that guilty pleas are entered voluntarily. And one would expect that, if duress is present in the plea-bargaining situation, then, just as the handing over of cash to the gunman is void of legal effect (as far as entitlement to the money is concerned), so no legal consequences should flow from the plea of guilty which is the product of duress. However, Rule 11 of the Federal Rules of Criminal Procedure requires the court to insure that a plea of guilty (or nolo contendere) is voluntary by "addressing the defendant personally in open court, determining that the plea is voluntary and not the result of force or promises *apart from a plea agreement*" (emphasis added). In two important cases (*North Carolina v. Alford* and *Brady v. United States*)[16] defendants agreed to plead guilty in order to avoid probable death sentences. Both accepted very long prison sentences. In both cases the Supreme Court decided that guilty pleas so entered were voluntary (through Brennan, Douglas, and Marshall dissented). In his dissent in *Alford*, Brennan writes: " . . . the facts set out in the majority opinion demonstrate that Alford was 'so gripped by fear of the death penalty' that his decision to plead guilty was not voluntary but was the 'product of duress as much so as choice reflecting physical constraint.' " In footnote 2 of the *Alford* opinion, the Court sets out the defendant's testimony given at the time of the entry of his plea of guilty before the trial court. That testimony deserves examination: "I pleaded guilty on second degree murder because they said there is too much evidence, but I ain't shot no man, but I take the fault for the other man. We never had an argument in our life and I just pleaded guilty because they said if I didn't they would gas me for it, and that is all." The rule to be followed in such cases is set out in *Brady*: "A plea of guilty entered by one fully aware of the direct consequences, including the actual value of any commitments made to him by the court, prosecutor or his own counsel, must stand unless induced by threats (or promises to discontinue improper harassment), misrepresentation (including unfilled or unfillable promises), or perhaps by promises that are by their very nature improper as having no proper relationship to the prosecutor's business (e.g. bribes)." Case law and the Federal Rules both hold that the standard exercise of prosecutorial discretion in order to secure a plea of guilty cannot be used to prove that such a plea is involuntary. Even where the defendant enters a guilty plea in order to avert his death at the hands of the state, as in *Alford*, the Court has not seen involuntariness. Nevertheless, it may be true that some guilty pleas are involuntary in virtue of prosecutorial inducement considered proper by the Supreme Court.

Regarding the elements of duress, let us compare the gunman situation with an example of plea bargaining in order to examine the voluntariness of the latter. Albert W. Alschuler, author of one of the most thorough studies of plea bargaining, describes an actual case:

San Francisco defense attorney Benjamin M. Davis recently represented a man charged with kidnapping and forcible rape. The defendant was innocent, Davis says, and after investigating the case Davis was confident of an acquittal. The prosecutor, who seems to have shared the defense attorney's opinion on this point, offered to permit a guilty plea to simple battery. Conviction on this charge would not have led to a greater sentence than thirty days' imprisonment, and there was every likelihood that the defendant would be granted probation. When Davis informed his client of this offer, he emphasized that conviction at trial seemed highly improbable. The defendant's reply was simple: "I can't take the chance."[17]

Both the gunman and the prosecutor require persons to make hard choices between a very certain smaller imposition and an uncertain greater imposition. In the gunman situation I must choose between the very certain loss of my money and the difficult-to-assess probability that my assailant is willing and able to kill me if I resist. As a defendant I am forced to choose between a very certain smaller punishment and a substantially greater punishment with a difficult-to-assess probability. As the size of the certain smaller imposition comes down and as the magnitude and probability of the larger imposition increases, it becomes more and more reasonable to choose the former. This is what seems to be occurring in Alschuler's example: "Davis reports that he is uncomfortable when he permits innocent defendants to plead guilty; but in this case it would have been playing God to stand in the defendant's way. The attorney's assessment of the outcome at trial can always be wrong, and it is hard to tell a defendant that 'professional ethics' require a course that may ruin his life." Davis's client must decide whether to accept a very certain, very minor punishment or to chance a ruined life. Of course the gunman's victim can try to overpower his assailant and the defendant can attempt to clear himself at trial. But the same considerations that will drive reasonable people to give in to the gunman compel one to accept the prosecutor's offer. Applying the second and third elements of duress, one can see that, like the gunman's act, the acts of the prosecutor can "operate coercively upon the will of the plaintiff, judged subjectively," and both the gunman's victim and the defendant may "have no adequate remedy to avoid the coercion except to give in." In both cases reasonable persons might well conclude (after considering the gunman's lethal weapon or the gas chamber) "I can't take the chance." A spineless person would not need to deliberate.

That prosecutors could exercise such duress apparently seemed plain to the authors of the *Restatement of Contracts*.[18] Their summarization of the law of contracts, adopted in 1932 by the American Law Institute, contained the following: "A threat of criminal prosecution . . . ordinarily is a threat of imprisonment and also . . . a threat of bringing disgrace upon the accused. Threats of this sort may be of such compelling force that acts done under their influence are coerced, and the better foundation there is for the prosecution, the greater is the coercion." While it is always true that even in the most desperate circum-

stances persons are free to reject the terms offered and risk the consequences, as Morris Raphael Cohen put it: "such choice is surely the very opposite of what men value as freedom."[19]

Indeed if one had to choose between being in the position of Davis's client and facing a fair-minded gunman, I think that it would be reasonable to prefer the latter. While the law permits one to recover money upon adverting to the forced choice of the gunman, it does not permit one to retract a guilty plea upon adverting to the forced choice of the prosecutor. This is the impact of *Brady* and Rule 11.

Note that the duress is not eliminated by providing defendants with counsel. While a good attorney may get better concessions and may help in the evaluation of options, in the end the defendant will still have to decide whether to settle for the smaller penalty or to risk a much heavier sentence. One does not eliminate the injustice in the gunman situation by providing victims with better advice.

Nor does it help matters to insure that promises of prosecutorial concessions are kept. The gunman who violates his part of the bargain—murdering his victims after they give over their money—has compounded his wrongdoing. Reputations for righteousness are not established by honoring such bargains.

Nor is it legitimate to distinguish the prosecutor from the gunman by saying that, while the gunman is threatening harm unless you hand over the cash, the prosecutor is merely promising benefits if you enter a guilty plea. For, in the proper context, threats and promises may be intertranslatable. Brandishing his pistol, the holdup man may promise to leave me unharmed if I hand over the cash. Similarly, the prosecutor may threaten to "throw the book" at me if I do not plead guilty to a lesser charge. In the proper context, one may be compelled to act by either form of words.

One might argue that not all "hard choices" are examples of duress. A doctor could offer to sell vital treatment for a large sum. After the patient has been cured it will hardly do for her to claim that she has been the victim of duress. The doctor may have forced the patient to choose between a certain financial loss and the risk of death. But surely doctors are not like gunmen.

Two important points need to be made in response to this objection. First, the doctor is not, one assumes, responsible for the diseased condition of the patient. The patient would be facing death even if she had never met the doctor. But this is not true in the case of the gunman, where both impositions are his work. And in this respect the prosecutor offering a plea bargain in a criminal case is like the gunman rather than like the doctor. For the state forces a choice between adverse consequences that it imposes. And, of course, one cannot say that in the defendant's wrongdoing he has brought his dreadful dilemma upon himself. To do so would be to ignore the good reasons there are for the presumption of innocence in dispositive criminal proceedings.

Second, our laws do not prohibit doctors from applying their healing skills to maximize their own wealth. They are free to contract to perform services in return for a fee. But our laws do severely restrict the state in its prosecution of criminal defendants. Those who framed our constitution were well aware of the great potential for abuse that the criminal law affords. Much of the constitution (especially the Bill of Rights) checks the activity of the state in this area. In particular, the Fifth Amendment provides that no person "shall be compelled in any criminal case to be a witness against himself." If I am right in judging that defendants like Alford and Davis's client do not act freely in pleading guilty to the facts of their cases, that the forced choice of the prosecutor may be as coercive as the forced choice of the gunman, that a defendant may be compelled to speak against himself (or herself) by a prosecutor's discretion inducing him to plead guilty, then, given the apparent constitutional prohibition of such compulsion, the prosecutor acts wrongfully in compelling such pleas. And in this manner it may be that the last element of duress, wrongfulness, can be established. But it is not my purpose here to establish the unconstitutionality of plea bargaining, for it is not necessary to reach unconstitutionality to grasp the wrongfulness of that institution. One need only reflect upon what justice amounts to in our system of criminal law. This is the task I will take up in the final section of this paper.

II

Not too long ago plea bargaining was an officially prohibited practice. Court procedures were followed to ensure that no concessions had been given to defendants in exchange for guilty pleas. But gradually it became widely known that these procedures had become charades of perjury, shysterism, and bad faith involving judges, prosecutors, defense attorneys and defendants. This was scandalous. But rather than cleaning up the practice in order to square it with the rules, the rules were changed in order to bring them in line with the practice.

There was a time when it apparently seemed plain that the old rules were the right rules. One finds in the *Restatement of Contracts:*[20] " . . . even if the accused is guilty and the process valid, so that as against the State the imprisonment is lawful, it is a wrongful means of inducing the accused to enter into a transaction. To overcome the will of another for the prosecutor's advantage is *an abuse of the criminal law which was made for another purpose*" (emphasis added). The authors of the *Restatement* do not tell us what they were thinking when they spoke of the purpose of the criminal law. Nonetheless it is instructive to conjecture and to inquire along the lines suggested by the *Restatement.*

Without going deeply into detail, I believe that it can be asserted without controversy that the liberal-democratic approach to criminal justice—and in particular the American criminal justice system—is an institutionalization of two principles. The first principle refers to the intrinsic point of systems of criminal justice.

A. Those (and only those) individuals who are clearly guilty of certain serious specified wrongdoings deserve an officially administered punishment which is proportional to their wrongdoing.

In the United States it is possible to see this principle underlying the activities of legislators specifying and grading wrongdoings which are serious enough to warrant criminalization and, further, determining the punishment appropriate to each offense; the activities of policemen and prosecutors bringing to trial those who are suspected of having committed such wrongdoings; the activities of jurors determining if defendants are guilty beyond a reasonable doubt; the activities of defense attorneys insuring that relevant facts in the defendant's favor are brought out at trial; the activities of judges seeing to it that proceedings are fair and that those who are convicted receive the punishment they deserve; and the activities of probation officers, parole officers, and prison personnel executing the sentences of the courts. All of these people play a part in bringing the guilty to justice.

But in liberal-democratic societies not everything is done to accomplish this end. A second principle makes reference to the limits placed upon the power of the state to identify and punish the guilty.

B. Certain basic liberties shall not be violated in bringing the guilty to justice.

This second principle can be seen to underlie the constellation of the constitutional checks on the activities of virtually every person playing a role in the administration of the criminal justice system.

Each of these principles is related to a distinctive type of injustice that can occur in the context of criminal law. An injustice can occur in the outcome of the criminal justice procedure. That is, an innocent defendant may be convicted and punished, or a guilty defendant may be acquitted or, if convicted, he or she may receive more or less punishment than is deserved. Because these injustices occur in the meting out of punishment to defendants who are being processed by the system, we can refer to them as internal injustices. They are violations of the first principle. On the other hand, there is a type of injustice which occurs when basic liberties are violated in the operation of the criminal justice system. It may be true that Star Chamber proceedings, torture, hostages, bills of attainder, dragnet arrests, unchecked searches, *ex post facto* laws, unlimited invasions of privacy, and an arsenal of other measures could be employed to bring more of the guilty to justice. But these steps lead to a dystopia where our most terrifying nightmares can come true. However we limit the activity of the criminal justice system in the interest of basic liberty, that limit can be overstepped. We can call such infringements upon basic liberties external injustices. They are violations of the second principle. If, for example, what I have suggested in the previous section is correct, then plea bargaining can bring about an external injustice with respect to a basic liberty secured by the Fifth Amendment. The remainder of this section will be concerned with internal injustice or violations of the first principle.

It is necessary to draw a further distinction between aberrational and systemic injustice. It may very well be that in the best criminal justice system that we are capable of devising human limitations will result in some aberrational injustice. Judges, jurors, lawyers, and legislators with the best of intentions may make errors in judgment that result in mistakes in the administration of punishment. But despite the knowledge that an unknown percentage of all dispositions of criminal cases are, to some extent, miscarriages of justice, it may still be reasonable to believe that a certain system of criminal justice is well calculated to avoid such results within the limits referred to by the second principle.[21] We can refer to these incorrect outcomes of a sound system of criminal justice as instances of aberrational injustice. In contrast, instances of systemic injustice are those that result from structural flaws in the criminal justice system itself. Here in-

correct outcomes in the operations of the system are not the result of human error. Rather, the system itself is not well calculated to avoid injustice. What would be instances of aberrational injustice in a sound system are not aberrations in an unsound system: they are a standard result.

This distinction has an analogy in the area of quality control. Two vials of antibiotic may be equally contaminated. But depending upon the process used to produce each, the contamination may be aberrational or systemic. The first sample may come from a factory where every conceivable step is taken to insure that such contamination will not take place. The second vial may come from a company which uses a cheap manufacturing process offering no protection against contamination. There is an element of tragedy if death results when all possible precautions have been taken: there just are limits to human capability at our present level of understanding. But where vital precautions are dropped in the name of expediency, the contamination that results is much more serious if only because we knew it would take place and we knew what could be done to prevent it. While we have every reason to believe that the first sample is pure, we have no reason to believe that the second sample is uncontaminated. Indeed, one cannot call the latter contamination accidental as one can in the first case. It would be more correct to call it an accident if contamination did not take place in the total absence of precaution.

Likewise, systematic injustice in the context of criminal law is a much more serious matter than aberrational injustice. It should not be forgotten that the criminal sanction is the most severe imposition that the state can visit upon one of its citizens. While it is possible to tolerate occasional error in a sound system, systematic carelessness in the administration of punishment is negligence of the highest order.

With this framework in mind, let us look at a particular instance of plea bargaining recently described by a legal aid defense attorney.[22] Ted Alston has been charged with armed robbery. Let us assume that persons who have committed armed robbery (in the way Alston is accused of having committed it) deserve five to seven years of prison. Alston's attorney sets out the options for him: "I told Alston it was possible, perhaps even probable, that if he went to trial he would be convicted and get a prison term of perhaps five to seven years. On the other hand, if he agreed to plead guilty to a low-grade felony, he would get a probationary sentence and not go to prison. The choice was his." Let us assume that Alston accepts the terms of the bargain and pleads guilty to a lesser offense. If Alston did commit the armed robbery, there is a violation of the first principle in that he receives far less punishment than he deserves. On the other hand, if Alston did not commit the armed robbery, there is still a violation of the first principle in that he is both convicted of and punished for a crime that he did not commit, a crime that no one seriously believes to be his distinctive wrongdoing. It is of course possible that while Alston did not commit the armed robbery, he did commit the lesser offense. But though justice would be done here, it would be an accident. Such a serendipitous result is a certain sign that what we have here is systemic injustice.

If we assume that legislatures approximate the correct range of punishment for each offense, that judges fairly sentence those who are convicted by juries, and that prosecutors reasonably charge defendants, then, barring accidents, justice will *never* be the outcome of the plea-bargaining procedure: the defendant who "cops a plea" will never receive the punishment which is deserved. Of course legislatures can set punishments too high, judges can oversentence those who are convicted by juries, and prosecutors can overcharge defendants. In these cases the guilty can receive the punishment they deserve through plea bargaining. But in these cases we compensate for one injustice by introducing others that unfairly jeopardize the innocent and those that demand trials.

In contrast to plea bargaining, the disposition of criminal cases by jury trial seems well calculated to avoid internal injustices even if these may sometimes occur. Where participants take their responsibilities seriously we have good reason to believe that the outcome is just, even when this may not be so. In contrast, with plea bargaining we have no reason to believe that the outcome is just even when it is.

I think that the appeal that plea bargaining has is rooted in our attitude toward bargains in general. Where both parties are satisfied with the terms of an agreement, it is improper to interfere. Generally speaking, prosecutors and defendants are pleased with the advantages they gain by negotiating a plea. And courts, which gain as well, are reluctant to vacate negotiated pleas where only "proper" inducements have been applied and where promises have been understood and kept. Such judicial neutrality may be commendable where entitlements are being exchanged. But the criminal justice system is not such a context. Rather it is one in which persons are justly given, not what they have bargained for, but what they deserve, irrespective of their bargaining position.

To appreciate this, let us consider another context in which desert plays a familiar role; the assignment of grades in an academic setting. Imagine a "grade bargain" negotiated between a grade-conscious student and a harried instructor. A term paper has been submitted and, after glancing at the first page, the instructor says that if he were to read the paper carefully, applying his usually rigid standards, he would probably decide to give the paper a grade of D. But if the student were to waive his right to a careful reading and conscientious critique, the instructor would agree to a grade of B. The grade-point average being more important to him than either education or justice in grading, the student happily accepts the B, and the instructor enjoys a reduced workload.

One strains to imagine legislators and administrators commending the practice of grade bargaining because it permits more students to be processed by fewer instructors. Teachers can be freed from the burden of having to read and to criticize every paper. One struggles to envision academicians arguing for grade bargaining in the way that jurists have defended plea bargaining, suggesting that a quick assignment of a grade is a more effective influence on the behavior of students, urging that grade bargaining is necessary to the efficient functioning of the schools. There can be no doubt that students who have negotiated a grade are more likely to accept and to understand the verdict of the instructor. Moreover, in recognition of a student's help to the school (by waiving both the reading and the critique), it is proper for the instructor to be lenient. Finally, a quickly assigned grade enables the guidance personnel and the registrar to respond rapidly and appropriately to the student's situation.

What makes all of this laughable is what makes plea bargaining outrageous. For grades, like punishments, should be deserved. Justice in retribution, like justice in grading, does not require that the end result be acceptable to the parties. To reason that because the parties are satisfied the bargain should stand is to be seriously confused. For bargains are out of place in contexts where persons are to receive what they deserve. And the American courtroom, like the American classroom, should be such a context.

In this section, until now I have been attempting to show that plea bargaining is not well calculated to insure that those guilty of wrongdoing will receive the punishment they deserve. But a further point needs to be made. While the conviction of the innocent would be a problem in any system we might devise, it appears to be a greater problem under plea bargaining. With the jury system the guilt of the defendant must be established in an adversary proceeding and it must be established beyond a reasonable doubt to each of the twelve jurors. This is very staunch protection against an aberrational conviction. But under plea bargaining the foundation for conviction need only include a factual basis for the plea (in the opinion of the judge) and the guilty plea itself. Considering the coercive nature of the circumstances surrounding the plea, it would be a mistake to attach much reliability to it. Indeed, as we have seen in *Alford*, guilty pleas are acceptable even when accompanied by a denial of guilt. And in a study of 724 defendants who had pleaded guilty, only

13.1 percent admitted guilt to an interviewer, while 51.6 percent asserted their innocence.[23] This leaves only the factual basis for the plea to serve as the foundation for conviction. Now it is one thing to show a judge that there are facts which support a plea of guilty and quite another to prove to twelve jurors in an adversary proceeding guilt beyond a reasonable doubt. Plea bargaining substantially erodes the standards for guilt and it is reasonable to assume that the sloppier we are in establishing guilt, the more likely it is that innocent persons will be convicted. So apart from having no reason whatever to believe that the guilty are receiving the punishment they deserve, we have far less reason to believe that the convicted are guilty in the first place than we would after a trial.

In its coercion of criminal defendants, in its abandonment of desert as the measure of punishment, and in its relaxation of the standards for conviction, plea bargaining falls short of the justice we expect of our legal system. I have no doubt that substantial changes will have to be made if the institution of plea bargaining is to be obliterated or even removed from its central position in the criminal justice system. No doubt we need more courts and more prosecutors. Perhaps ways can be found to streamline the jury trial procedure without sacrificing its virtues.[24] Certainly it would help to decriminalize the host of victimless crimes—drunkenness and other drug offenses, illicit sex, gambling and so on—in order to free resources for dealing with more serious wrongdoings. And perhaps crime itself can be reduced if we begin to attack seriously those social and economic injustices that have for too long sent their victims to our prisons in disproportionate numbers. In any case, if we are to expect our citizenry to respect the law, we must take care to insure that our legal institutions are worthy of that respect. I have tried to show that plea bargaining is not worthy, that we must seek a better way. Bargain justice does not become us.

NOTES

1. Marcia Chambers, "80% of City Felony Cases Settled by Plea Bargaining," *New York Times* (February 11, 1975), p. 1.
2. Tom Goldstein, "Backlog of Felonies Rose Sharply Here Despite Court Drive," *New York Times* (February 12, 1975), p. 1.
3. Often the judge will play an important role in these discussions, being called upon, for example, to indicate a willingness to go along with a bargain involving a reduction in sentence. A crowded calendar will make the bench an interested party.
4. In California, for example, armed robbers are technically guilty of kidnapping if they point a gun at their victim and tell him to back up. Thus, beyond the charge of armed robbery, they may face a charge of kidnapping which will be dropped upon entry of a guilty plea (see Albert W. Alschuler, "The Prosecutor's Role in Plea Bargaining," *University of Chicago Law Review* 36 (Fall 1968): 88).
5. Arthur Rosett, "The Negotiated Guilty Plea," *Annals of the American Academy of Political and Social Science* 374 (November 1967): 72.
6. Administrative Office of the United States Courts, *Federal Offenders in the United States District Courts* (Washington, D.C. 1970).
7. Ibid., pp. 57, 59.
8. Ibid., pp. 57, 65.
9. Ibid., p. 60.
10. 184 F. Supp. 679 (N.D. Ill. 1960).
11. Some of the most significant treatments of plea bargaining are Alschuler; Arnold Enker, "Perspectives on Plea Bargaining," in *Task Force Report: The Courts*, by the President's Commission on Law Enforcement and Administration of Justice (Washington, D.C., 1967), p. 108; "The Unconstitutionality of Plea Bargaining," *Harvard Law Review* 83 (April 1970); 1387; Donald J. Newman, *Conviction: The Determination of Guilt or Innocence without Trial* (Boston, 1966); Abraham S. Blumberg, *Criminal Justice* (Chicago, 1967); National Advisory Commission on Criminal Justice Standards and Goals, *Task Force Report: The Courts* (Washington, D.C., 1973): American Bar Association Project on Minimum Standards for Criminal Justice, *Standards Relating to Pleas of Guilty, Approved Draft* (New York, 1968).

12. Rosett, p. 71.

13. 392 F.2d 155 (1968).

14. 404 U.S. 257 (1971).

15. Dan B. Dobbs, *Handbook on the Law of Remedies* (Saint Paul, 1973), p. 658.

16. 400 U.S. 25 (1970) and 397 U.S. 742 (1970), respectively.

17. Alschuler, p. 61.

18. American Law Institute, *Restatement of Contracts* (Saint Paul, 1933), p. 652.

19. Morris Raphael Cohen, "The Basis of Contract," in *Law and the Social Order* (New York, 1933), p. 86.

20. American Law Institute, p. 652.

21. My discussion here owes much to John Rawls's treatment of "imperfect procedural justice" in his *A Theory of Justice* (Cambridge, 1971), pp. 85–86.

22. Robert Hermann, "The Case of the Jamaican Accent," *New York Times Magazine* (December 1, 1974), p. 93 (© The New York Times Company).

23. Blumberg, p. 91.

24. John Langbein has suggested that we look to the German legal system to see how this might be done. See his "Controlling Prosecutorial Discretion in Germany," *University of Chicago Law Review* 41 (Spring 1974): 439.

NO

Nick Schweitzer

PLEA BARGAINING: A PROSECUTOR'S VIEW

More than nine out of every ten cases I handle are disposed of by plea bargaining. And, to the best of my knowledge, except for Marco Polo-like reports from exotic foreign jurisdictions like Alaska and New Orleans, that ratio holds true for all prosecutors. Yet, despite the pervasiveness of the practice, plea bargaining often is criticized as improper—a conspiracy to emasculate the criminal justice system.

Plea bargaining is a useful, nay vital, tool. It is a response to a court system that never could accord the luxury of a trial to every criminal charge and civil suit brought before it. It is a practical way to dispose of matters that do not require the full solemnity of legal procedure. Plea bargaining in criminal cases is the equivalent of negotiation and mediation in civil cases. While the latter are praised and encouraged, the former is frequently condemned. Why?

At one level, academicians and other legal thinkers disapprove of prosecutors' unbridled discretion as not fitting into an orderly scheme. But, I see the criticism more often arising out of dissatisfaction with a particular case and expanding to the generalization that plea bargaining is bad. I find two basic reasons for such criticism. The first is that a particular plea-bargain genuinely may be "bad," which means that an offender is offered either a charge reduction or a sentence concession, or both, which is unmerited by the offender and unjustified by any necessity. Experience shows that such "bad" plea-bargains do occur in a small number of cases—generally for expedience, as explained later. The second source of criticism is much more common. This is where an interested party is dissatisfied with the outcome, finding it wholly inadequate to salve his or her injured feelings. I find that this is as likely to occur with a "good" plea-bargain, which is reasoned, conscientious and practical, as it is with a "bad" one.

The reason, I believe, lies in the differing expectations held by experienced criminal attorneys and the general public. Experienced attorneys know the inherent constraints and time-honored practices of our criminal justice

From Nick Schweitzer, "Plea Bargaining: A Prosecutor's View," *Wisconsin Bar Bulletin* (October 1988). Reprinted by permission of *Wisconsin Bar Bulletin*, the official publication of the State Bar of Wisconsin.

system, which imposed practical limits on the punishment of an offender even if she or he were convicted at trial. However, if the case happens to be disposed of by a negotiated plea, critics may ascribe all their frustrations and disappointments to the plea-bargain.

LOOKING AHEAD TO SENTENCING

Strange as it sounds, and despite all the criticism, an essential aspect of plea bargaining is the need to be fair. Plea negotiations, like the sentencing discretion of judges, reflect the need to individualize justice. Only the most naive person would think that a single determinate sentence awaits the end of any particular prosecution. For any given defendant, on any given charge, there is a range of penalties. Most criminal statutes carry a maximum penalty, and some a minimum penalty. However, all Wisconsin statutes, except that for first-degree murder, permit a range. In addition, sentencing options may include community service and probation as well as conditions on probation such as counseling, restitution, jail time and alcohol and drug treatment. Except in certain categories of cases for which sentencing guidelines have been set,[1] sentencing is a human decision. At some stage, some person must decide what sentence will deter future acts by this offender and by other potential offenders without being unduly harsh and at the same time sufficiently assuage the victim.

The sentencing decision is not the function of a trial. A trial is held to determine facts and the essential facts are truly at issue in only a small fraction of criminal cases. The majority of people charged with crimes are guilty and know

it, but before they plead guilty or no contest, they want to know what punishment they face. Often, the only argument is over one or more mitigating factors that do not rise to the level of legal defenses, so a trial in most criminal cases would be a waste of time. Sentencing is the bottom line for most defendants. If they can live with the sentence, most defendants are happy to save the court system and themselves the trouble of a trial. Generally, a bargain can be struck when the advantage to the defendant of an acceptable, known, sentence meets the advantage to the prosecutor of concluding the case for what it realistically is worth.

THE PROSECUTOR'S ROLE

The responsibility for sentencing ultimately lies with a judge. However, no judge has the time to check into the details of every felony, misdemeanor and ordinance that comes before the court. Court calendars being what they are, most judges want a recommendation from someone who already has taken the time to investigate the offense, the situation of any victims and the background of the defendant. A judge can accomplish this by ordering the local probation office to conduct a presentence investigation, but resources limit this option to only the more serious cases.

The prosecution and defense attorneys are in a position to review the offense, check the defendant's record and character, contact any victims and recommend an appropriate sentence. The prosecuting attorney knows the details of the offense and the defendant's prior record. The defense attorney knows the defendant and any mitigating factors. In most routine cases, these two lawyers are in the best position early on to discuss the merits of the case and are best able to find the time to negotiate before trial. If these two sides can reach agreement, the judge's decision can reasonably be reduced to review and ratification.

Another important reason for negotiation to take place at this level is the prosecutor's exclusive discretion to reduce or amend charges. A charge may be totally dismissed only with the court's approval.[2] However, the judge has no mandate to amend or reduce a charge. The discretion to amend charges is vested in the prosecutor to cover those rare cases where the wrong charge is issued.[3] This authority turns out to be even more useful in the frequent cases where some penalty is inappropriate. As an example, cooperative first offenders usually are offered some alternative, such as a county ordinance, that allows them to avoid a criminal record. This discretion to amend adds a second dimension to plea negotiations; the parties can consider not only the range of penalties associated with the original charge, but also the ranges associated with all related charges.

There are other reasons for a prosecutor to make concessions in return for a guilty or no contest plea. More often than not, a prosecutor will dismiss or read in one or more offenses for a defendant facing multiple charges. Usually, the prosecutor still will insist on a sentence consistent with the total number of offenses, but there is a general belief that reducing the number of convictions on the defendant's record will induce the defendant not to tie up the court system by trying all the cases. There also are cases in which the prosecutor faces some obstacle to conviction, other than the

defendant's innocence, such as an unavailable witness or a witness who would be compromised or traumatized by having to testify. In such cases, any conviction, even on a reduced charge, generally is seen as better than a dismissal, an acquittal or a Pyrrhic conviction. Then, there are the infrequent cases in which a concession is necessary to secure a defendant's testimony against a co-defendant in an unrelated case. Plea bargaining also can be used to expedite cases that would drag on for months or years. A prosecutor may agree to a charge or sentence concession in return for a speedy disposition that benefits a victim or quickly takes an offender out of circulation.

THE QUALITY OF THE BARGAIN

For all the above reasons, cases will continue to be settled at the trial attorneys' level. The real issue is the quality of the decisions made. Plea bargaining is a tool and its mark largely depends on the skill and care of the crafter. If the product is flawed, the fault lies less with the tool than with the user. The quality of the plea-bargain depends on the values, interests and abilities of the attorneys. If both sides are interested in finding a "just" sentence, the result is as likely to be "good" as that made by a conscientious judge. But if one or both sides are mainly interested in expedience, primarily want to "win" or have priorities unrelated to the merits of the defendant and the case, then the bargain may well be "bad." Unfortunately, it is true that prosecutors and defense attorneys make some "bad" plea-bargains. It also is true that judges can make sentencing decisions that are injudicious. Since the majority of cases are disposed of by negotiated plea, the opportunity for a "bad" decision by prosecutors is that much greater.

Two weaknesses exist in the plea bargaining process. First, it can become routine and thereby an end rather than a means. As stated earlier, very few cases crossing a prosecutor's desk deserve a trial. The majority of cases do settle and prosecutors develop a strong work habit of managing their caseload that way. As a result, a holdout case may be seen as a nuisance, causing plea bargaining to deteriorate into coercion, concession and compromise without regard for the merits of the case. The indiscriminate use of plea bargaining to clear court calendars justly has been condemned. But under pressure, a prosecutor's definition of a "reasonable" plea-bargain has an unfortunate tendency to expand.

Second, plea bargaining does not encourage participation by the victim. The criminal justice system historically has treated victims cavalierly. It is only with the recent development of victim/witness programs that victims' involvement is being encouraged.

Most victims want to have a voice in the outcome of a case, but this very seldom happens when cases are plea-bargained. Victims generally are left out because negotiations often are informal and unscheduled and talking to victims can be time-consuming and painful, as a victim's viewpoint often is very different from that of an experienced criminal attorney. Victims have difficulty accepting the concept of "what a case is worth" in criminal justice terms and understanding the realistic limitations on punishment. The prosecutor risks becoming the focus of the victim's anger, disappointment and abuse.

SUGGESTIONS

There are no standards or checks imposed on plea bargaining by statute or case law. In fact, courts strictly have avoided involvement in the process.[4] Whether to subject plea-bargaining to some degree of quality control is a policy decision balancing discretion and accountability. However, I offer a few suggestions to district attorneys and judges.

First, have set guidelines as have some D.A. offices. Well-understood policies for reductions and sentencing recommendations can limit very effectively the possibilities for poor judgment. Guidelines could be developed statewide, similar to the sentencing guidelines for judges, which set standard dispositions yet allow departure from the standards for good reason.

Second, plea-bargains could be reduced to writing and reviewed within the D.A.'s office before final agreement. Although this would add a step or two to the process, it would go a long way toward establishing uniformity, avoiding bad decisions and, if part of the policy, assuring that victims' views are considered.

Finally, any judge who is concerned about the quality of the plea-bargains brought before the court could develop questions for accepting a plea bargain, similar to those for the taking of a guilty plea. This allows the judge to play a more active role, or at least to signal that certain aspects of plea bargaining are open to scrutiny, without taking part in the actual negotiations. One question might ask the attorneys for justification of any reduction or sentencing recommendation. Another might ask whether a victim was involved and, if so, whether the victim has been consulted.

CONCLUSION

Despite my reservations about the potential and occasional weaknesses of plea bargaining, I defend the practice as a practical solution to some of the needs and pressures of today's criminal justice system. Plea bargaining is a vital part of the complex system of powers and responsibilities that has evolved in our efforts to make justice as equal, fair and efficient as resources permit. Without it, other parts of the system would have to absorb increased stress. Specifically, if we wanted judges to make all the decisions (even assuming that their decisions would uniformly be better), we would need more judges, more courtrooms, more jurors and more trials. This is not because defendants want trials but largely because most defendants will "plead in" only if they know ahead of time what sentence is likely to be imposed. Plea bargaining is essential until society decides to allocate sufficient resources to these ends. When exercised with a due regard to the case, the victim and the defendant, plea-bargains can result in outcomes as "just" as any available in our current system.

NOTES

1. State of Wisconsin Sentencing Commission, "Wisconsin Sentencing Guidelines Manual," (1985).
2. *State v. Kenyon*, 85 Wis. 2d 36, 270 N.W.2d 160 (1978).
3. Wis. Stat. § 971.29.
4. *See In the Matter of the Amendment of Rules of Civil & Criminal Procedure: Sections 971.07 & 971.08, Stats.*, 128 Wis. 2d 422, 383 N.W.2d 496 (1986); *State v. Erickson*, 53 Wis. 2d 474, 192 N.W.2d 872 (1972); *Rahhal v. State*, 52 Wis. 2d 144, 187 N.W.2d 800 (1971); *State v. Wolfe*, 46 Wis. 2d 478, 175 N.W.2d 216 (1970).

POSTSCRIPT

Should Plea Bargaining Be Abolished?

Plea bargaining, former Supreme Court chief justice Burger has stated, "is an essential component of the administration of criminal justice." What is more debatable is another statement by Burger that "properly administered, it is to be encouraged." We do not know how many innocent persons plead guilty in order to avoid a trial. On the other hand, abolitionists have difficulty describing what a workable replacement for plea bargaining would look like.

Interesting experiments to reform or abolish plea bargaining have taken place in Texas (see Weninger, "The Abolition of Plea Bargaining: A Case Study of El Paso County, Texas," 35 *UCLA Law Review* 265 (1987) and Callan, "An Experiment in Justice Without Plea Negotiation," 13 *Law and Society Review*, pp. 327–347, 1979); Alaska (see Rubinstein and White, "Plea Bargaining: Can Alaska Live Without It?" *Judicature*, December–January, 1979, pp. 267–279); and Arizona (see Berger, "The Case Against Plea Bargaining," *American Bar Association Journal*, p. 621, 1976). These and other alternatives to the plea bargaining system are examined in Alschuler, "Implementing the Criminal Defendant's Right to Trial: Alternatives to the Plea Bargaining System," 50 *University of Chicago Law Review* 931 (1983); Cohen and Doob, "Public Attitudes to Plea Bargaining," 32 *Criminal Law Quarterly* 85 (1989); "The Victim's Veto: A Way to Increase Victim Impact on Criminal Case Dispositions," 77 *California Law Review* 417 (1989); Fine, "Plea Bargaining: An Unnecessary Evil, 70 *Marquette Law Review* 615 (1987); Schulhofer, "Is Plea Bargaining Inevitable?" *Harvard Law Review* 1037 (1984); Note, "Constitutional Alternatives to Plea Bargaining: A New Waive," 132 *University of Pennsylvania Law Review* 327 (1984).

Plea bargaining has been the subject of a considerable number of Supreme Court cases. Among the most noteworthy are *Boykin v. Alabama*, 395 U.S. 238 (1969); *Brady v. U.S.*, 397 U.S. 742 (1970); *North Carolina v. Alford*, 400 U.S. 25 (1970); *Santobello v. New York*, 404 U.S. 257 (1971); and *Bordenkircher v. Hayes*, 434 U.S. 357 (1978). Each of these cases describes the plight of a particular defendant, but probably the most vivid account of the plea bargaining process is a journalist's description, see Mills, "I Have Nothing To Do With Justice," *Life Magazine*, March 12, 1971, reprinted in Bonsignore et al., *Before the Law* (Houghton Mifflin, 1979). A classroom simulation of the process, *Plea Bargaining: A Game of Criminal Justice*, is available from The Dushkin Publishing Group, Inc.

ISSUE 4

Is ADR (Alternative Dispute Resolution) Preferable to Litigation?

YES: Kenneth R. Feinberg, from "Mediation—A Preferred Method of Dispute Resolution," *Pepperdine Law Review* (vol. 16, 1989)

NO: Owen M. Fiss, from "Against Settlement," *Yale Law Journal* (vol. 93, 1984)

ISSUE SUMMARY

YES: Attorney Kenneth Feinberg describes the mediation process, including its informal, voluntary, and flexible nature, and argues that the process contains many advantages when compared to litigation.

NO: Professor Owen Fiss examines the nature and purpose of litigation and concludes that ADR should *not* be encouraged since litigation provides benefits for the public that are not obtainable through ADR.

> I saw that the litigation, if it were persisted in, would ruin the plaintiff and the defendant, who were relatives and both belonged to the same city . . . it might go on indefinitely and to no advantage of either party. . . . In the meantime, mutual ill-will was steadily increasing. . . . I also saw for the first time that the winning party never recovers all the cost incurred. This was more than I could bear. I felt that my duty was to befriend both parties and bring them together.
> —M. K. Gandhi,
> *Gandhi's Autobiography* (1948)

Mediation is a method of resolving disputes and conflicts that is very different from litigation. It is a means of dispute resolution that is rapidly growing in use in the United States. Unlike the adversary process, in which a lawyer's only aim is to help his client win, mediation stresses compromise and agreement between the parties. In addition, mediation encourages all parties to a dispute to participate actively in the settlement of their problems without being involved in a formal judicial proceeding.

Mediation is one of several techniques for settling disputes that constitute alternative dispute resolution (ADR). They are alternatives to litigation, which is viewed by supporters of ADR as being a process that is very costly and time-consuming, that typically ends with one party the winner and the other the loser, and that often makes the parties more hostile to each other at the end than they were at the beginning.

There was extraordinary growth in the use of alternatives to litigation in the 1980s. There are over seven hundred mediation programs in the United States today, compared with a handful that existed in the late 1970s. The most common ADR processes are negotiation, arbitration, and mediation. These processes differ from litigation in a number of ways.

1. They are more informal than litigation. Lawyers often are not present and rules of evidence do not have to be followed. Cases are settled more quickly and more cheaply.

2. They are generally held in private and the proceedings are confidential.

3. They are often voluntary, with the parties coming together because of a desire to settle the dispute out of court.

4. There is usually no appeal from a settlement reached through ADR.

There are also significant differences among the various ADR techniques, some of which are as different from each other as they are from litigation. Some ADR methods, for example, have some of the features of litigation and others do not. Negotiation is the ADR process that is least like litigation. There is no third party present to assist in the resolution of the problem and the parties are free to leave and break off negotiations at any time. Arbitration, on the other hand, is an ADR process that has some qualities in common with litigation. The parties agree ahead of time that the arbitrator has the authority to issue rulings and decide the case. Lawyers are often involved in presenting the case to the arbitrator. Arbitration will still typically be quicker than litigation and proceed less legalistically.

Mediation differs from arbitration in that a mediator does not have the power to issue rulings. Similar to negotiation, mediation works only when the settlement that is reached is acceptable to the parties involved. If either party is dissatisfied, there will be no settlement. Mediators will have different styles and some are more comfortable than others in making suggestions and indicating to the parties what they feel is fair. What is most important in increasing the likelihood that any settlement will last and that the parties will walk away pleased with the outcome is for them to believe that they have contributed to the nature of the settlement. The best settlements are those in which the parties come to understand the motives and needs of their opponents and have worked out a solution that benefits both sides. The mediator is much more interested than a judge in promoting communication and understanding and a complete airing of the circumstances that contributed to the dispute.

Should we encourage more cases to be resolved through mediation and fewer to go through the court system? Would anything be lost if cases that might have been resolved through litigation are instead diverted to a mediation project? This is a difficult public policy question that the authors of the following articles debate. Attorney Feinberg, who is an experienced mediator, points out many of the benefits of mediation. Professor Fiss, however, warns that there is a price to be paid for the quicker and cheaper settlements brought about through mediation.

YES
Kenneth R. Feinberg

MEDIATION—A PREFERRED METHOD OF DISPUTE RESOLUTION

I. INTRODUCTION

Burgeoning court dockets, spiraling litigation costs, and dissatisfaction with the traditional adversarial process have caused increased interest in and use of alternative dispute resolution mechanisms. A wide variety of such mechanisms has developed, including mediation, arbitration, mini-trials, summary jury trials, and numerous hybrid dispute resolution proceedings. Each of these methods of dispute resolution offers certain advantages over conventional litigation in particular cases.

Among the various alternative dispute resolution methods, mediation stands out as particularly advantageous. Mediation has several special features, including its informality, its flexibility and its completely voluntary and non-binding nature, that make it preferable not only to litigation but often to other alternative means of dispute resolution as well.

In this article, I will first direct the special advantages of mediation as a method of resolving disputes. I will then outline a specific procedure for the mediation of disputes that optimizes these advantages and that can serve as a model. The procedure is one that I developed and that I have used successfully on several occasions in a variety of disputes. Finally, I will discuss some remaining problems in the area of dispute resolution through mediation, that, unfortunately, act as obstacles to the more widespread use of this method of conflict resolution.

II. ADVANTAGES OF MEDIATION

A. Advantages Over Litigation

The problems associated with litigation are well documented.[1] Court costs and escalating legal fees make litigation a very expensive endeavor. The

From Kenneth R. Feinberg, "Mediation—A Preferred Method of Dispute Resolution," *Pepperdine Law Review,* vol. 16, Supplement (1989). Copyright © 1989 by the Pepperdine University School of Law. Reprinted by permission. Some notes omitted.

expense is compounded by the long delays caused by overcrowded court dockets and, sometimes, by dilatory procedural and legal tactics.

Even more problematic than the costs and delays associated with litigation are its inherent limitations as an effective means of dispute resolution. Litigation focuses on narrow issues determined by prefabricated legal doctrines. The outcome is limited by prior decisional criteria and by narrow, predefined legal remedies. These limitations rarely permit a full exploration of the factors underlying the dispute and a resolution of the problems in the relationship that led to the dispute between the parties. Indeed, the objective of litigation is not to resolve the dispute so much as it is to arrive at a decision about who is right and who is wrong.

Mediation, on the other hand, does not limit its focus to the discrete legal claims asserted by the parties. Mediation looks beyond the legal issues to explore the relationship between the parties in an attempt to find a true resolution to the problem between them. Furthermore, the potential outcomes of the mediation process are not limited to preexisting legal remedies, or by the requirement that one or the other party be found in the wrong. Thus, a wide range of creative "win-win" resolutions of the problems are possible.

Furthermore, the solution crafted through mediation is designed specifically for and will apply only to the particular dispute at hand. The outcome of a judicial procedure, on the other hand, will have binding legal effect on future related disputes. There are several reasons why parties may seek to avoid the establishment of judicial precedent, especially in new and uncertain areas of the law. Mediation offers the parties the desired ability to focus on resolution of a specific dispute without worrying about its impact on future disputes.

Another problem with litigation is that it places the parties in an extremely adversarial process over which they have little control. Litigation is controlled largely by the parties' lawyers, and proceedings are conducted using language unfamiliar to the parties. Encounters between the parties are rare and usually emotionally charged, tending to antagonize them further. Parties also feel alienated by the fact that the ultimate decision is not in their control, but rather in the hands of a single adjudicator—the judge.

Mediation, on the other hand, is a cooperative process through which the parties themselves fashion a mutually acceptable resolution to their dispute with the help of a neutral third party. Mediation is essentially a negotiation process that seeks a convergence among the parties rather than the polarization that characterizes litigation. It also gives the parties control over the outcome. In sum, mediation is preferable to litigation as a method of dispute resolution because, unlike litigation, mediation offers the parties to a dispute the opportunity to participate actively in a cooperative process designed to achieve a resolution to their problem that is not circumscribed by preexisting legal theories or remedies.

B. Advantages of Mediation Over Other Alternative Methods of Dispute Resolution

In addition to the qualities discussed above, mediation has several special features that make it preferable not only to litigation, but also to other forms of alternative dispute resolution.[2] Primary among these features are mediation's voluntary and non-binding nature, its informality, its flexibility, and its cost-effectiveness. The advantages of each of these qualities is discussed below.

1. Participation in Mediation Is Voluntary and Nonbinding

Perhaps the most attractive feature of mediation is the fact that participation in the process is completely voluntary and nonbinding. Both the initial decision to try mediation and the decision to continue participation in the process are left entirely to the parties. They retain complete control of the process from beginning to end. If either party is dissatisfied at any time with any aspect of the proceeding, that person can withdraw. The only commitment involved is to give it a try.

Furthermore, if the attempt at mediation fails, no alternative options have been foreclosed. Parties are free after mediation to engage in litigation or in other alternative methods of dispute resolution. Thus very little, if any, risk is involved. As one commentator put it, "[i]f it is going to work, it is going to work with some rapidity. If it's not going to work, you don't lose a lot finding out."

The fact that the decision to participate in mediation is risk-free makes people more willing to try it. This gives mediation a significant advantage among alternative dispute resolution techniques. As will be discussed in greater detail in section IV, the single greatest obstacle to successful development of alternative dispute resolution techniques is an unwillingness, especially among lawyers, to try alternatives to litigation. The voluntary and nonbinding nature of the mediation process helps overcome this unwillingness and therefore makes mediation especially attractive.

2. Mediation Is Informal

Another advantageous feature of mediation is the informality of the process. The exchange of thoughts and ideas through mediation is not constrained by predetermined rules of evidence or other rules that structure the presentation of information and other aspects of the proceedings. In mediation, parties are free to set their own rules and procedures and usually choose to forgo much of the formality associated with other forms of dispute resolution.

Mediation is considerably less formal than arbitration, for example. Arbitration involves several formal stages and in many respects resembles a trial. The parties make formal presentations of evidence and of arguments and sometimes submit briefs. Furthermore, ex parte communications between the arbitrator and the parties is prohibited. The mediator of a dispute, on the other hand, can communicate freely with each of the parties and can gather information in any form.

A mediation is also less formal than a summary jury trial, the structure of which, as indicated by its name, is modeled on a trial. In a summary jury trial, attorneys present formal arguments to a real judge and a real jury in court. The difference between such a proceeding and an actual trial is the lack of witness testimony and the advisory nature of the jury's verdict, not a lack of structure and formality. Similarly, the format of a mini-trial resembles a judicial proceeding. A mini-trial does not involve a judge or jury. Rather, presentations of the case are made by attorneys to the parties' executives in an effort to advance subsequent negotiations. The process, however, is highly structured. While the parties to a mediation can choose to incorporate a formal exchange of information or arguments, the parties are free to forgo such formalities and all trappings of courtroom proceedings.

3. Flexibility and Adaptability

Another advantageous feature of mediation is its adaptability to a vast, wide-ranging variety of disputes. There is a long history of using mediation to address labor and employment disputes. More recently, mediation has been applied successfully to resolve family disputes, community disputes, environmental disputes, landlord-tenant disputes, and even criminal matters. In my own particular experience as a mediator, cases involving commercial contractual disputes, construction defects, product liability claims arising out of government use of Agent Orange in Vietnam, antitrust claims, as well as allegations of larceny, embezzlement and RICO violations have all been satisfactorily resolved through mediation. Mediation can be tried in any kind of dispute. No law governs its availability or restricts its use. Moreover, it is suitable not only for disputes between two parties but also for multiparty disputes and even in class actions.[3]

Mediation also can be employed at any stage in a dispute, whether or not litigation is already pending. The parties can schedule a mediation soon (even within days) after the dispute arises. On the other hand, the parties can enter mediation after litigation commences. If litigation has already commenced and proceeded into discovery, the parties can draw on discovery materials. If mediation is begun before the parties reach the discovery stage, they can choose to incorporate a "mini-discovery" schedule into the mediation process.

This kind of procedural flexibility is one of mediation's foremost qualities and is one reason that mediation is adaptable to a wide variety of disputes. As one commentator has put it, "[a] mediation can proceed along any path and according to any format depending upon the circumstances of the case and the predilections of the mediator."[4] Furthermore, as indicated previously, a mediator is not constrained by rules governing formation of a record or appropriate forms of communications with the parties. A mediator is free to adopt operating procedures that fit the precise needs of the parties and can change those procedures at any time during the process if necessary.

Another reason that mediation is adaptable to a vast range of disputes is the ability of the parties to choose the mediator. The parties may, for example, seek out an individual who has had prior experience in resolving similar disputes. Or the parties in a dispute involving detailed technical issues may want to employ a mediator with technical expertise. This enables the parties to save the time they would otherwise spend on educating a factfinder, be it a judge, jury or arbitrator, about the technical aspects of their case.[5]

4. Cost-Effectiveness

The cost-effectiveness of mediation as a dispute resolution device is another attractive feature of mediation. Mediation is cost-effective in several respects. First, mediation generally requires little time when compared to such means of dispute resolution as litigation and arbitration.[6] Examples from my own experience as a mediator illustrate this. It took only three months to settle a ten-year-old anti-trust dispute between competitors in the telephone paging business. It took only ten days to resolve another dispute between a shipper and supplier. By saving time, the parties to the dispute minimize the costs—such as lost revenues and lost business opportunities—associated with diversion of staff and attention from ongoing business activities. Moreover, minimizing time means minimizing legal fees, which are often the most costly aspect of a business dispute.[7]

Mediation helps parties to minimize legal fees in other ways as well. Unlike both litigation and other alternative means of dispute resolution, mediation emphasizes participation by the parties themselves, rather than giving control over the process to lawyers. The parties may not even find it necessary to hire outside counsel. Indeed, my own experience in the mediation of business disputes indicates that direct dealings with the parties, as opposed to their attorneys, is more effective. Of course, the fee paid to the mediator, who is often a lawyer, may be substantial. This cost, however, is shared by the parties. Similarly, the parties can share other costs by, for example, mutually agreeing on experts to be consulted.[8]

Mediation also allows parties to avoid the emotional costs associated with such adversarial dispute resolution methods as litigation and arbitration. As one of my clients has commented publicly: "You don't expend as much emotional energy as you do in court, and that's a huge cost savings."[9]

The nonadversarial, cooperative nature of mediation and its focus on the needs of the parties also help parties to avoid the costs associated with damage or destruction of their business relationship. Adversarial processes often increase antagonism among the parties and damage or destroy the potential for a positive relationship. Mediation, on the other hand, seeks to encourage cooperation among the parties, not only with regard to the immediate dispute, but also with regard to structuring their relationship in the future. It thus leaves open the possibility of profitable future business among them. Some have suggested that going through the mediation process may even help parties avoid future disputes:

> Many commentators have compared the mediator to a catalyst, one who prompts action by others through identification of issues, clarification of facts, reason, and persuasion. In doing so, the mediator will help educate each party (at least those with a continuing relationship) not merely for the resolution of the present dispute, but for the resolution and even prevention of further disputes.[10]

Mediation's ability to help parties preserve opportunities for future business and to avoid the cost of future disputes is further evidence of its cost-effectiveness.

Finally, there are some indications that agreements arrived at through mediation have greater durability than those arrived at through adjudicatory proceedings, such as litigation or arbitration.[11] Unlike a court decree or arbitrator's award, the outcome of a mediation is one fashioned, and agreed to, by the parties themselves. No coercion is ever used since the mediator has no power to impose a settlement. Thus, as one commentator has stated: "By definition, a settlement reached through mediation is an efficient outcome; all the disputants and stakeholders prefer it to no agreement at all, or to any other feasible outcome."[12] In other words, mediation results in more stable agreements and, therefore, may enable parties to avoid costs associated with future noncompliance.

In sum, mediation is cost-effective because the process itself is economical and because the result of a successful mediation is often not only a durable agreement but a more stable relationship between the parties as well. . . .

IV. REMAINING PROBLEMS

Despite the many advantages of mediation as a method of dispute resolution, certain problems remain. Three problems in particular act as impediments to the more widespread use of mediation: (1) unwillingness to try mediation, (2) lack of institutionalized consideration of mediation as a dispute resolution option, and (3) legal uncertainty about the confidentiality of mediation.

A. Unwillingness to Try Mediation

The single greatest obstacle to the successful development of mediation in general, and to the initiation of any particular mediation, is unwillingness to try it. Despite repeated complaints about litigation, there is still a great deal of reluctance, especially among attorneys, to try such alternative methods of dispute resolution. There are several factors that may account for this unwillingness, including what one commentator termed "the deadening drag of status quoism."[13]

Perhaps the primary factor contributing toward unwillingness to try mediation is simply unfamiliarity with the process. This unfamiliarity stems largely from the lack of education, particularly in law school, about nonadversarial methods

of dispute resolution.[14] The standard law school curriculum trains students to be staunch advocates in an adversarial system and offers little, if any, opportunity to develop negotiating skills.

Law schools' adversarial emphasis as well as the litigious orientation of legal practice creates a mindset that is incompatible with mediation and negotiation. As one commentator explained:

> The lawyer's standard philosophical map is useful primarily where the assumptions upon which it is based— adversariness and amenability to solution by a general rule imposed by a third party—are valid. But when mediation is appropriate, these assumptions do not fit. The problem is that many lawyers . . . tend to suppose that these assumptions are germane in nearly any situation that they confront as lawyers. The map, and the litigation paradigm on which it is based, has a power all out of proportion to its utility. Many lawyers, therefore, tend not to recognize mediation as a viable means of reaching a solution; and worse, they see the kinds of unique solutions that mediation can produce as threatening to the best interests of their clients.[15]

This predisposition among lawyers against nonadversarial means of dispute resolution is a major impediment to the successful initiation of individual mediations and to the future growth of mediation as a dispute resolution technique.

Another reason that lawyers, and sometimes their clients, are hesitant to try mediation of a dispute is the fear of appearing weak to the other side. The above discussion of the many advantages of mediation, particularly among parties with an ongoing relationship, demonstrates that there are many reasons for preferring mediation over litigation, even for a party who would have a strong position in court. Nonetheless, there is a popular perception that suggesting any alternative method of dispute resolution implies a fear of the potential outcome of litigation. The underlying assumption of this perception is that litigation is the norm and that any alternative to litigation is the exception, reserved for exceptionally weak cases. If, however, alternatives to litigation were routinely considered and initiated by a given party, the other party would have no reason to associate an offer of mediation with weakness.

This brings us to the next issue—the need for businesses and other organizations to institutionalize consideration of mediation as a means of resolving a dispute.

B. The Need for Institutionalization

There has been a good deal of institutionalization by the courts and other governmental organizations of alternative methods of dispute resolution, including mediation.[16] Court-associated alternative dispute resolution programs, however, are focused primarily on the resolution of family disputes, neighborhood or community disputes, and criminal matters. They do not usually address commercial or business disputes.

Among corporations and other business entities, alternative methods of dispute resolution are generally used only on a piecemeal, case-by-case basis. Thus, mediation continues to be largely a "hit or miss" experimental device, alien to the normal decisionmaking process of a company or other organization. The challenge faced by advocates of mediation is to institutionalize it and make its consideration and use an integral part of an organization's process of decision-making about both pending and antici-pated disputes. In particular, what is needed is an in-house procedure to assure that every dispute is considered for mediation. . . .

Substantive Criteria for Referring Cases to ADR

Ultimately, successful institutionalization of the use of ADR will require companies to establish a presumption that all cases, with the very limited exceptions in which settlement is inappropriate and would convey the wrong message to potential adversaries, can be resolved through one or more ADR techniques. Realistically, however, it is helpful to develop substantive criteria that can be used in designating certain types of cases as particularly suitable for ADR treatment. My firsthand experience at mediation demonstrates that the following variables are critical in the decision to engage in ADR:

1. *Uncertainty of result.* Disputes in which the parties are either unsure of the likelihood of success after protracted litigation or confront the potential for great exposure (or minimal recovery) are well-suited for ADR consideration.

2. *Inefficiencies in time and money.* The likelihood of protracted litigation, with its attendant costs and diversion of lawyer and company official time, often corroborates the advantages of ADR. This factor is particularly important in contingent fee cases where the plaintiff's attorney sees advantages to a prompt settlement without the need to "bankroll" the litigation.

3. *A desire to expedite discovery, depositions or both.* ADR is often effective when the parties see an advantage to short-circuiting extensive discovery and/or depositions and desire to undertake "mini-discovery" followed by a settlement pro-

posal. This mini-discovery approach is particularly welcome in disputes where the settlement recommendation is non-binding, thus offering the parties a "free preview" of the case.

4. *The amount or importance of the controversy.* Most of the largest cases are eventually settled, in part because of reluctance to leave the decision to a court. High litigation costs, however, usually seem less important in a case involving very high stakes or a vital company interest. Thus, either or both parties may be reluctant to take part in a collaborate effort at an early stage. If so, the prospects are likely to be better after extensive discovery has taken place or the imminence of trial exerts pressure for settlement.

5. *Setting parameters for future conduct.* A settlement agreement can include provisions in the nature of injunctive relief that are enforceable as contractual obligations. If litigation is pending, such provisions can be incorporated in a consent decree.

6. *Suitability for neutral expert factfinding.* Whenever the parties find it necessary to retain technical, economic, or other experts, it may well be in their mutual interest to avoid the traditional battle of the experts by jointly retaining a neutral whose findings are advisory. These findings are likely to bring the parties much closer to settlement and, indeed, may enable the parties to avoid litigation altogether.

The above criteria can serve as useful guidelines in assessing the appropriateness of ADR techniques to a given dispute. Together with a presumption in favor of use of ADR in all cases, these considerations will help identify numerous cases in which a company can experiment with various ADR devices.

The company's experience with ADR techniques can then be applied to modify or refine the above criteria for assessing the ADR potential of a given dispute as well as other aspects of the company's ADR program. . . .

C. Confidentiality

Another problem associated with mediation as a method of dispute resolution is the legal uncertainty about the confidentiality of communications made in the mediation process. As a practical matter, the mutually agreed upon confidentiality of the mediation process is both an incentive for participation in the process and a critical ingredient for its success. Yet, as a legal matter, there is still considerable uncertainty about the extent to which communications made during the process of mediating a dispute are protected from disclosure in subsequent legal proceedings. This uncertainty about the confidentiality of mediation proceedings is cause for concern and may act as an impediment to the future development of mediation as a widespread method of dispute resolution.[17]

1. The Need for Confidentiality

Why is confidentiality critical to the success of mediation? First, the mediator of a dispute needs a broad and comprehensive understanding of the case, particularly if the mediator is called upon to fashion a settlement proposal. . . . In order to acquire this comprehensive understanding of the case, the mediator must look beyond the specific issues in dispute in an effort to illuminate and resolve the underlying causes of the dispute. This may require knowledge of proprietary information and/or information about internal corporate politics, which parties may be unwilling to share absent a credible assurance of confidentiality. The mediator must also understand the motives of the parties and their true needs, not merely their public bargaining positions. The parties must, therefore, feel free to advance tentative solutions and to make statements without fear that they will later be used as a basis for liability or as a measure of damage. This is particularly true in disputes involving uncertain areas of law, where limited abandonment of a firmly held legal position could be interpreted by others outside of the process as a tacit concession of the legal point. In sum, the success of a mediation hinges on candid, unrestricted dialogue and a free flow of information. In the absence of confidentiality, the exchange of information and ideas will be inhibited, severely curtailing the chance of fashioning a successful resolution to the dispute.

Second, the mediator must be perceived by the parties as completely neutral and impartial. This is necessary not only to ensure openness, but also to preserve the integrity of the mediation process. The presence of a neutral intermediary is, after all, the primary feature distinguishing mediation from conventional negotiation. Any suspicion that the mediator may become an adversary or witness against one of the parties in future litigation will undermine the parties' trust in the mediator. Such suspicions will cause parties to a mediation to take a cautious, adversarial stance vis-a-vis the mediator, making it difficult if not impossible for the mediator to create the cooperative atmosphere necessary for successful mediation.

Ultimately, the fear that mediators may be required to divulge information after a mediation would discourage people from entering into mediation at all. Thus,

ensuring confidentiality is linked directly to the public policy of encouraging resolution of disputes without resort to litigation. . . .

V. CONCLUSION

Those interested in using mediation to resolve disputes and in seeing mediation develop into a widely used means of conflict resolution still face problems, including the unwillingness of many to try mediation, the lack of institutionalized consideration of mediation as an alternative to litigation, and legal uncertainty about the confidentiality of the process. These problems, however, are not insurmountable and do not outweigh the important advantages of mediation as a means of resolving disputes. The many advantageous features of mediation include its cost-effectiveness, its informality, its flexibility, its adaptability to a variety of disputes, and its fully voluntary and nonbinding nature. . . .

In the final analysis, parties to a dispute should not hesitate to try mediation. Its potential for successfully resolving the dispute is great and the risk of failure is no more than to resort to the familiar course of litigation.

NOTES

1. *See generally* NATIONAL INSTITUTE FOR DISPUTE RESOLUTION, *Paths to Justice: Major Public Policy Issues of Dispute Resolution, Report of the Ad Hoc Panel on Dispute Resolution and Public Policy (Oct. 1983)*, in ACUS, SOURCEBOOK: FEDERAL AGENCY USE OF ALTERNATIVE MEANS OF DISPUTE RESOLUTION 5–53 (1987); DAUER, REPORT OF THE COMMITTEE ON CONFIDENTIALITY IN ALTERNATIVE DISPUTE RESOLUTION (CPR Oct. 1985); Hart, *Alternative Dispute Resolution: Negotiation, Mediation and Minitrial*, 37 FED'N INS. & CORP. COUNS. Q. 113, 114–16 (1987).
2. For descriptions and comparisons of various forms of alternative dispute resolution, *see* ACUS, *supra* note 1; Cooley, *Arbitration v. Media-*

tion: Explaining the Differences, 69 JUDICATURE 263 (1986); Hart, *supra* note 1; Sacks, *The Alternative Dispute Resolution Movement: Wave of the Future or Flash in the Pan?*, 26 ALBERTA L. REV. 233 (1988); AM. JUR. 2D, NEW TOPIC SERVICE, *Alternative Dispute Resolution* §§ 7–16 (1985).

3. *See generally* Phillips & Piazzva, *The Role of Mediation in Public Interest Disputes*, 34 HASTINGS L.J. 1231 (1983); Susskind & Ozawa, *Mediated Negotiation in the Public Sector*, 27 AM. BEHAV'L SCIENTIST 255 (1986).

4. Hart, *supra* note 1, at 119.

5. On the other hand, even in a case involving complex technical issues, the parties may not need a mediator with technical expertise. In mediation, it is the parties themselves who already have the requisite knowledge and make all the decisions. Unlike a judge or arbitrator, the mediator cannot impose a decision; thus, the mediator's technical understanding of the issues may not be crucial.

6. Estimates of the average duration of litigation and arbitration vary. *American Jurisprudence* reports that the average arbitration takes four to five months, while litigation may take several years. AM. JUR. 2D, *supra* note 2, § 7. Another source reports that the average duration from filing to trial in civil cases in federal courts throughout the United States is one and one-half years. Sacks, *supra* note 2, at 233. It can take up to six years to litigate a business dispute. THE FIRST ANNUAL JUDICIAL CONFERENCE OF THE UNITED STATES COURT OF APPEALS FOR THE FEDERAL CIRCUIT (May 20, 1983), *reprinted in* 100 F.R.D. 499, 521 (1984).

7. *See* ROGERS & SALEM, A STUDENT'S GUIDE TO MEDIATION AND THE LAW 45 (1987) (reporting that researchers have found that, on average, some 98% of a party's civil litigation expenses are attorney's fees).

8. *See* Liepmann, *Confidentiality in Environmental Mediation: Should Third Parties Have Access to the Process?*, 14 ENVTL. AFF. 93, 103 (1986).

9. Abramson, *Kenneth Feinberg Prospers by Getting Firms to Resolve Disputes Out of Court*, Wall St. J., Oct. 20, 1988, at B6, col. 1 (quoting William Von Glahn, an attorney for Williams Cos. in Tulsa, Okla.).

10. Henry & Lieberman, *Mediation: The Sleeping Giant of Business Dispute Resolution*, in THE MANAGER'S GUIDE TO RESOLVING LEGAL DISPUTES 59–60 (1985), *reprinted in* CPR LEGAL PROGRAM, PRACTICE GUIDE ON MEDIATION A1, A3–A4 (1988).

11. *See* Rogers & Salem, *supra* note 11, at 46; Susskind & Weinstein, *Toward a Theory of Environmental Dispute Resolution*, 9 BRIT. COLUM. ENVTL. AFF. L. REV. 311, 312–13 (1980-81); Note, *Protecting Confidentiality in Mediation*, 98 HARV. L. REV. 441, 444 n.25 (1984).

12. L. SUSSKIND, L. BACOW & M. WHEELER, RESOLVING ENVIRONMENTAL DISPUTES 2 (1983).

13. Sander, *Varieties of Dispute Processing*, 70 F.R.D. 79, 132 (1976) (address delivered at the National Conference on the Causes of Popular Dissatisfaction with the Administration of Justice).

14. *See generally* 4 ALTERNATIVES TO HIGH COST OF LITIGATION, *Academic Mismatch* 7 (Aug. 1986) (reporting on a recent survey of 6800 law students at seven northeastern law schools in which 58% responded that knowledge of negotiation and mediation was vital to practice but generally agreed that they did not learn about it in law school); Special Project, *Self-Help: Extrajudicial Rights, Privileges and Remedies in Contemporary American Society*, 37 VAND. L. REV. 845, 987–88 (1984).

15. Riskin, *Mediation and Lawyers*, 43 OHIO ST. L.J. 29, 45 (1982).

16. *See generally* Pou, *Federal Agency Use of "ADR": The Experience to Date*, in ACUS, *supra* note 1, at 101 (1987); Ray, Kestner, & Freedman, *Dispute Resolution: From Examination to Experimentation*, 65 MICH. B.J. 898 (1986); Smith, *Alternative Means of Dispute Resolution: Practices and Possibilities in the Federal Government*, 1984 MO. J. OF DISPUTE RESOLUTION 9.

17. A 1981 A.B.A. survey of mediation programs identified the question of whether statements made by participants during the mediation session could be used as evidence in subsequent legal proceedings as a predominant practical concern to alternative dispute resolution programs. Freedman, *Confidentiality: A Closer Look*, in A.B.A. SPECIAL COMMITTEE ON DISPUTE RESOLUTION, CONFIDENTIALITY IN MEDIATION: A PRACTITIONER'S GUIDE 47, 49 (1985).

NO

Owen M. Fiss

AGAINST SETTLEMENT

In a recent report to the Harvard Overseers, Derek Bok called for a new direction in legal education.[1] He decried "the familiar tilt in the law curriculum toward preparing students for legal combat," and asked instead that law schools train their students "for the gentler arts of reconciliation and accommodation."[2] He sought to turn our attention from the courts to "new voluntary mechanisms"[3] for resolving disputes. In doing so, Bok echoed themes that have long been associated with the Chief Justice,[4] and that have become a rallying point for the organized bar and the source of a new movement in the law. This movement . . . has even received its own acronym—ADR (Alternative Dispute Resolution). . . .

The advocates of ADR . . . exalt the idea of settlement more generally because they view adjudication as a process to resolve disputes. They act as though courts arose to resolve quarrels between neighbors who had reached an impasse and turned to a stranger for help. Courts are seen as an institutionalization of the stranger and adjudication is viewed as the process by which the stranger exercises power. The very fact that the neighbors have turned to someone else to resolve their dispute signifies a breakdown in their social relations; the advocates of ADR acknowledge this, but nonetheless hope that the neighbors will be able to reach agreement before the stranger renders judgment. Settlement is that agreement. It is a truce more than a true reconciliation, but it seems preferable to judgment because it rests on the consent of both parties and avoids the cost of a lengthy trial.

In my view, however, this account of adjudication and the case for settlement rest on questionable premises. I do not believe that settlement as a generic practice is preferable to judgment or should be institutionalized on a wholesale and indiscriminate basis. It should be treated instead as a highly problematic technique for streamlining dockets. Settlement is for me the civil analogue of plea bargaining: Consent is often coerced; the bargain may be struck by someone without authority; the absence of a trial and judgment renders subsequent judicial involvement troublesome; and although dockets are trimmed, justice may not be done. Like plea bargaining, settlement is a

From Owen M. Fiss, "Against Settlement," *Yale Law Journal*, vol. 93 (1984), pp. 1073–1090. Reprinted by permission of The Yale Law Journal Company and Fred B. Rothman & Company. Some notes omitted.

capitulation to the conditions of mass society and should be neither encouraged nor praised.

THE IMBALANCE OF POWER

By viewing the lawsuit as a quarrel between two neighbors, the dispute-resolution story that underlies ADR implicitly asks us to assume a rough equality between the contending parties. It treats settlement as the anticipation of the outcome of trial and assumes that the terms of settlement are simply a product of the parties' predictions of that outcome. In truth, however, settlement is also a function of the resources available to each party to finance the litigation, and those resources are frequently distributed unequally. Many lawsuits do not involve a property dispute between two neighbors, or between AT&T and the government (to update the story), but rather concern a struggle between a member of a racial minority and a municipal police department over alleged brutality, or a claim by a worker against a large corporation over work-related injuries. In these cases, the distribution of financial resources, or the ability of one party to pass along its costs, will invariably infect the bargaining process, and the settlement will be at odds with a conception of justice that seeks to make the wealth of the parties irrelevant.

The disparities in resources between the parties can influence the settlement in three ways. First, the poorer party may be less able to amass and analyze the information needed to predict the outcome of the litigation, and thus be disadvantaged in the bargaining process. Second, he may need the damages he seeks immediately and thus be induced to settle as a way of accelerating payment, even though he realizes he would get less now than he might if he awaited judgment. All plaintiffs want their damages immediately, but an indigent plaintiff may be exploited by a rich defendant because his need is so great that the defendant can force him to accept a sum that is less than the ordinary present value of the judgment. Third, the poorer party might be forced to settle because he does not have the resources to finance the litigation, to cover either his own projected expenses, such as his lawyer's time, or the expenses his opponent can impose through the manipulation of procedural mechanisms such as discovery. It might seem that settlement benefits the plaintiff by allowing him to avoid the costs of litigation, but this is not so. The defendant can anticipate the plaintiff's costs if the case were to be tried fully and decrease his offer by that amount. The indigent plaintiff is a victim of the costs of litigation even if he settles.

There are exceptions. Seemingly rich defendants may sometimes be subject to financial pressures that make them as anxious to settle as indigent plaintiffs. But I doubt that these circumstances occur with any great frequency. I also doubt that institutional arrangements such as contingent fees or the provision of legal services to the poor will in fact equalize resources between contending parties: The contingent fee does not equalize resources; it only makes an indigent plaintiff vulnerable to the willingness of the private bar to invest in his case. In effect, the ability to exploit the plaintiff's lack of resources has been transferred from rich defendants to lawyers who insist upon a hefty slice of the plaintiff's recovery as their fee. These lawyers, moreover, will only work for contingent fees in certain kinds of cases, such as personal-injury suits. And the contingent fee is of no avail when the defendant is the disadvantaged party. Governmental subsidies for legal services have a broader potential, but in the civil domain the battle for these subsidies was hard-fought, and they are in fact extremely limited, especially when it comes to cases that seek systemic reform of government practices.[5]

Of course, imbalances of power can distort judgment as well: Resources influence the quality of presentation, which in turn has an important bearing on who wins and the terms of victory. We count, however, on the guiding presence of the judge, who can employ a number of measures to lessen the impact of distributional inequalities. He can, for example, supplement the parties' presentations by asking questions, calling his own witnesses, and inviting other persons and institutions to participate as amici.[6] These measures are likely to make only a small contribution toward moderating the influence of distributional inequalities, but should not be ignored for that reason. Not even these small steps are possible with settlement. There is, moreover, a critical difference between a process like settlement, which is based on bargaining and accepts inequalities of wealth as an integral and legitimate component of the process, and a process like judgment, which knowingly struggles against those inequalities. Judgment aspires to an autonomy from distributional inequalities, and it gathers much of its appeal from this aspiration.

THE ABSENCE OF AUTHORITATIVE CONSENT

The argument for settlement presupposes that the contestants are individuals. These individuals speak for themselves and should be bound by the rules they generate. In many situations, however, individuals are ensnared in contractual relationships that impair their autonomy: Lawyers or insurance companies might, for example, agree to settlements that are in their interests but are not in the best interests of their clients, and to which their clients would not agree if the choice were still theirs.[7] But a deeper and more intractable problem arises from the fact that many parties are not individuals but rather organizations or groups. We do not know who is entitled to speak for these entities and to give the consent upon which so much of the appeal of settlement depends.

Some organizations, such as corporations or unions, have formal procedures for identifying the persons who are authorized to speak for them. But these procedures are imperfect: They are designed to facilitate transactions between the organization and outsiders, rather than to insure that the members of the organization in fact agree with a particular decision. Nor do they eliminate conflicts of interests. The chief executive officer of a corporation may settle a suit to prevent embarrassing disclosures about his managerial policies, but such disclosures might well be in the interest of the shareholders.[8] The president of a union may agree to a settlement as a way of preserving his power within the organization; for that very reason, he may not risk the dangers entailed in consulting the rank and file or in subjecting the settlement to ratification by the membership. Moreover, the representational procedures found in corporations, unions, or other private formal organizations are not universal. Much contemporary litigation, especially in the federal courts, involves governmental agencies,[9] and the procedures in those organizations for generating authoritative consent are far cruder than those in the corporate context. We are left to wonder, for example, whether the attorney general should be able to bind all state officials, some of whom are elected and thus have an independent mandate from the people, or even whether the incumbent attorney general should be able to bind his successors.[10]

These problems become even more pronounced when we turn from organizations and consider the fact that much contemporary litigation involves even more nebulous social entities, namely, groups. Some of these groups, such as ethnic or racial minorities, inmates of prisons, or residents of institutions for mentally retarded people, may have an identity or existence that transcends the lawsuit, but they do not have any formal organizational structure and therefore lack any procedures for generating authoritative consent. The absence of such a procedure is even more pronounced in cases involving a group, such as the purchasers of Cuisinarts between 1972 and 1982, which is constructed solely in order to create funds large enough to make it financially attractive for lawyers to handle the case.[11] . . .

THE LACK OF A FOUNDATION FOR CONTINUING JUDICIAL INVOLVEMENT

The dispute-resolution story trivializes the remedial dimensions of lawsuits and mistakenly assumes judgment to be the end of the process. It supposes that the judge's duty is to declare which neighbor is right and which wrong, and that this declaration will end the judge's involve-ment (save in that most exceptional situation where it is also necessary for him to issue a writ directing the sheriff to execute the declaration). Under these assumptions, settlement appears as an almost perfect substitute for judgment, for it too can declare the parties' rights. Often, however, judgment is not the end of a lawsuit but only the beginning. The involvement of the court may continue almost indefinitely. In these cases, settlement cannot provide an adequate basis for that necessary continuing involvement, and thus is no substitute for judgment.

The parties may sometimes be locked in combat with one another and view the lawsuit as only one phase in a long continuing struggle. The entry of judgment will then not end the struggle, but rather change its terms and the balance of power. One of the parties will invariably return to the court and again ask for its assistance, not so much because conditions have changed, but because the conditions that preceded the lawsuit have unfortunately not changed. This often occurs in domestic-relations cases, where the divorce decree represents only the opening salvo in an endless series of skirmishes over custody and support.

The structural reform cases that play such a prominent role on the federal docket provide another occasion for continuing judicial involvement. In these cases, courts seek to safeguard public values by restructuring large-scale bureaucratic organizations. The task is enormous, and our knowledge of how to restructure on-going bureaucratic organizations is limited. As a consequence, courts must oversee and manage the remedial process for a long time—maybe forever. This, I fear, is true of most school desegregation cases, some of which have been pending for twenty or thirty years. It is also true of antitrust cases that seek divestiture or reorganization of an industry. . . .

JUSTICE RATHER THAN PEACE

The dispute-resolution story makes settlement appear as a perfect substitute for judgment, as we just saw, by trivializing the remedial dimensions of a lawsuit, and also by reducing the social function of the lawsuit to one of resolving private disputes: In that story, settlement appears to achieve exactly the same purpose as judgment—peace between the parties—but at considerably less expense to society. The two quarreling neighbors turn to a court in order to resolve their dispute, and society makes courts available because it wants to aid in the achievement of their private ends or to secure the peace.

In my view, however, the purpose of adjudication should be understood in broader terms. Adjudication uses public resources, and employs not strangers chosen by the parties but public officials chosen by a process in which the public participates. These officials, like members of the legislative and executive branches, possess a power that has been defined and conferred by public law, not by private agreement. Their job is not to maximize the ends of private parties, nor simply to secure the peace, but to explicate and give force to the values embodied in authoritative texts such as the Constitution and statutes: to interpret those values and to bring reality into accord with them. This duty is not discharged when the parties settle.

In our political system, courts are reactive institutions. They do not search out interpretive occasions, but instead wait for others to bring matters to their attention. They also rely for the most part on others to investigate and present the law and facts. A settlement will thereby deprive a court of the occasion, and perhaps even the ability, to render an interpretation. A court cannot proceed (or not proceed very far) in the face of a settlement. To be against settlement is not to urge that parties be "forced" to litigate, since that would interfere with their autonomy and distort the adjudicative process; the parties will be inclined to make the court believe that their bargain is justice. To be against settlement is only to suggest that when the parties settle, society gets less than what appears, and for a price it does not know it is paying. Parties might settle while leaving justice undone. The settlement of a school suit might secure the peace, but not racial equality. Although the parties are prepared to live under the terms they bargained for, and although such peaceful coexistence may be a necessary precondition of justice, and itself a state of affairs to be valued, it is not justice itself. To settle for something means to accept less than some ideal.

I recognize that judges often announce settlements not with a sense of frustration or disappointment, as my account of adjudication might suggest, but with a sigh of relief. But this sigh should be seen for precisely what it is: It is not a recognition that a job is done, nor an acknowledgment that a job need not be done because justice has been secured. It is instead based on another sentiment altogether, namely, that another case has been "moved among," which is true whether or not justice has been done or even needs to be done. Or the sigh might be based on the fact that the agony of judgment has been avoided.

There is, of course, sometimes a value to avoidance, not just to the judge, who is thereby relieved of the need to make or enforce a hard decision, but also to society, which sometimes thrives by masking its basic contradictions. But will settlement result in avoidance when it is most appropriate? Other familiar avoidance devices, such as certiorari, at least promise a devotion to public ends, but settlement is controlled by the litigants, and is subject to their private motivations and all the vagaries of the bargaining process. There are also dangers to avoidance, and these may well outweigh any imagined benefits. Partisans of ADR—Chief Justice Burger, or even President Bok—may begin with a certain satisfaction with the status quo. But when one sees injustices that cry out for correction—as Congress did when it endorsed the concept of the private attorney general and as the Court of another era did when it sought to enhance access to the courts[12]—the value of avoidance diminishes and the agony of judgment becomes a necessity. Someone has to confront the betrayal of our deepest ideals and be prepared to turn the world upside down to bring those ideals to fruition.

THE REAL DIVIDE

To all this, one can readily imagine a simple response by way of confession and avoidance: We are not talking about *those* lawsuits. Advocates of ADR might insist that my account of adjudication, in contrast to the one implied by the dispute-resolution story, focuses on a rather narrow category of lawsuits. They could argue that while settlement may have only the most limited appeal with respect to those cases, I have not spoken to the "typical" case. My response is twofold.

First, even as a purely quantitative matter, I doubt that the number of cases I am referring to is trivial. My universe includes those cases in which there are significant distributional inequalities; those in which it is difficult to generate authoritative consent because organizations or social groups are parties or because the power to settle is vested in autonomous agents; those in which the court must continue to supervise the parties after judgment; and those in which justice needs to be done, or to put it more modestly, where there is a genuine social need for an authoritative interpretation of law. I imagine that the number of cases that satisfy one of these four criteria is considerable; in contrast to the kind of case portrayed in the dispute-resolution story, they probably dominate the docket of a modern court system.

Second, it demands a certain kind of myopia to be concerned only with the number of cases, as though all cases are equal simply because the clerk of the court assigns each a single docket number. All cases are not equal. The Los Angeles desegregation case,[13] to take one example, is not equal to the allegedly more typical suit involving a property dispute or an automobile accident. The desegregation suit consumes more resources, affects more people, and provokes far greater challenges to the judicial power. The settlement movement must introduce a qualitative perspective; it must speak to these more "significant" cases, and demonstrate the propriety of settling them. Otherwise it will soon be seen as an irrelevance, dealing with trivia rather than responding to the very conditions that give the movement its greatest sway and saliency.

Nor would sorting cases into "two tracks," one for settlement, and another for judgment, avoid my objections. Settling automobile cases and leaving discrimination or antitrust cases for judgment might remove a large number of cases from the dockets, but the dockets will nevertheless remain burdened with the cases that consume the most judicial resources and represent the most controversial exercises of the judicial power. A "two track" strategy would drain the argument for settlement of much of its appeal. I also doubt whether the "two track" strategy can be sensibly implemented. It is impossible to formulate adequate criteria for prospectively sorting cases. The problems of settlement are not tied to the subject matter of the suit, but instead stem from factors that are harder to identify, such as the wealth of the parties, the likely post-judgment history of the suit, or the need for an authoritative interpretation of law. . . . Settlement is a poor substitute for judgment; it is an even poorer substitute for the withdrawal of jurisdiction.

. . . [M]ost ADR advocates make no effort to distinguish between different types of cases or to suggest that "the gentler arts of reconciliation and accommodation" might be particularly appropriate for one type of case but not for another. They lump all cases together. This suggests that what divides me from the partisans of ADR is not that we are concerned with different universes of cases, that Derek Bok, for example, focuses on boundary quarrels while I see only desegregation suits. I suspect instead that what divides us is much deeper and stems from our understanding of the purpose of the civil law suit and its place in society. It is a difference in outlook.

Someone like Bok sees adjudication in essentially private terms: The purpose of lawsuits and the civil courts is to resolve disputes, and the amount of litigation we encounter is evidence of the needlessly combative and quarrelsome character of Americans. Or as Bok put it, using a more diplomatic idiom: "At bottom, ours is a society built on individualism, competition, and success."[14] I, on the other hand, see adjudication in more public terms: Civil litigation is an institutional arrangement for using state power to bring a recalcitrant reality closer to our chosen ideals. We turn to the courts because we need to, not because of some quirk in our personalities. We train our students in the tougher arts so that they may help secure all that the law promises, not because we want them to become gladiators or because we take a special pleasure in combat.

To conceive of the civil lawsuit in public terms as America does might be unique. I am willing to assume that no other country—including Japan, Bok's new paragon[15]—has a case like *Brown v. Board of Education*[16] in which the judicial power is used to eradicate the caste structure. I am willing to assume that no other country conceives of law and uses law in quite the way we do. But this should be a source of pride rather than shame. What is unique is not the problem, that we live short of our ideals, but that we alone among the nations of the world seem willing to do something about it. Adjudication American-style is not a reflection of our combativeness but rather a tribute to our inventiveness and perhaps even more to our commitment.

NOTES

1. Bok, *A Flawed System*, HARV. MAG., May-June 1983, at 38, *reprinted in* N.Y. ST. B.J., Oct. 1983, at 8, N.Y. ST. B.J., Nov. 1983, at 31; *excerpted in* 33 J. LEGAL EDUC. 570 (1983).

2. Bok, *supra* note 1, at 45.

3. *Id.*

4. *See, e.g.*, Burger, *Isn't There a Better Way?*, 68 A.B.A. J. 274 (1982); Burger, *Agenda for 2000 A.D.—A Need for Systematic Anticipation*, 70 F.R.D. 83, 93–96 (1976).

5. *See* 42 U.S.C. § 2996f(b)(3), (6), (8), (9) (Supp. V 1981) (restricting use of Legal Services Corporation funds for, *inter alia*, political, abortion-rights, and desegregation litigation).

6. In a case challenging conditions in Texas' state prison system, for example, Judge Justice ordered the United States to appear as an amicus curiae "[i]n order to investigate the facts alleged in the prisoners' complaints, to participate in such civil action with the full rights of a party thereto, and to advise this Court at all stages of the proceedings as to any action deemed appropriate by it." *In re* Estelle, 516 F.2d 480, 482 (5th Cir. 1975) (quoting unpublished district court order), *cert. denied*, 426 U.S. 925 (1976). The decree which was eventually entered found systemic constitutional violations and ordered sweeping changes in the state's prisons. *See Ruiz v. Estelle*, 503 F. Supp. 1265 (S.D. Tex. 1980), *motion to stay order granted in part and denied in part*, 650 F.2d 555 (5th Cir. 1981), *add'l motion to stay order granted in part and denied in part*, 666 F.2d 854 (5th Cir. 1982).

7. In *Glazer v. J.C. Bradford & Co.*, 616 F.2d 167 (5th Cir. 1980), for example, the court held that the plaintiff was bound by his attorney's offer of settlement simply because he had earlier instructed his attorney to investigate the possibility of settling the case.

8. In *Wolf v. Barkes*, 348 F.2d 994 (2d Cir. 1965), *cert. denied*, 382 U.S. 941 (1966), Curtis Publishing Company, one of whose stockholders had brought a derivative suit against several corporate officers alleging mismanagement and waste, settled privately with those officers. This settlement effectively eliminated the stockholders' ability to get an accounting of managerial behavior.

9. According to Judge Gilbert Merritt, almost half of the cases in the Sixth Circuit involve suits against government agencies or officials. Merritt, *Owen Fiss in Paradise Lost: The Judicial Bureaucracy in the Administrative State*, 92 YALE L.J. (1983) (forthcoming).

10. In March of this year, the Civil Rights Division announced its intention to support the position of white municipal employees in Birmingham, Alabama, who are attacking the city's affirmative action policy, even though that policy was initiated under a consent decree that the Division had previously negotiated and obtained in a suit to eliminate discrimination against blacks, *United States v. Jefferson County*, Civ. Act. No. 75-P-0666-S (N.D. Ala. Aug. 21, 1981) (approving consent decree). *See U.S. to Support Whites in Suits On Bias Decree*, N.Y. Times, Mar. 5, 1984, at A1, col. 2.

In the fall of 1982, the Reagan Administration announced that it would not defend the Internal Revenue Service's policy of withholding tax-exempt status from private educational institutions that discriminated on the basis of race. The IRS had initiated the policy after a three-judge district court had issued an injunction prohibiting the IRS from exempting such schools. *Green v. Kennedy*, 309 F. Supp. 1127 (D.D.C.), *appeal dismissed sub nom. Cannon v. Green*, 398 U.S. 956 (1970). The Supreme Court appointed a private attorney, William Coleman, essentially to defend the decree when the Reagan Administration announced its position. *See Bob Jones Univ. v. United States*, 102 S. Ct. 1965 (1982) ("invit[ing]" Coleman to brief and argue case "in support of the judgments below"), 103 S. Ct. 2017 (1983) (affirming IRS' policy); N.Y. Times, Apr. 20, 1982, at A1, col. 5; *id.* at D21, col. 1 (describing government's actions and Coleman's appointment).

11. *See In re* Cuisinart Food Processor Antitrust Litig., [1982–83 Transfer Binder] TRADE REG. REP. (CCH) ¶ 65,680 (D. Conn. Oct. 24, 1983).

12. For a discussion of the Supreme Court's decisions during the 1960's and early 1970's suggesting that access to the courts and the opportunity to litigate are essential due process rights, see Michelman, *The Supreme Court and Litigation Access Fees* (pts. 1 & 2), 1973 DUKE L.J. 1153, 1974 DUKE L.J. 527.

13. *See Crawford v. Board of Educ.*, 46 Cal. App. 3d 872, 120 Cal. Rptr. 334 (Ct. App. 1975), *aff'd*, 17 Cal. 3d, 551 P.2d 28, 130 Cal. Rptr. 724 (1976). For a recent recounting of the history of the 20 years of litigation, see *Crawford v. Board of Educ.*, 103 S. Ct. 3211, 3214–15 (1982).

14. Bok, *supra* note 1, at 42.

15. *Id.* at 41. As to the validity of the comparisons and a more subtle explanation of the determinants of litigiousness, see Haley, *The Myth of the Reluctant Litigant*, 4 J. JAPANESE STUD. 359, 389 (1978) ("Few misconceptions about Japan have been more widespread or as pernicious as the myth of the special reluctance of the Japanese to litigate."); *see also* Galanter, *Reading the Landscape of Disputes: What We Know and Don't Know (And Think We Know) About Our Allegedly Contentious and Litigious Society*, 31 UCLA L. REV. 4, 57–59 (1983) (paucity of lawyers in Japan due to restrictions on number of attorneys admitted to practice rather than to non-litigousness).

16. 347 U.S. 483 (1954); 349 U.S. 294 (1955).

POSTSCRIPT

Is ADR (Alternative Dispute Resolution) Preferable to Litigation?

These articles raise one question considered in Issue 1 on legal ethics—namely, what are the goals of the legal process? The attractiveness of mediation is that it does such an excellent job of fostering communication between hostile parties and of allowing them to work through their differences. But, as Fiss argues, law is designed to do more than help the particular disputants in a case. The resolution of disputes through law sends a message to all of us indicating what the norms of our society are and should be, what is acceptable behavior and what is not. When disputes are mediated privately, as occurs with most ADR processes, the public is left out. Having read the preceding articles, consider whether this is a problem that is insurmountable or whether there are ways to determine which kinds of problems should be settled in court and which might be resolved through ADR.

In the late 1960s and early 1970s, a common rallying cry was the phrase "law and order." The solution to disorder and to conflict was to have more law. It would have been inconceivable for many to believe that one could have more order with less law. Since that time, we have become more skeptical about the power of our institutions. We are also more knowledgeable about the strengths and weaknesses of the law. The growth of ADR reflects this increased level of both skepticism and knowledge. The increased use of ADR presents us with more choices in how disputes may be settled. It also provides us with a more complicated system of dispute resolution, since we no longer automatically run to court to solve a problem but instead ask which of several available methods is most appropriate.

Modern life is characterized by increased options and choices. Our range of alternatives in both ideas and material goods have been expanded and making choices is not easy. We are no longer able to react to some social problem or dispute with the attitude of "there ought to be a law." We are more sensitive today to the limits of law and to the strengths of some alternatives to law. We also have to be very careful to know when it is appropriate to use some alternative in lieu of law and when it is not.

Further information about the practice and theory of ADR can be found in Fisher and Ury, *Getting To Yes* (1981); J. Auerbach, *Justice Without Law* (1983); Goldberg, Green, and Sander, *Dispute Resolution* (1985); and L. Singer, *Settling Disputes* (1989).

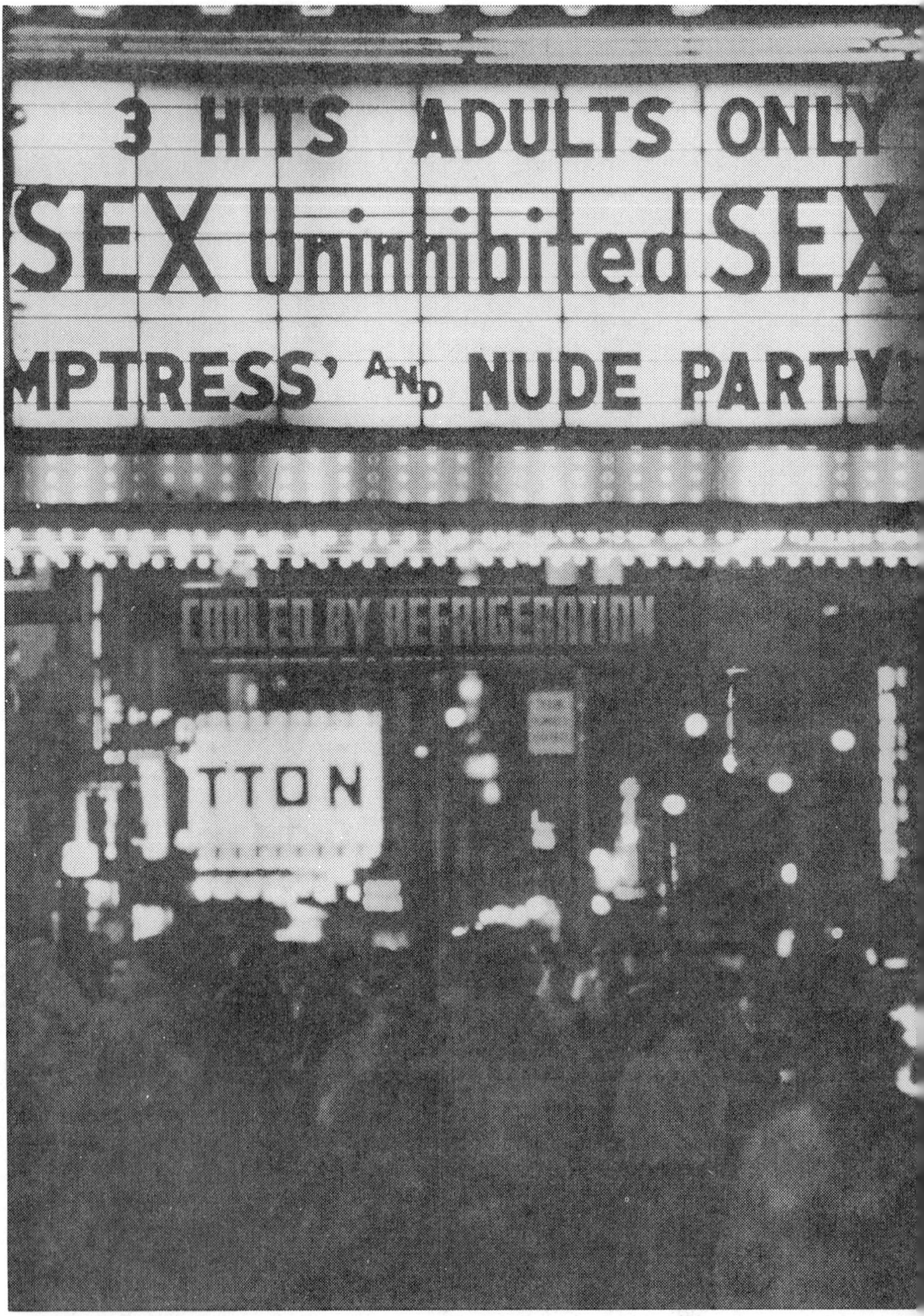
3 HITS ADULTS ONLY
SEX Uninhibited SEX
MPTRESS' AND NUDE PARTY
COOLED BY REFRIGERATION
TTON

PART 2

Law and Social Values

In any democratic society, the laws must reflect some consensus concerning the values of that society. Some of these values are clearly and easily determined. Laws against murder and theft, for example, command respect and acceptance and reflect widely held values.

In an increasingly complex, diverse, and technologically advanced society, however, questions of how best to protect individual rights of minorities and those with unpopular views inspire intense emotional debate. The delicate balance between the interests of the society as a whole and the liberties of individuals goes to the heart of the nature of law.

Is Drug Use Testing Permitted Under the Fourth Amendment?

Should Student Newspapers Be Censored?

Religious Displays on Public Property: Do They Violate the Constitution?

Is Abortion Protected by the Constitution?

Should Pornography Be Protected by the First Amendment?

Is Affirmative Action Constitutional?

Can States Restrict the Right to Die?

103

ISSUE 5

Is Drug Use Testing Permitted Under the Fourth Amendment?

YES: Anthony Kennedy from Majority Opinion, *National Treasury Employees Union v. Von Raab*, U.S. Supreme Court (1989)

NO: Antonin Scalia, from Dissenting Opinion, *National Treasury Employees Union v. Von Raab*, U.S. Supreme Court (1989)

ISSUE SUMMARY

YES: Supreme Court justice Anthony Kennedy believes that drug tests of Customs Service officials are reasonable under the Fourth Amendment to the Constitution, even when there is no probable cause or individualized suspicion.
NO: Justice Antonin Scalia, in dissent, argues that the Customs Service rules were not justified, served no reasonable purpose, and are unnecessary invasions of privacy.

Assume that you have recently completed your education and have applied for a job at a local public high school. You submitted a written application and have been invited for an interview. When you appear at school department headquarters, the receptionist tells you that prior to the interview you will have to provide a urine sample, which will be tested for the presence of drugs. If the test shows traces of certain drugs, your application for employment will be denied. What would be your response to such a request? Would you take the test? Do you have any objections or concerns about such tests? Do you think such practices should be allowed?

As public concern about drug abuse in this country has grown, drug use testing is becoming increasingly common. More than a quarter of all *Fortune* 500 companies test employees for drug use. Professional and college athletes are tested. The Department of Defense began mandatory urinalysis for members of the armed forces in 1982, and it claims that drug use has been cut in half as a result. Yet, critics argue, drug tests are often inaccurate and administered improperly, innocent people are hurt, privacy is invaded unduly, and testing programs are often a substitute for long-range solutions involving education or treatment.

In trying to develop a legal response to expanded proposals for drug use testing, consider the circumstances that courts might find significant in the hypothetical example above:

1. *Private or public institution*   The case described above involves a government agency as employer. The Constitution provides more protection to citizens from governmental invasions of privacy than from similar acts by private employers. Even if the Fourth Amendment, which protects against unreasonable searches and seizures, were held to bar drug use testing by the government, private employers might still be allowed to conduct such tests. Unless privacy or civil rights laws are found to be applicable, legislation, either by states or by the Congress, would probably be necessary to regulate private drug testing.

2. *Test reliability*   Urine tests give false positive results between five and twenty percent of the time. In addition, some over-the-counter drugs and even some foods have been known to trigger positive readings. If you had a cold the day of your interview and took a Contac or Sudafed pill that morning, your test might suggest the presence of amphetamines. Thus, urine tests will identify all illegal users but will also direct suspicion on some innocent persons. More expensive follow-up tests can be used to separate the legal from the illegal drug users, but sometimes action is made merely on the basis of the first urine screen. Should this be permitted? How much suspicion of drug use should be required to allow some action to be taken?

3. *Privacy*   In thinking about the drug testing process, you might be concerned with two different privacy issues. The most obvious is the intrusiveness of the testing procedure itself. In addition, however, drug use testing raises the question of whether employers have a legitimate interest in off-the-job activities of employees. A positive reading by the most commonly used urine tests will not reveal when the drug was used. Drug traces may remain in the urine for days or weeks. Thus, the employer often is not testing for drugs that were consumed on the job or are affecting job performance. Should it be lawful for employers to concern themselves with the off-hours activities of employees, even if they are illegal?

Drug use testing is becoming increasingly common. Many, if not most, individuals can live their lives without being fingerprinted or experiencing a lie detector test, but drug use testing is something that is becoming more difficult to avoid. It is a condition of employment in much of the private sector and in a variety of public sector occupations. It is a test that is of value only if given periodically and without notice. In the following opinion by Justice Anthony Kennedy, a majority of the Supreme Court finds that nothing in the Constitution bars such testing programs. In a very vigorous response, Justice Antonin Scalia, one of the most conservative members of the current Supreme Court, accuses the majority of needlessly invading privacy and weakening the Fourth Amendment.

YES

Anthony Kennedy

MAJORITY OPINION

NATIONAL TREASURY EMPLOYEES UNION, et al., v WILLIAM VON RAAB, **Commissioner, United States Customs Service**

Justice Kennedy delivered the opinion of the Court.

We granted certiorari to decide whether it violates the Fourth Amendment for the United States Customs Service to require a urinalysis test from employees who seek transfer or promotion to certain positions.

I
A

The United States Customs Service, a bureau of the Department of the Treasury, is the federal agency responsible for processing persons, carriers, cargo, and mail into the United States, collecting revenue from imports, and enforcing customs and related laws. An important responsibility of the Service is the interdiction and seizure of contraband, including illegal drugs. In 1987 alone, Customs agents seized drugs with a retail value of nearly 9 billion dollars. In the routine discharge of their duties, many Customs employees have direct contact with those who traffic in drugs for profit. Drug import operations, often directed by sophisticated criminal syndicates, may be effected by violence or its threat. As a necessary response, many Customs operatives carry and use firearms in connection with their official duties.

In December 1985, respondent, the Commissioner of Customs, established a Drug Screening Task Force to explore the possibility of implementing a drug screening program within the Service. After extensive research and consultation with experts in the field, the Task Force concluded "that drug screening through urinalysis is technologically reliable, valid and accurate." Citing this conclusion, the Commissioner announced his intention to require drug tests of employees who applied for, or occupied, certain positions

From *National Treasury Employees Union et al. v. William Van Raab,* 109 S.Ct. 1384, 103 L.Ed. 2d 685 (1989). Some notes and case citations omitted.

within the Service. The Commissioner stated his belief that "Customs is largely drug-free," but noted also that "unfortunately no segment of society is immune from the threat of illegal drug use." Drug interdiction has become the agency's primary enforcement mission, and the Commissioner stressed that "there is no room in the Customs Service for those who break the laws prohibiting the possession and use of illegal drugs."

In May 1986, the Commissioner announced implementation of the drug-testing program. Drug tests were made a condition of placement or employment for positions that meet one or more of three criteria. The first is direct involvement in drug interdiction or enforcement of related laws, an activity the Commissioner deemed fraught with obvious dangers to the mission of the agency and the lives of customs agents. The second criterion is a requirement that the incumbent carry firearms, as the Commissioner concluded that "[p]ublic safety demands that employees who carry deadly arms and are prepared to make instant life or death decisions be drug free." The third criterion is a requirement for the incumbent to handle "classified" material, which the Commissioner determined might fall into the hands of smugglers if accessible to employees who, by reason of their own illegal drug use, are susceptible to bribery or blackmail.

After an employee qualifies for a position covered by the Customs testing program, the Service advises him by letter that his final selection is contingent upon successful completion of drug screening. An independent contractor contacts the employee to fix the time and place for collecting the sample. On reporting for the test, the employee must produce photographic identification and remove any outer garments, such as a coat or a jacket, and personal belongings. The employee may produce the sample behind a partition, or in the privacy of a bathroom stall if he so chooses. To ensure against adulteration of the specimen, or substitution of a sample from another person, a monitor of the same sex as the employee remains close at hand to listen for the normal sounds of urination. Dye is added to the toilet water to prevent the employee from using the water to adulterate the sample.

Upon receiving the specimen, the monitor inspects it to ensure its proper temperature and color, places a tamper-proof custody seal over the container, and affixes an identification label indicating the date and the individual's specimen number. The employee signs a chain-of-custody form, which is initialed by the monitor, and the urine sample is placed in a plastic bag, sealed, and submitted to a laboratory.[1]

The laboratory tests the sample for the presence of marijuana, cocaine, opiates, amphetamines, and phencyclidine. Two tests are used. An initial screening test uses the enzyme-multiplied-immunoassay technique (EMIT). Any specimen that is identified as positive on this initial test must then be confirmed using gas chromatography/mass spectrometry (GC/MS). Confirmed positive results are reported to a "Medical Review Officer," "[a] licensed physician . . . who has knowledge of substance abuse disorders and has appropriate medical training to interpret and evaluate the individual's positive test result together with his or her medical history and any other relevant biomedical information." HHS Reg § 1.2, 53 Fed Reg 11980 (1988); HHS Reg § 2.4(g), id., at 11983. After verifying the positive result, the Medical Review Officer transmits it to the agency.

Customs employees who test positive for drugs and who can offer no satisfactory explanation are subject to dismissal from the Service. Test results may not, however, be turned over to any other agency, including criminal prosecutors, without the employee's written consent.

B

Petitioners, a union of federal employees and a union official, commenced this suit in the United States District Court for the Eastern District of Louisiana on behalf of current Customs Service employees who seek covered positions. Petitioners alleged that the Custom Service drug-testing program violated, inter alia, the Fourth Amendment. The District Court agreed. 649 F Supp. 380 (1986). The court acknowledged "the legitimate governmental interest in a drug-free work place and work force," but concluded that "the drug testing plan constitutes an overly intrusive policy of searches and seizures without probable cause or reasonable suspicion, in violation of legitimate expectations of privacy." Id., at 387. The court enjoined the drug testing program, and ordered the Customs Service not to require drug tests of any applicants for covered positions.

A divided panel of the United States Court of Appeals for the Fifth Circuit vacated the injunction. 816 F2d 170 (1987). The court agreed with petitioners that the drug screening program, by requiring an employee to produce a urine sample for chemical testing, effects a search within the meaning of the Fourth Amendment. The court held further that the searches required by the Commissioner's directive are reasonable under the Fourth Amendment. It first noted that the "[t]he Service has attempted to minimize the

intrusiveness of the search" by not requiring visual observation of the act of urination and by affording notice to the employee that he will be tested. Id., at 177. The court also considered it significant that the program limits discretion in determining which employees are to be tested, ibid., and noted that the tests are an aspect of the employment relationship. Id., at 178.

The court further found that the Government has a strong interest in detecting drug use among employees who meet the criteria of the Customs program. It reasoned that drug use by covered employees casts substantial doubt on their ability to discharge their duties honestly and vigorously, undermining public confidence in the integrity of the Service and concomitantly impairing the Service's efforts to enforce the drug laws. Illicit drug users, the court found, are susceptible to bribery and blackmail, may be tempted to divert for their own use portions of any drug shipments they interdict, and may, if required to carry firearms, "endanger the safety of their fellow agents, as well as their own, when their performance is impaired by drug use." Ibid. "Considering the nature and responsibilities of the jobs for which applicants are being considered at Customs and the limited scope of the search," the court stated, "the exaction of consent as a condition of assignment to the new job is not unreasonable." Id., at 179.

The dissenting judge concluded that the Customs program is not an effective method for achieving the Service's goals. He argued principally that an employee "given a five day notification of a test date need only abstain from drug use to prevent being identified as a user." Id., at 184. He noted also that persons already employed in sensitive positions are not subject to the test. Ibid. Because he did not believe the Customs program can achieve its purposes, the dissenting judge found it unreasonable under the Fourth Amendment.

We granted certiorari. 485 US _____, 99 L Ed 2d 232, 108 S Ct 1072 (1988). We now affirm so much of the judgment of the court of appeals as upheld the testing of employees directly involved in drug interdiction or required to carry firearms. We vacate the judgment to the extent it upheld the testing of applicants for positions requiring the incumbent to handle classified materials, and remand for further proceedings.

II

In *Skinner v Railway Labor Executives' Assn.*, ante, at _____, 103 L Ed 2d 639, 109 S Ct _____, decided today, we hold that federal regulations requiring employees of private railroads to produce urine samples for chemical testing implicate the Fourth Amendment, as those tests invade reasonable expectations of privacy. Our earlier cases have settled that the Fourth Amendment protects individuals from unreasonable searches conducted by the government, even when the Government acts as an employer, and, in view of our holding in Railway Labor Executives that urine tests are searches, it follows that the Customs Service's drug testing program must meet the reasonableness requirement of the Fourth Amendment.

While we have often emphasized, and reiterate today, that a search must be supported, as a general matter, by a warrant issued upon probable cause, our decision in Railway Labor Executives reaffirms the longstanding principle that neither a warrant nor probable cause, nor, indeed, any measure of individualized suspicion, is an indispensable component of reasonableness in every circumstance. As we note in Railway Labor Executives, our cases establish that where a Fourth Amendment intrusion serves special governmental needs, beyond the normal need for law enforcement, it is necessary to balance the individual's privacy expectations against the Government's interests to determine whether it is impractical to require a warrant or some level of individualized suspicion in the particular context.

It is clear that the Customs Service's drug testing program is not designed to serve the ordinary needs of law enforcement. Test results may not be used in a criminal prosecution of the employee without the employee's consent. The purposes of the program are to deter drug use among those eligible for promotion to sensitive positions within the Service and to prevent the promotion of drug users to those positions. These substantial interests, no less than the Government's concern for safe rail transportation at issue in Railway Labor Executives, present a special need that may justify departure from the ordinary warrant and probable cause requirements. . . .

B

Even where it is reasonable to dispense with the warrant requirement in the particular circumstances, a search ordinarily must be based on probable cause. Our cases teach, however, that the probable-cause standard " 'is peculiarly related to criminal investigations.' " In particular, the traditional probable-cause standard may be unhelpful in analyzing the reasonableness of routine administrative functions, especially where the Government seeks to *prevent* the development of hazardous conditions or to detect violations that rarely generate articulable grounds for searching any particular place or person. Cf. *Camara v Municipal Court*, 387 US, at 535–536, 18 L Ed 2d 930, 87 S Ct 1727 (noting that building code inspections, unlike searches conducted pursuant to a criminal investigation, are designed "to prevent even the unintentional development of conditions which are hazardous to public health and safety"); *United States v Martinez-Fuerte*, 428 US, at 557, 49 L Ed 2d 1116, 96 S Ct 3074 (noting that requiring particularized suspicion before routine stops on major highways near the Mexican border "would be impractical because the flow of traffic tends to be too heavy to allow the particularized study of a given car that would enable it to be identified as a possible carrier of illegal aliens"). Our precedents have settled that, in certain limited circumstances, the Government's need to discover such latent or hidden conditions, or to prevent their development, is sufficiently compelling to justify the intrusion on privacy entailed by conducting such searches without any measure of individualized suspicion. We think the Government's need to conduct the suspicionless searches required by the Customs program outweighs the privacy interests of employees engaged directly in drug interdiction, and of those who otherwise are required to carry firearms.

The Customs Service is our Nation's first line of defense against one of the greatest problems affecting the health and welfare of our population. We have adverted before to "the veritable national crisis in law enforcement caused by smuggling of illicit narcotics." *United States v Montoya de Hernandez*, 473 US 531, 538, 87 L Ed 2d 381, 105 S Ct 3304 (1985).

See also *Florida v Royer*, 460 US 491, 513, 75 L Ed 2d 229, 103 S Ct 1319 (Blackmun, J., dissenting). Our cases also reflect the traffickers' seemingly inexhaustible repertoire of deceptive practices and elaborate schemes for importing narcotics. e.g., *United States v Montoya de Hernandez*, supra, at 538–539, 87 L Ed 2d 381, 105 S Ct 3304; *United States v Ramsey*, 431 US 606, 608–609, 52 L Ed 2d 617, 97 S Ct 1972 (1977). The record in this case confirms that, through the adroit selection of source locations, smuggling routes, and increasingly elaborate methods of concealment, drug traffickers have managed to bring into this country increasingly large quantities of illegal drugs. The record also indicates, and it is well known, that drug smugglers do not hesitate to use violence to protect their lucrative trade and avoid apprehension.

Many of the Service's employees are often exposed to this criminal element and to the controlled substances they seek to smuggle into the country. The physical safety of these employees may be threatened, and many may be tempted not only by bribes from the traffickers with whom they deal, but also by their own access to vast sources of valuable contraband seized and controlled by the Service. The Commissioner indicated below that "Customs [o]fficers have been shot, stabbed, run over, dragged by automobiles, and assaulted with blunt objects while performing their duties." At least nine officers have died in the line of duty since 1974. He also noted that Customs officers have been the targets of bribery by drug smugglers on numerous occasions, and several have been removed from the Service for accepting bribes and other integrity violations. Id., at 114. See also Customs USA, Fiscal Year 1987, at 31 (reporting internal investigations that resulted in the arrest of 24 employees and 54 civilians); Customs USA, Fiscal Year 1986, p 32 (reporting that 334 criminal and serious integrity investigations were conducted during the fiscal year, resulting in the arrest of 37 employees and 17 civilians); Customs USA, Fiscal Year 1985, at 32 (reporting that 284 criminal and serious integrity investigations were conducted during the 1985 fiscal year, resulting in the arrest of 15 employees and 51 civilians).

It is readily apparent that the Government has a compelling interest in ensuring that front-line interdiction personnel are physically fit, and have unimpeachable integrity and judgment. Indeed, the Government's interest here is at least as important as its interest in searching travelers entering the country. We have long held that travelers seeking to enter the country may be stopped and required to submit to a routine search without probable cause, or even founded suspicion, "because of national self protection reasonably requiring one entering the country to identify himself as entitled to come in, and his belongings as effects which may be lawfully brought in." *Carroll v United States*, 267 US 132, 154, 69 L Ed 543, 45 S Ct 280, 39 ALR 790 (1985). This national interest in self protection could be irreparably damaged if those charged with safeguarding it were, because of their own drug use, unsympathetic to their mission of interdicting narcotics. A drug user's indifference to the Service's basic mission or, even worse, his active complicity with the malefactors, can facilitate importation of sizable drug shipments or block apprehension of dangerous criminals. The public interest demands effective measures to bar drug users from positions directly involving the interdiction of illegal drugs.

The public interest likewise demands effective measures to prevent the promotion of drug users to positions that require the incumbent to carry a firearm, even if the incumbent is not engaged directly in the interdiction of drugs. Customs employees who may use deadly force plainly "discharge duties fraught with such risks of injury to others that even a momentary lapse of attention can have disastrous consequences." Railway Labor Executives, ante at 103 L Ed 2d 639. We agree with the Government that the public should not bear the risk that employees who may suffer from impaired perception and judgment will be promoted to positions where they may need to employ deadly force. Indeed, ensuring against the creation of this dangerous risk will itself further Fourth Amendment values, as the use of deadly force may violate the Fourth Amendment in certain circumstances. See *Tennessee v Garner*, 471 US 1, 7–12, 85 L Ed 2d 1, 105 S Ct 1694 (1985).

Against these valid public interests we must weigh the interference with individual liberty that results from requiring these classes of employees to undergo a urine test. The interference with individual privacy that results from the collection of a urine sample for subsequent chemical analysis could be substantial in some circumstances. We have recognized, however, that the "operational realities of the workplace" may render entirely reasonable certain work-related intrusions by supervisors and co-workers that might be viewed as unreasonable in other contexts. While these operational realities will rarely affect an employee's expectations of privacy with respect to searches of his person, or of personal effects that the employee may bring to the workplace, it is plain that certain forms of public employment may diminish privacy expectations even with respect to such personal searches. Employees of the United States Mint, for example, should expect to be subject to certain routine personal searches when they leave the workplace every day. Similarly, those who join our military or intelligence services may not only be required to give what in other contexts might be viewed as extraordinary assurances of trustworthiness and probity, but also may expect intrusive inquiries into their physical fitness for those special positions. Cf. *Snepp v United States*, 444 US 507, 509, n 3, 62 L Ed 2d 704, 100 S Ct 763 (1980); *Parker v Levy*, 417 US 733, 758, 41 L Ed 2d 439, 94 S Ct 2547 (1974); *Committee for GI Rights v Callaway*, 171 US App DC 73, 84, 518 F 2d 466, 477 (1975).

We think Customs employees who are directly involved in the interdiction of illegal drugs or who are required to carry firearms in the line of duty likewise have a diminished expectation of privacy in respect to the intrusions occasioned by a urine test. Unlike most private citizens or government employees in general, employees involved in drug interdiction reasonably should expect effective inquiry into their fitness and probity. Much the same is true of employees who are required to carry firearms. Because successful performance of their duties depends uniquely on their judgment and dexterity, these employees cannot reasonably expect to keep from the Service personal information that bears directly on their fitness. While reasonable tests designed to elicit this information doubtless infringe some privacy expectations, we do not believe these expectations outweigh the Government's compelling interests in safety and in the integrity of our borders.[2]

Without disparaging the importance of the governmental interests that support the suspicionless searches of these employees, petitioners nevertheless contend that the Service's drug testing program is unreasonable in two particulars. First, petitioners argue that the program is unjustified because it is not based on a belief that testing will reveal any drug use by covered employees. In pressing this argument, petitioners point out that the Service's testing scheme was not implemented in response to any perceived drug problem among Customs employees, and that the program actually has not led to the discovery of a significant number of drug users. Counsel for petitioners informed us at oral argument that no more than 5 employees out of 3,600 have tested positive for drugs. Second, petitioners contend that the Service's scheme is not a "sufficiently productive mechanism to justify [its] intrusion upon Fourth Amendment interests," *Delaware v Prouse*, 440 US, at 648, 658–659, 59 L Ed 2d 660, 99 S Ct 1391, because illegal drug users can avoid detection with ease by temporary abstinence or by surreptitious adulteration of their urine specimens. These contentions are unpersuasive.

Petitioners' first contention evinces an unduly narrow view of the context in which the Service's testing program was implemented. Petitioners do not dispute, nor can there be doubt, that drug abuse is one of the most serious problems confronting our society today. There is little reason to believe that American workplaces are immune from this pervasive social problem, as is amply illustrated by our decision in Railway Labor Executives. See also *Masino v United States*, 589 F2d 1048, 1050 (Ct Cl 1978) (describing marijuana use by two Customs Inspectors). Detecting drug impairment on the part of employees can be a difficult task, especially where, as here, it is not feasible to subject employees and their work-product to the kind of day-to-day scrutiny that is the norm in more traditional office environments. Indeed, the almost unique mission of the Service gives the Government a compelling interest in ensuring that many of these covered employees do not use drugs even off-duty, for such use creates risks of bribery and blackmail against which the Government is entitled to guard. In light of the extraordinary safety and national security hazards that would attend the promotion of drug users to positions that require the carrying of firearms or the interdiction of controlled substances, the Service's policy of deterring drug users from seeking such promotions cannot be deemed unreasonable.

The mere circumstance that all but a few of the employees tested are entirely innocent of wrongdoing does not impugn the program's validity. The same is likely to be true of householders who are required to submit to suspicionless housing code inspections, see *Camara v Municipal Court*, 387 US 523, 18 L Ed 2d 930, 87 S Ct 1727 (1967), and of motorists who are stopped at the checkpoints we approved in *United States v Martinez-Fuerte*, 428 US 543, 49 L Ed 2d 1116, 96 S Ct 3074 (1976). The Service's program is designed to prevent the promotion of drug users to sensitive positions as much as it is designed to detect those employees who use drugs. Where, as here, the possible harm against which the Government seeks to guard is substantial, the need to prevent its occurrence furnishes an ample justification for reasonable searches calculated to advance the Government's goal.[3]

We think petitioners' second argument—that the Service's testing program

is ineffective because employees may attempt to deceive the test by a brief abstention before the test date, or by adulterating their urine specimens—overstates the case. As the Court of Appeals noted, addicts may be unable to abstain even for a limited period of time, or may be unaware of the "fade-away effect" of certain drugs. 816 F2d, at 180. More importantly, the avoidance techniques suggested by petitioners are fraught with uncertainty and risks for those employees who venture to attempt them. A particular employee's pattern of elimination for a given drug cannot be predicted with perfect accuracy, and, in any event, this information is not likely to be known or available to the employee. Petitioners' own expert indicated below that the time it takes for particular drugs to become undetectable in urine can vary widely depending on the individual, and may extend for as long as 22 days. Thus, contrary to petitioners' suggestion, no employee reasonably can expect to deceive the test by the simple expedient of abstaining after the test date is assigned. Nor can he expect attempts at adulteration to succeed, in view of the precautions taken by the sample collector to ensure the integrity of the sample. In all the circumstances, we are persuaded that the program bears a close and substantial relation to the Service's goal of deterring drug users from seeking promotion to sensitive positions.

In sum, we believe the Government has demonstrated that its compelling interests in safeguarding our borders and the public safety outweigh the privacy expectations of employees who seek to be promoted to positions that directly involve the interdiction of illegal drugs or that require the incumbent to carry a firearm. We hold that the testing of these employees is reasonable under the Fourth Amendment.

C

We are unable, on the present record, to assess the reasonableness of the Government's testing program insofar as it covers employees who are required "to handle classified material." We readily agree that the Government has a compelling interest in protecting truly sensitive information from those who, "under compulsion of circumstances or for other reasons, . . . might compromise [such] information." *Department of the Navy v Egan*, 98 L Ed 2d 918, 108 S Ct 818 (1988). See also *United States v Robel*, 389 US 258, 267, 19 L Ed 2d 508, 88 S Ct 419 (1967) ("We have recognized that, while the Constitution protects against invasions of individual rights, it does not withdraw from the Government the power to safeguard its vital interests . . . The Government can deny access to its secrets to those who would use such information to harm the Nation"). We also agree that employees who seek promotions to positions where they would handle sensitive information can be required to submit to a urine test under the Service's screening program, especially if the positions covered under this category require background investigations, medical examinations, or other intrusions that may be expected to diminish their expectations of privacy in respect of a urinalysis test. Cf. Department of the *Navy v Egan*, supra, at 98 L Ed 2d 918, 108 S Ct 818 (noting that the Executive branch generally subjects those desiring a security clearance to "a background investigation that varies according to the degree of adverse effect the applicant could have on the national security").

It is not clear, however, whether the category defined by the Service's testing directive encompasses only those Customs employees likely to gain access to sensitive information. Employees who are tested under the Service's scheme include those holding such diverse positions as "Accountant," "Accounting Technician," "Animal Caretaker," "Attorney (All)," "Baggage Clerk," "Co-op Student (All)," "Electric Equipment Repairer," "Mail Clerk/Assistant," and "Messenger." We assume these positions were selected for coverage under the Service's testing program by reason of the incumbent's access to "classified" information, as it is not clear that they would fall under either of the two categories we have already considered. Yet it is not evident that those occupying these positions are likely to gain access to sensitive information, and this apparent discrepancy raises in our minds the question whether the Service has defined this category of employees more broadly than necessary to meet the purposes of the Commissioner's directive.

We cannot resolve this ambiguity on the basis of the record before us, and we think it is appropriate to remand the case to the court of appeals for such proceedings as may be necessary to clarify the scope of this category of employees subject to testing. Upon remand the court of appeals should examine the criteria used by the Service in determining what materials are classified and in deciding whom to test under this rubric. In assessing the reasonableness of requiring tests of these employees, the court should also consider pertinent information bearing upon the employees' privacy expectations, as well as the supervision to which these employees are already subject.

III

Where the Government requires its employees to produce urine samples to be analyzed for evidence of illegal drug use, the collection and subsequent chemical analysis of such samples are searches that must meet the reasonableness requirement of the Fourth Amendment. Because the testing program adopted by the Customs Service is not designed to serve the ordinary needs of law enforcement, we have balanced the public interest in the Service's testing program against the privacy concerns implicated by the tests, without reference to our usual presumption in favor of the procedures specified in the Warrant Clause, to assess whether the tests required by Customs are reasonable.

We hold that the suspicionless testing of employees who apply for promotion to positions directly involving the interdiction of illegal drugs, or to positions which require the incumbent to carry a firearm, is reasonable. The Government's compelling interests in preventing the promotion of drug users to positions where they might endanger the integrity of our Nation's borders or the life of the citizenry outweigh the privacy interests of those who seek promotion to these positions, who enjoy a diminished expectation of privacy by virtue of the special, and obvious, physical and ethical demands of those positions. We do not decide whether testing those who apply for promotion to positions where they would handle "classified" information is reasonable because we find the record inadequate for this purpose.

The judgment of the Court of Appeals for the Fifth Circuit is affirmed in part and vacated in part, and the case is remanded for further proceedings consistent with this opinion.

It is so ordered.

NOTES

1. After this case was decided by the Court of Appeals, 816 F2d 170 (CA5 1987), the United States Department of Health and Human Services, in accordance with recently enacted legislation, Pub L 100-71, § 503, 101 Stat 468–471, promulgated regulations (hereinafter HHS Regulations or HHS Reg) governing certain federal employee drug testing programs. 53 Fed Reg 11979 (1988). To the extent the HHS Regulations add to, or depart from, the procedures adopted as part of a federal drug screening program covered by Pub L 100-71, the HHS Regulations control. Pub L 100-71, § 503(b)(2)(B), 101 Stat. 470. Both parties agree that the Customs Service's drug testing program must conform to the HHS Regulations. See Brief for Petitioners 6, n 8; Brief for Respondents 4–5, and n 4. We therefore consider the HHS Regulations to the extent they supplement or displace the Commissioner's original directive. See *California Bankers Assn. v Shultz*, 416 US 21, 53, 39 L Ed 2d 812, 94 S Ct 1494 (1974); *Thorpe v Housing Authority*, 393 US 268, 281–282, 21 L Ed 2d 474, 89 S Ct 518, 49 Ohio Ops 2d 374 (1969).

One respect in which the original Customs directive differs from the now-prevailing regime concerns the extent to which the employee may be required to disclose personal medical information. Under the Service's original plan, each tested employee was asked to disclose, at the time the urine sample was collected, any medications taken within the last 30 days, and to explain any circumstances under which he may have been in legitimate contact will illegal substances within the last 30 days. Failure to provide this information at this time could result in the agency not considering the effect of medications or other licit contacts with drugs on a positive test result. Under the HHS Regulations, an employee need not provide information concerning medications when he produces the sample for testing. He may instead present such information only after he is notified that his specimen tested positive for illicit drugs, at which time the Medical Review Officer reviews all records made available by the employee to determine whether the positive indication could have been caused by lawful use of drugs. See HHS Reg § 2.7, 53 Fed Reg 11985–11986 (1988).

2. The procedures prescribed by the Customs Service for the collection and analysis of the requisite samples do not carry the grave poten-

tial for "arbitrary and oppressive interference with the privacy and personal security of individuals." *United States v Martinez-Fuerte*, 428 US 543, 554, 49 L Ed 2d 1116, 96 S Ct 3074 (1976), that the Fourth Amendment was designed to prevent. Indeed, these procedures significantly minimize the program's intrusion on privacy interests. Only employees who have been tentatively accepted for promotion or transfer to one of the three categories of covered positions are tested, and applicants know at the outset that a drug test is a requirement of those positions. Employees are also notified in advance of the scheduled sample collection, thus reducing to a minimum any "unsettling show of authority," *Delaware v Prouse*, 440 US 648, 657, 59 L Ed 2d 660, 99 S Ct 1391 (1979), that may be associated with unexpected intrusions on privacy. Cf. *United States v Martinez-Fuerte*, supra, at 559, 49 L Ed 2d 1116, 96 S Ct 3074 (noting that the intrusion on privacy occasioned by routine highway checkpoints is minimized by the fact that motorists "are not taken by surprise as they know, or may obtain knowledge of, the location of the checkpoints and will not be stopped elsewhere"); *Wyman v James*, 400 US 309, 320–321, 27 L Ed 2d 408, 91 S Ct 381 (1971) (providing a welfare recipient with advance notice that she would be visited by a welfare caseworker minimized the intrusion on privacy occasioned by the visit). There is no direct observation of the act of urination, as the employee may provide a specimen in the privacy of a stall.

Further, urine samples may be examined only for the specified drugs. The use of samples to test for any other substances is prohibited. See HHS Reg § 2.1(c), 53 Fed Reg 11980 (1988). And, as the court of appeals noted, the combination of EMIT and GC/MS tests required by the Service is highly accurate, assuming proper storage, handling, and measurement techniques. 816 F2d, at 181. Finally, an employee need not disclose personal medical information to the Government unless his test result is positive, and even then any such information is reported to a licensed physician. Taken together, these procedures significantly minimize the intrusiveness of the Service's drug screening program.

3. The point is well illustrated also by the Federal Government's practice of requiring the search of all passengers seeking to board commercial airliners, as well as the search of their carry-on luggage, without any basis for suspecting any particular passenger of an untoward motive. Applying our precedents dealing with administrative searches, see, e.g., *Camara v Municipal Court*, the lower courts that have considered the question have consistently concluded that such searches are reasonable under the Fourth Amendment. As Judge Friendly explained in a leading case upholding such searches: "When the risk is the jeopardy to hundreds of human lives and millions of dollars of property inherent in the pirating or blowing up of a large airplane, that danger *alone* meets the test of reasonableness, so long as the search is conducted in good faith for the purpose of preventing hijacking or like damage and with reasonable scope and the passenger has been given advance notice of his liability to such a search so that he can avoid it by choosing not to travel by air." *United States v Edwards*, 498 F2d 496, 500 (CA2 1974) (emphasis in original). See also *United States v Skipwith*, 482 F2d 1272, 1275–1276 (CA5 1973); *United States v Davis*, 482 F2d 893, 907–912 (CA9 1973).

It is true, as counsel for petitioners pointed out at oral argument, that these air piracy precautions were adopted in response to an observable national and international hijacking crisis. Tr of Oral Arg 13. Yet we would not suppose that, if the validity of these searches be conceded, the Government would be precluded from conducting them absent a demonstration of danger as to any particular airport or airline. It is sufficient that the Government have a compelling interest in preventing an otherwise pervasive societal problem from spreading to the particular context.

Nor would we think, in view of the obvious deterrent purpose of these searches, that the validity of the government's airport screening program necessarily turns on whether significant numbers of putative air pirates are actually discovered by the searches conducted under the program. In the 15 years the program has been in effect, more than 9.5 *billion* persons have been screened, and over 10 *billion* pieces of luggage have been inspected. See Federal Aviation Administration, Semiannual Report to Congress on the Effectiveness of The Civil Aviation Program (Nov. 1988) (Exhibit 6). By far the overwhelming majority of those persons who have been searched, like Customs employees who have been tested under the Service's drug screening scheme, have proved entirely innocent—only 42,000 firearms have been detected during the same period. Ibid. When the Government's interest lies in deterring highly hazardous conduct, a low incidence of such conduct, far from impugning the validity of the scheme for implementing this interest, is more logically viewed as a hallmark of success. See *Bell v Wolfish*, 441 US 520, 559, 60 L Ed 2d 447, 99 S Ct 1861 (1979).

MINORITY OPINION OF ANTONIN SCALIA

Justice Scalia, with whom Justice Stevens joins, dissenting.

The issue in this case is not whether Customs Service employees can constitutionally be denied promotion, or even dismissed, for a single instance of unlawful drug use, at home or at work. They assuredly can. The issue here is what steps can constitutionally be taken to *detect* such drug use. The Government asserts it can demand that employees perform "an excretory function traditionally shielded by great privacy," *Skinner v Railway Labor Executives' Assn.*, ante, at 103 L Ed 2d 6539, while "a monitor of the same sex . . . remains close at hand to listen for the normal sounds," ante, at 103 L Ed 2d 699, and that the excretion thus produced be turned over to the Government for chemical analysis. The Court agrees that this constitutes a search for purposes of the Fourth Amendment—and I think it obvious that it is a type of search particularly destructive of privacy and offensive to personal dignity.

Until today this Court had upheld a bodily search separate from arrest and without individualized suspicion of wrongdoing only with respect to prison inmates, relying upon the uniquely dangerous nature of that environment. See *Bell v Wolfish*, 441 US 520, 558–560, 60 L Ed 2d 447, 99 S Ct 1861 (1979). Today, in *Skinner*, we allow a less intrusive bodily search of railroad employees involved in train accidents. I joined the Court's opinion there because the demonstrated frequency of drug and alcohol use by the targeted class of employees, and the demonstrated connection between such use and grave harm, rendered the search a reasonable means of protecting society. I decline to join the Court's opinion in the present case because neither frequency of use nor connection to harm is demonstrated or even likely. In my view the Customs Service rules are a kind of immolation of privacy and human dignity in symbolic opposition to drug use.

The Fourth Amendment protects the "right of the people to be secure in their persons, houses, papers, and effects, against unreasonable searches and seizures." While there are some absolutes in Fourth Amendment law, as

From *National Treasury Employees Union et al. v. William Van Raab*, 109 S.Ct. 1384, 103 L.Ed. 2d 685 (1989). Some case citations omitted.

soon as those have been left behind and the question comes down to whether a particular search has been "reasonable," the answer depends largely upon the social necessity that prompts the search. Thus, in upholding the administrative search of a student's purse in a school, we began with the observation (documented by an agency report to Congress) that "[m]aintaining order in the classroom has never been easy, but in recent years, school disorder has often taken particularly ugly forms: drug use and violent crime in the schools have become major social problems." *New Jersey v T. L. O.* 469 US 325, 339, 83 L Ed 2d 720, 105 S Ct 733 (1985). When we approved fixed checkpoints near the Mexican border to stop and search cars for illegal aliens, we observed at the outset that "the Immigration and Naturalization Service now suggests there may be as many as 10 or 12 million aliens illegally in the country," and that "[i]nterdicting the flow of illegal entrants from Mexico poses formidable law enforcement problems." *United States v Martinez-Fuerte,* 428 US 543, 551–552, 49 L Ed 2d 1116, 96 S Ct 3074 (1976). And the substantive analysis of our opinion today in *Skinner* begins, "[t]he problem of alcohol use on American railroads is as old as the industry itself," and goes on to cite statistics concerning that problem and the accidents it causes, including a 1979 study finding that "23% of the operating personnel were 'problem drinkers' " *Skinner,* ante, at 103 L Ed 2d 639.

The Court's opinion in the present case, however, will be searched in vain for real evidence of a real problem that will be solved by urine testing of Customs Service employees. Instead, there are assurances that "[t]he Customs Service is our Nation's first line of defense against one of the greatest problems affecting the health and welfare of our population," ante, at 103 L Ed 2d 704; that "[m]any of the Service's employees are often exposed to [drug smugglers] and to the controlled substances they seek to smuggle into the country," ante, at 103 L Ed 2d 704; that "Customs officers have been the targets of bribery by drug smugglers on numerous occasions, and several have been removed from the Service for accepting bribes and other integrity violations," Ibid.; that "the Government has a compelling interest in ensuring that front-line interdiction personnel are physically fit, and have unimpeachable integrity and judgment," ibid.; that the "national interest in self protection could be irreparably damaged if those charged with safeguarding it were, because of their own drug use, unsympathetic to their mission of interdicting narcotics," ante, at 103 L Ed 2d 705; and that "the public should not bear the risk that employees who may suffer from impaired perception and judgment will be promoted to positions where they may need to employ deadly force," ibid. To paraphrase Churchill, all this contains much that is obviously true, and much that is relevant; unfortunately, what is obviously true is not relevant, and what is relevant is not obviously true. The only pertinent points, it seems to me, are supported by nothing but speculation, and not very plausible speculation at that. It is not apparent to me that a Customs Service employee who uses drugs is significantly more likely to be bribed by a drug smuggler, any more than a Customs Service employee who wears diamonds is significantly more likely to be bribed by a diamond smuggler—unless, perhaps, the addiction to drugs is so severe, and requires so much money to maintain, that it would be detectable even without benefit of a urine test. Nor is it apparent to me that Customs officers who use drugs will be appreciably less "sympathetic" to their drug-interdiction mission, any more than police officers who exceed the speed limit in their private cars are appreciably less sympathetic to their mission of enforcing the traffic laws. (The only difference is that the Customs officer's individual efforts, if they are irreplaceable, can theoretically affect the availability of his own drug supply—a prospect so remote as to be an absurd basis of motivation.) Nor, finally, is it apparent to me that urine tests will be even marginally more effective in preventing gun-carrying agents from risking "impaired perception and judgment" than is their current knowledge that, if impaired, they may be shot dead in unequal combat with unimpaired smugglers—unless, again, their addiction is so severe that no urine test is needed for detection.

What is absent in the Government's justifications—notably absent, revealingly absent, and as far as I am concerned dispositively absent—is the recitation of *even a single instance* in which any of the speculated horribles actually occurred: an instance, that is, in which the cause of bribe-taking, or of poor aim, or of unsympathetic law enforcement, or of compromise of classified information, was drug use. Although the Court points out that several employees have in the past been removed from the Service for accepting bribes and other integrity violations, and that at least nine officers have died in the line of duty since 1974, ante, at 103 L Ed 2d 704, there is no indication whatever that these incidents were related to drug use by Service employees. Perhaps concrete evidence of the severity

of a problem is unnecessary when it is so well known that courts can almost take judicial notice of it; but that is surely not the case here. The Commissioner of Customs himself has stated that he "believe[s] that Customs is largely drug-free," that "[t]he extent of illegal drug use by Customs employees was not the reason for establishing this program," and that he "hope[s] and expect[s] to receive reports of very few positive findings through drug screening." App 10, 15. The test results have fulfilled those hopes and expectations. According to the Service's counsel, out of 3,600 employees tested, no more than 5 tested positive for drugs. See ante, at 103 L Ed 2d 707.

The Court's response to this lack of evidence is that "[t]here is little reason to believe that American workplaces are immune from [the] pervasive social problem" of drug abuse. Ante, at 103 L Ed 2d 707. Perhaps such a generalization would suffice if the workplace at issue could produce such catastrophic social harm that no risk whatever is tolerable—the secured areas of a nuclear power plant, for example, see *Rushton v Nebraska Public Power District*, 844 F2d 562 (CA8 1988). But if such a generalization suffices to justify demeaning bodily searches, without particularized suspicion, to guard against the bribing or blackmailing of a law enforcement agent, or the careless use of a firearm, then the Fourth Amendment has become frail protection indeed. In *Skinner, Bell, T. L. O.,* and *Martinez-Fuerte*, we took pains to establish the existence of special need for the search or seizure—a need based not upon the existence of a "pervasive social problem" combined with speculation as to the effect of that problem in the field at issue, but rather upon well known or well demonstrated evils *in that field*, with well known or well demonstrated consequences. In *Skinner*, for example, we pointed to a long history of alcohol abuse in the railroad industry, and noted that in an 8-year period 45 train accidents and incidents had occurred because of alcohol- and drug-impaired railroad employees, killing 34 people, injuring 66, and causing more than $28 million in property damage. Ante, at 103 L Ed 2d 639. In the present case, by contrast, not only is the Customs Service thought to be "largely drug-free," but the connection between whatever drug use may exist and serious social harm is entirely speculative. Except for the fact that the search of a person is much more intrusive than the stop of a car, the present case resembles *Delaware v Prouse*, 440 US 648, 59 L Ed 2d 660, 99 S Ct 1391 (1979), where we held that the Fourth Amendment prohibited random stops to check drivers' licenses and motor vehicle registration. The contribution of this practice to highway safety, we concluded, was "marginal at best" since the number of licensed drivers that must be stopped in order too find one unlicensed one "will be large indeed." Id., at 660, 59 L Ed 2d 660, 99 S Ct 1391.

Today's decision would be wrong, but at least of more limited effect, if its approval of drug testing were confined to that category of employees assigned specifically to drug interdiction duties. Relatively few public employees fit that description. But in extending approval of drug testing to that category consisting of employees who carry firearms, the Court exposes vast numbers of public employees to this needless indignity. Logically, of course, if those who carry guns can be treated in this fashion, so can all others whose work, if performed under the influence of drugs, may en-

danger others—automobile drivers, operators of other potentially dangerous equipment, construction workers, school crossing guards. A similarly broad scope attaches to the Court's approval of drug testing for those with access to "sensitive information."[1] Since this category is not limited to Service employees with drug interdiction duties, nor to "sensitive information" specifically relating to drug traffic, today's holding apparently approves drug testing for all federal employees with security clearances—or, indeed, for all federal employees with valuable confidential information to impart. Since drug use is not a particular problem in the Customs Service, employees throughout the government are no less likely to violate the public trust by taking bribes to feed their drug habit, or by yielding to blackmail. Moreover, there is no reason why this super-protection against harms arising from drug use must be limited to public employees; a law requiring similar testing of private citizens who use dangerous instruments such as guns or cars, or who have access to classified information would also be constitutional.

There is only one apparent basis that sets the testing at issue here apart from all these other situations—but it is not a basis upon which the Court is willing to rely. I do not believe for a minute that the driving force behind these drug-testing rules was any of the feeble justifications put forward by counsel here and accepted by the Court. The only plausible explanation, in my view, is what the Commissioner himself offered in the concluding sentence of his memorandum to Customs Service employees announcing the program: "Implementation of the drug screening program would set an important example in our country's struggle with this most serious threat to our national health and security." App 12. Or as respondent's brief to this Court asserted: "if a law enforcement agency and its employees do not take the law seriously, neither will the public on which the agency's effectiveness depends." Brief for United States 36. What better way to show that the Government is serious about its "war on drugs" than to subject its employees on the front line of that war to this invasion of their privacy and affront to their dignity? To be sure, there is only a slight chance that it will prevent some serious public harm resulting from Service employee drug use, but it will show to the world that the Service is "clean," and—most important of all—will demonstrate the determination of the Government to eliminate this scourge of our society! I think it obvious that this justification is unacceptable; that the impairment of individual liberties cannot be the means of making a point; that symbolism, even symbolism for so worthy a cause as the abolition of unlawful drugs, cannot validate an otherwise unreasonable search.

There is irony in the Government's citation, in support of its position, of Justice Brandeis's statement in *Olmstead v United States*, 277 US 438, 485, 72 L Ed 944, 48 S Ct 564, 66 ALR 376 (1928) that "[f]or good or for ill, [our Government] teaches the whole people by its example." Brief for the United States 36. Brandeis was there *dissenting* from the Court's admission of evidence obtained through an unlawful Government wiretap. He was not praising the Government's example of vigor and enthusiasm in combating crime, but condemning its example that "the end justified the means," 277 US, at 485, 72 L Ed 944, 48 S Ct 564, 66 ALR 376. An even more apt

quotation from that famous Brandeis dissent would have been the following:

"[I]t is . . . immaterial that the intrusion was in aid of law enforcement. Experience should teach us to be most on our guard to protect liberty when the Government's purposes are beneficent. Men born to freedom are naturally alert to repel invasion of their liberty by evil-minded rulers. The greatest dangers to liberty lurk in insidious encroachment by men of zeal, well-meaning but without understanding." Id., at 479, 72 L Ed 944, 48 S Ct 564, 66 ALR 376.

Those who lose because of the lack of understanding that begot the present exercise in symbolism are not just the Customs Service employees, whose dignity is thus offended, but all of us—who suffer a coarsening of our national manners that ultimately give the Fourth Amendment its content, and who become subject to the administration of federal officials whose respect for our privacy can hardly be greater than the small respect they have been taught to have for their own.

NOTES

1. The Court apparently approves application of the urine tests to personnel receiving access to "sensitive information." Ante, at 103 L Ed 2d 710. Since, however, it is unsure whether "classified material" is "sensitive information," it remands with instructions that the court of appeals "examine the criteria used by the Service in determining what materials are classified and in deciding whom to test under this rubric." Ante, at 103 L Ed 2d 710. I am not sure what these instructions mean. Surely the person who classifies information *always* considers it "sensitive" in some sense—and the Court does not indicate what particular sort of sensitivity is crucial. Moreover, it seems to me most unlikely that "the criteria used by the Service in determining what materials are classified" are any different from those prescribed by the President in his Executive Order on the subject, see Exec Order No. 12356, 3 CFR 166 (1982 Comp)—and if there is a

difference it is probably unlawful, see § 5.4(b)(2), id., at 177. In any case, whatever idiosyncratic standards for classification the Customs Service might have would seem to be irrelevant, inasmuch as the rule at issue here is not limited to material classified *by the Customs Service*, but includes (and may well apply principally to) material classified elsewhere in the Government—for example, in the Federal Bureau of Investigation, the Drug Enforcement Administration or the State Department—and conveyed to the Service. See App 24-25.

POSTSCRIPT

Is Drug Use Testing Permitted Under the Fourth Amendment?

The pressure to pursue drug testing programs is political, economic, and technological. Drug abuse has surfaced a principal domestic concern of voters. Economically, government studies claim that drug abuse costs employers between $30–40 billion in property damage, quality control, absenteeism, employee theft, and increased insurance costs. Widely divergent estimates of narcotics traffic range from $27 to $110 billion. In addition, technologies for drug testing that are cheaper and more revealing but seem less intrusive are being developed. Would the objection to drug testing be as strong if the test consisted of cutting and analyzing one or two hairs rather than obtaining a urine specimen? The new technologies that will become available for testing, and the new technologies that already exist for communicating private information, guarantee that there will be a growing amount of litigation during the next few years.

The number of cases involving the legality of drug use testing is proliferating. In addition to customs officials, courts have allowed such tests for jockeys, *Shoemaker v. Handel*, 795 F. 2d 1136 (1986); prison employees, *McDonell v. Hunter*, 809 F. 2d 1302 (1987); and school bus drivers, *Division 241 Amalgamated Transit Union v. Sucsy*, 538 F. 2d 1264 (1976). Testing has not been allowed for firefighters, *Capua v. City of Plainfield*, 643 F. Supp. 1507 (1986). For a state court case that ruled that teachers may not be tested without particularized suspicion, see *Patchogue-Medford Congress of Teachers v. Board of Education*, 70 N.Y. 2d 57, 517 N.Y.S. 2d 456, 510 N.E. 2d 325 (1987). A landmark case that allowed forcibly obtained blood tests in drunk driving tests was *Schmerber v. California*, 86 S.Ct. 1826 (1966).

Recent analyses of drug use testing can be found in "Alternative Challenges to Drug Testing of Government Employees: Options After *Von Raab* and *Skinner*," 58 *George Washington Law Review* 148 (1989); "Testing for Drug Use in the American Workplace: A Symposium," 11 *Nova Law Review* 291 (1987); Morrow, "Drug Testing in the Workplace: Issues for the Arbitrator," 4 *Journal of Dispute Resolution* 273 (1989); Leeson, "The Drug Testing of College Athletes," 16 *Journal of College and University Law* 325 (1989); Edward Adams, "Random Drug Testing of Government Employees: A Constitutional Procedure," 54 *University of Chicago Law Review* 1335 (1987); and Yale Kamisar, "The Fourth Amendment in an Age of Drug and AIDS Testing," *New York Times Magazine*, September 13, 1987. J. M. Chaiken and M. R. Chaiken, in *Varieties of Criminal Behavior* (Rand Co., 1982), studied the history of drug abuse among career criminals.

ISSUE 6

Should Student Newspapers Be Censored?

YES: Byron White, from Majority Opinion, *Hazelwood v. Kuhlmeier,* U.S. Supreme Court (1988)

NO: Stephen Arons, from "Censorship Undermines Education," *An Original Essay Written for This Volume* (1990)

ISSUE SUMMARY

YES: Supreme Court justice Byron White believes that school officials act under proper authority when they choose to censor school publications, or any other school-sponsored activities, because they, as well as parents and teachers, are responsible for safeguarding the values expressed by their schools.

NO: Stephen Arons, a professor of legal studies at the University of Massachusetts, argues that Justice White's decision in *Hazelwood v. Kuhlmeier* ignores the ways in which "majority-dominated schooling" can undermine education. To him, the policies of our schools and the opinions of our courts should teach us that "freedom of intellect and spirit" are necessary to a democracy.

The universality of public education in the United States, or at least the attempt to educate 100% of the children aged 6–18, seems a given in the 1990s. We might forget that in many parts of the world access to formal educational institutions was restricted to very small segments of the society—the nobility, the rich, or only boys and men. Even today, many children remain estranged from the educational system of their country.

As educational systems became more universal, they have also assumed more of the responsibility for preparing children for future life, and more demands have been made of teachers and administrators. The school environment is different from what it once was, partly because children are less sheltered than they used to be. They have easier access to information and to ideas from which they were previously restricted. Professor Joshua Meyrowitz has described how

> in the first half of the twentieth century, childhood was considered a time of innocence and isolation. The child was sheltered from the nasty realities of life.

The child was dressed differently from adults. There were separate "languages" for children and adults; there were words and topics—such as birth, death, sex, and money—that were considered unfit for children's ears. And there was a strict age-grading system, supported by the structure of the school, that designated what a child of any given age should know and do.[1]

The modern family is different from what the family used to be and the conditions under which children are raised are different from what they once were. It should not be surprising, therefore, that conflict and controversy seem to be occurring with more frequency in the school setting.

The issue debated in the articles that follow is whether or not and under what conditions a student newspaper may be censored by school authorities. Supreme Court justice Byron White, in an opinion from an actual legal case, believes that control by the authorities is legitimate. Professor Stephen Arons, on the other hand, suggests that censorship is antithetical to the goals of education.

The conflicting attitudes of the parties involved in the case—the teacher, principal, students, and community—are typical of clashing viewpoints that arise in the school arena. On one side are the students. They wrote a newspaper as part of a school course and included articles that they thought were enlightening and relevant to their lives. Certainly, the subjects of the controversial articles, teenage pregnancy and the impact of divorce, are timely and of serious concern to high school students.

Competing with the rights of the students are the concerns of Mr. Reynolds, the school principal. He has broad responsibilities in his position. He must guard the safety and welfare of his students while monitoring curriculum, teacher performance, parental requests, and the needs of individual students. As you read Justice White's opinion in the case, assess how legitimate you think Mr. Reynolds's concerns are and whether they should take precedence over the asserted rights of the students.

The kind of situation described in the following articles, in which constitutional rights are subverted to the will of the majority, raises questions in many people's minds about what the limits of public education's authority should be. As one tries to answer this question, an even more profound question emerges—what are the goals of public education?

NOTES

1. Meyrowitz, *No Sense of Place* (1985), p. 227.

YES

Byron White

MAJORITY OPINION OF BYRON WHITE

HAZELWOOD SCHOOL DISTRICT v. CATHY KUHLMEIER

This case concerns the extent to which educators may exercise editorial control over the contents of a high school newspaper produced as part of the school's journalism curriculum.

I

Petitioners are the Hazelwood School District in St. Louis County, Missouri; various school officials; Robert Eugene Reynolds, the principal of Hazelwood East High School, and Howard Emerson, a teacher in the school district. Respondents are three former Hazelwood East students who were staff members of Spectrum, the school newspaper. They contend that school officials violated their First Amendment rights by deleting two pages of articles from the May 13, 1983, issue of Spectrum.

Spectrum was written and edited by the Journalism II class at Hazelwood East. The newspaper was published every three weeks or so during the 1982–1983 school year. More than 4,500 copies of the newspaper were distributed during that year to students, school personnel, and members of the community.

The Board of Education allocated funds from its annual budget for the printing of Spectrum. These funds were supplemented by proceeds from sales of the newspaper. The printing expenses during the 1982–1983 school year totaled $4,668.50; revenue from sales was $1,166.84. The other costs associated with the newspaper—such as supplies, textbooks, and a portion of the journalism teacher's salary—were borne entirely by the Board.

The Journalism II course was taught by Robert Stergos for most of the 1982–1983 academic year. Stergos left Hazelwood East to take a job in private industry on April 29, 1983, when the May 13 edition of Spectrum was nearing completion, and petitioner Emerson took his place as newspaper adviser for the remaining weeks of the term.

From *Hazelwood School District v. Cathy Kuhlmeier*, 484 U.S. 260, 108 S.Ct. 562, 98 L.Ed. 2d 592 (1988). Some notes and case citations omitted.

The practice at Hazelwood East during the spring 1983 semester was for the journalism teacher to submit page proofs of each Spectrum issue to Principal Reynolds for his review prior to publication. On May 10, Emerson delivered the proofs of the May 13 edition to Reynolds, who objected to two of the articles scheduled to appear in that edition. One of the stories described three Hazelwood East students' experiences with pregnancy; the other discussed the impact of divorce on students at the school.

Reynolds was concerned that, although the pregnancy story used false names "to keep the identity of these girls a secret," the pregnant students still might be identifiable from the text. He also believed that the article's references to sexual activity and birth control were inappropriate for some of the younger students at the school. In addition, Reynolds was concerned that a student identified by name in the divorce story had complained that her father "wasn't spending enough time with my mom, my sister and I" prior to the divorce, "was always out of town on business or out late playing cards with the guys," and "always argued about everything" with her mother. Reynolds believed that the student's parents should have been given an opportunity to respond to these remarks or to consent to their publication. He was unaware that Emerson had deleted the student's name from the final version of the article.

Reynolds believed that there was no time to make the necessary changes in the stories before the scheduled press run and that the newspaper would not appear before the end of the school year if printing were delayed to any significant extent. He concluded that his only options under the circumstances were to publish a four-page newspaper instead of the planned six-page newspaper, eliminating the two pages on which the offending stories appeared, or to publish no newspaper at all. Accordingly, he directed Emerson to withhold from publication the two pages containing the stories on pregnancy and divorce.[1] He informed his superiors of the decision, and they concurred.

Respondents subsequently commenced this action in the United States District Court for the Eastern District of Missouri seeking a declaration that their First Amendment rights had been violated, injunctive relief, and monetary damages. After a bench trial, the District Court denied an injunction, holding that no First Amendment violation had occurred. 607 F. Supp. 1450 (1985).

The District Court concluded that school officials may impose restraints on students' speech in activities that are " 'an integral part of the school's education function' "—including the publication of a school-sponsored newspaper by a journalism class—so long as their decision has " 'a substantial and reasonable basis.' " Id., at 1466 (quoting Frasca v. Andrews, 463 F. Supp. 1043, 1052 (EDNY 1979)). The court found that Principal Reynolds' concern that the pregnant students' anonymity would be lost and their privacy invaded was "legitimate and reasonable," given "the small number of pregnant students at Hazelwood East and several identifying characteristics that were disclosed in the article." The court held that Reynolds' action was also justified "to avoid the impression that [the school] endorses the sexual norms of the subjects" and to shield younger students from exposure to unsuitable material. The deletion of the article on divorce was seen by the court as a reasonable response to the invasion of privacy concerns raised by the named student's remarks. Because the article did not indicate that the student's parents had been offered an opportunity to respond to her allegations, said the court, there was cause for "serious doubt that the article complied with the rules of fairness which are standard in the field of journalism and which were covered in the textbook used in the Journalism II class." Furthermore, the court concluded that Reynolds was justified in deleting two full pages of the newspaper, instead of deleting only the pregnancy and divorce stories or requiring that those stories be modified to address his concerns, based on his "reasonable belief that he had to make an immediate decision and that there was no time to make modifications to the articles in question."

The Court of appeals for the Eighth Circuit reversed. 795 F. 2d 1368 (1986). The court held at outset that Spectrum was not only "a part of the school adopted curriculum," but also a public forum, because the newspaper was "intended to be and operated as a conduit for student viewpoint." The court then concluded that Spectrum's status as a public forum precluded school officials from censoring its contents except when " 'necessary to avoid material and substantial interference with school work or discipline . . . or the rights of others.' " Id., at 1374 (quoting Tinker v. Des Moines Independent Community School Dist., 393 U. S. 503, 511 (1969)).

The Court of Appeals found "no evidence in the record that the principal could have reasonably forecast that the censored articles or any materials in the censored articles would have materially disrupted classwork or given rise to substantial disorder in the school." School officials were entitled to censor the articles on the ground that they invaded the rights of others, according to the court, only if publication of the articles could have resulted in tort liability to the school. The court concluded that no tort action for libel or invasion of privacy could have been maintained against the school by the subjects of the two articles or by their families. Accordingly, the court held that school officials had violated respondents' First Amendment rights by deleting the two pages of the newspaper.

We granted certiorari, and we now reverse.

II

Students in the public schools do not "shed their constitutional rights to freedom of speech or expression at the schoolhouse gate." Tinker, supra, at 506. They cannot be punished merely for expressing their personal views on the school premises—whether "in the cafeteria, or on the playing field, or on the campus during the authorized hours," id., at 512-513—unless school authorities have reason to believe that such expression will "substantially interfere with the work of the school or impinge upon the rights of other students." Id., at 509.

We have nonetheless recognized that the First Amendment rights of students in the public schools "are not automatically coextensive with the rights of adults in other settings," Bethel School District No. 403 v. Fraser (1986), and must be "applied in light of the special characteristics of the school environment." Tinker, supra, at 506; cf. New Jersey v. T. L. O., 469 U. S.325, 341-343 (1985). A school need not tolerate student speech that is inconsistent with its "basic educational mission," *Fraser, supra,* at——, even though the government could not censor similar speech outside the school. Accordingly, we held in *Fraser* that a student could be disciplined for having delivered a speech that was "sexually explicit" but not legally obscene at an official school assembly, because the school was entitled to "disassociate itself" from the speech in a manner that would demonstrate to others that such vulgarity is "wholly inconsistent with the 'fundamental values' of public school education." *Ibid.* We thus recognized that "[t]he determination of what manner of speech in the classroom or in school assembly is inappropriate properly rests with the school board," *id.,* at——, rather than with the federal courts. It is in this context that respondents' First Amendment claims must be considered.

A

We deal first with the question whether Spectrum may appropriately be characterized as a forum for public expression. The public schools do not possess all of the attributes of streets, parks, and other traditional public forums that "time out of mind, have been used for purposes of assembly, communicating thoughts between citizens, and discussing public questions." *Hague v. CIO,* 307 U. S. 496, 515 (1939). Cf. *Widmar v. Vincent,* 454 U. S. 263, 267–268, n. 5 (1981). Hence, school facilities may be deemed to be public forums only if school authorities have "by policy or by practice" opened those facilities "for indiscriminate use by the general public," *Perry Education Assn. v. Perry Local Educators' Assn.,* 460 U. S. 37, 47 (1983), or by some segment of the public, such as student organizations. *Id.,* at 46, n. 7 (citing *Widmar v. Vincent*).

If the facilities have instead been reserved for other intended purposes, "communicative or otherwise," then no public forum has been created, and school officials may impose reasonable restrictions on the speech of students, teachers, and other members of the school community. *Ibid.* "The government does not create a public forum by inaction or by permitting limited discourse, but only by intentionally opening a nontraditional forum for public discourse." *Cornelius v. NAACP Legal Defense & Educational Fund, Inc.,* 473 U. S. 788, 802 (1985).

The policy of school officials toward Spectrum was reflected in Hazelwood School Board Policy 348.51 and the Hazelwood East Curriculum Guide. Board Policy 348.51 provided that "[s]chool sponsored publications are developed within the adopted curriculum and its educational implications in regular classroom activities." The Hazelwood East Curriculum Guide described the Journalism II course as a "laboratory situation in which the students publish the school newspaper applying skills they have learned in Journalism I." The lessons that were to be learned from the Journalism II course, according to the Curriculum Guide, included development of journalistic skills under deadline pressure, "the legal, moral, and ethical restrictions imposed upon journalists within the school community," and "responsibility and acceptance of criticism for articles of opinion." Journalism II was taught by a faculty member during regular class hours. Students received grades and academic credit for their performance in the course.

School officials did not deviate in practice from their policy that production of Spectrum was to be part of the educational curriculum and a "regular classroom activit[y]." The District Court found that Robert Stergos, the journalism teacher during most of the 1982–1983 school year, "both had the authority to exercise and in fact exercised a great deal of control over *Spectrum.*" 607 F. Supp., at 1453. For example, Stergos selected the editors of the newspaper, scheduled publication dates, decided the number of pages for each issue, assigned story ideas to class members, advised students on the development of their stories, reviewed the use of quotations, edited stories, selected and edited the letters to the editor, and dealt with the printing company. Many of these decisions were made without consultation with the Journalism II students. The District Court thus found it "clear that Mr. Stergos was the final authority with respect to almost every aspect of the production and publication of *Spectrum,* including its content." Moreover, after each Spectrum issue had been finally approved by Stergos or his successor, the issue still had to be reviewed by Principal Reynolds prior to publication. Respondents' assertion that they had believed that they could publish "practically anything" in Spectrum was therefore dismissed by the District Court as simply "not credible." These factual findings are amply supported by the record, and were not rejected as clearly erroneous by the Court of Appeals.

The evidence relied upon by the Court of Appeals in finding Spectrum to be a public forum, 795 F. 2d, at 1372–1373, is equivocal at best. For example, Board Policy 348.51, which stated in part that "[s]chool sponsored student publications will not restrict free expression or diverse viewpoints within the rules of responsible journalism," also stated that such publications were "developed within the adopted curriculum and its educational implications." One might reasonably infer from the full text of Policy 348.51 that school officials retained ultimate control over what constituted "responsible journalism" in a school-sponsored newspaper. Although the Statement of Policy published in the September 14, 1982, issue of Spectrum declared that "*Spectrum,* as a student-press publication, accepts all rights implied by the First Amendment," this statement, understood in the context of the paper's role in the school's curriculum, suggests at most that the administration will not interfere with the students' exercise of those First Amendment rights that attend the publication of a school-sponsored newspaper. It does not reflect an intent to expand those rights by converting a curricular newspaper into a public forum.[2] Finally, that students were permitted to exercise some authority over the contents of Spectrum was fully consistent with the Curriculum Guide objective of teaching the Journalism II students "leadership responsibilities as issue and page editors." A decision to teach leadership skills in the context of a classroom activity hardly implies a decision to relinquish school control over that activity. In sum, the evidence relied upon by the Court of Appeals fails to demonstrate the "clear intent to create a public forum," *Cornelius,* 473 U. S., at 802, that existed in cases in which we found public forums to have been created. School officials did not evince either "by policy or by practice," *Perry Education Assn.,* 460 U. S., at 47, any intent to open the pages of Spectrum to "indiscriminate use," by its student reporters and editors, or by the student body generally. Instead, they "reserve[d] the forum for its intended purpos[e]," as a supervised learning experience for journalism students. Accordingly, school officials were entitled to regulate the contents of Spectrum in any reasonable manner. It is this standard, rather than our decision in *Tinker*, that governs this case.

B

The question whether the First Amendment requires a school to tolerate particular student speech—the question that we addressed in *Tinker*—is different from the question whether the First Amendment requires a school affirmatively to promote particular student speech. The former question addresses educators' ability to silence a student's personal expression that happens to occur on the school premises. The latter question concerns educators' authority over school-sponsored publications, theatrical productions, and other expressive activities that students, parents, and members of the public might reasonably perceive to bear the imprimatur of the school. These activities may fairly be characterized as part of the school curriculum, whether or not they occur in a traditional classroom setting, so long as they are supervised by faculty members and designed to impart particular knowledge or skills to student participants and audiences.[3]

Educators are entitled to exercise greater control over this second form of student expression to assure that participants learn whatever lessons the activity is designed to teach, that readers or listeners are not exposed to material that may be inappropriate for their level of maturity, and that the views of the individual speaker are not erroneously attributed to the school. Hence, a school may in its capacity as publisher of a school newspaper or producer of a school play "disassociate itself," *Fraser*, 478 U. S., at——, not only from speech that would "substantially interfere with [its] work . . . or impinge upon the rights of other students," *Tinker*, 393 U. S., at 509, but also from speech that is, for example, ungrammatical, poorly written, inadequately researched, biased or prejudiced, vulgar or profane, or unsuitable for immature audiences.[4] A school must be able to set high standards for the student speech that is disseminated under its auspices—standards that may be higher than those demanded by some newspaper publishers or theatrical producers in the "real" world—and may refuse to disseminate student speech that does not meet those standards. In addition, a school must be able to take into account the emotional maturity of the intended audience in determining whether to disseminate student speech on potentially sensitive topics, which might range from the existence of Santa Claus in an elementary school setting to the particulars of teenage sexual activity in a high school setting. A school must also retain the authority to refuse to sponsor student speech that might reasonably be perceived to advocate drug or alcohol use, irresponsible sex, or conduct otherwise inconsistent with "the shared values of a civilized social order," *Fraser*, *supra*, at——, or to associate the school with any position other than neutrality on matters of political controversy. Otherwise, the schools would be unduly constrained from fulfilling their role as "a principal instrument in awakening the child to cultural values, in preparing him for later professional training, and in helping him to adjust normally to his environment." *Brown v. Board of Education*, 347 U. S. 483, 493 (1954).

Accordingly, we conclude that the standard articulated in *Tinker* for determining when a school may punish student expression need not also be the standard for determining when a school may refuse to lend its name and resources to the dissemination of student expression.[5] Instead, we hold that educators do not offend the First Amendment by exercising editorial control over the style and content of student speech in school-sponsored expressive activities so long as their actions are reasonably related to legitimate pedagogical concerns.[6]

This standard is consistent with our oft-expressed view that the education of the Nation's youth is primarily the responsibility of parents, teachers, and state and local school officials, and not of federal judges. It is only when the decision to censor a school-sponsored publication, theatrical production, or other vehicle of student expression has no valid educational purpose that the First Amendment is so "directly and sharply implicate[d]," as to require judicial intervention to protect students' constitutional rights.[7]

III

We also conclude that Principal Reynolds acted reasonably in requiring the deletion from the May 13 issue of Spectrum of the pregnancy article, the divorce article, and the remaining articles that were to appear on the same pages of the newspaper.

The initial paragraph of the pregnancy article declared that "[a]ll names have been changed to keep the identity of these girls a secret." The principal concluded that the students' anonymity was not adequately protected, however, given the other identifying information in the article and the small number of pregnant students at the school. Indeed, a teacher at the school credibly testified that she could positively identify at least one of the girls and possibly all three. It is likely that many students at Hazelwood East would have been at least as successful in identifying the girls. Reynolds therefore could reasonably have feared that the article violated whatever pledge of anonymity had been given to the pregnant students. In addition, he could reasonably have been concerned that the article was not sufficiently sensitive to the privacy interests of the students' boyfriends and parents, who were discussed in the article but who were given no opportunity to consent to its publication or to offer a response. The article did not contain graphic accounts of sexual activity. The girls did comment in the article, however, concerning their sexual histories and their use or nonuse of birth control. It was not unreasonable for the principal to have concluded that such frank talk was inappropriate in a school-sponsored publication distributed to 14-year-old freshmen and presumably taken home to be read by students' even younger brothers and sisters.

The student who was quoted by name in the version of the divorce article seen by Principal Reynolds made comments sharply critical of her father. The principal could reasonably have concluded that an individual publicly identified as an inattentive parent—indeed, as one who chose "playing cards with the guys" over home and family—was entitled to an opportunity to defend himself as a matter of journalistic fairness. These concerns were shared by both of Spectrum's faculty advisers for the 1982–1983 school year, who testified that they would not have allowed the article to be printed without deletion of the student's name.[8]

Principal Reynolds testified credibly at trial that, at the time that he reviewed the proofs of the May 13 issue during an extended telephone conversation with Emerson, he believed that there was no time to make any changes in the articles, and that the newspaper had to be printed immediately or not at all. It is true that Reynolds did not verify whether the necessary modifications could still have been made in the articles, and that Emerson did not volunteer the information that printing could be delayed until the changes were made. We nonetheless agree with the District Court that the decision to excise the two pages containing the problematic articles was reasonable given the particular circumstances of this case. These circumstances included the very recent replacement of Stergos by Emerson, who may not have been entirely familiar with Spectrum editorial and production procedures, and the pressure felt by Reynolds to make an immediate decision so that students would not be deprived of the newspaper altogether.

In sum, we cannot reject as unreasonable Principal Reynolds' conclusion that neither the pregnancy article nor the divorce article was suitable for publication in Spectrum. Reynolds could reasonably have concluded that the students who had written and edited these articles had not sufficiently mastered those portions of the Journalism II curriculum that pertained to the treatment of controversial issues and personal attacks, the need to protect the privacy of individuals whose most intimate concerns are to be revealed in the newspaper, and "the legal, moral, and ethical restrictions imposed upon journalists within [a] school community" that includes adolescent subjects and readers. Finally, we conclude that the principal's decision to delete two pages of Spectrum, rather than to delete only the offending articles or to require that they be modified, was reasonable under the circumstances as he understood them. Accordingly, no violation of First Amendment rights occurred.[9]

The judgment of the Court of Appeals for the Eighth Circuit is therefore

Reversed.

NOTES

1. The two pages deleted from the newspaper also contained articles on teenage marriage, runaways, and juvenile delinquents, as well as a general article on teenage pregnancy. Reynolds testified that he had no objection to these articles and that they were deleted only because they appeared on the same pages as the two objectionable articles.

2. The Statement also cited *Tinker v. Des Moines Independent Community School Dist.*, 393 U. S. 503 (1969), for the proposition that "[o]nly speech that " 'materially and substantially interferes with the requirements of appropriate discipline' can be found unacceptable and therefore be prohibited." App. 26. This portion of the Statement does not, of course, even accurately reflect our holding in *Tinker*. Furthermore, the Statement nowhere expressly extended the *Tinker* standard to the news and feature articles contained in a school-sponsored newspaper. The dissent apparently finds as a fact that the Statement was published annually in Spectrum; however, the District Court was unable to conclude that the Statement appeared on more than one occasion. In any event, even if the Statement says what the dissent believes that it says, the evidence that school officials never intended to designate Spectrum as a public forum remains overwhelming.

3. The distinction that we draw between speech that is sponsored by the school and speech that is not is fully consistent with *Papish v. Board of Curators*, 410 U. S. 667 (1973) *(per curiam)*, which involved an off-campus "underground" newspaper that school officials merely had allowed to be sold on a state university campus.

4. The dissent perceives no difference between the First Amendment analysis applied in *Tinker* and that applied in *Fraser*. We disagree.

The decision in *Fraser* rested on the "vulgar," "lewd," and "plainly offensive" character of a speech delivered at an official school assembly rather than on any propensity of the speech to "materially disrupt[] classwork or involve[] substantial disorder or invasion of the rights of others." 393 U. S., at 513. Indeed, the *Fraser* Court cited as "especially relevant" a portion of Justice Black's dissenting opinion in *Tinker* "disclaim-[ing] any purpose . . . to hold that the Federal Constitution compels the teachers, parents and elected school officials to surrender control of the American public school system to public school students." 478 U. S., at——(citing 393 U. S., at 522). Of course, Justice Black's observations are equally relevant to the instant case.

5. We therefore need not decide whether the Court of Appeals correctly construed *Tinker* as precluding school officials from censoring student speech to avoid "invasion of the rights of others," 393 U. S., at 513, except where that speech could result in tort liability to the school.

6. We reject respondents' suggestion that school officials be permitted to exercise prepublication control over school-sponsored publications only pursuant to specific written regulations. To require such regulations in the context of a curricular activity could unduly constrain the ability of educators to educate. We need not now decide whether such regulations are required before school officials may censor publications not sponsored by the school that students seek to distribute on school grounds. See *Baughman v. Freienmuth*, 478 F. 2d 1345 (CA4 1973); *Shanley v. Northwest Independent School Dist., Bexar Cty., Tex.* 462 F. 2d 960 (CA5 1972); *Eisner v. Stamford Board of Education*, 440 F. 2d 803 (CA2 1971).

7. A number of lower federal courts have similarly recognized that educators' decisions with regard to the content of school-sponsored newspapers, dramatic productions, and other expressive activities are entitled to substantial deference. See, *e. g., Nicholson v. Board of Education Torrance Unified School Dist.*, 682 F. 2d 858 (CA9 1982); *Seyfried v. Walton*, 668 F. 2d 214 (CA3 1981); *Trachtman v. Anker*, 563 F. 2d 512 (CA2 1977), cert. denied, 435 U. S. 925 (1978); *Frasca v. Andrews*, 463 F. Supp. 1043 (EDNY 1979). We need not now decide whether the same degree of deference is appropriate with respect to school-sponsored expressive activities at the college and university level.

8. The reasonableness of Principal Reynolds' concerns about the two articles was further substantiated by the trial testimony of Martin Duggan, a former editorial page editor of the St. Louis Globe Democrat and a former college journalism instructor and newspaper adviser. Duggan testified that the divorce story did not meet journalistic standards of fairness and balance because the father was not given an opportunity to respond, and that the pregnancy story was not appropriate for publication in a high school newspaper because it was unduly intrusive into the privacy of the girls, their parents, and their boyfriends. The District Court found Duggan to be "an objective and independent witness" whose testimony was entitled to significant weight. 607 F. Supp. 1450, 1461 (ED Mo. 1985).

9. It is likely that the approach urged by the dissent would as a practical matter have far more deleterious consequences for the student press than does the approach that we adopt today. The dissent correctly acknowledges "[t]he State's prerogative to dissolve the student newspaper entirely." It is likely that many public schools would do just that rather than open their newspapers to all student expression that does not threaten "materia[l] disrup[tion of] classwork" or violation of "rights that are protected by law," regardless of how sexually explicit, racially intemperate, or personally insulting that expression otherwise might be.

NO

Stephen Arons

DOES SCHOOL CENSORSHIP UNDERMINE EDUCATION?

[State-controlled education] is a mere contrivance for moulding people to be exactly like one another: and as the mould in which it casts them is that which pleases the predominant power in the government, whether this be a monarch, a priesthood, an aristocracy, or the majority of the existing generation, in proportion as it is efficient and successful, it establishes a despotism over the mind . . .

—John Stuart Mill, 1859

The school has become the established church of secular times.

—Ivan Illich, 1974

The majority opinion in *Hazelwood v. Kuhlmeier* is bad First Amendment law and worse education policy. It distorts the Court's landmark ruling in *Tinker v. Des Moines,* and it teaches the nation's public school students that the principles of the First Amendment are empty slogans to be learned but not lived, taught but not practiced.

Mr. Justice Brennan's dissenting opinion in *Hazelwood*,[1] had it prevailed, would have made better First Amendment law. It is consistent with the Court's earlier view that public school students do not "shed their constitutional rights to freedom of speech or expression at the schoolhouse gate," *Tinker v. Des Moines,* 393 US at 506, and it teaches that "unthinking contempt for individual rights is intolerable from any state official" (*Hazelwood,* 56 USLW at 4087).

But even Brennan's eloquent dissent is inadequate because, like all Supreme Court cases in this area, it fails to address the deep contradiction between the majoritarian structure of compulsory schooling and the principles of freedom of belief and expression which lie at the heart of the U.S. Constitution and Bill of Rights. The most basic lesson to be learned from majority and dissenting opinions in *Hazelwood* is that the structure of

American schooling itself amounts to a system of censorship which undermines both education and the First Amendment.

To grasp the basic flaw in the opinions and in the school structure they legitimize, it is necessary to recognize the historical tension between the majority's impulse to re-create itself and the First Amendment principle that freedom of thought is an individual's most important liberty.

One hundred and sixty years ago, the French lawyer and aristocrat Alexis De Tocqueville wrote what remains the most perceptive, and perhaps the most prophetic commentary ever written about the United States, *Democracy In America*. In it he warned the nation whose experiment with democracy he so admired about the tension between freedom of thought and the "tyranny of the majority."

"Thought is an invisible and subtle power that mocks all the efforts of tyranny," he wrote. But because the majority can become a tyrant in a democracy, De Tocqueville warned that he knew of "no country in which there is so little independence of mind and real freedom of discussion as in America." His description of the means by which majorities controlled thought in 1830 is an uncomfortably accurate prediction of the way in which majorities in the late twentieth century stifle freedom of thought by controlling the schools:

Monarchs had, so to speak, materialized oppression; the democratic republics of the present day have rendered it as entirely an affair of the mind as the will which it is intended to coerce. Under the absolute sway of one man the body was attacked in order to subdue the soul; but the soul escaped . . . Such is not the course adopted by tyranny in democratic republics; there the body is left free, and the soul is enslaved. The master no longer says: 'You shall think as I do or you shall die'; but he [majority as tyrant] says 'You are free to think differently from me and to retain your life, your property, and all that you possess; but you are henceforth a stranger among your people.'
(*Democracy in America*, Vol. 1, p. 274)

This perception, that in a democracy political and social majorities can coercively perpetuate their own views and assumptions without resorting to physical oppression, is still disturbing to a people who regard freedom of expression as sacred. That public schooling, intended to spread and support democracy, should become an agency of this majoritarian tyranny over the mind is still more disturbing. But the idea that the governmental manipulation of public thinking might make even a democracy into a political perpetual-motion machine was not new with De Tocqueville. The Framers of the Constitution and the Bill of Rights two generations earlier had seen clearly that if the sphere of intellect and belief were not withdrawn from majority control, individual development and political exchange would be crippled and the entire democratic experiment would collapse. They understood history's lesson. If non-violent dissent—the right to form, hold and express beliefs disturbing to the majority—were not a right of citizenship, the idea that governments derive their legitimacy from the consent of the governed would become a mockery. The "first freedom," which outlaws majority control of thought and belief, thus became the linchpin of American democracy and an essential counterweight to the tyranny of the majority against which De Tocqueville warned.

Compulsory, universal, publicly-supported schooling—which was virtually unknown in both 1789 and 1830—has since become ubiquitous in the U.S. For much of the twentieth century it has been structured as an agency of government which gives expression to the values of the political majority in the socialization of the rising generation. Most Americans have expected the overt and hidden curricula of the public schools to teach not only the three R's, but to pass on to children the values, attitudes, assumptions, and beliefs of the local and national culture. During this time America has become more pluralistic, not homogenous, in spite of claims about the "melting pot." As a result, the transmission of culture through schooling has become a source of continuous conflict.[2]

A dilemma has thus been created about how to protect freedom of thought and belief in an institution which is designed to inculcate the values of the majority in the minds of a captive audience which includes the children of dissenters. One hundred years of school conflict have implicitly raised the question, how should the principles of the First Amendment be applied to a public school system whose content is controlled by political majorities?

In 1925 the U.S. Supreme Court gave its first and most important answer to this problem. In *Pierce v. Society of Sisters*, 268 US 510, it found unconstitutional an Oregon statute which required that children of compulsory school age attend only public schools. The statute had been passed at the urging of the KKK to insure the "Americanism" of post-World War I children. In affirming the right of private schools to exist and the right of parents to choose them as an alternative to government schooling, the Court declared that "the child is not the mere creature of the state." It thereby wrote into the Constitution what appeared to be a right of families to choose the values with which their children would be inculcated:

> The fundamental theory of liberty upon which all governments in this Union repose excludes any general power of the state to standardize its children by forcing them to accept instruction from public teachers only. (268 US at 535)

But the opinion was not based upon the First Amendment, which had not yet been made applicable to the states; and the content of the newly-articulated right was vague at best.[3] As the cost of non-government schooling and the tax burden of government schooling both increased, the right to choose an alternative to the public schools became less and less meaningful to most Americans. As a result, the conflict between cultural transmission and individual freedoms of belief and expression was more and more focused upon the content of public schools.

That this conflict has become imbedded in the very structure of public schooling—in which the majority controls the value content of the schooling of all the children who cannot choose an alternative—was perhaps expressed most clearly in the Supreme Court's 1982 landmark decision, *Island Trees v. Pico*, 102 S. Ct. 2799. In *Pico* the Court held unconstitutional a local school board's removal of books from the school library. The Board had banned nine books, with later approval from a majority of the electorate, because it disliked the ideas those books contained. At the same time that the *Pico* Court was reaffirming the First

Amendment rights of high school students to read and acquire knowledge free of majority tyranny, however, it made the following statement about the proper role of schooling:

> We are therefore in full agreement with petitioners that local school boards must be permitted " 'to establish and apply their curriculum in such a way as to transmit community values' and that 'there is a legitimate and substantial community interest in promoting respect for authority and traditional values be they social, moral, or political.' (102 S. Ct. at 2806)

The Court did not suggest whose traditional values or authority were to be inculcated by local schools in a pluralistic society. Nor did it suggest how the First Amendment freedoms of intellect and belief of students and their families were to be protected from hostile majorities within the public schools. Indeed the Court could not have addressed these issues in any way other than by declaring that each family has an equal right of school choice regardless of income, a declaration that would have required the complete revamping of the political and financial structure of American education.[4]

The difficulty the U.S. Supreme Court has had in applying First Amendment principles of freedom of expression and belief to public schools—an institution the Court defines as an instrument of the political majority in imposing itself upon young minds—indicates that the contradiction between majoritarian schooling and the First Amendment is built into the structure of the school system. Over the last 50 years, the Court has sought to strike a balance between the desire for social cohesion and the respect for dissent for which De Tocqueville implicitly

called. But *Hazelwood* is an example of the failure to strike this balance successfully, and of the impossibility of so doing without providing equality of school choice to all families.

Hazelwood distorts the balance between freedom of the mind and bureaucratic control in the nation's schools. It is the latest in a long string of Supreme Court decisions which ignore the multiple ways in which majority-dominated schooling undermines education and cripples individual freedom. *Hazelwood* is wrongly decided and if the underlying problem for intellectual freedom is to be recognized, the opinion needs public criticism.

In the 1968 case of *Tinker v. Des Moines*, the Court invalidated the suspensions of high school students who had silently protested the war in Vietnam by wearing black armbands to school. In so ruling, the Court created a standard which permitted education officials to infringe upon student expression at school only if those officials had evidence that the challenged expression would materially and substantially interfere with school work or discipline:

> In our system, students may not be regarded as closed circuit recipients of only that which the state chooses to communicate. They may not be confined to the expression of those sentiments that are officially approved. (89 S. Ct. at 739 (1968)).

The case was a victory for freedom of expression and belief for students because the standard of judgment articulated by the Court required substantial evidence that the censorship was needed to preserve order within the classroom or school. But the Court's opinion took back much of what it granted to these dissenting students, for it allowed the school authorities to define the nature of the order to be preserved. By imposing an ever more rigid and intrusive order upon students and teachers—for example by forbidding talking in the halls and at lunch and by providing no space, time, or public forum for students to exchange views beyond answers called for in class—the school authorities could justify additional censorship without running afoul of the *Tinker* test.

Nevertheless, the *Tinker* test did provide some protection to dissenting students. The damage done by the *Hazelwood* case is not simply in what happened to the reporters and editors of the Hazelwood *Spectrum*, but that the Court effectively replaced even the modest *Tinker* standard with a grant of power to school officials which would make even an old world communist party official envious:

> . . .we hold that educators do not offend the First Amendment by exercising editorial control over the style and content of student speech in school-sponsored expressive activities so long as their actions are *reasonably related to legitimate pedagogical concerns.* [emphasis added] (56 USLW at 4082)

This standard of judgment suggests that by defining the content of curriculum and by making every activity at school a part of that curriculum, school officials (who are responsible only to local political majorities) become entitled to control the content of student expression and may endlessly restrict the spectrum of knowledge and opinion available to students in school. *Hazelwood* equates censorship with good pedagogy, and converts the narrowing of young minds into a legally acceptable form of education. Justice Brennan's dissent is more blunt:

> If mere incompatibility with the school's pedagogical message were a constitu-

tionally sufficient justification for the suppression of student speech, school officials could . . . convert[. . .] our public schools into 'enclaves of totalitarianism', that 'strangle the free mind at its source'. (56 USLW at 4084)

In creating a new test of pedagogical compatibility for lower courts to apply in judging student claims of unconstitutional censorship, the Supreme Court has taught a lesson of its own to the nation's high school students: While at school students are once again "mere creatures of the State." Some students will no doubt see even deeper lessons here—lessons of distrust, of fear of democracy, of intolerance for dissent; and lessons of disingenuous reasoning, of lack of courage and conviction in the face of controversy, and of the importance of timidity and ignorance over freedom of inquiry and individual development. Justice Brennan again:

> Instead of 'teaching children to respect the diversity of ideas that is fundamental to the American system,' and 'that our Constitution is a living reality, not parchment preserved under glass,' the Court today 'teaches youth to discount important principles of our government as mere platitudes.' (56 USLW at 4087)

That the lower courts have learned this lesson all too well is demonstrated by two cases handed down by federal courts of appeal in 1989. In *Poling v. Murphy*, 872 F2d 757, the court found no First Amendment problem with a high school principal's disqualifying a student from a ballot for school council president because the student, Dean Poling, had made a campaign speech deemed "discourteous" by the school administration. Using the new *Hazelwood* test, the appeals court found that a student council campaign speech delivered at a school assembly was sufficiently related to the school's pedagogy to permit censorship of its content and electoral disqualification for violation of the censor's standard of politeness. Up until just about the same time, Poling could have learned this same civics lesson on any street-corner in eastern Europe.

The second case, *Virgil v. Columbia County*, 862 F2d 1517, extends *Hazelwood* to the banning of great literature from high school texts. The enlightened majority of Columbia County, Florida had decided that Chaucer's "Miller's Tale" and Aristophanes' "Lysistrata" were "vulgar and sexually explicit" and ought therefore to be banned from classroom use. Turning back the constitutional claims of a dissenting minority of parents in the same school system, the court applied the "relatively lenient *Hazelwood* test" and found that elective courses and collections of great literature were part of the curriculum which could be censored by school officials for any reason they described as pedagogical. Plainly *Hazelwood* has become a blank check written to local officials who wish to "use public schools to inculcate fundamental values" approved by political majorities.

The use of the schools to reduce the life of the mind to a maze of politically-specified and bureaucratically-administered regulations teaches more than just a political lesson. In allowing local bias to subdue intellectual freedom and universally-recognized literature, *Virgil* converts what De Tocqueville stated as a fact about American literature in 1830 into a grim prediction about American thought in the Twenty-first century:

> If America has not as yet had any great writers, the reason is given in these facts; there can be no literary genius without freedom of opinion, and free-

dom of opinion does not exist in America. (De Tocqueville, V1p275)

Neither can there be any meaningful education or political democracy without freedom of opinion. The *Hazelwood* case and its progeny may be harbingers of what is in store for freedom of intellect and spirit in the schools and in the culture generally. *Hazelwood* is such a distortion of the balance of power between schooling-as-liberation and schooling-as-compulsory-socialization, that it exposes the fundamental First Amendment flaw in the Court's conception of both education and freedom of the mind.

The First Amendment should be read to protect both the formation and expression of belief and opinion in the nation's schools. The lesson of education policy and of constitutional opinion ought to be that individual freedom of intellect and spirit are not only the highest of human aspirations, but absolute necessities for the healthy functioning of a constitutional democracy.

Both the U.S. Supreme Court and the Hazelwood, Missouri School Board would have better served the nation's ideals, its schools, and its Constitution had they heeded Justice Robert Jackson's lesson in striking down the compulsory flag salute in the schools of 1943:

> As governmental pressure toward unity becomes greater, so strife becomes more bitter as to whose unity it shall be. Probably no division of our people could proceed from any provocation than from finding it necessary to choose what doctrine and whose program public educational officials shall compel youth to unite in embracing. Ultimate futility of such attempts to compel coherence is the lesson of every such effort . . . Compulsory unification

of opinion achieves only the unanimity of the graveyard.

West Va. v. Barnette, 319 US at 641

NOTES

1. 56 USLW 4083.

2. The history of American schooling struggles is well chronicled in, for example, David Tyack's *The One Best System* and in Nasaw's *Schooled To Order* and Ravitch's *The Great School Wars*.

3. For a thorough explication of the legal significance of *Pierce* see Arons, "The Separation of School and State: *Pierce* Reconsidered" in 46 Harv. Ed. Rev. 76 (1976).

4. This restructuring is the subject of current debates over school choice in the US and has been at the heart of proposals over the past twenty years for tuition vouchers, tax credits and aid to non-government schools. See, e.g. Chubb, *Politics, Markets & America's Schools*, Brookings, 1990 and Arons, *Compelling Belief: The Culture of American Schooling*, Univ. of Mass. Press, 1986.

POSTSCRIPT

Should Student Newspapers Be Censored?

Education is something that you should be something of an expert in. After all, you have been in school for ten, twelve, or more years. You have been exposed to many different teachers and have probably been in several different schools. Were Principal Reynolds's concerns legitimate and more important than the interest of the students? With whose view of education, Justice White's or Professor Arons's, are you more in agreement? What do you believe is the purpose of public education—the communication of information, fostering certain attitudes about our society, or promoting more values and a particular way of Life? Is school free inquiry and, if so, can students be educated to the fullest where inquiry is not really free? Finally, should any attention be paid to the concerns of the community? Should unpopular or controversial views be restricted because some or even many members of the community might be offended?

The *Hazelwood* case, not surprisingly, has led to new cases of conflict involving majoritarian control of public school curricula and activities. As this volume was being prepared, the news media contained reports of the following: Some students at a California high school claimed they were being harassed by administrators for publishing an "underground" newspaper critical of teachers and administrators, and a Delaware school board was reconsidering its policy of tearing "objectionable" stories out of a high school literature text. Entire stories by James Baldwin, Ralph Ellison, and Bernard Malamud had been ripped out. A California school district decided to stop using "Little Red Riding Hood" in the elementary school because the little girl in the story brings her grandmother a bottle of wine and "that condones the use of alcohol." One irony in the reporting of these stories is that, at the same time, freedom of the press was generally expanding in Eastern Europe, and the Soviet legislature had passed a new law eliminating state censorship and guaranteeing the right of any organization or individual to start a publication.

Other recent cases involving access to information in educational settings are *Bethel v. Fraser*, 106 S.Ct. 3159 (1986) which stated that speech containing "offensive and indecent" language given at a high school political assembly was unprotected by the First Amendment; *Searcey v. Harris,* 888 F. 2d 1314 (1989), regarding restrictions on access of military and nonmilitary groups to Atlanta schools; and *Virgil v. School Board of Columbia County,* 862 F. 2d 1517 (1989), about removal from a high school curriculum of a textbook that contained excerpts from Aristophanes' *Lysistrata* and Chaucer's *The Miller's Tale.*

Recent writings about the issues raised in this chapter are Note, "Textbook Removal Decisions and the First Amendment—A Better Balance," 62 *Temple Law Review* 1317 (1989); Stewart, "The First Amendment, The Public Schools, and the Inculcation of Community Values," 18 *Journal of Law & Education* 23 (1989); Abrams and Goodman, "End of an Era? The Decline of Student Press Rights in the Wake of *Hazelwood School District v. Kuhlmeier,*" 1988 *Duke Law Journal* 706; Arons, *Compelling Belief: The Culture of American Schooling* (1986); Yudof, *When Government Speaks* (1983); and Schimmel and Fischer, *Parents, Schools, and the Law* (1987).

ISSUE 7

Religious Displays on Public Property: Do They Violate the Constitution?

YES: Harry Blackmun, from Majority Opinion, *County of Allegheny v. American Civil Liberties Union,* U.S. Supreme Court (1989)

NO: Anthony Kennedy, from Dissenting Opinion, *County of Allegheny v. American Civil Liberties Union,* U.S. Supreme Court (1989)

ISSUE SUMMARY

YES: Supreme Court justice Harry Blackmun argues that a crèche and a menorah on public property constitute a public endorsement of religion and violates the First Amendment.
NO: Justice Anthony Kennedy disagrees and argues that the First Amendment does not prohibit public celebration of events that have a secular and religious nature.

An Easter egg hunt on the White House lawn. Christmas as a national holiday. Prayers opening legislative sessions of state legislatures. If you were a judge and the above practices were challenged as being unconstitutional, how would you rule?

The First Amendment to the Constitution states that "Congress shall make no law respecting an establishment of religion, or prohibiting the free exercise thereof." Interpreting these words and applying them in particular cases has been exceedingly difficult for the courts. What, for example, does "respecting an establishment of religion" mean? Is any governmental involvement or support for religion, direct or indirect, small or great, barred by this phrase?

While the courts have struggled to keep church and state separate, they have also recognized that it would be impossible to have an absolute prohibition on the celebration of religious values and holidays. Cases continue to be brought, therefore, challenging the courts to determine how the words of the Constitution and the standards of prior cases should be applied to the facts of the new case.

The clearest and most well known of the establishment of religion cases are the school prayer decisions. In 1963, in *School District of Abington Township, Pennsylvania v. Schempp,* 374 U.S. 203, the Supreme Court ruled that it was unconstitutional to require students to open the school day by reading biblical passages and reciting the Lord's Prayer. A year earlier, in *Engel v. Vitale*, 370 U.S. 421 (1962), the Supreme Court had ruled that recitation of the New York Regent's Prayer was unconstitutional. This prayer read, "Almighty God, we acknowledge our dependence upon Thee, and we beg thy blessings upon us, our parents, our teachers, and our country."

The Supreme Court has attempted to make its decision in this area appear less subjective by considering the following three questions:

1. Does the statute have a secular legislative purpose?
2. Does its principal effect advance or inhibit religion?
3. Does the statute foster an excessive governmental entanglement with religion?

Using this standard, the courts have upheld some questionable practices, such as blue laws and the loaning of secular textbooks to parochial schools, but have struck down other statutes, such as the Kentucky law that required posting the Ten Commandments in the classroom (see *Stone v. Graham*, 101 S.Ct. 192, 1980). More generally, the Court has upheld prayers at the beginning of a legislative session, the existence of after-school religious clubs, and tuition tax credits for parochial schools. Yet, using the same test, it has held unconstitutional a statute requiring a moment of silence in public schools, remedial programs for parochial schools, and a law requiring the teaching of "creation science" whenever evolution was taught.

The many cases involving religion that have been considered by the Supreme Court in the past twenty-five years indicate that the task of defining precisely what role religion should have in government-sponsored activities is extraordinarily difficult. Religion has not been banned from public life. "In God We Trust" appears on our coins, prayers are said at presidential inaugurations, Christmas is a national holiday, the lighting of the national Christmas tree at the White House is a newsworthy event, and tax exemptions are given to religious institutions. It is probably still accurate, as a Supreme Court justice once wrote, that "we are a religious people whose institutions presuppose a Supreme Being." It is also true, however, that many religious activities may not be sponsored by the government.

The following readings concern a type of controversy that has occurred fairly often in recent years. Are cities and towns allowed to erect public displays in commemoration of religious holidays? The following case was the second such case decided by the Court within a five-year period. This suggests not only a tension in the Court about what is lawful but the difficult questions that are inherent in such cases.

145

YES

Harry Blackmun

MAJORITY OPINION OF
HARRY BLACKMUN

This litigation concerns the constitutionality of two recurring holiday displays located on public property in downtown Pittsburgh. The first is a crèche placed on the Grand Staircase of the Allegheny County Courthouse. The second is a Chanukah menorah placed just outside the City-County Building, next to a Christmas tree and a sign saluting liberty. The Court of Appeals for the Third Circuit ruled that each display violates the Establishment Clause of the First Amendment because each has the impermissible effect of endorsing religion. 842 F.2d 655 (1988). We agree that the crèche display has that unconstitutional effect but reverse the Court of Appeals' judgment regarding the menorah display.

I

A

The County Courthouse is owned by Allegheny County and is its seat of government. It houses the offices of the County Commissioners, Controller, Treasurer, Sheriff, and Clerk of Court. Civil and criminal trials are held there. The "main," "most beautiful," and "most public" part of the courthouse is its Grand Staircase, set into one arch and surrounded by others, with arched windows serving as a backdrop.

Since 1981, the county has permitted the Holy Name Society, a Roman Catholic group, to display a crèche in the County Courthouse during the Christmas holiday season. Christmas, we note perhaps needlessly, is the holiday when Christians celebrate the birth of Jesus of Nazareth, whom they believe to be the Messiah. Western churches have celebrated Christmas Day on December 25 since the fourth century. As observed in this Nation, Christmas has a secular as well as a religious dimension.[1]

The crèche in the County Courthouse, like other crèches, is a visual representation of the scene in the manger in Bethlehem shortly after the

From *County of Allegheny v. American Civil Liberties Union,* 109 S.Ct. 3086 (1989). Some notes and case citations omitted.

birth of Jesus, as described in the Gospels of Luke and Matthew. The crèche includes figures of the infant Jesus, Mary, Joseph, farm animals, shepherds, and wise men, all placed in or before a wooden representation of a manger, which has at its crest an angel bearing a banner that proclaims, "Gloria in Excelsis Deo!"

During the 1986–1987 holiday season, the crèche was on display on the Grand Staircase from November 26 to January 9. It had a wooden fence on three sides and bore a plaque stating: "This Display Donated by the Holy Name Society." Sometime during the week of December 2, the county placed red and white poinsettia plants around the fence. The county also placed a small evergreen tree, decorated with a red bow, behind each of the two endposts of the fence. These trees stood alongside the manger backdrop, and were slightly shorter than it was. The angel thus was at the apex of the crèche display. Altogether, the crèche, the fence, the poinsettias, and the trees occupied a substantial amount of space on the Grand Staircase. No figures of Santa Claus or other decorations appeared on the Grand Staircase.

The county uses the crèche as the setting for its annual Christmas-carole program. During the 1986 season, the county invited high school choirs and other musical groups to perform during weekday lunch hours from December 3 through December 23. The county dedicated this program to world peace and to the families of prisoners-of-war and of persons missing-in-action in Southeast Asia.

Near the Grand Staircase is an area of the County Courthouse known as the "gallery forum" used for art and other cultural exhibits. The crèche, with its fence-and-floral frame, however, was distinct and not connected with any exhibit in the gallery forum. In addition, various departments and offices within the County Courthouse had their own Christmas decorations, but these also are not visible from the Grand Staircase.

B

The City-County Building is separate and a block removed from the County Courthouse and, as the name implies, is jointly owned by the city of Pittsburgh and Allegheny County. The city's portion of the building houses the city's principal offices, including the Mayor's. The city is responsible for the building's Grant Street entrance which has three rounded arches supported by columns.

For a number of years, the city has had a large Christmas tree under the middle arch outside the Grant Street entrance. Following this practice, city employees on November 17, 1986, erected a 45-foot tree under the middle arch and decorated it with lights and ornaments. A few days later, the city placed at the foot of the tree a sign bearing the Mayor's name and entitled "Salute to Liberty." Beneath the title, the sign stated:

> "During this holiday season, the City of Pittsburgh salutes liberty. Let these festive lights remind us that we are the keepers of the flame of liberty and our legacy of freedom."

At least since 1982, the city has expanded its Grant Street holiday display to include a symbolic representation of Chanukah, an 8-day Jewish holiday that begins on the 25th day of the Jewish lunar month of Kislev. The 25th of Kislev usually occurs in December, and thus Chanukah is the annual Jewish holiday that falls closest to Christmas Day each year. In 1986, Chanukah began at sundown on December 26.

According to Jewish tradition, on the 25th of Kislev in 164 B.C.E. (before the common era), the Maccabees rededicated the Temple of Jerusalem after recapturing it from the Greeks, or, more accurately, from the Greek-influenced Seleucid Empire, in the course of a political rebellion. Chanukah is the holiday which celebrates that event. The early history of the celebration of Chanukah is unclear; it appears that the holiday's central ritual—the lighting of lamps—was well established long before a single explanation of that ritual took hold.

The Talmud explains the lamp-lighting ritual as a commemoration of an event that occurred during the rededication of the Temple. The Temple housed a seven-branch menorah, which was to be kept burning continuously. When the Maccabees rededicated the Temple, they had only enough oil to last for one day. But, according to the Talmud, the oil miraculously lasted for eight days (the length of time it took to obtain additional oil). To celebrate and publicly proclaim this miracle, the Talmud prescribes that it is a mitzvah (*i.e.*, a religious deed or commandment), for Jews to place a lamp with eight lights just outside the entrance to their homes during the eight days of Chanukah. . . .

Chanukah, like Christmas, is a cultural event as well as a religious holiday. Indeed, the Chanukah story always has had a political or national as well as a religious dimension: it tells of national heroism in addition to divine intervention. Also, Chanukah, like Christmas, is a winter holiday; according to some historians, it was associated in ancient times with the winter solstice. Just as some Americans celebrate Christmas without regard to its religious significance, some nonreligious American Jews celebrate Chanukah as an expression of ethnic identity, and "as a cultural or national event, rather than as a specifically religious event."

The cultural significance of Chanukah varies with the setting in which the holiday is celebrated. In contemporary Israel, the nationalist and military aspects of the Chanukah story receive special emphasis. In this country, the tradition of giving Chanukah gelt has taken on greater importance because of the temporal proximity of Chanukah to Christmas. Indeed, some have suggested that the proximity of Christmas accounts for the social prominence of Chanukah in this country. Whatever the reason, Chanukah is observed by American Jews to an extent greater than its religious importance would indicate: in the hierarchy of Jewish holidays, Chanukah ranks fairly low in religious significance. This socially heightened status of Chanukah reflects its cultural or secular dimension.

On December 22 of the 1986 holiday season, the city placed at the Grant Street entrance to the City-County Building an 18-foot Chanukah menorah of an abstract tree-and-branch design. The menorah was placed next to the city's 45-foot Christmas tree, against one of the columns that supports the arch into which the tree was set. The menorah is owned by Chabad, a Jewish group, but is stored, erected, and removed each year by the city. The tree, the sign, and the menorah were all removed on January 13.

II

This litigation began on December 10, 1986, when respondents, the Greater Pittsburgh Chapter of the American Civil Liberties Union and seven local residents, filed suit against the county and the city, seeking permanently to enjoin the county from displaying the crèche in the County Courthouse and the city from displaying the menorah in front of the City-County Building. Respondents claim that the displays of the crèche and the menorah each violate the Establishment Clause of the First Amendment, made applicable to state governments by the Fourteenth Amendment. . . .

On May 8, 1987, the District Court denied respondent's request for a permanent injunction. Relying on *Lynch v. Donnelly, supra,* the court stated that "the crèche was but part of the holiday decoration of the stairwell and a foreground for the high school choirs which entertained each day at noon." Regarding the menorah, the court concluded that "it was but an insignificant part of another holiday display." The court also found that "the displays had a secular purpose" and "did not create an excessive entanglement of government with religion."

Respondents appealed, and a divided panel of the Court of Appeals reversed. 842 F.2d 655 (CA3 1988). Distinguishing *Lynch v. Donnelly,* the panel majority determined that the crèche and the menorah must be understood as endorsing Christianity and Judaism. The court observed: "Each display was located at or in a public building devoted to core functions of government." The court also stated: "Further, while the menorah was placed near a Christmas tree, neither the crèche nor the menorah can reasonably be deemed to have been subsumed by a larger display of non-religious items." Because the impermissible effect of endorsing religion was a sufficient basis for holding each display to be in violation of the Establishment Clause under *Lemon v. Kurtzman,* 403 U.S. 602, 91 S.Ct. 2105, 29 L.Ed. 2d 745 (1971), the Court of Appeals did not consider whether either one had an impermissible purpose or resulted in an unconstitutional entanglement between government and religion. . . .

III

A

This Nation is heir to a history and tradition of religious diversity that dates from the settlement of the North American continent. Sectarian differences among various Christian denominations were central to the origins of our Republic. Since then, adherents of religions too numerous to name have made the United States their home, as have those whose beliefs expressly exclude religion.

Precisely because of the religious diversity that is our national heritage, the Founders added to the Constitution a Bill of Rights, the very first words of which declare: "Congress shall make no law respecting an establishment of religion, or prohibiting the free exercise thereof. . . . " Perhaps in the early days of the Republic these words were understood to protect only the diversity within Christianity, but today they are recognized as guaranteeing religious liberty and equality to "the infidel, the atheist, or the adherent of a non-Christian faith such as Islam or Judaism." *Wallace v. Jaffree,* 472 U.S. 38, 52, 105 S.Ct. 2479, 2487, 86 L.Ed.2d 29 (1985). It is settled law that no government official in this Nation may violate these fundamental constitutional rights regarding matters of conscience.

In the course of adjudicating specific cases, this Court has come to understand the Establishment Clause to mean that government may not promote or affiliate itself with any religious doctrine or organization,[2] may not discriminate among persons on the basis of their religious beliefs and practices, may not delegate a governmental power to a religious institution, and may not involve itself too deeply in such an institution's affairs. Although "the myriad, subtle ways in which Establishment Clause values can be eroded," *Lynch v. Donnelly*, 465 U.S., at 694, 104 S.Ct., at 1370 (O'CONNOR, J., concurring), are not susceptible to a single verbal formulation, this Court has attempted to encapsulate the essential precepts of the Establishment Clause. Thus, in *Everson v. Board of Education*, 330 U.S. 1, 67 S.Ct. 504, 91 L.Ed. 711 (1947), the Court gave this often-repeated summary:

"The 'establishment of religion' clause of the First Amendment means at least this: Neither a state nor the Federal Government can set up a church. Neither can pass laws which aid one religion, aid all religions, or prefer one religion over another. Neither can force nor influence a person to go to or remain away from church against his will or force him to profess a belief or disbelief in any religion. No person can be punished for entertaining or professing religious beliefs or disbeliefs, for church attendance or non-attendance. No tax in any amount, large or small, can be levied to support any religious activities or institutions, whatever they may be called, or whatever form they may adopt to teach or practice religion. Neither a state nor the Federal Government can, openly or secretly, participate in the affairs of any religious organizations or groups and *vice versa*." *Id.*, at 15–16, 67 S.Ct., at 511–512.

In *Lemon v. Kurtzman, supra,* the Court sought to refine these principles by focusing on three "tests" for determining whether a government practice violates the Establishment Clause. Under the *Lemon* analysis, a statute or practice which touches upon religion, if it is to be permissible under the Establishment Clause, must have a secular purpose; it must neither advance nor inhibit religion in its principal or primary effect; and it must not foster an excessive entanglement with religion. 403 U.S., at 612–613, 91 S.Ct., at 2111. This trilogy of tests has been applied regularly in the Court's later Establishment Clause cases.

Our subsequent decisions further have refined the definition of governmental action that unconstitutionally advances religion. In recent years, we have paid particularly close attention to whether the challenged governmental practice either has the purpose or effect of "endorsing" religion, a concern that has long had a place in our Establishment Clause jurisprudence. Thus, in *Wallace v. Jaffree*, 472 U.S., at 60, 105 S.Ct., at 2491, the Court held unconstitutional Alabama's moment-of-silence statute because it was "enacted . . . for the sole purpose of expressing the State's endorsement of prayer activities." The Court similarly invalidated Louisiana's "Creationism Act" because it "endorses religion" in its purpose. *Edwards v. Aguillard*, 482 U.S. 578, 593, 107 S.Ct. 2573, 2582, 96 L.Ed. 2d 510 (1987). And the educational program in *School District of Grand Rapids v. Ball*, 473 U.S. 373, 389–392, 105 S.Ct. 3216, 3225–3227, 87 L.Ed.2d 267 (1985), was held to violate the Establishment Clause because of its "endorsement" effect. See also *Texas Monthly, Inc. v. Bullock*, 489 U.S. ——, ——, 109 S.Ct. 890, 901, 103 L.Ed.2d 1 (1989) (plurality opinion) (tax exemption limited to religious periodicals "effectively endorses religious belief").

Of course, the word "endorsement" is not self-defining. Rather, it derives its meaning from other words that this Court has found useful over the years in interpreting the Establishment Clause. Thus, it has been noted that the prohibition against governmental endorsement of religion "preclude[s] government from conveying or attempting to convey a message that religion or a particular religious belief is *favored or preferred."* Wallace v. Jaffree, 472 U.S., at 70, 105 S.Ct., at 2497 (O'CONNOR, J., concurring in judgment) (emphasis added). . . . Moreover, the term "endorsement" is closely linked to the term "promotion," *Lynch v. Donnelly,* 465 U.S., at 691, 104 S.Ct., at 1368 (O'CONNOR, J., concurring), and this Court long since has held that government "may not . . . promote one religion or religious theory against another or even against the militant opposite." *Epperson v. Arkansas,* 393 U.S. 97, 104, 89 S.Ct. 266, 270, 21 L.Ed.2d 228 (1968). See also *Wallace v. Jaffree,* 472 U.S., at 59–60, 105 S.Ct., at 2491 (using the concepts of endorsement, promotion, and favoritism interchangeably).

Whether the key word is "endorsement," "favoritism," or "promotion," the essential principle remains the same. The Establishment Clause, at the very least, prohibits government from appearing to take a position on questions of religious belief or from "making adherence to a religion relevant in any way to a person's standing in the political community." *Lynch v. Donnelly,* 465 U.S., at 687, 104 S.Ct., at 1366 (O'CONNOR, J., concurring).

B

We have had occasion in the past to apply Establishment Clause principles to the government's display of objects with religious significance. In *Stone v. Graham,* 449 U.S. 39, 101 S.Ct. 192, 66 L.Ed.2d 199 (1980), we held that the display of a copy of the Ten Commandments on the walls of public classrooms violates the Establishment Clause. Closer to the facts of this litigation is *Lynch v. Donnelly, supra,* in which we considered whether the city of Pawtucket, R.I., had violated the Establishment Clause by including a crèche in its annual Christmas display, located in a private park within the downtown shopping district. By a 5–4 decision in that difficult case, the Court upheld inclusion of the crèche in the Pawtucket display, holding, *inter alia,* that the inclusion of the crèche did not have the impermissible effect of advancing or promoting religion.

The rationale of the majority opinion in *Lynch* is none too clear: the opinion contains two strands, neither of which provides guidance for decision in subsequent cases. First, the opinion states that the inclusion of the crèche in the display was "no more an advancement or endorsement of religion" than other "endorsements" this Court has approved in the past, 465 U.S., at 683, 104 S.Ct., at 1364—but the opinion offers no discernible measure for distinguishing between permissible and impermissible endorsements. Second, the opinion observes that any benefit the government's display of the crèche gave to religion was no more than "indirect, remote, and incidental," *ibid.*—without saying how or why.

Although Justice O'CONNOR joined the majority opinion in *Lynch,* she wrote a concurrence that differs in significant respects from the majority opinion. The main difference is that the concurrence provides a sound analytical framework for evaluating governmental use of religious symbols.

First and foremost, the concurrence squarely rejects any notion that this Court will tolerate some government endorsement of religion. Rather, the concurrence recognizes any endorsement of religion as "invalid," *id.*, at 690, 104 S.Ct., at 1368, because it "sends a message to nonadherents that they are outsiders, not full members of the political community, and an accompanying message to adherents that they are insiders, favored members of the political community." *Id.*, at 688, 104 S.Ct., at 1367.

Second, the concurrence articulates a method for determining whether the government's use of an object with religious meaning has the effect of endorsing religion. The effect of the display depends upon the message that the government's practice communicates: the question is "what viewers may fairly understand to be the purpose of the display." *Id.*, at 692, 104 S.Ct., at 1369. That inquiry, of necessity, turns upon the context in which the contested object appears: "a typical museum setting, though not neutralizing the religious content of a religious painting, negates any message of endorsement of that content." *Ibid.* The concurrence thus emphasizes that the constitutionality of the crèche in that case depended upon its "particular physical setting," *ibid.*, and further observes: "Every government practice must be judged in its unique circumstances to determine whether it [endorses] religion." *Id.*, at 694, 104 S.Ct., at 1370.

The concurrence applied this mode of analysis to the Pawtucket crèche, seen in the context of that city's holiday celebration as a whole. In addition to the crèche, the city's display contained: a Santa Claus House with a live Santa distributing candy; reindeer pulling Santa's sleigh; a live 40-foot Christmas tree strung with lights; statues of carolers in old-fashioned dress; candy-striped poles; a "talking" wishing well; a large banner proclaiming "SEASONS GREETINGS"; a miniature "village" with several houses and a church; and various "cut-out" figures, including those of a clown, a dancing elephant, a robot, and a teddy bear. See 525 F.Supp. 1150, 1155 (RI 1981). The concurrence concluded that both because the crèche is "a traditional symbol" of Christmas, a holiday with strong secular elements, and because the crèche was "displayed along with purely secular symbols," the crèche's setting "changes what viewers may fairly understand to be the purpose of the display" and "negates any message of endorsement" of "the Christian beliefs represented by the crèche." 465 U.S., at 692, 104 S.Ct., at 1369.

The four *Lynch* dissenters agreed with the concurrence that the controlling question was "whether Pawtucket ha[d] run afoul of the Establishment Clause by endorsing religion through its display of the crèche." *Id.*, at 698, n. 3, 104 S.Ct., at 1372, n. 3 (BRENNAN, J., dissenting). The dissenters also agreed with the general proposition that the context in which the government uses a religious symbol is relevant for determining the answer to that question. *Id.*, at 705–706, 104 S.Ct., at 1376–1377. They simply reached a different answer: the dissenters concluded that the other elements of the Pawtucket display did not negate the endorsement of Christian faith caused by the presence of the crèche. They viewed the inclusion of the crèche in the city's overall display as placing "the government's imprimatur of approval on the particular religious beliefs exemplified by the crèche." *Id.*, at 701, 104 S.Ct., at 1374. Thus, they stated: "The effect on minority religious groups, as well as on those who may reject all religion, is to convey the message that their views are not similarly worthy of public recognition nor entitled to public support." *Ibid.*

Thus, despite divergence at the bottom line, the five Justices in concurrence and dissent in *Lynch* agreed upon the relevant constitutional principles: the government's use of religious symbolism is unconstitutional if it has the effect of endorsing religious beliefs, and the effect of the government's use of religious symbolism depends upon its context. These general principles are sound, and have been adopted by the Court in subsequent cases. Since *Lynch*, the Court has made clear that, when evaluating the effect of government conduct under the Establishment Clause, we must ascertain whether "the challenged governmental action is sufficiently likely to be perceived by adherents of the controlling denominations as an endorsement, and by the nonadherents as a disapproval, of their individual religious choices." *Grand Rapids*, 473 U.S., at 390, 105 S.Ct., at 3226. Accordingly, our present task is to determine whether the display of the crèche and the menorah, in their respective "particular physical settings," has the effect of endorsing or disapproving religious beliefs.

IV

We turn first to the county's crèche display. There is no doubt, of course, that the crèche itself is capable of communicating a religious message. Indeed, the crèche in this lawsuit uses words, as well as the picture of the nativity scene, to make its religious meaning unmistakably clear. "Glory to God in the Highest!" says the angel in the crèche—Glory to God because of the birth of Jesus. This praise to God in Christian terms is indisputably religious—indeed sectarian—just as it is when said in the Gospel or in a church service.

Under the Court's holding in *Lynch*, the effect of a crèche display turns on its setting. Here, unlike in *Lynch*, nothing in the context of the display detracts from the crèche's religious message. The *Lynch* display comprised a series of figures and objects, each group of which had its own focal point. Santa's house and his reindeer were objects of attention separate from the crèche, and had their specific visual story to tell. Similarly, whatever a "talking" wishing well may be, it obviously was a center of attention separate from the crèche. Here, in contrast, the crèche stands alone: it is the single element of the display on the Grand Staircase.

The floral decoration surrounding the crèche cannot be viewed as somehow equivalent to the secular symbols in the overall *Lynch* display. The floral frame, like all good frames, serves only to draw one's attention to the message inside the frame. The floral decoration surrounding the crèche contributes to, rather than detracts from, the endorsement of religion conveyed by the crèche. It is as if the county had allowed the Holy Name Society to display a cross on the Grand Staircase at Easter, and the county had surrounded the cross with Easter lilies. The county could not say that surrounding the cross with traditional flowers of the season would negate the endorsement of Christianity conveyed by the cross on the Grand Staircase. Its contention that the traditional Christmas greens negate the endorsement effect of the crèche fares no better.

Nor does the fact that the crèche was the setting for the county's annual Christmas carole-program diminish its religious meaning. First, the carole program in 1986 lasted only from December 3 to December 23 and occupied at most two hours a day. JEV 28. The effect of the crèche on those who viewed it when the choirs were not singing—the vast majority of the time—cannot be negated by the presence of the choir program. Second, because some of the caroles performed at the site of the crèche were religious in nature, those caroles were more likely to augment the religious quality of the scene than to secularize it.

Furthermore, the crèche sits on the Grand Staircase, the "main" and "most beautiful part" of the building that is the seat of county government. No viewer could reasonably think that it occupies this location without the support and approval of the government. Thus, by permitting the "display of the crèche in this particular physical setting," Lynch, 465 U.S., at 692, 104 S.Ct., at 1369 (O'CONNOR, J., concurring), the county sends an unmistakable message that it supports and promotes the Christian praise to God that is the crèche's religious message.

The fact that the crèche bears a sign disclosing its ownership by a Roman Catholic organization does not alter this conclusion. On the contrary, the sign simply demonstrates that the government is endorsing the religious message of that organization, rather than communicating a message of its own. But the Establishment Clause does not limit only the religious content of the government's own communications. It also prohibits the government's support and promotion of religious communications by religious organizations. See, e.g., Texas Monthly, supra (government support of the distribution of religious messages by religious organizations violates the Establishment Clause). Indeed, the very concept of "endorsement" conveys the sense of promoting someone else's message. Thus, by prohibiting government endorsement of religion, the Establishment Clause prohibits precisely what occurred here: the government's lending its support to the communication of a religious organization's religious message.

Finally, the county argues that it is sufficient to validate the display of the crèche on the Grand Staircase that the display celebrates Christmas, and Christmas is a national holiday. This argument obviously proves too much. It would allow the celebration of the Eucharist inside a courthouse on Christmas Eve. While the county may have doubts about the constitutional status of celebrating the Eucharist inside the courthouse under the government's auspices, this Court does not. The government may acknowledge Christmas as a cultural phenomenon, but under the First Amendment it may not observe it as a Christian holy day by suggesting that people praise God for the birth of Jesus.

In sum, Lynch teaches that government may celebrate Christmas in some manner and form, but not in a way that endorses Christian doctrine. Here, Allegheny County has transgressed this line. It has chosen to celebrate Christmas in a way that has the effect of endorsing a patently Christian message: Glory to God for the birth of Jesus Christ. Under Lynch, and the rest of our cases, nothing more is required to demonstrate a violation of the Establishment Clause. The display of the crèche in this context, therefore, must be permanently enjoined. . . .

C

Although Justice KENNEDY repeatedly accuses the Court of harboring a "latent hostility" or "callous indifference" toward religion, nothing could be further from the truth, and the accusations could be said to be as offensive as they are absurd. Justice KENNEDY apparently has misperceived a respect for religious pluralism, a respect commanded by the Constitution, as hostility or indifference to religion. No misperception could be more antithetical to the values embodied in the Establishment Clause.

Justice KENNEDY's accusations are shot from a weapon triggered by the following proposition: if government may celebrate the secular aspects of Christmas, then it must be allowed to celebrate the religious aspects as well because, otherwise, the government would be discriminating against citizens who celebrate Christmas as a religious, and not just a secular, holiday. This proposition, however, is flawed at its foundation. The government does not discriminate against any citizen on the basis of the citizen's religious faith if the government is secular in its functions and operations. On the contrary, the Constitution mandates that the government remain secular, rather than affiliating itself with religious beliefs or institutions, precisely in order to avoid discriminating among citizens on the basis of their religious faiths.

A secular state, it must be remembered, is not the same as an atheistic or antireligious state. A secular state establishes neither atheism nor religion as its official creed. Justice KENNEDY thus has it exactly backwards when he says that enforcing the Constitution's requirement that government remain secular is a prescription of orthodoxy. It follows directly from the Constitution's proscription against government affiliation with religious beliefs or institutions that there is no orthodoxy on religious matters in the secular state. Although Justice KENNEDY accuses the Court of "an Orwellian rewriting of history," perhaps it is Justice KENNEDY himself who has slipped into a form of Orwellian newspeak when he equates the constitutional command of secular government with a prescribed orthodoxy.

To be sure, in a pluralistic society there may be some would-be theocrats, who wish that their religion were an established creed, and some of them perhaps may be even audacious enough to claim that the lack of established religion discriminates against their preferences. But this claim gets no relief, for it contradicts the fundamental premise of the Establishment Clause itself. The antidiscrimination principle inherent in the Establishment Clause necessarily means that would-be discriminators on the basis of religion cannot prevail.

For this reason, the claim that prohibiting government from celebrating Christmas as a religious holiday discriminates against Christians in favor of nonadherents must fail. Celebrating Christmas as a religious, as opposed to a secular, holiday, necessarily entails professing, proclaiming, or believing that Jesus of Nazareth, born in a manger in Bethlehem, is the Christ, the Messiah. If the government celebrates Christmas as a religious holiday (for example, by issuing an official proclamation saying: "We rejoice in the glory of Christ's birth!"), it means that the government really is declaring Jesus to be the Messiah, a specifically Christian belief. In contrast, confining the government's own celebration of Christmas to the holiday's secular aspects does *not* favor the religious beliefs of non-Christians over those of Christians. Rather, it simply permits the government to acknowledge the holiday without expressing an allegiance to Christian beliefs, an allegiance that would truly favor Christians over non-Christians. To be sure, some Christians may wish to see the government proclaim its allegiance to Christianity in a religious celebration of Christmas, but the Constitution does not permit the gratification of that desire, which would contradict the " 'logic of secular liberty' " it is the purpose of the Establishment Clause to protect. See *Larson v. Valente*, 456 U.S., at 244, 102 S.Ct., at 1683, quoting B. Bailyn, The Ideological Origins of the American Revolution 265 (1967).

Of course, not all religious celebrations of Christmas located on government property violate the Establishment Clause. It obviously is not unconstitutional, for example, for a group of parishioners from a local church to go caroling through a city park on any Sunday in Advent or for a Christian club at a public university to sing caroles during their Christmas meeting. Cf. *Widmar v. Vincent*, 454 U.S. 263, 102 S.Ct., 269, 70 L.Ed.2d 440 (1981). The reason is that activities of this nature do not demonstrate the government's allegiance to, or endorsement of, the Christian faith.

Equally obvious, however, is the proposition that not all proclamations of Christian faith located on government property are permitted by the Establishment Clause just because they occur during the Christmas holiday season, as the example of a Mass in the courthouse surely illustrates. And once the judgment has been made that a particular proclamation of Christian belief, when disseminated from a particular location on government property, has the effect of demonstrating the government's endorsement of Christian faith, then it necessarily follows that the practice must be enjoined to protect the constitutional rights of those citizens who follow some creed other than Christianity. It is thus incontrovertible that the Court's decision today, premised on the determination that the crèche display on the Grand Staircase demonstrates the county's endorsement of Christianity, does not represent a hostility or indifference to religion but, instead, the respect for religious diversity that the Constitution requires.

VI

The display of the Chanukah menorah in front of the City-County Building may well present a closer constitutional question. The menorah, one must recognize, is a religious symbol: it serves to commemorate the miracle of the oil as described in the Talmud. But the menorah's message is not exclusively religious. The menorah is the primary visual symbol for a holiday that, like Christmas, has both religious and secular dimensions.

Moreover, the menorah here stands next to a Christmas tree and a sign saluting liberty. While no challenge has been made here to the display of the tree and the sign, their presence is obviously relevant in determining the effect of the menorah's display. The necessary result of placing a menorah next to a Christmas tree is to create an "overall holiday setting" that represents both Christmas and Chanukah—two holidays, not one.

The mere fact that Pittsburgh displays symbols of both Christmas and Chanukah does not end the constitutional inquiry. If the city celebrates both Christmas and Chanukah as religious holidays, then it violates the Establishment Clause. The simultaneous endorsement of Judaism and Christianity is no less constitutionally infirm than the endorsement of Christianity alone.

Conversely, if the city celebrates both Christmas and Chanukah as secular holidays, then its conduct is beyond the reach of the Establishment Clause. Because government may celebrate Christmas as a secular holiday,[3] it follows that government may also acknowledge Chanukah as a secular holiday. Simply put, it would be a form of discrimination against Jews to allow Pittsburgh to celebrate Christmas as a cultural tradition while simultaneously disallowing the city's acknowledgment of Chanukah as a contemporaneous cultural tradition.

Accordingly, the relevant question for Establishment Clause purposes is whether the combined display of the tree, the sign, and the menorah has the effect of endorsing both Christian and Jewish faiths, or rather simply recognizes that both Christmas and Chanukah are part of the same winter-holiday season, which has attained a secular status in our society. Of the two interpretations of this particular display, the latter seems far more plausible and is also in line with *Lynch*.[4]

The Christmas tree, unlike the menorah, is not itself a religious symbol. Although Christmas trees once carried religious connotations, today they typify the secular celebration of Christmas. See *ACLU of Illinois v. City of St. Charles*, 794 F.2d 265, 271 (CA7), cert. denied, 479 U.S. 961, 107 S.Ct. 458, 93 L.Ed.2d 403 (1986); L. Tribe, *American Constitutional Law* 1295 (2d ed. 1988) (Tribe).[5] Numerous Americans place Christmas trees in their homes without subscribing to Christian religious beliefs, and when the city's tree stands alone in front of the City-County Building, it is not considered an endorsement of Christian faith. Indeed, a 40-foot Christmas tree was one of the objects that validated the crèche in *Lynch*. The widely accepted view of the Christmas tree as the preeminent secular symbol of the Christmas holiday season serves to emphasize the secular component of the message communicated by other elements of an accompanying holiday display, including the Chanukah menorah.

The tree, moreover, is clearly the predominant element in the city's display. The 45-foot tree occupies the central position beneath the middle archway in front of the Grant Street entrance to the City-County Building; the 18-foot menorah is positioned to one side. Given this configuration, it is much more sensible to interpret the meaning of the menorah in light of the tree, rather than *vice versa*. In the shadow of the tree, the menorah is readily understood as simply a recognition that Christmas is not the only traditional way of observing the winter-holiday season. In these circumstances, then, the combination of the tree and the menorah communicates, not a simultaneous endorsement of both Christian and Jewish faith, but instead, a secular celebration of Christmas coupled with an acknowledgment of Chanukah as a contemporaneous alternative tradition.

Although the city has used a symbol with religious meaning as its representation of Chanukah, this is not a case in which the city has reasonable alternatives that are less religious in nature. It is difficult to imagine a predominantly secular symbol of Chanukah that the city could place next to its Christmas tree. An

18-foot dreidel would look out of place, and might be interpreted by some as mocking the celebration of Chanukah. The absence of a more secular alternative symbol is itself part of the context in which the city's actions must be judged in determining the likely effect of its use of the menorah. Where the government's secular message can be conveyed by two symbols, only one of which carries religious meaning, an observer reasonably might infer from the fact that the government has chosen to use the religious symbol that the government means to promote religious faith. But where, as here, no such choice has been made, this inference of endorsement is not present.

The Mayor's sign further diminishes the possibility that the tree and the menorah will be interpreted as a dual endorsement of Christianity and Judaism. The sign states that during the holiday season the city salutes liberty. Moreover, the sign draws upon the theme of light, common to both Chanukah and Christmas as winter festivals, and links that theme with this Nation's legacy of freedom, which allows an American to celebrate the holiday season in whatever way he wishes, religiously or otherwise. While no sign can disclaim an overwhelming message of endorsement, an "explanatory plaque" may confirm that in particular contexts the government's association with a religious symbol does not represent the government's sponsorship of religious beliefs. Here, the Mayor's sign serves to confirm what the context already reveals: that the display of the menorah is not an endorsement of religious faith but simply a recognition of cultural diversity.

Given all these considerations, it is not "sufficiently likely" that residents of Pittsburgh will perceive the combined display of the tree, the sign, and the menorah as an "endorsement" or "disapproval . . . of their individual religious choices." *Grand Rapids*, 473 U.S., at 390, 105 S.Ct., at 3226. While an adjudication of the display's effect must take into account the perspective of one who is neither Christian nor Jewish, as well as of those who adhere to either of these religions, *ibid.*, the constitutionality of its effect must also be judged according to the standard of a "reasonable observer." See *Witters v. Washington Dept. of Services for the Blind*, 474 U.S. 481, 493, 106 S.Ct. 748, 755, 88 L.Ed.2d 846 (1986) (O'CONNOR, J., concurring in part and concurring in judgment); see also Tribe, at 1296 (challenged government practices should be judged "from the perspective of a 'reasonable non-adherent' "). When measured against this standard, the menorah need not be excluded from this particular display. The Christmas tree alone in the Pittsburgh location does not endorse Christian belief; and, on the facts before us, the addition of the menorah "cannot fairly be understood to" result in the simultaneous endorsement of Christian and Jewish faiths. *Lynch*, 465 U.S., at 693, 104 S.Ct., at 1370 (O'CONNOR, J., concurring). On the contrary, for purposes of the Establishment Clause, the city's overall display must be understood as conveying the city's secular recognition of different traditions for celebrating the winter-holiday season.[6]

The conclusion here that, in this particular context, the menorah's display does not have an effect of endorsing religious faith does not foreclose the possibility that the display of the menorah might violate either the "purpose" or "entanglement" prong of the *Lemon* analysis. These issues were not addressed by the Court of Appeals and may be considered by that court on remand.[7]

VII

Lynch v. Donnelly confirms, and in no way repudiates, the longstanding constitutional principle that government may not engage in a practice that has the effect of promoting or endorsing religious beliefs. The display of the crèche in the County Courthouse has this unconstitutional effect. The display of the menorah in front of the City-County Building, however, does not have this effect, given its "particular physical setting."

The judgment of the Court of Appeals is affirmed in part and reversed in part, and the cases are remanded for further proceedings.

It is so ordered.

NOTES

1. "[T]he Christmas holiday in our national culture contains both secular and sectarian elements." Lynch v. Donnelly, 465 U.S. 668, 709, and n. 15, 104 S.Ct. 1355, 1378, and n. 15, 79 L.Ed.2d 604 (1984) (BRENNAN, J., dissenting). It has been suggested that the cultural aspect of Christmas in this country now exceeds the theological significance of the holiday. See J. Barnett, The American Christmas, a Study in National Culture 23 (1954) ("by the latter part of the last century, the folk-secular aspects of Christmas were taking precedence over its religious ones") (Barnett).

2. A State may neither allow public-school students to receive religious instruction on public-school premises, McCollum v. Board of Education, 333 U.S. 203, 68 S.Ct. 461, 92 L.Ed. 649 (1948), nor allow religious-school students to receive state-sponsored education in their religious schools. School District of Grand Rapids v. Ball, 473 U.S. 373, 105 S.Ct. 3216, 87 L.Ed.2d 267 (1985). Similarly unconstitutional is state-sponsored prayer in public schools. Abington School District v. Schempp, 374 U.S. 203, 83 S.Ct. 1560, 10 L.Ed.2d 844 (1963); Engel v. Vitale, 370 U.S. 421, 82 S.Ct. 1261, 8 L.Ed.2d 601 (1962). And the content of a public school's curriculum may not be based on a desire to promote religious beliefs. Edwards v. Aguillard, 482 U.S. 578, 107 S.Ct. 2573, 96 L.Ed.2d 510 (1987); Epperson v. Arkansas, 393 U.S. 97, 89 S.Ct. 266, 21 L.Ed.2d 228 (1968). For the same reason, posting the Ten Commandments on the wall of a public-school classroom violates the Establishment Clause. Stone v. Graham, 449 U.S. 39, 101 S.Ct. 192, 66 L.Ed.2d 199 (1980).

3. It is worth recalling here that no member of the Court in Lynch suggested that government may not celebrate the secular aspects of Christmas. On the contrary, the four dissenters there stated: "If public officials . . . participate in the secular celebration of Christmas—by, for example, decorating public places with such secular images as wreaths, garlands, or Santa Claus figures—they move closer to the limits of their constitutional power but nevertheless remain within the boundaries set by the Establishment Clause." 465 U.S., at 710–711, 104 S.Ct., at 1379 (BRENNAN, J., dissenting) (emphasis in original).

4. It is distinctly implausible to view the combined display of the tree, the sign, and the menorah as endorsing Jewish faith alone. During the time of this litigation, Pittsburgh had a population of 387,000, of which approximately 45,000 were Jews. Statistical Abstract of the United States 34 (1988); When a city like Pittsburgh places a symbol of Chanukah next to a symbol of Christmas, the result may be a simultaneous endorsement of Christianity and Judaism (depending upon the circumstances of the display). But the city's addition of a visual representation of Chanukah to its pre-existing Christmas display cannot reasonably be understood as an endorsement of Jewish—yet not Christian—belief. Thus, unless the combined Christmas-Chanukah display fairly can be seen as a double endorsement of Christian and Jewish faiths, it must be viewed as celebrating both holidays without endorsing either faith.

The conclusion that Pittsburgh's combined Christmas-Chanukah display cannot be interpreted as endorsing Judaism alone does not mean, however, that it is implausible, as a general matter, for a city like Pittsburgh to endorse a minority faith. The display of a menorah alone might well have that effect.

5. See also Barnett, at 141–142 (describing the Christmas tree, along with gift-giving and Santa Claus, as those aspects of Christmas which have become "so intimately identified with national life" that immigrants feel the need to adopt these customs in order to be a part of American culture). Of course, the tree is capable of taking on a religious significance if it is decorated with religious symbols. Cf. Gilbert, "The Season of Good Will and Inter-religious Tension," 24 Reconstructionist 13 (1958) (considering the Christmas tree, without the Star of Bethlehem, as one of "the cultural aspects of Christmas celebration").

6. This is not to say that the combined display of a Christmas tree and a menorah is constitutional wherever it may be located on government

property. For example, when located in a public school, such a display might raise additional constitutional considerations. Cf. *Edwards v. Aguillard*, 482 U.S., at 583–584, 107 S.Ct., at 2577 (Establishment Clause must be applied with special sensitivity in the public-school context).

7. In addition, nothing in this opinion forecloses the possibility that on other facts a menorah display could constitute an impermissible endorsement of religion. Indeed, there is some evidence in this record that in the past Chabad lit the menorah in front of the City-County Building in a religious ceremony that included the recitation of traditional religious blessings. See App. 281. Respondents, however, did not challenge this practice, there are no factual findings on it, and the Court of Appeals did not consider it in deciding that the display of a menorah in this location necessarily endorses Judaism. See 842 F.2d, at 662.

There is also some suggestion in the record that Chabad advocates the public display of menorahs as part of its own proselytizing mission, but again there have been no relevant factual findings that would enable this Court to conclude that Pittsburgh has endorsed Chabad's particular proselytizing message. Of course, nothing in this opinion forecloses a challenge to a menorah display based on such factual findings.

NO

DISSENTING OPINION OF
ANTHONY KENNEDY

Justice KENNEDY, concurring in the judgment in part and dissenting in part. The majority holds that the County of Allegheny violated the Establishment Clause by displaying a crèche in the county courthouse, because the "principal or primary effect" of the display is to advance religion within the meaning of *Lemon v. Kurtzman*, 403 U.S. 602, 612–613, 91 S.Ct. 2105, 2111, 29 L.Ed.2d 745 (1971). This view of the Establishment Clause reflects an unjustified hostility toward religion, a hostility inconsistent with our history and our precedents, and I dissent from this holding. The crèche display is constitutional, and, for the same reasons, the display of a menorah by the city of Pittsburgh is permissible as well. . . .

I

In keeping with the usual fashion of recent years, the majority applies the *Lemon* test to judge the constitutionality of the holiday displays here in question. I am content for present purposes to remain within the *Lemon* framework, but do not wish to be seen as advocating, let alone adopting, that test as our primary guide in this difficult area. Persuasive criticism of *Lemon* has emerged. See *Edwards v. Aguillard*, 482 U.S. 578, 636–640, 107 S.Ct. 2573, 2605–2607, 96 L.Ed.2d 510 (1987) (SCALIA, J., dissenting); *Aguilar v. Felton*, 473 U.S. 402, 426–430, 105 S.Ct. 3232, 3245–3247, 87 L.Ed.2d 290 (1985) (O'CONNOR, J., dissenting); *Wallace v. Jaffree*, 472 U.S. 38, 108–113, 105 S.Ct. 2479, 2516–2519, 86 L.Ed.2d 29 (1985) (REHNQUIST, J., dissenting); *Roemer v. Maryland Bd. of Public Works*, 426 U.S. 736, 768–769, 96 S.Ct. 2337, 2355, 49 L.Ed.2d 179 (1976) (WHITE, J., concurring in judgment). Our cases often question its utility in providing concrete answers to Establishment Clause questions, calling it but a " 'helpful signpos[t]' " or " 'guidelin[e]' ", to assist our deliberations rather than a comprehensive test. *Mueller v. Allen*, 463 U.S. 388, 394, 103 S.Ct. 3062, 3066, 77 L.Ed.2d 721 (1983) (quoting *Hunt v. McNair*, 413 U.S. 734, 741, 93 S.Ct. 2868, 2873, 37 L.Ed.2d 923 (1973));

From County of Allegheny v. American Civil Liberties Union, 109 S.Ct. 3086 (1989). Some notes and case citations omitted.

Committee for Public Education v. Nyquist, 413 U.S. 756, 773, n. 31, 93 S.Ct. 2955, 2965, n. 31, 37 L.Ed.2d 948 (1973) (quoting *Tilton v. Richardson,* 403 U.S. 672, 677–678, 91 S.Ct. 2091, 2095, 29 L.Ed.2d 790 (1971)); see *Lynch v. Donnelly,* 465 U.S. 668, 679, 104 S.Ct. 1355, 1362, 79 L.Ed.2d 604 (1984) ("we have repeatedly emphasized our willingness to be confined to any single test or criterion in this sensitive area"). Substantial revision of our Establishment Clause doctrine may be in order; but it is unnecessary to undertake that task today, for even the *Lemon* test, when applied with proper sensitivity to our traditions and our caselaw, supports the conclusion that both the crèche and the menorah are permissible displays in the context of the holiday season.

The only *Lemon* factor implicated in this case directs us to inquire whether the "principal or primary effect" of the challenged government practice is "one that neither advances nor inhibits religion." 403 U.S., at 612, 91 S.Ct., at 2111. The requirement of neutrality inherent in that formulation has sometimes been stated in categorical terms. For example, in *Everson v. Board of Education,* 330 U.S. 1, 67 S.Ct. 504, 91 L.Ed. 711 (1947), the first case in our modern Establishment Clause jurisprudence, Justice Black wrote that the Clause forbids laws "which aid one religion, aid all religions, or prefer one religion over another." *Id.,* at 15–16, 67 S.Ct., at 511. We have stated that government "must be neutral in matters of religious theory, doctrine, and practice" and "may not aid, foster, or promote one religion or religious theory against another or even against the militant opposite." *Epperson v. Arkansas,* 393 U.S. 97, 103–104, 89 S.Ct. 266, 269–270, 21 L.Ed.2d 228 (1968). And we have spoken of a prohibition against conferring an " 'imprimatur of state ap-

proval' " on religion, *Mueller v. Allen, supra,* 463 U.S. at 399, 103 S.Ct., at 3069 (quoting *Widmar v. Vincent,* 454 U.S. 263, 274, 102 S.Ct. 269, 276, 70 L.Ed.2d 440 (1981)), or "favor[ing] the adherents of any sect or religious organization." *Gillette v. United States,* 401 U.S. 437, 450, 91 S.Ct. 828, 836, 28 L.Ed.2d 168 (1971).

These statements must not give the impression of a formalism that does not exist. Taken to its logical extreme, some of the language quoted above would require a relentless extirpation of all contact between government and religion. But that is not the history or the purpose of the Establishment Clause. Government policies of accommodation, acknowledgment, and support for religion are an accepted part of our political and cultural heritage. As Chief Justice Burger wrote for the Court in *Walz v. Tax Comm'n,* 397 U.S. 664, 90 S.Ct. 1409, 25 L.Ed.2d 697 (1970), we must be careful to avoid "[t]he hazards of placing too much weight on a few words or phrases of the Court," and so we have "declined to construe the Religion Clauses with a literalness that would undermine the ultimate constitutional objective as illuminated by history." *Id.,* at 670–671, 90 S.Ct., at 1412.

Rather than requiring government to avoid any action that acknowledges or aids religion, the Establishment Clause permits government some latitude in recognizing and accommodating the central role religion plays in our society. Any approach less sensitive to our heritage would border on latent hostility toward religion, as it would require government in all its multifaceted roles to acknowledge only the secular, to the exclusion and so to the detriment of the religious. A categorical approach would install federal courts as jealous guardians of an absolute "wall of separation,"

NO Anthony Kennedy / 163

sending a clear message of disapproval. In this century, as the modern administrative state expands to touch the lives of its citizens in such diverse ways and redirects their financial choices through programs of its own, it is difficult to maintain the fiction that requiring government to avoid all assistance to religion can in fairness be viewed as serving the goal of neutrality.

Our cases reflect this understanding. In *Zorach v. Clauson*, 343 U.S. 306, 72 S.Ct. 679, 96 L.Ed. 954 (1952), for example, we permitted New York City's public school system to accommodate the religious preferences of its students by giving them the option of staying in school or leaving to attend religious classes for part of the day. Justice Douglas wrote for the Court:

"When the state encourages religious instruction . . . it follows the best of our traditions. For it then respects the religious nature of our people and accommodates the public service to their spiritual needs. To hold that it may not would be to find in the Constitution a requirement that the government show a callous indifference to religious groups. That would be preferring those who believe in no religion over those who do believe." *Id.*, at 313–314, 72 S.Ct., at 683–684.

Nothing in the First Amendment compelled New York City to establish the release-time policy in *Zorach*, but the fact that the policy served to aid religion, and in particular those sects that offer religious education to the young, did not invalidate the accommodation. Likewise, we have upheld government programs supplying textbooks to students in parochial schools, *Board of Education v. Allen*, 392 U.S. 236, 88 S.Ct. 1923, 20 L.Ed.2d 1060 (1968), providing grants to church-sponsored universities and colleges, *Roemer v. Maryland Bd. of Public Works*, 426 U.S. 736, 96 S.Ct. 2337, 49 L.Ed.2d 179 (1976); *Tilton v. Richardson*, 403 U.S. 672, 91 S.Ct. 2091, 29 L.Ed.2d 790 (1971), and exempting churches from the obligation to pay taxes, *Walz v. Tax Comm'n*, *supra*. These programs all have the effect of providing substantial benefits to particular religions, see, *e.g.*, *Tilton*, *supra*, 403 U.S., at 679, 91 S.Ct., at 2096 (grants to church-sponsored educational institutions "surely aid" those institutions), but they are nonetheless permissible. As Justice Goldberg wrote in *Abington School District v. Schempp*:

"It is said, and I agree, that the attitude of government toward religion must be one of neutrality. But untutored devotion to the concept of neutrality can lead to invocation or approval of results which partake not simply of that noninterference and noninvolvement with the religious which the Constitution commands, but of a brooding and pervasive devotion to the secular and a passive, or even active, hostility to the religious. Such results are not only not compelled by the Constitution, but, it seems to me, are prohibited by it.

Neither government nor this Court can or should ignore the significance of the fact that a vast portion of our people believe in and worship God and that many of our legal, political and personal values derive historically from religious teachings. Government must inevitably take cognizance of the existence of religion. . . ." 374 U.S. 203, 306, 83 S.Ct. 1560, 1615, 10 L.Ed.2d 844 (1963) (Goldberg, J., concurring, joined by Harlan, J.).

. . . Our cases disclose two limiting principles: government may not coerce anyone to support or participate in any religion or its exercise; and it may not, in the guise of avoiding hostility or callous indifference, give direct benefits to religion in such a degree that it in fact "establishes a [state] religion or religious faith, or tends to do so." *Lynch v. Donnelly, supra*, 465 U.S., at 678, 104 S.Ct., at 1361. These two principles, while distinct, are not unrelated, for it would be difficult indeed to establish a religion without some measure of more or less subtle coercion, be it in the form of taxation to supply the substantial benefits that would sustain a state-established faith, direct compulsion to observance, or governmental exhortation to religiosity that amounts in fact to proselytizing.

It is no surprise that without exception we have invalidated actions that further the interests of religion through the coercive power of government. Forbidden involvements include compelling or coercing participation or attendance at a religious activity, see *Engel v. Vitale*, 370 U.S. 421, 82 S.Ct. 1261, 8 L.Ed.2d 601 (1962); *McGowan v. Maryland, supra*, 366 U.S., at 452, 81 S.Ct., at 1118 (discussing *McCollum v. Board of Education, supra*), requiring religious oaths to obtain government office or benefits, *Torcaso v. Watkins*, 367 U.S. 488, 81 S.Ct. 1680, 6 L.Ed.2d 982 (1961), or delegating government power to religious groups, *Larkin v. Grendel's Den, Inc.*, 459 U.S. 116, 103 S.Ct. 505, 74 L.Ed.2d 297 (1982). The freedom to worship as one pleases without government interference or oppression is the great object of both the Establishment and the Free Exercise Clauses. Barring all attempts to aid religion through government coercion goes far toward attainment of this object. . . .

In determining whether there exists an establishment, or a tendency toward one, we refer to the other types of church-state contacts that have existed unchallenged throughout our history, or that have been found permissible in our caselaw. In *Lynch*, for example, we upheld the city of Pawtucket's holiday display of a crèche, despite the fact that "the display advance[d] religion in a sense." We held that the crèche conferred no greater benefit on religion than did governmental support for religious education, legislative chaplains, "recognition of the origins of the [Christmas] Holiday itself as 'Christ's Mass,' " or many other forms of symbolic or tangible governmental assistance to religious faiths that are ensconced in the safety of national tradition. And in *Marsh v. Chambers*, we found that Nebraska's practice of employing a legislative chaplain did not violate the Establishment Clause, because "legislative prayer presents no more potential for establishment than the provision of school transportation, beneficial grants for higher education, or tax exemptions for religious organizations." 463 U.S., at 791, 103 S.Ct., at 3335 (citations omitted). Non-coercive government action within the realm of flexible accommodation or passive acknowledgment of existing symbols does not violate the Establishment Clause unless it benefits religion in a way more direct and more substantial than practices that are accepted in our national heritage.

II

These principles are not difficult to apply to the facts of the case before us. In permitting the displays on government property of the menorah and the crèche, the city and county sought to do no more than "celebrate the season," and to acknowledge, along with many of their citizens, the historical background and the religious as well as secular nature of the Chanukah and Christmas holidays. This interest falls well within the tradition of government accommodation and acknowledgment of religion that has marked our history from the beginning. It cannot be disputed that government, if it chooses, may participate in sharing with its citizens the joy of the holiday season, by declaring public holidays, installing or permitting festive displays, sponsoring celebrations and parades, and providing holiday vacations for its employees. All levels of our government do precisely that. As we said in *Lynch,* "Government has long recognized—indeed it has subsidized—holidays with religious significance." 465 U.S., at 676, 104 S.Ct., at 1360.

If government is to participate in its citizens' celebration of a holiday that contains both a secular and a religious component, enforced recognition of only the secular aspect would signify the callous indifference toward religious faith that our cases and traditions do not require; for by commemorating the holiday only as it is celebrated by nonadherents, the government would be refusing to acknowledge the plain fact, and the historical reality, that many of its citizens celebrate its religious aspects as well. Judicial invalidation of government's attempts to recognize the religious underpinnings of the holiday would signal not neutrality but a pervasive intent to insulate government from all things religious. The Religion Clauses do not require government to acknowledge these holidays or their religious component; but our strong tradition of government accommodation and acknowledgment permits government to do so.

There is no suggestion here that the government's power to coerce has been used to further the interests of Christianity or Judaism in any way. No one was compelled to observe or participate in any religious ceremony or activity. Neither the city nor the county contributed significant amounts of tax money to serve the cause of one religious faith. The crèche and the menorah are purely passive symbols of religious holidays. Passersby who disagree with the message conveyed by these displays are free to ignore them, or even to turn their backs, just as they are free to do when they disagree with any other form of government speech.

There is no realistic risk that the crèche or the menorah represent an effort to proselytize or are otherwise the first step down the road to an establishment of religion.[1] *Lynch* is dispositive of this claim with respect to the crèche, and I find no reason for reaching a different result with respect to the menorah. Both are the traditional symbols of religious holidays that over time have acquired a secular component. Without ambiguity, *Lynch* instructs that "the focus of our inquiry must be on the [religious symbol] in the context of the [holiday] season," 465 U.S., at 679, 104 S.Ct., at 1362. In that context, religious displays that serve "to celebrate the Holiday and to depict the origins of that Holiday" give rise to no Establishment Clause concern. If Congress and the state legislatures do not run afoul of the Establishment Clause when they begin each day with a state-sponsored prayer for divine guidance offered by a chaplain whose salary is paid at government expense, I cannot comprehend how a menorah or a crèche, displayed in the limited context of the holiday season, can be invalid.

Respondents say that the religious displays involved here are distinguishable from the crèche in *Lynch* because they are located on government property and are not surrounded by the candy canes, reindeer, and other holiday paraphernalia that were a part of the display in *Lynch*. Nothing in Chief Justice Burger's opinion for the Court in *Lynch* provides support for these purported distinctions. After describing the facts, the *Lynch* opinion makes no mention of either of these factors. It concentrates instead on the significance of the crèche as part of the entire holiday season. Indeed, it is clear that the Court did not view the secular aspects of the display as somehow subduing the religious message conveyed by the crèche, for the majority expressly rejected the dissenters' suggestion that it sought " 'to explain away the clear religious import of the crèche,' " or had "equated the crèche with a Santa's house or reindeer." *Id.*, 465 U.S., at 685, n. 12, 104 S.Ct., at 1365, n. 12. Crucial to the Court's conclusion was not the number, prominence, or type of secular items contained in the holiday display but the simple fact that, when displayed by government during the Christmas season, a crèche presents no realistic danger of moving government down the forbidden road toward an establishment of religion. Whether the crèche be surrounded by poinsettias, talking wishing wells, or carolers, the conclusion remains the same, for the relevant context is not the items in the display itself but the season as a whole.

The fact that the crèche and menorah are both located on government property, even at the very seat of government, is likewise inconsequential. In the first place, the *Lynch* Court did not rely on the fact that the setting for Pawtucket's display was a privately owned park, and it is difficult to suggest that anyone could

have failed to receive a message of government sponsorship after observing Santa Claus ride the city fire engine to the park to join with the Mayor of Pawtucket in inaugurating the holiday season by turning on the lights of the city-owned display. See *Donnelly v. Lynch*, 525 F.Supp. 1150, 1156 (RI 1981). Indeed, the District Court in *Lynch* found that "people might reasonably mistake the Park for public property," and rejected as "frivolous" the suggestion that the display was not directly associated with the city. *Id.*, at 1176, and n. 35. . . .

If *Lynch* is still good law—and until today it was—the judgment below cannot stand. I accept and indeed approve both the holding and the reasoning of Chief Justice Burger's opinion in *Lynch*, and so I must dissent from the judgment that the crèche display is unconstitutional. On the same reasoning, I agree that the menorah display is constitutional.

III

The majority invalidates display of the crèche, not because it disagrees with the interpretation of *Lynch* applied above, but because it chooses to discard the reasoning of the *Lynch* majority opinion in favor of Justice O'CONNOR's concurring opinion in that case. It has never been my understanding that a concurring opinion "suggest[ing] a clarification of our . . . doctrine," *Lynch*, 465 U.S., at 687, 104 S.Ct., at 1366 (O'CONNOR, J., concurring), could take precedence over an opinion joined in its entirety by five Members of the Court. As a general rule, the principle of *stare decisis* directs us to adhere not only to the holdings of our prior cases, but also to their explications of the governing rules of law. Since the majority does not state its intent to overrule *Lynch*, I find its refusal to apply the reasoning of that decision quite confusing.

Even if *Lynch* did not control, I would not commit this Court to the test applied by the majority today. The notion that cases arising under the Establishment Clause should be decided by an inquiry into whether a " 'reasonable observer' " may " 'fairly understand' " government action to " 'sen[d] a message to non-adherents that they are outsiders, not full members of the political community,' " is a recent, and in my view most unwelcome, addition to our tangled Establishment Clause jurisprudence. *Ante*, at 3102, 3114. Although a scattering of our cases have used "endorsement" as another word for "preference" or "imprimatur," the endorsement test applied by the majority had its genesis in Justice O'CONNOR's concurring opinion in *Lynch*. . . .

For the reasons expressed below, I submit that the endorsement test is flawed in its fundamentals and unworkable in practice. The uncritical adoption of this standard is every bit as troubling as the bizarre result it produces in the case before us.

A

I take it as settled law that, whatever standard the Court applies to Establishment Clause claims, it must at least suggest results consistent with our precedents and the historical practices that, by tradition, have informed our First Amendment jurisprudence. It is true that, for reasons quite unrelated to the First Amendment, displays commemorating religious holidays were not commonplace in 1791. See generally J. Barnett, The American Christmas: A Study in National Cul-

ture 2–11 (1954). But the relevance of history is not confined to the inquiry into whether the challenged practice itself is a part of our accepted traditions dating back to the Founding. . . .

If the endorsement test, applied without artificial exceptions for historical practice, reached results consistent with history, my objections to it would have less force. But, as I understand that test, the touchstone of an Establishment Clause violation is whether nonadherents would be made to feel like "outsiders" by government recognition or accommodation of religion. Few of our traditional practices recognizing the part religion plays in our society can withstand scrutiny under a faithful application of this formula.

Some examples suffice to make plain my concerns. Since the Founding of our Republic, American Presidents have issued Thanksgiving Proclamations establishing a national day of celebration and prayer. The first such proclamation was issued by President Washington at the request of the First Congress, and "recommend[ed] and assign[ed]" a day "to be devoted by the people of these States to the service of that great and glorious Being who is the beneficent author of all the good that was, that is, or that will be," so that "we may then unite in most humbly offering our prayers and supplications to the great Lord and Ruler of Nations, and beseech Him to . . . promote the knowledge and practice of true religion and virtue. . . . " 1 J. Richardson, A Compilation of Messages and Papers of the Presidents, 1789–1897, p. 64 (1899). Most of President Washington's successors have followed suit,[2] and the forthrightly religious nature of these proclamations has not waned with the years. President Franklin D. Roosevelt went so far as to "suggest a nationwide reading of the Holy Scriptures during the period from Thanksgiving Day to Christmas" so that "we may bear more earnest witness to our gratitude to Almighty God." Presidential Proclamation No. 2629, 58 Stat. 1160. It requires little imagination to conclude that these proclamations would cause nonadherents to feel excluded, yet they have been a part of our national heritage from the beginning.[3]

The Executive has not been the only Branch of our Government to recognize the central role of religion in our society. The fact that this Court opens its sessions with the request that "God save the United States and this honorable Court" has been noted elsewhere. See *Lynch*, 465 U.S., at 677, 104 S.Ct., at 1361. The Legislature has gone much further, not only employing legislative chaplains, see 2 U.S.C. § 61d, but also setting aside a special prayer room in the Capitol for use by Members of the House and Senate. The room is decorated with a large stained glass panel that depicts President Washington kneeling in prayer; around him is etched the first verse of the 16th Psalm: "Preserve me, O God, for in Thee do I put my trust." Beneath the panel is a rostrum on which a Bible is placed; next to the rostrum is an American Flag. See We the People: The Story of the United States Capitol 122 (1978). Some endorsement is inherent in these reasonable accommodations, yet the Establishment Clause does not forbid them.

The United States Code itself contains religious references that would be suspect under the endorsement test. Congress has directed the President to "set aside and proclaim a suitable day each year . . . as a National Day of Prayer, on which the people of the United States may turn to God in prayer and meditation at churches, in groups, and as individuals." 36 U.S.C. § 169h. This statute does not require anyone to pray, of course, but it is a straightforward endorsement of the concept of "turn[ing] to God in prayer." Also by statute, the Pledge of Allegiance to the Flag describes the United States as "one Nation under God." 36 U.S.C. § 172. To be sure, no one is obligated to recite this phrase, see *West Virginia State Board of Education v. Barnette*, 319 U.S. 624, 63 S.Ct. 1178, 87 L.Ed. 1628 (1943), but it borders on sophistry to suggest that the " 'reasonable' " atheist would not feel less than a " 'full membe[r] of the political community' " every time his fellow Americans recited, as part of their expression of patriotism and love for country, a phrase he believed to be false. Likewise, our national motto, "In God we trust," 36 U.S.C. § 186, which is prominently engraved in the wall above the Speaker's dais in the Chamber of the House of Representatives and is reproduced on every coin minted and every dollar printed by the Federal Government, 31 U.S.C. §§ 5112(d)(1), 5114(b), must have the same effect.

If the intent of the Establishment Clause is to protect individuals from mere feelings of exclusion, then legislative prayer cannot escape invalidation. It has been argued that "[these] government acknowledgments of religion serve, in the only ways reasonably possible in our culture, the legitimate secular purposes of solemnizing public occasions, expressing confidence in the future, and encouraging the recognition of what is worthy of appreciation in society." *Lynch, supra,* 465 U.S., at 693, 104 S.Ct., at 1369 (O'CONNOR, J., concurring). I fail to see why prayer is the only way to convey these messages; appeals to patriotism, moments of silence, and any number of other approaches would be as effective, were the only purposes at issue the ones described by the *Lynch* concurrence. Nor is it clear to me why "encouraging the recognition of what is worthy of appreciation in society" can be characterized as a purely secular purpose, if it can be achieved only through religious prayer. No doubt prayer is "worthy of appreciation," but that is most assuredly not because it is secular. Even accepting the secular-solemnization explanation at face value, moreover, it seems incredible to suggest that the average observer of legislative prayer who either believes in no religion or whose faith rejects the concept of God would not receive the clear message that his faith is out of step with the political norm. Either the endorsement test must invalidate scores of traditional practices recognizing the place religion holds in our culture, or it must be twisted and stretched to avoid inconsistency with practices we know to have been permitted in the past, while condemning similar practices with no greater endorsement effect simply by reason of their lack of historical antecedent.[4] Neither result is acceptable.

B

In addition to disregarding precedent and historical fact, the majority's approach to government use of religious symbolism threatens to trivialize constitutional adjudication. By mischaracterizing the Court's opinion in *Lynch* as an endorsement-in-context test, the majority embraces a jurisprudence of minutiae. A reviewing court must consider whether the city has included Santas, talking wishing wells, reindeer, or other secular symbols as "a center of attention separate from the crèche." After determining whether these centers of attention are sufficiently "separate" that each "had their specific visual story to tell," the court must then measure their proximity to the crèche. A community that wishes to construct a constitutional display must also take care to avoid floral frames or other devices that might insulate the crèche from the sanitizing effect of the secular portions of the display. The majority also notes the presence of evergreens near the crèche that are identical to two small evergreens placed near official county signs. After today's decision, municipal greenery must be used with care.

Another important factor will be the prominence of the setting in which the display is placed. In this case, the Grand Staircase of the county courthouse proved too resplendent. Indeed, the Court finds that this location itself conveyed an "unmistakable message that [the county] supports and promotes the Christian praise to God that is the crèche's religious message."

My description of the majority's test, though perhaps uncharitable, is intended to illustrate the inevitable difficulties with its application.[5] This test could provide workable guidance to the lower courts, if ever, only after this Court has decided a long series of holiday display cases, using little more than intuition and a tape measure. Deciding cases on the basis of such an unguided examination of marginalia is irreconcilable with the imperative of applying neutral principles in constitutional adjudication. "It would be appalling to conduct litigation under the Establishment Clause as if it were a trademark case, with experts testifying about whether one display is really like another, and witnesses testifying they were offended—but would have been less so were the crèche five feet closer to the jumbo candy cane." *American Jewish Congress v. Chicago,* 827 F.2d 120, 130 (CA7 1987) (Easterbrook, J., dissenting). . . .

The result the Court reaches in this case is perhaps the clearest illustration of the unwisdom of the endorsement test. Although Justice O'CONNOR disavows Justice BLACKMUN's suggestion that the minority or majority status of a religion is relevant to the question whether government recognition constitutes a forbidden endorsement, the very nature of the endorsement test, with its emphasis on the feelings of the objective observer, easily lends itself to this type of inquiry. If there be such a person as the "reasonable observer," I am quite certain that he or she will take away a salient message from our holding in this case: the Supreme Court of the United States has concluded that the First Amendment creates classes of religions based on the relative numbers of their adherents. Those religions enjoying the largest following must be consigned to the status of least-favored faiths so as to avoid any possible risk of offending members of minority religions. I would be the first to admit that many questions arising under the Establishment Clause do not admit of easy answers, but whatever the Clause requires, it is not the result reached by the Court today.

IV

The approach adopted by the majority contradicts important values embodied in the Clause. Obsessive, implacable resistance to all but the most carefully scripted and secularized forms of accommodation requires this Court to act as a censor, issuing national decrees as to what is orthodox and what is not. What is orthodox, in this context, means what is secular; the only Christmas the State can acknowledge is one in which references to religion have been held to a minimum. The Court thus lends its assistance to an Orwellian rewriting of history as many understand it. I can conceive of no judicial function more antithetical to the First Amendment.

A further contradiction arises from the majority's approach, for the Court also assumes the difficult and inappropriate task of saying what every religious symbol means. Before studying this case, I had not known the full history of the menorah, and I suspect the same was true of my colleagues. More important, this history was, and is, likely unknown to the vast majority of people of all faiths who saw the symbol displayed in Pittsburgh. Even if the majority is quite right about the history of the menorah, it hardly follows that this same history informed the observers' view of the symbol and the reason for its presence. This Court is ill-equipped to sit as a national theology board, and I question both the widsom and the constitutionality of its doing so. Indeed, were I required to choose between the approach taken by the majority and a strict separationist view, I would have to respect the consistency of the latter.

The case before us is admittedly a troubling one. It must be conceded that, however neutral the purpose of the city and county, the eager proselytizer may seek to use these symbols for his own ends. The urge to use them to teach or to taunt is always present. It is also true that some devout adherents of Judaism or Christianity may be as offended by the holiday display as are nonbelievers, if not more so. To place these religious symbols in a common hallway or sidewalk, where they may be ignored or even insulted, must be distasteful to many who cherish their meaning.

For these reasons, I might have voted against installation of these particular displays were I a local legislative official. But we have no jurisdiction over matters of taste within the realm of constitutionally permissible discretion. Our role is enforcement of a written Constitution. In my view, the principles of the Establishment Clause and our Nation's historic traditions of diversity and pluralism allow communities to make reasonable judgments respecting the accommodation or acknowledgment of holidays with both cultural and religious aspects. No constitutional violation occurs when they do so by displaying a symbol of the holiday's religious origins.

I dissent.

NOTES

1. One can imagine a case in which the use of passive symbols to acknowledge religious holidays could present this danger. For example, if a city chose to recognize, through religious displays, every significant Christian holiday while ignoring the holidays of all other faiths, the argument that the city was simply recognizing certain holidays celebrated by its citizens without establishing an official faith or applying pressure to obtain adherents would be much more difficult to maintain. On the facts of this case, no such unmistakable and continual preference for one faith has been demonstrated or alleged.

2. In keeping with his strict views of the degree of separation mandated by the Establishment Clause, Thomas Jefferson declined to follow this tradition. See 11 Writings of Thomas Jefferson 429 (A. Lipscomb ed. 1904).

3. Similarly, our presidential inaugurations have traditionally opened with a request for divine blessing. At our most recent such occasion, on January 20, 1989, thousands bowed their heads in prayer to this invocation:

"Our Father and our God, Thou hast said blessed is the nation whose God is the Lord,

"We recognize on this historic occasion that we are a nation under God. This faith in God is our foundation and our heritage. . . ."

4. If the majority's test were to be applied logically, it would lead to the elimination of all nonsecular Christmas caroling in public buildings or, presumably, anywhere on public property. It is difficult to argue that lyrics like "Good Christian men, rejoice," "Joy to the world! the Savior reigns," "This, this is Christ the King," "Christ, by highest heav'n adored," and "Come and behold Him, Born the King of angels," have acquired such a secular nature that nonadherents would not feel "left out" by a government-sponsored or approved program that included these carols. See W. Ehret & G. Evans, The International Book of Christmas Carols 12, 28, 30, 46, 318 (1963). We do not think for a moment that the Court will ban such carol programs, however. Like Thanksgiving Proclamations, the reference to God in the Pledge of Allegiance, and invocations to God in sessions of Congress and of this Court, they constitute practices that the Court will not proscribe, but that the Court's reasoning today does not explain.

5. Justice BLACKMUN and Justice O'CONNOR defend the majority's test by suggesting that the approach followed in *Lynch* would require equally difficult line-drawing. It is true that the *Lynch* test may involve courts in difficult line-drawing in the unusual case where a municipality insists on such extreme use of religious speech that an establishment of religion is threatened. Only adoption of the absolutist views that either *all* government involvement with religion is permissible, or that *none* is, can provide a bright line in all cases. That price for clarity is neither exacted nor permitted by the Constitution. But for the most part, Justice BLACKMUN's and Justice O'CONNOR's objections are not well taken. As a practical matter, the only cases of symbolic recognition likely to arise with much frequency are those involving simple holiday displays, and in that context *Lynch* provides unambiguous guidance. I would follow it. The majority's test, on the other hand, demands the Court to draw exquisite distinctions from fine detail in a wide range of cases. The anomalous result the test has produced here speaks for itself.

POSTSCRIPT

Religious Displays on Public Property: Do They Violate the Constitution?

Why should church and state be separate? Is there any danger to be feared from public religious displays? It is probably fair to say that behind the debates over this issue and the ongoing controversy over prayer in the schools are differing interpretations of the history of religion. Does religion bring us to a higher level of existence, or is it a system that will oppress dissidents, nonbelievers, and members of minority faiths? Almost everyone has an opinion on this question, and most can find some historical support for their positions. Ironically, the same historical circumstance may even be used to support opposing points of view. For example, at a congressional hearing on school prayer, the following testimony was introduced.

> When I was educated in German public schools, they provided as part of the regular curriculum separate religious instruction for children of the three major faiths. At that time, all children in public schools from the ages of 6 to 18 were required not merely to recite a prayer at the beginning of each school session but to receive religious instruction twice a week. That system contin-ued in the following decades. . . .
> Did that program effectively teach morality to the German people? If it did, it would be difficult to explain the rise of Hitler and the total moral collapse and even depravity of the German people, which resulted in the torture and death of millions of Jews and Christians.[1]

Yet another witness, however, testifying in support of prayer in the schools, quoted the report of the President's Commission on the Holocaust, which wrote that "the Holocaust could not have occurred without the collapse of certain religious norms; increasing secularity fueled a devaluation of the image of the human being created in the likeness of God."[2]

Relevant cases concerning religion in the public schools are *McCollum v. Board of Education*, 333 U.S. 203 (1948), about religious instruction on school property; and *Zorach v. Clauson*, 343 U.S. 306 (1952), regarding free time from school for religious instruction off school property; and *Board of Education of the Westside Community Schools v. Mergens*, 110 S. Ct. 2356 (1990), regarding the use of school premises for an after-school religious club. The pro-prayer lobby has had its greatest failure in cases involving schools or children, the area where it would probably most like to see change (see, for example, *Wallace v. Jaffree*, 105 S.Ct. 2479, 1985), which ruled the Alabama moment of silence statute unconstitutional; or *Edwards v. Aquillard*, 107 S.Ct. 2573 (1987), prohibiting the teaching of "creation science."

NOTES

1. Statement by Joachim Prinz, quoted in testimony of Nathan Dershowitz, *Hearings on Prayer in Public Schools and Buildings*, Committee on the Judiciary, House of Representatives, August 19, 1980.

2. Statement of Juda Glasner, *Hearings on Prayer in Public Schools and Buildings*, Committee on the Judiciary, House of Representatives, July 30, 1980.

ISSUE 8

Is Abortion Protected by the Constitution?

YES: Harry Blackmun, from Majority Opinion, *Roe v. Wade*, U.S. Supreme Court (1973)

NO: Brief for the United States as Amicus Curiae, from *Webster v. Reproductive Services*, U.S. Supreme Court (1989)

ISSUE SUMMARY

YES: Supreme Court justice Harry Blackmun refers to historical attitudes, medical opinion, and legal precedent to defend the right of abortion.
NO: The solicitor general argues that *Roe v. Wade* should be overturned since Justice Blackmun's model is not warranted by the Constitution and too much discretion is removed from the states.

One of the strengths of our judicial process, lawyers often claim, is that it encourages logical and objective solutions to problems and reduces the influence of emotion and whim. By proceeding slowly, by applying abstract legal rules, by relying on professional lawyers and restricting the lay person's role, it is asserted that impartiality and neutrality will be achieved and that explosive issues will be defused. The legal process works this kind of magic often, but it has clearly failed to do so with regard to the issue of abortion. Abortion remains as newsworthy and important a subject today as it was when the landmark case of *Roe v. Wade* was decided in 1973.

Perceptions of the abortion issue differ. For the courts, it is a constitutional issue, meaning that the focus is on whether laws restricting abortion deny a woman due process of law under the Fourteenth Amendment. Part of the reason courts have been unable to defuse the abortion issue is that they have not persuaded the public to see the subject only in these terms. How we define or categorize an issue frequently determines our conclusions about the subject. For example, do we view abortion as an issue affecting women, and thus as an example of sex discrimination? Or do we think primarily of the fetus, and thus conclude that what is occurring is murder? Do we look at abortion from a religious perspective, thinking of how the legal codes of Western religion treat the subject? Is it a question of privacy and of preventing the state from intruding into the affairs and personal decisions of citizens? Is it a matter of health, of preventing injuries and death to women who undergo illegal abortions? Is it an issue of discrimination against the poor, who may need the state to subsidize abortions, or even racial discrimination, because a higher proportion of poor women are black? How abortion is described can be all-important. One writer, for example, has written, "The real question is not, 'How can we justify abortion?' but, 'How can we justify compulsory childbearing?' " (Cisler, "Unfinished Business: Birth Control and Women's Liberation," in Morgan, ed. *Sisterhood is Powerful*, 1970). From reading the way this question is worded, it is not difficult to figure out this person's point of view.

The landmark decision of *Roe v. Wade*, 410 U.S. 113 (1973) was handed down on January 23, 1973. In the majority opinion, Justice Blackmun wrote that states may not prohibit abortions during the first trimester, that abortions may be regulated but not prohibited during the second trimester, and that abortions may be prohibited during the last trimester. In the fifteen years since *Roe v. Wade* there have been many attempts to circumvent, narrow, delay, or avoid the Court's ruling. These attempts have resulted in additional Supreme Court rulings. Four of the most important cases are the following:

1. *Harris v. McCrae*, 100 S.Ct. 2671 (1980)   In a 5–4 decision in 1980, the Supreme Court upheld a federal law that prohibited the federal government from reimbursing states for providing Medicaid abortions to women, except under specified circumstances. The majority held that the law did not illegally discriminate against the poor nor did it violate the doctrines of separation of church and state merely because the restrictions coincided with Roman Catholic religious beliefs.

2. *H. L. v. Matheson*, 101 S.Ct. 1164 (1981)   In a 6–3 decision, the Supreme Court upheld a Utah statute that required a physician to "notify, if possible," the parents or guardian of a minor upon whom an abortion is to be performed. Previous decisions had ruled that for a state to permit a blanket, unreviewable parental veto of a child's abortion was unconstitutional, but the Court felt that requiring mere notice was a proper exercise of state power.

3. *Webster v. Reproductive Health Services*, 109 S. Ct. 3040 (1989)   The Court refused to overturn *Roe v. Wade*, but it allowed states to impose more restrictions, such as one that required doctors, when a woman is more than twenty weeks pregnant, to perform tests "to determine if the unborn child is viable." The five-member majority included four votes to overturn *Roe*. Justice O'Connor, the critical fifth vote, was unwilling to overturn *Roe* but felt the Missouri law was constitutional since it did not place an "undue burden" on the woman's right. This perspective meant that future cases would have to review other state statutes, perhaps more restrictive than the Missouri statute, to determine whether or not they were an "undue burden."

4. *Hodgson v. Minnesota*, 58 U.S. L.W. 4597 (1990)   The Court decided that states could require minors to notify both parents before obtaining an abortion, even if the minor lived with only one parent. The minor did have to be provided with an option of getting permission from a judge, instead of from her parents.

YES

Harry Blackmun

ABORTION AND FREEDOM

Mr. Justice Blackmun delivered the opinion of the Court.

This Texas federal appeal and its Georgia companion, *Doe v. Bolton*, 410 U.S. 179, 93 S.Ct. 739, 35 L.Ed.2d 201, present constitutional challenges to state criminal abortion legislation. . . . We forthwith acknowledge our awareness of the sensitive and emotional nature of the abortion controversy, of the vigorous opposing views, even among physicians, and of the deep and seemingly absolute convictions that the subject inspires. One's philosophy, one's experiences, one's exposure to the raw edges of human existence, one's religious training, one's attitudes toward life and family and their values, and the moral standards one establishes and seeks to observe, are all likely to influence and to color one's thinking and conclusions about abortion.

In addition, population growth, pollution, poverty, and racial overtones tend to complicate and not to simplify the problem.

Our task, of course, is to resolve the issue by constitutional measurement, free of emotion and of predilection. We seek earnestly to do this, and, because we do, we have inquired into, and in this opinion place some emphasis upon, medical and medical-legal history and what that history reveals about man's attitudes toward abortion procedure over the centuries. . . .

The Texas statutes that concern us here [make] it a crime to "procure an abortion," or to attempt one, except with respect to "an abortion procured or attempted by medical advice for the purpose of saving the life of the mother." Similar statutes are in existence in a majority of the States. . . .

The principal thrust of appellant's attack on the Texas statutes is that they improperly invade a right, said to be possessed by the pregnant woman, to choose to terminate her pregnancy. Appellant would discover this right in the concept of personal "liberty" embodied in the Fourteenth Amendment's Due Process Clause; or in personal, marital, familial, and sexual privacy said to be protected by the Bill of Rights or its penumbras; or among those rights reserved to the people by the Ninth Amendment. Before addressing this claim, we feel it desirable briefly to survey, in several aspects, the history of abortion, for such insight as that history may afford us, and then to examine the States' purposes and interests behind the criminal abortion laws.

From *Roe v. Wade*, 410 U.S. 113 (1973).

It perhaps is not generally appreciated that the restrictive criminal abortion laws in effect in a majority of States today are of relatively recent vintage. Those laws, generally proscribing abortion or its attempt at any time during pregnancy except when necessary to preserve the pregnant woman's life, are not of ancient or even of common-law origin. Instead, they derive from statutory changes effected, for the most part, in the latter half of the 19th century.

1. *Ancient attitudes.* These are not capable of precise determination. We are told that at the time of the Persian Empire abortifacients were known and that criminal abortions were severely punished. We are also told, however that abortion was practiced in Greek times as well as in the Roman Era, and that "it was resorted to without scruple." The Ephesian, Soranos, often described as the greatest of the ancient gynecologists, appears to have been generally opposed to Rome's prevailing free-abortion practices. He found it necessary to think first of the life of the mother, and he resorted to abortion when, upon this standard, he felt the procedure advisable. Greek and Roman law afforded little protection to the unborn. If abortion was prosecuted in some places, it seems to have been based on a concept of a violation of the father's right to his offspring. Ancient religion did not bar abortion.

2. *The Hippocratic Oath.* What then of the famous Oath that has stood so long as the ethical guide of the medical profession and that bears the name of the great Greek (460(?)–377(?) B.C., who has been described as the Father of Medicine, the "wisest and the greatest practitioner of his art," and the "most important and most complete medical personality of antiquity," who dominated the medical schools of his time, and who typified the sum of the medical knowledge of the past? The Oath varies somewhat according to the particular translation, but in any translation the content is clear. "I will give no deadly medicine to anyone if asked, nor suggest any such counsel; and in like manner I will not give to a woman a pessary to produce abortion," or "I will neither give a deadly drug to anybody if asked for it, nor will I make a suggestion to this effect. Similarly, I will not give to a woman an abortive remedy."

Although the Oath is not mentioned in any of the principal briefs in this case or in *Doe v. Bolton*, 410 U.S. 179, 93 S.Ct. 739, 35 L.Ed.2d 201, it represents the apex of the development of strict ethical concepts in medicine, and its influence endures to this day. Why did not the authority of Hippocrates dissuade abortion practice in his time and that of Rome? . . .

Dr. Edelstein [concludes] that the Oath originated in a group representing only a small segment of Greek opinion and that it certainly was not accepted by all ancient physicians. He points out that medical writings down to Galen (A.D. 130–200) "give evidence of the violation of almost every one of its injunctions." But with the end of antiquity a decided change took place. Resistance against suicide and against abortion became common. The Oath came to be popular. The emerging teachings of Christianity were in agreement with the Pythagorean ethic. The Oath "became the nucleus of all medical ethics" and "was applauded as the embodiment of truth." . . .

This, it seems to us, is a satisfactory and acceptable explanation of the Hippocratic Oath's apparent rigidity. It enables us to understand, in historical context, a long-accepted and revered statement of medical ethics.

3. *The common law.* It is undisputed that at common law, abortion performed *before* "quickening"—the first recognizable movement of the fetus *in utero,* appearing usually from the 16th to the 18th week of pregnancy—was not an indictable offense. The absence of a common-law crime for pre-quickening abortion appears to have developed from a confluence of earlier philosophical, theological, and civil and canon law concepts of when life begins. These disciplines variously approached the question in terms of the point at which the embryo or fetus became "formed" or recognizably human, or in terms of when a "person" came into being, that is, infused with a "soul" or "animated." A loose consensus evolved in early English law that these events occurred at some point between conception and live birth. This was "mediate animation." Although Christian theology and the canon law came to fix the point of animation at 40 days for a male and 80 days for a female, a view that persisted until the 19th century, there was otherwise little agreement about the precise time of formation or animation. There was agreement, however, that prior to this point the fetus was to be regarded as part of the mother, and its destruction, therefore, was not homicide. Due to continued uncertainty about the precise time when animation occurred, to the lack of any empirical basis for the 40–80-day view, and perhaps to Aquinas' definition of movement as one of the two first principles of life, Bracton focused upon quickening as the critical point. The significance of quickening was echoed by later common-law scholars and found its way into the received common law in this country.

Whether abortion of a *quick* fetus was a felony at common law, or even a lesser crime, is still disputed. Bracton, writing early in the 13th century, thought it homicide. But the later and predominant view, following the great common-law scholars, has been that it was, at most, a lesser offense. . . . [In] all the reported cases, dictum (due probably to the paucity of common-law prosecutions for post-quickening abortion), makes it now appear doubtful that abortion was ever firmly established as a common-law crime even with respect to the destruction of a quick fetus.

4. *English statutory law.* England's first criminal abortion statute came in 1803. It made abortion of a quick fetus, § 1, a capital crime, but in § 2 it provided lesser penalties for the felony of abortion before quickening, and thus preserved the "quickening" distinction. This contrast was continued in the general revision of 1828. It disappeared, however, together with the death penalty, [in 1837] and did not reappear in the Offenses Against the Person Act of 1861, that formed the core of English anti-abortion law until the liberalizing reforms of 1967. In 1929, the Infant Life (Preservation) Act, came into being. Its emphasis was upon the destruction of "the life of a child capable of being born alive." It made a willful act performed with the necessary intent a felony. It contained a proviso that one was not to be found guilty of the offense "unless it is proved that the act which caused the death of the child was not done in good faith for the purpose only of preserving the life of the mother." . . .

Recently, Parliament enacted a new abortion law. This is the Abortion Act of 1967. The Act permits a licensed physician to perform an abortion where two other licensed physicians agree (a) "that the continuance of the pregnancy would involve risk to the life of the pregnant woman, or of injury to the physical or mental health of the pregnant woman or any existing children of her family, greater than if the pregnancy were terminated," or (b) "that there is a substantial risk that if the child were born it would suffer from such physical or mental abnormalities as to be seriously handicapped." The Act also provides that, in making this determination, "account may be taken of the pregnant woman's actual or reasonable foreseeable environment." It also permits a physician, without the concurrence of others, to terminate a pregnancy where he is of the good-faith opinion that the abortion "is immediately necessary to save the life or to prevent grave permanent injury to the physical or mental health of the pregnant woman."

5. *The American law.* In this country, the law in effect in all but a few States until mid-19th century was the pre-existing English common law. Connecticut, the first State to enact abortion legislation, adopted in 1821 that part of Lord Ellenborough's Act that related to a woman "quick with child." The death penalty was not imposed. Abortion before quickening was made a crime in that State only in 1860. In 1828, New York enacted legislation that in two respects, was to serve as a model for early anti-abortion statutes. First, while barring destruction of an unquickened fetus as well as a quick fetus, it made the former only a misdemeanor, but the latter second-degree manslaughter. Second, it incorporated a concept of therapeutic abortion by providing that an abortion was excused if it "shall have been necessary to preserve the life of such mother, or shall have been advised by two physicians to be necessary for such purpose." By 1840, when Texas had received the common law, only eight American States had statutes dealing with abortion. It was not until after the War Between the States that legislation began generally to replace the common law. Most of these initial statutes dealt severely with abortion after quickening but were lenient with it before quickening. . . .

Gradually, in the middle and late 19th century the quickening distinction disappeared from the statutory law of most States and the degree of the offense and the penalties were increased. By the end of the 1950's a large majority of the jurisdictions banned abortion, however and whenever performed, unless done to save or preserve the life of the mother. The exceptions, Alabama and the District of Columbia, permitted abortion to preserve the mother's health. Three States permitted abortions that were not "unlawfully" performed or that were not "without lawful justification," leaving interpretation of those standards to the courts. In the past several years, however, a trend toward liberalization of abortion statutes has resulted in adoption, by about one-third of the States, of less stringent laws. . . .

It is thus apparent that at common law, at the time of the adoption of our Constitution, and throughout the major portion of the 19th century, abortion was viewed with less disfavor than under most American statutes currently in effect. Phrasing it another way, a woman enjoyed a substantially broader right to terminate a pregnancy than she does in most States today. At least with respect to the early stage of pregnancy, and very possibly without such a limitation, the opportunity to make this choice was present in this country well into the 19th century. Even later, the law continued for some time to treat less punitively an abortion procured in early pregnancy.

6. *The position of the American Medical Association.* The anti-abortion mood prevalent in this country in the late 19th century was shared by the medical profession. Indeed, the attitude of the profession may have played a significant role in the enactment of stringent criminal abortion legislation during that period.

An AMA Committee on Criminal Abortion was appointed in May 1857. It presented its report to the Twelfth Annual Meeting. That report observed that the Committee had been appointed to investigate criminal abortion "with a view to its general suppression." It deplored abortion and its frequency and it listed three causes of "this general demoralization":

> "The first of these causes is a widespread popular ignorance of the true character of the crime—a belief, even among mothers themselves, that the fetus is not alive till after the period of quickening.
> "The second of the agents alluded to is the fact that the professionals themselves are frequently supposed careless of foetal life. . . .
> "The third reason of the frightful extent of this crime is found in the grave defects of our laws, both common and statute, as regards the independent and actual existence of the child before birth, as a living being. These errors, which are sufficient in most instances to prevent conviction, are based, and only based, upon mistaken and exploded medical dogmas. With strange inconsistency, the law fully acknowledges the foetus in utero and its inherent rights, for civil purposes; while personally and as criminally affected, it fails to recognize it, and to its life as yet denies all protection."

The Committee then offered, and the Association adopted, resolutions protesting "against such unwarrantable destruction of human life," calling upon state legislatures to revise their abortion laws, and requesting the cooperation of state medical societies "in pressing the subject."

In 1871 a long and vivid report was submitted by the Committee on Criminal Abortion. It ended with the observation, "We had to deal with human life. In a matter of less importance we could entertain no compromise. An honest judge on the bench would call things by their proper names. We could do no less." It proffered resolutions, adopted by the Association, recommending, among other things, that it "be unlawful and unprofessional for any physician to induce abortion or premature labor, without the concurrent opinion of at least one respectable consulting physician, and then always with a view to the safety of the child—if that be possible," and calling "the attention of the clergy of all denominations to the perverted views of morality entertained by a large class of females—aye, and men also, of this important question."

Except for periodic condemnation of the criminal abortionist, no further formal AMA action took place until 1967. In that year, the Committee on Human Reproduction urged the adoption of a stated policy of opposition to induced abortion, except when there is "documented medical evidence" of a threat to the health or life of the mother, or that the child "may be born with incapacitating physical deformity or mental deficiency," or that a pregnancy "resulting from legally established statutory or forcible rape or incest may constitute a threat to the mental or physical health of the patient," two other physicians "chosen because of their recognized professional competency have examined the patient and have concurred in writing," and the procedure "is performed in a hospital accredited by the Joint Commission on Accreditation of Hospitals." The providing of medical information by physicians to state legislatures in their consideration of legislation regarding therapeutic abortion was "to be considered consistent with the principles of ethics of the American Medical Association." This recommendation was adopted by the House of Delegates.

In 1970, after the introduction of a variety of proposed resolutions, and of a report from its Board of Trustees, a reference committee noted "polarization of the medical profession on this controversial issue"; division among those who had testified; a difference of opinion among AMA councils and committees; "the remarkable shift in testimony" in six months, felt to be influenced "by the rapid changes in state laws and by the judicial decisions which tend to make abortion more freely available"; and a feeling "that this trend will continue." On June 25, 1970, the House of Delegates adopted preambles and most of the resolutions proposed by the reference committee. The preambles emphasized "the best interests of the patient," "sound clinical judgment," and "informed patient consent," in contrast to "mere acquiescence to the patient's demand." The resolutions asserted that abortion is a medical procedure that should be performed by a licensed physician in an accredited hospital only after consultation with two other physicians and in conformity with state law, and that no party to the procedure should be required to violate personally held moral principles.

7. *The position of the American Public Health Association.* In October 1970, the Executive Board of the APHA adopted Standards for Abortion Services. These were five in number.

"a. Rapid and simple abortion referral must be readily available through state and local public health departments, medical societies, or other nonprofit organizations.

"b. An important function of counseling should be to simplify and expedite the provision of abortion services; it should not delay the obtaining of these services.

"c. Psychiatric consideration should not be mandatory. As in the case of other specialized medical services, psychiatric consultation should be sought for definite indications and not on a routine basis.

"d. A wide range of individuals from appropriately trained, sympathetic volunteers to highly skilled physicians may qualify as abortion counselors.

"e. Contraception and/or sterilization should be discussed with each abortion patient." . . .

Three reasons have been advanced to explain historically the enactment of criminal abortion laws in the 19th century and to justify their continued existence.

It has been argued occasionally that these laws were the product of a Victorian social concern to discourage illicit sexual conduct. Texas, however, does not advance this justification in the present case, and it appears that no court or commentator has taken the argument seriously. The appellants and *amici* contend, moreover, that this is not a proper state purpose at all and suggest that, if it were, the Texas statutes are overbroad in protecting it since the law fails to distinguish between married and unwed mothers.

A second reason is concerned with abortion as a medical procedure. When most criminal abortion laws were first enacted, the procedure was a hazardous one for the woman. This was particularly true prior to the development of antisepsis. Antiseptic techniques, of course, were based on discoveries by Lister, Pasteur, and others first announced in 1867, but were not generally accepted and employed until about the turn of the century. Abortion mortality was high. Even after 1900, and perhaps until as late as the development of antibiotics in the 1940's, standard modern techniques such as dilation and curettage were not nearly so safe as they are today. Thus, it has been argued that a State's real concern in enacting a criminal abortion law was to protect the pregnant woman, that is, to restrain her from submitting to a procedure that placed her life in serious jeopardy.

Modern medical techniques have altered this situation. Appellants and various *amici* refer to medical data indicating that abortion in early pregnancy, that is, prior to the end of the first trimester, although not without its risk, is now relatively safe. Mortality rates for women undergoing early abortions, where the procedure is legal, appear to be as low as or lower than the rates for normal childbirth. Consequently, any interest of the State in protecting the woman from an inherently hazardous procedure, except when it would be equally dangerous for her to forgo it, has largely disappeared. Of course, important state interests in the areas of health and medical standards do remain. The State has a legitimate interest in seeing to it that abortion, like any other medical procedure, is performed under circumstances that insure maximum safety for the patient. This interest obviously extends at least to the performing physician and his staff, to the facilities involved, to the availability of after-care, and to adequate provision for any complication or emergency that might arise. The prevalence of high mortality rates at illegal "abortion mills" strengthens, rather than weakens, the State's interest in regulating the conditions under which abortions are performed. Moreover, the risk to the woman increases as her pregnancy continues. Thus, the State retains a definite interest in protecting the woman's own health and safety when an abortion is proposed at a late stage of pregnancy.

The third reason is the State's interest—some phrase it in terms of duty—in protecting prenatal life. Some of the argument for this justification rests on the theory that a new human life is present from the moment of conception. The State's interest and general obligation to protect life then extends, it is argued, to prenatal life. Only when the life of the pregnant mother herself is at stake, balanced against the life she carries within her, should the interest of the embryo or fetus not prevail. Logically, of course, a legitimate state interest in this area need not stand or fall on acceptance of the belief that life begins at conception or at some other point prior to live birth. In assessing the State's interest, recognition may be given to the less rigid claim that as long as at least *potential* life is involved, the State may assert interests beyond the protection of the pregnant woman alone.

Parties challenging state abortion laws have sharply disputed in some courts the contention that a purpose of these laws, when enacted, was to protect prenatal life. Pointing to the absence of legislative history to support the contention, they claim that most state laws were designed solely to protect the woman. Because medical advances have lessened this concern, at least with respect to abortion in early pregnancy, they argue that with respect to such abortions the laws can no longer be justified by any state interest. There is some scholarly support for this view of original purpose. The few state courts called upon to interpret their laws in the late 19th and early 20th centuries did focus on the State's interest in protecting the woman's health rather than in preserving the embryo and fetus. Proponents of this view point out that in many States, including Texas, by statute or judicial interpretation, the pregnant woman herself could not be prosecuted for self-abortion or for cooperating in an abortion performed upon her by another. They claim that adoption of the "quickening" distinction through received common law and state statutes tacitly recognizes the greater health hazards inherent in late abortion and impliedly repudiates the theory that life begins at conception.

It is with these interests, and the weight to be attached to them, that this case is concerned.

The Constitution does not explicitly mention any right of privacy. In a line of decisions, however, going back perhaps as far as *Union Pacific R. Co. v. Botsford*, 141 U.S. 250, 251, 11 S.Ct. 1000, 1001, 35 L.Ed. 734 (1891), the Court has recognized that a right of personal privacy, or a guarantee of certain areas or zones of privacy, does exist under the Constitution. In varying contexts, the Court or individual Justices have, indeed, found at least the roots of that right in the First Amendment, [in] the Fourth and Fifth Amendments, [in] the penumbras of the Bill of Rights, [in] the Ninth Amendment, or in the concept of liberty guaranteed by the first section of the Fourteenth Amendment. . . . These decisions make it clear that only personal rights that can be deemed "fundamental" or "implicit

in the concept of ordered liberty," [are] included in this guarantee of personal privacy. They also make it clear that the right has some extension to activities relating to marriage, [procreation,] [contraception,] [family relationships,] [and] child rearing and education.

This right of privacy, whether it be founded in the Fourteenth Amendment's concept of personal liberty and restrictions upon state action, as we feel it is, or, as the District Court determined, in the Ninth Amendment's reservation of rights to the people, is broad enough to encompass a woman's decision whether or not to terminate her pregnancy. The detriment that the State would impose upon the pregnant woman by denying this choice altogether is apparent. Specific and direct harm medically diagnosable even in early pregnancy may be involved. Maternity, or additional offspring, may force upon the woman a distressful life and future. Psychological harm may be imminent. Mental and physical health may be taxed by child care. There is also the distress for all concerned, associated with the unwanted child, and there is the problem of bringing a child into a family already unable, psychologically and otherwise, to care for it. In other cases, as in this one, the additional difficulties and continuing stigma of unwed motherhood may be involved. All these are factors the woman and her responsible physician necessarily will consider in consultation.

On the basis of elements such as these, appellant and some *amici* argue that the woman's right is absolute and that she is entitled to terminate her pregnancy at whatever time, in whatever way, and for whatever reason she alone chooses. With this we do not agree. Appellant's arguments that Texas either has no valid interest at all in regulating the abortion decision, or no interest strong enough to support any limitation upon the woman's sole determination, are unpersuasive. The Court's decisions recognizing a right of privacy also acknowledge that some state regulation in areas protected by that right is appropriate. As noted above, a State may properly assert important interests in safeguarding health, in maintaining medical standards, and in protecting potential life. At some point in pregnancy, these respective interests become sufficiently compelling to sustain regulation of the factors that govern the abortion decision. The privacy right involved, therefore, cannot be said to be absolute. In fact, it is not clear to us that the claim asserted by some *amici* that one has an unlimited right to do with one's body as one pleases bears a close relationship to the right of privacy previously articulated in the Court's decisions. . . .

We, therefore, conclude that the right of personal privacy includes the abortion decision, but that this right is not unqualified and must be considered against important state interests in regulation. . . .

Where certain "fundamental rights" are involved, the Court has held that regulation limiting these rights may be justified only by a "compelling state interest," [and] that legislative enactments must be narrowly drawn to express only the legitimate state interests at stake. . . .

The District Court held that the appellee failed to meet his burden of demonstrating that the Texas statute's infringement upon Roe's rights was necessary to support a compelling state interest, and that, although the appellee presented "several compelling justifications for state presence in the area of abortions," the statutes outstripped these justifications and swept "far beyond any areas of compelling state inter-

est." 314 F.Supp., at 1222, 1223, appellant and appellee both contest that holding. Appellant, as has been indicated, claims an absolute right that bars any state imposition of criminal penalties in the area. Appellee argues that the State's determination to recognize and protect prenatal life from and after conception constitutes a compelling state interest. As noted above, we do not agree fully with either formulation.

A. The appellee and certain *amici* argue that the fetus is a "person" within the language and meaning of the Fourteenth Amendment. In support of this, they outline at length and in detail the well-known facts of fetal development. If this suggestion of personhood is established, the appellant's case, of course, collapses, for the fetus' right to life would then be guaranteed specifically by the Amendment. The appellant conceded as much on reargument. On the other hand, the appellee conceded on reargument that no case could be cited that holds that a fetus is a person within the meaning of the Fourteenth Amendment.

The Constitution does not define "person" in so many words. Section 1 of the Fourteenth Amendment contains three references to "person." The first, in defining "citizens" speaks of "persons born or naturalized in the United States." The word also appears both in the Due Process Clause and in the Equal Protection Clause. "Person" is used in other places in the Constitution: in the listing of qualifications for Representatives and Senators; . . . in the Apportionment Clause; . . . in the Migration and Importation provision; . . . in the Emolument Clause; . . . in the Electors provisions; . . . in the provision outlining qualifications for the office of President; . . . in the Extradition provisions; . . . and the superseded Fugitive Slave Clause; and in the Fifth, Twelfth, and Twenty-second Amendments, as well as in . . . the Fourteenth Amendment. But in nearly all these instances, the use of the word is such that it has application only postnatally. None indicates, with any assurance, that it has any possible prenatal application.[1]

All this, together with our observation, *supra*, that throughout the major portion of the 19th century prevailing legal abortion practices were far freer than they are today, persuades us that the word "person," as used in the Fourteenth Amendment, does not include the unborn. . . .

This conclusion, however, does not of itself fully answer the contentions raised by Texas, and we pass on to other considerations.

B. The pregnant woman cannot be isolated in her privacy. She carries an embryo and, later, a fetus, if one accepts the medical definitions of the developing young in the human uterus. The situation therefore is inherently different from marital intimacy, or bedroom possession of obscene material, or marriage, or procreation, or education, with which *Eisenstadt* and *Griswold, Stanley, Loving, Skinner* and *Pierce* and *Meyer* were respectively concerned. As we have intimated above, it is reasonable and appropriate for a State to decide that at some point in time another interest, that of health of the mother or that of potential human life, becomes significantly involved. The woman's privacy is no longer sole and any right of privacy she possesses must be measured accordingly.

Texas urges that, apart from the Fourteenth Amendment, life begins at conception and is present throughout pregnancy, and that, therefore, the State has a compelling interest in protecting that life from the after conception. We need not resolve the difficult question of when life begins. When those trained in the respective disciplines of medicine, philosophy, and theology are unable to arrive at any consensus, the judiciary, at this point in the development of man's knowledge, is not in a position to speculate as to the answer.

It should be sufficient to note briefly the wide divergence of thinking on this most sensitive and difficult question. There has always been strong support for the view that life does not begin until live birth. This was the belief of the Stoics. It appears to be the predominant, though not the unanimous, attitude of the Jewish faith. It may be taken to represent also the position of a large segment of the Protestant community, insofar as that can be ascertained; organized groups that have taken a formal position on the abortion issue have generally regarded abortion as a matter for the conscience of the individual and her family. As we have noted, the common law found greater significance in quickening. Physicians and their scientific colleagues have regarded that event with less interest and have tended to focus either upon conception, upon live birth, or upon the interim point at which the fetus becomes "viable," that is, potentially able to live outside the mother's womb, albeit with artificial aid. Viability is usually placed at about seven months (28 weeks) but may occur earlier, even at 24 weeks. The Aristotelian theory of "mediate animation," that held sway throughout the Middle Ages and the Renaissance in Europe, continued to be official Roman Catholic dogma until the 19th century, despite opposition to this "ensoulment" theory from those in the Church who would recognize the existence of life from the moment of conception. The latter is now, of course, the official belief of the Catholic Church. As one brief *amicus* discloses, this is a view strongly held by many non-Catholics as well, and by many physicians. Substantial problems for precise definition of this view are posed, however, by new embryological data that purport to indicate that conception is a "process" over time, rather than an event, and by new medical techniques such as menstrual extraction, the "morning-after" pill, implantation of embryos, artificial insemination, and even artificial wombs.

In areas other than criminal abortion, the law has been reluctant to endorse any theory that life, as we recognize it, begins before live birth or to accord legal rights to the unborn except in narrowly defined situations and except when the rights are contingent upon live birth. For example, the traditional rule of tort law denied recovery for prenatal injuries even though the child was born alive. That rule has been changed in almost every jurisdiction. In most States, recovery is said to be permitted only if the fetus was viable, or at least quick, when the injuries were sustained, though few courts have squarely so held. In a recent development, generally opposed by the commentators, some States permit the parents of a stillborn child to maintain an action for wrongful death because of prenatal injuries. Such an action, however, would appear to be one to vindicate the parents' interest and is thus consistent with the view that the fetus, at most, represents only the potentiality of life. Similarly, unborn children have been recognized as acquiring rights or interests by way of inheritance or other devolution of property, and have been represented by guardians *ad litem*. Perfection of the interests involved, again, has generally been contingent upon live birth. In short, the unborn have never been recog-

nized in the law as persons in the whole sense.

In view of all this, we do not agree that, by adopting one theory of life, Texas may override the rights of the pregnant woman that are at stake. We repeat, however, that the State does have an important and legitimate interest in preserving and protecting the health of the pregnant woman, whether she be a resident of the State or a non-resident who seeks medical consultation and treatment there, and that it has still *another* important and legitimate interest in protecting the potentiality of human life. These interests are separate and distinct. Each grows in substantiality as the woman approaches term and, at a point during pregnancy, each becomes "compelling."

With respect to the State's important and legitimate interest in the health of the mother, the "compelling" point, in the light of present medical knowledge, is at approximately the end of the first trimester. This is so because of the now-established medical fact . . . that until the end of the first trimester mortality in abortion may be less than mortality in normal childbirth. It follows that, from and after this point, a State may regulate the abortion procedure to the extent that the regulation reasonably relates to the preservation and protection of maternal health. Examples of permissible state regulation in this area are requirements as to the qualifications of the person who is to perform the abortion; as to the licensure of that person; as to the facility in which the procedure is to be performed, that is, whether it must be a hospital or may be a clinic or some other place of less-than-hospital status; as to the licensing of the facility; and the like.

This means, on the other hand, that, for the period of pregnancy prior to this "compelling" point, the attending physician, in consultation with his patient, is free to determine, without regulation by the State, that, in his medical judgment, the patient's pregnancy should be terminated. If that decision is reached, the judgment may be effectuated by an abortion free of interference by the State.

With respect to the State's important and legitimate interest in potential life, the "compelling" point is at viability. This is so because the fetus then presumably has the capability of meaningful life outside the mother's womb. State regulation protective of fetal life after viability thus has both logical and biological justification. If the State is interested in protecting fetal life after viability, it may go so far as to proscribe abortion during that period, except when it is necessary to preserve the life or health of the mother.

Measured against these standards, Art. 1196 of the Texas Penal Code, in restricting legal abortions to those "procured or attempted by medical advice for the purpose of saving the life of the mother," sweeps too broadly. The statute makes no distinction between abortions performed early in pregnancy and those performed later, and it limits to a single reason, "saving" the mother's life, the legal justification for the procedure. The statute, therefore, cannot survive the constitutional attack made upon it here.

To summarize and to repeat:

1. A state criminal abortion statute of the current Texas type, that excepts from criminality only a *life-saving* procedure on behalf of the mother, without regard to pregnancy stage and without recognition of the other interests involved, is violative of the Due Process Clause of the Fourteenth Amendment.

(a) For the stage prior to approximately the end of the first trimester, the abortion decision and its effectuation must be left to the medical judgment of the pregnant woman's attending physician.

(b) For the stage subsequent to approximately the end of the first trimester, the State, in promoting its interest in the health of the mother, may, if it chooses, regulate the abortion procedure in ways that are reasonably related to maternal health.

(c) For the stage subsequent to viability, the State in promoting its interest in the potentiality of human life may, if it chooses, regulate, and even proscribe, abortion except where it is necessary, in appropriate medical judgment, for the preservation of the life or health of the mother.

NOTES

1. When Texas urges that a fetus is entitled to Fourteenth Amendment protection as a person, it faces a dilemma. Neither in Texas nor in any other State are all abortions prohibited. Despite broad proscription, an exception always exists. The exception contained in Art. 1196, for an abortion procured or attempted by medical advice for the purpose of saving the life of the mother, is typical. But if the fetus is a person who is not to be deprived of life without due process of law, and if the mother's condition is the sole determinant, does not the Texas exception appear to be out of line with the Amendment's command?

There are other inconsistencies between Fourteenth Amendment status and the typical abortion statute. It has already been pointed out [that] in Texas the woman is not a principal or an accomplice with respect to an abortion upon her. If the fetus is a person, why is the woman not a principal or an accomplice? Further, the penalty for criminal abortion specified by Art. 1195 is significantly less than the maximum penalty for murder prescribed by Art. 1257 of the Texas Penal Code. If the fetus is a person, may the penalties be different?

NO

Brief for the United States as Amicus Curiae

WEBSTER v. REPRODUCTIVE SERVICES

Appellants have asked this Court to reconsider its decision in *Roe v. Wade*, 410 U.S. 113 (1973). The United States has previously filed briefs as amicus curiae in *City of Akron v. Akron Center for Reproductive Health*, 462 U.S. 416 (1983), and *Thornburgh v. American College of Obstetricians and Gynecologists*, 476 U.S. 747 (1986), questioning the regime of judicial review established by *Roe v. Wade*. The United States continues to believe that *Roe v. Wade* unduly restricts the proper sphere of legislative authority in this area and should be overruled by this Court. . . .

STATEMENT

In 1986, the State of Missouri passed a statute regulating abortions. The first section of the statute contains a general "finding" by the state legislature that "[t]he life of each human being begins at conception," and a requirement that all state laws be interpreted to provide unborn children with all the rights of other persons "subject only to the Constitution of the United States, and decisional interpretations thereof by the United States Supreme Court" (Mo. Stat. Ann. @ 1.205.1–2). Among its various other provisions, the statute requires that, prior to performing an abortion on any woman whom a physician has reason to believe is 20 or more weeks pregnant, the physician must determine whether the fetus is viable by performing "such medical examinations and tests as are necessary to make a finding of the gestational age, weight, and lung maturity of the unborn child" (@ 188.029). The statute also provides that no public funds, employees, or facilities may be used for the purpose of "encouraging or counseling" a woman to have an abortion not necessary to save her life or for "performing or assisting" an abortion not necessary to save the life of the mother (@@ 188.205, 188.210, 188.215).

Five publicly employed physicians and nurses and two nonprofit corporations brought a class action challenging the constitutionality of these and

From Brief for the United States as Amicus Curiae, *Webster v. Reproductive Services*, 109 S.Ct. 3040 (1989). Some case citations omitted.

other provisions of the Missouri statute. The district court held the challenged provisions unconstitutional and the court of appeals affirmed. The court of appeals concluded that Missouri's declaration that life begins at conception was "simply an impermissible state adoption of a theory of when life begins to justify its abortion regulations." The court of appeals rejected Missouri's reliance on the declaration's caveat requiring compatibility with the Constitution and Supreme Court precedent on the ground that a mere recitation of the Supremacy Clause "cannot . . . validate state laws that are in fact incompatible with the constitution."[1]

The court further concluded that the requirement that physicians perform viability tests is an unconstitutional legislative intrusion on a matter of medical skill and judgment. The court found that tests to determine fetal weight at 20 weeks are unreliable, inaccurate, and would add $125 to $250 to the cost of an abortion. And the court determined that "amniocentesis, the only method available to determine lung maturity, is contrary to accepted medical practice until 28–30 weeks of gestation, expensive, and imposes significant health risks for both the pregnant woman and the fetus."

The court of appeals also invalidated the provision prohibiting the use of public funds for "encouraging or counseling a woman to have an abortion not necessary to save her life" (Mo. Ann. Stat. @ 188.205), finding that provision both overly vague and inconsistent with the right to abortion recognized in *Roe v. Wade*, 410 U.S. 113 (1973).[2] "[T]he statute is vague," the court stated, "because the word 'counsel' is fraught with ambiguity; its range is incapable of objective measurement." In addition, the court

held, the prohibition "is an unacceptable infringement of the woman's fourteenth amendment right to choose an abortion after receiving the medical information necessary to exercise the right knowingly and intelligently." The court rejected as "completely inapt" the analogy to the bans on the use of public funds to perform or assist abortions upheld in *Harris v McRae*, 448 U.S. 297 (1980), and *Maher v. Roe*, 432 U.S. 464 (1977). "Missouri," the court concluded, "is not simply declining to fund abortions when it forbids its doctors to encourage or counsel women to have abortions. Instead, it is erecting an obstacle in the path of women seeking full and uncensored medical advice about alternatives to childbirth."

Finally, the court of appeals struck down Missouri's prohibition on the use of public facilities and public employees "to perform or assist an abortion not necessary to save the life of the mother." Mo. Stat. Ann. @@ 188.210, 188.215. The court distinguished this Court's cases holding that the government need not provide funding for elective abortions on the grounds that "[t]here is a fundamental difference between providing direct funding to effect the abortion decision and allowing staff physicians to perform abortions at an existing publicly owned hospital." The court noted that all of the public facilities' costs in providing abortion services, including the costs of employees' services, are recouped from funds provided by the patient. Hence, the court stated, the question at issue is not whether the State is required to fund abortions but whether "the state creates an undue burden or obstacle to the free exercise of the right to choose an abortion" when it prohibits the use of public facilities and public employees to perform or assist abortions.

SUMMARY OF ARGUMENT

Roe v. Wade, as the Court is well aware, has been intensely controversial from the day it was decided. That controversy is more than simply a reflection of the deep divisions in American society over the underlying question of abortion. Rather, the controversy has, in substantial measure, been a product of the decision itself. *Roe* rests on assumptions that are not firmly grounded in the Constitution; it adopts an unworkable framework tying permissible state regulation of abortion to particular periods in pregnancy; and it has allowed courts to usurp the function of legislative bodies in weighing competing social, ethical, and scientific factors in reaching a judgment as to how much state regulation is appropriate in this highly sensitive area. In similar circumstances, the Court has "not hesitated" to overrule a prior interpretation of the Constitution. *Garcia v. San Antonio Metro. Transit Auth.*, 469 U.S. 528, 557 (1985). It should do so here as well.

The Court's decision in *Roe v. Wade* rests upon two key premises—that there is a fundamental right to abortion and that the States do not have a compelling interest in protecting prenatal human life throughout pregnancy. Neither premise, however, is supportable. The fundamental right to abortion can draw no support from the text of the Constitution or from history. Even assuming that the various "privacy" cases relied upon by *Roe* establish a generalized right to privacy, it does not follow that the abortion decision is encompassed within such a right. Abortion involves the destruction of the fetus, and is therefore "different in kind from the decision not to conceive in the first place" (*Thornburgh v. American College of Obstetricians and Gynecologists*, 476

U.S. 747, 792 n.2 (1986) (White, J. dissenting)). *Roe's* other critical assumption—that a State that wishes to regulate abortion does not have a compelling interest in protecting prenatal life throughout pregnancy—is similarly lacking in any logical or historical foundation. "[P]otential life is no less potential in the first weeks of pregnancy than it is at viability or afterward." *Akron*, 462 U.S. at 461 (O'Connor, J. dissenting).

Roe's flaws are both illustrated and compounded by the manner in which the Court sought to implement its unfounded premises. The Court in *Roe* erected a framework for reviewing abortion regulations based on the division of pregnancy into three trimesters, with different types of state regulation permitted in each trimester. The dividing lines were grounded not in any principle of constitutional law, but rather in medical findings. As a consequence, the lines must either become increasingly arbitrary over time or change as medical technology changes. Debate over these and other issues has spawned extensive litigation and has put the Court in the position of reviewing medical and operational practices beyond its competence.

We therefore believe that the time has come for the Court to abandon its efforts to impose a comprehensive solution to the abortion question. Under the Constitution, legislative bodies cannot impose irrational constraints on a woman's procreative choice. But, within those broad confines, the appropriate scope of abortion regulation "should be left with the people and to the political processes the people have devised to govern their affairs." *Doe v. Bolton*, 410 U.S. 179, 222 (1973) (White, J., dissenting). Other Western countries have, through the legislative process, reached reasonable accommodations of the competing interests involved in the abortion controversy. There is no reason to believe that American legislatures, if basic decision-making responsibility were returned to them, would not similarly arrive at humane solutions.

Even if the Court is not inclined to reconsider *Roe v. Wade*, we believe that the court below erred in striking down provisions of the Missouri statute prohibiting the use of public funds to counsel a woman to have an abortion and the use of public facilities and public employees to perform abortions. Through these provisions, the State of Missouri has placed no obstacles in the path of women seeking to obtain an abortion. The State has simply chosen not to encourage or assist abortions in any respect. That is a permissible choice even assuming the continued vitality of *Roe v. Wade*.

TEXT: ARGUMENT
I. ROE v. WADE SHOULD BE RECONSIDERED AND, UPON RECONSIDERATION, OVERRULED

Appellants have asked the Court to reconsider the approach to determining the constitutionality of abortion regulations established in *Roe v. Wade*, 410 U.S. 113 (1973). We think this case presents a proper occasion for such a reconsideration. . . . [T]hose provisions of the Missouri statute related to abortion counseling and the use of state facilities and personnel to perform abortions should be upheld even assuming the continued validity of *Roe*. But other provisions of the Missouri statute appear to reflect legislative choices foreclosed by *Roe*. In particular, the provision mandating the performance of certain viability tests when a woman is 20 or more weeks pregnant and the declaration that human life begins at conception are in tension with the severe limitations imposed by *Roe* on the ability of the States to adopt any measures to protect prenatal life prior to viability.[3] We accordingly agree with the State of Missouri that a consideration of the constitutionality of these provisions raises the question whether *Roe v. Wade* should be reconsidered.

A. We recognize of course that the principle of stare decisis serves important purposes in our legal system. It promotes the evenhanded, predictable, and consistent development of legal principles; it fosters reliance on judicial rules; and it contributes to the fact and appearance of integrity in our judicial system. See, e.g., *Vasquez v. Hillery*, 474 U.S. 254, 265–266 (1986); *Thomas v. Washington Gas Light Co.*, 448 U.S. 261, 272 (1980) (plurality opinion). Those considerations must be given due weight in this as in any other area of the law. See *Akron*, 462 U.S. at 420 n.1.

Nonetheless, as Justice Frankfurter explained, "stare decisis is a principle of policy and not a mechanical formula of adherence to the latest decision, however recent and questionable, when such adherence involves collision with a prior doctrine more embracing in its scope, intrinsically sounder, and verified by experience." *Helvering v. Hallock*, 309 U.S. 106, 119 (1940). Furthermore, it is well settled that stare decisis has less force in constitutional litigation, where, short of a constitutional amendment, this Court is the only body capable of effecting a needed change. *Monell v. Department of Social Services*, 436 U.S. 658, 696 (1978); *Glidden Co. v. Zdanok*, 370 U.S. 530, 543 (1962). For that reason, "[i]t is . . . not only [the Court's] prerogative but also [its] duty to re-examine a precedent where its reasoning or understanding of the Constitution is fairly called into question." *Mitchell v. W.T. Grant Co.*, 416 U.S. 600, 627–628 (1974) (Powell, J., concurring). See also *Solorio v. United States*, No. 85-1581 (June 25, 1987), slip op. 15; *Continental T.V., Inc. v. GTE Sylvania Inc.*, 433 U.S. 36, 58 n.30 (1977); *Erie R.R. v. Tompkins*, 304 U.S. 64, 77–78 (1938).

Although this Court has never adopted a "rigid formula" for determining when a prior construction of the Constitution should be overruled (*Vasquez*, 474 U.S. at 266), it has identified several factors that bear on this inquiry. One question of obvious importance is whether the prior ruling is inconsistent with basic assumptions about the nature of the Constitution or established methods for giving effect to its key provisions. See *Garcia v. San Antonio Metro. Transit Auth.*, 469 U.S. at 547–555; *New Orleans v. Dukes*, 427 U.S. 297, 306 (1976); *West Virginia State Bd. of Ed. v. Barnette*, 319 U.S. 624 (1943); *Erie R.R. v. Tompkins*, 304 U.S. at 78–80. Another factor that is clearly relevant is whether the prior rule has proved to be unworkable, has bred confusion, or has led to unforeseen or anomalous results. See *Solorio*, slip op. at 12–14; *Garcia*, 469 U.S. at 537–547; *Erie R.R. v. Tompkins*, 304 U.S. at 74–78. Finally, the Court has stated that prior decisions, even if of fairly recent vintage, should be reconsidered if they "disserve principles of democratic self-governance." *Garcia*, 469 U.S. at 547. Taken together, these factors strongly suggest that the regime of judicial review established by *Roe v. Wade* should be abandoned.

B. The decision in *Roe v. Wade* rests on two crucial but highly problematic premises: that a woman has a fundamental right to decide whether or not to terminate her pregnancy and that the States do not have a compelling interest in protecting prenatal human life throughout the term of a woman's pregnancy. See *Thornburgh*, 476 U.S. at 796 (White, J., dissenting). The first premise—that the right to an abortion is fundamental—means that abortion regulation is subject to strict scrutiny and, thus, that the State must demonstrate that it has a compelling interest before it may burden that right. The second premise—that the State does not have a compelling interest in protecting fetal life throughout pregnancy—yields the conclusion that, except for regulations designed to preserve the health of the mother, the Constitution prohibits any effort by the State to regulate or discourage abortion in the early months of pregnancy. Neither of those essential premises, however, is tenable.

1. All Members of this Court who have addressed the issue agree "that a woman's ability to choose an abortion is a species of 'liberty' that is subject to the general protections of the Due Process Clause." *Thornburgh*, 476 U.S. at 790 (White, J., dissenting). See also *Roe*, 410 U.S. at 173 (Rehnquist, J., dissenting). The presence of such a liberty interest, however, ordinarily means only that any state regulation affecting that interest must be procedurally fair and must bear a rational relation to valid state objectives. See *Williamson v. Lee Optical Co.*, 348 U.S. 483, 491 (1955). In order to subject state regulation to the far more demanding requirements of strict scrutiny, it is necessary to show that it interferes with a "fundamental" constitutional right. The abortion decision, however, cannot be counted as a "fundamental" constitutional right under any of the traditional means used to identify such rights.[4]

The primary source for fundamental rights lies in the provisions of the Constitution other than the Fourteenth Amendment itself. "[T]he Court is on relatively firm ground when it deems certain of the liberties set forth in the Bill of Rights to be fundamental and therefore finds them incorporated in the Fourteenth Amendment's guarantee that no State may deprive any person of liberty without due process of law." *Thornburgh*, 476 U.S. at 790 (White, J., dissenting). All of the "privacy" cases that preceded *Roe v. Wade*—and upon which the Court relied in *Roe*—are explicable in terms of some other constitutional command beyond the generalized interest in "liberty" secured by the Fourteenth Amendment. They were rooted in accepted principles, whether of equal protection,[5] or of freedom of expression at the core of the First Amendment,[6] or of freedom from unreasonable searches assured by the Fourth Amendment.[7] In contrast, the right to abortion identified in *Roe* was grounded only in the liberty clause of the Fourteenth Amendment. As this Court recently reaffirmed, "[t]he Court is most vulnerable and comes nearest to illegitimacy when it deals with judge-made constitutional law having little or no cognizable roots in the language or design of the Constitution." *Bowers v. Hardwick*, 478 U.S. 186, 194 (1986).

In addition to rights secured by specific provisions of the Constitution, the Court has indicated that an interest will be deemed to be constitutionally fundamental if it is "implicit in the concept of ordered liberty" (*Palko v. Connecticut*, 302 U.S. 319, 325 (1937)) or "deeply rooted in this Nation's history and tradition" (*Moore v. East Cleveland*, 431 U.S. 492, 503 (1977) (opinion of Powell, J.)). See *Bowers*, 478 U.S. at 191–192. It cannot be credibly argued, however, that the abortion decision forms a part of any historically rec-

ognized right that is fundamental in this sense. As the Court in *Roe* acknowledged in its review of the history of abortion regulation (410 U.S. at 129–141), and as Justice Rehnquist emphasized in his dissent (id. at 174–176 & n.1), state laws condemning or limiting abortion were very common at the time the Fourteenth Amendment was adopted.[8] "By the time of the adoption of the Fourteenth Amendment in 1868, there were at least 36 laws enacted by state or territorial legislatures limiting abortion. While many States have amended or updated their laws, 21 of the laws on the books in 1868 remain in effect today." Id. at 174–176 (Rehnquist, J., dissenting).[9] Against this background, the right to abortion cannot be described as one that is "deeply rooted in this Nation's history and tradition" or "implicit in the concept of ordered liberty." Compare *Bowers v. Hardwick*, 478 U.S. at 192–194 (rejecting claim that there is a fundamental right to engage in homosexual sodomy based in part on discussion of criminal sodomy laws existing "[i]n 1868, when the Fourteen Amendment was ratified").

The most plausible source of support for a fundamental right to abortion lies in the Court's "privacy" decisions that antedate *Roe*. But even assuming that cases like *Griswold v. Connecticut*, 381 U.S. 479 (1965), and *Eisenstadt v. Baird*, 405 U.S. 438 (1972), establish a general right to privacy or personal autonomy under the Fourteenth Amendment, see *Carey v. Population Services International*, 431 U.S. 678, 684–686 (1977), it does not follow that the abortion decision is encompassed within such a right. "The pregnant woman," this Court acknowledged (*Roe*, 410 U.S. at 159), "cannot be isolated in her privacy." Her decision to seek an abortion is "inherently different" from decisions concerning marital privacy and the use of contraceptives because it "involves the purposeful termination of a potential life" (*Harris v. McRae*, 448 U.S. at 325). As Justice White has observed (*Thornburgh*, 476 U.S. at 792 n.2):

> That the decision involves the destruction of the fetus renders it different in kind from the decision not to conceive in the first place. This difference does not go merely to the weight of the state interest in regulating abortion; it affects as well the characterization of the liberty interest itself. For if the liberty to make certain decisions with respect to contraception without governmental constraint is "fundamental," it is not only because those decisions are "serious" and "important" to the individual, but also because some value of privacy or individual autonomy that is somehow implicit in the scheme of ordered liberties established by the Constitution supports a judgment that such decisions are none of the government's business. The same cannot be said where, as here, the individual is not "isolated in her privacy."

If a woman does not have a fundamental constitutional right to choose an abortion, then the *Roe* framework collapses. Absent such a right, abortion regulations, like other forms of regulation that affect general liberty interests, should be upheld as long as they are procedurally fair and bear some rational relationship to a permissible governmental goal.

2. Equally central to the *Roe* holding was the Court's determination that a State that chooses to regulate abortion does not have a compelling interest in preserving fetal life throughout the term of pregnancy. The Court acknowledged (410 U.S. at 154) that a woman's right to terminate her pregnancy "is not unqualified and must be considered against important state interests . . . in safeguarding health, in maintaining medical standards, and in protecting potential life." But the Court concluded that these interests are not present in the same degree from conception to birth; instead, the court found (id. at 162–163) that they "grow in substantiality as the woman approaches term." Especially critical in this regard was the Court's conclusion that "the State's important and legitimate interest in potential life" does not become "compelling," i.e., sufficiently weighty to overcome the fundamental right to abortion, until the fetus has reached the point of viability (id. at 163).

The assumption that a State's asserted interest in protecting prenatal life is qualitatively different at different periods of pregnancy is debatable at best. As Justice O'Connor has observed, "potential life is no less potential in the first weeks of pregnancy than it is at viability or afterward." *Akron*, 462 U.S. at 461 (O'Connor, J., dissenting) (emphasis in original). See also *Thornburgh*, 476 U.S. at 795 (White, J., dissenting). But even if there is a core of common sense in the notion that a State's legitimate interest in prenatal life "grows in substantiality" along with the development of the fetus, it does not follow that this interest should not be regarded as compelling throughout pregnancy. An interest may be sufficiently weighty to be compelling in the constitutional sense even if subsequently it takes on even greater urgency.

The problem with the Court's treatment of the State's interest in fetal life is that it is not rooted in any analysis of what interests have been historically recognized as compelling. Deciding what is a "compelling" state interest is a little like deciding whether or not a particular value is "fundamental." Judges have not been left "free to roam where unguided speculation might take them." *Poe v. Ullman*, 367 U.S. 497, 542 (1961) (Harlan, J., dissenting). See *New York v. Ferber*, 458 U.S. 747, 756–758 (1982) (citing prior judicial decisions, legislative findings, and the enactment of legislation by "virtually all" States and the United States as relevant factors in identifying a compelling interest). The historical record here is clear. The tenor and contemporaneous understanding of the anti-abortion laws enacted from the mid-Nineteenth Century up to the time of the decision in *Roe v. Wade* leave little doubt that they were directed not only at protecting maternal health, but also at what was widely viewed as a moral evil comprehending the destruction of actual or nascent human life. See J. Mohr, *Abortion in America* (1978). Moreover, the historical record reveals that this interest has been consistently asserted by the States throughout the term of pregnancy, not just after viability or "quickening" or some other arbitrary line of demarcation.[10]

If a State that wishes to regulate abortion has a compelling interest in protecting prenatal life throughout pregnancy, then *Roe*'s framework cannot survive. For even if there is a fundamental right to abortion, that right may be overridden by the State's compelling interest in protecting prenatal life. Laws that impinge upon fundamental rights are not automatically invalid; rather, they will survive strict scrutiny if they are "narrowly drawn to express only the legitimate state interests at stake." *Roe v. Wade*, 410 U.S. at 155 (citing cases). If a State's interest in protecting prenatal life is compelling throughout pregnancy, then abortion regulation designed to advance that interest in a rational manner should be permissible throughout pregnancy.

C. The untenable nature of *Roe*'s premises is demonstrated and compounded by the unworkable framework the Court adopted to implement those premises. To provide a framework for delimiting the permissible scope of abortion regulation, *Roe* divided pregnancy into three trimesters, with radically different consequences for state regulatory power in each. During the first trimester, both "the abortion decision and its effectuation must be left to the medical judgment of the pregnant woman's attending physician" (410 U.S. at 164). During the second trimester, the State "may, if it chooses, regulate the abortion procedure in ways that are reasonably related to maternal health" (ibid.). After viability, the State "may, if it chooses, regulate, and even proscribe, abortion except where it is necessary, in appropriate medical judgment, for the preservation of the life or health of the mother" (id. at 165).

This analytical framework has proved to be "a completely unworkable method of accommodating the conflicting personal rights and compelling state interests that are involved in the abortion context." *Akron*, 462 U.S. 454 (O'Connor, J., dissenting). For example, it is difficult to grasp why the compelling quality of a State's interest in safeguarding maternal health should undergo a radical change at the end of the first trimester. Indeed, "[t]he fallacy inherent in the *Roe* framework is apparent: just because the State has a compelling interest in ensuring maternal safety once an abortion may be more dangerous than childbirth, it simply does not follow that the State has no interest before that point that justifies state regulation to ensure that first-trimester abortions are performed as safely as possible" (id. at 460 (emphasis in original)).

The Court in *Roe* chose the end of the first trimester as a crucial point based on its determination—basically one of legislative fact—that "in the light of present medical knowledge . . . until the end of the first trimester mortality in abortion may be less than mortality in normal childbirth" (410 U.S. at 149, 163). However, "developments in the past decade, particularly the development of a much safer method for performing second-trimester abortions, . . . have extended the period in which abortions are safer than childbirth (*Akron*, 462 U.S. at 429 n.11). The fact that the Court in *Akron*, despite this evidence, found it "prudent" to retain the end of the first trimester as the sharply determinative point demonstrates the essential arbitrariness of the framework: the Court "simply concluded that a line must be drawn . . . and proceeded to draw that line" (*Garcia*, 469 U.S. at 543).

It was similarly arbitrary for the Court in *Roe* to determine that the State's legitimate interest "in protecting prenatal life" (410 U.S. at 150, 153–154) undergoes a constitutionally significant transformation at the point of fetal viability. The Court defined "viability" as the point when the fetus is "potentially able to live outside the mother's womb, albeit with artificial aid." 410 U.S. at 160; see *Colautti*, 439 U.S. at 387. There is no obvious constitutional connection between the ability of a fetus to survive outside the womb with artificial support and the magnitude of a State's lawful concern to protect future life. As Justice O'Connor said in her *Akron* dissent, "potential life is no less potential in the first weeks of pregnancy than it is at viability or afterward. . . . The choice of viability as the point at which the state interest in potential life becomes compelling is no less

arbitrary than choosing any point before viability or any point afterward" (462 U.S. at 461 (emphasis in original)). "[T]he State's interest, if compelling after viability, is equally compelling before viability." *Thornburgh*, 476 U.S. at 795 (White, J., dissenting).

The "viability" standard is particularly unworkable as a constitutional reference point because, as the Court has acknowledged, the point when a fetus may survive outside the womb with artificial aid changes with "advancements in medical skill" (*Colautti*, 439 U.S. at 387). The "increasingly earlier fetal viability" demonstrated in recent scientific studies (462 U.S. at 457 (O'Connor, J., dissenting)) is the product of improvements in medical techniques, not of any change in our perceptions about how fully developed or worthy of life a fetus is at any point in time. It is disturbing to attribute constitutional significance to a point which, besides being in motion rather than being fixed, moves in response to advances in medical science rather than in response to forces more familiar to traditional judicial analysis. And it is troubling to contemplate a constitutional doctrine that would permit the State's power to regulate to vary from community to community—or from hospital to hospital—depending on the availability of sophisticated medical technology.

The arbitrary nature of *Roe*'s analytical framework is also reflected in the increasingly complex linedrawing of its progeny. A State may require that certain information be furnished to a woman by a physician or his assistant (*Akron*, 462 U.S. at 448), but it may not require that such information be furnished to her by the physician himself (id. at 449). A State may require that second-trimester abortions be performed in clinics (*Simopoulos v. Virginia,* 462 U.S. 506 (1983)), but may not require that they be performed in hospitals (*Akron,* 462 U.S. at 437–439). As each set of these subtle distinctions has been crafted, still more unanswered questions have been posed. During the decade and a half since *Roe v. Wade,* the adversaries in the abortion debate have come back again and again, asking this Court to spin an ever finer web of regulations.[11] The adversaries are back again today, and they are sure to return.

D. At the heart of the abortion controversy lies a divisive conflict between a woman's interest in procreative choice and the State's interest in protecting the life of an unborn child and promoting respect for life generally. This is not the kind of conflict that is amenable to judicial resolution. If a "principled" resolution of this conflict is to be reached, it can only be by adopting a moral theory of the sanctity of the person, or a theory of when human life begins—neither of which can be derived through ordinary processes of adjudication.[12] Failing such a resolution, it will be necessary to reach an accommodation among the competing interests involved. Under our democratic system of government such an accommodation can be reached only through the political process. As long as the various factions continue to look to the courts, however, a constructive dialogue will be impossible.[13]

The proper role of a court in reviewing abortion legislation is neither to substitute its judgment for that of the legislature, nor to abdicate. Instead, as long as such legislation is procedurally fair and does not violate any of the specific prohibitions of the Bill of Rights, a court should simply ask whether the resolution reached by the legislature is rational—whether it is reasonably related to the advancement of legitimate governmental objectives. That standard of review is deferential, but it is not toothless. Compare, e.g., *Cleburne v. Cleburne Living Center, Inc.,* 473 U.S. 432, 446–447 (1985); *United States Dept. of Agriculture v. Moreno,* 413 U.S. 528, 534 (1973). The important point is that the resolution of the abortion controversy, including any compromise, must come from the legislature; it cannot be imposed by the courts from above.

It is possible to envision a standard of review more deferential than that adopted by *Roe v. Wade,* yet more stringent than rationality review, such as the "undue burden" analysis thoroughly delineated by Justice O'Connor in her separate opinions in *Akron* and *Thornburgh,* and urged in our brief in *Akron.* On reflection, however, we believe that any such intermediate standard would inevitably fall prey to the same difficulties that have beset the *Roe* framework. The concept of an "undue burden" obviously is not self-defining; in giving effect to such a concept, the Court would be required to develop a new regime of substantive abortion rights. Like the regime it would replace, this new system would lack any moorings in the Constitution and would quickly reintroduce the arbitrary line-drawing characteristic of *Roe.* And because it would hold forth the promise of continued and intensive (albeit not strict) judicial arbitration of the competing interests, it would undermine the attempts of the legislative branch to negotiate a compromise among those interests. If such a political resolution of the abortion controversy is ever to become a reality, the Court must unequivocally announce its intention to allow the States to act "free from the suffocating power of the federal judge, purporting to act in the name of the Constitution." *Planned Parenthood of Missouri v. Danforth*, 428 U.S. at 93 (White, J., dissenting).[14]

In a recent study of the abortion laws of 20 Western countries, a leading comparative law scholar reported two striking conclusions. M. A. Glendon, *Abortion and Divorce in Western Law: American Failures, European Challenges* (1987). First, under the abortion regime established by *Roe*, "we have less regulation of abortion in the interest of the fetus than any other Western nation. . . ." *Id.* at 2.[15] The fact that the regime established by *Roe* is out of step with the legislative judgment of virtually every other country with which we share a common cultural tradition by itself suggests that the decision ought to be reconsidered. Second, and more fundamentally, "[t]o a greater extent than in any other country, our courts have shut down the legislative process of bargaining, education, and persuasion on the abortion issue." *Id.* at 2.[16] The survey indicates that democratic legislatures are full capable of reaching a resolution of the competing interests in the abortion controversy. Indeed, the fact that this issue touches or can touch nearly everyone's life—not just those representing a special interest or defending a discrete and insular minority—means that it should be capable of resolution through the process of political dialogue. In short, unless the American political culture is somehow radically different from that of other countries with which we share a common heritage, it would appear that there is nothing inherent in the abortion controversy, or the sharply conflicting interests and viewpoints in this area, that makes it uniquely resistant to legislative resolution.

Under the Constitution, legislative bodies cannot impose irrational constraints on a woman's procreative choice. But within those broad confines, the proper scope of abortion regulation "should be left with the people and to the political processes the people have devised to govern their affairs." *Doe v. Bolton*, 410 U.S. at 222 (White, J., dissenting). The effect of the decisions in *Roe* and its progeny has been "to withdraw from community concern a range of subjects with which every society in civilized times has found it necessary to deal." *Poe v. Ullman*, 376 U.S. at 546 (Harlan, J., dissenting). The time has come to end this "difficult and continuing venture in substantive due process." *Planned Parenthood of Missouri v. Danforth*, 428 U.S. at 92 (White, J., dissenting).

NOTES

1. Judge Arnold dissented from this aspect of the decision below, contending that Missouri's declaration of when life begins should be upheld "insofar as it relates to subjects other than abortion," such as "creating causes of action against persons other than the mother" for wrongful death or bringing fetuses within the protection of the criminal law.

2. In addition to banning the use of public funds to encourage or counsel a woman to have an abortion, the Missouri statute also forbids any public employee acting within the scope of his public employment to encourage or counsel a woman to have an abortion not necessary to save her life and forbids the use of any facilities for that purpose. See Mo. Stat. Ann. @@ 188.210, 188.215. Although the court of appeals also struck down those provisions, the State of Missouri has not appealed from this aspect of the judgment below.

3. The mandated viability tests (Mo. Stat. Ann. @ 188.029) are aimed at promoting the State's interest in the life of the unborn child rather than in maternal health. To the extent that these tests add to the cost of an abortion prior to the end of the second trimester, they may run afoul of the rigid trimester approach mandated in *Roe*. See *City of Akron v. Akron Center for Reproductive Health*, 462 U.S. 416, 434–438 (1983). They may also run afoul of the Court's repeated admonition that the determination of viability is to be left wholly to "the judgment of the attend-

ing physician on the particular facts of the case before him." *Colautti v. Franklin,* 439 U.S. 379, 388–389 (1979).See also *Planned Parenthood of Missouri v. Danforth,* 428 U.S. 52, 64 (1976). The provisions of the statute setting forth a general "finding" by the state legislature that "[t]he life of each human being begins at conception," and a requirement that all state laws be interpreted to provide unborn children with all the rights of other persons "subject only to the Constitution of the United States, and decisional interpretations thereof by the United States Supreme Court" (Mo. Stat. Ann. @ 1.205.1–2), may run afoul of the Court's assertion that "a State may not adopt one theory of when life begins to justify its regulation of abortions." *Akron,* 462 U.S. at 444. It may also—to the extent it provides unborn children with property rights and the protection of state tort and criminal laws—place a burden of uncertain scope on the performance of abortions by supplying a general principle that would fill in whatever interstices may be present in existing abortion precedents.

4. This judgment is shared by a broad spectrum of constitutional scholars. See, e.g., A. Cox, *The Court and the Constitution* 322–338 (1987); J. Ely, *Democracy and Distrust* 2–3, 248 n.52 (1980); A. Bickel, *The Morality of Consent* 27–29 (1975); Gunther, "Some Reflections on the Judicial Role: Distinctions, Roots, and Prospects," 1979 *Wash. U.L.Q.* 817, 819; Burt, "The Constitution of the Family," 1979 *Sup. Ct. Rev.* 329, 371–373; Epstein, "Substantive Due Process by Any Other Name: The Abortion Cases," 1973 *Sup. Ct. Rev.* 159; Wellington, "Common Law Rules and Constitutional Double Standards: Some Notes on Adjudication," 83 *Yale L.J.* 221, 297–311 (1973).

5. *Skinner v. Oklahoma,* 316 U.S. 535, 538 (1942) (criminal sterilization act violated equal protection by distinguishing without an adequate basis between persons convicted of larceny and embezzlement); *Loving v. Virginia,* 388 U.S. 1, 12 (1967) (statute prohibiting interracial marriages involved "invidious racial discriminations"); *Eisenstadt v. Baird,* 405 U.S. 438, 446–455 (1972) (statute prohibiting distribution of contraceptives violated equal protection by treating married and unmarried women differently without a rational basis).

6. *Meyer v. Nebraska,* 262 U.S. 390, 400 (1923) (invalidating law prohibiting the teaching of foreign languages in private elementary schools because "[m]ere knowledge of the German language cannot reasonably be regarded as harmful"); *Pierce v. Society of Sisters,* 268 U.S. 510 (1925) (invalidating statute requiring all children to attend public schools); *Prince v. Massachusetts,* 321 U.S. 158, 164 (1944) (prosecution of Jehovah's Witness under statute prohibiting sale by minors of periodicals implicates but does not violate freedom of religion); *Stanley v. Georgia,* 394 U.S. 557 (1969) (invalidating criminal conviction for mere possession of obscene films in defendant's home).

7. As one commentator has explained, this Court's decision in *Griswold v. Connecticut,* 381 U.S. 479 (1965), invalidating a statute regulating the use of contraceptives, as opposed to their manufacture or sale, indicated an underlying concern that enforcement of the statute "would have been virtually impossible without the most outrageous sort of governmental prying into the privacy of the home." Ely, "The Wages of Crying Wolf: A Comment on *Roe v. Wade,*" 82 *Yale L.J.* 920, 929–930 (1973) (emphasis in original). A statute limiting a medical procedure performed by a doctor in a clinic or hospital is simply not analogous; abortion statutes could obviously be enforced without the necessity of repulsive searches. Fourth Amendment policies accordingly provide no support for the holding in *Roe v. Wade.*

8. Indeed, the period between 1860 and 1880 witnessed "the most important burst of anti-abortion legislation in the nation's history." J. Mohr, *Abortion in America* 200 (1978).

9. Prior to the mid-Nineteenth Century, the legal status of abortion was more uncertain. It is clear, however, that the abortion of a fetus after "quickening" was regarded as criminal at common law. *Roe,* 410 U.S. at 132–136. And the earliest English abortion statute, adopted in 1803, made abortion a criminal offense throughout pregnancy. *Id.* at 136.

10. Prior to concluding that a State does not have a compelling interest in prenatal life throughout pregnancy, the Court in *Roe* observed that Nineteenth Century English and American law typically treated abortion after quickening as a more serious crime than an abortion performed before quickening. 410 U.S. at 136–139. Obviously, however, the fact that an abortion performed in the early months of pregnancy was regarded as "only" a misdemeanor, rather than a felony, does not support the conclusion that the State has no compelling interest in preventing abortion in the earlier period. See *Mohr, supra,* at 200 ("most of the legislation passed between 1860 and 1880 explicitly accepted the [regular physicians'] assertions that the interruption of gestation at any point in pregnancy should be a crime and that the state itself should try actively to restrict the practice of abortion") (emphasis supplied). That conclusion is further undermined by the Court's observation that, "[b]y the end of the 1950's, a large majority of the jurisdictions banned abortion, however and whenever performed, unless done to save or preserve the life of the mother." *Id.* at 139 (emphasis supplied).

11. Between the decision in *Roe* and 1985, state legislatures enacted more than 250 statutes regulating abortion. Wardle, "Rethinking *Roe v. Wade*," 1985 *B.Y.U.L. Rev.* 231, 247.

12. *Roe* specifically declined to adopt either type of theory. The Court stated (410 U.S. at 154): "it is not clear to us that the claim asserted by some amici that one has an unlimited right to do with one's body as one pleases bears a close relationship to the right of privacy previously articulated in the Court's decisions. The Court has refused to recognize an unlimited right of this kind in the past. *Jacobson v. Massachusetts*, 197 U.S. 11 (1905) (vaccination); *Buck v. Bell*, 274 U.S. 200 (1927) (sterilization)." And the Court declined to address the question of when life may be said to begin (410 U.S. at 159): "We need not resolve the difficult question of when life begins. When those trained in the respective disciplines of medicine, philosophy, and theology are unable to arrive at any consensus, the judiciary, at this point in the development of man's knowledge, is not in a position to speculate as to the answer."

13. The Court's continuing effort to oversee virtually all elements of the abortion controversy has seriously distorted the nature of abortion legislation. Because *Roe* and its progeny have resolved most of the central questions about the permissible scope of abortion regulation, legislative action in this area has been relegated to relatively peripheral issues. And because legislators know that whatever they enact in this area will be subject to de novo review by the courts, they have little incentive to try to moderate their positions. The result, all too often, has been statutes that are significant primarily because of their highly "inflammatory" symbolic content—such as fetal description requirements and humane disposal provisions. *Thornburgh*, 476 U.S. at 762 n.10. This process has undermined the accountability of legislative bodies, and has disserved the courts and the Constitution. As James Bradley Thayer once observed, the "tendency of a common and easy resort" to the power of judicial review "is to dwarf the political capacity of the people, and to deaden its sense of moral responsibility." J. B. Thayer, *John Marshall* 106–107 (1901). See also *Plyler v. Doe*, 457 U.S. 202, 253–254 (1982) (Burger, J., dissenting); *United States v. Richardson*, 418 U.S. 166, 188 (1974) (Powell, J., concurring).

14. If the Court does adopt an "undue burden" analysis, we think the appropriate characterization of the liberty interest that must not be burdened is not a "right to abortion," but rather an interest in procreational choice—"whether or not to beget or bear a child" (*Carey v. Population Services International*, 431 U.S. 678, 685 (1977)). Thus, in asking whether any particular state regulation imposes an undue burden, the relevant question would be whether a woman has been afforded a meaningful opportunity to avoid an unwanted pregnancy, taking into account all of the options available to her, including abstinence and contraception. Under this type of analysis, a regulation that prohibits the use of abortion as a form of routine family planning might not be regarded as imposing an undue burden, because it could not be said in this context that a woman lacks a meaningful opportunity to exercise procreational choice. On the other hand, a regulation that prohibits abortion in cases of rape or incest presumably would entail an undue burden, because in such cases, where the pregnancy is the result of coercion, a woman has not been afforded a meaningful opportunity to avoid pregnancy through alternative means. We reiterate, however, that these judgments are more appropriately drawn by legislatures rather than courts.

15. Professor Glendon reports that two countries (Belgium and Ireland) have blanket prohibitions against abortion in their criminal law, subject only to the defense of necessity. Four countries (Canada, Portugal, Spain, and Switzerland) permit abortion only in early pregnancy and only in restricted circumstances, as where there is a serious danger to the pregnant woman's health, a likelihood of serious disease or defect in the fetus, or where the pregnancy resulted from rape or incest. Eight countries (England, Finland, France, West Germany, Iceland, Italy, Luxembourg, and the Netherlands) permit abortion in early pregnancy in a wider variety of circumstances that pose a particular hardship for the pregnant woman. Five countries (Austria, Denmark, Greece, Norway, and Sweden) permit elective abortions in early pregnancy, though abortions are strictly limited thereafter. Glendon, supra, at 13–15 & Table 1. Only in the United States is elective abortion permitted until viability. *Ibid.*

16. After the publication of Glendon's book, the Canadian Supreme Court struck down its abortion law on grounds similar to those stated in *Roe v. Wade*. See *Morgentaler v. Her Majesty the Queen*, 1 S.C.R. 30, 44 D.L.R. 4th 385 (1988). The West German high court, by contrast, had earlier struck down a law liberalizing access to abortion on the grounds that "life developing within the womb is constitutionally protected." See Judgment of Feb. 25, 1975, 39 BVerfGE 1 (quoted in Glendon, supra, at 26).

POSTSCRIPT

Is Abortion Protected by the Constitution?

Whether *Roe v. Wade* is overturned is only partly a matter of legal analysis. It is also a matter of politics, of personality, of values, and of judicial philosophy. The legal question focuses on whether a majority of the Supreme Court will continue to accept Justice Blackmun's analysis and his conclusion that the Constitution contains a privacy right that protects the woman's decision. But whether *Roe* is reversed will also be affected by who is on the Court and, currently at least, as aging liberal justices are replaced by more conservative justices, this prospect is becoming more likely.

There is some irony in this, since the vague terms "conservative" and "strict constructionist" are generally taken to mean that such judges are more prone to maintain consistent links with past decisions, to give more weight to the words of prior decisions and less weight to policy considerations. Because of this, such judges might be expected to follow a prior case, such as *Roe*, even if they might not have voted with the majority in the original case. As the makeup of the current Supreme Court changes, it will be interesting to see what the position of new appointees is toward overrruling prior cases.

What would be the consequences of a decision overturning *Roe*? The current state of great controversy over abortion would certainly not decline. Quite the contrary. The reason for this is that reversing *Roe* would mean that each state could permit or restrict abortion as it wished to do. The main contention of the justices who wish to overturn *Roe* is not necessarily that abortion should be banned, but that this decision should be left to the states, and that it is not a constitutional issue. Such a position means that the political process will have to deal with the issue more than it does now, and this is not likely to defuse the issue.

Recent writings about abortion include Tribe, *Abortion: The Clash of Absolutes* (1990); Note, "Judicial Restraint and the Non-decision in *Webster v. Reproductive Health Services*," 13 *Harvard Journal of Law & Public Policy* 263 (1990); Novick, "Justice Holmes and *Roe v. Wade*," 25 *Trial* 58 (December, 1989); and Symposium on Abortion, *University of Pennsylvania Law Review* v. 138 (1989). The story of the *Roe* case is recounted in Faux, *Roe v. Wade: The Untold Story of the Landmark Supreme Court Decision That Made Abortion Legal* (1988).

ISSUE 9

Should Pornography Be Protected by the First Amendment?

YES: Sarah Evans Barker, from *American Booksellers Association, Inc., v. Hudnut,* U.S. Court of Appeals for the Seventh Circuit (1984)

NO: Andrea Dworkin, from *Amicus Curiae, American Booksellers Association, Inc., v. Hudnut,* U.S. Court of Appeals for the Seventh Circuit (1984)

ISSUE SUMMARY

YES: Judge Sarah Evans Barker outlines her opinion that the ordinances banning pornography as a violation of the civil rights of women are unconstitutional infringements on freedom of speech.

NO: Author Andrea Dworkin maintains that pornography should not be constitutionally protected because it is destructive, abusive, and detrimental to women, and violates their civil rights.

In April 1984, the city of Indianapolis, urged on by an unusual alliance between feminists and the conservative right, passed an ordinance banning the distribution of pornography within the city limits. Several groups in Indianapolis went to court, arguing that the new law interfered with their rights of free speech and free press as guaranteed by the First Amendment. In November, 1984, Judge Sarah Evans Barker of the Federal District Court ruled that the law was indeed a violation of the Constitution. Her decision was affirmed by the Court of Appeals, 771 F. 2d 323 (1984), and sustained by the Supreme Court, 106 S.Ct. 1172 (1986). The following readings contain Judge Barker's opinion and a brief filed by Andrea Dworkin in the Court of Appeals arguing that Judge Barker was wrong in declaring the law unconstitutional.

From a legal point of view, what is perhaps most significant about the pornography litigation is that the courts refused to recognize another exception to the First Amendment. The First Amendment does not provide absolute protection to everything that is spoken or printed. The most common example of unprotected speech is obscenity. Obscene publications have been deemed to contribute so little to society that the courts have held the First Amendment to be essentially irrelevant to obscene publications. Similarly, "fighting words," in which someone advocates illegal acts "where such advocacy is directed to inciting or producing imminent lawless action and is likely to incite or produce such action," can sometimes be punished. In general, however, constitutional theory holds that the solution to speech that someone does not like is more speech. According to the Supreme Court,

> a function of speech . . . is to invite dispute. It may indeed best serve its high purpose when it induces a condition of unrest, creates dissatisfaction with conditions as they are, or even stirs people to anger. Speech is often provocative and challenging. It may strike at prejudices and preconceptions and have profound unsettling effects.

The main issue, in obscenity cases that are brought to court, is whether the material meets the standards that have been developed to define obscenity. The conclusion that obscene expression is constitutionally unprotected was affirmed more than thirty years ago. The struggle for judges since then has been to construct a precise definition of obscenity so that judges, authors, and publishers will know when a publication is legally obscene and when it is not. This has been a mighty and not particularly successful struggle, and you will see mention in the following readings of the various definitions that have been tried and then abandoned by the Supreme Court.

The legal assault on pornography, in order for it to be successful, must not only define pornography in a clear manner, but must also persuade the courts that pornography is so damaging and contributes so little to our society that nothing will be lost if it is suppressed. It would have been surprising if the antipornography movement had won a complete victory in its first lawsuit. What will be worth noting is whether other judges, even if they reject the approach used in Indianapolis, suggest that the sale and production of pornography might be restricted in some other way.

While the courts have generally resisted attempts to restrict offensive art and expression, political pressure to combat pornography has been increasing. In 1989 and 1990, there were frequent newsworthy attempts to suppress a wide variety of forms of expression, such as the exhibit of photographs by the late Robert Mapplethorpe and the records of the rap music group 2 Live Crew. Efforts were made to require special warning labels on record albums, to prosecute some television executives for transmitting allegedly obscene films by satellite to Alabama, and to impose restrictions on artists who receive grants from the National Endowment for the Arts. These examples suggest that courts will continue to be very busy trying to distinguish protected from unprotected forms of expression.

YES

Sarah Evans Barker

PORNOGRAPHY AND FIRST AMENDMENT RIGHTS

This case comes to the Court amidst heated public and private debate over the problems of pornography and sex discrimination in American society. In apparent response to the perceived urgency and seriousness of these issues, the Indianapolis City-County Council debated and enacted an ordinance with subsequent amendments which sought to deal with both of these conditions by limiting the availability in Indianapolis of materials which depict the sexually explicit subordination of women. The Council defined pornography as the graphic depiction of the sexually explicit subordination of women and then declared pornography a discriminatory practice. By way of outlawing this practice, it then forbade most of the specific acts necessary to produce, sell, or distribute such material.

It is difficult to quarrel either with the Council's underlying concern (that pornography and sex discrimination are harmful, offensive, and inimical to and inconsistent with enlightened approaches to equality) or with its premise that some legislative controls are in order. But beyond that, it is in fact outside the rightful purview of this Court to enter the public debate over whether and to what extent these conditions constitute a real social harm. It is also beyond the purview of the Court to substitute its judgment for that of the legislative body, either in defining the acceptable community standards in these areas or in imposing appropriate sanctions for behavior which violate those standards.

Thus, the Court's duty in this circumstance is a narrow one. That duty is to assess the constitutionality of the legislative enactment: to determine whether the Ordinance, however well-motivated or otherwise meritorious it may be, unconstitutionally diminishes, violates, or otherwise derrogates our fundamental freedoms as a people.

This litigation, therefore, requires the Court to weigh and resolve the conflict between the First Amendment guarantees of free speech, on the one hand, and the Fourteenth Amendment right to be free from sex-based discrimination, on the other hand. In addition, the Court must determine

From U.S. Court of Appeals for the Seventh Circuit, *American Booksellers Association, Inc. v. William H. Hudnut III*, 598 F.Supp. 1316, 106 S.Ct. 1172 (1984).

whether the Indianapolis enactment meets the due process requirements of the Fifth and Fourteenth Amendments.

The plaintiffs in this lawsuit request the Court "to preliminarily and permanently enjoin enforcement of, and to declare facially unconstitutional, void and of no effect, City County General Ordinances No. 24 and 35, 1984 (together hereinafter referred to as the "Ordinance"), on the grounds that it is unconstitutional under the United States Constitution. . . .

Plaintiffs have cited numerous reasons to support their claim for relief. They first contend that the Ordinance severely restricts the availability, display and distribution of constitutionally protected, non-obscene materials, in violation of the First and Fourteenth Amendments. More specifically, they claim that the regulatory restraints of the Ordinances are not limited merely to unprotected speech, such as obscenity. As a result, plaintiffs contend that they will be forced under the Ordinance to remove from availability in Indianapolis materials which are in fact protected by the First Amendment.

Plaintiffs also contend that in seeking to ban speech directed to the general public because it is highly offensive to many, the Ordinances violate established Supreme Court precedents which preclude the banning of speech simply because its contents may be socially or politically offensive to the majority. . . .

The defendants admit in their answer that the scope of the Ordinance goes beyond regulating obscene materials. However, they assert, such action does not violate the Constitution. Defendants deny every other allegation that the plaintiffs' rights as guaranteed by the United States Constitution are violated by this Ordinance. . . .

FIRST AMENDMENT REQUIREMENTS

This Ordinance cannot be analyzed adequately without first recognizing this: the drafters of the Ordinance have used what appears to be a legal term of art, "pornography," but have in fact given the term a specialized meaning which differs from the meanings ordinarily assigned to that word in both legal and common parlance. In Section 16–3(v) (page 6), the Ordinance states:

> "Pornography shall mean the sexually explicit subordination of women, graphically depicted, whether in pictures or in words, that includes one or more of the following . . . "

There follows at that point a listing of five specific presentations of women in various settings which serve as examples of "pornography" and as such further define and describe that term under the Ordinance.

As is generally recognized, the word "pornography" is usually associated, and sometimes synonomous, with the word, "obscenity." "Obscenity" not only has its own separate and specialized meaning in the law, but in laymen's use also, and it is a much broader meaning than the definition given the word "pornography" in the Ordinance which is at issue at this action. There is thus a considerable risk of confusion in analyzing this ordinance unless care and precision are used in that process.

The Constitutional analysis of this Ordinance requires a determination of several underlying issues: first, the Court must determine whether the Ordinance imposes restraints on speech or behavior (content versus conduct); if the Ordinance is found to regulate speech, the

Court must next determine whether the subject speech is protected or not protected under the First Amendment; if the speech which is regulated by this Ordinance is protected speech under the Constitution, the Court must then decide whether the regulation is constitutionally permissible as being based on a compelling state interest justifying the removal of such speech from First Amendment protections.

Do the Ordinances Regulate Speech or Behavior (Content or Conduct)?

It appears to be central to the defense of the Ordinance by defendants that the Court accept their premise that the City-County Council has not attempted to regulate speech, let alone protected speech. Defendants repeat throughout the briefs the incantation that their Ordinance regulates conduct, not speech. They contend (one senses with a certain sleight of hand) that the production, dissemination, and use of sexually explicit words and pictures *is* the actual subordination of women and not an expression of ideas deserving of First Amendment protection. . . .

Defendants claim support for their theory by analogy, arguing that it is an accepted and established legal distinction that has allowed other courts to find that advocacy of a racially "separate but equal" doctrine in a civil rights context is protected speech under the First Amendment though "segregation" is not constitutionally protected behavior. Accordingly, defendants characterize their Ordinance here as a civil rights measure, through which they seek to prevent the distribution, sale, and exhibition of "pornography," as defined in the Ordinance, in order to regulate and control the underlying unacceptable conduct.

The content-versus-conduct approach espoused by defendants is not persuasive, however, and is contrary to accepted First Amendment principles. Accepting as true the City-County Council's finding that pornography conditions society to subordinate women, the means by which the Ordinance attempts to combat this sex discrimination is nonetheless through the regulation of speech.

For instance, the definition of pornography, the control of which is the whole thrust of the Ordinance, states that it is "the sexually explicit subordination of women, graphically *depicted*, whether in *pictures* or in *words*, that includes one or more of the following:" (emphasis supplied) and the following five descriptive subparagraphs begin with the words, "Women are *presented* . . ." (emphasis supplied).

The unlawful acts and discriminatory practices under the Ordinance are set out in Section 16–3(g):

"(4) Trafficking in pornography: the production, sale, exhibition, or distribution of pornography. [Subparagraphs omitted here]
(5) Coercion into pornographic performance: coercing, intimidating or fraudulently inducing any person . . . into performing for pornography. . . . [Subparagraphs omitted here]
(6) Forcing pornography on a person: . . .
(7) Assault or physical attack due to pornography: the assault, physical attack, or injury of any woman, man, child or transsexual in a way that is directly caused by specific pornography. . . . "

Section (7), *supra*, goes on to provide a cause of action in damages against the perpetrators, makers, distributors, sellers and exhibitors of pornography and injunctive relief against the further exhibition, distribution or sale of pornography.

In summary, therefore, the Ordinance establishes through the legislative findings that pornography causes a tendency to commit these various harmful acts, and outlaws the pornography (that is, the "depictions"), the activities involved in the production of pornography, and the behavior caused by or resulting from pornography.

Thus, though the purpose of the Ordinance is cast in civil rights terminology—"to prevent and prohibit all discriminatory practices of sexual subordination or inequality through pornography" (Section 16-1(b)(8))—it is clearly aimed at controlling the content of the speech and ideas which the City-County Council has found harmful and offensive. Those words and pictures which depict women in sexually subordinate roles are banned legislation. Despite defendants' attempt to redefine offensive speech as harmful action, the clear wording of the Ordinance discloses that they seek to control speech, and those restrictions must be analyzed in light of applicable constitutional requirements and standards.

Is the Speech Regulated by the Ordinance Protected or Unprotected Speech Under the First Amendment?

The First Amendment provides that government shall make no law abridging the freedom of speech. However, "the First and Fourteenth Amendments have never been thought to give absolute protection to every individual to speak whenever or wherever he pleases or to use any form of address in any circumstances that he chooses." *Cohen v. California*, 403 U.S. 15, 19, 91 S.Ct. 1780, 1785, 29 L.Ed.2d 284 (1971). Courts have recognized only a "relatively few categories of

instances," *id.* at 19–20, 91 S.Ct. at 1785, where the government may regulate certain forms of individual expression. The traditional categories of speech subject to permissible government regulation include "the lewd and obscene, the profane, the libelous, and the insulting or 'fighting' words—those which by their very utterance inflict injury or tend to incite an immediate breach of the peace." *Chaplinsky v. State of New Hampshire*, 315 U.S. 568, 572, 62 S.Ct. 766, 769, 86 L.Ed. 1031 (1942). In addition, the Supreme Court has recently upheld legislation prohibiting the dissemination of material depicting children engaged in sexual conduct. *New York v. Ferber*, 458 U.S. 747, 102 S.Ct. 3348, 73 L.Ed.2d 1113 (1982).

Having found that the Ordinance at issue here seeks to regulate speech (and not conduct), the next question before the Court is whether the Ordinance, which seeks to restrict the distribution, sale, and exhibition of "pornography" as a form of sex discrimination against women, falls within one of the established categories of speech subject to permissible government regulation, that is, speech deemed to be unprotected by the First Amendment.

It is clear that this case does not present issues relating to profanity, libel, or "fighting words." In searching for an analytical "peg," the plaintiffs argue that the Ordinance most closely resembles obscenity, and is, therefore, subject to the requirements set forth in *Miller v. California*, 413 U.S. 15, 93 S.Ct. 2607, 37 L.Ed.2d 419 (1973). . . . But the defendants admit that the scope of the Ordinance is not limited to the regulation of legally obscene material as defined in *Miller*. . . . In fact, defendants concede that the "pornography" they seek to control goes beyond obscenity, as defined by the Supreme Court and excepted from First Amendment protections. Accordingly, the parties agree that the materials encompassed in the restrictions set out in the Ordinance include to some extent what have traditionally been protected materials.

The test under *Miller* for determining whether material is legal obscenity is:

"(a) whether 'the average person, applying contemporary community standards would find that the work, taken as a whole, appeals to the prurient interest, . . . ; (b) whether the work depicts or describes, in a patently offensive way a sexual conduct specifically defined by the applicable state law; and (c) whether the work, taken as a whole, lacks serious literary, artistic, political, or scientific value.". . .

It is obvious that this three-step test is not directly applicable to the present case, because, as has been noted, the Ordinance goes beyond legally obscene material in imposing its controls. The restrictions in the Indianapolis ordinance reach what has otherwise traditionally been regarded as protected speech under the *Miller* test. Beyond that, the Ordinance does not speak in terms of a "community standard" or attempt to restrict the dissemination of material that appeals to the "prurient interest." Nor has the Ordinance been drafted in a way to limit only distributions of "patently offensive" materials. Neither does it provide for the dissemination of works which, though "pornographic," may have "serious literary, artistic, political or scientific value." Finally, the Ordinance does not limit its reach to "hard core sexual conduct," though conceivably "hard core" materials may be included in its proscriptions.

Because the Ordinance spans so much more broadly in its regulatory scope than merely "hard core" obscenity by limiting the distribution of "pornography," the proscriptions in the Ordinance intrude with defendants' explicit approval into areas of otherwise protected speech. Under ordinary constitutional analysis, that would be sufficient grounds to overturn the Ordinance, but defendants argue that this case is not governed by any direct precedent, that it raises a new issue for the Court and even though the Ordinance regulates protected speech, it does so in a constitutionally permissible fashion.

Does Established First Amendment Law Permit the Regulation Provided for in the Ordinance of Otherwise Protected Speech? In conceding that the scope of this Ordinance extends beyond constitutional limits, it becomes clear that what defendants actually seek by enacting this legislation is a newly-defined class of constitutionally unprotected speech, labeled "pornography" and characterized as sexually discriminatory.

Defendants vigorously argue that *Miller* is not the " 'constitutional divide' separating protected from unprotected expression in this area." . . . Defendants point to three cases which allegedly support their proposition that *Miller* is not the exclusive guideline for disposing of pornography/obscenity cases, and that the traditional obscenity test should not be applied in the present case. *See New York v. Ferber*, 458 U.S. 747, 102 S.Ct. 3348, 73 L.Ed.2d 1113 (1982); *FCC v. Pacifica Foundation*, 438 U.S. 726, 98 S.Ct. 3026, 57 L.Ed.2d 1073 (1978); *Young v. American Mini Theatres, Inc.*, 427 U.S. 50, 96 S.Ct. 2440, 49 L.Ed.2d 310 (1976).

Defendants first argue that the Court must use the same reasoning applied by the Supreme Court in *New York v. Ferber, supra,* which upheld a New York statute prohibiting persons from promoting child pornography by distributing material which depicted such activity, and carve out another similar exception to protected speech under the First Amendment.

Defendants can properly claim some support for their position in *Ferber.* There the Supreme Court allowed the states "greater leeway" in their regulation of pornographic depictions of children in light of the State's compelling interest in protecting children who, without such protections, are extraordinarily vulnerable to exploitation and harm. The Court stated in upholding the New York statute:

"The prevention of sexual exploitation and abuse of children constitutes a government objective of surpassing importance. The legislative findings accompanying passage of the New York laws reflect this concern. . . ."

The Supreme Court continued in *Ferber* by noting that the *Miller* standard for legal obscenity does not satisfy the unique concerns and issues posed by child pornography where children are involved; it is irrelevant, for instance, that the materials sought to be regulated contain serious literary, artistic, political or scientific value. In finding that some speech, such as that represented in depictions of child pornography, is outside First Amendment protections, the *Ferber* court stated:

"When a definable class of material, such as that covered by § 263.15, bears so heavily and pervasively on the welfare of children engaged in its production, we think the balance of competing interests is clearly struck and that it is permissible to consider these materials as without the protection of the First Amendment.". . .

Defendants, in the case at bar, argue that the interests of protecting women from sex-based discrimination are analogous to and every bit as compelling and fundamental as those which the Supreme Court upheld in *Ferber* for the benefit of children. But *Ferber* appears clearly distinguishable from the instant case on both the facts and law.

As has already been shown, the rationale applied by the Supreme Court in *Ferber* appears intended to apply solely to child pornography cases. In *Ferber,* the court recognized "that a state's interest in 'safeguarding the physical and psychological well-being of a minor' is 'compelling.' *Globe Newspaper v. Superior Court,* 457 U.S. 596, 607, 102 S.Ct. 2613, 2621, 73 L.Ed.2d 248 (1982)." 102 S.Ct. at 3354. *See also, FCC v. Pacifica Foundation, supra; Prince v. Massachusetts,* 321 U.S. 158, 168, 64 S.Ct. 438, 443, 88 L.Ed. 645 (1944); *Ginsberg v. New York,* 390 U.S. 629, 88 S.Ct. 1274, 20 L.Ed.2d 195 (1968). Also, the obscenity standard in *Miller* is appropriately abandoned in child pornography cases because it "[does] not reflect the State's particular and more compelling interest in prosecuting those who promote the sexual exploitations of children." *Id.* Since a state's compelling interest in preventing child pornography outweighs an individual's First Amendment rights, the Supreme Court held that "the states are entitled to greater leeway in the regulation of pornographic depictions of children." *Id.* 102 S.Ct. at 3354.

In contrast, the case at bar presents issues more far reaching than those in *Ferber.* Here, the City-County Council found that the distribution, sale, and exhibition of words and pictures depicting the subordination of women is a form of sex discrimination and as such is appropriate for governmental regulation. The state has a well-recognized interest in preventing sex discrimination, and, defendants argue, it can regulate speech to accomplish that end.

But the First Amendment gives primacy to free speech and any other state interest (such as the interest of sex based equality under law) must be so compelling as to be fundamental; only then can it be deemed to outweigh the interest of free speech. This Court finds no legal authority or public policy argument which justifies so broad an incursion into First Amendment freedoms as to allow that which defendants attempt to advance here. *Ferber* does not open the door to allow the regulation contained in the Ordinance for the reason that adult women as a group do not, as a matter of public policy or applicable law, stand in need of the same type of protection which has long been afforded children. This is true even of women who are subject to the sort of inhuman treatment defendants have described and documented to the Court in support of this Ordinance. The Supreme Court's finding in *Ferber* of the uncontroverted state interest in "safeguarding the physical and psychological well being of a minor" and its resultant characterization of that interest as "compelling," 102 S.Ct. 3348, 3354, is an interest which inheres to children and is not an interest which is readily transferrable to adult women as a class. Adult women generally have the capacity to protect themselves from participating in and being personally victimized by pornography, which makes the State's interest in safeguarding the physical and psychological well-being of women by prohibiting "the sexually explicit subordination of women, graphically depicted, whether in pictures or in words" not so compelling as to sacrifice the guarantees of the First Amendment. . . .

The second case relied upon by defendants to support their contention that *Miller* is not controlling in the present case is *FCC v. Pacifica Foundation*, 438 U.S. 726, 98 S.Ct. 3026, 57 L.Ed.2d 1073 (1978). According to defendants, *Pacifica* exemplifies the Supreme Court's refusal to make obscenity the sole legal basis for regulating sexually explicit conduct.

In *Pacifica*, the Supreme Court was faced with the question of whether a broadcast of patently offensive words dealing with sex and excretion may be regulated on the basis of their content. 438 U.S. at 745, 98 S.Ct. at 3038. The Court held that this type of speech was not entitled to absolute constitutional protection in every context. *Id.* at 747, 98 S.Ct. at 3039. Since the context of the speech in *Pacifica* was broadcasting, it was determined only to be due "the most limited First Amendment protection." *Id.* at 748, 98 S.Ct. at 3040. The reason for such treatment was twofold:

"First, the broadcast media have established a uniquely pervasive presence in all the lives of all Americans. Patently offensive, indecent material presented over the airwaves confronts the citizen, not only in public, but also in the privacy of the home, where the individual's right to be left alone plainly outweighs the First Amendment rights of an intruder." Second, broadcasting is uniquely accessible to children, even those too young to read . . ."

Although the defendants correctly point out that the Supreme Court did not use the traditional obscenity test in *Pacif-*

ica, this Court is not persuaded that the rule enunciated there is applicable to the facts of the present case. The Ordinance does not attempt to regulate the airwaves; in terms of its restrictions, it is not even remotely concerned with the broadcast media. The reasons for the rule in *Pacifica,* that speech in certain contexts should be afforded minimal First Amendment protection, are not present here, since we are not dealing with a medium that "invades" the privacy of the home. In contrast, if an individual is offended by "pornography," as defined in the Ordinance, the logical thing to do is avoid it, an option frequently not available to the public with material disseminated through broadcasting.

In addition, the Ordinance is not written to protect children from the distribution of pornography, in contrast to the challenged FCC regulation in *Pacifica.* Therefore, the peculiar state interest in protecting the "well being of its youth," *id.* at 649, 98 S.Ct. at 3040 (quoting *Ginsberg v. New York,* 390 U.S. 629, 88 S.Ct. 1274, 20 L.Ed.2d 195 (1968)), does not underlie this Ordinance and cannot be called upon to justify a decision by this Court to uphold the Ordinance.

The third case cited by defendants in support of their proposition that the traditional obscenity standard in *Miller* should not be used to overrule the Ordinance is *Young v. American Mini Theatres, Inc.,* 427 U.S. 50, 96 S.Ct. 2440, 49 L.Ed.2d 310 (1976). In *Young* the Supreme Court upheld a city ordinance that restricted the location of movie theatres featuring erotic films. The Court, in a plurality opinion, stated that "[e]ven though the First Amendment protects communication in this area from total suppression, we hold that the State may legitimately use the content of these ma-

terials as the basis for placing them in a different classification from other motion pictures." 427 U.S. at 71–72, 96 S.Ct. at 2452. The Court concluded that the city's interest in preserving the character of its neighborhoods justified the ordinance which required that adult theaters be separated, rather than concentrated, in the same areas as it is permissible for other theaters to do without limitation. *Id.* at 71, 96 S.Ct. at 2452–53.

Young is distinguishable from the present case because we are not here dealing with an attempt by the City-County Council to restrict the time, place, and manner in which "pornography" may be distributed. Instead, the Ordinance prohibits completely the sale, distribution, or exhibition of material depicting women in a sexually subordinate role, at all times, in all places and in every manner.

The Ordinance's attempt to regulate speech beyond one of the well-defined exceptions to protected speech under the First Amendment is not supported by other Supreme Court precedents. The Court must, therefore, examine the underlying premise of the Ordinance: that the State has so compelling an interest in regulating the sort of sex discrimination imposed and perpetuated through "pornography" that it warrants an exception to free speech.

Is Sex Discrimination a Compelling State Interest Justifying an Exception to First Amendment Protections?
It is significant to note that the premise of the Ordinance is the sociological harm, *i.e.,* the discrimination, which results from "pornography" to degrade women as a class. The Ordinance does not presume or require specifically defined, identifiable victims for most of it

proscriptions. The Ordinance seeks to protect adult women, as a group, from the diminution of their legal and sociological status as women, that is, from the discriminatory stigma which befalls women as *women* as a result of "pornography." On page one of the introduction to defendants' *Amicus* Brief, counsel explicitly argues that the harm which underlies this legislation is the "harm to the treatment and *status* of women . . . on the basis of sex." . . .

This is a novel theory advanced by the defendants, an issue of first impression in the courts. If this Court were to accept defendants' argument—that the State's interest in protecting women from the humiliation and degradation which comes from being depicted in a sexually subordinate context is so compelling as to warrant the regulation of otherwise free speech to accomplish that end—one wonders what would prevent the City-County Council (or any other legislative body) from enacting protections for other equally compelling claims against exploitation and discrimination as are presented here. Legislative bodies, finding support, here, could also enact legislation prohibiting other unfair expression —the publication and distribution of racist material, for instance, on the grounds that it causes racial discrimination,[1] or legislation prohibiting ethnic or religious slurs on the grounds that they cause discrimination against particular ethnic or religious groups, or legislation barring literary depictions which are uncomplimentary or oppressive to handicapped persons on the grounds that they cause discrimination against that group of people, and so on. If this Court were to extend to this case the rationale in *Ferber* to uphold the Amendment, it would signal so great a potential encroachment

upon First Amendment freedoms that the precious liberties reposed within those guarantees would not survive. The compelling state interest, which defendants claim gives constitutional life to their Ordinance, though important and valid as that interest may be in other contexts, is not so fundamental an interest as to warrant a broad intrusion into otherwise free expression.

Defendants contend that pornography is not deserving of constitutional protection because its harms victimize all women. It is argued that "pornography" not only negatively effects [sic] women who risk and suffer the direct abuse of its production,[2] but also, those on whom violent pornography is forced through such acts as compelled performances of "dangerous acts such as being hoisted upside down by ropes, bound by ropes and chains, hung from trees and scaffolds or having sex with animals. . . ." Defendants' Memorandum In Support To Plaintiffs' Motion For Summary Judgment, pp. 3–4. It is also alleged that exposure to pornography produces a negative impact on its viewers, causing in them an increased willingness to aggress toward women, *ibid.* at p. 4, and experience self-generated rape fantasies, increases in sexual arousal and a rise in the self-reported possibility of raping. *Ibid.* at p. 6. In addition, it causes discriminatory attitudes and behavior toward all women. *Ibid.*, at pp. 11–12. The City-County Council, after considering testimony and social research studies, enacted the Ordinance in order to "combat" pornography's "concrete and tangible harms to women." *Ibid.* at p. 13.

Defendants rely on *Paris Adult Theatre I v. Slaton*, 413 U.S. 49, 93 S.Ct. 2628, 37 L.Ed.2d 446 (1973), to justify their regulation of "pornography." In that case the

Supreme Court held "that there are legitimate state interests at stake in stemming the tide of commercialized obscenity . . . [which] include the interest of the public in the quality of life and the total community environment, the tone of commerce in the great city centers, and, possibly, the public safety itself." 413 U.S. at 57–58, 93 S.Ct. at 2635.

The Georgia Legislature had determined that in that case exposure to obscene material adversely affected men and women, that is to say, society as a whole. Although the petitioners argued in that case that there was no scientific data to conclusively prove that proposition, the Court said, "[i]t is not for us to resolve empirical uncertainties underlying state legislation, save in the exceptional case where that legislation plainly impinges upon rights protected by the constitution itself." *Id.* at 60, 93 S.Ct. at 2636–37 (footnote omitted).

In *Slaton*, the Georgia Legislature sought to regulate "obscenity," an accepted area of unprotected speech. *See Miller v. California*, 413 U.S. 15, 93 S.Ct. 2607, 37 L.Ed.2d 419 (1973). The Court specifically found that "nothing precludes the State of Georgia from the regulation of the allegedly obscene material exhibited in *Paris Adult Theatre I or II*, provided that the applicable Georgia law, as written or authoritatively interpreted by the Georgia courts, meets the First Amendment standards set forth in *Miller v. California* . . ." 413 U.S. at 69, 93 S.Ct. at 2642 (citations omitted).

Based on this reasoning, defendants argue that there is more than enough "empirical" evidence in the case at bar to support the City-County Council's conclusion that "pornography" harms women in the same way obscenity harms people, and, therefore, this Court should not question the legislative finding. As has already been acknowledged, it is not the Court's function to question the City-County Council's legislative finding. The Court's solitary duty is to ensure that the Ordinance accomplishes its purpose without violating constitutional standards or impinging upon constitutionally protected rights. In applying those tests, the Court finds that the Ordinance cannot withstand constitutional scrutiny.

It has already been noted that the Ordinance does not purport to regulate legal obscenity, as defined in *Miller.* Thus, although the City-County Council determined that "pornography" harms women, this Court must and does declare the Ordinance invalid without being bound by the legislative findings because "pornography," as defined and regulated in the Ordinance, is constitutionally protected speech under the First Amendment and such an exception to the First Amendment protections is constitutionally unwarranted.[3] This Court cannot legitimately embark on judicial policymaking, carving out a new exception to the First Amendment simply to uphold the Ordinance, even when there may be many good reasons to support legislative action. To permit every interest group, especially those who claim to be victimized by unfair expression, their own legislative exceptions to the First Amendment so long as they succeed in obtaining a majority of legislative votes in their favor demonstrates the potentially predatory nature of what defendants seek through this Ordinance and defend in this lawsuit.

It ought to be remembered by defendants and all others who would support such a legislative initiative that, in terms of altering sociological patterns, much as alteration may be necessary and desirable, free speech, rather than being the enemy, is a long-tested and worthy ally. To deny free speech in order to engineer social change in the name of accomplishing a greater good for one sector of our society erodes the freedoms of all and, as such, threatens tyranny and injustice for those subjected to the rule of such laws. The First Amendment protections presuppose the evil of such tyranny and prevent a finding by this Court upholding the Ordinance. . . .

SUMMARY

For the foregoing reasons, the Court finds that the Ordinance regulates speech protected by the First Amendment and is, therefore, in violation of the United States Constitution. The Ordinance's proscriptions are not limited to categories of speech, such as obscenity or child pornography, which have been excepted from First Amendment protections and permit some governmental regulation. The City-County Council, in defining and outlawing "pornography" as the graphically depicted subordination of women, which it then characterizes as sex discrimination, has sought to regulate expression, that is, to suppress speech. And although the State has a recognized interest in prohibiting sex discrimination, that interest does not outweigh the constitutionally protected interest of free speech. For these reasons the Ordinance does not withstand this constitutional challenge.

NOTES

1. In *Beauharnais v. Illinois*, 343 U.S. 250, 72 S.Ct. 725, 96 L.Ed. 919 (1952), the Supreme Court upheld an Illinois libel statute prohibiting the dissemination of materials promoting racial or religious hatred and which tended to produce a breach of the peace and riots. It has been recognized that "the rationale of that decision turns quite plainly on the strong tendency of the prohibited utterances to cause violence and disorder." *Collin v. Smith*, 578 F.2d 1197, 1204 (7th Cir. 1978). The Supreme Court has recognized breach of the peace as the traditional justification for upholding a criminal libel statute. *Beauharnais*, 343 U.S. at 254, 72 S.Ct. at 729. Therefore, a law preventing the distribution of material that causes racial discrimination, an attitude, would be upheld under this analysis. Further, the underlying reasoning of the *Beauharnais* opinion, that the punishment of libel raises no constitutional problems, has been questioned in many recent cases. *See Collin, supra,* 578 F.2d at 1205, and cases cited therein.

2. The defendants point to social research data, as well as graphic personal accounts of individuals, in support of their position that "women are recruited into all forms of sexual exploitation through physical force, psychological coercion, drugs and economic exigencies." Defendants' Memorandum In Support To Plaintiffs' Motion For Summary Judgment, p. 2.

3. Defendants again rely on *Young v. American Mini Theatres, Inc.*, 427 U.S. 50, 96 S.Ct. 2440, 49 L.Ed.2d 310 (1976), contending that since the legislation in that case was upheld upon a single affidavit of a sociologist that the location of adult movie theatres had a disruptive impact on the community, the Ordinance should be upheld because there is more than enough data to demonstrate that pornography harms women. As discussed above in subpart B, however, the legislation in *Young* sought to regulate the place where pornography could be distributed, not to completely ban its distribution. Thus *Young* is not controlling.

NO

Andrea Dworkin

THE OPPRESSION OF PORNOGRAPHY

I am co-author with Catharine A. MacKinnon of the Indianapolis legislation defining pornography as a violation of women's civil rights; the author of *Pornography: Men Possessing Women* (1981), *Woman Hating* (1974), and many articles on pornography; a lecturer at universities on pornography; a speaker at rallies protesting pornography; and an organizer involved in demonstrating against pornography. I have spent the last thirteen years analyzing the impact of pornography on women's social status and the role of pornography in sexual abuse. . . .

PORNOGRAPHY IS A CENTRAL ELEMENT
IN THE OPPRESSION OF WOMEN

Judge Barker says that pornography as defined in the Ordinance is constitutionally protected speech. This means that the abuse of women in pornography, the trafficking in women that constitutes the bulk of pornography, the coercion of women required to make pornography, the abuses of women inevitably resulting from pornography, and the inequality created by pornography all have constitutional protection. Women cannot function as citizens in this world of social and sexual predation.

The Ordinance characterizes pornography as "a discriminatory practice based on sex." Speech and action are meshed in this discrimination, which is a system of sexual exploitation constructed on sex-based powerlessness and which generates sex-based abuse. The presence of speech cannot be used to immunize discrimination and sexual abuse from legal remedy.

When pornography is photographic, it is indisputably action. It gets perceived as speech because the woman in the photograph is effectively rendered an object or commodity by the pornography; the perception of the photograph as speech in itself denies the human status of the woman in it. The so-called speech belongs to whomever took or sold the photograph—the pornographer—not to the woman used in it, to whom things were done as if she were an object or commodity, and who indeed continues to be sold as an

From U.S. Court of Appeals for the Seventh Circuit, *American Booksellers Association, Inc. v. William H. Hudnut III*, 598 F.Supp. 1316, 106 S.Ct. 1172 (1984).

object or commodity. The woman is excluded from recognizably human dialogue by the uses to which she is put. The courts reify this injustice when they take the photograph to be real speech and do not recognize the woman in it as a real person who, by virtue of being human, is necessarily being used in ways antagonistic to full human status. The court accepts the pornographers' misogyny as its own if it holds that the pornographers' exploitation of a woman's body is an appropriate use of her: that what she is entitled to as a human being is properly expressed in these uses to which she is put.

The actions immortalized in pornography are not ideas, thoughts, or fantasies. The vocabulary of "sexual fantasy," often applied to pornography as a genre, is in fact the language of prostitution, where the act that the man wants done and pays to get done is consistently referred to as his "fantasy," as if it never happens in the real world. He goes to a prostitute and pays her money so that she will do what he tells her to do, and it is this *act* that is called "fantasy."

Similarly, in pornography, *acts* done to or by women are called "speech," even though the woman is doing an act dictated by what is required to sexually gratify men. Her body is a commodity in itself. Her body is also the literal language of the so-called publisher, who in reality is a pimp trafficking in women. Because the pimp introduces a camera into the trafficking, his whole process of exploiting the woman's body is protected as "speech."

The First Amendment predated the invention of the camera. The founding fathers could never have considered that there might be physical rights of people trampled on by rights of speech: that in protecting a photograph, for instance, one might be protecting an actual act of torture. In pornography, photographs are made with real women. These photographs are then used on real women, to get them to do the acts the real women in the photographs are doing.

The hostility and discrimination produced by written pornography is just as real. In written pornography, the vocabularies of sex and violence are inextricably combined, so that erection and orgasm are produced as pleasurable responses to sexual abuse. This behaviorally conditions men to sex as dominance over and violence against women. The nature of written pornography is definable and distinct enough from all other written material that it can be isolated as well as recognized. Sexually explicit and abusive male dominance, conveyed in repeated acts of rape, torture, and humiliation, is the entire substance of written pornography. *See* Smith, *The Social Content of Pornography*, 26 J. Communication 16 (1976). It is impossible, however, to separate the effects of written pornography from the effects of photographic pornography.

Obscenity law recognizes the incredible physical impact of this kind of sexually explicit material, written and photographic, on men—an impact so different from the impact of any known form of "speech" that the Supreme Court has repeatedly held that obscenity is not speech, even though it is words and pictures. *See*, e.g., *Roth v. United States*, 354 U.S. 476, 485 (1957). The standard of "prurient interest" suggests the kind of line that the Court wants to draw between "speech" and "not speech" even with regard to words and pictures. "Prurient" means "itch" or "itching"; it is derived from the Sanscrit "he burns."

If he itches, let alone burns, the power and urgency of his response is not socially innocuous. Pornography creates the physiologically real conviction in men that women want abuse; that women are whores by nature; that women want to be raped and humiliated; that women get sexual pleasure from pain; even that women get sexual pleasure from being maimed or killed. . . . Obscenity law is premised on the inevitability of male sexual response to sexually explicit verbal and visual stimuli; it occurs in a world of concrete male dominance, obscenity law itself originating in a context of legalized male ownership of women.

Judicial decisions reflect and perpetuate the focus on male response, by wholly ignoring women, both in and outside the pornography. The statutory definition of pornography in the Ordinance articulates for the first time in the law how pornography both uses and impacts on women in particular, which is what distinguishes it as a uniquely destructive phenomenon. Pornography is appropriately recognized as an energetic agent of male domination over women. Pornography creates a devastating relationship between the status of some women, who are particularly powerless and vulnerable to abuse, and the status of all women. The vicious exploitation through sex of some women in pornography as entertainment establishes a sexual imperative in which forcing sex on any woman is justified. The bad treatment of some women in pornography justifies the second-class status of all women in society, because the bad treatment is presented as an appropriate response to the human worthlessness of women as such. Only *some* Christians had to be slaughtered as public entertainment in Roman circuses for all Christians and all Romans to understand who could be hurt, harassed, and persecuted with *de facto* impunity.

Pornographers draw on and benefit from particularly cruel aspects of women's vulnerability. Incest and child sexual abuse produce between two-thirds and three-quarters of the women who get exploited in pornography. *See* James and Heyerding, *Early Sexual Experiences and Prostitution*, 134 Am. J. Psychiatry 1381 (1977); Silbert and Pines, *Pornography and Sexual Abuse of Women*, 10 Sex Roles 857 (1984); Senate Committee on the Judiciary, Subcommittee on Juvenile Justice, *A Hearing to Consider the Effects of Pornography on Children and Women* (Aug. 8, 1984) (testimony of Katherine Brady). The ownership of a girl by her father or other adult male, including sexual ownership of her, is deeply implicated in the continuing vulnerability of adult women to the sexual abuse of pornography. It is not possible to draw a firm line between the uses of children in pornography, recognized in *New York v. Ferber*, 458 U.S. 747 (1982), and the uses of women in pornography, since so many of the women are habituated to sexual abuse, even first used in pornography, as children. The court must not accept the pornographers' propaganda, which insists that these women have made a career choice as free and equal adults for pornographic exploitation. The ownership of women and children by adult men is historically linked (for example, in the power of the Roman *paterfamilias*); and it is empirically and sociologically linked in the abuse of women and children in pornography.

Pornography is deeply implicated in rape, *see* Minneapolis Hearings, Sess. III (Dec. 13, 1983) at 11 (testimony of Bill Neiman), 14 (testimony of Susan Graack),

18 *et seq.* (testimony of Carol LaFavor); in battery, *see id.* at 21 (testimony of Wanda Richardson), 27 *et seq.* (testimony of Donna Dunn); in incest, *see id.* at 69 *et seq.* (testimony of Charlotte Castle); in forced prostitution, *see id.* at 75 *es seq.* (testimony of Sue Santa). Pornography is also a consistent phenomenon in the lives of serial killers. *See* S. Michaud and J. Aynesworth, *The Only Living Witness* 104, 105, 115, 118, 130 (1983) (Ted Bundy); T. Schwarz, *The Hillside Strangler* 152–153 (1982); T. Sullivan and P. Maiken, *Killer Clown: The John Wayne Gacy Murders* 28, 29, 218, 223; P. Johnson, *On Iniquity* 39, 52, 80, 81 (1967) (Moors murders); E. Williams, *Beyond Belief* 135, 143, 148–156 (1968) (Moors murders); G. Burn, ' . . . *somebody's husband, somebody's son': The Story of Peter Sutcliffe* 113–116, 123 (1984) (Yorkshire Ripper).

Pornography presents the rape and torture of women as entertainment. This is surely the nadir of social worthlessness.

PORNOGRAPHERS' RIGHTS OF EXPRESSION ARE OUTWEIGHED BY WOMEN'S RIGHTS TO EQUALITY

The Expression of Ideas Through Injurious Acts Is Not Constitutionally Protected

It is wrong to say, as Judge Barker did, that pornography as defined in the Ordinance expresses ideas and is therefore protected speech, unless one is prepared to say that murder or rape or torture with an ideology behind it also expresses ideas and might well be protected on that account. Most acts express ideas. Most systems of exploitation or inequality express ideas. Segregation expressed

an idea more eloquently than any book-about the inferiority of black people ever did. Yet the Supreme Court overturned segregation—after protecting it for a very long time—because the Court finally grasped its harm to people. The difference between the Court's view in *Plessy v. Ferguson*, 163 U.S. 537, 551 (1896), that segregation harmed blacks "solely because the colored race chooses to put that construction upon it," and its view in *Brown v. Bd. of Education of Topeka*, 347 U.S. 483, 494 (1954) that segregation "generates a feeling of inferiority as to their status in the community that may affect their hearts and minds in a way unlikely ever to be undone," is dramatic and instructive. The fact that the idea segregation expressed would suffer because the idea required the practice for much of its persuasive power did not afford segregation constitutional protection: attempts to invoke First Amendment justifications have been thoroughly repudiated. . . . An effort to claim that segregation was protected as first amendment "speech" because it has a point of view and an ideology would be a transparent use of the First Amendment to shield a practice of inequality; and such a claim for pornography is similarly transparent. Exploitation cannot be protected because it expresses the idea that the people being exploited are inferior or worthless as human beings or deserve to be exploited. All exploitation fundamentally expresses precisely that idea.

The Sexual Exploitation of Women Perpetuated by Pornography Negates Women's Rights to Equality

In her decision, Judge Barker says that "[a]dult women generally have the capacity to protect themselves from participating in and being personally victimized by pornography." The fault, she suggests, is with the individual who is hurt, and no legal remedy is justified. Adult men generally have the capacity to protect themselves from being murdered; yet murderers are not excused because they only succeed in murdering men who are dumb enough, weak enough, or provocative enough to get killed. Indeed, no one ever thinks of male victims of violence in those terms at all. Yet that valuation of women hurt by pornography is implicit in Judge Barker's misogynistic logic.

It is not true that women can protect ourselves from being victimized by pornography. Pornography's effect on our civil status—the way it creates attitudes and behaviors of discrimination against us—is beyond personal remedy. Pornography's role in generating sexual abuse is beyond our capacities as individuals to stop or moderate, especially with no legal recourse against its production, sale, exhibition, or distribution. Sexual abuse is endemic in this country. One-fifth to one-third of all women have an unwanted sexual encounter with an adult male as children; one woman in a hundred has had a sexual experience as a child with her father or step-father; it is estimated that 16,000 new cases of father-daughter incest are initiated each year. See J. Herman, *Father-Daughter Incest* 12–14 (1982). Studies and police and hospital records in different localities suggest that battery occurs in one-third to one-half of all marriages. See R. Langley and R. Levy, *Wife Beating* 4–11 (1977); D. Russell, *Rape in Marriage* 98–100 (1982). A documented forcible rape occurs every seven minutes; and rape remains one of the most underreported violent crimes. See Federal Bureau of Investigation, *Uniform Crime Reports for the United States* at 5, 14 (1983). Studies continue to be done in all areas of sexual abuse, including sexual harassment, marital rape, and prostitution; and the figures showing frequency of abuse increase as the descriptions of violence become more precise and the political efforts of feminists provide a context in which to comprehend the abuse.

The place of pornography in actually producing the scenarios and behaviors that constitute that mass of sexual abuse is increasingly documented, especially by victims. Coercion of women into pornography is expanding as the market for live women expands, especially in video pornography. Women in homes do not have the real social and economic power to keep men from using pornography on them or making them participate in it. There has been an increased use of cameras in actual rapes, with the subsequent appearance of the photographs on the commercial pornography market. Pornography itself is also being used as a form of sexual assault: the public violation of a woman—photographs made against her will or by fraud or without her knowledge, then published as public rape. Her forced exposure, like rape, is an act of hostility and humiliation. With the normalization of pornography, women who have pictures of themselves used against them as sexual abuse have no social or legal credibility to assert that rights of privacy were violated, because they appear indistinguishable from other women in similar photographs whose active compliance is presumed.

The statutory definition of pornography in the Ordinance, far from being "vague," delineates the structure of actual, concrete material produced and sold as pornography by the $8-billion-a-year pornography industry. *See U.S. News and World Report*, June 4, 1984, at 84–85. No adult bookstore has any problem knowing what to stock. No consumer has any problem knowing what to buy. No pornography theatre has any trouble knowing what to show. The so-called books are produced by formula, and they do not vary ever in their nature, content, or impact. They cannot be confused with the language of any writer I have ever read, including Jean Genet and Jerzy Kosinski, who are particularly graphic about rape and hate women. It may be difficult to believe that the definition is accurate and clear, because it may be difficult to believe that we are actually living in a country where the material described in the statutory definition is being produced, especially with live people. Nevertheless, we do. Or perhaps one effect of using $8 billion of pornography a year is that the basic premise of this law appears bizarre by contrast with the pornography: that women are human beings with rights of equality; and that being hurt by pornography violates those rights.

The Elimination of Sex Discrimination Is a Compelling State Interest That Is Furthered by the Ordinance

Sex discrimination keeps more than half the population from being able to enjoy the full benefits of free speech, because they are too poor to buy speech, too silenced through sexual abuse to articulate in a credible way their own experiences, too despised because of their sex to be able to achieve the public significance required to exercise speech in a technologically advanced society. The First Amendment protects speech already articulated and published from state interference. It does nothing to empower those who have been systematically excluded—especially on the bases of sex and race—from pragmatic access to the means of speech.

The First Amendment is nearly as old as this country. The eradication of sex discrimination is new as a compelling state interest, perhaps causing Judge Barker to underestimate its importance. . . . Without vigorous action in behalf of equality, women will never be able to exercise the speech that the First Amendment would then protect.

State governments were not held to the proscriptions on government in the First Amendment until the Supreme Court held that the due process clause of the Fourteenth Amendment incorporated First Amendment standards. *See, e.g., Fiske v. Kansas*, 274 U.S. 380 (1927). Nevertheless, the simple reality is that the First Amendment and its values of free speech existed in harmony with both legal slavery and legal segregation. No effective legal challenge to those systems of racial subordination was mounted under the rubric of freedom of expression, even though in both systems reading and writing were at issue. In slavery, laws prohibited teaching slaves to read or write. *See* K. Stampp, *The Peculiar Institution* 208 (1956). In segregation, separate-but-equal education assured that blacks remained widely illiterate; then literacy tests were used to screen voters, so that blacks could not qualify to vote. *See Oregon v. Mitchell*, 400 U.S. 112, 132–33 (1970) (Black, J.); *Gaston County v. United States*, 395 U.S. 285 (1969). *Cf. Griggs v. Duke Power Company*, 401 U.S. 424, 430 (1971) (inferior segregated education hurts blacks where employer uses non-job-related educational criteria for employment decisions). Rights of speech, association, and religion (being kept out of certain churches, for instance, by state law), were simply denied blacks. The Civil War Amendments are an institutional acknowledgment that powerlessness is not cured simply by "more speech"; first amendment values alone could not fulfill constitutional ambitions for dignity and equity that reside in principles of justice not abrogated even by sadistic political institutions like slavery. The Fourteenth Amendment, however, purposefully used the word "male" in its guarantee of voting rights, U.S. Const. amend. XIV, §2, to rule out any possible application of equality rights to women's social and political condition. The right to vote, won in 1920, gave women the most mundane recognition of civil existence as citizens. U.S. Const., amend. XIX. The equality principles underlying the Fourteenth Amendment were even then not applied to women until 1971. *Reed v. Reed*, 404 U.S. 71 (1971).

The absolute, fixed, towering importance of the First Amendment and the absolute, fixed insignificance of sex discrimination and of equality of interests in Judge Barker's decision is a direct consequence of how late women came into this legal system as real citizens. Equality must be the legal priority for any group excluded from constitutional protections for so long and stigmatized as inferior. Yet the historical worthlessness of women—which is why our interests are not as old as this country—undermines any claim we make to having rights that must be taken as fundamental: equality for women is seen as trivial, faddish. The First Amendment, by contrast, is fundamental—a behemoth characterized by longevity, constancy, and familiarity. Because women have been silenced, and because women have been second-class, our equality claims are seen as intrinsically inferior. The opposite should be the case. Those whom the law has helped to keep out by enforcing conditions of inferiority, servitude, and debasement should, by virtue of that involuntary but intensely destructive exclusion, have the court's full attention when asserting any equality claim.

This must certainly be true when speech rights are asserted in behalf of pornographers, since the speech of the pornographers is exercised largely through sexual abuse and is intricately interwoven with physical assault and injury. The First Amendment here is clearly being used to shield those who are not only powerful but also cruel and cynical. The victims, targeted on the basis of sex, must ask for relief from systematic sexual predation through a recognition of equality rights, because only equality stands up against the injury of longstanding exclusion from constitutional protections. Judge Barker holds that only expression matters, even when the expression is trafficking in women; equality does not matter, and the systematic harms of inequality and abuse suffered by women on a massive scale do not matter. This view of the First Amendment relies on historical inequities to establish modern constitutional priorities.

The courts must, instead, give real weight to equality interests, because of their historical exclusion from the original Bill of Rights. The deformities of the social system caused by that exclusion destroy justice, which requires symmetry, equity, and balance. By refusing to give equality values any weight when in conflict with free speech values, Judge Barker allows speech to function as if it were a military arsenal: hoarded by men for over two centuries, it is now used to bludgeon women, who have been without it and have none in reserve; we do not even have slingshots against Goliath. If equality interests can never matter against first amendment challenges, then speech becomes a weapon used by the haves against the have-nots; and the First Amendment, not balanced against equality rights of the have-nots, becomes an intolerable instrument of dispossession, not a safeguard of human liberty. The real exclusion of women from public discourse has allowed men to accumulate speech as a resource of power; and with that power, men have articulated values and furthered practices that have continued to debase women and to justify that debasement. The First Amendment, then, in reality, operates to the extreme detriment of those who do not have the power of socially and politically real speech. In this case, Judge Barker is saying that real people being tortured are properly not persons with rights of equality that are being violated; but, because a picture has been taken, are the abstract speech of those who exploit them. She is saying that the victim in the photograph is properly silent, even if gagged; that the victim's historical exclusion from speech need not, cannot, and should not be changed by vigorous legislative and judicial commitments to equality. She is saying that the woman's body is properly seen as the man's speech; and, in this corrupt logic, that the picture that in fact documents the abuse of a human being is to be dignified as an idea that warrants legal protection. Equality is indeed meaningless in this arrangement of power; and speech is a nightmare with a victim whose humanity is degraded by both the pornographers and the court.

The Pornographers Degrade the First Amendment

The pornographers also degrade the First Amendment by using it as a shield to protect sexual abuse and sexual trafficking. If the court allows these parasites an impenetrable shield of absolute protection because they use pictures and words as part of the sexual abuse they perpetrate and promote, there is really no end to the possible manipulations of the First Amendment to protect like forms of exploitation. All any exploiter has to do is to interject speech into any practice of exploitation, however malignant, and hide the whole practice behind the First Amendment. By isolating the speech elements in other practices of discrimination and asserting their absolute protection, the discrimination could be made to disappear. Consider, for example, a common situation in sexual harassment in employment, where a "speech" element—a sexual proposition from a supervisor—is part of a chain of events leading to an adverse employment consequence. *See*, e.g., *Tomkins v. Public Serv. Elec. & Gas Co.*, 568 F.2d 1044, 1045 (3d Cir. 1977), in which a conversation over lunch was a crucial component of the Title VII violation. No court has held that the mere presence of words in the process of discrimination turns the discrimination into protected activity. The speech is part of the discrimination. The Constitution places no value on discrimination. . . .

If the First Amendment is not to protect those who have power against the just claims of those who need equality; if pornography is sexual exploitation and produces sexual abuse and discrimination; then the Ordinance is more than justified. It saves our constitutional system from the indignity of protecting sex-based abuse. It exonerates principles of equity by allowing them vitality and potency. It shows that law can actively help the powerless and not be paralyzed by the cynical manipulations of sadists and profiteers. It is an appropriate and care-fully balanced response to a social harm of staggering magnitude.

CONCLUSION

For the foregoing reasons, the judgment of the District Court should be reversed.

POSTSCRIPT

Should Pornography Be Protected
by the First Amendment?

The antipornography forces have not been very successful in the courts, but they may have won at least one battle in the war. The pornography issue has attracted the attention of politicians and attempts to regulate content seem destined to continue. It will be very interesting to follow the continuing clashes between First Amendment rights and those favoring restrictions on pornographic material to see whether the process of law will be influenced by the public debate.

It is also worth keeping in mind that the problem is no longer mainly one of books, magazines, and film. Pornographic videotapes are one of the fastest-growing segments of the videotape market. The growth in this market has undoubtedly influenced many of those who fear the effects of pornography. Should different standards apply to tapes? Should the fact that they can be viewed in the privacy of one's home make them less or more of a public concern? Congress and the Federal Communications Commission have attempted to establish penalties recently for both dial-a-porn services and for "indecent" speech on radio and television. The ease of making and copying videotapes makes pornographic tapes a more difficult regulatory target. The relationship between the development of new communications technology and the pornography explosion is discussed in Katsh, *The Electronic Media and The Transformation of Law* (1989), pp. 181–189. The Supreme Court addressed the dial-a-porn issue in *Sable Communications of Cal., Inc. v. FCC,* 109 S.Ct. 2829 (1989).

The *Hudnut* case is discussed in Paul Brest and Ann Vandenberg, "Politics, Feminism, and the Constitution: The Anti-Pornography Movement in Minneapolis," 39 *Stanford Law Review* 607 (1987); Rebecca Benson, "Pornography and the First Amendment: *American Booksellers v. Hudnut,*" 9 *Harvard Women's Law Journal* 153 (1986); Final Report, Attorney General's Commission on Pornography (1986); Downs, *The New Politics of Pornography* (1989); C. MacKinnon, *Toward a Feminist Theory of the State* (1989); and C. MacKinnon, *Feminism Unmodified* (1989).

Recent writings on the problem of pornography include Symposium, *Law & Contemp. Probs.* v. 51 (Winter 1988); Hawkins and Zimring, *Pornography in a Free Society* (1989); C. McKinnion, "Pornography, Civil Rights, and Speech," 20 *Harvard Civil Rights–Civil Liberties Law Review* 1 (1985); A. Dworkin, *Pornography: Men Possessing Women* (1981); A. Dworkin, "Against The Male Flood: Censorship, Pornography and Equality," 8 *Harvard Women's Law Journal* 1 (1985); Note, "Feminism, Pornography and the Law," 133 *University of Pennsylvania Law Review* 497 (1985); and Note, "Anti-Pornography Laws and First Amendment Values," 98 *Harvard Law Review* 460 (1984). Child pornography was dealt with by the Supreme Court in *New York v. Ferber*, 458 U.S. 747. The most relevant obscenity case is *Miller v. California*, 413 U.S. 15 (1973).

ISSUE 10

Is Affirmative Action Constitutional?

YES: Thurgood Marshall, from Dissenting Opinion, *Regents of the University of California v. Allan Bakke,* U.S. Supreme Court (1978)

NO: Potter Stewart, from Dissenting Opinion, *Fullilove v. Klutznick,* U.S. Supreme Court (1980)

ISSUE SUMMARY

YES: Supreme Court justice Thurgood Marshall points to past discrimination and argues that we must find a way to compensate for the years of disadvantage.
NO: Justice Potter Stewart contends that the law and the Constitution must not discriminate on the basis of race, for whatever reason.

The most widely publicized Supreme Court case of the late 1970s was that of the *Regents of the University of California v. Allan Bakke,* 438 U.S. 265 (1978). Bakke had been denied admission to the medical school of the University of California at Davis even though he had ranked higher than some minority applicants who were admitted to the school. He sued, asserting that the affirmative action program, which reserved sixteen of one hundred places for minority students, discriminated against him because of his race and that "reverse discrimination" of this sort violated his constitutional right to equal protection of the laws.

In its decision, the Supreme Court held that Bakke should prevail and be admitted to the medical school. Rigid quotas, it was ruled, were indeed prohibited by the Constitution. More importantly, however, the Court also indicated that affirmative action programs that did not impose quotas would be permissible. Thus, if the University of California had an admissions program that gave some preference to an ethnic or racial group and that took race or sex into account along with test scores, geographical origins, extracurricular activities, etc., it would have been upheld. It is fair to say, therefore, that although Bakke won, the principle of affirmative action without rigid quotas also won.

The *Bakke* case, as is often the case with Supreme Court decisions, raised as many questions as it answered. It inevitably led to cases involving the validity of affirmative action programs in contexts different from that in *Bakke.* In *United Steelworkers v. Weber,* 443 U.S. 193 (1979), the Steelworkers

Union and the Kaiser Aluminum and Chemical Co. negotiated a collective bargaining agreement that set aside fifty percent of trainee positions for blacks, until their low percentage (two percent) among Kaiser craft employees rose to approximate their percentage (thirty-nine percent) in the local labor force. This case included a strict quota, but the Supreme Court upheld the program since it did not involve state action and was, according to Justice Powell, "adopted voluntarily" (even though it was begun in response to criticism by the Federal Office of Contract Compliance).

In 1989, in a case that did involve government, the Court ruled that a municipal public works program that allotted thirty percent of the funds for minority contractors was unconstitutional (*City of Richmond v. J. A. Croson Co.*, 109 S.Ct. 706, 1989). In the absence of some specific evidence of discrimination, such a program was held to violate the white contractors' rights to equal protection of the law. The case has been a major blow to local governmental efforts to increase minority involvement in construction, although similar programs mandated by Congress are still constitutional.

Should the law permit otherwise equal applicants to be treated differently on the basis of sex, race, or ethnic background? In the following excerpt from his dissenting opinion in the *Bakke* case, Justice Marshall argues that such a practice is necessary to remedy past injuries. In his dissent in the *Fullilove* case, Justice Stewart asserts that such preferences are impermissible and unconstitutional forms of discrimination.

In their opinions, the justices outline the legal reasons and principles for and against affirmative action programs. Yet, more is involved in these cases than the development of a consistent body of law. Affirmative action is an experiment that tests the power of law. In his exceptional book about the 1954 school desegregation cases, *Simple Justice*, Richard Kluger describes discussions in 1929 about what strategies could be used to promote the legal rights of southern blacks. At that time, Roger Baldwin of the American Civil Liberties Union expressed some skepticism that the law could be used to this end "because forces that keep the Negro under subjection will find some way of accomplishing their purposes, law or no law." Such an attitude toward affirmative action programs and their real impact upon institutions might not be inappropriate today. Affirmative action is legally required of public institutions and many private ones, but it is not yet clear that any substantial change has resulted. Nor is it clear that the judges of the Supreme Court agree on standards that would govern affirmative action plans that differ from the ones already ruled upon.

YES

Thurgood Marshall

COMPENSATION FOR PAST DISCRIMINATION

Mr. Justice Marshall dissenting.

I do not agree that petitioner's admissions program violates the Constitution. For it must be remembered that, during most of the past 200 years, the Constitution as interpreted by this Court did not prohibit the most ingenious and pervasive forms of discrimination against the Negro. Now, when a State acts to remedy the effects of that legacy of discrimination, I cannot believe that this same Constitution stands as a barrier.

I

A. Three hundred and fifty years ago, the Negro was dragged to this country in chains to be sold into slavery. Uprooted from his homeland and thrust into bondage for forced labor, the slave was deprived of all legal rights. It was unlawful to teach him to read; he could be sold away from his family and friends at the whim of his master; and killing or maiming him was not a crime. The system of slavery brutalized and dehumanized both master and slave.[1]

The denial of human rights was etched into the American Colonies' first attempts at establishing self-government. When the colonists determined to seek their independence from England, they drafted a unique document cataloguing their grievances against the King and proclaiming as "self-evident" that "all men are created equal" and are endowed "with certain unalienable Rights," including those to "Life, Liberty and the pursuit of Happiness." The self-evident truths and the unalienable rights were intended, however, to apply only to white men. An earlier draft of the Declaration of Independence, submitted by Thomas Jefferson to the Continental Congress, had included among the charges against the King that

"[h]e has waged cruel war against human nature itself, violating its most sacred rights of life and liberty in the persons of a distant people who never

From *Regents of the University of California v. Allan Bakke*, 98 S.Ct. 2733, 438 U.S. 265, 57 L.Ed. 2d 750 (1978).

offended him, captivating and carrying them into slavery in another hemisphere, or to incur miserable death in their transportation thither." Franklin 88.

The Southern delegation insisted that the charge be deleted; the colonists themselves were implicated in the slave trade, and inclusion of this claim might have made it more difficult to justify the continuation of slavery once the ties to England were severed. Thus, even as the colonists embarked on a course to secure their own freedom and equality, they ensured perpetuation of the system that deprived a whole race of those rights.

The implicit protection of slavery embodied in the Declaration of Independence was made explicit in the Constitution, which treated a slave as being equivalent to three-fifths of a person for purposes of apportioning representatives and taxes among the States. Art. I, § 2. The Constitution also contained a clause ensuring that the "Migration or Importation" of slaves into the existing States would be legal until at least 1808, Art. I, § 9, and a fugitive slave clause requiring that when a slave escaped to another State, he must be returned on the claim of the master, Art. IV, § 2. In their declaration of the principles that were to provide the cornerstone of the new Nation, therefore, the Framers made it plain that "we the people," for whose protection the Constitution was designed, did not include those whose skins were the wrong color. As Professor John Hope Franklin has observed, Americans "proudly accepted the challenge and responsibility of their new political freedom by establishing the machinery and safeguards that insured the continued enslavement of blacks." Franklin 100.

The individual States likewise established the machinery to protect the sys-tem of slavery through the promulgation of the Slave Codes, which were designed primarily to defend the property interest of the owner in his slave. The position of the Negro slave as mere property was confirmed by this Court in *Dred Scott v. Sandford,* 19 How. 393, 15 L.Ed. 691 (1857), holding that the Missouri Compromise—which prohibited slavery in the portion of the Louisiana Purchase Territory north of Missouri—was unconstitutional because it deprived slave owners of their property without due process. The Court declared that under the Constitution a slave was property, and "[t]he right to traffic in it, like an ordinary article of merchandise and property, was guaranteed to the citizens of the United States. . . ." *Id.,* at 451. The Court further concluded that Negroes were not intended to be included as citizens under the Constitution but were "regarded as beings of an inferior order . . . altogether unfit to associate with the white race, either in social or political relations; and so far inferior, that they had no rights which the white man was bound to respect. . . ." *Id.,* at 407.

B. The status of the Negro as property was officially erased by his emancipation at the end of the Civil War. But the long-awaited emancipation, while freeing the Negro from slavery, did not bring him citizenship or equality in any meaningful way. Slavery was replaced by a system of "laws which imposed upon the colored race onerous disabilities and burdens, and curtailed their rights in the pursuit of life, liberty, and property to such an extent that their freedom was of little value." *Slaughter-House Cases,* 16 Wall 36, 70, 21 L.Ed. (1873). Despite the passage of the Thirteenth, Fourteenth, and Fifteenth Amendments, the Negro was systematically denied the rights those Amendments were supposed to secure. The combined actions and inactions of the State and Federal Governments maintained Negroes in a position of legal inferiority for another century after the Civil War.

The Southern States took the first steps to re-enslave the Negroes. Immediately following the end of the Civil War, many of the provisional legislatures passed Black Codes, similar to the Slave Codes, which, among other things, limited the rights of Negroes to own or rent property and permitted imprisonment for breach of employment contracts. Over the next several decades, the South managed to disenfranchise the Negroes in spite of the Fifteenth Amendment by various techniques, including poll taxes, deliberately complicated balloting processes, property and literacy qualifications, and finally the white primary.

Congress responded to the legal disabilities being imposed in the Southern States by passing the Reconstruction Acts and the Civil Rights Acts. Congress also responded to the needs of the Negroes at the end of the Civil War by establishing the Bureau of Refugees, Freedmen, and Abandoned Lands, better known as the Freedmen's Bureau, to supply food, hospitals, land, and education to the newly freed slaves. Thus, for a time it seemed as if the Negro might be protected from the continued denial of his civil rights and might be relieved of the disabilities that prevented him from taking his place as a free and equal citizen.

That time, however, was short-lived. Reconstruction came to a close, and, with the assistance of this Court, the Negro was rapidly stripped of his new civil rights. In the words of C. Vann Woodward: "By narrow and ingenious

interpretation [the Supreme Court's] decisions over a period of years had whittled away a great part of the authority presumably given the government for protection of civil rights." Woodward 139.

The Court began by interpreting the Civil War Amendments in a manner that sharply curtailed their substantive protections. See, e.g., *Slaughter-House Cases, supra; United States v. Reese,* 92 U.S. 214, 23 L.Ed. 563 (1876); *United States v. Cruikshank,* 92 U.S. 542, 23 L.Ed. 588 (1876). Then in the notorious *Civil Rights Cases,* 109 U.S. 3, 3 S.Ct. 18, 27 L.Ed. 835 (1883), the Court strangled Congress' efforts to use its power to promote racial equality. In those cases the Court invalidated sections of the Civil Rights Act of 1875 that made it a crime to deny equal access to "inns, public conveyances, theatres and other places of public amusement." *Id.,* at 10, 3 S.Ct., at 20. According to the Court, the Fourteenth Amendment gave Congress the power to proscribe only discriminatory action by the State. The Court ruled that the Negroes who were excluded from public places suffered only an invasion of their social rights at the hands of private individuals, and Congress had no power to remedy that. *Id.,* at 24–25, 3 S.Ct., at 31. "When a man has emerged from slavery, and by the aid of beneficent legislation has shaken off the inseparable concomitants of that state," the Court concluded, "there must be some stage in the progress of his elevation when he takes the rank of a mere citizen, and ceases to be the special favorite of the laws. . . ." *Id.,* at 25, 3 S.Ct, at 31. As Mr. Justice Harlan noted in dissent, however, the Civil War Amendments and Civil Rights Acts did not make the Negroes the "special favorite" of the laws but instead "sought to accomplish in reference to that race . . . —what had already been done in every State of the Union for the white race—to secure and protect rights belonging to them as freemen and citizens; nothing more." *Id.*, at 61, 3 S.Ct, at 57.

The Court's ultimate blow to the Civil War Amendments and to the equality of Negroes came in *Plessy v. Ferguson*, 163 U.S. 537, 16 S.Ct. 1138, 41 L.Ed. 256 (1896). In upholding a Louisiana law that required railway companies to provide "equal but separate" accommodations for whites and Negroes, the Court held that the Fourteenth Amendment was not intended "to abolish distinctions based upon color, or to enforce social, as distinguished from political equality, or a commingling of the two races upon terms unsatisfactory to either." *Id.*, at 544, 16 S.Ct., at 1140. Ignoring totally the realities of the positions of the two races, the Court remarked:

> "We consider the underlying fallacy of the plaintiff's argument to consist in the assumption that the enforced separation of the two races stamps the colored race with a badge of inferiority. If this be so, it is not by reason of anything found in the act, but solely because the colored race chooses to put that construction upon it." *Id.*, at 551, 16 S.Ct., at 1143.

Mr. Justice Harlan's dissenting opinion recognized the bankruptcy of the Court's reasoning. He noted that the "real meaning" of the legislation was "that colored citizens are so inferior and degraded that they cannot be allowed to sit in public coaches occupied by white citizens." *Id.*, at 560, 16 S.Ct., at 1147. He expressed his fear that if like laws were enacted in other States, "the effect would be in the highest degree mischievous." *Id.*, at 563, 16 S.Ct., at 1148. Although slavery would

have disappeared, the States would retain the power "to interfere with the full enjoyment of the blessings of freedom; to regulate civil rights, common to all citizens, upon the basis of race; and to place in a condition of legal inferiority a large body of American citizens . . ." *Ibid.*

The fears of Mr. Justice Harlan were soon to be realized. In the wake of *Plessy*, many States expanded their Jim Crow laws, which had up until that time been limited primarily to passenger trains and schools. The segregation of the races was extended to residential areas, parks, hospitals, theaters, waiting rooms, and bathrooms. These were even statutes and ordinances which authorized separate phone booths for Negroes and whites, which required that textbooks used by children of one race be kept separate from those used by the other, and which required that Negro and white prostitutes be kept in separate districts. In 1898, after *Plessy*, the Charlestown News and Courier printed a parody of Jim Crow laws:

> " 'If there must be Jim Crow cars on the railroads, there should be Jim Crow cars on the street railways. Also on all passenger boats. . . . If there are to be Jim Crow cars, moreover, there should be Jim Crow waiting saloons at all stations, and Jim Crow eating houses. . . . There should be Jim Crow sections of the jury box, and a separate Jim Crow dock and witness stand in every court—and a Jim Crow Bible for colored witnesses to kiss.' " Woodward 68.

The irony is that before many years had passed, with the exception of the Jim Crow witness stand, "all the improbable applications of the principle suggested by the editor in derision had been put into practice—down to and including the Jim Crow Bible." *Id.*, at 69.

Nor were the laws restricting the rights of Negroes limited solely to the Southern States. In many of the Northern States, the Negro was denied the right to vote, prevented from serving on juries, and excluded from theaters, restaurants, hotels, and inns. Under President Wilson, the Federal Government began to require segregation in government buildings; desks of Negro employees were curtained off; separate bathrooms and separate tables in the cafeterias were provided; and even the galleries of the Congress were segregated. When his segregationist policies were attacked, President Wilson responded that segregation was "not humiliating but a benefit" and that he was "rendering [the Negroes] more safe in their possession of office and less likely to be discriminated against." Kluger 91.

The enforced segregation of the races continued into the middle of the 20th century. In both World Wars, Negroes were for the most part confined to separate military units; it was not until 1948 that an end to segregation in the military was ordered by President Truman. And the history of the exclusion of Negro children from white public schools is too well known and recent to require repeating here. That Negroes were deliberately excluded from public graduate and professional schools—and thereby denied the opportunity to become doctors, lawyers, engineers, and the like—is also well established. It is of course true that some of the Jim Crow laws (which the decisions of this Court had helped to foster) were struck down by this Court in a series of decisions leading up to *Brown v. Board of Education*, 347 U.S. 483, 74 S.Ct. 686, 98 L.Ed. 873 (1954). See, e.g., *Morgan*

v. Virginia, 328 U.S. 373, 66 S.Ct. 1050, 90 L.Ed. 1317 (1946); *Sweatt v. Painter*, 339 U.S. 629, 70 S.Ct. 848, 94 L.Ed. 1114 (1950); *McLaurin v. Oklahoma State Regents*, 339 U.S. 637, 70 S.Ct. 851, 94 L.Ed. 1149 (1950). Those decisions, however, did not automatically end segregation, nor did they move Negroes from a position of legal inferiority to one of equality. The legacy of years of slavery and of years of second-class citizenship in the wake of emancipation could not be so easily eliminated.

II

The position of the Negro today in America is the tragic but inevitable consequence of centuries of unequal treatment. Measured by any benchmark of comfort or achievement, meaningful equality remains a distant dream for the Negro.

A Negro child today has a life expectancy which is shorter by more than five years than that of a white child. The Negro child's mother is over three times more likely to die of complications in childbirth, and the infant mortality rate for Negroes is nearly twice that for whites. The median income of the Negro family is only 60% that of the median of a white family, and the percentage of Negroes who live in families with incomes below the poverty line is nearly four times greater than that of whites.

When the Negro child reaches working age, he finds that America offers him significantly less than it offers his white counterpart. For Negro adults, the unemployment rate is twice that of whites, and the unemployment rate for Negro teenagers is nearly three times that of white teenagers. A Negro male who completes four years of college can expect a median annual income of merely $110 more than a white male who has only a high school diploma. Although Negroes represent 11.5% of the population, they are only 1.2% of the lawyers, and judges, 2% of the physicians, 2.3% of the dentists, 1.1% of the engineers and 2.6% of the college and university professors.

The relationship between those figures and the history of unequal treatment afforded to the Negro cannot be denied. At every point from birth to death the impact of the past is reflected in the still disfavored position of the Negro.

In light of the sorry history of discrimination and its devastating impact on the lives of Negroes, bringing the Negro into the mainstream of American life should be a state interest of the highest order. To fail to do so is to ensure that America will forever remain a divided society.

III

I do not believe that the Fourteenth Amendment requires us to accept that fate. Neither its history nor our past cases lend any support to the conclusion that a university may not remedy the cumulative effects of society's discrimination by giving consideration to race in an effort to increase the number and percentage of Negro doctors.

A. This Court long ago remarked that

"in any fair and just construction of any section or phrase of these [Civil War] amendments, it is necessary to look to the purpose which we have said was the pervading spirit of them all, the evil which they were designed to remedy. . . ." *Slaughter-House Cases*, 16 Wall., at 72.

It is plain that the Fourteenth Amendment was not intended to prohibit measures designed to remedy the effects of the Nation's past treatment of Negroes. The Congress that passed the Fourteenth Amendment is the same Congress that passed the 1866 Freedmen's Bureau Act, an Act that provided many of its benefits only to Negroes. Act of July 16, 1866, ch. 200, 14 Stat. 173; see *supra*, at 2800. Although the Freedmen's Bureau legislation provided aid for refugees, thereby including white persons within some of the relief measures, 14 Stat. 174; see also Act of Mar. 3, 1865, ch. 90, 13 Stat. 507, the bill was regarded, to the dismay of many Congressmen, as "solely and entirely for the freedmen, and to the exclusion of all other persons. . . ." Cong. Globe, 39th Cong., 1st Sess., 544 (1866) (remarks of Rep. Taylor). See also *id.*, at 634–635 (remarks of Rep. Chanler). Indeed, the bill was bitterly opposed on the ground that it "undertakes to make the Negro in some respects . . . superior . . . and gives them favors that the poor white boy in the North cannot get." *Id.*, at 401 (remarks of Sen. McDougall). See also *id.*, at 319 (remarks of Sen. Hendricks); *id.*, at 362 (remarks of Sen. Saulsbury); *id.*, at 397 (remarks of Sen. Willey); *id.*, at 544 (remarks of Rep. Taylor). The bill's supporters defended it— not by rebutting the claim of special treatment—but by pointing to the need for such treatment:

"The very discrimination it makes between 'destitute and suffering' Negroes, and destitute and suffering white paupers, proceeds upon the distinction that, in the omitted case, civil rights and immunities are already sufficiently protected by the possession of political power, the absence of which in the case provided for necessitates governmental protection." *Id.*, at App. 75 (remarks of Rep. Phelps).

Despite the objection to the special treatment the bill would provide for Negroes, it was passed by Congress. *Id.*, at 421, 688. President Johnson vetoed this bill and also a subsequent bill that contained some modifications; one of his principle objections to both bills was that they gave special benefits to Negroes. 8 Messages and Papers of the Presidents 3596, 3599, 3620, 3623 (1897). Rejecting the concerns of the President and the bill's opponents, Congress overrode the President's second veto. Cong. Globe, 39th Cong., 1st Sess., 3842, 3850 (1866).

Since the Congress that considered and rejected the objections to the 1866 Freedmen's Bureau Act concerning special relief to Negroes also proposed the Fourteenth Amendment, it is inconceivable that the Fourteenth Amendment was intended to prohibit all race-conscious relief measures. It "would be a distortion of the policy manifested in that amendment, which was adopted to prevent state legislation designed to perpetuate discrimination on the basis of race or color." *Railway Mail Assn. v. Corsi*, 326 U.S. 88, 94, 65 S.Ct. 1483, 1487, 89 L.Ed. 2072 (1945), to hold that it barred state action to remedy the effects of that discrimination. Such a result would pervert the intent of the Framers by substituting abstract equality for the genuine equality the Amendment was intended to achieve.

B. As has been demonstrated in our joint opinion, this Court's past cases establish the constitutionality of race-conscious remedial measures. Beginning with the school desegregation cases, we recognized that even absent a judicial or legislative finding of constitutional violation, a school board constitutionally could consider the race of students in making school-assignment decisions.

See *Swann v. Charlotte-Mecklenburg Board of Education*, 402 U.S. 1, 16, 91 S. Ct. 1267, 1276, 28 L.Ed.2d 554 (1971); *McDaniel v. Barresi*, 402 U.S. 39, 41, 91 S.Ct. 1287, 1288, 28 L.Ed.2d 582 (1971). We noted, moreover, that a

> "flat prohibition against assignment of students for the purpose of creating a racial balance must inevitably conflict with the duty of school authorities to disestablish dual school systems. As we have held in *Swann*, the Constitution does not compel any particular degree of racial balance or mixing, but when past and continuing constitutional violations are found, some ratios are likely to be useful as starting points in shaping a remedy. An absolute prohibition against use of such a device—even as a starting point—contravenes the implicit command of *Green v. County School Board*, 391 U.S. 430 [88 S.Ct. 1689, 20 L.Ed.2d 716] (1968), that all reasonable methods be available to formulate an effective remedy." *Board of Education v. Swann*, 402 U.S. 43, 46, 91 S.Ct. 1284, 1286, 28 L.Ed.2d 586 (1971).

As we have observed, "[a]ny other approach would freeze the status quo that is the very target of all desegregation processes." *McDaniel v. Barresi, supra*, 402 U.S. at 41, 91 S.Ct. at 1289.

Only last Term, in *United Jewish Organizations v. Carey*, 430 U.S. 144, 97 S.Ct. 996, 51 L.Ed. 229 (1977), we upheld a New York reapportionment plan that was deliberately drawn on the basis of race to enhance the electoral power of Negroes and Puerto Ricans; the plan had the effect of diluting the electoral strength of the Hasidic Jewish community. We were willing in *UJO* to sanction the remedial use of a racial classification even though it disadvantaged otherwise "innocent" individuals. In another case last Term, *Califano v. Webster*, 430 U.S. 313,

97 S.Ct. 1192, 51 L.Ed.2d 360 (1977), the Court upheld a provision in the Social Security laws that discriminated against men because its purpose was "the permissible one of redressing our society's longstanding disparate treatment of women.' " *Id.*, at 317, 97 S.Ct. at 1195, quoting *Califano v. Goldfarb*, 430 U.S. 199, 209, n. 8, 97 S.Ct. 1021, 1028, 51 L.Ed.2d 270 (1977) (plurality opinion). We thus recognized the permissibility of remedying past societal discrimination through the use of otherwise disfavored classifications. . . .

IV

While I applaud the judgment of the Court that a university may consider race in its admissions process, it is more than a little ironic that, after several hundred years of class-based discrimination against Negroes, the Court is unwilling to hold that a class-based remedy for that discrimination is permissible. In declining to so hold, today's judgment ignores the fact that for several hundred years Negroes have been discriminated against, not as individuals, but rather solely because of the color of their skins. It is unnecessary in 20th-century America to have individual Negroes demonstrate that they have been victims of racial discrimination; the racism of our society has been so pervasive that none, regardless of wealth or position, has managed to escape its impact. The experience of Negroes in America has been different in kind, not just in degree, from that of other ethnic groups. It is not merely the history of slavery alone but also that a whole people were marked as inferior by the law. And that mark has endured. The dream of America as the great melting pot has not been realized for the Negro; be-

cause of his skin color he never even made it into the pot.

These differences in the experiences of the Negro make it difficult for me to accept that Negroes cannot be afforded greater protection under the Fourteenth Amendment where it is necessary to remedy the effects of past discrimination. In the *Civil Rights Cases, supra,* the Court wrote that the Negro emerging from slavery must cease "to be the special favorite of the laws." 109 U.S., at 25, 3 S.Ct., at 31, see *supra,* at 2800. We cannot in light of the history of the last century yield to that view. Had the Court in that decision and others been willing to "do for human liberty and the fundamental rights of American citizenship, what it did . . . for the protection of slavery and the rights of the masters of fugitive slaves," 109 U.S., at 53, 3 S.Ct., at 51 (Harlan, J., dissenting), we would not need now to permit the recognition of any "special wards."

Most importantly, had the Court been willing in 1896, in *Plessy v. Ferguson,* to hold that the Equal Protection Clause forbids differences in treatment based on race, we would not be faced with this dilemma in 1978. We must remember, however, that the principle that the "constitution is color-blind" appeared only in the opinion of the lone dissenter. 163 U.S., at 559, 16 S.Ct., at 1146. The majority of the Court rejected the principle of color-blindness, and for the next 58 years, from *Plessy* to *Brown v. Board of Education,* ours was a Nation where, *by law,* an individual could be given "special" treatment based on the color of his skin.

It is because of a legacy of unequal treatment that we now must permit the institutions of this society to give consideration to race in making decisions about who will hold the positions of influence, affluence, and prestige in America. For far too long, the doors to those positions have been shut to Negroes. If we are ever to become a fully integrated society, one in which the color of a person's skin will not determine the opportunities available to him or her, we must be willing to take steps to open those doors. I do not believe that anyone can truly look into America's past and still find that a remedy for the effects of that past is impermissible.

It has been said that this case involves only the individual, Bakke, and this University. I doubt, however, that there is a computer capable of determining the number of persons and institutions that may be affected by the decision in this case. For example, we are told by the Attorney General of the United States that at least 27 federal agencies have adopted regulations requiring recipients of federal funds to take "affirmative action to overcome the effects of conditions which resulted in limiting participation . . . by persons of a particular race, color, or national origin." Supplemental Brief for United States as *Amicus Curiae* 16 (emphasis added). I cannot even guess the number of state and local governments that have set up affirmative-action programs, which may be affected by today's decision.

I fear that we have come full circle. After the Civil War our Government started several "affirmative action" programs. This Court in the *Civil Rights Cases* and *Plessy v. Ferguson* destroyed the movement toward complete equality. For almost a century no action was taken, and this nonaction was with the tacit approval of the courts. Then we had *Brown v. Board of Education* and the Civil Rights Acts of Congress, followed by numerous affirmative-action programs. *Now*, we have this Court again stepping in, this time to stop affirmative-action programs of the type used by the University of California.

NOTES

1. The history recounted here is perhaps too well known to require documentation. But I must acknowledge the authorities on which I rely in retelling it. J. Franklin, *From Slavery to Freedom* (4th ed. 1974) (hereinafter Franklin); R. Kluger, *Simple Justice* (1975) (hereinafter Kluger); C. Woodward, *The Strange Career of Jim Crow* (3d ed. 1974) (hereinafter Woodward).

NO

Potter Stewart

THE CONSTITUTION AND DISCRIMINATION

Mr. Justice Stewart, with whom Mr. Justice Rehnquist joins, dissenting.

"Our Constitution is color-blind, and neither knows nor tolerates classes among citizens. . . . The law regards man as man, and takes no account of his surroundings or of his color. . . ." Those words were written by a Member of this Court 84 years ago. *Plessy v. Ferguson*, 163 U.S. 537, 16 S.Ct. 1138, 1146, 41 L.Ed. 256 (Harlan, J., dissenting). His colleagues disagreed with him, and held that a statute that required the separation of people on the basis of their race was constitutionally valid because it was a "reasonable" exercise of legislative power and had been "enacted in good faith for the promotion [of] the public good. . . ." *Id.*, at 550, 16 S.Ct., at 1143. Today, the Court upholds a statute that accords a preference to citizens who are "Negroes, Spanish-speaking, Orientals, Indians, Eskimos, and Aleuts," for much the same reasons. I think today's decision is wrong for the same reason that *Plessy v. Ferguson* was wrong, and I respectfully dissent.

A

The equal protection standard of the Constitution has one clear and central meaning—it absolutely prohibits invidious discrimination by government. That standard must be met by every State under the Equal Protection Clause of the Fourteenth Amendment. . . . And that standard must be met by the United States itself under the Due Process Clause of the Fifth Amendment. . . . Under our Constitution, any official action that treats a person differently on account of his race or ethnic origin is inherently suspect and presumptively invalid. . . .

The hostility of the Constitution to racial classifications by government has been manifested in many cases decided by this Court. . . . And our cases have made clear that the Constitution is wholly neutral in forbidding such racial discrimination, whatever the race may be of those who are its victims. In *Anderson v. Martin*, 375 U.S. 399, 84 S.Ct. 454, 11 L.Ed.2d 430, for instance,

From *Fullilove v. Klutznick*, 100 S.Ct. 2758, 448 U.S. 448, 65 L.Ed. 2d 902 (1980).

the Court dealt with a state law that required that the race of each candidate for election to public office be designated on the nomination papers and ballots. Although the law applied equally to candidates of whatever race, the Court held that it nonetheless violated the constitutional standard of equal protection. "We see *no relevance*," the Court said, "in the State's pointing up the race of the candidate as bearing upon his qualifications for office." *Id.*, at 403, 84 S.Ct., at 456 (emphasis added). Similarly, in *Loving v. Virginia, supra,* and *McLaughlin v. Florida, supra,* the Court held that statutes outlawing miscegenation and interracial cohabitation were constitutionally invalid, even though the laws penalized all violators equally. The laws were unconstitutional for the simple reason that they penalized individuals solely because of their race, whatever their race might be. . . .

This history contains one clear lesson. Under our Constitution, the government may never act to the detriment of a person solely because of that person's race. The color of a person's skin and the country of his origin are immutable facts that bear no relation to ability, disadvantage, moral culpability, or any other characteristics of constitutionally permissible interest to government. "Distinctions between citizens solely because of their ancestry are by their very nature odious to a free people whose institutions are founded upon the doctrine of equality." *Hirabayashi v. United States,* 320 U.S. 81, 100, 63 S.Ct. 1375, 1385, 87 L.Ed. 1774, quoted in *Loving v. Virginia, supra,* 388 U.S., at 11, 87 S.Ct., at 1823. In short, racial discrimination is by definition invidious discrimination.

The rule cannot be any different when the persons injured by a racially biased law are not members of a racial minority. The guarantee of equal protection is "universal in [its] application, to all persons . . . without regard to any differences of race, of color, or of nationality." *Yick Wo v. Hopkins,* 118 U.S. 356, 369, 6 S.Ct. 1064, 1070, 30 L.Ed. 220. . . . The command of the equal protection guarantee is simple but unequivocal: In the words of the Fourteenth Amendment, "No State shall . . . deny to *any* person . . . the equal protection of the laws." Nothing in this language singles out some "persons" for more "equal" treatment than others. Rather, as the Court made clear in *Shelley v. Kraemer,* 334, U.S. 1, 22, 68 S.Ct. 836, 846, 92 L.Ed. 1161 the benefits afforded by the Equal Protection Clause "are, by its terms, guaranteed to the individual. [They] are personal rights." From the perspective of a person detrimentally affected by a racially discriminatory law, the arbitrariness and unfairness is entirely the same, whatever his skin color and whatever the law's purpose, be it purportedly "for the promotion of the public good" and otherwise.

No one disputes the self-evident proposition that Congress has broad discretion under its Spending Power to disburse the revenues of the United States as it deems best and to set conditions on the receipt of the funds disbursed. No one disputes that Congress has the authority under the Commerce Clause to regulate contracting practices on federally funded public works projects, or that it enjoys broad powers under § 5 of the Fourteenth Amendment "to enforce by appropriate legislation" the provisions of that Amendment. But these self-evident truisms do not begin to answer the question before us in this case. For in the exercise of its powers,

Congress must obey the Constitution just as the legislatures of all the States must obey the Constitution in the exercise of their powers. If a law is unconstitutional, it is no less unconstitutional just because it is a product of the Congress of the United States.

B

On its face, the minority business enterprise (MBE) provision at issue in this case denies the equal protection of the law. The Public Works Employment Act of 1977 directs that all project construction shall be performed by those private contractors who submit the lowest competitive bids and who meet established criteria of responsibility. 42 U.S.C. § 6705(e)(1) (1976 ed. Supp. I). One class of contracting firms—defined solely according to the racial and ethnic attributes of their owners—is, however, excepted from the full rigor of these requirements with respect to a percentage of each federal grant. The statute, on its face and in effect, thus bars a class to which the petitioners belong from having the opportunity to receive a government benefit, and bars the members of that class solely on the basis of their race or ethnic background. This is precisely the kind of law that the guarantee of equal protection forbids.

The Court's attempt to characterize the law as a proper remedial measure to counteract the effects of past or present racial discrimination is remarkably unconvincing. The Legislative Branch of government is not a court of equity. It has neither the dispassionate objectivity nor the flexibility that are needed to mold a race-conscious remedy around the single objective of eliminating the effects of past or present discrimination.

But even assuming that Congress has the power, under § 5 of the Fourteenth Amendment or some other constitutional provision, to remedy previous illegal racial discrimination, there is no evidence that Congress has in the past engaged in racial discrimination in its disbursement of federal contracting funds. The MBE provision thus pushes the limits of any such justification far beyond the equal protection standard of the Constitution. Certainly, nothing in the Constitution gives Congress any greater authority to impose detriments on the basis of race than is afforded the Judicial Branch. And a judicial decree that imposes burdens on the basis of race can be upheld only where its sole purpose is to eradicate the actual effects of illegal race discrimination. . . .

The provision at issue here does not satisfy this condition. Its legislative history suggests that it had at least two other objectives in addition to that of counteracting the effects of past or present racial discrimination in the public works construction industry. One such purpose appears to have been to assure to minority contractors a certain percentage of federally funded public works contracts. But, since the guarantee of equal protection immunizes from capricious governmental treatment "persons"—not "races," it can never countenance laws that seek racial balance as a goal in and of itself. "Preferring members of any group for no reason other than race or ethnic origin is discrimination for its own sake. This the Constitution forbids." *Regents of the University of California v. Bakke*, 438 U.S. 265, 307, 98 S.Ct. 2733, 2757, 57 L.Ed.2d 750 (opinion of Powell, J.). Second, there are indications that the MBE provision may have been enacted to compensate for the effects of social, educational, and economic disadvantage. No race, however, has a monopoly on social, educational, or economic disadvantage, and any law that indulges in such a presumption clearly violates the constitutional guarantee of equal protection. Since the MBE provision was in whole or in part designed to effectuate objectives other than the elimination of the effects of racial discrimination, it cannot stand as a remedy that comports with the strictures of equal protection, even if it otherwise could.

C

The Fourteenth Amendment was adopted to ensure that every person must be treated equally by each State regardless of the color of his skin. The Amendment promised to carry to its necessary conclusion a fundamental principle upon which this Nation had been founded—that the law would honor no preference based on lineage. Tragically, the promise of 1868 was not immediately fulfilled, and decades passed before the States and the Federal Government were finally directed to eliminate detrimental classifications based on race. Today, the Court derails this achievement and places its imprimatur on the creation once again by government of privileges based on birth.

The Court, moreover, takes this drastic step without, in my opinion, seriously considering the ramifications of its decision. Laws that operate on the basis of race require definitions of race. Because of the Court's decision today, our statute books will once again have to contain laws that reflect the odious practice of delineating those qualities that make one person a Negro and make another white. Moreover, racial discrimination, even "good faith" racial discrimination, is inevitably a two-edged sword. "[P]referential programs may only reinforce common stereotypes holding that certain groups are unable to achieve success without special protection based on a factor having no relationship to individual worth." *University of California Regents v. Bakke, supra,* 438 U.S., at 298, 98 S.Ct., at 2753 (opinion of Powell, J.). Most importantly, by making race a relevant criterion once again in its own affairs, the Government implicitly teaches the public that the apportionment of rewards and penalties can legitimately be made according to race—rather than according to merit or ability—and that people can, and perhaps should, view themselves and others in terms of their racial characteristics. Notions of "racial entitlement" will be fostered, and private discrimination will necessarily be encouraged. . . .

There are those who think that we need a new Constitution, and their views may someday prevail. But under the Constitution we have, one practice in which government may never engage is the practice of racism—not even "temporarily" and not even as an "experiment."

POSTSCRIPT

Is Affirmative Action Constitutional?

One of the major surprises of the 1989–90 Supreme Court term occurred on its last day. The Court, by a 5–4 vote, upheld a federal affirmative action program that gave minorities some preferences in obtaining braodcasting licenses. The purpose of increasing diversity in voices and opinions on the air was held to be a valid one. In Addition, the majority felt that Congress has more discretion than state or local governments to adopt programs that take race into account (*Metro Broadcasting v. FCC*, 58 U.S.L.W. 5053, 1990).

The study of the question of affirmative action calls for an interdisciplinary approach. Justices Marshall and Stewart focus primarily on the legal issue of whether such programs violate the Fourteenth Amendment guarantee of equal protection of the laws. Yet beyond the legal issue are philosophical problems of morality and justice, economic issues involving employment and the distribution of scarce resources, and sociological and psychological analyses of racism and sexism.

Affirmative action programs force us to take an honest look at our own attitudes and at the nature of our society. What are the attitudes and practices of our institutions with respect to race and sex? What would we like such attitudes and practices to be in the future? What means should be employed to move us from the current state of affairs to where we would like to be?

Recent litigation in the affirmative action area is discussed in Devins, "Affirmative Action After Reagan," 68 *Tex. L. Rev.* 353 (1989); "Constitutional Scholars' Statement on Affirmative Action After *City of Richmand v. J. A. Croson Co.*," 98 *Yale Law Journal* 1711 (1989); Fried, "Affirmative Action After *City of Richmond v. J. A. Croson Co.*: A Response to the Scholars' Statement," 99 *Yale Law Journal* 155 (1989); and Schwartz, "The 1986 and 1987 Affirmative Action Cases: It's All Over But the Shouting," 86 *Michigan Law Review* 524 (1987). One of the most enlightening law review articles defending affirmative action is Wasserstrom, "Racism, Sexism and Preferential Treatment: An Approach to the Topics," 24 *UCLA Law Review*, pp. 581–622 (1977). A history of the *Bakke* case is found in Dreyfuss and Lawrence, *The Bakke Case: The Politics of Inequality* (Harcourt Brace Jovanovich, 1979).

ISSUE 11

Can States Restrict the Right to Die?

YES: William Rehnquist, from Majority Opinion, *Cruzan v. Director, Missouri Department of Health,* U.S. Supreme Court (1990)

NO: William J. Brennan, Jr., from Dissenting Opinion, *Cruzan v. Director, Missouri Department of Health,* U.S. Supreme Court (1990)

ISSUE SUMMARY

YES: Chief Justice William Rehnquist recognizes that a competent individual may refuse medical treatment but requires a showing of clear and convincing proof of the individual's wishes before allowing the termination of feeding to an incompetent person.

NO: Justice William Brennan argues that the Court is erecting too high a standard for allowing the individual's wishes to be followed and that Nancy Cruzan did indeed wish to have her feeding discontinued.

> To please no one will I prescribe a deadly drug, nor give advice which may cause death. . . .
>
> *—Oath of Hippocrates*

When a dispute gets to court, the issues before the court tend to be framed differently from the way they are stated in the popular press or in discussions among individuals. Legal discussions in court emphasize different issues from discussions among lay people even when the topic is the same. For example, the substantive question of what the result should be in a particular case, the kind of debate that one often finds on editorial pages of newspapers, may not be the main question in a legal case. Instead, the legal question for the court may be what is the proper procedure to follow, or who has the right or authority to do something, leaving the decision of whether or not to perform the act up to the person who has won the case.

One of the most publicized cases of the 1970s involved twenty-one-year-old Karen Ann Quinlan. Miss Quinlan was in a coma, her doctors did not believe she would ever come out of the coma, and all believed, erroneously it turned out, that if her respirator were removed she would stop breathing. The question the court focused on was who had authority over the respirator and who should bear the responsibility for what was done. The court did not answer the question of whether the respirator should be disconnected in this case, and left this tormenting problem to the party that prevailed in the case.

Soon after the decision, Miss Quinlan's parents authorized the removal of the respirator. Contrary to what had been predicted, this did not result in her death. She survived another nine years before succumbing in 1985.

The process followed in the Quinlan case, and in the Cruzan case that follows, illustrates a basic distinction made by the law. The law prohibits active euthanasia, in which death results from some positive act, such as a lethal injection. "Mercy killings" fall into this category and can be prosecuted as acts of homicide. The law is more tolerant of passive euthanasia, in which death results from the failure to act or on the removal of life-saving equipment. As you read the following opinions, you should consider whether this is a reasonable distinction to make.

While modern debates about euthanasia can be traced back more than one hundred years, the necessity for the legal system to become involved is more recent. Not all of these cases raise the same issues. The Quinlan case involved a person who was neither legally dead nor, according to medical opinion, ever likely to regain consciousness. She was unable to make the decision herself and the key question was whose interests needed to be given priority and how the interests of the individual should be protected. The following case, in that it involves the termination of feeding rather than the removal of life support equipment, is more difficult. Or is it? Due to advances in medical technology, some of the traditional distinctions made in this area are not as clear as they once were. As Alexander Capron, a professor of law at the University of Southern California and a knowledgeable observer in this area, has written,

> The growing medicalization of death also meant that human interventions replaced natural processes. If pneumonia was once the old man's friend, his companion now is an antibiotic; if cardiopulmonary arrest once meant inevitable death, now the cries of 'Code Blue' echo down hospital corridors, as nurses and physicians race to the bedside to jump-start hearts with drugs and electric paddles, and to reinflate lungs with artificial pumps. We have gotten to the point . . . when in the age of miracle drugs and surgical derring-do, no illness can be said to have a natural course. There is no such thing as a 'natural' death. Somewhere along the way for just about every patient, death is forestalled by human choice and human action, or death is allowed to occur because of human choice. Life-support techniques make death a matter of human choice and hence a matter that provokes ethical concern. Who should make the choice? When? And on what grounds?

The *Cruzan* case that follows was probably the most discussed Supreme Court decision of the 1989–90 term. Nancy Cruzan, age 32, had been in a coma for the last seven years. She is one of an estimated 10,000 persons in the United States in a "vegetative state." She had left no explicit directions on whether or not she would like to continue to be fed and receive treatment if she were ever to be in such a condition. Should her parents be allowed to make this decision under such circumstances? How clear should an incompetent person's wishes be before the parents are allowed to make a decision?

YES

William Rehnquist

MAJORITY OPINION OF
WILLIAM REHNQUIST

CHIEF JUSTICE REHNQUIST delivered the opinion of the Court.

Petitioner Nancy Beth Cruzan was rendered incompetent as a result of severe injuries sustained during an automobile accident. Co-petitioners Lester and Joyce Cruzan, Nancy's parents and co-guardians, sought a court order directing the withdrawal of their daughter's artificial feeding and hydration equipment after it became apparent that she had virtually no chance of recovering her cognitive faculties. The Supreme Court of Missouri held that because there was no clear and convincing evidence of Nancy's desire to have life-sustaining treatment withdrawn under such circumstances, her parents lacked authority to effectuate such a request. We granted certiorari, and now affirm.

On the night of January 11, 1983, Nancy Cruzan lost control of her car as she traveled down Elm Road in Jasper County, Missouri. The vehicle overturned, and Cruzan was discovered lying face down in a ditch without detectable respiratory or cardiac function. Paramedics were able to restore her breathing and heartbeat at the accident site, and she was transported to a hospital in an unconscious state. An attending neurosurgeon diagnosed her as having sustained probable cerebral contusions, compounded by significant anoxia (lack of oxygen). The Missouri trial court in this case found that permanent brain damage generally results after 6 minutes in an anoxic state; it was estimated that Cruzan was deprived of oxygen from 12 to 14 minutes. She remained in a coma for approximately three weeks and then progressed to an unconscious state in which she was able to orally ingest some nutrition. In order to ease feeding and further the recovery, surgeons implanted a gastrostomy feeding and hydration tube in Cruzan with the consent of her then husband. Subsequent rehabilitative efforts proved unavailing. She now lies in a Missouri state hospital in what is commonly referred to as a persistent vegetative state: generally, a condition in which a person exhibits motor reflexes but evinces no indications of significant cognitive function.[1]

From *Nancy Beth Cruzan v. Director, Missouri Department of Health*, 58 L.W. 4916 (1990). Some notes and case citations omitted.

The State of Missouri is bearing the cost of her care.

After it had become apparent that Nancy Cruzan had virtually no chance of regaining her mental faculties her parents asked hospital employees to terminate the artificial nutrition and hydration procedures. All agree that such a removal would cause her death. The employees refused to honor the request without court approval. The parents then sought and received authorization from the state trial court for termination. The court found that a person in Nancy's condition had a fundamental right under the State and Federal Constitutions to refuse or direct the withdrawal of "death prolonging procedures." The court also found that Nancy's "expressed thoughts at age twenty-five in somewhat serious conversation with a housemate friend that if sick or injured she would not wish to continue her life unless she could live at least halfway normally suggests that given her present condition she would not wish to continue on with her nutrition and hydration."

The Supreme Court of Missouri reversed by a divided vote. The court recognized a right to refuse treatment embodied in the common-law doctrine of informed consent, but expressed skepticism about the application of that doctrine in the circumstances of this case. *Cruzan v. Harmon*, 760 S. W. 2d 408, 416–417 (Mo. 1988) (en banc). The court also declined to read a broad right of privacy into the State Constitution which would "support the right of a person to refuse medical treatment in every circumstance," and expressed doubt as to whether such a right existed under the United States Constitution. *Id.*, at 417–418. It then decided that the Missouri Living Will statute, Mo. Rev. State. § 459.010 *et seq.* (1986), embodied a state policy strongly favoring the preservation of life. 760 S. W. 2d, at 419–420. The court found that Cruzan's statements to her roommate regarding her desire to live or die under certain conditions were "unreliable for the purpose of determining her intent," *id.*, at 424, "and thus insufficient to support the co-guardians claim to exercise substituted judgment on Nancy's behalf." *Id.*, at 426. It rejected the argument that Cruzan's parents were entitled to order the termination of her medical treatment, concluding that "no person can assume that choice for an incompetent in the absence of the formalities required under Missouri's Living Will statutes or the clear and convincing, inherently reliable evidence absent here." *Id.*, at 425. The court also expressed its view that "[b]road policy questions bearing on life and death are more properly addressed by representative assemblies" than judicial bodies. *Id.*, at 426.

We granted certiorari to consider the question of whether Cruzan has a right under the United States Constitution which would require the hospital to withdraw life-sustaining treatment from her under these circumstances. . . .

Before the turn of the century, this Court observed that "[n]o right is held more sacred, or is more carefully guarded, by the common law, than the right of every individual to the possession and control of his own person, free from all restraint or interference of others, unless by clear and unquestionable authority of law." *Union Pacific R. Co. v. Botsford*, 141 U.S. 250, 251 (1891). This notion of bodily integrity has been embodied in the requirement that informed consent is generally required for medical treatment. Justice Cardozo, while on the Court of Appeals of New York, aptly described this doctrine: "Every human being of adult years and sound mind has a right to determine what shall be done with his own body; and a surgeon who performs an operation without his patient's consent commits an assault, for which he is liable in damages." *Schloendorff v. Society of New York Hospital*, 211 N. Y. 125, 129–30, 105 N. E. 92, 93 (1914). The informed consent doctrine has become firmly entrenched in American tort law.

The logical corollary of the doctrine of informed consent is that the patient generally possesses the right not to consent, that is, to refuse treatment. Until about 15 years ago and the seminal decision in *In re Quinlan*, 70 N. J. 10, 355 A. 2d 647, cert. denied *sub nom.*, *Garger v. New Jersey*, 429 U.S. 922 (1976), the number of right-to-refuse-treatment decisions were relatively few.[2] Most of the earlier cases involved patients who refused medical treatment forbidden by their religious beliefs, thus implicating First Amendment rights as well as common law rights of self-determination.[3] More recently, however, with the advance of medical technology capable of sustaining life well past the point where natural forces would have brought certain death in earlier times, cases involving the right to refuse life-sustaining treatment have burgeoned. See 760 S. W. 2d, at 412, n. 4 (collecting 54 reported decisions from 1976–1988).

In the *Quinlan* case, young Karen Quinlan suffered severe brain damage as the result of anoxia, and entered a persistent vegetative state. Karen's father sought judicial approval to disconnect his daughter's respirator. The New Jersey Supreme Court granted the relief, holding that Karen had a right of privacy grounded in the Federal Constitution to terminate treatment. *In re Quinlan*, 70 N. J., at 38–42, 355 A. 2d at 662–664. Recog-

nizing that this right was not absolute, however, the court balanced it against asserted state interests. Noting that the State's interest "weakens and the individual's right to privacy grows as the degree of bodily invasion increases and the prognosis dims," the court concluded that the state interests had to give way in that case. *Id.*, at 41, 355 A. 2d, at 664. The court also concluded that the "only practical way" to prevent the loss of Karen's privacy right due to her incompetence was to allow her guardian and family to decide "whether she would exercise it in these circumstances." *Ibid.*

After *Quinlan*, however, most courts have based a right to refuse treatment either solely on the common law right to informed consent or on both the common law right and a constitutional privacy right. See L. Tribe, American Constitutional Law § 15–11, p. 1365 (2d ed. 1988). In *Superintendent of Belchertown State School v. Saikewicz*, 373 Mass. 728, 370 N. E. 2d 417 (1977), the Supreme Judicial Court of Massachusetts relied on both the right of privacy and the right of informed consent to permit the withholding of chemotherapy from a profoundly-retarded 67-year-old man suffering from leukemia. *Id.*, at 737–738, 370 N. E. 2d, at 424. Reasoning that an incompetent person retains the same rights as a competent individual "because the value of human dignity extends to both," the court adopted a "substituted judgment" standard whereby courts were to determine what an incompetent individual's decision would have been under the circumstances. *Id.*, at 745, 752–753, 757–758, 370 N. E. 2d, at 427, 431, 434. Distilling certain state interests from prior case law—the preservation of life, the protection of the interests of innocent third parties, the prevention of suicide, and the maintenance of the ethical integrity of the medical profession—the court recognized the first interest as paramount and noted it was greatest when an affliction was curable, "as opposed to the State interest where, as here, the issue is not whether, but when, for how long, and at what cost to the individual [a] life may be briefly extended." *Id.*, at 742, 370 N. E. 2d, at 426.

In *In re Storar* 52 N. Y. 2d 363, 420 N. E. 2d 64, cert. denied, 454 U.S. 858 (1981), the New York Court of Appeals declined to base a right to refuse treatment on a constitutional privacy right. Instead, it found such a right "adequately supported" by the informed consent doctrine. *Id.*, at 376–377, 420 N. E. 2d, at 70. In *In re Eichner* (decided with *In re Storar*, *supra*) an 83-year-old man who had suffered brain damage from anoxia entered a vegetative state and was thus incompetent to consent to the removal of his respirator. The court, however, found it unnecessary to reach the question of whether his rights could be exercised by others since it found the evidence clear and convincing from statements made by the patient when competent that he "did not want to be maintained in a vegetable coma by use of a respirator." *Id.*, at 380, 420 N. E. 2d, at 72. In the companion *Storar* case, a 52-year-old man suffering from bladder cancer had been profoundly retarded during most of his life. Implicitly rejecting the approach taken in *Saikewicz*, *supra*, the court reasoned that due to such life-long incompetency, "it is unrealistic to attempt to determine whether he would want to continue potentially life prolonging treatment if he were competent." 52 N. Y. 2d, at 380, 420 N. E. 2d, at 72. As the evidence showed that the patient's required blood transfusions did not involve excessive pain and without them his mental and physical abilities would deteriorate, the court concluded that it should not "allow an incompetent patient to bleed to death because someone, even someone as close as a parent or sibling, feels that this is best for one with an incurable disease." *Id.*, at 382, 420 N. E. 2d, at 73.

Many of the later cases build on the principles established in *Quinlan*, *Saikewicz* and *Storar/Eichner*. For instance, in *In re Conroy*, 98 N. J. 321, 486 A. 2d 1209 (1985), the same court that decided *Quinlan* considered whether a nasogastric feeding tube could be removed from an 84-year-old incompetent nursing-home resident suffering irreversible mental and physical ailments. While recognizing that a federal right of privacy might apply in the case, the court, contrary to its approach in *Quinlan*, decided to base its decision on the common-law right to self-determination and informed consent. 98 N. J., at 348, 486 A. 2d, at 1223. "On balance, the right to self-determination ordinarily outweighs any countervailing state interests, and competent persons generally are permitted to refuse medical treatment, even at the risk of death. Most of the cases that have held otherwise, unless they involved the interest in protecting innocent third parties, have concerned the patient's competency to make a rational and considered choice." *Id.*, at 353–354, 486 A. 2d, at 1225.

Reasoning that the right of self-determination should not be lost merely because an individual is unable to sense a violation of it, the court held that incompetent individuals retain a right to refuse treatment. It also held that such a right could be exercised by a surrogate decisionmaker using a "subjective" standard when there was clear evidence that the incompetent person would have exercised it. Where such evidence was lacking, the court held that an individual's right could still be involved in certain circumstances under objective "best interest" standards. *Id.*, at 361–368, 486 A. 2d, at 1229–1233. Thus, if some trustworthy evidence existed that the individual would have wanted to terminate treatment, but not enough to clearly establish a person's wishes for purposes of the subjective standard, and the burden of a prolonged life from the experience of pain and suffering markedly outweighed its satisfactions, treatment could be terminated under a "limited-objective" standard. Where no trustworthy evidence existed, and a person's suffering would make the administration of life-sustaining treatment inhumane, a "pure-objective" standard could be used to terminate treatment. If none of these conditions obtained, the court held it was best to err in favor of preserving life. *Id.*, at 364–368, 486 A. 2d, at 1231–1233.

The court also rejected certain categorical distinctions that had been drawn in prior refusal-of-treatment cases as lacking substance for decision purposes: the distinction between actively hastening death by terminating treatment and passively allowing a person to die of a disease; between treating individuals as an initial matter versus withdrawing treatment afterwards; between ordinary versus extraordinary treatment; and between treatment by artificial feeding versus other forms of life-sustaining medical procedures. *Id.*, at 369–374, 486 N. E. 2d, at 1233–1237. As to the last item, the court acknowledged the "emotional significance" of food, but noted that feeding by implanted tubes is a "medical procedur[e] with inherent risks and possible side effects, instituted by skilled health-care providers to compensate for impaired physical functioning"

which analytically was equivalent to artificial breathing using a respirator. *Id.*, at 373, 486 A 2d, at 1236.[4]

In contrast to *Conroy*, the Court of Appeals of New York recently refused to accept less than the clearly expressed wishes of a patient before permitting the exercise of her right to refuse treatment by a surrogate decisionmaker. *In re Westchester County Medical Center on behalf of O'Connor*, 531 N. E. 2d 607 (1988) (*O'Connor*). There, the court, over the objection of the patient's family members, granted an order to insert a feeding tube into a 77-year-old woman rendered incompetent as a result of several strokes. While continuing to recognize a common-law right to refuse treatment, the court rejected the substituted judgment approach for asserting it "because it is inconsistent with our fundamental commitment to the notion that no person or court should substitute its judgment as to what would be an acceptable quality of life for another. Consequently, we adhere to the view that, despite its pitfalls and inevitable uncertainties, the inquiry must always be narrowed to the patient's expressed intent, with every effort made to minimize the opportunity for error." *Id.*, at 530, 531 N. E. 2d, at 613 (citation omitted). The court held that the record lacked the requisite clear and convincing evidence of the patient's expressed intent to withhold life-sustaining treatment. *Id.*, at 531–534, 531 N. E. 2d, at 613–615. . . .

In *In re Estate of Longeway*, 123 Ill. 2d 33, 549 N. E. 2d 292 (1989), the Supreme Court of Illinois considered whether a 76-year-old woman rendered incompetent from a series of strokes had a right to the discontinuance of artificial nutrition and hydration. Noting that the boundaries of a federal right of privacy were uncertain, the court found a right to refuse treatment in the doctrine of informed consent. *Id.*, at 43–45, 549 N. E. 2d, at 296–297. The court further held that the State Probate Act impliedly authorized a guardian to exercise a ward's right to refuse artificial sustenance in the event that the ward was terminally ill and irreversibly comatose. *Id.*, at 45–47, 549 N. E. 2d, at 298. Declining to adopt a best interests standard for deciding when it would be appropriate to exercise a ward's right because it "lets another make a determination of a patient's quality of life," the court opted instead for a substituted judgment standard. *Id.*, at 49, 549 N. E. 2d, at 299. Finding the "expressed intent" standard utilized in *O'Connor, supra*, too rigid, the court noted that other clear and convincing evidence of the patient's intent could be considered. 133 Ill. 2d, at 50–51, 549 N. E. 2d, at 300. The court also adopted the "consensus opinion [that] treats artificial nutrition and hydration as medical treatment." *Id.*, at 42, 549 N. E. 2d, at 296. Cf. *McConnell v. Beverly Enterprises-Connecticut, Inc.*, 209 Conn. 692, 705, 553 A. 2d 596, 603 (1989) (right to withdraw artificial nutrition and hydration found in the Connecticut Removal of Life Support Systems Act, which "provid[es] functional guidelines for the exercise of the common law and constitutional rights of self-determination"; attending physician authorized to remove treatment after finding that patient is in a terminal condition, obtaining consent of family, and considering expressed wishes of patient).[5]

As these cases demonstrate, the common-law doctrine of informed consent is viewed as generally encompassing the right of a competent individual to refuse medical treatment. Beyond that, these decisions demonstrate both similarity and diversity in their approach to deci-

sion of what all agree is a perplexing question with unusually strong moral and ethical overtones. State courts have available to them for decision a number of sources—state constitutions, statutes, and common law—which are not available to us. In this Court, the question is simply and starkly whether the United States Constitution prohibits Missouri from choosing the rule of decision which it did. This is the first case in which we have been squarely presented with the issue of whether the United States Constitution grants what is in common parlance referred to as a "right to die." We follow the judicious counsel of our decision in *Twin City Bank v. Nebeker*, 167 U.S. 197, 202 (1897), where we said that in deciding "a question of such magnitude and importance . . . it is the [better] part of wisdom not to attempt, by any general statement, to cover every possible phase of the subject."

The Fourteenth Amendment provides that no State shall "deprive any person of life, liberty, or property, without due process of law." The principle that a competent person as a constitutionally protected liberty interest in refusing unwanted medical treatment may be inferred from our prior decisions. In *Jacobson v. Massachusetts*, 197 U.S. 11, 24–30 (1905), for instance, the Court balanced an individual's liberty interest in declining an unwanted smallpox vaccine against the State's interest in preventing disease. . . .

Just this Term, in the course of holding that a State's procedures for administering antipsychotic medication to prisoners were sufficient to satisfy due process concerns, we recognized that prisoners possess "a significant liberty interest in avoiding the unwanted administration of antipsychotic drugs under the Due Process Clause of the Fourteenth Amendment." *Washington v. Harper,* (1990) ("The forcible injection of medication into a nonconsenting person's body represents a substantial interference with that person's liberty"). Still other cases support the recognition of a general liberty interest in refusing medical treatment. *Vitek v. Jones,* 445 U.S. 480, 494 (1980) (transfer to mental hospital coupled with mandatory behavior modification treatment implicated liberty interests); *Parham v. J.R.,* 442 U.S. 584, 600 (1979) ("a child, in common with adults, has a substantial liberty interest in not being confined unnecessarily for medical treatment").

But determining that a person has a "liberty interest" under the Due Process Clause does not end the inquiry; "whether respondent's constitutional rights have been violated must be determined by balancing his liberty interests against the relevant state interests." *Youngberg v. Romeo,* 457 U.S. 307, 321 (1982). See also *Mills v. Rogers,* 457 U.S. 291, 299 (1982).

Petitioners insist that under the general holdings of our cases, the forced administration of life-sustaining medical treatment, and even of artificially-delivered food and water essential to life, would implicate a competent person's liberty interest. Although we think the logic of the cases discussed above would embrace such a liberty interest, the dramatic consequences involved in refusal of such treatment would inform the inquiry as to whether the deprivation of that interest is constitutionally permissible. But for purposes of this case, we assume that the United States Constitution would grant a competent person a constitutionally protected right to refuse lifesaving hydration and nutrition.

Petitioners go on to assert that an incompetent person should possess the same right in this respect as is possessed by a competent person. They rely primarily on our decisions in *Parham v. J. R., supra,* and *Youngberg v. Romeo,* 457 U.S. 307 (1982). In *Parham,* we held that a mentally disturbed minor child had a liberty interest in "not being confined unnecessarily for medical treatment," 442 U.S. at 600, but we certainly did not intimate that such a minor child, after commitment, would have a liberty interest in refusing treatment. In *Youngberg,* we held that a seriously retarded adult had a liberty interest in safety and freedom from bodily restraint, 457 U.S., at 320. *Youngberg,* however, did not deal with decisions to administer or withhold medical treatment.

The difficulty with petitioners' claim is that in a sense it begs the question: an incompetent person is not able to make an informed and voluntary choice to exercise hypothetical right to refuse treatment or any other right. Such a "right" must be exercised for her, if at all, by some sort of surrogate. Here, Missouri has in effect recognized that under certain circumstances a surrogate may act for the patient in electing to have hydration and nutrition withdrawn in such a way as to cause death, but it has established a procedural safeguard to assure that the action of the surrogate conforms as best it may to the wishes expressed by the patient while competent. Missouri requires that evidence of the incompetent's wishes as to the withdrawal of treatment be proved by clear and convincing evidence. The question, then, is whether the United States Constitution forbids the establishment of this procedural requirement by the State. We hold that it does not.

Whether or not Missouri's clear and convincing evidence requirement comports with the United States Constitution depends in part on what interests the State may properly seek to protect in this situation. Missouri relies on its interest in the protection and preservation of human life, and there can be no gainsaying this interest. As a general matter, the States—indeed, all civilized nations—demonstrate their commitment to life by treating homicide as serious crime. Moreover, the majority of States in this country have laws imposing criminal penalties on one who assists another to commit suicide. We do not think a State is required to remain neutral in the face of an informed and voluntary decision by a physically-able adult to starve to death.

But in the context presented here, a State has more particular interests at stake. The choice between life and death is a deeply personal decision of obvious and overwhelming finality. We believe Missouri may legitimately seek to safeguard the personal element of this choice through the imposition of heightened evidentiary requirements. It cannot be disputed that the Due Process Clause protects an interest in life as well as an interest in refusing life-sustaining medical treatment. Not all incompetent patients will have loved ones available to serve as surrogate decisionmakers. And even where family members are present, "[t]here will, of course, be some unfortunate situations in which family members will not act to protect a patient." *In re Jobes*, 108 N. J. 394, 419, 529 A. 2d 434, 477 (1987). A State is entitled to guard against potential abuses in such situations. Similarly, a State is entitled to consider that a judicial proceeding to make a determination regarding an incompetent's wishes may very well not be an adversarial one, with the added guarantee of accurate factfinding that the adversary process brings with it. Finally, we think a State

may properly decline to make judgments about the "quality" of life that a particular individual may enjoy, and simply assert an unqualified interest in the preservation of human life to be weighed against the constitutionally protected interests of the individual.

In our view, Missouri has permissibly sought to advance these interests through the adoption of a "clear and convincing" standard of proof to govern such proceedings. "The function of a standard of proof, as that concept is embodied in the Due Process Clause and in the realm of factfinding, is to 'instruct the factfinder concerning the degree of confidence our society thinks he should have in the correctness of factual conclusions for a particular type of adjudication.' " *Addington v. Texas*, 441 U.S. 418, 423 (1979) (quoting *In re Winship*, 397 U.S. 358, 370 (1970) (Harlan, J., concurring)). "This Court has mandated an intermediate standard of proof—'clear and convincing evidence'—when the individual interests at stake in a state proceeding are both 'particularly important' and 'more substantial than mere loss of money.' " *Santosky v. Kramer*, 455 U.S. 745, 756 (1982) (quoting *Addington, supra*, at 424). Thus, such a standard has been required in deportation proceedings, *Woodby v. INS*, 385 U.S. 276 (1966), in denaturalization proceedings, *Schneiderman v. United States*, 320 U.S. 118 (1943), in civil commitment proceedings, *Addington, supra*, and in proceedings for the termination of parental rights. *Santosky, supra*,[6] Further, this level of proof, "or an even higher one, has traditionally been imposed in cases involving allegations of civil fraud, and in a variety of other kinds of civil cases involving such issues as . . . lost wills, oral contracts to make bequests, and the like." *Woodby, supra*, at 285, n. 18.

We think it self-evident that the interests at stake in the instant proceedings are more substantial, both on an individual and societal level, than those involved in a run-of-the-mine civil dispute. But not only does the standard of proof reflect the importance of a particular adjudication, it also serves as "a societal judgment about how the risk of error should be distributed between the litigants." *Santosky, supra,* 455 U.S. at 755; *Addington, supra,* at 423. The more stringent the burden of proof a party must bear, the more that party bears the risk of an erroneous decision. We believe that Missouri may permissibly place an increased risk of an erroneous decision on those seeking to terminate an incompetent individual's life-sustaining treatment. An erroneous decision not to terminate results in a maintenance of the status quo; the possibility of subsequent developments such as advancments in medical science, the discovery of new evidence regarding the patient's intent, changes in the law, or simply the unexpected death of the patient despite the administration of life-sustaining treatment, at least create the potential that a wrong decision will eventually be corrected or its impact mitigated. An erroneous decision to withdraw life-sustaining treatment, however, is not susceptible of correction. In *Santosky,* one of the factors which led the Court to require proof by clear and convincing evidence in a proceeding to terminate parental rights was that a decision in such a case was final and irrevocable. *Santosky, supra,* at 759. The same must be said of the decision to discontinue hydration and nutrition of a patient such as Nancy Cruzan, which all agree will result in her death.

It is also worth noting that most, if not all, States simply forbid oral testimony entirely in determining the wishes of parties in transactions which, while important, simply do not have the consequences that a decision to terminate a person's life does. At common law and by statute in most States, the parole evidence rule prevents the variations of the terms of a written contract by oral testimony. The statute of frauds makes unenforceable oral contracts to leave property by will, and statutes regulating the making of wills universally require that those instruments be in writing. See 2 A. Corbin, Contracts § 398, pp. 360–361 (1950); 2 W. Page, Law of Wills § § 19.3–19.5, pp. 61–71 (1960). There is no doubt that statutes requiring wills to be in writing, and statutes of frauds which require that a contract to make a will be in writing, on occasion frustrate the effectuation of the intent of a particular decedent, just as Missouri's requirement of proof in this case may have frustrated the effectuation of the not-fully-expressed desires of Nancy Cruzan. But the Constitution does not require general rules to work faultlessly; no general rule can.

In sum, we conclude that a State may apply a clear and convincing evidence standard in proceedings where a guardian seeks to discontinue nutrition and hydration of a person diagnosed to be in a persistent vegetative state. We note that many courts which have adopted some sort of substituted judgment procedure in situations like this, whether they limit consideration of evidence to the prior expressed wishes of the incompetent individual, or whether they allow more general proof of what the individual's decision would have been, require a clear and convincing standard of proof for such evidence.

The Supreme Court of Missouri held that in this case the testimony adduced at trial did not amount to clear and convincing proof of the patient's desire to have hydration and nutrition withdrawn. In so doing, it reversed a decision of the Missouri trial court which had found that the evidence "suggest[ed]" Nancy Cruzan would not have desired to continue such measures, but which had not adopted the standard of "clear and convincing evidence" enunciated by the Supreme Court. The testimony adduced at trial consisted primarily of Nancy Cruzan's statements made to a housemate about a year before her accident that she would not want to live should she face life as a "vegetable," and other observations to the same effect. The observations did not deal in terms with withdrawal of medical treatment or of hydration and nutrition. We cannot say that the Supreme Court of Missouri committed constitutional error in reaching the conclusion that it did.[7]

Petitioners alternatively contend that Missouri must accept the "substituted judgment" of close family members even in the absence of substantial proof that their views reflect the views of the patient. They rely primarily upon our decisions in *Michael H. v. Gerald D.*, 491 U.S.——(1989), and *Parham v. J. R.*, 442 U.S. 584 (1979). But we do not think these cases support their claim. In *Michael H.*, we *upheld* the constitutionality of California's favored treatment of traditional family relationships; such a holding may not be turned around into a constitutional requirement that a State *must* recognize the primacy of those relationships in a situation like this. And in *Parham*, where the patient was a minor, we also *upheld* the constitutionality of a state scheme in which parents made certain decisions for mentally ill minors. Here again petitioners would seek to turn a decision which allowed a State to rely on family decisionmaking into a constitutional requirement that the State recognize such decisionmaking. But constitutional law does not work that way.

No doubt is engendered by anything in this record but that Nancy Cruzan's mother and father are loving and caring parents. If the State were required by the United States Constitution to repose a right of "substituted judgment" with anyone, the Cruzans would surely qualify. But we do not think the Due Process Clause requires the State to repose judgment on these matters with anyone but the patient herself. Close family members may have a strong feeling—a feeling not at all ignoble or unworthy, but not entirely disinterested, either—that they do not wish to witness the continuation of the life of a loved one which they regard as hopeless, meaningless, and even degrading. But there is no automatic assurance that the view of close family members will necessarily be the same as the patient's would have been had she been confronted with the prospect of her situation while competent. All of the reasons previously discussed for allowing Missouri to require clear and convincing evidence of the patient's wishes lead us to conclude that the state may choose to defer only to those wishes, rather than confide the decision to close family members.[8]

The judgment of the Supreme Court of Missouri is

Affirmed.

NOTES

1. The State Supreme Court, adopting much of the trial court's findings, described Nancy Cruzan's medical condition as follows:
" . . .(1) [H]er respiration and circulation are not artificially maintained and are within the normal

limits of a thirty-year-old female; (2) she is oblivious to her environment except for reflexive responses to sound and perhaps painful stimuli; (3) she suffered anoxia of the brain resulting in a massive enlargement of the ventricles filling with cerebrospinal fluid in the area where the brain has degenerated and [her] cerebral cortical atrophy is irreversible, permanent, progressive and ongoing; (4) her highest cognitive brain function is exhibited by her grimacing perhaps in recognition of ordinarily painful stimuli, indicating the experience of pain and apparent response to sound; (5) she is a spastic quadriplegic; (6) her four extremities are contracted with irreversible muscular and tendon damage to all extremities; (7) she has no cognitive or reflexive ability to swallow food or water to maintain her daily essential needs and . . . she will never recover her ability to swallow sufficient [sic] to satisfy her needs. In sum, Nancy is diagnosed as in a persistent vegetative state. She is not dead. She is not terminally ill. Medical experts testified that she could live another thirty years." *Cruzan v. Harmon,* 760 S. W. 2d 408, 411 (Mo. 1989) (en banc) (quotations omitted; footnote omitted).

In observing that Cruzan was not dead, the court referred to the following Missouri statute: "For all legal purposes, the occurrence of human death shall be determined in accordance with the usual and customary standards of medical practice, provided that death shall not be determined to have occurred unless the following minimal conditions have been met:

"(1) When respiration and circulation are not artificially maintained, there is an irreversible cessation of spontaneous respiration and circulation; or

"(2) When respiration and circulation are artificially maintained, and there is total irreversible cessation of all brain function, including the brain stem and that such determination is made by a licensed physician." Mo. Rev. Stat. § 194.005 (1986).

Since Cruzan's respiration and circulation were not being artificially maintained, she obviously fit within the first proviso of the statute.

Dr. Fred Plum, the creator of the term "persistent vegetative state" and a renowned expert on the subject, has described the "vegetative state" in the following terms:

" 'Vegetative state describes a body which is functioning entirely in terms of its internal controls. It maintains temperature. It maintains heart beat and pulmonary ventilation. It maintains digestive activity. It maintains reflex activity of muscles and nerves for low level conditioned responses. But there is no behavioral evidence of either self-awareness or awareness of the surroundings in a learned manner.' " *In re Jobes,* 108 N. J. 394, 403, 529 A. 2d 434, 438 (1987).

See also Brief for American Medical Association et al., as *Amici Curiae,* 6 ("The persistent vegetative state can best be understood as one of the conditions in which patients have suffered a loss of consciousness").

2. See generally Karnezis, Patient's Right to Refuse Treatment Allegedly Necessary to Sustain Life, 93 A. L. R. 3d 67 (1979) (collecting cases); Cantor, A Patient's Decision to Decline Life-Saving Medical Treatment: Bodily Integrity Versus the Preservation of Life, 26 Rutgers L. Rev. 228, 229, and n. 5 (1973) (noting paucity of cases).

3. See Chapman, The Uniform Rights of the Terminally Ill Act: Too Little, Too Late?, 42 Ark. L. Rev. 319, 324, n. 15 (1989); see also F. Rozovsky, Consent to Treatment, A Practical Guide 415–423 (2d ed. 1984).

4. In a later trilogy of cases, the New Jersey Supreme Court stressed that the analytic framework adopted in *Conroy* was limited to elderly, incompetent patients with shortened life expectancies, and established alternative approaches to deal with a different set of situations. See *In re Farrell,* 108 N. J. 335, 529 A. 2d 404 (1987) (37-year-old competent mother with terminal illness had right to removal of respirator based on common law and constitutional principles which overrode competing state interests); *In re Peter,* 108 N.J. 365, 529 A. 2d 419 (1987) (65-year-old woman in persistent vegetative state had right to removal of nasogastric feeding tube—under *Conroy* subjective test, power of attorney and hearsay testimony constituted clear and convincing proof of patient's intent to have treatment withdrawn); *In re Jobes,* 108 N. J. 394, 529 A. 2d 434 (1987) (31-year-old woman in persistent vegetative state entitled to removal of jejunostomy feeding tube—even though hearsay testimony regarding patient's intent insufficient to meet clear and convincing standard of proof, under *Quinlan,* family or close friends entitled to make a substituted judgment for patient).

5. Besides the Missouri Supreme Court in *Cruzan* and the courts in *McConnell, Longeway, Drabick, Bouvia, Barber, O'Connor, Conroy, Jobes,* and *Peter, supra,* appellate courts of at least four other States and one Federal District Court have specifically considered and discussed the issue of withholding or withdrawing artificial nutrition and hydration from incompetent individuals. See *Gray v. Romeo,* 697 F. Supp. 580 (RI 1988); *In re Gardner,* 534 A. 2d 947 (Me. 1987); *In re Grant,* 109 Wash. 2d 545, 747 P. 2d 445 (Wash. 1987); *Brophy v. New England Sinai Hospital, Inc.,* 398 Mass. 417, 497 N. E. 2d 626 (1986); *Corbett v. D'Alessandro,* 487 So. 2d 368 (Fla. App. 1986). All of these courts permitted or would permit the termination of such measures based on rights

grounded in the common law, or in the State or Federal Constitution.

6. We recognize that these cases involved instances where the government sought to take action against an individual. See *Price Waterhouse v. Hopkins*, 490 U.S.___, ___(1989) (plurality opinion). Here, by contrast, the government seeks to protect the interests of an individual, as well as its own institutional interests, in life. We do not see any reason why important individual interests should be afforded less protection simply because the government finds itself in the position of defending them. "[W]e find it significant that . . . the defendant rather than the plaintiff" seeks the clear and convincing standard of proof—"suggesting that this standard ordinarily serves as a shield rather than . . . a sword." *Id.*, at ___ . That it is the government that has picked up the shield should be of no moment.

7. The clear and convincing standard of proof has been variously defined in this context as "proof sufficient to persuade the trier of fact that the patient held a firm and settled commitment to the termination of life supports under the circumstances like those presented," *In re Westchester County Medical Center on behalf of O'Connor*, 72 N. Y. 2d 517, 531, N. E. 2d 607, 613 (1988) (*O'Connor*), and as evidence which "produces in the mind of the trier of fact a firm belief or conviction as to the truth of the allegations sought to be established, evidence so clear, direct and weighty and convincing as to enable [the factfinder] to come to a clear conviction, without hesitancy, of the truth of the precise facts in issue." *In re Jobes*, 108 N. J. at 407–408, 529 A. 2d, at 441 (quotation omitted). In both of these cases the evidence of the patient's intent to refuse medical treatment was arguably stronger than that presented here. The New York Court of Appeals and the Supreme Court of New Jersey, respectively, held that the proof failed to meet a clear and convincing threshold. See *O'Connor, supra*, at 526–534, 531 N. E. 2d, at 610–615; *Jobes, supra*, at 442–443.

8. We are not faced in this case with the question of whether a State might be required to defer to the decision of a surrogate if competent and probative evidence established that the patient herself had expressed a desire that the decision to terminate life-sustaining treatment be made for her by that individual. Petitioners also adumbrate in their brief a claim based on the Equal Protection Clause of the Fourteenth Amendment to the effect that Missouri has impermissibly treated incompetent parties differently from competent ones, citing the statement in *Cleburne v. Cleburne Living Center, Inc.*, 473 U.S. 432, 439 (1985), that the clause is "essentially a direction that all persons similarly situated should be treated alike." The differences between the choice made *by* a competent person to refuse medical treatment, and the choice made *for* an incompetent person by someone else to refuse medical treatment, are so obviously different that the State is warranted in establishing rigorous procedures for the latter class of cases which do not apply to the former class.

NO

William J. Brennan, Jr.

DISSENTING OPINION OF
WILLIAM J. BRENNAN, JR.

: . . JUSTICE BRENNAN, . . . dissenting.

"Medical technology has effectively created a twilight zone of suspended animation where death commences while life, in some form, continues. Some patients, however, want no part of a life sustained only by medical technology. Instead, they prefer a plan of medical treatment that allows nature to take its course and permits them to die with dignity."[1]

Nancy Cruzan has dwelt in that twilight zone for six years. She is oblivious to her surroundings and will remain so. Her body twitches only reflexively, without consciousness. The areas of her brain that once thought, felt, and experienced sensations have degenerated badly and are continuing to do so. The cavities remaining are filling with cerebrospinal fluid. The " 'cerebral cortical atrophy is irreversible, permanent, progressive and ongoing.' " "Nancy will never interact meaningfully with her environment again. She will remain in a persistent vegetative state until her death." Because she cannot swallow, her nutrition and hydration are delivered through a tube surgically implanted in her stomach.

A grown woman at the time of the accident, Nancy had previously expressed her wish to forgo continuing medical care under circumstances such as these. Her family and her friends are convinced that this is what she would want. A guardian ad litem appointed by the trial court is also convinced that this is what Nancy would want. See 760 S. W. 2d, at 444 (Higgins, J., dissenting from denial of rehearing). Yet the Missouri Supreme Court, alone among state courts deciding such a question, has determined that an irreversibly vegetative patient will remain a passive prisoner of medical technology—for Nancy, perhaps for the next 30 years. See *id.*, at 424, 427.

Today the Court, while tentatively accepting that there is some degree of constitutionally protected liberty interest in avoiding unwanted medical treatment, including life-sustaining medical treatment such as artificial

From *Nancy Beth Cruzan v. Director, Missouri Department of Health*, 58 L.W. 4916 (1990). Some notes and case citations omitted.

nutrition and hydration, affirms the decision of the Missouri Supreme Court. The majority opinion, as I read it, would affirm that decision on the ground that a State may require "clear and convincing" evidence of Nancy Cruzan's prior decision to forgo life-sustaining treatment under circumstances such as hers in order to ensure that her actual wishes are honored. Because I believe that Nancy Cruzan has a fundamental right to be free of unwanted artificial nutrition and hydration, which right is not outweighed by any interests of the State, and because I find that the improperly biased procedural obstacles imposed by the Missouri Supreme Court impermissibly burden that right, I respectfully dissent. Nancy Cruzan is entitled to choose to die with dignity.

I

A

"[T]he timing of death—once a matter of fate—is now a matter of human choice." Office of Technology Assessment Task Force, Life Sustaining Technologies and the Elderly 41 (1988). Of the approximately two million people who die each year, 80% die in hospitals and long-term care institutions,[2] and perhaps 70% of those after a decision to forgo life-sustaining treatment has been made.[3] Nearly every death involves a decision whether to undertake some medical procedure that could prolong the process of dying. Such decisions are difficult and personal. They must be made on the basis of individual values, informed by medical realities, yet within a framework governed by law. The role of the courts is confined to defining that framework, delineating

the ways in which government may and may not participate in such decisions.

The question before this Court is a relatively narrow one: whether the Due Process Clause allows Missouri to require a now-incompetent patient in an irreversible persistent vegetative state to remain on life-support absent rigorously clear and convincing evidence that avoiding the treatment represents the patient's prior, express choice. If a fundamental right is at issue, Missouri's rule of decision must be scrutinized under the standards this Court has always applied in such circumstances. As we said in *Zablocki v. Redhail*, 434 U.S. 374, 388 (1978), if a requirement imposed by a State "significantly interferes with the exercise of a fundamental right, it cannot be upheld unless it is supported by sufficiently important state interests and is closely tailored to effectuate only those interests." . . .

B

The starting point of our legal analysis must be whether a competent person has a constitutional right to avoid unwanted medical care. Earlier this Term, this Court held that the Due Process Clause of the Fourteenth Amendment confers a significant liberty interest in avoiding unwanted medical treatment. *Washington v. Harper*, (1990). Today, the Court concedes that our prior decisions "support the recognition of a general liberty interest in refusing medical treatment." The Court, however, avoids discussing either the measure of that liberty interest or its application by assuming, for purposes of this case only, that a competent person has a constitutionally protected liberty interest in being free of unwanted artificial nutrition and hydration. JUSTICE

O'CONNOR's opinion is less parsimonious. She openly affirms that "the Court has often deemed state incursions into the body repugnant to the interests protected by the Due Process Clause," that there is a liberty interest in avoiding unwanted medical treatment and that it encompasses the right to be free of "artificially delivered food and water."

But if a competent person has a liberty interest to be free of unwanted medical treatment, as both the majority and JUSTICE O'CONNOR concede, it must be fundamental. "We are dealing here with [a decision] which involves one of the basic civil rights of man." *Skinner v. Oklahoma ex rel. Williamson*, 316 U.S. 535, 541 (1942) (invalidating a statute authorizing sterilization of certain felons). Whatever other liberties protected by the Due Process Clause are fundamental, "those liberties that are 'deeply rooted in this Nation's history and tradition' " are among them. *Bowers v. Hardwick*, 478 U.S. 186, 192 (1986) (quoting *Moore v. East Cleveland, supra*, at 503 (plurality opinion).

The right to be free from medical attention without consent, to determine what shall be done with one's own body, *is* deeply rooted in this Nation's traditions, as the majority acknowledges. This right has long been "firmly entrenched in American tort law" and is securely grounded in the earliest common law. *Ibid*. See also *Mills v. Rogers*, 457 U.S. 291, 294, n. 4 (1982) ("the right to refuse any medical treatment emerged from the doctrines of trespass and battery, which were applied to unauthorized touchings of a physician"). " 'Anglo-American law starts with the premise of thoroughgoing self determination. It follows that each man is considered to be master of his own body, and he may, if he be of sound mind, expressly prohibit the performance of lifesaving surgery, or other medical treatment.' " *Natanson v. Kline*, 186 Kan. 393, 406–407, 350 P. 2d 1093, 1104 (1960). "The inviolability of the person" has been held as "sacred" and "carefully guarded" as any common law right. *Union Pacific R. Co. v. Botsford*, 141 U.S. 250, 251–252 (1891). Thus, freedom from unwanted medical attention is unquestionably among those principles "so rooted in the traditions and conscience of our people as to be ranked as fundamental." *Snyder v. Massachusetts*, 291 U.S. 97, 105 (1934).

That there may be serious consequences involved in refusal of the medical treatment at issue here does not vitiate the right under our common law tradition of medical self-determination. It is "a well-established rule of general law . . . that it is the patient, not the physician, who ultimately decides if treatment—any treatment—is to be given at all. . . . The rule has never been qualified in its application by either the nature or purpose of the treatment, or the gravity of the consequences of acceding to or foregoing it." *Tune v. Walter Reed Army Medical Hospital*, 602 F. Supp. 1452, 1455 (DC 1985). See also *Downer v. Veilleux*, 322 A. 2d 82, 91 (Me. 1974). . . .

No material distinction can be drawn between the treatment to which Nancy Cruzan continues to be subject—artificial nutrition and hydration—and any other medical treatment. The artificial delivery of nutrition and hydration is undoubtedly medical treatment. The technique to which Nancy Cruzan is subject—artificial feeding through a gastrostomy tube—involves a tube implanted surgically into her stomach through incisions in her abdominal wall. It may obstruct the intestinal tract, erode and pierce the stomach wall or cause leakage of the stomach's contents into the abdominal cavity. See Page, Andrassy, & Sandler, Techniques in Delivery of Liquid Diets, in Nutrition in Clinical Surgery 66–67 (M. Deitel 2d ed. 1985). The tube can cause pneumonia from reflux of the stomach's contents into the lung. See Bernard & Forlaw, Complications and Their Prevention, in Enteral and Tube Feeding 553 (J. Rombeau & M. Caldwell eds. 1984). Typically, and in this case, commercially prepared formulas are used, rather than fresh food. The type of formula and method of administration must be experimented with to avoid gastrointestinal problems. The patient must be monitored daily by medical personnel as to weight, fluid intake and fluid output; blood tests must be done weekly.

Artificial delivery of food and water is regarded as medical treatment by the medical profession and the Federal Government.[4] According to the American Academy of Neurology, "[t]he artificial provision of nutrition and hydration is a form of medical treatment . . . analogous to other forms of life-sustaining treatment, such as the use of the respirator. When a patient is unconscious, both a respirator and an artificial feeding device serve to support or replace normal bodily functions that are compromised as a result of the patient's illness." Position of the American Academy of Neurology on Certain Aspects of the Care and Management of the Persistent Vegetative State Patient, 39 Neurology 125 (Jan. 1989). See also Council on Ethical and Judicial Affairs of the American Medical Association, Current Opinions, Opinion 2.20 (1989) ("Life-prolonging medical treatment includes medication and artificially or technologically supplied respiration, nutrition or hydration"); President's Commission 88 (life-sustaining treatment includes respirators, kidney dialysis machines, special feeding procedures). The Federal Government permits the cost of the medical devices and formulas used in enteral feeding to be reimbursed under Medicare. The formulas are regulated by the Federal Drug Administration as "medical foods," and the feeding tubes are regulated as medical devices.

Nor does the fact that Nancy Cruzan is now incompetent deprive her of her fundamental rights. See Youngberg v. Romeo, 457 U.S. 307, 315–316, 319 (1982) (holding that severely retarded man's liberty interests in safety, freedom from bodily restraint and reasonable training survive involuntary commitment); Parham v. J. R., 442 U.S. 584, 600 (1979) (recognizing a child's substantial liberty interest in not being confined unnecessarily for medical treatment); Jackson v. Indiana, 406 U.S. 715, 730, 738 (1972) (holding that Indiana could not violate the due process and equal protection rights of a mentally retarded deaf mute by committing him for an indefinite amount of time simply because he was incompetent to stand trial on the criminal charges filed against him). As the majority recognizes, the question is not whether an incompetent has constitutional rights, but how such rights may be exercised. As we explained in Thompson v. Oklahoma, 487 U.S. 815 (1988), "[t]he law must often adjust the manner in which it affords rights to those whose status renders them unable to exercise choice freely and rationally. Children, the insane, and those who are irreversibly ill with loss of brain function, for instance, all retain 'rights,' to be sure, but often such rights are only meaningful as they are exercised by agents acting with the best interests of their principals in mind." Id., at 825, n. 23 (emphasis added). "To deny [its] exercise because the patient is unconscious or incompetent would be to deny the right." *Foody v. Manchester Memorial Hospital*, 40 Conn. Super. 127, 133, 482 A. 2d 713, 718 (1984). . . .

III

This is not to say that the State has no legitimate interests to assert here. As the majority recognizes, Missouri has a *parens patriae* interest in providing Nancy Cruzan, now incompetent, with as accurate as possible a determination of how she would exercise her rights under these circumstances. Second, if and when it is determined that Nancy Cruzan would want to continue treatment, the State may legitimately assert an interest in providing that treatment. But *until* Nancy's wishes have been determined, the only state interest that may be asserted is an interest in safeguarding the accuracy of that determination.

Accuracy, therefore, must be our touchstone. Missouri may constitutionally impose only those procedural requirements that serve to enhance the accuracy of a determination of Nancy Cruzan's wishes or are at least consistent with an accurate determination. The Missouri "safeguard" that the Court upholds today does not meet that standard. The determination needed in this context is whether the incompetent person would choose to live in a persistent vegetative state on life-support or to avoid this medical treatment. Missouri's rule of decision imposes a markedly asymmetrical evidentiary burden. Only evidence of specific statements of treatment choice made by the patient when competent is admissible to support a finding that the patient, now in a persistent vegetative state, would wish to avoid further medical treatment. Moreover, this evidence

must be clear and convincing. No proof is required to support a finding that the incompetent person would wish to continue treatment.

A

The majority offers several justifications for Missouri's heightened evidentiary standard. First, the majority explains that the State may constitutionally adopt this rule to govern determinations of an incompetent's wishes in order to advance the State's substantive interests, including its unqualified interest in the preservation of human life. Missouri's evidentiary standard, however, cannot rest on the State's own interest in a particular substantive result. To be sure, courts have long erected clear and convincing evidence standards to place the greater risk of erroneous decisions on those bringing disfavored claims. In such cases, however, the choice to discourage certain claims was a legitimate, constitutional policy choice. In contrast, Missouri has not such power to disfavor a choice by Nancy Cruzan to avoid medical treatment, because Missouri has no legitimate interest in providing Nancy with treatment until it is established that this represents her choice. Just as a State may not override Nancy's choice directly, it may not do so indirectly through the imposition of a procedural rule. . . .

The majority claims that the allocation of the risk of error is justified because it is more important not to terminate life-support for someone who would wish it continued than to honor the wishes of someone who would not. An erroneous decision to terminate life-support is irrevocable, says the majority, while an erroneous decision not to terminate "results in a maintenance of the status quo." But, from the point of view of the patient, an erroneous decision in either direction is irrevocable. An erroneous decision to terminate artificial nutrition and hydration, to be sure, will lead to failure of that last remnant of physiological life, the brain stem, and result in complete brain death. An erroneous decision not to terminate life-support, however, robs a patient of the very qualities protected by the right to avoid unwanted medical treatment. His own degraded existence is perpetuated; his family's suffering is protracted; the memory he leaves behind becomes more and more distorted.

Even a later decision to grant him his wish cannot undo the intervening harm. But a later decision is unlikely in an event. "[T]he discovery of new evidence," to which the majority refers, is more hypothetical than plausible. The majority also misconceives the relevance of the possibility of "advancements in medical science," by treating it as a reason to force someone to continue medical treatment against his will. The possibility of a medical miracle is indeed part of the calculus, but it is a part of the *patient's* calculus. If current research suggests that some hope for cure or even moderate improvement is possible within the life-span projected, this is a factor that should be and would be accorded significant weight in assessing what the patient himself would choose.[5] . . .

C

I do not suggest that States must sit by helplessly if the choices of incompetent patients are in danger of being ignored. Even if the Court had ruled that Missouri's rule of decision is unconstitutional, as I believe it should have, States would nevertheless remain free to fashion procedural protections to safeguard the interests of incompetents under these circumstances. The Constitution provides merely a framework here: protections must be genuinely aimed at ensuring decisions commensurate with the will of the patient, and must be reliable as instruments to that end. Of the many states which have instituted such protections, Missouri is virtually the only one to have fashioned a rule that lessens the likelihood of accurate determinations. In contrast, nothing in the Constitution prevents States from reviewing the advisability of a family decision, by requiring a court proceeding or by appointing an impartial guardian ad litem. . . .

D

Finally, I cannot agree with the majority that when it is not possible to determine what choice an incompetent patient would make, a State's role as *parens patriae* permits the State automatically to make that choice itself. . . . Under fair rules of evidence, it is improbable that a court could not determine what the patient's choice would be. Under the rule of decision adopted by Missouri and upheld today by this Court, such occasions might be numerous. But in neither case does it follow that it is constitutionally acceptable for the State invariably to assume the role of deciding for the patient. A State's legitimate interest in safeguarding a patient's choice cannot be furthered by simply appropriating it.

The majority justifies its position by arguing that, while close family members may have a strong feeling about the question, "there is no automatic assurance that the view of close family members will necessarily be the same as the patient's would have been had she been confronted with the prospect of her situation while competent." I cannot quarrel with this observation. But it leads only to another question: Is there any reason to suppose that a State is *more* likely to make the choice that the patient would have made than someone who knew the patient intimately? To ask this is to answer it. As the New Jersey Supreme Court observed: "Family members are best qualified to make substituted judgments for incompetent patients not only because of their peculiar grasp of the patient's approach to life, but also because of their special bonds with him or her. . . . It is . . . they who treat the patient as a person, rather than a symbol of a cause." *In re Jobes*, 108 N. J. 394, 416, 529 A. 2d 434, 445 (1987). The State, in contrast, is a stranger to the patient.

A State's inability to discern an incompetent patient's choice still need not mean that a State is rendered powerless to protect that choice. But I would find that the Due Process Clause prohibits a State from doing more than that. A State may ensure that the person who makes the decision on the patient's behalf is the one whom the patient himself would have selected to make that choice for him. And a State may exclude from consideration anyone having improper motives. But a State generally must either repose the choice with the person whom the patient himself would most likely have chosen as proxy or leave the decision to the patient's family.[6]

IV

As many as 10,000 patients are being maintained in persistent vegetative states in the United States, and the number is expected to increase significantly in the near future. Medical technology, developed over the past 20 or so years, is often capable of resuscitating people after they have stopped breathing or their hearts have stopped beating. Some of those people are brought fully back to life. Two decades ago, those who were not and could not swallow and digest food, died. Intravenous solutions could not provide sufficient calories to maintain people for more than a short time. Today, various forms of artificial feeding have been developed that are able to keep people metabolically alive for years, even decades. See Spencer & Palmisano, Specialized Nutritional Support of Patients— A Hospital's Legal Duty?, 11 Quality Rev. Bull. 160, 160–161 (1985). In addition, in this century, chronic or degenerative ailments have replaced communicable diseases as the primary causes of death. See R. Weir, Abating Treatment with Critically Ill Patients 12–13 (1989); President's Commission 15–16. The 80% of Americans who die in hospitals are "likely to meet their end . . . 'in a sedated or comatose state; betubed nasally, abdominally and intravenously; and far more like manipulated objects than like moral subjects.' "[7] A fifth of all adults surviving to age 80 will suffer a progressive dementing disorder prior to death. See Cohen & Eisdorfer, Dementing Disorders, in The Practice of Geriatrics 194 (E. Calkins, P. Davis, & A, Ford eds. 1986).

"[L]aw, equity and justice must not themselves quail and be helpless in the face of modern technological marvels presenting questions hitherto unthought of." *In re Quinlan*, 70 N. J. 10, 44, 355 A. 2d 647, 665, cert. denied, 429 U.S. 922 (1976). The new medical technology can reclaim those who would have been irretrievably lost a few decades ago and restore them to active lives. For Nancy Cruzan, it failed, and for others with wasting incurable disease it may be doomed to failure. In these unfortunate situations, the bodies and preferences and memories of the victims do not escheat to the State; nor does our Constitution permit the State or any other government to commandeer them. No singularity of feeling exists upon which such a government might confidently rely as *parens patriae*. The President's Commission, after years of research, concluded:

"In few areas of health care are people's evaluations of their experiences so varied and uniquely personal as in their assessments of the nature and value of the processes associated with dying. For some, every moment of life is of inestimable value; for others, life without some desired level of mental or physical ability is worthless or burdensome. A moderate degree of suffering may be an important means of personal growth and religious experience to one person, but only frightening or despicable to another." President's Commission 276.

Yet Missouri and this Court have displaced Nancy's own assessment of the processes associated with dying. They have discarded evidence of her will, ignored her values, and deprived her of the right to a decision as closely approximating her own choice as humanly possible. They have done so disingenuously in her name, and openly in Missouri's own. That Missouri and this Court may truly be motivated only by concern for incompetent patients makes no matter. As one of our most prominent jurists warned us decades ago: "Experience should teach us to be most on our guard to protect liberty when the government's

purposes are beneficent. . . . The greatest dangers to liberty lurk in insidious encroachment by men of zeal, well meaning but without understanding." *Olmstead v. United States*, 277 U.S. 438, 479 (1928) (Brandeis, J., dissenting).

I respectfully dissent.

NOTES

1. *Rasmussen v. Fleming*, 154 Arix. 207, 211, 741 P. 2d 674, 678 (1987) (en banc).

2. See President's Commission for the Study of Ethical Problems in Medicine and Biomedical and Behavioral Research, Deciding to Forego Life Sustaining Treatment 15, n. 1, and 17–18 (1983) (hereafter President's Commission).

3. See Lipton, Do-Not-Resuscitate Decisions in a Community Hospital: Incidence, Implications and Outcomes, 256 JAMA 1164, 1168 (1986).

4. The Missouri court appears to be alone among state courts to suggest otherwise, 760 S. W. 2d, at 419 and 423, although the court did not rely on a distinction between artificial feeding and other forms of medical treatment. *Id.*, at 423. See, *e. g.*, *Delio v. Westchester County Medical Center*, 129 App. Div. 2d 1, 19, 516 N. Y. S. 2d 677, 689 (1987) ("review of the decisions in other jurisdictions . . . failed to uncover a single case in which a court confronted with an application to discontinue feeding by artificial means has evaluated medical procedures to provide nutrition and hydration differently from other type of life-sustaining procedures").

5. For Nancy Cruzan, no such cure or improvement is in view. So much of her brain has deteriorated and been replaced by fluid, that apparently the only medical advance that could restore consciousness to her body would be a brain transplant.

6. Only in the exceedingly rare case where the State cannot find any family member or friend who can be trusted to endeavor genuinely to make the treatment choice the patient would have made does the State become the legitimate surrogate decisionmaker.

7. Fadiman, The Liberation of Lolly and Gronky, Life Magazine, Dec. 1986, p. 72 (quoting medical ethicist Joseph Fletcher).

POSTSCRIPT

Can States Restrict the Right to Die?

The fundamental concern in right to die cases, indeed in most civil liberties cases, is the fear of what will happen in the next case. In other words, a judge may avoid doing what seems reasonable in one case if his ruling could be used to reach a less desirable result in a future case with slightly different facts. Lawyers refer to this as the "slippery slope." If euthanasia is justified in a case where the patient is terminally ill and in severe pain, it may be allowed in a later case where, as in *Cruzan*, the patient is in an unrecoverable state but not in pain. Perhaps euthanasia would be extended to handicapped newborns or to the senile.

Underlying the slippery slope argument in these cases, as in the abortion cases, is the fear of what might happen if life in some instances is not considered to be sacred. A member of the prosecution staff at the Nuremberg trials of Nazi doctors who participated in the killing of "incurables" and the "useless" traced the origin of Nazi policy to

> a subtle shift in emphasis in the basic attitude of the physicians. It started with the acceptance of the attitude, basic in the euthanasia movement, that there is such a thing as the life not worthy to be lived. This attitude in its early stages concerned itself merely with the severely and chronically sick. Gradually, the sphere of those to be included in this category was enlarged to encompass the socially unproductive, the ideologically unwanted, the racially unwanted and finally all non-Germans. But it is important to realize that the infinitely small wedged-in lever from which this entire trend received its impetus was the attitude toward the unrehabilitatable sick. (Kamisar, see below)

Considering the decisions in the *Cruzan* case, how do you feel about the slippery slope argument? Does the majority opinion, by allowing alert and competent patients to choose to remove feeding tubes, start us down the slippery slope? Does establishing a "clear and convincing" standard effectively halt the slide down the slope? Even if you feel that the slide down the slope has not begun, it is also true that there will be more cases to follow *Cruzan*. For example, what if there is disagreement between hospital and family officials about whether the patient's wishes are "clear and convincing?" What happens if the patient is conscious but in great pain and receiving large doses of pain medication? Who are the parties who should be entitled to be heard if a case gets to court? What is to be done if there is disagreement among family members?

One effect of the Court's opinion is to encourage the use of living wills. Forty states and the District of Columbia have statutes permitting living wills, which allow individuals to specify in advance what treatment they would wish to receive. Most of these statutes apply only in cases of terminal illness, but the statutes are likely to be changed in the light of the *Cruzan* decision. Since less than half of the U.S. population have regular wills, the living will is unlikely to provide a total solution to the problem.

Other recent cases involving the withdrawal of treatment are *In the matter of Mary O'Connor,* 72 N.Y. 2d 517 (1988); *Brophy v. New England Sinai Hospital,* 497 N.E. 2d 626 (1986); *In re Conroy,* 486 A. 2d 1209 (1985); *Bovia v. The Superior Court of Los Angeles County,* 225 California Reporter 297 (1986); and *In re Quinlan,* 355 A. 2d 647 (1976). Recent analyses include "The Care of the Dying: A Symposium on the Case of Betty Wright," 17 *Law, Medicine and Health Care,* pp. 207–233 (1989); Weir, *Abating Treatment with Critically Ill Patients* (1989); Wennberg, *Terminal Choices: Euthanasia, Suicide and the Right to Die* (1989); Rhoden, "Litigating Life and Death," 102 *Harvard Law Review* 375 (1988); Note; "Judicial Postponement of Death Recognition: The Tragic Case of Mary O'Connor," 15 *American Journal of Law and Medicine* 301 (1990); Alexander Capron, "Legal and Ethical Problems in Decisions for Death," 14 *Law, Medicine and Health Care* 141 (1987); Norman Cantor, *Legal Frontiers of Death and Dying* (Indiana University Press, 1987); and *Guidelines on the Termination of Life-sustaining Treatment and the Care of the Dying: A Report by the Hastings Center* (1987).

Further worthwhile reading on euthanasia and the right to die may be found in Y. Kamisar, "Some Non-Religious Views Against Proposed 'Mercy Killing' Legislation," 42 *Minnesota Law Review* 969 (1958); *President's Commission for the Study of Ethical Problems in Medicine, Deciding to Forgo Lifesaving Treatment* (Washington, 1983); J. Lyon, *Playing God in the Nursery* (New York, 1985); and R. Weir, *Selective Treatment of Handicapped Newborns* (New York, 1984).

PART 3

Law and Crime

Crime is a fact of life for many citizens in the United States, and the social, economic, and psychic costs are high for individual victims and society as a whole. Every society has to contend with those members who refuse to adhere to the established rules of behavior; how criminals are treated is often one standard for judging a society's fairness and compassion.

The debates in this section address issues concerning the treatment of criminals and the legal rights of the accused as well as the rights of citizens to be free from fear.

Should the Death Penalty
 Be Abolished?

Should the Exclusionary Rule
 Be Abolished?

Should Drugs Be Legalized?

Should a National Gun Control Policy
 Be Established?

DNA Profiling: Should It Be Used to
 Convict Criminals?

Should the Insanity Defense Be
 Abolished?

ISSUE 12

Should the Death Penalty Be Abolished?

YES: Michael L. Radelet, from Statement before the Subcommittee on Criminal Justice of the House Judiciary Committee, *Hearings on the Death Penalty,* U.S. House of Representatives (July 16, 1987)

NO: Report of the Senate Judiciary Committee, from "Establishing Constitutional Procedures for the Imposition of Capital Punishment," *Congressional Record* (January 17, 1980)

ISSUE SUMMARY

YES: Michael Radelet, a professor of sociology at the University of Florida, is concerned about the growing acceptance of capital punishment in the United States and questions the state court's ability to correctly decide who should get the death penalty.
NO: The Judiciary Committee of the U.S. Senate reports on the need for capital punishment, both for its deterrent effect and as a means to protect society.

Unlike some of the issues in this book, capital punishment has a long history. For example, in 428 B.C., Thucydides recorded the following arguments by Cleon, in support of the death penalty:

> Punish them as they deserve, and teach your other allies by a striking example that the penalty of rebellion is death. Let them once understand this and you will not so often have to neglect your enemies while you are fighting with your confederates.

In response, Diodotus wrote:

> All states and individuals are alike prone to err, and there is no law that will prevent them, or why should men have exhausted the list of punishments in search of enactments to protect them from evil doers? It is probable that in early times the penalties for the greatest offenses were less severe, and that as these were disregarded, the penalty of death has been by degrees in most cases arrived at, which is itself disregarded in like manner. Either some means of terror more terrible than this must be discovered, or it must be owned that this restraint is useless. . . .
> We must make up our minds to look for our protection not to legal terrors but to careful administration. . . . Good policy against an adversary is superior to the blind attacks of brute force.

During the last two decades, the Supreme Court has been confronted with death penalty cases almost every year. The most significant decision was that of *Furman v. Georgia*, 408 U.S. 238, decided in 1972. Furman, a twenty-six-year-old black man, had killed a homeowner during a break-in and was sentenced to death. In a 5–4 decision, the Court overturned the sentence. It held that the procedure used by Georgia (and most other states at that time) was "cruel and unusual" and therefore a violation of the Eighth Amendment of the Constitution. At the heart of the case was the fact that Georgia law left it up to the discretion of the jury to decide whether or not the death penalty was appropriate in a particular case. Two justices, Marshall and Brennan, believed that the death penalty under any circumstances violated the cruel and unusual punishment clause. The three other justices in the majority, however, felt that the death penalty was not in itself unconstitutional but that the manner in which it was applied in this case was unlawful. They felt that leaving the sentence up to the jury led it to be "wantonly" and "freakishly" imposed and "pregnant with discrimination."

The short-term impact of the *Furman* case was to remove all individuals sentenced under pre-*Furman* laws from death row. The long-term message of the decision, however, was that the death penalty was lawful if the procedure that was employed limited the discretion of the person(s) meting out the punishment.

Since 1972, thirty-seven states have enacted new death penalty statutes. The following cases illustrate some of the difficulties involved in developing a consistent standard through a case-by-case approach.

1. *Gregg v. Georgia*, 428 U.S. 153 (1976)   After *Furman*, Georgia enacted a new statute retaining the death penalty for murder and five other crimes. Guilt or innocence was determined at a trial and then a second hearing or trial was held for the jury to determine whether the death penalty should be applied. The law set up procedures that were intended to limit the jury's discretion and that required higher court review of the sentence with the hope that this would reduce the incidence of discrimination and prejudice. In a 7–2 decision, this law was upheld by the Supreme Court.

2. *Lockett v. Ohio*, 438 U.S. 586 (1978)   Ohio law prevented the jury from considering any mitigating circumstances other than those specifically enumerated in the statute. The Supreme Court held that this law was unconstitutional.

3. *Coker v. Georgia*, 433 U.S. 584 (1977)   The Supreme Court held that the death penalty may not be imposed on persons convicted of rape. The case suggests that the death penalty is unconstitutional if a death did not take place as a result of the defendant's actions.

What these cases indicate is that the death penalty is lawful and not "cruel and unusual" if the victim has been killed, if the statute provides the defendant the opportunity to present mitigating circumstances, if the statute lists aggravating circumstances that must be considered, and if it requires appellate review. These procedural requirements have been imposed mainly to reduce the possibility of discriminatory application of the death penalty.

YES

Michael L. Radelet

STATEMENT OF MICHAEL L. RADELET

It would be only a slight overstatement to say that for the last fifteen years, the policy of most states on capital punishment has been to enact laws that would allow the execution of as many prisoners as our Constitution would allow. The result is that as we speak today there are over 1,900 death row inmates in our country, and it now seems that the only way out of the corner into which we have painted ourselves will be to execute at rates heretofore unseen in our nation's history. And, even if present rates double to a national pace of one execution per week, we will still not eliminate our current backlog of death row inmates until the year 2023.

Like slavery, our contemporary executions have thus far been exclusively a southern phenomenon. There have been 83 executions in the U.S. in the last 15 years. Two of these were in Indiana, two were in Nevada, and one took place in Utah. Each of these, however, occurred after the defendant fired his attorney and dropped his appeals. Excluding these consensual executions, the remaining 78 executions have all occurred in the former states of the Confederacy, and nine of the eleven states of the former Confederacy have executed at least one of these defendants. I hasten to add, however, that numerous northern and western states are trying their best to change this pattern.

Mr. Chairman, you and your colleagues are aware of the fact that whether it be through lynching or legally-imposed capital punishment, the threat or use of death as a punishment has been a powerful means of class and race intimidation throughout American history. In the nineteenth century, statutes that explicitly considered race were not uncommon. In Virginia, for example, the statutes of 150 years ago listed five capital crimes for whites but 70 for black slaves (Bowers, 1984:140). Today, Watt Espy, our country's foremost death penalty historian, uses records of state compensations to slave owners to learn how many slaves were executed. Of the 15,000 executions in our history for which we now have some information, a project on which I am currently working indicates there are only 29 cases in which a white was executed for killing a black. Most of these cases involved

From U.S. House. Committee on the Judiciary. Subcommittee on Criminal Justice. *Death Penalty.* Hearing, July 16, 1987. Washington, D.C.: Government Printing Office, 1987. (Serial No. 142)

defendants who also killed whites or killers of slaves who angered the victim's owner because the death of his slave represented an economic loss. There are no cases in our history in which a white was executed for the rape of a black woman.

The most significant (and arguably the only) progress made in the last 20 years in reducing racial disparities in executions was a 1977 Supreme Court decision that outlawed the death penalty for those convicted of rape (*Coker v. Georgia*, 433 U.S. 485). If we examine only executions for murder, we learn that between 1930 and 1967, 50.1 percent of the executions involved nonwhites (U.S. Department of Justice, 1986:12). Today, 49.3 percent of those on death row, all of whom stand convicted of murder, are nonwhite (NAACP Legal Defense and Educational Fund, 1987). Thus, all the efforts to revise death penalty statutes in the last 20 years and allegedly make them more fair have reduced the relevant minority population by less than one percent.

Mr. Chairman, I am not among those who can rest comfortably with the simplistic observation that the main reason why blacks are sentenced to death and executed at rates higher than their representation in our population is because blacks have a higher homicide rate. That observation, we all know, is true. But any thorough understanding of the problem of race and capital punishment must begin with a consideration of the racism that even the strongest death penalty advocates would agree plagued at least the first 150 years of our history. The plain fact is that the disproportionate rates of involvement of blacks in homicides can only be explained by this legacy of racism and its historical role in the destruction of black family structure

(Ryan, 1976). Although I realize that this is not news to you, the effects of the history of racism in this country will take generations to remove. And today no responsible person could argue that the chances of dying at the hands of the executioner are as high for the sons of the affluent and powerful as they are for those born into poor, black, or single-parent households. To pick parents who are drug addicts, alcoholics, or child abusers would also help increase a newborn infant's odds of eventually dying at the hands of our government. In short, our electric chairs will not be color blind until every American is truly born with an equal chance of dying in them. One could easily take the position that even if the criminal justice system was completely neutral in its administration of the death penalty, opposition to the punishment would still be warranted until the effects of our history of racism are eradicated and blacks no longer have disproportionate rates of involvement in violent crimes.

Nonetheless, the scholarly research on race and the death penalty does not directly explore this dimension of the problem. Instead, the research on race and capital punishment starts by recognizing that blacks have higher per capita rates of involvement in criminal homicides than do whites. The question for researchers thus becomes: given this differential involvement, or controlling for differential involvement, is there a differential response by the criminal justice system?

Using different methodologies, different data sets, and different states, researchers for diverse backgrounds and universities have answered the question affirmatively (Radelet and Vandiver, 1986). In fact, there have been no major studies on death sentencing patterns conducted in the last fifteen years that have failed to find a significant race effect. Even Arnold Barnett (1985), in his creative and thought-provoking reanalysis of data from Georgia, does not suggest that race is immaterial, although he accords it a smaller explanatory role than have other researchers. The evidence of racial disparities comes to us from a far wider geographical area than the evidence reviewed by the Supreme Court in its 1987 *McCleskey* decision (107 S.Ct. 1756).

Last year, this Subcommittee heard from three scholars whose work has examined this question: William Bowers, Samuel Gross, and David Baldus (Subcommittee on Criminal Justice, 1987). Bowers and his colleague Glenn Pierce (1980) examined over 16,000 homicide cases in Florida, Georgia, Texas, and Ohio and found that black defendants convicted of killing whites were more likely to receive the death penalty than were defendants in any of the other three racial categories. Similar patterns emerged when their analysis was restricted to homicides involving felony circumstances. Gross and Mauro (1984) used the FBI's Supplemental Homicide Reports to examine sentencing patterns in eight states: Arkansas, Florida, Georgia, Illinois, Mississippi, North Carolina, Oklahoma, and Virginia. They found "remarkably stable and consistent" discrimination, based on victim's race, in all the states, and these results held when several other factors which might affect sentencing decisions were statistically controlled. This Subcommittee has also heard from David Baldus, whose well-known work is, by any measure, the best study of capital sentencing ever conducted (Baldus et al., 1983; 1985; 1986). As you know, Professor

Baldus concluded that the odds of a death sentence for those charged with killing whites in Georgia were, after statistically controlling for 39 other factors, still 4.3 times higher than the odds of a death sentence for those charged with killing blacks. . . .

My records indicate, believe it or not, that since Florida's current death penalty statute took effect in December, 1972, there have been 490 death sentences or resentences handed out in the Sunshine State. While approximately 44 percent of the homicide victims in Florida over the last 15 years have been black, only about 10 percent of those sentenced to death were condemned for killing blacks (Radelet, 1985). My own work has focused on this disparity, and I am sorry to report that the reason for the skewed distribution is not simply that homicides with white victims tend to be more aggravated than are homicides with black victims.

In 1981, for example, I examined 637 Florida homicide cases (Radelet, 1981). I first restricted this sample to homicides between strangers, thus avoiding the objection that those who kill blacks may be more likely to kill family members, and thus less likely to be selected for execution, than those who kill whites. I found that, among stranger-killings, 14 percent of those with white victims and 5.4 percent of those with black victims were eventually condemned. Even after I further restricted this analysis to those who were indicted for first-degree murder, 16.5 percent of those with white victims and 10 percent of those with black victims were condemned.

In 1983, Margaret Vandiver and I explored the question of whether or not the members of the Florida Supreme Court were correcting these racial disparities in sentencing when they reviewed death penalty cases on direct appeal (Radelet and Vandiver, 1983). They are not. Our data set included the first 145 cases reviewed by the court under Florida's current death penalty statute. Because so few defendants with black victims were condemned, we could not ascertain the importance of victim's race at this decision point. We found, however, that black defendants with female victims were the most likely group to have their death sentences affirmed.

In 1985, I teamed up with Glenn Pierce to scrutinize prosecutorial discretion in a sample of 1,017 Florida homicides. We compared police and prosecutorial classifications of the homicides, as each had classified the homicide as a felony, possible felony, or nonfelony. We found a strong tendency for prosecutors to treat cases more severely in their upgrading and downgrading patterns if the cases had white victims and/or black defendants (Radelet and Pierce, 1985).

I should also mention that even when a person is sentenced to death for killing a black, extraneous factors may explain the outcome. In 1984, despite objections from the family of his victim, James Dupree Henry was executed for killing a black man in Orlando. Michael Mello and I examined all the press coverage of this crime in the pages of the *Orlando Sentinel* in the three-month period between the date of the homicide and the date of Henry's condemnation. Despite the fact that the victim was a leading civil rights activist in central Florida, his murder attracted only a small article in the second section of the newspaper. But three days later, when a white police officer was slightly wounded while taking Henry into custody, the case became front-page headlines. Our analysis revealed that over the next three months, the wounding of the police officer received over twice as much press coverage than the actual murder. While one case does not make a pattern, in this one the evidence was clear that the newspaper thought the assault on the white police officer was more newsworthy than was the murder of the prominent black citizen.

More evidence of racial disparities in death sentencing comes to us from South Carolina. In 1982, Joseph Jacoby and Raymond Paternoster, in an analysis of 205 homicide cases from the first 29 months after South Carolina's present death penalty statute was enacted, discovered that "(d)efendants who were charged with killing whites were 3.2 times more likely to have prosecutors seek the death penalty than those charged with killing blacks" (1982:384). Paternoster (1983; 1984) later extended that body of research to include all homicides with at least one aggravating factor in South Carolina through December 31, 1981. Again, similar patterns emerged. In addition, this work revealed that cases from rural areas were more likely than those from urban jurisdictions to end in a sentence of death.

The troubling correlations between race and death sentencing are not only found in the south, albeit the energies of researchers interested in this issue have focused on the south because of its high frequency of condemnations. But similar patterns can also be found elsewhere. In a study of 32 states, the *Dallas Times Herald* (Nov. 17, 1985) found that a murderer convicted of killing a white is almost three times more likely to receive a death sentence than if a black had been the victim. In California, 2.6 percent of those with black victims were condemned compared to 6.3 percent of those who killed whites. In Illinois it was 3.4 percent to 9.9 percent. In Maryland it was 1 percent vs. 7.3 percent. While some states (such as Pennsylvania) appear to be an exception to this pattern, the results indicate that a Baldus-type study using sophisticated control variables in most other states, northern and western states included, would expose disparities similar to those already revealed in the south.

The member of this Subcommittee are quite aware that the pro-death penalty response to these correlations is to acknowledge their existence, but then to argue that they can be explained by legally-relevant variables left out of the equations. Yet, when similar statistical models fail to find a deterrent effect of the death penalty, these same death penalty advocates are quick to argue that a correlation could be found if the models were more sophisticated, and that we should continue to execute as long as there is a chance of deterrence. When it deals with race they argue the correlations found by almost everyone can be explained away, and when it comes to deterrence they argue the lack of correlations found by almost everyone can be explained away. A slight chance of deterrence makes them pro-death penalty; a strong chance of racial bias is treated as irrelevant. Alternatively, death penalty advocates claim that statistical demonstration of racial disparities does not show intent to discriminate, but in the next breath go on to claim that the few statistical studies that allege to show a deterrent effect do measure intent: executions reduce the intent to murder. In this sense, when comparing the reactions to the studies of race with the studies of deterrence, death penalty ad-

vocates seem to want to have their cake and eat it, too.

Parenthetically, I have attached a statement made three years ago by every criminologist at the University of Florida, expressing our conclusion that there is no credible research at all that supports the contention that the threat or use of the death penalty is or has been a deterrent to homicide. We have all heard some politicians and a couple of economists argue that death has deterrent powers over and above life imprisonment, but I know of virtually no criminologists who would advance such a claim.

Mr. Chairman, I understand that other witnesses today will show this Subcommittee the problem of racial disparities in the administration of the death penalty overlaps with the ever-present risk that we are now taking of executing the innocent. As you know, for the last four years Professor Hugo Adam Bedau and I have been conducting research on miscarriages of justice in potentially capital cases. The results of that project will be available in a 200-page paper to be published by *Stanford Law Review* in November. In it we describe 350 cases in which innocent defendants were convicted of murder, or sentenced to death for rape, during this century. In over 300 of these cases, the state itself implicitly or explicitly admitted that a miscarriage had occurred. In 23 cases, a defendant we count as innocent was eventually executed.

Sadly, our results indicate not only that we have executed the innocent in the past, but also that it is a virtual certainty that at least some of the prisoners on death row today are innocent, and some of them will be executed. Further, the problem is far more likely to affect our minority population than white defendants. Of our 350 cases, 48 percent involve minority defendants, clearly indicating that they are easy targets for these judicial blunders. And, of course, no person can guess how many innocent prisoners, whether they be minorities or not, are among those not lucky enough to have their innocence acknowledged prior to execution. I would like to give you three brief examples of the unlucky defendants, and one final one where the defendant was lucky enough to be removed from death row before it was too late.

In 1937, a black man named Roosevelt Collins was convicted of raping a white woman in Alabama, sentenced to death after four minutes of jury deliberation, and executed. His testimony that the so-called victim had consented caused a near-riot in the courtroom. Subsequent interviews with several jurors and the trial judge revealed that they all believed that Collins was telling the truth, but that he deserved to die simply from "messin' around" with a white woman.

In 1945, a similar case occurred in Florida. William Henry Anderson was executed only five months after his arrest, with no appeal, perhaps in part because the sheriff wrote to the governor, "I would appreciate special attention in this case before some sympathizing organization gets hold of it." Anderson had been telling his friends and family about his affair with the so-called victim for several months before they were discovered and she cried rape. Even then, she had not resisted, screamed, or used a pistol that was at her disposal to resist Anderson's advances.

In 1974, a black man named James Adams was convicted of killing a white rancher in Florida; ten years later he was executed. In the month before the execution, a skilled investigator thoroughly destroyed the state's case. Among the evidence uncovered was that a hair sample found clutched in the victim's hand, which in all likelihood had come from the assailant, did not match Adams's hair. Nonetheless, our then-Governor and now Senator Bob Graham would not grant even a short stay so these questions could be resolved. To this day, Senator Graham refuses to discuss this case.

Finally, I would like to tell you about another Florida case in which I was involved. In 1984, a black man named Tony Peek was convicted of murdering a white woman in Bartow. I was asked to testify on racial disparities in Florida's death penalty during the sentencing phase of his trial. When I arrived there, I learned that the trial judge had disqualified himself from the penalty phase because he had referred to the defendant's family as "niggers." Nonetheless, the new judge would not allow me to testify in front of the jury on the issue of race, claiming that such testimony was irrelevant. Peek was sentenced to death. In 1986, the Florida Supreme Court ordered a new trail on an unrelated issue (488 So.2d 52). At the end of its opinion, the court wrote:

> For future guidance of the bench, we believe that we should address the circumstances requiring the original trial judge in this case to disqualify himself after the completion of the guilt phase of the trail. The disqualification resulted from comments made by the trial judge immediately after the appellant was convicted and as the trial judge and attorneys were discussing procedure for the penalty phase. The defense attorney stated the trial judge commented: "Since the nigger mom and dad are here anyway, why don't we go ahead and do the penalty phase today instead of having to subpoena them back at cost to the state." Another per-

son heard the comment as: "Since the niggers are here, maybe we can go ahead with the sentencing phase." As a result of these statements, the defendant moved to disqualify the trial judge. The trial judge disqualified himself from the penalty phase and the chief judge of the circuit presided for the remainder of the trial.

Trial judges not only must be impartial in their own minds, but also must convey the image of impartiality to the parties and the public. Judges must make sure that their statements, both on and off the bench, are proper and do not convey an image of prejudice or bias to any person or any segment of the community. . . . We write about this incident to emphasize the need for all judges to be constantly vigilant about their comments and demeanor both inside and outside the courtroom to assure that their impartiality may not "reasonably be questioned" (488 So.2d 52, 56).

Note that the court was more concerned about the appearance of neutrality than its actual reality. Note too that the court did not even refer to the judge, Thomas M. Langston, by name. At retrial in 1987, Peek was able to introduce convincing alibi evidence, and he was acquitted and released from death row.

I would like to stress to this Subcommittee that the problem of condemning the innocent is not a problem that has been solved by the new death penalty statutes enacted over the last fifteen years. Our files now include 24 cases in which a defendant sentenced to death in the last fifteen years has now been freed from death row because of doubts about guilt, and one other, James Adams, who was executed despite such doubts. We already include Joseph Green Brown in this sad tally; the cases of Edward Earl Johnson and Clarence Brandley, about which other speakers will teach us today, may indeed be others to add. The nets of the criminal justice system itself prove there are fish in this lake, but how many these nets do not catch can never be known or estimated.

Mr. Chairman, I would like to conclude my remarks by making the argument that the political feasibility of ending capital punishment in the immediate future is more realistic than many politicians might expect. I do so by pointing to the latest national Gallup Opinion Report that we have on this subject (Gallup, 1986). In that national poll, Gallup found that 70 percent of the respondents supported the death penalty for murder. However, the poll also found that public support for the death penalty declines dramatically—from 70 percent to 55 percent—if life imprisonment without the possibility of parole were given as an alternative. Many states already have such an option. Further, a similar decline in support, from 70 percent to 56 percent, would occur if the respondents were convinced that the death penalty had no deterrent effects. Combining these, Gallup reports that only 43 percent of the public would still favor death over life imprisonment if executions have no deterrent effect. Mr. Chairman, with these data I submit to you that the prospects for ending the injustice of the death penalty are not as slim as some of its advocates would want us to believe.

REFERENCES

Baldus, D. C., Pulaski, C., and Woodworth, G. (1983) "Comparative review of death sentences: An empirical review of death sentences." Journal of Criminal Law and Criminology 74:661–753.

Baldus, D. C., Woodworth, G., and Pulaski, C. A. (1985) "Monitoring and evaluating contemporary death sentencing systems: Lessons from Georgia." University of California-Davis Law Review 18:1375–1407.

Baldus, D. C., Pulaski, C. A., and Woodworth, G. (1986) "Arbitrariness and discrimination in the administration of the death penalty: A challenge to state supreme courts." Stetson Law Review 15:133–261.

Barnett, A. (1985) "Some distribution patterns for the Georgia death sentence." University of California-Davis Law Review 18:1327–1374.

Bowers, W. J. (1984) Legal Homicide: Death as Punishment in America, 1864–1982. Boston: Northeastern University Press.

Bowers, W. J. and Pierce, G. L. (1980) "Arbitrariness and discrimination under post-Furman capital statutes." Crime and Delinquency 26:563–635.

Gallup, G. (Jan.–Feb., 1986) "The death penalty." The Gallup Report, Nos. 244–245, 10–16.

Gross, S. R. and Mauro, R. (1984) "Patterns of death: An analysis of racial disparities and homicide victimization." Stanford Law Review 37:27–153.

Jacoby, J. E. and Paternoster, R. (1982) "Sentencing disparity and jury packing: Further challenges to the death penalty." Journal of Criminal Law and Criminology 73:379–387.

NAACP Legal Defense Fund (May 1, 1987) "Death Row, U.S.A." Unpublished compilation.

Paternoster, R. (1983) "Race of victim and location of crime: The decision to seek the death penalty in South Carolina." Journal of Criminal Law and Criminology 74:754–785.

Paternoster, R. (1984) "Prosecutorial discretion in requesting the death penalty: A case of victim-based racial discrimination." Law and Society Review 18:437–478.

Radelet, M. L. (1981) "Racial characteristics and the imposition of the death penalty." American Sociological Review 46:918–927.

Radelet, M. L. (1985) "Rejecting the jury: The imposition of the death penalty in Florida." University of California-Davis Law Review 18:1409–1431.

Radelet, M. L. and Vandiver, M. (1983) "The Florida Supreme Court and death penalty appeals." Journal of Criminal Law and Criminology 74:913–926.

Radelet, M. L., Vandiver, M., and Berardo, F. M. (1983) "Families, prisons, and death row inmates: The human impact of structured uncertainty." Journal of Family Issues 4:593–612.

Radelet, M. L. and Pierce, G. L. (1985) "Race and prosecutorial discretion in homicide cases." Law and Society Review 19:587–621.

Radelet, M. L. and Barnard, G. W. (1986) "Ethics and the psychiatric determination of competency to be executed." Bulletin of the American Academy of Psychiatry and the Law 14:37–53.

Radelet, M. L. and Mello, M. (1986) "Executing those who kill blacks: An unusual case study." Mercer Law Review 37:911–925.

Radelet, M.L. and Vandiver, M. (1986) "Race and capital punishment: An overview of the issues." Crime and Social Justice 25:94–113.

Ryan, W. (1976) Blaming the Victim. N.Y.: Vintage Books.

Subcommittee on Criminal Justice, Committee on the Judiciary, U.S. House of Representatives (1987) Hearings on H. R. 2837 and H. R. 343, Serial No. 133. Washington, D.C: U.S. Government Printing Office.

U.S. Department of Justice (1986) Capital Punishment, 1983 (NCJ-99561). Washington, D.C.: U.S. Government Printing Office.

ESTABLISHING CONSTITUTIONAL PROCEDURES FOR THE IMPOSITION OF CAPITAL PUNISHMENT

. . . Despite the explicit approval by the Supreme Court for the death penalty as an appropriate sanction under the Eighth Amendment of the Constitution, the basic issue of the use of the death penalty is so important that the Committee feels compelled to reiterate here the justifications for its use in heinous crimes under the particular circumstances provided in S. 114.

The conclusion in favor of the retention of capital punishment for these crimes has its basis in the belief that the primary responsibility of society is the protection of its members so that they may live out their lives in peace and safety. Indeed, this is one of the main reasons why any society exists. Where the safety of its citizenry can no longer be guaranteed, society's basic reason for being disappears. In providing its members protection, society must do what is necessary to deter those who would break its laws and punish those who do so in an appropriate manner. It is the Committee's conclusion that capital punishment applied to the most serious offenses fulfills these functions.

The question of the deterrent effect of capital punishment has probably been the one point most debated by those favoring the abolition of the penalty and those desiring its retention. Several studies have been conducted purporting to show the absence of any correlation between the existence of the penalty and the number of capital crimes committed in a particular jurisdiction. The argument then follows that, since there exists no such relationship, the penalty serves no legitimate social purpose and should not be imposed.

If the absence of any correlation between the existence of the penalty and the frequency of capital crimes could actually be proved by these studies, the argument for abolition would be much stronger. Although entitled to consideration, however, the value of these studies is seriously diminished by the unreliability of the statistical evidence used, the contrary experience of

From Report of the Senate Judiciary Committee, "Establishing Constitutional Procedures for the Imposition of Capital Punishment," *Congressional Record* (January 17, 1980).

those in the field of law enforcement, and the inherent logic of the deterrent power of the threat of death.

With regard to the statistical evidence, the first and most obvious point is that those who are, in fact, deterred by the threat of the death penalty and do not commit murder are not included in the statistical data. There is no way to determine the number of such people. Secondly, even those favoring abolition agree that the available evidence on the subject of deterrence is, at best, inadequate. For example, Hugo Adam Bedau has described the difficulty in obtaining accurate data in this way:

> In a word, there is no exact information anywhere as to the volume of capital crimes in the United States. Difficult as it is to specify the capital laws for the nation as a whole, it is impossible with the present sort of criminal statistics to specify the exact amount of capital crimes for even one jurisdiction in even one year for even one crime.[1]

[. . .] In the absence of reliable statistical evidence, great weight must be placed on the experience of those who are most frequently called upon to deal with murderers and potential murderers and who are thus in the best position to judge the effectiveness of the remedy— our law enforcement officials. The vast majority of these officials continue to favor the retention of the death penalty as a deterrent to violent crime. As Sheriff Peter Pitchess of Los Angeles County testified before the California Senate Committee on the Judiciary:

> I can tell you that the overwhelming majority of people in law enforcement— the ones who are dealing with these criminals, the ones who are seeing them not as statistics but real live human beings, and who are studying their

human behavior—are overwhelmingly convinced that capital punishment is a deterrent.[2]

The Honorable J. Edgar Hoover, the late Director of the Federal Bureau of Investigation, declared that:

> [t]he professional law enforcement officer is convinced from experience that the hardened criminal has been and is deterred from killing based on the prospect of the death penalty.[3]

In his testimony before the Subcommittee on Criminal Law and Procedures on S. 1401, Mr. Edward J. Kiernan, President of the International Conference of Police Associations and a police officer with 30 years of service, discussed the criminal's fear of the death penalty and declared that:

> sometimes the specter of that fear will stay a trigger finger at the critical moment.[4]

In this testimony on S. 1401, Mr. Arlen Specter, the district attorney of Philadelphia, stated:

> I believe the death penalty is an effective deterrent against murder. I say that based upon more than 7 years as district attorney of Philadelphia, and dealing with a great many cases in that capacity. We have the frequent occurrence in the criminal courts of Philadelphia where professional burglars have expressed themselves on the point of not carrying a weapon on a burglary because of their concern there may be a scuffle, there may be a dispute, the weapon may be used and death may result, and prior to *Furman*, they may face the possibility of capital punishment.[5]

The issue, for our purposes here, has been definitely resolved by the Supreme Court in *Gregg* where it concluded that it is appropriate for a legislature to consider deterrence as a justification for the imposition of the death penalty:

> Although some of the studies suggest that the death penalty may not function as a significantly greater deterrent than lesser penalties, there is no convincing empirical evidence either supporting or refuting this view. We may nevertheless assume safely that there are murderers, such as those who act in passion, for whom the threat of death has little or no deterrent effect. But for many others, the death penalty undoubtedly is a significant deterrent. There are carefully contemplated murders, such as murder for hire, where the possible penalty of death may well enter into the cold calculus that precedes the decision at act. And there are some categories of murder, such as murder by a life prisoner, where other sanctions may not be adequate.[6]

A frequently made argument in opposition to the idea of the death penalty as a deterrent is that most homicides are crimes of passion against which no penalty constitutes a true deterrent. Although it is true that many murders are indeed the result of passion, it is equally true that a very large number are the result of premeditation. Moreover, logic suggests that consequences can influence conduct motivated by passion. As pointed out by the late Senator John L. McClellan:

> It is sometimes said deterrence will not work with homicide, since murders are committed in the heat of passion, when the individual does not consider the consequences of his actions. This is true in some cases, but not all. As I have noted, of all murders committed in 1971, 27.5 percent were either known or suspected to have taken place during the commission of a felony. Premedita-

tion, not passion, motivated these crimes. There were no situations of uncontrollable rage.

> Where reason is present, the thought that one consequence of an individual's action is the forfeiture of his own life will, in most instances, serve as a deterrent.

> Experience has proven this point. Recently, former criminal court Judge Samuel Leibowitz of New York, an eminent jurist who presided over many capital cases explained that, when he asked hardened criminals why they would not shoot their way out to escape capture, they would inevitably reply, "I was afraid of the hot seat, Judge."

> Indeed, even in situations involving passion, the knowledge that murder will result in the swift termination of the murderer's own life must necessarily encourage restraint and self-control.[7]

Coupled with the great weight of experience is the inherent rationality of a deterrent effect. Senator DeConcini has observed that he doubts that deterrence can ever be empirically proven or disproven and "[u]ltimately, only the inherent logic that the threat of loss of one's life is a deterrent justifies capital punishment."[8] Clearly a person will be slow to undertake an action that will result in the loss of something which he values highly. Since life itself is the most highly prized possession an individual has, he will be most hesitant to engage in conduct which will result in its forfeiture. In the words of Mr. Richard E. Gerstein before the Section of Criminal Law of the American Bar Association:

> It is clear that for normal human beings no other punishment deters so effectively from committing murder as the punishment of death . . . [S]ince peo-

ple fear death more than anything else, the death penalty is the most effective deterrent.[9]

But the death penalty ought not be thought of solely in terms of individual deterrence. It also has value in terms of social or general deterrence as well. By associating the penalty with the crimes for which it is inflicted, society is made more aware of the horror of those crimes, and there is instilled in its members the desire to avoid such conduct.

The incapacitating effect of capital punishment is clear. Obviously those who suffer this penalty are unable to commit similar crimes in the future. The question, then, becomes one of necessity. Is the death penalty necessary to adequately protect society in the future from the possible actions of those who have already committed capital crimes? The Committee is of the opinion that, in certain circumstances, it is.

In some cases, imprisonment is simply not a sufficient safeguard against the future actions of criminals. Some criminals are incorrigibly anti-social and will remain potentially dangerous to society for the rest of their lives. Mere imprisonment offers these people the possibility of escape or, in some cases, release on parole through error or oversight. Even if they are successfully imprisoned for life prison itself is an environment presenting dangers to guards, inmates and others. In each of these cases, society is the victim. Basically, there is no satisfactory alternative sentence for these individuals. Life imprisonment without parole, although at first appearing to be a reasonable answer, is in reality highly unsatisfactory. Such a sentence greatly increases the danger to guards and to other prisoners who come into contact with those who have been so sentenced. Mr. Wallace Re-

idt, former director of the Maryland Department of Parole and Probation, expressed it in this way:

> If capital punishment is abolished, there will be considerable pressure to prevent parole in life terms and there will be removed what I believe is a great deterrent in the handling of prisoners in institutions.
>
> Most persons connected with institutions feel that unless there is some fear of punishment or hope of reward that a good many lifetermers would cause a great deal of trouble in the institutions and make the work of prison officials much more dangerous than it now is.[10]

It cannot be overemphasized that it is not the Committee's desire to see capital punishment utilized as an alternative to efforts at rehabilitation. This simply is not the case. The members of the Committee recognize that still greater attempts must be made to enable our prison system to achieve its goal of restoring productive and useful individuals to society. We here discuss only a minute class of extremely dangerous persons.

The Committee finds also that capital punishment serves the legitimate function of retribution. This is distinct from the concept of revenge in the sense of the "eye for an eye" mentality; rather it is through retribution that society expresses its outrage, and sense of revulsion, toward those who undermine the foundations of civilized society by contravening its laws. It reflects the fact that criminals have not simply inflicted injury upon discrete individuals; they have also weakened the often tenuous bonds that hold communities together.

The retributive function of punishment in general, and capital punishment in particular, was discussed by Lord Justice Denning before the British Royal Commission on Capital Punishment:

> The punishment inflicted for grave crimes should adequately reflect the revulsion felt by the great majority of citizens for them. It is a mistake to consider the objects of punishment as being deterrent or reformative or preventive and nothing else. The ultimate justification of any punishment is not that it is a deterrent, but that it is the emphatic denunciation by the community of a crime; and from this point of view, there are some murders which, in the present state of public opinion, demand the most emphatic denunciation of all, namely the death penalty,[11]

Similarly, Justice Holmes wrote in "The Common Law":

> The first requirement of a sound body of law is that it should correspond with the actual feelings and demands of the community, whether right or wrong.

It is the view of the committee that these feelings rightly and justly warrant the imposition of capital punishment under such circumstances.

That men who take the lives of others in an unjustified manner may sometimes be subject to the extreme sanction of capital punishment reflects a social consensus that places great sanctity on the value of human life. It is a consensus that holds that individual offenders are responsible and accountable beings, having it within themselves to conduct themselves in a civilized manner. It is also a consensus that holds that there is no offense more repugnant and more heinous than the deprivation of an innocent person's life.

Murder does not simply differ in magnitude from extortion or burglary or property destruction offenses; it differs in kind. Its punishment ought to also differ in kind. It must acknowledge the inviolability and dignity of innocent human life. It must, in short, be proportionate. The Committee has concluded that, in the relatively narrow range of circumstances outlined in this bill, that the penalty of death satisfies that standard.

Apart from its legitimacy as one of the purposes of punishment, questions have arisen with respect to the constitutional validity of retribution as a basis for punishment, specifically capital punishment. This question was addressed by the Supreme Court in the *Gregg* case:

> In part, capital punishment is an expression of society's moral outrage at particularly offensive conduct. This function may be unappealing to many, but it is essential in an ordered society that asks its citizens to rely on legal processes rather than self-help to vindicate their wrongs.
>
> "The instinct for retribution is part of the nature of man, and channelling that instinct in the administration of criminal justice serves an important purpose in promoting the stability of a free society governed by law. When people begin to believe that organized society is unwilling or unable to impose upon criminal offenders the punishment they 'deserve,' then there are sown the seeds of anarchy—of self-help, vigilante justice, and lynch law." *Furman v. Georgia, supra* at 308 (Stewart, J., concurring).
>
> "Retribution is no longer the dominant objective of the criminal law," *Williams v. New York* 337 U.S. 241, 248 (1949), but neither is it a forbidden objective nor one inconsistent with our respect for the dignity of men. *Furman v. Georgia,* 408 U.S. at 394-5 (Burger, J. dissenting); id. at 452-4 (Powell, J., dissenting); *Powell v. Texas* 392 U.S. at 531, 535-6. Indeed, the decision that capital punishment may be the appropriate sanction in extreme cases is an expres-

sion of the community's belief that certain crimes are themselves so grievous an affront to humanity that the only adequate response may be the penalty of death.[12]

It is the conclusion of this Committee that it is not enough to proclaim the sanctity and import of innocent life. This must be, and can only be secured by, a society that is willing to impose its highest penalty upon those who threaten such life. As observed by Professor Walter Berns:

> We think that some criminals must be made to pay for their crimes with their lives, and we think that we, the survivors of the world they violated, may legitimately extract that payment because we, too, are their victims. By punishing them, we demonstrate that there are laws that bind men across generations as well as across (and within) nations, that we are not simply isolated individuals, each pursuing his selfish interests. . . .[13]

An argument that is often asserted in favor of abolition of capital punishment concerns the dangers of executing the innocent. It is pointed out that if such an error occurs, it is irremediable. The argument is then made that, since the cost of such a mistake is so great, the risk of permitting the death penalty to be imposed at all is unacceptable.

The Committee finds this argument to be without great weight, particularly in light of the procedural safeguards for criminal defendants mandated by the Supreme Court in recent years. The Court's decision with respect to the rights of the individual, particularly those expanding the right to counsel, together with the precautions taken by any court in a capital case, have all but reduced the danger or error in these cases to that of a mere

theoretical possibility. Indeed, the Committee is aware of no case where an innocent man has been put to death. Admittedly, however, due to the fallible nature of man, this possibility does continue to exist. Insofar as it does, it is the opinion of the Committee that this minimal risk is justified by the protection afforded to society by the death penalty. As stated in the minority report of the Massachusetts Special Commission:

> We do not feel, however, that the mere possibility of error, which can never be completely ruled out, can be urged as a reason why the right of the state to inflict the death penalty can be questioned in principle. . . . All that can be expected of [human authorities] is that they take every reasonable precaution against the danger of error. When this is done by those who are charged with the application of the law, the likelihood that errors will be made descends to an irreducible minimum. If errors are then made, this is the necessary price that must be paid within a society which is made up of human beings and whose authority is exercised not by angels but by men themselves. It is not brutal or unfeeling to suggest that the danger of miscarriage of justice must be weighed against the far greater evils for which the death penalty aims to provide effective remedies. . . .[14]

NOTES

1. "The Death Penalty in America, an Anthology," Hugo Adam Bedau, ed., p. 56, Doubleday (1964).

2. Hearings, report and testimony on Senate bill No. 1, Second Extraordinary Session, which proposed to abolish the death penalty in California and to substitute life imprisonment, without possibility of parole. California Legislature, Senate Committee on the Judiciary, p. 150 (1960).

3. "The Uniform Crime Reports of the United States," Federal Bureau of Investigation, p. 14 (1959).

4. Senate Hearings (1973) at 157.

5. Id. at 70.

6. *Gregg v. Georgia*, at 185–86 (footnotes omitted).

7. See *supra* note 4 at 2–3.

8. See Senate Hearings (1977) at 51.

9. American Bar Association, Section of Criminal Law, 1959 proceedings, p. 16 (1960).

10. Maryland Committee on Capital Punishment, Report, p. 23 (1962).

11. Quoted by Richard C. Donnelly, "Capital Punishment," inserted in 106 Cong. Rec. at p. A6284 (daily ed. Aug. 14, 1960). See also Walter Berns, "For Capital Punishment," Harper's Magazine, April 1979, p. 15; Ernest van den Haag, "The Collapse of the Case Against Capital Punishment," National Review, Mar. 31, 1978, p. 395; Sidney Hook, "The Death Sentence," The New Leader, Apr. 3, 1961, p. 18; Jacques Barzun, "In Favor of Capital Punishment," The American Scholar, Spring 1962, p. 181, reprinted in Hugo A. Bedau (ed.), "The Death Penalty in America," Anchor Books, 1967.

12. *Gregg v. Georgia*, at 183–84 (footnotes omitted).

13. Walter Berns, "For Capital Punishment," Harper's Magazine, p. 15, April 1979.

14. McClellan, Grant S., ed., "Capital Punishment," p. 81 (1961).

POSTSCRIPT

Should the Death Penalty Be Abolished?

We are in a new era in the history of capital punishment. The death penalty is constitutional and almost twenty-four hundred persons are on death row, a larger number than at any time since a national count was begun. In the first edition of this book, published in 1982, I wrote that "Although only four persons have been executed in the past fifteen years, this situation seems certain to change in the next two years as appeals in many cases are exhausted." There has indeed been an increase in executions, although the rise has not been as fast as some had been predicting. One hundred and thirty-seven persons had been executed as of the summer of 1990.

Appeals still are time-consuming, a situation that some Supreme Court justices have complained about. As a result of the appeals process, the number of persons on death row is still growing by about one hundred and fifty a year. When the first edition of this book was prepared, there were more than a thousand people on death row, less than half the number today. The increase in the death row population means, of course, that there are more people sentenced to death each year than there are executions. The slow pace of executions has been a source of great frustration to some Supreme Court justices and Congress has been urged to pass legislation that would restrict when inmates on death row may raise new *habeas corpus* claims in court.

The Supreme Court has made several notable and controversial decisions in recent years involving the death penalty. These include *Penry v. Lyunaugh*, 109 S.Ct. 2934 (1989), in which the Court ruled that mentally retarded murderers may be executed, and *Stanford v. Kentucky*, 109 S.Ct. 2969 (1989), in which the Court ruled that persons as young as sixteen years of age may be executed. There are approximately thirty minors currently on death row.

The most comprehensive collection of materials on both the pros and cons of capital punishment is H. Bedau, ed., *The Death Penalty in America*, 3d ed. (Oxford University Press, 1982). Other interesting works on the subject include F. Zimring and G. Hawkins, *Capital Punishment and the American Agenda* (1989); Brown and Adler, *Public Justice, Private Mercy: A Governor's Education on Death Row* (1989); H. Bedau, *Death Is Different: Studies in the Morality, Law, and Politics of Capital Punishment* (Northeastern University Press, 1987); W. Berns, *For Capital Punishment: Crime and the Morality of the Death Penalty* (Basic books, 1979); E. van den Haag and J. P. Conrad, *The Death Penalty: A Debate* (Plenum, 1983); and L. L. Black, *Capital Punishment: The Inevitability of Caprice and Mistake* (Norton, 1974). M. Meltsner's *Cruel and Unusual: The Supreme Court and Capital Punishment* (Random House, 1973) describes the history of the *Furman* case.

ISSUE 13

Should the Exclusionary Rule Be Abolished?

YES: Malcolm Richard Wilkey, from "The Exclusionary Rule: Why Suppress Valid Evidence?" *Judicature* (November 1978)

NO: Yale Kamisar, from "The Exclusionary Rule in Historical Perspective: The Struggle to Make the Fourth Amendment More Than 'an Empty Blessing,' " *Judicature* (February 1979)

ISSUE SUMMARY

YES: U.S. Court of Appeals judge Malcolm Wilkey raises objections to the exclusionary rule on the grounds that it may suppress evidence and allow the guilty to go free.
NO: Professor Yale Kamisar argues that the exclusionary rule is necessary to prevent abuses by police and to protect citizens' rights.

The Fourth Amendment to the Constitution provides that "the right of the people to be secure in their persons, houses, papers, and effects against unreasonable searches and seizures, shall not be violated, and no Warrants shall issue, but upon probable cause. . . ." Thus, if the police wish to search someone's property, they must first persuade a judge that probable cause exists to believe that a crime has been committed and that the evidence sought will be found in the place to be searched. The warrant requirement is the key constitutional element restricting the power of the police to decide unilaterally to invade the privacy of someone's home.

What should happen if the police conduct an illegal search and, as a result, discover incriminating evidence? According to the exclusionary rule, such evidence may not be introduced at a trial or be considered by a jury in considering guilt or innocence. If no other evidence of guilt exists, therefore, the defendant will go free. If there is enough other evidence of the defendant's guilt, he may still be convicted.

The exclusionary rule is over seventy years old. It is not required by the Constitution nor mentioned in it. Rather, courts have imposed it because they felt it was the most workable and feasible way to deter illegal police conduct and maintain an honest system of law enforcement. In the following articles, Yale Kamisar, a noted criminal law scholar, argues that this rationale is still valid and that the rule should be maintained. Federal Court of Appeals judge Malcolm Wilkey, on the other hand, asserts that society can no longer bear the costs that the rule brings, that guilty persons escape prosecution because of it, and that illegal police conduct is not deterred.

The articles mention a number of legal cases that should be understood since they describe the historical development of the rule:

1. *Weeks v. United States*, 232 U.S. 383 (1914)   The United States Supreme Court imposed the exclusionary rule for the first time and ruled that illegally seized evidence could not be used in the federal courts. Such evidence, however, could still be used in criminal cases in state courts unless the state decided on its own to require the exclusionary rule in its courts. Although a few states did impose the exclusionary rule, most did not. The New York Court of Appeals, for example, rejected the rule, with Judge Cardozo refusing to accept the proposition that "the criminal is to go free because the constable has blundered" (*People v. Defore*, 150 N.E. 585, 1926).

2. *Wolf v. Colorado*, 338 U.S. 25 (1949)   The Supreme Court ruled that due process of law under the Fourteenth Amendment is denied individuals who are illegally searched. But the Court refused to require state courts to impose or apply the exclusionary rule. Thus, the Court held that "in a prosecution in a State court for a State crime the Fourteenth Amendment does not forbid the admission of evidence obtained by an unreasonable search and seizure."

3. *Rochin v. California*, 342 U.S. 165 (1952) and *Irvine v. California*, 347 U.S. 128 (1954)   These two cases involved particularly blatant Fourth Amendment violations by the police. The defendants were convicted, but the Supreme Court refused, as in *Wolf*, to require states to follow the exclusionary rule. Rochin's conviction, however, was reversed because the police action was "shocking to the conscience."

4. *Mapp v. Ohio*, 367 U.S. 643 (1961)   Miss Dollree Mapp was convicted of possession of obscene materials after the police conducted a search of her home without a search warrant. The Supreme Court decided to overrule the *Wolf* decision and require state courts to apply the exclusionary rule. The Court cited a well-known statement by Justice Brandeis that "if the government becomes a lawbreaker, it breeds contempt for the law; it invites every man to become a law unto himself; it invites anarchy." As you read the following articles, consider whether Justice Brandeis's statement is still valid. (A fascinating description of the facts of the *Mapp* case is contained in Fred Friendly and Martha Elliot's, *The Constitution: That Delicate Balance* [Random House, 1984].)

YES

Malcolm Richard Wilkey

WHY SUPPRESS VALID EVIDENCE?

America is now ready to confront frankly and to examine realistically both the achievements and social costs of the policies which have been so hopefully enacted in the past 40 years. That reappraisal has made the most headlines in regard to economic and fiscal matters. It is imperative that this honest reappraisal include the huge social costs which American society—alone in the civilized world—pays as a result of our unique exclusionary rule of evidence in criminal cases.

We can see that huge social cost most clearly in the distressing rate of street crimes—assaults and robberies with deadly weapons, narcotics trafficking, gambling and prostitution—which flourish in no small degree simply because of the exclusionary rule of evidence. To this high price we can rightfully add specific, pernicious police conduct and lack of discipline—the very opposite of the objectives of the rule itself. . . .

Though scholars have been shedding more and more light on this problem, few people have considered the enormous social cost of the exclusionary rule, and fewer still have thought about possible alternatives to the rule. I propose to do both those things in this article.

THE RULE'S MYSTIQUE

What is the exclusionary rule? It is a judge-made rule of evidence, originated in 1914 by the Supreme Court in *Weeks v. United States*, which bars "the use of evidence secured through an illegal search and seizure." It is not a rule required by the Constitution. No Supreme Court has ever held that it was. As Justice Black once said,

> [T]he Fourth Amendment does not itself contain any provision expressly precluding the use of such evidence and I am extremely doubtful that such a provision could properly be inferred from nothing more than the basic command against unreasonable searches and seizures.

The greatest obstacle to replacing the exclusionary rule with a rational process, which will both protect the citizenry by controlling the police and

From Malcolm Richard Wilkey, "The Exclusionary Rule: Why Suppress Valid Evidence?" *Judicature* (November 1978). Copyright © 1978 by Ambassador Malcolm R. Wilkey. Reprinted by permission.

avoid rewarding the criminal, is the powerful, unthinking emotional attachment to the rule. The mystique and misunderstanding of the rule causes not only many ordinary citizens but also judges and lawyers to feel (not think) that the exclusionary rule was enshrined in the Constitution by the Founding Fathers, and that to abolish it would do violence to the whole sacred Bill of Rights. They appear totally unaware that the rule was not employed in U.S. courts during the first 125 years of the Fourth Amendment, that it was devised by the judiciary in the assumed absence of any other method of controlling the police, and that no other country in the civilized world has adopted such a rule.

Realistically, the exclusionary rule can probably never be abolished until both the public and the Supreme Court are satisfied that there is available in our legal system a reasonably workable alternative. Unfortunately, the converse may also be true—we will never have any alternative in operation until the rule is abolished. So long as we keep the rule, the police are not going to investigate and discipline their own men, and thus sabotage prosecutions by invalidating the admissibility of vital evidence.

HOW THE RULE WORKS

The impact of the exclusionary rule may not be immediately apparent from the simple phrase of the *Wolf* decision that it bars "the use of evidence seized through an illegal search and seizure." It may help to consider three examples to see how the exclusionary rule needlessly frustrates police and prosecutors trying to do a very difficult job on the streets of our cities.

In *U.S. v. Montgomery*, two police officers on auto patrol in a residential neighborhood at 6 P.M. on a winter day saw Montgomery driving his car in a way that suggested he was "sizing up" the area. When they stopped and identified him, they learned by radio that an arrest warrant was outstanding against him. Before taking him into custody, the officers searched him for weapons and found a .38 caliber bullet in his pants pocket, a magnum revolver loaded with six rounds and an unregistered, sawed-off shotgun with shells in the car.

A trial court convicted him of illegal possession of firearms, but the Court of Appeals (2–1) reversed, holding that no probable cause existed for stopping Montgomery in the first place, and that all evidence discovered thereafter was the product of an illegal search and seizure. Applying the exclusionary rule, the court suppressed as evidence the revolver and the sawed-off shotgun, which made it impossible to convict Montgomery or to retry the case.

Montgomery is an example of typical routine police work, which many citizens would think of as needed reasonable effort to prevent crime. But now look at *U.S. v. Willie Robinson*, a similar case with a different result. A policeman stopped Robinson for a minor traffic violation and discovered that license bureau records indicated his license was probably a forgery. Four days later, the same officer spotted Robinson about 2 A.M. and arrested him for driving with a forged credential.

Since police regulations required him to take Robinson into custody, the officer began a pat down or frisk for dangerous weapons. Close inspection of the cigarette package in the outer pocket of the man's jacket revealed heroin. Robinson was convicted of heroin possession but the Court of Appeals held 5–4 that, in light of the exclusionary rule, the search of Robinson was illegal and the heroin evidence must be suppressed. The Supreme Court reversed, holding that probable cause existed for the search, the evidence was legally obtained, and it could be offered in evidence. The High Court reinstated the original conviction.

This is one search and seizure case which turned out, in my view, correctly. But it took a U.S. District Court suppression hearing, a 2–1 panel decision in the Court of Appeals, a 5–4 decision in the court *en banc*, and a 6–3 decision of the Supreme Court to confirm the validity of the on-the-spot judgment of a lone police officer exercised at 2 A.M. on a Washington Street—five years and eight months earlier.

In *Coolidge v. New Hampshire*, a 14-year-old girl was found with her throat slit and a bullet in her head eight days after she had disappeared. Police contacted the wife of a suspect whose car was like one seen near the crime, and she gave them her husband's guns. Tests proved that one of the weapons had fired the fatal bullet.

Invoking his statutory authority, the attorney general of the state issued a warrant for the arrest of the suspect and the seizure of his car. Coolidge was captured and convicted. But the Supreme Court reversed the conviction on the grounds that the warrant was defective, the search of the auto unreasonable and vacuum sweepings from the auto (which matched the victim's clothing) were inadmissible. Why? Because the attorney general who issued the warrant had personally assumed direction of the investigation and thus was not a "neutral and detached magistrate."

Observe that here the conviction was reversed because of a defect in the warrant, not because of any blunder. Errors of law by either the attorney preparing the affidavit and application for the warrant or the magistrate in issuing the warrant frequently invalidate the entire search that the police officers make, relying in good faith on the warrant; those errors cause the suppression of the evidence and the reversal of the conviction. How does the exclusionary rule improve police conduct in such cases?

THE COURT'S RATIONALE

Deterrence: During the rule's development, the Supreme Court has offered three main reasons for the rule. The principal and almost sole theory today is that excluding the evidence will punish the police officers who made the illegal search and seizure or otherwise violated the constitutional rights of the defendant, and thus deter policemen from committing the same violation again. The flaw in this theory is that there is absolutely no empirical data that excluding evidence against a defendant has anything to do with either punishing police officers or thereby deterring them from future violations.

Chief Justice Burger has flatly asserted " . . . there is no empirical evidence to support the claim that the rule actually deters illegal conduct of law enforcement officials," and the Supreme Court has never sought to adduce such empirical evidence in support of the rule. Probably such a connection can never be proved, for as a matter of logical analysis "the exclusionary rule is well tailored to deter the prosecutor from illegal conduct. But the prosecutor is not the guilty party in an illegal arrest or search and seizure, and he rarely has any measure of control over the police who are responsible."

Privacy: From *Weeks* (1914) to *Mapp* (1961) the rule was also justified as protecting the privacy of the individual against illegal searches and seizures as guaranteed by the Fourth Amendment. The Supreme Court later downgraded the protection of privacy rationale, perhaps because of the obvious defect that the rule purports to do nothing to recompense innocent victims of Fourth Amendment violations, and the gnawing doubt as to just what right of privacy guilty individuals have in illegal firearms, contraband narcotics and policy betting slips—the frequent objects of search and seizure.

Judicial integrity: A third theme of the Supreme Court's justifying rationale, now somewhat muted, is that the use of illegally obtained evidence brings the court system into disrepute. In *Mapp* Justice Clark referred to "that judicial integrity so necessary in the true administration of justice," which was reminiscent of Justice Brandeis dissenting in *Burdeau v. McDowell*, " . . . respect for law will not be advanced by resort, in its enforcement, to means which shock the common man's sense of decency and fair play."

THE IMPACT OF THE RULE

It is undeniable that, as a result of the rule, the most valid, conclusive, and irrefutable factual evidence is excluded from the knowledge of the jury or consideration by the judge. As Justice Cardozo predicted in 1926, in describing the complete irrationality of the exclusionary rule:

The criminal is to go free because the constable has blundered. . . . A room is searched against the law, and the body of a murdered man is found. . . . The privacy of the home has been infringed, and the murderer goes free.

Fifty years later Justice Powell wrote for the Court:

The costs of applying the exclusionary rule even at trial and on direct review are well known: . . . the physical evidence sought to be excluded is typically reliable and often the most probative evidence bearing on the guilt or innocence of the defendant. . . . Application of the rule thus deflects the truthfinding process and often frees the guilty. The disparity in particular cases between the error committed by the police officer and the windfall afforded the guilty defendant by application of the rule is contrary to the idea of proportionality that is essential to the concept of justice.

I submit that justice is, or should be, a truth-seeking process. The court has a duty to the accused to see that he receives a fair trial; the court also has a duty to society to see that all the truth is brought out; only if all the truth is brought out can there be a fair trial. The exclusionary rule results in a complete distortion of the truth. Undeniable facts, of the greatest importance, are forever barred—facts such as Robinson's heroin, Montgomery's sawed-off shotgun and pistol, the bullet fired from Coolidge's gun and the sweepings from his car which contained items from the dead girl's clothes.

If justice is a truth-seeking process, it is all important that *there is never any question of reliability* in exclusionary rule cases involving material evidence, as the three examples illustrate. We rightly exclude evidence whenever its reliability is questionable—a coerced or induced confession, for example, or a faulty line-up for identification of the suspect. We exclude it because it is inherently unreliable, not because of the illegality of obtaining it. An illegal search in no way reduces the reliability of the evidence.

There have been several empirical studies on the effects of the exclusionary rule in five major American cities—Boston, Chicago, Cincinnati, New York and Washington, D.C.—during the period from 1950 to 1971. These have been recently collected and analyzed, along with other aspects of the exclusionary rule and its alternatives, by Professor Steven Schlesinger in his book *Exclusionary Injustice: The Problem of Illegally Obtained Evidence.*

Three of these studies concluded that the exclusionary rule was a total failure in its primary task of deterring illegal police activity and that it also produced other highly undesirable side effects. The fourth study, which said the first three were too harsh in concluding that the rule was totally ineffective, still said: "Nonetheless, the inconclusiveness of our findings is real enough; they do not nail down an argument that the exclusionary rule has accomplished its task."

Schlesinger and others regard the study by Dallin Oakes as perhaps the most comprehensive ever undertaken, both in terms of data and the breadth of analysis of the rule's effects. Oakes concluded:

> As a device for directly deterring illegal searches and seizures by the police, the exclusionary rule is a failure. . . . The harshest criticism of the rule is that it is ineffective. It is the sole means of enforcing the essential guarantees of freedom from unreasonable arrests and searches and seizures by law enforcement officers, and it is a failure in that vital task.

Spiotto made a comparative study of both the American exclusionary rule and the existing Canadian tort alternative, taking Chicago and Toronto as comparable metropolitan areas. He found that an

> empirical study [of narcotics and weapons cases] indicates that, over a 20-year period in Chicago, the proportion of cases in which there were motions to suppress evidence allegedly obtained illegally increased significantly. This is the opposite result of what would be expected if the rule had been efficacious in deterring police misconduct.

Three studies conducted between 1950 and 1971 show a substantial increase in motions to suppress in both narcotics and gun offenses. The increase from 1950 to 1971 can fairly be attributed to the impact of *Mapp* (1961) on search and seizure in the state courts.

CRITICISMS OF THE RULE

By this point, we should be able to see that the exclusionary rule actually produces many effects opposite from those that the Court intended to produce. No matter what rationale we consider, the rule in its indiscriminate workings does far more harm than good and, in many respects, it actually prevents us from dealing with the real problems of Fourth Amendment violations in the course of criminal investigations.

In the eyes of the Supreme Court, the first and primary rationale of the exclusionary rule is deterrence. I submit that all available facts and logic show that excluding the most reliable evidence does absolutely nothing to punish and thus deter the official wrongdoer, but the inevitable and certain result is that the guilty criminal defendant goes free.

The second—now rather distant second—rationale in the eyes of the Court has been the protection of privacy. I submit a policy of excluding incriminating evidence can never protect an innocent victim of an illegal search against whom no incriminating evidence is discovered. The only persons protected by the rule are the guilty against whom the most serious reliable evidence should be offered. It cannot be separately argued that the innocent person is protected *in the future* by excluding evidence against the criminal *now*, for this is only the deterrent argument all over again.

The third rationale found in the past opinions of the Court is that the use of illegally obtained evidence brings our court system into disrepute. I submit that the exclusion of valid, probative, undeniably truthful evidence undermines the reputation of and destroys the respect for the entire judicial system.

Ask any group of laymen if they can understand why a pistol found on a man when he is searched by an officer should not be received in evidence when the man is charged with illegal possession of a weapon, or why a heroin package found under similar circumstances should not be always received in evidence when he is prosecuted for a narcotics possession, and I believe you will receive a lecture that these are outrageous technicalities of the law which the American people should not tolerate. If you put the same issue to a representative group of lawyers and judges, I predict you would receive a strong preponderance of opinions supporting the lay view, although from those heavily imbued with a mystique of the exclusionary rule as of almost divine origin you would doubtless hear some support.

The rationale of protecting judicial integrity is also inconsistent with the behavior of the courts in other areas of the criminal law. For example, it is well settled that courts will try defendants who have been illegally seized and brought before them. In *Ker v. Illinois*, a defendant kidnapped in Peru was brought by force to Illinois for trial; in *Mahon v. Justice* the accused was forcibly abducted from West Virginia for trial in Kentucky; and in *Frisbie v. Collins*, the defendant was forcibly seized in Illinois for trial in Michigan. Said the *Frisbie* court:

This court has never departed from the rule announced in *Ker v. Illinois* . . . that the power of the court to try a person for crime is not impaired by the fact that he had been brought within the court's jurisdiction by reason of 'forcible abduction.'

Why should there be an exclusionary rule for illegally seized evidence when there is no such exclusionary rule for illegally seized people? Why should a court be concerned about the circumstances under which the murder weapon has been obtained, while it remains unconcerned about the circumstances under which the murderer himself has been apprehended? It makes no sense to argue that the admission of illegally seized evidence somehow signals the judiciary's condonation of the violation of rights when the judiciary's trial of an illegally-seized *person* is not perceived as signaling such condonation.

OTHER DEFECTS OF THE RULE

The rule does not simply fail to meet its declared objectives; it suffers from five other defects, too. One of those defects is that it uses an undiscriminating, meat-ax approach in the most sensitive areas of the administration of justice. It totally fails to discriminate between the degrees of culpability of the officer or the degrees of harm to the victim of the illegal search and seizure.

It does not matter whether the action of the officer was grossly willful and flagrant or whether he was conscientiously using his very best judgment under difficult circumstances; the result is the same: the evidence is out. The rule likewise fails to distinguish errors of judgment which cause no harm or inconvenience to the individual whose person or premises are searched, except for the discovery of valid incriminating evidence, from flagrant violations of the Fourth Amendment as in *Mapp* or *Rochin.* Chief Justice Burger's point in *Bivens* is undeniable:

> . . . society has at least as much right to expect rationally graded responses from judges in place of the universal 'capital punishment' we inflict on all evidence when police error is shown in its acquisition.

Another defect is that the rule makes no distinction between minor offenses and more serious crimes. The teenage runner caught with policy slips in his pocket and the syndicate hit man accused of first degree murder are each automatically set free by operation of the exclusionary rule, without any consideration of the impact on the community. Customarily, however, we apply different standards to crimes which vary as to seriousness, both in granting bail before trial and in imposing sentence afterwards.

A third problem is that, strangely, a rule which is supposed to discipline and improve police conduct actually results in encouraging highly pernicious police behavior. A policeman is supposed to tell the truth, but when he knows that describing the search truthfully will taint the evidence and free the suspect, the policeman is apt to feel that he has a "higher duty" than the truth. He may perjure himself to convict the defendant.

Similarly, knowing that evidence of gambling, narcotics or prostitution is hard to obtain under the present rules of search and seizure, the policeman may feel that he can best enforce the law by stepping up the incidence of searches and seizures, making them frequent enough to be harassing, with no idea of ultimate prosecution. Or, for those policemen inclined *ab initio* to corruption, the exclusionary rule provides a fine opportunity to make phony raids on establishments, deliberately violating the standards of the Fourth Amendment and immunizing the persons and premises raided—while making good newspaper headlines for active law enforcement.

Fourth, the rule discourages internal disciplinary action by the police themselves. Even if police officials know that an officer violated Fourth Amendment standards in a particular case, few of them will charge the erring officer with a Fourth Amendment violation: it would sabotage the case for the prosecution before it even begins. The prosecutor hopes the defendant will plea bargain and thus receive some punishment, even if the full rigor of the law cannot be imposed because of the dubious validity of the search. Even after the defendant has been convicted or has pleaded guilty, it would be dangerous to discipline the officer—months or years later—because the offender might come back seeking one of the now popular post-conviction remedies.

Finally, the existence of the federally imposed exclusionary rule makes it virtually impossible for any state, not only the federal government, to experiment with any other methods of controlling police. One unfortunate consequence of *Mapp* was that it removed from the states both the incentive and the opportunity to deal with illegal search and seizure by means other than suppression. Justice Harlan, in commenting on the evil impact of the federal imposition of the exclusionary rule on the states, observed:

> Another [state], though equally solicitous of constitutional rights, may choose to pursue one purpose at a time, allowing all evidence relevant to guilt to be brought into a criminal trial, and dealing with constitutional infractions by other means.

ALTERNATIVES TO THE RULE

The excuse given for the persistence of the exclusionary rule in this country is that there is no effective alternative to make the police obey the law in regard to unreasonable searches and seizures. If this excuse did not come from such respected sources, one would be tempted to term it an expression of intellectual bankruptcy.

"No effective alternative"? How do all the other civilized countries control their police? By disciplinary measures against the erring policeman, by effective civil damage action against both the policeman and the government—not by freeing the criminal. Judging by police conduct in England, Canada and other nations, these measures work very well. Why does the United States alone rely upon the irrational exclusionary rule?

It isn't necessary. Justice Frankfurter in *Wolf* (1949) noted that none of the 10 jurisdictions in the British Commonwealth had held evidence obtained by an illegal search and seizure inadmissible, and "the jurisdictions which have rejected the *Weeks* doctrine have not left the right to privacy without other means of protection. . . ." Justice Harlan in his dissent in *Mapp* noted the wisdom of allowing all evidence to be brought in and "dealing with constitutional infractions by other means." Justice Black, concurring in *Mapp*, noted that the Fourth Amendment did not itself preclude the use of illegally obtained evidence.

In his dissent in *Bivens*, Chief Justice Burger suggested that Congress provide that Fourth Amendment violations be made actionable under the Federal Tort Claims Act, or something similar. Senator Lloyd Bentsen and other members of Congress have put forward proposals to abolish the rule and substitute the liability of the federal government toward the victims of illegal searches and seizures, both those innocent and those guilty of crimes.

THE PURPOSES OF AN ALTERNATIVE

Before examining what mechanism we might adopt in place of the exclusionary rule as a tool for enforcing the rights guaranteed by the Fourth Amendment, let us see clearly what objectives we desire to achieve by such alternatives.

The *first* objective, in sequence and perhaps in the public consciousness of those who are aware of the shortcomings of the rule, is to prevent the unquestionably guilty from going free from all punishment for their crime—to put an end to the ridiculous situation that the murderer goes free because the constable has blundered. Let me reiterate: the exclusionary rule, as applied to tangible evidence, has never prevented an innocent person from being convicted.

Second, the system should provide effective guidance to the police as to proper conduct under the Fourth Amendment. When appellate courts rule several years after the violation, their decisions are not only years too late, but usually far too obscure for the average policeman to understand. They are remote in both time and impact on the policeman at fault. Immediate guidance to the policeman as to his error, with an appropriate penalty, is obviously more effective, in contrast to simply rewarding the criminal.

Third sequentially, but first in value, the mechanism should protect citizens from Fourth Amendment violations by law enforcement officers. (I say sequentially, because it is necessary first to abolish the exclusionary rule and then to provide guidance to the police.) If police receive immediate and meaningful rulings, accompanied by prompt disciplinary penalties, they will be effectively deterred from future wrongful action and citizens will thus be effectively protected.

Fourth, the procedure should provide effective and meaningful compensation to those citizens, particularly innocent victims of illegal searches and seizures. This the present exclusionary rule totally fails to do. Only the guilty person who has suffered an illegal search and seizure receives some form of compensation—an acquittal, which is usually in gross disproportion to the injury inflicted on him by an illegal search and seizure. Thus, under the present irrational exclusionary rule system, the guilty are over-rewarded by a commutation of all penalties for crimes they did commit and the innocent are never compensated for the injuries they suffered.

THE MAGNITUDE OF THE OFFENSE

Fifth, it should be an objective of any substitute for the exclusionary rule to introduce comparative values into what is now a totally arbitrary process and inflexible penalty. Under the exclusionary rule, the "penalty" is the same irrespective of the offense. If an officer barely oversteps the line on probable cause and seizes five ounces of heroin from a peddler on the street corner, or an officer without a warrant and without probable cause barges into a home and seizes private papers, the result is automatic—the evidence is barred, the accused is freed, and this is all the "punishment" the officer receives.

Surely the societal values involved in the two incidents are of a totally different magnitude. The error of the officer in dealing with narcotics peddlers should not be overlooked, his misapprehension of the requirement of probable cause should be called to his attention quickly in a way which he will remember, but actual punishment should be relatively minimal. In the instance of an invalid seizure of private papers in the home, the officer should be severely punished for such a gross infraction of Fourth Amendment rights.

The exclusionary rule is applied automatically now when there is no illegal action by investigative officers and hence no possible deterrence to future police misconduct. For example, where government agents have dutifully applied to a judge or magistrate for a search warrant, and executed the warrant in strict conformity with its terms, a warrant which later proves defective will force the judge later to exclude the evidence illegally seized. All that is involved in these instances is a legal error on the part of the judge, magistrate, or perhaps the attorney who drew the papers. It is absurd to say that the court subsequently is "punishing" or attempting to "deter" the judge, magistrate, or attorney who made the legal error by suppressing the evidence and letting the accused go free, but this is what happens now.

It these are valid objectives in seeking a substitute procedure for the exclusionary rule as a method of enforcing Fourth Amendment rights, there seem to be two general approaches which might well be combined in one statute—internal discipline by the law enforcement authorities themselves, and external control by the courts or an independent review board.

INTERNAL DISCIPLINE

Disciplinary action against the offending law enforcement officer could be initiated by the law enforcement organization itself or by the person whose Fourth Amendment rights had been allegedly violated. The police could initiate action either within the regular command structure or by an overall disciplinary board outside the hierarchy of command. Many law enforcement organizations have such disciplinary boards now and they could be made mandatory by statute in all federal law enforcement agencies. Wherever they may be located, the organization would require action to be taken following the seizure of material evidence, if the criminal trial or an independent investigation showed a violation of the Fourth Amendment standards.

The person injured could also initiate action leading to internal discipline of the offending officer by complaint to the agency disciplinary board. Each enforcement agency or department could establish a process to hear and decide the complaint, providing both a penalty for the offending officer (if the violation were proved) and government compensation to the injured party.

This procedure would cover numerous cases in which citizens suffer violations of Fourth Amendment rights, but in which no court action results. The injured party could choose this administrative remedy in lieu of court action, but any award in the administrative proceedings would be taken into account by a court later if a citizen, dissatisfied with the award, instituted further legal action.

The penalty against the officer would be tailored to fit his own culpability; it might be a reprimand, a fine, a delay in promotion, a suspension, or discharge. Factors bearing upon the extent of the penalty would include the extent to which the violation was willful, the manner in which it deviated from approved conduct, the degree to which it invaded the privacy of the injured party, and the extent to which human dignity and societal values were breached.

Providing compensation to the injured party from the government is necessary, for it is simply realistic to make the government liable for the wrongful acts of its agent in order to make the prospect of compensation meaningful. Policemen traditionally are not wealthy and the government has a deep purse. Moreover, higher administrative officials and irate taxpayers may be expected to react adversely to losses resulting from the misconduct of policemen and to do something about their training and exercise of responsibilities.

EXTERNAL CONTROL

When a prosecutor tries a defendant in the wake of a violation of Fourth Amendment rights, the court could conduct a mini-trial of the offending officer after the violation is alleged and proof outlined in the principal criminal case. This mini-trial would be similar to a hearing on a motion to suppress now, but it would be conducted after the main criminal case. The burden would be on the injured party to prove, by preponderance of the evidence, that the officer violated his Fourth Amendment rights. The policeman could submit his case to either the judge or the jury who heard the main criminal case.

By initiating the "trial" of the officer immediately following the criminal case in which he was charged with misconduct, the court could determine the question of his violation speedily and economically. Presumably both the judge and jury have been thoroughly familiarized with the facts of the main case and are able to put the conduct of the officer in perspective.

Such a mini-trial would provide an outside disciplinary force that the injured party could utilize in lieu of internal discipline by the agency. Any previous administrative action taken against the officer would be considered by the judge and jury, if a penalty were to be assessed as a result of the mini-trial. The same factors bearing on the penalty to the officer and compensation to the injured party as discussed under the administrative remedy would be relevant in the mini-trial.

In those instances where police violate Fourth Amendment rights but the prosecutor does not bring charges against the suspect, the wronged party should be able to bring a statutory civil action against the government and the officer. Both would be named as defendants: the officer to defend against any individual penalty, the government to be able to respond adequately in damages to the injured party if such were found. Many instances of Fourth Amendment violation now go unnoticed because no criminal charge is brought and the injured party is not in position to bring a *Bivens*-type suit for the alleged constitutional violation. The burden of proof on the factors in regard to penalty and compensation would be the same as in a mini-trial following the principal criminal case, as discussed above.

The creation of this civil remedy could be accomplished by simple amendment to the present Federal Tort Claims Act. This is the procedure followed in many other countries, among them Canada.

> . . . the remedy in tort has proved reasonably effective; Canadian juries are quick to resent illegal activity on the part of the police and to express that resentment by a proportionate judgment for damages.

Disciplinary punishment and civil penalties directly against the erring officer involved would certainly provide a far more effective deterrent than the Supreme Court has created in the exclusionary rule. The creation of a civil remedy for violations of privacy, whether or not the invasion resulted in a criminal prosecution, would provide a remedy for the innocent victims of Fourth Amendment violations which the exclusionary rule has never pretended to give. And the rationale that the "government should not 'profit' from its own agent's misconduct" would disappear completely if erring officers were punished and injured parties compensated when there was a Fourth Amendment violation. If such a law and procedure were enforced, there would be no remaining objection to the subject of search and seizure still receiving his appropriate punishment for his crime.

CONCLUSION

All of the above was written before I read Professor Kamisar's ["Is the exclusionary rule an 'illogical' or 'unnatural' interpretation of the Fourth Amendment?" 62 Judicature 66.] It is apparent that our respective positions are widely divergent. After pondering his statement, I believe it fair to say that he must attempt to defend his position on one of two grounds, and that on analysis neither is defensible.

First, if Professor Kamisar believes that the Fourth Amendment necessarily mandates the exclusionary rule, then he ought to cite Supreme Court authority for this position. Nowhere in his article does he do so. It is undeniable that at no time in the Court's history has a majority in any case ever so held, and I do not believe that any more than two individual justices in the Court's history have so expressed themselves. In contrast, numerous justices, both favoring and opposing the rule, have stated that the rule itself is *not* mandated by the Fourth Amendment.

Second, if Professor Kamisar's article is intended only to say that under the Constitution we have a choice of methods to enforce the ban against "unreasonable searches and seizures," and that the exclusionary rule is a good choice only because of "the imperative of judicial integrity," then I submit both logic and experience in this country and all other countries refutes this. If the Su-

preme Court or the Congress has a choice of methods under the Constitution, then it simply will not do to rest the choice of exclusionary rule solely on the high principle of "judicial integrity" and to ignore the pragmatic result, the failure to achieve the objective of enforcement and the other pernicious side effects discussed above, which themselves strongly discredit judicial integrity.

If we have a choice, to attempt to justify the continuation of the exclusionary rule on this basis is to be stubbornly blind to 65 years of experience. If we have a choice, to insist on continuing a method of enforcement with as many demonstrated faults as the exclusionary rule is to be blindly stubborn. If we have a choice, let us calmly and carefully consider the available alternatives, draw upon the experience of other nations with systems of justice similar to our own, and by abolishing the rule permit in the laboratories of our 51 jurisdictions the experimentation with various possible alternatives promising far more than the now discredited exclusionary rule.

NO ·   Yale Kamisar

THE STRUGGLE TO MAKE
THE FOURTH AMENDMENT
MORE THAN AN EMPTY BLESSING

In the 65 years since the Supreme Court adopted the exclusionary rule, few critics have attacked it with as much vigor and on as many fronts as did Judge Malcolm Wilkey in his recent *Judicature* article, "The exclusionary rule: why suppress valid evidence?" (November 1978).

According to Judge Wilkey, there is virtually nothing good about the rule and a great deal bad about it. He thinks the rule is partly to blame for "the distressing rate of street crimes." He tells us that it "discourages internal disciplinary action by the police themselves"; actually results in "encouraging highly pernicious police behavior" (e.g., perjury, harassment and corruption); "makes it virtually impossible for any state, not only the federal government, to experiment with any methods of controlling police"; and "undermines the reputation of and destroys the respect for the entire judicial system."

Judge Wilkey claims, too, that the rule "dooms" "every scheme of gun control . . . to be totally ineffective in preventing the habitual use of weapons in street crimes." Until we rid ourselves of this rule, he argues, "the criminal can parade in the street with a great bulge in his pocket or a submachine gun in a blanket under his arm" and "laugh in the face of the officer who might wish to search him for it."

UNTHINKING, EMOTIONAL ATTACHMENT?

Why, then, has the rule survived? "The greatest obstacle to replacing the exclusionary rule with a rational process," Judge Wilkey maintains, is "the powerful, unthinking emotional attachment" to the rule. If you put the issue to a representative group of lawyers and judges, he concedes, "you would doubtless hear some support" for the rule, but only from those "heavily imbued with a mystique of the exclusionary rule as of almost divine origin."

From Yale Kamisar, "The Exclusionary Rule in Historical Perspective: The Struggle to Make the Fourth Amendment More Than 'an Empty Blessing,' " *Judicature* (February 1979). Copyright © 1979 by Yale Kamisar. Reprinted by permission of the author.

It is hard to believe that nothing more substantial than "unthinking emotional attachment" or mystical veneration accounts for support for the rule by Justices Holmes and Brandeis [and,] more recently, by such battlescarred veterans as Roger Traynor, Earl Warren and Tom Clark.

In the beginning, Judge Traynor was not attached to the rule, emotionally or otherwise. Indeed, in 1942 he wrote the opinion of the California Supreme Court reaffirming the admissibility of illegally-seized evidence. But by 1955, it became apparent to Traynor that illegally seized evidence "was being offered and admitted as a routine procedure" and "it became impossible to ignore the corollary that illegal searches and seizures were also a routine procedure, subject to no effective deterrent."

> [W]ithout fear of criminal punishment or other discipline, law enforcement officers . . . casually regard [illegal searches and seizures] as nothing more than the performance of their ordinary duties for which the City employs and pays them.

In light of these circumstances, Traynor overruled the court's earlier decision.

And consider Earl Warren. During the 24 years he spent in state law enforcement work in California (as deputy district attorney, district attorney and attorney general), California admitted illegally seized evidence. Indeed, Warren was the California Attorney General who successfully urged Judge Traynor and his brethren to reaffirm that rule in 1942. In 1954, during his first year as Chief Justice of the United States, he heard a case involving police misconduct so outrageous as to be "almost incredible if it were not admitted" (the infamous *Irvine* case), but he resisted the tempta-

tion to impose the exclusionary rule on the states, even in such extreme cases. It was not until 1961 that he joined in the opinion for the Court in *Mapp*, which imposed the rule on the states.

Chief Justice Warren knew the exclusionary rule's limitations as a tool of judicial control, but at the end of an extraordinary public career—in which he had served more years as a prosecutor than any other person who has ascended to the Supreme Court—Warren observed:

> [I]n our system, evidentiary rulings provide the context in which the judicial process of inclusion and exclusion approves some conduct as comporting with constitutional guarantees and disapproves other actions by state agents. A ruling admitting evidence in a criminal trial, we recognize, has the necessary effect of legitimizing the conduct which produced the evidence, while an application of the exclusionary rule withholds the constitutional imprimatur.

The author of the *Mapp* opinion, Tom Clark, was, of course, U.S. Attorney General for four years before he became a Supreme Court justice and he was assistant attorney general in charge of the criminal division before that. Evidently, nothing in his experience gave Clark reason to believe that the rule had "handcuffed" federal officials or would cripple state law enforcement. And he never changed his views about the need for the exclusionary rule during his 18 years on the Court or the 10 years he spent in the administration of justice following his retirement. Indeed, shortly before his death, he warmly defended *Mapp* and *Weeks*.

Moreover, nothing in Justice Clark's career suggests that he endorsed *Mapp* out of "sentimentality" or in awe of the "divine origins" of the exclusionary rule. More likely, he was impressed with the failure of *Wolf* and *Irvine* to stimulate any meaningful alternative to the exclusionary rule in the more than 20 states that still admitted illegally seized evidence at the time of *Mapp*.

I do not mean to suggest that Judge Wilkey's views on the exclusionary rule are aberrational among lawyers and judges; many members of the bench and bar share his deep distress with the rule. Indeed, when Judge Wilkey asks us to abolish the exclusionary rule now—without waiting for a meaningful alternative to emerge—he but follows the lead of Chief Justice Burger, who recently maintained:

> [T]he continued existence of the rule, as presently implemented, inhibits the development of rational alternativest. . . .
> It can no longer be assumed that other branches of government will act while judges cling to this Draconian, discredited device in its present absolutist form.

Because so many share Judge Wilkey's hostility to the exclusionary rule, it is important to examine and to evaluate Wilkey's arguments at some length. Only then can we determine whether the rule is as irrational and pernicious as he and other critics maintain—and whether we can abolish it before we have developed an alternative.

CRIME AND THE RULE

A year before the California Supreme Court adopted the exclusionary rule on its own—and years before the "revolution" in American criminal procedure began—William H. Parker, the Chief of the Los Angeles Police Department, said:

> [O]ur most accurate crime statistics indicate that crime rates rise and fall on the tides of economic, social, and political cycles with embarrassingly little attention to the most determined efforts of our police.

Almost as soon as the California Supreme Court adopted the exclusionary rule, though, Chief Parker began blaming the rule for the high rate of crime in Los Angeles, calling it "catastrophic as far as efficient law enforcement is concerned," and insisting "that the imposition of the exclusionary rule has rendered the people powerless to adequately protect themselves against the criminal army."

Such criticism of the *Cahan* rule was only a preview of the attack on *Mapp*. Chief Justice Traynor, speaking about the debate following the *Mapp* decision, rightly observed that: "Articulate comment about [*Mapp*] . . . was drowned out in the din about handcuffing the police.

Thus, it is not surprising that Judge Wilkey would claim on his very first page that "[w]e can see [the] huge social cost [of *Weeks* and *Mapp*] most clearly in the distressing rate of street crimes . . . which flourish in no small degree simply because of the exclusionary rule." Nevertheless, it is disappointing to hear a critic repeat this charge, because after 65 years of debate, there was reason to hope that this criticism, at least, would no longer be made. As Professor James Vorenberg pointed out, shortly after he completed his two years of service as Executive Director of the President's Commission on Law Enforcement and Administration of Justice:

> What the Supreme Court does has practically no effect on the amount of crime in this country, and what the

police do has far less effect than is generally realized.

Even Professor Dallin Oaks (now a university president), upon whose work Judge Wilkey relies so heavily, advised a decade ago:

> The whole argument about the exclusionary rule 'handcuffing' the police should be abandoned. If this is a negative effect, then it is an effect of the constitutional rules, not an effect of the exclusionary rule as the means chosen for their enforcement.
>
> Police officials and prosecutors should stop claiming that the exclusionary rule prevents effective law enforcement. In doing so they attribute far greater effect to the exclusionary rule than the evidence warrants, and they are also in the untenable position of urging that the sanction be abolished so that they can continue to violate the [constitutional] rules with impunity.

A WEAK LINK

Over the years, I have written about the impact of *Cahan*, *Mapp* and other decisions on crime rates and police-prosecution efficiency. I will not restate my findings again, especially since Judge Wilkey has presented no statistical support for his assertion. I would, however, like to summarize a few points:

•Long before the exclusionary rule became law in the states—indeed, long before any of the procedural safeguards in the federal Constitution was held applicable to the states—invidious comparisons were made between the rate of crime in our nation and the incidence of crime in others.

Thus, in 1911, the distinguished ex-president of Cornell University, Andrew D. White, pointed out that, although London's population was two million larger than New York's, there were 10 times more murders in New York. And in 1920, Edwin W. Sims, the first head of the Chicago Crime Commission, pointed out that "[d]uring 1919 there were more murders in Chicago (with a population of three million) than in the entire British Isles (with a population of forty million)." This history ought to raise some doubts about the alleged causal link between the high rate of crime in America and the exclusionary rule.

•England and Wales have not experienced anything like the "revolution" in American criminal procedure which began at least as early as the 1961 *Mapp* case. Nevertheless, from 1955–65 (a decade which happened to be subjected to a most intensive study), the number of indictable offenses against the person in England and Wales increased 162 percent. How do opponents of the exclusionary rule explain such increases in countries which did not suffer from the wounds the Warren Court supposedly inflicted upon America?

•In the decade before *Mapp*, Maryland admitted illegally seized evidence in all felony prosecutions; Virginia, in all cases. District of Columbia police, on the other hand, were subject to both the exclusionary rule and the *McNabb-Mallory* rule, a rule which "hampered" no other police department during this period. Nevertheless, during this decade the felony rate per 100,000 population increased much more in the three Virginia and Maryland suburbs of the District (69 percent) than in the District itself (a puny one percent).

•The predictions and descriptions of near-disaster in California law enforcement which greeted the 1955 *Cahan* decision find precious little empirical support. The percentage of narcotics convictions did drop almost 10 points (to 77 percent), but only possession cases were significantly affected. Meanwhile, both the rate of arrests and felony complaints filed for narcotics offenses actually increased! Thus, in 1959–60, 20 percent more persons were convicted of narcotics offenses in California superior courts than in the record conviction percentage years before *Cahan*.

The overall felony conviction rate was 84.5 percent for the three years before *Cahan*, 85.4 percent for the *Cahan* year and 86.4 percent in the three years after *Cahan* (even including the low narcotic percentages). Conviction rates for murder, manslaughter, felony assault, rape, robbery and burglary remained almost the same, though the number of convicted felons rose steadily.

The exclusionary rule, to be sure, does free some "guilty criminals" (as would an effective tort remedy that inhibited the police from making illegal searches and seizures in the first place), but very rarely are they robbers or murderers. Rather they are "offenders caught in the everyday world of police initiated vice and narcotics enforcement . . ."

> Though critics of the exclusionary rule sometimes sound as though it constitutes the main loophole in the administration of justice, the fact is that it is only a minor escape route in a system that filters out far more offenders through police, prosecutorial, and judicial discretion than it tries, convicts and sentences. . . .
>
> Moreover, the critics' concentration on the formal issue of conviction tends to overlook the very real sanctions that are imposed even on defendants who 'escape' via the suppression of evidence [e.g., among the poor, most suffer at least several days of imprisonment, regardless of the ultimate verdict; many

lose their jobs as a result and have a hard time finding another]. . . .

> When one considers that many convictions in the courts that deal with large numbers of motions to suppress often amount to small fines, suspended sentences, and probation, the distinction between conviction and escape becomes even more blurred.

AN UNDEMONSTRATED CONNECTION

. . . Judge Wilkey hints darkly that there is a "connection" between America's high crime rate and its "unique" exclusionary rule. So far as I am aware, no one has been able to demonstrate such a connection on the basis of the annual *Uniform Crime Reports* or any other statistical data. In Michigan, for example, the rate of violent crime seems to have fluctuated without regard to the life and death of the state's "anti-exclusionary" proviso.

From 1960–64, the robbery rate increased only slightly in the Detroit Metropolitan Statistical Area but it quadrupled from 1964 to 1970 (from 152.5 per 100,000 to 648.5). When the Michigan Supreme Court struck down the state's "anti-exclusionary" proviso in 1970, the robbery rate fell (to 470.3 per 100,000 in 1973), climbed (to 604.2 in 1975), then dropped again (to 454.3 in 1977, the lowest it has been since the 1960's).

From 1960–64, the murder and nonnegligent manslaughter rate remained almost the same in the Detroit area, but it rose extraordinarily the next six years (5.0 in 1964 to 14.7 in 1970). In the next four years it continued to climb (but less sharply) to 20.2 in 1974. Then it dropped to 14.1 in 1977, the lowest it has been since the 1960's.

Finally, I must take issue with Judge Wilkey's case of the criminal who "parade[s] in the streets with a great bulge in his pocket or a submachine gun in a blanket under his arm," "laugh[ing] in the face of the officer who might wish to search him for it." If American criminals "know the difficulties of the police in making a valid search," as Judge Wilkey tells us, they know, too, that the exclusionary rule has "virtually no applicability" in "large areas of police activity which do not result in criminal prosecutions" and that confiscation of weapons is one of them. (The criminal might get back his blanket, but not the submachine gun).

Moreover, it is not at all clear that an officer who notices a "great bulge" in a person's pocket or, as in the recent *Mimms* case, a "large bulge" under a person's sports jacket, lacks lawful authority to conduct a limited search for weapons. Indeed, *Mimms* seems to say that a policeman *does* have the authority under such circumstances. Even if I am wrong, however, even if the Fourth Amendment does not permit an officer to make such a limited search for weapons, *abolishing the exclusionary rule wouldn't change that*. If an officer now lacks the lawful authority to conduct a "frisk" under these circumstances, he would still lack the lawful authority to do so if the rule were abolished. This is a basic point, one that I shall focus on in the next section.

A BASIC CONFUSION

In my earlier *Judicature* article, I pointed out how police and prosecutors have treated the exclusionary rule as if it were itself the guaranty against unreasonable search and seizure (which is one good reason for retaining the rule). At several places Judge Wilkey's article reflects the same confusion.

He complains, for example, that if a search or frisk turns up a deadly weapon, that weapon cannot be used in evidence if the officer lacked the constitutionally required cause for making the search or frisk in the first place. But this is really an attack on the constitutional guaranty itself, not the exclusionary rule. Prohibiting the use of illegally seized evidence may be poor "public relations" because by then we know who the criminal is, but an *after-the-fact* prohibition

> prevents convictions in no greater degree than would effective prior direction to police to search only by legal means . . . [T]he maintenance of existing standards by means of exclusion is not open to attack unless it can be doubted whether the standards themselves are necessary.

If we replace the exclusionary rule with "disciplinary punishment and civil penalties directly against the erring officer involved," as Judge Wilkey proposes, and if these alternatives "would certainly provide a far more effective deterrent than . . . the exclusionary rule," as the judge assures us, the weapon still would not be brought in as evidence in the case he poses because the officer would not *make* the search or frisk if he lacked the requisite cause to do so.

Judge Wilkey points enviously to England, where "the criminals know that the police have a right to search them *on the slightest suspicion*, and they know that if a weapon is found they will be prosecuted" (emphasis added). But what is the relevance of this point in an article discussing the exclusionary rule and its alternatives? Abolishing the rule would not confer a *right* on our police to search "on the slightest suspicion;" it would not affect lawful police practices in any way. Only a change in the substantive law of search and seizure can do that. . . . And replacing the exclusionary rule with a statutory remedy against the government would not bring about an increase in unlawful police activity if the alternative were equally effective—and Judge Wilkey expects it to be "a far more effective deterrent."

I venture to say that Judge Wilkey has confused the *content* of the law of search seizure (which proponents of the exclusionary rule need not, and have not always, defended) with the *exclusionary rule*—which "merely states the consequences of a breach of whatever principles might be adopted to control law enforcement officers." The confusion was pointed out more than 50 years ago by one who had the temerity to reply to the great Wigmore's famous criticism of the rule. Every student of the problem knows Wigmore's views on this subject, but very few are familiar with Connor Hall's reply. It is worth recalling:

> When it is proposed to secure the citizen his constitutional rights by the direct punishment of the violating officer, we must assume that the proposer is honest, and that he would have such consistent prosecution and such heavy punishment of the offending officer as would cause violations to cease and thus put a stop to the seizure of papers and other tangible evidence through unlawful search.
>
> If this, then, is to be the result, no evidence in any appreciable number of cases would be obtained through unlawful searches, and the result would be the same, so far as the conviction of criminals goes, as if the constitutional right was enforced by a return of the evidence.

Then why such anger in celestial breasts? Justice can be rendered inefficient and the criminal classes coddled by the rule laid down in *Weeks* only upon the assumption that the officer will not be directly punished, but that the court will receive the fruits of his lawful acts, will do no more than denounce and threaten him with jail or the penitentiary and, at the same time, with its tongue in its cheek, give him to understand how fearful a thing it is to violate the Constitution. This has been the result previous to the rule adopted by the Supreme Court, and that is what the courts are asked to continue.

. . . If punishment of the officer is effective to prevent unlawful searches, then equally by this is justice rendered inefficient and criminals coddled. It is only by violations that the great god Efficiency can thrive.

WAITING FOR ALTERNATIVES

Judge Wilkey makes plain his agreement with Chief Justice Burger that "the continued existence of [the exclusionary rule] . . . inhibits the development of rational alternatives" and that "incentives for developing new procedures or remedies will remain minimal or nonexistent so long as the exclusionary rule is retained in its present form."

Thus, Judge Wilkey warns that "we will never have any alternative in operation until the rule is abolished. So long as we keep the rule, the police are not going to investigate and discipline their men, and thus sabotage prosecutions by invalidating the admissibility of vital evidence. . . ." He argues the *Mapp* "removed from the states both the incentive and the opportunity to deal with illegal search and seizure by means other than suppression." And he concludes his first article with these words:

[L]et us . . . by abolishing the rule permit in the laboratories of our fifty-one jurisdictions the experimentation with the various possible alternatives promising far more than the now discredited exclusionary rule.

In light of our history, these comments (both the Chief Justice's and Judge Wilkey's) are simply baffling. First, the fear of "sabotaging" prosecutions has never inhibited law enforcement administrators from disciplining officers for committing the "many unlawful searches of homes and automobiles of innocent people which turn up nothing incriminating, in which no arrest is made, about which courts do nothing, and about which we never hear."

Second, both defenders of the rule and its critics recognize that

there are large areas of police activity which do not result in criminal prosecutions [e.g., arrest or confiscation as a punitive sanction (common in gambling and liquor law violations), illegal detentions which do not result in the acquisition of evidence, unnecessary destruction of property]—hence the rule has virtually no applicability and no effect in such situations.

Whatever the reason for the failure to discipline officers for "mistakes" in these "large areas of police activities," it cannot be the existence of the exclusionary rule.

Finally, and most importantly, *for many decades* a majority of the states had no exclusionary rule but *none of them* developed any meaningful alternative. Thirty-five years passed between the time the federal courts adopted the exclusionary rule and the time *Wolf* was decided in 1949, but none of the 31 states which still admitted illegally seized evidence had established an alternative method of controlling the police. Twelve more years passed before *Mapp* imposed the rule on the state courts, but none of the 24 states which still rejected the exclusionary rule had instituted an alternative remedy. This half-century of post-*Weeks* "freedom to experiment" did not produce any meaningful alternative to the exclusionary rule anywhere.

DISPARITY BETWEEN FACT AND THEORY

Of course, few critics of the exclusionary rule have failed to suggest alternative remedies that *might be devised* or that *warranted study*. None of them has become a reality.

In 1922, for example, Dean Wigmore maintained that "the natural way to do justice" would be to enforce the Fourth Amendment directly "by sending for the high-handed, overzealous marshal who had searched without a warrant, imposing a 30-day imprisonment for his contempt of the Constitution, and then proceeding to affirm the sentence of the convicted criminal." Nothing ever came of that proposal. Another critic of the rule suggested that a civil rights office be established, independent of the regular prosecutor, "charged solely with the responsibility of investigating and prosecuting alleged violations of the Constitution by law-enforcement officials." Nothing came of that proposal either.

Judge Wilkey recognizes that "policemen traditionally are not wealthy," but "[t]he government has a deep purse." Thus, as did Chief Justice Burger in his *Bivens* dissent, Judge Wilkey proposes that in lieu of the exclusion of illegally seized evidence there be a statutory remedy against the government itself to afford meaningful compensation and restitution for the victims of police illegality. Two leading commentators, Caleb Foote and Edward Barrett, Jr., made the same suggestion 20 years ago, but none of the many states that admitted illegally seized evidence at the time seemed interested in experimenting along these lines.

Indeed, the need for, and the desirability of, a statutory remedy against the government itself was pointed out at least as long ago as 1936. In a famous article published that year, Jerome Hall noted that the prospects of satisfying a judgment against a police officer were so poor that the tort remedy in the books "collapses at its initial application to fact." Said Hall:

> [W]here there is liability (as in the case of the policeman), the fact of financial irresponsibility is operative and, presumably, conclusive; while, where financial responsibility exists (as in the case of a city), there is no liability.

"This disparity between theory and fact, between an empty shell of relief and substantial compensation," observed Professor Hall—43 years ago—"could not remain unnoticed."

This disparity—no longer unnoticed, but still uncorrected—has troubled even the strongest critics of the rule. Thus, more than 35 years ago, J. A. C. Grant suggested "implement[ing] the law covering actions for trespass, even going so far as to hold the government liable in damages for the torts of its agents." And William Plumb, Jr., accompanied his powerful attack on the rule with a similar suggestion.

MAPP'S TRAUMATIC EFFECTS

At the time of Plumb's article, the admissibility of illegally-seized evidence had "once more become a burning question in New York." Delegates to the 1938 constitutional convention had defeated an effort to write the exclusionary rule into the constitution, but only after a long and bitter debate. The battle then moved to the legislature, where bills were pending to exclude illegally obtained, or at least illegally wiretapped, evidence.

Against this background, Plumb offered a whole basketful of alternative to the rule and he said the state legislature "should make a thorough study of the problem of devising effective direct remedies [such as those he had outlined] to make the constitutional guarantee 'a real, not an empty blessing.'" But nothing happened.

Otherwise why would a New York City Police Commissioner say of *Mapp* some 20 years later:

> I can think of no decision in recent times in the field of law enforcement which had such a dramatic effect as this. . . . I was immediately caught up in the entire problem of reevaluating our procedures which had followed the *Defore* rule, and modifying, amending, and creating new policies and new instructions for the implementation of *Mapp*. The problems were manifold. [Supreme Court decisions such as *Mapp*] create tidal waves and earthquakes which require rebuilding of our institutions sometimes from their very foundations upward. Retraining sessions had to be held from the very top administrators down to each of the thousands of foot patrolmen. . . ."

In theory, *Defore*, which rejected the exclusionary rule in New York, had not expanded lawful police powers one iota. Nor, in theory, had *Mapp* reduced these powers. What was an illegal search before *Defore* was still an illegal search. What was an unlawful arrest before *Mapp* was still an unlawful arrest.

The *Defore* rule, of course, was based largely upon the premise that New York did not need to adopt the exclusionary rule because existing remedies were adequate to effectuate the guaranty against illegal search and seizure. Cardozo said that:

> The officer might have been resisted[!], or sued for damages or even prosecuted for oppression. He was subject to removal or other discipline at the hands of his superiors.

Why, then, did *Mapp* have such a "dramatic" and "traumatic" effect? Why did it necessitate "creating new policies?" What were the old policies like? Why did it necessitate retraining sessions from top to bottom? What was the *old* training like? What did the commissioner mean when he said that before *Mapp* his department had "followed the *Defore* rule?"

> On behalf of the New York City Police Department as well as law enforcement in general, I state unequivocally that every effort was directed and is still being directed at compliance with and implementation of *Mapp*. . . .

Isn't it peculiar to talk about police "compliance with" and "implementation of" a *remedy* for a violation of a body of law the police were supposed to be complying with and implementing all along? Why did the police have to make such strenuous efforts to comply with *Mapp* unless they had not been complying with the Fourth Amendment?

> Flowing from the *Mapp* case is the issue of defining probable cause to constitute a lawful arrest and subsequent search and seizure.

Doesn't this issue flow from the Fourth Amendment itself? Isn't that what the Fourth Amendment is all about?

The police reaction to *Mapp* demonstrates the unsoundness of the underlying premise of *Defore*. Otherwise why, at a post-Mapp training session on the law of search and seizure, would Leonard Reisman, then the New York Deputy Police Commissioner in charge of legal matters, comment:

> The *Mapp* case was a shock to us. We had to reorganize our thinking, frankly. Before this, nobody bothered to take out search warrants. Although the U.S. Constitution requires warrants in most cases, the U.S. Supreme Court had ruled [until 1961] that evidence obtained without a warrant—illegally if you will—was admissible in state courts. So the feeling was, why bother?

NO INCENTIVE FOR CHANGE

As I have already indicated, critics of the exclusionary rule have often made proposals for effectuating the Fourth Amendment by means other than the exclusionary rule—but almost always as a *quid pro quo* for rejecting or repealing the rule. Who has ever heard of a police-prosecution spokesman urging—or a law enforcement group supporting—an effective "direct remedy" for illegal searches and seizures in a jurisdiction which *admitted* illegally seized evidence? Abandoning the exclusionary rule without waiting for a meaningful alternative (as Judge Wilkey and Chief Justice Burger would have us do) will not furnish an incentive for devising an alternative, but *relieve* whatever pressure there now exists for doing so.

I spoke in my earlier article of the great symbolic value of the exclusionary rule. Abolition of the exclusionary rule, after the long, bitter struggle to attain it, would be even more important as a symbol.

During the 12-year reign of *Wolf*, some state judges

> remained mindful of the cogent reasons for the admission of illegally obtained evidence and clung to the fragile hope that the very brazenness of lawless police methods would bring on effective deterrents other than the exclusionary rule.

Their hope proved to be in vain. *Wolf* established the "underlying constitutional doctrine" that "the Federal Constitution, by virtue of the Fourteenth Amendment, prohibits unreasonable searches and seizures by state officers" (though it did not require exclusion of the resulting evidence); *Irvine* warned that if the state "defaulted and there were no demonstrably effective deterrents to unreasonable searches and seizures in lieu of the exclusionary rule, the Supreme Court might yet decide that they had not complied with 'minimal standards' of due process." But neither *Wolf* nor *Irvine* stimulated a single state legislature or a single law enforcement agency to demonstrate that the problem could be handled in other ways.

The disappointing 12 years between *Wolf* and *Mapp* give added weight to Francis Allen's thoughtful commentary on the *Wolf* case at the time it was handed down:

> This deference to local authority revealed in the *Wolf* case stands in marked contrast to the position of the court in other cases arising within the last decade involving rights 'basic to a free society.' It seems safe to assert that in no other area of civil liberties litigation is there evidence that the court has construed the obligations of federalism

to require so high a degree of judicial self-abnegation.

> . . . [I]n no other area in the civil liberties has the court felt justified in trusting to public protest for protection of basic personal rights. Indeed, since the rights of privacy are usually asserted by those charged with crime and since the demands of efficient law enforcement are so insistent, it would seem that reliance on public opinion in these cases can be less justified than in almost any other. . . .

Now Judge Wilkey asks us to believe that the resurrection of *Wolf* (and evidently the overruling of the 65-year-old *Weeks* case as well) will permit "the laboratories of our 51 jurisdictions" to produce meaningful alternatives to the exclusionary rule. His ideological ally, Chief Justice Burger, is even more optimistic. He asks us to believe that a return to the pre-exclusionary rule days "would inspire a surge of activity toward providing some kind of statutory remedy for persons injured by police mistakes or misconduct."

And to think that Judge Wilkey accuses *defenders* of the exclusionary rule of being "stubbornly blind to 65 years of experience"!

POSTSCRIPT

Should the Exclusionary Rule Be Abolished?

Judge Wilkey is not the only federal judge opposed to the exclusionary rule. The most famous judicial critic is former Supreme Court chief justice Warren Burger. Justice Burger's opposition to the rule, however, has not led to an overturning of *Mapp* or *Weeks*, at least not yet. But during the past eighteen years, there have been a substantial number of cases in which the Court considered the rule and restricted its scope. Thus, while the rule can still be invoked by a defendant at a criminal trial, it cannot be used at a grand jury proceeding (see *United States v. Calandra*, 414 U.S. 338, 1974), in a *habeas corpus* proceeding by a state prisoner (see *Stone v. Powell*, 428 U.S. 465, 1976), when the illegal search is conducted on someone other than the defendant (see *United States v. Payner*, 447 U.S. 727, 1980), or when the illegal search was conducted outside the United States (see *U.S. v. Verdugo-Urguidez*, 110 S.Ct. 1056, 1990). The most noteworthy recent case in which the exclusionary rule was upheld was *James v. Illinois*, 110 S.Ct. 648 (1990), where the Court refused to allow the use of illegally seized evidence to impeach the credibility of a defense witness if the defendant does not testify.

The Court has approved a good faith exception to the rule in cases where the police officer believed that he was acting lawfully, even though the warrant may have been defective or procured illegally (*Massachusetts v. Sheppard*, 104 S.Ct. 3424, 1984). It has also ruled that search warrants are not required for school officials to search school lockers if there are reasonable grounds for believing the search will reveal evidence of criminal behavior (*New Jersey v. T. L. O., A Juvenile*, 105 S.Ct. 733, 1985). The Burger and Rehnquist courts have generally been lenient in upholding police law enforcement practices and the policy of limiting the defendant's opportunities for invoking the exclusionary rule seems likely to continue. This is an effective approach for those opposed to the exclusionary rule, particularly when one considers the fact that most cases are plea bargained and do not get to trial, where the police search could be scrutinized by a judge.

In part, the resistance to the exclusionary rule is based on a belief that it does not deter illegal police conduct. An interesting debate on the subject, which examines many of the relevant research studies, is found in a series of articles in *Judicature:* B. Canon, "The Exclusionary Rule: Have Critics Proven That It Doesn't Deter Police?" pp. 398–403, March 1979, and Steven S. Schlesinger, "The Exclusionary Rule: Have Proponents Proven That It Is a Deterrent to Police?" pp. 404–409, March 1979. Recent articles include Nelson, "The Paradox of the Exclusionary Rule," *The Public Interest,* Summer, 1989, p. 117; and Note, "The Future of the Exclusionary Rule and the Development of State Constitutional Law," 1987 *Wisconsin Law Review* 377 (1987).

ISSUE 14

Should Drugs Be Legalized?

YES: Ethan A. Nadelmann, from "The Case for Legalization," *The Public Interest* (vol. 92, 1988)

NO: Steven Brill, from "Should We Give Up?" *The American Lawyer* (March 1990)

ISSUE SUMMARY

YES: Professor Ethan Nadelmann claims that drug enforcement policies are not working and will never be effective and that legalizing drugs would eliminate many of the costs brought about by the war on drugs.

NO: Publisher and journalist Steven Brill maintains that government should not abdicate its responsibility, that legalization would make the drug problem worse, and that some segments of the population would be devastated if enforcement were stopped.

One can hardly miss the impact of illegal drugs on the fabric of American life. If you watch the local evening news, there is evidence of increasing incidents of violent crime in urban neighborhoods, with most of the victims being young. The lure of the "get very rich quick" life-style of drug dealers has tempted many poor teenagers into a life of violence, even against their own families. It is hard to believe that a child would turn the family apartment into a "shooting gallery" or sell all the family possessions for money to purchase drugs. But it has happened and when the parents have protested, the children have even turned their wrath against them.

According to the article in this issue by Steven Brill, one-fifth of the 3,000 babies born in New York City's Harlem Hospital this year will be born to addicted mothers. That is a staggering figure, particularly because these 600 children will be among hundreds of other similarly afflicted children born in urban hospitals across the nation.

What is even more harrowing is the description of the crack-addicted mothers in Brill's article. It makes one shiver to think about what will be the future of the children of these mothers. Fifty percent go into foster care. But a hundred percent need to go to school, and many such children are now entering the public education systems around the nation. What educators are facing are children who exhibit serious neurological and learning problems that may condemn them to a lifelong struggle to attain any learning.

How much can be hoped for of a child who is part of the foster care system, who is from a desperately poor family, and who cannot attend to a task for any length of time?

Lest one erroneously think that only poor children are the victims of the drug epidemic, the names Gooden, Zaccaro, and Belushi, among others, have been linked to drugs. Athletes such as Dwight Gooden of the New York Mets have had their careers jeopardized by drug use. The 1984 Democratic candidate for vice president of the United States, Geraldine Ferraro, had to listen to testimony against her son, John Zaccaro, when he was tried for drug trafficking.

Men and women in all walks of life are using drugs regularly and while engaging in their professions. A March 1988 *New York Times*/CBS poll indicated that, at that time, Americans were far more worried about the impact of drugs on their lives than about problems of Mid-East peace or terrorism abroad. Americans should be worried, because the drug problem is not just the problem of the poor teenager in Detroit or Philadelphia. In Massachusetts recently, a mother was tried for leaving her two small children alone in an apartment, to which they set fire and in which they died. Her defense was astonishing—she asked for leniency because she was an addict and had to leave her home to get a fix.

What is the solution to this situation that is ripping apart our society? In the following article, Professor Ethan Nadelmann argues that the approaches currently being used, such as drug use testing (Issue 5), are all wrong. He says we should legalize drugs and expand non-legal approaches to treatment and prevention. He believes that only through legalization of these drugs can we get a grip on the situation. Present approaches, which rely heavily on the police and court systems, are not putting much of a dent in either the rate of use or the supply of drugs. In fact, the prices of drugs are declining, while potency of street drugs is increasing. Furthermore, our present system is draining the government coffers of billions of dollars while urban street crime increases.

Steven Brill, an attorney and journalist, argues in "Should We Give Up?" for continuing the illegal status and consequent punishments attached to using and selling drugs. He cites some chilling evidence on the results of drug addiction and argues for more money and more effort going to treat addiction, thereby reducing the demand for drugs and the devastating effects that addiction has not only on the addict but on everyone else in the addict's life. Brill dismisses the arguments of Nadelmann and others that legalization would have greater benefit in poor neighborhoods where drugs and crime are linked.

YES

Ethan A. Nadelmann

THE CASE FOR LEGALIZATION

What can be done about the "drug problem"? Despite frequent proclamations of war and dramatic increases in government funding and resources in recent years, there are many indications that the problem is not going away and may even be growing worse. During the past year alone, more than thirty million Americans violated the drug laws on literally billions of occasions. Drug-treatment programs in many cities are turning people away for lack of space and funding. In Washington, D.C., drug-related killings, largely of one drug dealer by another, are held responsible for a doubling in the homicide rate over the past year. In New York and elsewhere, courts and prisons are clogged with a virtually limitless supply of drug-law violators. In large cities and small towns alike, corruption of policemen and other criminal-justice officials by drug traffickers is rampant. . . .

If there were a serious public debate on this issue, far more attention would be given to one policy option that has just begun to be seriously considered, but which may well prove more successful than anything currently being implemented or proposed: legalization. Politicians and public officials remain hesitant even to mention the word, except to dismiss it contemptuously as a capitulation to the drug traffickers. Most Americans perceive drug legalization as an invitation to drug-infested anarchy. Even the civil-liberties groups shy away from this issue, limiting their input primarily to the drug-testing debate. The minority communities in the ghetto, for whom repealing the drug laws would promise the greatest benefits, fail to recognize the costs of our drug-prohibition policies. And the typical middle-class American, who hopes only that his children will not succumb to drug abuse, tends to favor any measures that he believes will make illegal drugs less accessible to them. Yet when one seriously compares the advantages and disadvantages of the legalization strategy with those of current and planned policies, abundant evidence suggests that legalization may well be the optimal strategy for tackling the drug problem. . . .

There is, of course, no single legalization strategy. At one extreme is the libertarian vision of virtually no government restraints on the production

From Ethan A. Nadelmann, "The Case for Legalization," *The Public Interest*, vol. 92, no. 3 (1988). Copyright © 1988 by Ethan A. Nadelmann. Reprinted by permission of the author. Some notes omitted.

and sale of drugs or any psychoactive substances, except perhaps around the fringes, such as prohibiting sales to children. At the other extreme is total government control over the production and sale of these goods. In between lies a strategy that may prove more successful than anything yet tried in stemming the problems of drug abuse and drug-related violence, corruption, sickness, and suffering. It is one in which government makes most of the substances that are now banned legally available to competent adults, exercises strong regulatory powers over all large-scale production and sale of drugs, makes drug-treatment programs available to all who need them, and offers honest drug-education programs to children. This strategy, it is worth noting, would also result in a new benefit to public treasuries of at least ten billion dollars a year, and perhaps much more.

There are three reasons why it is important to think about legalization scenarios, even though most Americans remain hostile to the idea. First, current drug-control policies have failed, are failing, and will continue to fail, in good part because they are fundamentally flawed. Second, many drug-control efforts are not only failing, but also proving highly costly and counter-productive; indeed, many of the drug-related evils that Americans identify as part and parcel of the "drug problem" are in fact caused by our drug-prohibition policies. Third, there is good reason to believe that repealing many of the drug laws would not lead, as many people fear, to a dramatic rise in drug abuse. In this essay I expand on each of these reasons for considering the legalization option. Government efforts to deal with the drug problem will succeed only if the rhetoric and crusading mentality that now dominate drug policy are replaced by reasoned and logical analysis.

WHY CURRENT DRUG POLICIES FAIL

Most proposals for dealing with the drug problem today reflect a desire to point the finger at those most removed from one's home and area of expertise. New York Mayor Ed Koch, Florida Congressman Larry Smith, and Harlem Congressman Charles Rangel, who recognize government's inability to deal with the drug problem in the cities, are among the most vocal supporters of punishing foreign drug-producing countries and stepping up interdiction efforts. Foreign leaders and U.S. State Department and drug-enforcement officials stationed abroad, on the other hand, who understand all too well why it is impossible to crack down successfully on illicit drug production outside the United States, are the most vigorous advocates of domestic enforcement and demand-reduction efforts within the United States. In between, those agencies charged with drug interdiction, from the Coast Guard and U.S. Customs Service to the U.S. military, know that they will never succeed in capturing more than a small percentage of the illicit drugs being smuggled into the United States. Not surprisingly, they point their fingers in both directions. The solution, they promise, lies in greater source-control efforts abroad and greater demand-reduction efforts at home. . . .

By most accounts, the dramatic increase in drug-enforcement efforts over the past few years has had little effect on the illicit drug market in the United States. The mere existence of drug-prohibition laws, combined with a minimal level of law-enforcement resources, is sufficient to maintain the price of illicit drugs at a level significantly higher than it would be if there were no such laws. Drug laws and enforcement also reduce the availability of illicit drugs, most notably in parts of the United States where demand is relatively limited to begin with. Theoretically, increases in drug-enforcement efforts should result in reduced availability, higher prices, and lower purity of illegal drugs. That is, in fact, what has happened to the domestic marijuana market (in at least the first two respects). But in general the illegal drug market has not responded as intended to the substantial increases in federal, state, and local drug-enforcement efforts.

Cocaine has sold for about a hundred dollars a gram at the retail level since the beginning of the 1980s. The average purity of that gram, however, has increased from 12 to 60 percent. Moreover, a growing number of users are turning to "crack," a potent derivative of cocaine that can be smoked; it is widely sold in ghetto neighborhoods now for five to ten dollars per vial. Needless to say, both crack and the 60 percent pure cocaine pose much greater threats to users than did the relatively benign powder available eight years ago. Similarly, the retail price of heroin has remained relatively constant even as the average purity has risen from 3.9 percent in 1983 to 6.1 percent in 1986. Throughout the southwestern part of the United States, a particularly potent form of heroin known as "black tar" has become increasingly prevalent. And in many cities, a powerful synthetic opiate, Dilaudid, is beginning to compete with heroin as the preferred opiate. The growing number of heroin-related hospital emergencies and deaths is directly related to these developments.

All of these trends suggest that drug-enforcement efforts are not succeeding and may even be backfiring. There are numerous indications, for instance, that a growing number of marijuana dealers in both the producer countries and the United States are switching to cocaine dealing, motivated both by the promise of greater profits and by government drug-enforcement efforts that place a premium on minimizing the bulk of the illicit product (in order to avoid detection). It is possible, of course, that some of these trends would be even more severe in the absence of drug laws and enforcement. At the same time, it is worth observing that the increases in the potency of illegal drugs have coincided with decreases in the potency of legal substances. Motivated in good part by health concerns, cigarette smokers are turning increasingly to lower-tar and -nicotine tobacco products, alcohol drinkers from hard liquor to wine and beer, and even coffee drinkers from regular to decaffeinated coffee. This trend may well have less to do with the nature of the substances than with their legal status. It is quite possible, for instance, that the subculture of illicit-drug use creates a bias or incentive in favor of riskier behavior and more powerful psychoactive effects. If this is the case, legalization might well succeed in reversing today's trend toward more potent drugs and more dangerous methods of consumption. . . .

THE FAILURE OF INTERNATIONAL DRUG CONTROL

Many drug-enforcement officials and urban leaders recognize the futility of domestic drug-enforcement efforts and place their hopes in international control efforts. Yet these too are doomed to fail—

for numerous reasons. First, marijuana and opium can be grown almost anywhere, and the coca plant, from which cocaine is derived, is increasingly being cultivated successfully in areas that were once considered inhospitable environments. Wherever drug-eradication efforts succeed, other regions and countries are quick to fill the void; for example, Colombian marijuana growers rapidly expanded production following successful eradication efforts in Mexico during the mid-1970s. Today, Mexican growers are rapidly taking advantage of recent Colombian government successes in eradicating marijuana in the Guajira peninsula. Meanwhile, Jamaicans and Central Americans from Panama to Belize, as well as a growing assortment of Asians and Africans, do what they can to sell their own marijuana in American markets. And within the United States, domestic marijuana production is believed to be a multi-billion-dollar industry, supplying between 15 and 50 percent of the American market.

This push-down/pop-up factor also characterizes the international heroin market. At various points during the past two decades, Turkey, Mexico, Southeast Asia (Burma, Thailand, and Laos), and Southwest Asia (Pakistan, Afghanistan, and Iran) have each served as the principal source of heroin imported into the United States. During the early 1970s, Mexican producers rapidly filled the void created by the Turkish government's successful opium-control measures. Although a successful eradication program during the latter part of the 1970s reduced Mexico's share of the U.S. market from a peak of 87 percent in 1975, it has since retained at least a one-third share in each year. Southwest Asian producers, who had played no role in supplying the American market as late as 1976, were able to supply over half the American market four years later. Today, increasing evidence indicates that drug traffickers are bringing unprecedented quantities of Southeast Asian heroin into the United States. . . .

No illicit drug is as difficult to keep out of the United States as heroin. The absence of geographical limitations on where it can be cultivated is just one minor obstacle. American heroin users consume an estimated six tons of heroin each year. The sixty tons of opium required to produce that heroin represent just 2–3 percent of the estimated 2–3,000 tons of illicit opium produced during each of the past few years. Even if eradication efforts combined with what often proves to be the opium growers' principal nemesis—bad weather—were to eliminate three-fourths of that production in one year, the U.S. market would still require just 10 percent of the remaining crop. Since U.S. consumers are able and willing to pay more than any others, the chances are good that they would still obtain their heroin. In any event, the prospects for such a radical reduction in illicit opium production are scanty indeed. . . .

THE COSTS OF PROHIBITION

The fact that drug-prohibition laws and policies cannot eradicate or even significantly reduce drug abuse is not necessarily a reason to repeal them. They do, after all, succeed in deterring many people from trying drugs, and they clearly reduce the availability and significantly increase the price of illegal drugs. These accomplishments alone might warrant retaining the drug laws, were it not for the fact that these same laws are also responsible for much of what Americans identify as the "drug problem." Here the analogies to alcohol and tobacco are worth noting. There is little question that we could reduce the health costs associated with use and abuse of alcohol and tobacco if we were to criminalize their production, sale, and possession. But no one believes that we could eliminate their use and abuse, that we could create an "alcohol-free" or "tobacco-free" country. Nor do most Americans believe that criminalizing the alcohol and tobacco markets would be a good idea. Their opposition stems largely from two beliefs: that adult Americans have the right to choose what substances they will consume and what risks they will take; and that the costs of trying to coerce so many Americans to abstain from those substances would be enormous. It was the strength of these two beliefs that ultimately led to the repeal of Prohibition, and it is partly due to memories of that experience that criminalizing either alcohol or tobacco has little support today.

Consider the potential consequences of criminalizing the production, sale, and possession of all tobacco products. On the positive side, the number of people smoking tobacco would almost certainly decline, as would the health costs associated with tobacco consumption. Although the "forbidden fruit" syndrome would attract some people to cigarette smoking who would not otherwise have smoked, many more would likely be deterred by the criminal sanction, the moral standing of the law, the higher cost and unreliable quality of the illicit tobacco, and the difficulties involved in acquiring it. Non-smokers would rarely if ever be bothered by the irritating habits of their fellow citizens. The anti-tobacco laws would discourage some people from ever starting to smoke, and would induce others to quit.

On the negative side, however, millions of Americans, including both tobacco addicts and recreational users, would no doubt defy the law, generating a massive underground market and billions in profits for organized criminals. Although some tobacco farmers would find other work, thousands more would become outlaws and continue to produce their crops covertly. Throughout Latin America, farmers and gangsters would rejoice at the opportunity to earn untold sums of gringo greenbacks, even as U.S. diplomats pressured foreign governments to cooperate with U.S. laws. Within the United States, government helicopters would spray herbicides on illicit tobacco fields; people would be rewarded by the government for informing on their tobacco-growing, -selling, and -smoking neighbors; urine tests would be employed to identify violators of the anti-tobacco laws; and a Tobacco Enforcement Administration (the T.E.A.) would employ undercover agents, informants, and wiretaps to uncover tobacco-law violators. Municipal, state, and federal judicial systems would be clogged with tobacco traffickers and "abusers." "Tobacco-related murders" would increase dramatically as criminal organizations competed with one another for turf and markets. Smoking would become an act of youthful rebellion, and no doubt some users would begin to experiment with more concentrated, potent, and dangerous forms of tobacco. Tobacco-related corruption would infect all levels of government, and respect for the law would decline noticeably. Government expenditures on tobacco-law enforcement would climb rapidly into the billions of dollars, even as budget balancers longingly recalled the almost ten billion dollars per year in tobacco taxes earned by the federal and state governments prior to prohibition. Finally, the State of North Carolina might even secede again from the Union.

This seemingly far-fetched tobacco-prohibition scenario is little more than an extrapolation based on the current situation with respect to marijuana, cocaine, and heroin. In many ways, our predicament resembles what actually happened during Prohibition. Prior to Prohibition, most Americans hoped that alcohol could be effectively banned by passing laws against its production and supply. During the early years of Prohibition, when drinking declined but millions of Americans nonetheless continued to drink, Prohibition's supporters placed their faith in tougher laws and more police and jails. After a few more years, however, increasing numbers of Americans began to realize that laws and policemen were unable to eliminate the smugglers, bootleggers, and illicit producers, as long as tens of millions of Americans continued to want to buy alcohol. At the same time, they saw that more laws and policemen seemed to generate more violence and corruption, more crowded courts and jails, wider disrespect for government and the law, and more power and profits for the gangsters. Repeal of Prohibition came to be seen not as a capitulation to Al Capone and his ilk, but as a means of both putting the bootleggers out of business and eliminating most of the costs associated with the prohibition laws.

Today, Americans are faced with a dilemma similar to that confronted by our forebears sixty years ago. Demand for illicit drugs shows some signs of abating, but no signs of declining significantly. Moreover, there are substantial reasons to doubt that tougher laws and policing

have played an important role in reducing consumption. Supply, meanwhile, has not abated at all. Availability of illicit drugs, except for marijuana in some locales, remains high. Prices are dropping, even as potency increases. And the number of drug producers, smugglers, and dealers remains sizable, even as jails and prisons fill to overflowing. As was the case during Prohibition, the principal beneficiaries of current drug policies are the new and old organized-crime gangs. The principal victims, on the other hand, are not the drug dealers, but the tens of millions of Americans who are worse off in one way or another as a consequence of the existence and failure of the drug-prohibition laws. . . .

COSTS TO THE TAXPAYER

Since 1981, federal expenditures on drug enforcement have more than tripled—from less than one billion dollars a year to about three billion. According to the National Drug Enforcement Policy Board, the annual budgets of the Drug Enforcement Administration (DEA) and the Coast Guard have each risen during the past seven years from about $220 million to roughly $500 million. During the same period, FBI resources devoted to drug enforcement have increased from $8 million a year to over $100 million; U.S. Marshals resources from $26 million to about $80 million; U.S. Attorney resources from $20 million to about $100 million; State Department resources from $35 million to $100 million; U.S. Customs resources from $180 million to over $400 million; and Bureau of Prison resources from $77 million to about $300 million. Expenditures on drug control by the military and the intelligence agencies are more difficult to calculate, although by all accounts they have increased by at least the same magnitude, and now total hundreds of millions of dollars per year. Even greater are the expenditures at lower levels of government. In a 1987 study for the U.S. Customs Service by Wharton Econometrics, state and local police were estimated to have devoted 18 percent of their total investigative resources, or close to five billion dollars, to drug-enforcement activities in 1986. This represented a 19 percent increase over the previous year's expenditures. All told, 1987 expenditures on all aspects of drug enforcement, from drug eradication in foreign countries to imprisonment of drug users and dealers in the United States, totalled at least ten billion dollars.

Of course, even ten billion dollars a year pales in comparison with expenditures on military defense. Of greater concern than the actual expenditures, however, has been the diversion of limited resources—including the time and energy of judges, prosecutors, and law-enforcement agents, as well as scarce prison space—from the prosecution and punishment of criminal activities that harm far more innocent victims than do violations of the drug laws. Drug-law violators account for approximately 10 percent of the roughly 800,000 inmates in state prisons and local jails, and more than one-third of the 44,000 federal prison inmates. These proportions are expected to increase in coming years, even as total prison populations continue to rise dramatically.[1] Among the 40,000 inmates in New York State prisons, drug-law violations surpassed first-degree robbery in 1987 as the number one cause of incarceration, accounting for 20 percent of the total prison population. The U.S. Sentencing Commission has estimated that, largely as a consequence of the Anti-Drug Abuse Act passed by Congress in 1986, the proportion of federal inmates incarcerated for drug violations will rise from one-third of the 44,000 prisoners sentenced to federal-prison terms today to one-half of the 100,000 to 150,000 federal prisoners anticipated in fifteen years. The direct costs of building and maintaining enough prisons to house this growing population are rising at an astronomical rate. The opportunity costs, in terms of alternative social expenditures forgone and other types of criminals not imprisoned, are perhaps even greater. . . .

DRUGS AND CRIME

The drug/crime connection is one that continues to resist coherent analysis, both because cause and effect are so difficult to distinguish and because the role of the drug-prohibition laws in causing and labelling "drug-related crime" is so often ignored. There are four possible connections between drugs and crime, at least three of which would be much diminished if the drug-prohibition laws were repealed. First, producing, selling, buying, and consuming strictly controlled and banned substances is itself a crime that occurs billions of times each year in the United States alone. In the absence of drug-prohibition laws, these activities would obviously cease to be crimes. Selling drugs to children would, of course, continue to be criminal, and other evasions of government regulation of a legal market would continue to be prosecuted; but by and large the drug/crime connection that now accounts for all of the criminal-justice costs noted above would be severed.

Second, many illicit-drug users commit crimes such as robbery and burglary, as well as drug dealing, prostitution, and numbers running, to earn enough money to purchase the relatively high-priced illicit drugs. Unlike the millions of alcoholics who can support their habits for relatively modest amounts, many cocaine and heroin addicts spend hundreds and even thousands of dollars a week. If the drugs to which they are addicted were significantly cheaper—which would be the case if they were legalized—the number of crimes committed by drug addicts to pay for their habits would, in all likelihood, decline dramatically. Even if a legal-drug policy included the imposition of relatively high consumption taxes in order to discourage consumption, drug prices would probably still be lower than they are today.

The third drug/crime connection is the commission of crimes—violent crimes in particular—by people under the influence of illicit drugs. This connection seems to have the greatest impact upon the popular imagination. Clearly, some drugs do "cause" some people to commit crimes by reducing normal inhibitions, unleashing aggressive and other antisocial tendencies, and lessening the sense of responsibility. Cocaine, particularly in the form of crack, has gained such a reputation in recent years, just as heroin did in the 1960s and 1970s, and marijuana did in the years before that. Crack's reputation for inspiring violent behavior may or may not be more deserved than those of marijuana and heroin; reliable evidence is not yet available. No illicit drug, however, is as widely associated with violent behavior as alcohol. According to Justice Department statistics, 54 percent of all jail inmates convicted of violent crimes in 1983 reported having used alcohol just prior to committing their offense. The impact of drug legalization on this drug/crime connection is the most difficult to predict. Much would depend on overall rates of drug abuse and changes in the nature of consumption, both of which are impossible to predict. It is worth noting, however, that a shift in consumption from alcohol to marijuana would almost certainly contribute to a decline in violent behavior.

The fourth drug/crime link is the violent, intimidating, and corrupting behavior of the drug traffickers. Illegal markets tend to breed violence—not only because they attract criminally-minded individuals, but also because participants in the market have no resort to legal institutions to resolve their disputes. During Prohibition, violent struggles between bootlegging gangs and hijackings of booze-laden trucks and sea vessels were frequent and notorious occurrences. Today's equivalents are the booby traps that surround some marijuana fields, the pirates of the Caribbean looking to rip off drug-laden vessels en route to the shores of the United States, and the machine-gun battles and executions carried out by drug lords—all of which occasionally kill innocent people. Most law-enforcement officials agree that the dramatic increases in urban murder rates during the past few years can be explained almost entirely by the rise in drug-dealer killings.

Perhaps the most unfortunate victims of the drug-prohibition policies have been the law-abiding residents of America's ghettos. These policies have largely proven futile in deterring large numbers of ghetto dwellers from becoming drug abusers, but they do account for much of what ghetto residents identify as the drug problem. In many neighborhoods, it often seems to be the aggressive gun-toting drug dealers who upset law-abiding residents far more than the addicts nodding out in doorways. Other residents, however, perceive the drug dealers as heroes and successful role models. In impoverished neighborhoods, they often stand out as symbols of success to children who see no other options. At the same time, the increasingly harsh criminal penalties imposed on adult drug dealers have led to the widespread recruitment of juveniles by drug traffickers. Formerly, children started dealing drugs only after they had been using them for a while; today the sequence is often reversed: many children start using illegal drugs now only after working for older drug dealers. And the juvenile-justice system offers no realistic options for dealing with this growing problem.

The conspicuous failure of law-enforcement agencies to deal with this drug/crime connection is probably most responsible for the demoralization of neighborhoods and police departments alike. Intensive police crackdowns in urban neighborhoods do little more than chase the menace a short distance away to infect new areas. By contrast, legalization of the drug market would drive the drug-dealing business off the streets and out of the apartment buildings, and into legal, government-regulated, tax-paying stores. It would also force many of the gun-toting dealers out of business, and would convert others into legitimate businessmen. Some, of course, would turn to other types of criminal activities, just as some of the bootleggers did following Prohibition's repeal. Gone, however, would be the unparalleled financial temptations that lure so many people from all sectors of society into the drug-dealing business. . . .

PHYSICAL AND MORAL COSTS

Perhaps the most paradoxical consequence of the drug laws is the tremendous harm they cause to the millions of drug users who have not been deterred from using illicit drugs in the first place. Nothing resembling an underground Food and Drug Administration has arisen to impose quality control on the illegal-drug market and provide users with accurate information on the drugs they consume. Imagine that Americans could not tell whether a bottle of wine contained 6 percent, 30 percent, or 90 percent alcohol, or whether an aspirin tablet contained 5 or 500 grams of aspirin. Imagine, too, that no controls existed to prevent winemakers from diluting their product with methanol and other dangerous impurities, and that vineyards and tobacco fields were fertilized with harmful substances by ignorant growers and sprayed with poisonous herbicides by government agents. Fewer people would use such substances, but more of those who did would get sick. Some would die.

The above scenario describes, of course, the current state of the illicit drug market. Many marijuana smokers are worse off for having smoked cannabis that was grown with dangerous fertilizers, sprayed with the herbicide paraquat, or mixed with more dangerous substances. Consumers of heroin and the various synthetic substances sold on the street face even severer consequences, including fatal overdoses and poisonings from unexpectedly potent or impure drug supplies. More often than not, the quality of a drug addict's life depends greatly upon his or her access to reliable supplies. Drug-enforcement operations that succeed in temporarily disrupting supply networks are thus a double-edged sword: they encourage some addicts to seek admission into drug-treatment programs, but they oblige others to seek out new and hence less reliable suppliers; the result is that more, not fewer, drug-related emergencies and deaths occur. . . .

[U]ltimately the moral quality of laws must be judged not by how those laws are intended to work in principle, but by how they function in practice. When laws intended to serve a moral end inflict great damage on innocent parties, we must rethink our moral positions.

Because drug-law violations do not create victims with an interest in notifying the police, drug-enforcement agents rely heavily on undercover operations, electronic surveillance, and information provided by informants. These techniques are indispensable to effective law enforcement, but they are also among the least palatable investigative methods employed by the police. The same is true of drug testing: it may be useful and even necessary for determining liability in accidents, but it also threatens and undermines the right of privacy to which many Americans believe they are entitled. There are good reasons for requiring that such measures be used sparingly. . . .

THE BENEFITS OF LEGALIZATION

Repealing the drug-prohibition laws promises tremendous advantages. Between reduced government expenditures on enforcing drug laws and new tax revenue from legal drug production and sales, public treasuries would enjoy a net benefit of at least ten billion dollars a year, and possibly much more. The quality of urban life would rise significantly. Homicide rates would decline. So would robbery and burglary rates. Organized criminal groups, particularly the newer ones that have yet to diversify out of drugs, would be dealt a devastating setback. The police, prosecutors, and courts would focus their resources on combatting the types of crimes

that people cannot walk away from. More ghetto residents would turn their backs on criminal careers and seek out legitimate opportunities instead. And the health and quality of life of many drug users—and even drug abusers—would improve significantly.

All the benefits of legalization would be for naught, however, if millions more Americans were to become drug abusers. Our experience with alcohol and tobacco provides ample warnings. Today, alcohol is consumed by 140 million Americans and tobacco by 50 million. All of the health costs associated with abuse of the illicit drugs pale in comparison with those resulting from tobacco and alcohol abuse. In 1986, for example, alcohol was identified as a contributing factor in 10 percent of work-related injuries, 40 percent of suicide attempts, and about 40 percent of the approximately 46,000 annual traffic deaths in 1983. An estimated eighteen million Americans are reported to be either alcoholics or alcohol abusers. The total cost of alcohol abuse to American society is estimated at over 100 billion dollars annually. Alcohol has been identified as the direct cause of 80,000 to 100,000 deaths annually, and as a contributing factor in an additional 100,000 deaths. The health costs of tobacco use are of similar magnitude. In the United States alone, an estimated 320,000 people die prematurely each year as a consequence of their consumption of tobacco. By comparison, the National Council on Alcoholism reported that only 3,562 people were known to have died in 1985 from use of all illegal drugs combined. Even if we assume that thousands more deaths were related in one way or another to illicit drug abuse but not reported as such, we are still left with the conclusion that all of the health costs of marijuana, cocaine, and heroin combined amount to only a small fraction of those caused by tobacco and alcohol.

Most Americans are just beginning to recognize the extensive costs of alcohol and tobacco abuse. At the same time, they seem to believe that there is something fundamentally different about alcohol and tobacco that supports the legal distinction between those two substances, on the one hand, and the illicit ones, on the other. The most common distinction is based on the assumption that the illicit drugs are more dangerous than the licit ones. Cocaine, heroin, the various hallucinogens, and (to a lesser extent) marijuana are widely perceived as, in the words of the President's Commission on Organized Crime, "inherently destructive to mind and body." They are also believed to be more addictive and more likely to cause dangerous and violent behavior than alcohol and tobacco. All use of illicit drugs is therefore thought to be abusive; in other words, the distinction between use and abuse of psychoactive substances that most people recognize with respect to alcohol is not acknowledged with respect to the illicit substances. . . .

DEALING WITH DRUGS' DANGERS

. . . It is important to think about the illicit drugs in the same way we think about alcohol and tobacco. Like tobacco, many of the illicit substances are highly addictive, but can be consumed on a regular basis for decades without any demonstrable harm. Like alcohol, most of the substances can be, and are, used by most consumers in moderation, with little in the way of harmful effects; but like alcohol, they also lend themselves to abuse by a minority of users who become addicted or otherwise harm themselves or others as a consequence. And as is the case with both the legal substances, the psychoactive effects of the various illegal drugs vary greatly from one person to another. To be sure, the pharmacology of the substance is important, as is its purity and the manner in which it is consumed. But much also depends upon not only the physiology and psychology of the consumer, but also his expectations regarding the drug, his social milieu, and the broader cultural environment—what Harvard University psychiatrist Norman Zinberg has called the "set and setting" of the drug. It is factors such as these that might change dramatically, albeit in indeterminate ways, were the illicit drugs made legally available.

CAN LEGALIZATION WORK?

It is thus impossible to predict whether legalization would lead to much greater levels of drug abuse, and exact costs comparable to those of alcohol and tobacco abuse. The lessons that can be drawn from other societies are mixed. China's experience with the British opium pushers of the nineteenth century, when millions became addicted to the drug, offers one worst-case scenario. The devastation of many native American tribes by alcohol presents another. On the other hand, the legal availability of opium and cannabis in many Asian societies did not result in large addict populations until recently. Indeed, in many countries U.S.-inspired opium bans imposed during the past few decades have paradoxically contributed to dramatic increases in heroin consumption among Asian youth. Within the United States, the decriminalization of marijuana by about a dozen states during the 1970s did not lead to increases in marijuana consumption. In the Netherlands, which went even further in decriminalizing cannabis during the 1970s, consumption has actually declined significantly. The policy has succeeded, as the government intended, in making drug use boring. Finally, late nineteenth-century America was a society in which there were almost no drug laws or even drug regulations—but levels of drug use then were about what they are today. Drug abuse was considered a serious problem, but the criminal-justice system was not regarded as part of the solution.

There are, however, reasons to believe that none of the currently illicit substances would become as popular as alcohol or tobacco, even if they were legalized. Alcohol has long been the principal intoxicant in most societies, including many in which other substances have been legally available. Presumably, its diverse properties account for its popularity—it quenches thirst, goes well with food, and promotes appetite as well as sociability. The popularity of tobacco probably stems not just from its powerful addictive qualities, but from the fact that its psychoactive effects are sufficiently subtle that cigarettes can be integrated with most other human activities. The illicit substances do not share these qualities to the same extent, nor is it likely that they would acquire them if they were legalized. Moreover, none of the illicit substances can compete with alcohol's special place in American culture and history. . . .

It is important to stress what legalization is not. It is not a capitulation to the drug dealers—but rather a means to put them out of business. It is not an endorsement of drug use—but rather a recognition of the rights of adult Americans to make their own choices free of the fear of criminal sanctions. It is not a repudiation of the "just say no" approach—but rather an appeal to government to provide assistance and positive inducements, not criminal penalties and more repressive measures, in support of that approach. It is not even a call for the elimination of the criminal-justice system from drug regulation—but rather a proposal for the redirection of its efforts and attention.

There is no question that legalization is a risky policy, since it may lead to an increase in the number of people who abuse drugs. But that is a risk—not a certainty. At the same time, current drug-control policies are failing, and new proposals promise only to be more costly and more repressive. We know that repealing the drug-prohibition laws would eliminate or greatly reduce many of the ills that people commonly identify as part and parcel of the "drug problem." Yet legalization is repeatedly and vociferously dismissed, without any attempt to evaluate it openly and objectively. The past twenty years have demonstrated that a drug policy shaped by exaggerated rhetoric designed to arouse fear has only led to our current disaster. Unless we are willing to honestly evaluate our options, including various legalization strategies, we will run a still greater risk: we may never find the best solution for our drug problems.

NOTES

1. The total number of state and federal prison inmates in 1975 was under 250,000; in 1980 it was 350,000; and in 1987 it was 575,000. The projected total for 2000 is one million. . . .

NO

Steven Brill

SHOULD WE GIVE UP?

On the Lower East Side of Manhattan Benito Sanchez is panhandling for drug money while wheeling his girlfriend's 3-year-old in a stroller. According to subsequent police reports, passersby notice that the motionless little girl isn't napping. She's stiff. Dead. Sanchez had beaten her the night before because she wouldn't stop crying. A police investigation reveals that Sanchez was high on crack at the time. (After plea bargaining to manslaughter he is sentenced to eight-and-a-third to twenty-five years in prison.)

In midtown, Earl Caple brings his one-month-old baby to the emergency room at Bellevue Hospital because her vagina is bleeding. He later tells police he raped her while he was high on crack because she wouldn't stop crying. (He pleads guilty to assault in the first degree and gets five to fifteen years.)

Uptown, in the neonatal care ward on the fourth floor of Harlem Hospital, David Bateman, the doctor who runs the unit, talks almost drearily about the crack mothers who, he says, "have no maternal instinct. . . . They smoke the stuff while they're pregnant," which typically makes the babies underdeveloped at birth. "Then," he adds, "when we have to keep the babies here in the unit because they've got some sort of problem, the mothers leave and often don't come back. Or you'll see them once in thirty or forty days come in at midnight with sunglasses on, giggling, looking for their baby. . . . With the poorest, most desperate mothers in this area who have babies who have to remain here, you don't see that kind of neglect. Unless they're on crack."

Across the country, . . . illegal drugs, particularly crack, are poisoning us in so many ways, in so many places, and with such nightmarish results that it's as if Frankenstein, or Muammar Qaddafi, had broken into our water supply.

Whether we can fight back and enforce the laws against these drugs would seem, therefore, to be a pivotal test for what we have always thought was the sturdiest, surest legal system on earth.

Yet Dr. Bateman, the man who treats the premature babies of the cracked-out mothers with the sunglasses, isn't so sure we should spend our time worrying about enforcing the law.

Steven Brill is the editor in chief of *The American Lawyer*. This article is republished with permission from March 1990 issue of *The American Lawyer*. Copyright © 1990 by *The American Lawyer*.

And as I listened over the last several weeks to people like him and to others who favor legalization more strongly, I almost joined their side. Almost.

"Sure, I hate the people who sell this stuff," Bateman says. "But so what? I'm not sure that even if we hang them all up by their toes and pelt them with tomatoes, it will do any good. There will just be someone else to take their place. . . . This is a medical and social problem, not a legal problem, but it's become caught up in politics. . . . And so we have the rhetoric of a war on drugs and drug dealers, when we should probably legalize it and focus on the medical and social problems."

Bateman has been at Harlem Hospital for nine years. He is anything but cavalier about drugs and what drug abuse has wrought in America's most famous center of the underclass. He sees the horror of it all every day.

"Crack has produced social devastation," he says. "What you see is shockingly abnormal maternal behavior. The complete absence of a maternal instinct. . . . Mothers who have no thought of taking their babies home when they leave."

A good percentage of those crack babies can't go home, anyway, because of what their mothers' drug habit has done to them in the womb. Bateman says that before 1985 approximately 3 percent of the babies born at Harlem Hospital had mothers who were using addictive illegal drugs. By 1986, when crack—which because it is smoked is more popular with women than injectable heroin—had begun its full sweep through the ghetto, the number had risen to 15 percent. By 1988 it was 20 percent.

Which is where it is now: One fifth of the 3,000 babies born in Harlem Hospital this year will be born of mothers addicted to drugs, usually crack.

Crack babies, explains Bateman, are often premature and almost always physically smaller—in everything from bone size to weight to brain size—than normal babies. "And the evidence so far," he adds, "is spotty, but the ones we've watched so far don't seem to catch up as they get older," meaning that they will probably stay smaller, with less fully developed brains and other faculties.

Bateman says that nationally the birth rate of "small, premature babies," which are defined as babies weighing three pounds, four ounces or less at birth is about 1 percent. At Harlem Hospital it is now 3.5 percent.

Nationally, about 7 percent of all babies require intensive hospital care after birth; according to Bateman, the rate at Harlem Hospital in the nine years he has been there has jumped from 13 percent to 24 percent, an increase he attributes almost exclusively to crack.

The mothers of these crack babies—mothers who traditionally have formed the core of the nuclear family in the ghetto—have been so robbed of maternal instinct, or their living situations are so unsustainable, that 50 percent of all the babies Bateman treats in the neonatal unit go into foster care, where they typically become wards of the state.

The ones who do go home are likely to be shell-shocked by mothers whose moods swing from euphoria to violent paranoia and whose promiscuity is a predictable side effect of the addiction. These children are the faces behind the avalanche of child abuse cases reported in New York and other urban areas. According to New York Court of Appeals chief judge Sol Wachtler's 1989 annual report on the state of the judiciary, child abuse cases have exploded by 232 percent in the last four years in New York

City. "Those numbers are the cost of crack, pure and simple," says Wachtler. "It's as if this drug's effects were designed by the devil."

Bateman asserts that "much of what you've read in the newspapers about crack babies suffering the shakes or other pain is garbage, part of the drug war rhetoric." But he says he is "willing to concede" the bona fides of recent studies at the National Institute on Drug Abuse in Washington, D.C., that have asserted that prenatal exposure to crack interferes with babies' emotional development in a way that may leave them permanently handicapped in developing basic employment skills and close human relationships—"flat moods and emotional poverty," The New York Times called it in a September 1989 article. "That wouldn't surprise me." Bateman says. "It's an awful drug."

Across the country, the best data is that there are now 30,000–50,000 crack babies born every year. Almost 1,000 a week. More than 100 a day. Parentless, or living with an addicted mother. Underdeveloped. Probably less capable of normal emotional attachments. Future zombies.

Nonetheless, Bateman argues that "spending all this money and energy and rhetoric on putting people in jail just hasn't worked. . . . You can go right around the corner from this hospital and buy crack," he adds (an assertion I found to be true when I left him that afternoon), "and you always will be able to until we treat the social causes and the medical causes of addiction."

"When I talk about legalization, people tell me I should go visit the crack babies in Harlem Hospital," says federal district court judge Robert Sweet, who lately has assumed a leading public role among a growing group of public figures who favor legalization. "Well, what I tell them is that those crack babies are there now with the present system. What we have now just doesn't work."

Sweet, 67, is a former federal prosecutor, deputy mayor of New York under John Lindsay, and partner at Skadden, Arps, Slate, Meagher & Flom. He's a serious, thoughtful man, and a highly regarded judge (and no bleeding heart) near the end of his career. As such he is above the suspicion one might harbor about a politician who might be eager to ride this issue to greater glory. In fact, Sweet's first public pronouncement on legalization was in what he thought was a private dinner speech; only when his remarks generated a story in The New York Times did he allow himself to be nudged into the limelight enough to defend his position.

But he does defend it, and persuasively.

"The other day," he begins, "I had to sentence a kid about twenty years old to the five-year mandatory minimum that this new statute requires . . . because he was caught steering someone to a sale of a few hundred dollars' worth of crack. . . . The kid was an addict. . . . And I felt like leaning over the bench and saying to him. 'Why didn't you just get high off of alcohol.' . . .

"It's the profit from the stuff being illegal that drives the whole market. . . . This kid was encouraged to be an addict because some pusher could make money off of him. . . . He was a gofer, who was swept up in this. . . .

"Why did he get into it? Because he saw a way to make some easy dollars. He saw the only way for him to make some easy dollars. . . .

"We need to deal with the problem of desperation that these people face, but first we have to take the economics and the corruption out of it. Treat it like a disease."

"But don't you hate the idea of people being allowed to sell something that kills other people?" I asked. "How can you make that legal? How would you feel about our society and our rule of law if you could walk up to someone at a cocktail party and ask him what he did for a living and he said matter-of-factly, 'Oh, I sell crack in Harlem'?"

"Well, how do you feel if you see Edgar Bronfman at a cocktail party . . . or Larry Tisch," Sweet replied, referring, respectively, to the chairman of Joseph E. Seagram & Sons, Inc., and to the chairman of the Loews Corporation (in addition to CBS), which owns the Lorillard Tobacco Company. "Alcohol and tobacco kill more people, but we don't outlaw it because we are willing to let people be responsible for their own conduct. . . .

"It's all a question of responsibility," Sweet adds. "We tend to want to push responsibility up, from the individual to society as a whole, or to government. But it doesn't work. . . .

"How many times do you hear of someone being indicted for attempted suicide? What we do is try to treat people who attempt to commit suicide, just as we try to treat alcoholics."

As I said, he is persuasive.

In fact, Sweet's point could be carried further: We attempt to persuade and treat people who abuse alcohol and tobacco because these people are as often as not white and middle-class. But heroin and crack are mostly the province of the nonwhite underclass. And because this kind of suicidal drug abuse is a symptom of their desperation—desperation for which the rest of us are arguably responsible—we need to criminalize it rather than face it and treat it: If we call it

criminal conduct, then it's not our fault. And if we call it criminal conduct we can send in the police rather than the more expensive doctors and other therapists.

Similarly, it could be argued (and Sweet, in fact, seems to be arguing) that criminalization amounts to nothing less than the worst kind of racist paternalism: People in the ghetto are incapable of being responsible for themselves; they need the long arm of our law to help them save themselves.

One of Sweet's key allies on the legalization side is Ethan Nadelmann, a 32-year-old Harvard-trained lawyer and an assistant professor of politics and public affairs at Princeton's Woodrow Wilson School. . . . Nadelmann's writing is credited with persuading many of the recent enlistees to the legalization side, such as former Secretary of State George Schulz and Baltimore Mayor Kurt Schmoke.

In a compelling September 1989 article in *Science* magazine the professor—who, unlike Sweet, does seem eager to have this issue be his ticket to regular appearances on ABC's *Nightline*—notes that, despite all of our law enforcement efforts against cocaine, the price has actually come down in the last decade even as the purity of a typical gram of the stuff has quintupled.

Worse, crack is a particularly cheap but potent form of cocaine. (Indeed, the development of this cheap, smokeable, baking soda-based "junk food" form of cocaine in the mid-1980s was a seminal breakthrough for the drug marketers, equivalent to the development of the microchip for information processing.) Thus, there is almost no hope of putting its price beyond the reach of a potential addict.

Nor is there much hope for eradicating it at its source in South America; Nadelmann says that only 700 square miles of the roughly 2.5 million square miles of farmland in South America that are arid enough to grow cocaine are now used for that crop, which means there is lots of room for the growers to move around.

Meanwhile, at home we are spending what Nadelmann says is more than $10 billion a year to enforce laws that fill our prisons, clog our courts with arrests that are mostly for possession, preoccupy our police, and do little to curb drug abuse, while enriching and encouraging a $10–50 billion black market that, says Nadelmann, would be devastated by legalization.

And we do all of that, Nadelmann points out, while we allow the sale of cigarettes, when "an estimated 320,000 people die prematurely each year as a consequence of their consumption of tobacco." Similarly, we tolerate alcohol, despite the fact that booze is a "contributing factor in . . . 40 percent of suicide attempts and about 40 percent of the 46,000 . . . traffic deaths in 1983," and that "no illicit drug . . . is as strongly associated with violent behavior as is alcohol. According to Justice Department statistics, 54 percent of all jail [sic] inmates convicted of violent crimes in 1983 reported having used alcohol just prior to committing their offense."

("We're not sure yet of what crack does to babies," adds Bateman of Harlem Hospital. "But there is one drug we are certain of, and that's alcohol. We have identified a clear fetal syndrome associated with babies whose mothers are alcoholics; the babies are often retarded.")

"All of the health costs of marijuana, cocaine, and heroin combined amount to only a small fraction of those caused by either of these two licit substances," Nadelmann adds, referring to tobacco and alcohol.

"Legalization of drugs," Nadelmann concludes, "would yield its greatest benefit in the ghettos, where it would sever much of the drug-crime connection, seize the market away from the criminals, de-glorify involvement in the illicit drug business, help redirect the work ethic from illegitimate to legitimate employment opportunities, help stem the transmission of AIDS in I.V. drug users, and significantly improve the safety, health, and well-being of those who do use and abuse drugs" because "billions in new revenues" from taxes on the newly legal drugs would fund treatment programs, and because the drugs would be dispensed in a setting that would guarantee their purity and safety.

But what kind of setting?

Nadelmann's article seems to be missing a page in this regard; he tells us nothing of how the legalization scheme would work.

But Sweet says, "Addicts would go into a government-licensed store, maybe a pharmacy. They would have to register, and they'd get their drugs [which would be manufactured by legitimate drug companies] at the same time that they would be encouraged to enroll in treatment."

The more one ponders Sweet's scenario, the easier it is to see why Nadelmann chose to avoid the issue of how legalization would work. For it's here that the whole appealing, facile argument begins to crumble.

Let's remember that crack is a particularly fiendish drug.

"Two or three hits can turn many people into addicts," says Dr. Mitchell Rosenthal, who helped pioneer the Phoenix House drug treatment centers in New York in the late 1960s, and who now treats 1,400 addicts as inpatients and 300 more as outpatients at ten treatment centers in New York and California.

Adds Rosenthal: "When you take one hit, you want to binge. You want five or ten more hits. You have to keep going until you drop with exhaustion, because the high is so quick—straight to the brain—but so short—maybe a few minutes—and the down is so terrible that you have to keep going. . . . And when you're on crack you will do all kinds of violent, antisocial things. It is not like heroin, where you nod off."

So, will our friendly government dispensary keep giving out hits?

If not, won't the black market be out there ready and willing to help the binging crack addict?

"Bars don't serve drunks," says Sweet. Sure, but many drunks don't usually feel compelled, physically, to keep drinking, or if they do they can go home and raid their own bars. Are we going to sell crack addicts large enough amounts for them to store at home? Besides, do we really want to hold up our "success" in controlling binging drunks as our standard for crack addicts?

Asked about that, Nadelmann says, "I haven't really worked out the details, but there could be two scenarios. . . . One idea might be just to sell cocaine in powder form to see if snorting it will satisfy crack addicts."

Which, of course, it won't. And which will allow the purchasers to buy some baking soda and go into the black market crack business for themselves—good perhaps for our balance of trade (with Colombia) but absurd as a way of controlling the problem.

"Another alternative," the professor continues, "would be, yes, to sell them unlimited quantities of crack. At least that would drive out the black market. . . . Look at it this way: Suppose to get crack you had to walk up to the counter at a government store and there was a sign that says, 'You have a sixty percent chance of becoming addicted, and a one in two thousand chance of dying from one dose.' Wouldn't that setting send a different message than what we now have, where kids are pushed into it for fast money?"

Speaking of kids, what about minors? Will they be allowed, or will the black market serve them, too?

Sweet, again, points to liquor. But do we want today's teenage alcohol problem to be matched by a teenage crack problem?

Nadelmann says, "Sure, there would be a black market for kids, but it would be less than what we have now." Really? With everyone else allowed to buy unlimited quantities from the neighborhood dispensary, everyone else could be a black marketeer.

What about pregnant women? Will we serve them? Will we force them to have abortions? "Those are tough questions," Nadelmann says.

And who's going to come in and register at these dispensaries, anyway, rather than go to the black market? If the lure for signing up (and being fingerprinted, too, says Sweet) will be that they'll save money, then what will happen to Nadelmann's "billions" in tax revenue? How much below the current price of $5 per hit can the government go and still collect its taxes?

Asked about that, Nadelmann says that he still hasn't "worked out all the details of sale and price, or location."

But it's all in the details, a reality that seemed to dawn on Nadelmann as I questioned him further and he backpedaled, asserting that "at this point I'm probably only arguing that we *experiment* with legalization, beginning, probably, just with marijuana . . . or just in one isolated community."

In short, it is impossible to imagine any legalization scheme that would eliminate, or even make a dent in, the black market. All that legalization is likely to do is make crack more available and less forbidding to the vast majority of people, including ghetto residents, who are now deterred by the stigma and the relative inaccessibility that results from its being illegal, and who might experiment with it if they could walk into a store and get it.

"To me it seems horrible to contemplate selling heroin or cocaine over the counter," says "Steve," a former big-firm lawyer-addict. . . . "Sure, some people try drugs because they are illegal and there's a thrill in that," he continues. "But a lot more would be tempted if it were legal. You have to assume that."

In that regard, Nadelmann and Sweet can be hoisted on their own liquor and tobacco analogies and all the accompanying statistics. Maybe the reason that the death and illness numbers attached to tobacco and the death, sickness, and violence numbers attached to alcohol are so high is because they *are* legal. Do we want to find out how many more people would try crack if it were legal?

"I wouldn't let crack be sold at seven cents a piece in vending machines," says Nadelmann. "And we shouldn't do that with cigarettes either." Fine, but should we take it from the back alleys of the ghetto to the friendly neighborhood dispensary? Won't the increased availability and the elimination of the stigma of illegality create thousands, even millions, of new addicts who will now be free to try it?

Nadelmann attempts to deal with this point in his article by noting that studies show that most people who tried cocaine and marijuana in the 1960s and 1970s did not become addicted. But that was before crack cocaine. It was when cocaine was snorted and therefore far less potent, addictive, and dangerous, an obvious point that Nadelmann ignores, and which he dismissed in our conversation by saying that "we shouldn't let one drug like crack" that is "temporarily popular" dictate our whole drug policy.

Yet the overriding reality of drug abuse in the 1990s is that with scientific advances there are likely to be more types of fiendish drugs like crack coming on line. "Ice," now in vogue on the West Coast and in Hawaii, is the latest example. Crack and ice and the drugs we haven't heard of yet are the realities we have to assume when we consider legalization.

"Brian," a lawyer-addict from Skadden, Arps . . . , says he is "torn" by the question of legalization, but on balance favors it, because "the stigma of it being illegal makes people like me afraid to seek help. There was a time when a partner asked me what was wrong with me and I so wanted to tell him, but was afraid because I was breaking the law."

Perhaps, but he did ultimately seek treatment, and many more of his colleagues today are alcohol abusers, in part because the barriers to initial use aren't there.

Leaving aside the question of whether Nadelmann's numbers make a good case for making alcohol and tobacco illegal rather than making crack legal, it seems clear that there are differences between alcohol and tobacco that compel the conclusion that at least crack should be illegal.

First, to the extent that tobacco has victims other than the user, we can control that victimization, as we are now starting to do, by prohibiting smoking in places where nonsmokers will have their lungs polluted. Second, not all smokers automatically die or have their lives ruined, the way almost all crack users do. Third, while tobacco is addictive, cigarette addicts and potential addicts are far more capable of being persuaded to end their habits, as we know from all the data showing recent declines in smoking.

As for alcohol, we can't claim to be very good at controlling victimization of others, but there is some evidence that tougher enforcement of drunk driving laws is helping in at least that area. (Similarly, although the fetal alcohol syndrome cited by Bateman of Harlem Hospital is horrendous, he concedes that pregnant women apparently give up their drinking enough and that the syndrome is rare enough that he sees "fewer than ten babies a year" with that problem.)

Also, we can agree that not all drinkers become alcohol addicts, let alone die or ruin their lives as a result of their drinking. And as with tobacco, there is some evidence that people are being weaned off alcohol as its dangers become clearer and more clearly articulated.

So it may not make sense—indeed, it may be emblematic of the bankruptcy of our principles as a nation—that beer and cigarette maker Phillip Morris Companies, Inc., was listed last month in a *Fortune* poll of the business community as the second-most-admired corporation in America, or that a man like cigarette peddler Henry Kravis, whose LBO partnership owns RJR/Nabisco, is one of the darlings of New York society. But alcohol and tobacco aren't crack.

The point is that when Judge Sweet says, "Are we going to ban red meat because it causes heart attacks?" we ought to say that there is not one all-encompassing principle at work in our society that says we allow everything or we allow nothing. Rather, there is a continuum, a line, and a place where we draw the line. We will draw the line between products we will tolerate freely and leave for people to make their own decisions about (like red meat), products we will tolerate with some controls on who can buy them and how they can be marketed (cigarettes, prescription drugs, cars, and guns someday, one hopes), and products we won't tolerate at all, with the line-drawing based on weighing the costs and the benefits of that product and how likely it is that those using the product will be able to make rational decisions about it and will not victimize others if they make the wrong decision.

Sweet argues that the purpose of law is to direct itself to those areas where people hurt others, not themselves. Even on that basis, the case for the current legal prohibition against crack is clear. Selling it clearly hurts others. That's easy. But buying it hurts others too, because it sustains the marketplace for the sellers. And just possessing it—the most difficult legal prohibition to rationalize on Sweet's theoretically reasonable terms—also hurts others because its use so predictably makes the user uncontrollably antisocial, be it in terms of child abuse, fetal abuse, or random violent crime.

Rosenthal of Phoenix House is a lot less theoretical about it, and for good reason: "Comparing crack to alcohol or tobacco is like comparing a BB gun to a shotgun," he says. "Adding another chemical to what's already legal out there that is by many magnitudes more potent would be mindless. . . .

"Nadelmann and Sweet think that if we give these drugs to people they'll achieve some kind of equilibrium," Rosenthal continues heatedly. "That they won't be criminals. That they won't be antisocial. That their crime is because of the money they need for drugs. Well, I've seen people with unlimited money come in here who had enough to buy all the drugs they wanted and they didn't stabilize. They weren't in that social equilibrium that Sweet and Nadelmann think they'll find. . . .

"They figure that maybe we can't solve the problem, but that if we just give the addict what he's asking for, he'll settle down and be a nice fella and won't bother us. Well, he won't be a nice fella, and he will bother us. He'll be violent. He'll be paranoid. He'll binge. He'll need twenty or thirty crack vials a day, and he'll never reach that equilibrium."

A young black woman from Brooklyn named Kelly, who is being treated for crack addiction at Phoenix House, puts it this way: "When you have one vial, you scheme to get the second. If you have ten, when you get to the ninth you think about what you can sell—your body, the TV set, anything—to get the eleventh. You look at a TV set and say, 'The TV, who needs it? I'll sell it.' The next day . . . after you've passed out, you get up and say, 'What happened to the TV?' . . . Legalize crack and let me be able to buy it anytime, and I'd have a home with no furniture, and I'd die."

"I feel so bad about this legalization theory," adds Rosenthal, whose program claims a 60 percent success rate for its patients, who include all varieties of addicts. "I have never met a drug user who's untreatable. But I have met plenty who don't want treatment. And one way you get them to want it is to say, 'You can't have drugs.' "

Conversely, Rosenthal notes that "you can't treat people for addiction and give them drugs."

Kelly adds, "Legalize it, and this place would be empty. You'd be telling me, 'It's okay to do crack. It's legal.' So why be here?"

The fact is that for all the talk about current enforcement not working, it may, in fact, be working. "We've clearly made progress with mainstream America," says Rosenthal. "Drug use is down in mainstream America."

And Bateman of Harlem Hospital concedes that the rate of drug abusing mothers has "leveled off at twenty percent since last year and may even be dropping a bit," an assessment that echoes an observation by noted criminologist James Q. Wilson in a recent article in *Commentary* that despite the argument for legalization of heroin in the 1970s—that law enforcement wasn't working—heroin addiction in fact has leveled off since 1972, while it has escalated in England, where the drug is legally administered to addicts.

But the more important point is that we haven't really tried to do what we need to do to bring that percentage of addicted mothers below 20 percent. As Manhattan district attorney Robert Morgenthau puts it, "We haven't tried enforcement, so how do we know if it will work?"

Morgenthau points out that despite President Bush's drug war rhetoric, the entire federal Drug Enforcement Agency consists of 2,600 agents across the country—roughly half of the police force in the Bronx—and that the new money in the President's drug war chest totals $39 million, to be spread among the 50 states.

"There are two cheap answers to drugs," says Morgenthau. "Legalization and the death penalty. The real answer is the expensive answer: real money for real enforcement and real treatment programs."

"People can be treated, if they want to be treated," adds Rosenthal. "And one of the ways you get them to want to be treated is to have the foot of the law up their ass, to have them facing prosecution if they don't go into treatment. . . . If we weren't so wimpy about this, we could make progress."

What's the way to be unwimpy?

"Well, we know from studies that seventy to eighty percent of all those arrested have a drug problem," Rosenthal says. "Right now, we have eight thousand people a week arraigned in New York, and seventy percent of them are addicts. And it's the same in every city across the country. But do we test them? No. We should test them, and then make treatment a condition of their release."

That, of course, means billions for new treatment facilities, but, as Rosenthal notes, "We're putting them in prison anyway. It wouldn't cost more to treat them."

On this front, too, there is progress. For example, in New York, Governor Mario Cuomo has started a program whereby 2,450 of the state's 52,000 prison beds in the next year will be converted to drug treatment beds.

But the real progress will only come when efforts like this aren't an exception. If we discovered that Muammar Qaddafi was contaminating our water supply with a poison that made millions of us paranoid, violent, and incapable of fulfilling any obligations to loved ones, we would post police and national guardsmen everywhere necessary. And we would treat all the victims.

We wouldn't write off the victims, let alone set up dispensaries for the poisoned water.

"If Bob Sweet found out that his fourteen-year-old daughter was using crack, he wouldn't want the government to help her get it," says Rosenthal. "He'd be knocking on my door to get her into a drug-free program, and he'd do whatever he had to do to force her into it. Why should he have a different solution for someone else's fourteen-year-old daughter?"

Rosenthal is right. We can't write off anyone's daughter. We can't just write off those communities where the desperation is highest and, therefore, the reach for an escape the most frequent. This is one instance where the politicians' rhetoric would actually match reality. For this would be the genocide that many black political leaders have labeled it to be. And in the process we would also encourage the poisoning among those not in the underclass who are now more likely to be deterred by the illegality of drugs like crack.

Nor as a society should we commit the most destabilizing act in a system built on the rule of law—the abandonment of a law because it takes too much resolve to enforce it.

If for a year or two it takes cops on half the street corners of America, let's do it. . . . Let's put cops, or troops, on that block next to Dr. Bateman's hospital. And if it takes investments in treatment equal to 20 or 30 percent of what we're paying to bail out the Charlie Keatings of the world, let's do that, too. If it takes another 30 or 40 percent of what we're spending to bail out the S&Ls to provide real educational and job opportunity for the people whose desperation drove them to crack in the first place, let's do that too.

Or, at least, let's try.

In the coming months the arguments for legalization, supported by an eye-catching coalition of respected thinkers from the right and left, are going to be increasingly in vogue. For the liberals, the lure will be the notion of enlightened treatment taking the place of a storm-trooper police effort that features wiretaps and stool pigeons and the incarceration of desperate people "swept up," to use Sweet's words, in this activity. For conservatives the lure will be a Chicago School kind of argument, that we should let people decide for themselves in the great marketplace out there what they want to do to themselves.

But liberals should understand that legalization represents the ultimate abdication of governmental responsibility, a decision to give the underclass (and ultimately everyone else) whatever drugs they want, with whatever consequences to themselves and their families, as long as they won't bother us with crime. (Indeed, liberals should understand that the fact that addicts commit crimes against the mainstream is probably the only reason there is any broad-based constituency at all today for providing drug treatment.)

And conservatives should know that legalization represents the ultimate throwing in of the towel, the ultimate abandonment of the notion that we're serious about being a society based on the rule of law. For we'd be getting rid of the law simply because we've found that it's hard to enforce.

"You don't solve this by saying, 'There's nothing I can do, so let's put a government label on crack and give it out at the government crack house,' " says Rosenthal. "If you do, there will be more instability, more violence, more child abuse. And the addicts will stand there at the crack house and take the stuff until they drop dead."

POSTSCRIPT

Should Drugs Be Legalized?

The question of whether or not illicit drugs should be legalized is an extremely difficult one and one that will continue to confront us. Current public opinion surveys find that the "legalizing" option has insignificant public support. But another few years of drug-related violence and complaints by judges and court administrators that drug cases are clogging the courts could bring about a shift in public attitudes. (Drug cases account for 44 percent of criminal trials and 50 percent of criminal appeals in the federal courts. See Martin, "Drugs, Crime, and Urban Trial Court Management: The Unintended Consequences of the War on Drugs," 8 *Law and Policy Review* 117 [1990].)

It should be emphasized that one choice is not necessarily the easy one and the other the hard one. The "legalizers" are occasionally depicted as advocates of a free market of drugs, of letting individuals make decisions about personal use of drugs, and of letting the market regulate the price of a product that now has an artificially elevated price. But most "legalizers" are, in fact, asking that government involvement in dealing with the drug problem continue. To suggest a noncriminal approach to drugs is not to advocate a hands-off approach. As Nadelmann makes clear, treatment is needed and education is needed. It is not all that clear that this would be cheaper than the current approach.

It would also not necessarily be easier. Other than complete legalization, where drugs might be as readily available as aspirin, most approaches call for some regulation by the state. Choices would have to be made among these alternatives, ranging from outlawing sales to minors to requiring medical prescriptions for some drugs to establishing clinics that would distribute the drugs. Each of these alternatives would raise questions about free access and about effects on the black market for drugs.

Recent writings on the legalization question include Moore, "Drugs: Getting a Fix on the Problem and the Solution," 8 *Yale Law and Policy Review* 8 (1990); Kaplan, "Taking Drugs Seriously," *Public Interest*, Summer, 1988, p. 42; and Wilson, "Against the Legalization of Drugs," *Commentary*, February, 1990, p. 21. Cloud, "Cocaine, Demand, and Addiction: A Study of the Possible Convergence of Rational Theory and National Policy," 42 *Vanderbilt Law Review* 725 (1989), contains a discussion of the legislative history of prevention and treatment programs. Packer, *The Limits of the Criminal Sanction* (1968) analyzes problems associated with legal enforcement of moral norms. The myths and realities of the Prohibition era are examined in Clark, *Deliver Us from Evil* (1976) and Kyvig, ed., *Law, Alcohol and Order: Perspective on National Prohibition* (1985).

ISSUE 15

Should a National Gun Control Policy Be Established?

YES: Mark Udulutch, from "The Constitutional Implications of Gun Control and Several Realistic Gun Control Proposals," *American Journal of Criminal Law* (vol. 19, 1989)

NO: James D. Wright, from "Second Thoughts About Gun Control," *Public Interest* (Spring 1988)

ISSUE SUMMARY

YES: Law student Mark Udulutch examines the gun control problem and asserts that gun control is necessary and that effective and enforceable federal regulations are feasible.
NO: Professor of sociology James Wright concludes, after examining how guns are used, that banning guns would not be beneficial.

Unlike previous assassinations or attempted assassinations, the attempt on President Reagan's life in 1981 did not lead to a widespread debate about gun control. The issue that captured public discussion was the insanity defense raised by John Hinckley (see Issue 17). Probably because President Reagan opposed gun control legislation, Hinckley's act did little to further the cause of gun control on the federal level. In fact, there have been some efforts to weaken federal limitations on interstate purchases of handguns. There have been recent attempts by cities and towns to restrict handguns, but some of these, such as those in San Francisco, have been invalidated by the courts, and their impact is necessarily limited.

The issue of handgun regulation is interesting partly because there is a history of gun control laws, both in this country and abroad, that can be looked to for guidance. Such an examination suggests that there are cultural traditions and attitudes toward violence that need to be considered in evaluating why some gun legislation is effective and some is not.

One of the most frequently mentioned legal justifications for permitting individuals to possess handguns is the Second Amendment to the Constitution. This amendment states that:

A well regulated Militia, being necessary to the security of a free State, the right of the people to keep and bear Arms, shall not be infringed.

Yet, due to court interpretations of the meaning of these words, the Amendment has become almost irrelevant to the issue of gun control. Certainly, one convicted of violating a firearms statute is unlikely to win his or her case by relying on the Second Amendment.

Although many people are familiar with the last half of the Amendment, the crucial words are contained in the first part. The right to bear arms is not absolute. Rather, it is a right related to the need for a state militia. This was the ruling of the Supreme Court in the case of *United States v. Miller,* 307 U.S. 174 (1939), the only case interpreting the Second Amendment as it relates to the federal government. In that case, two men were charged in federal court with transporting an unregistered sawed-off shotgun and violating the National Firearms Act. The defendants claimed that they were protected by the Second Amendment and won in the trial court. The Supreme Court, however, interpreted the rights granted by the Second Amendment differently. Justice McReynolds wrote,

> In the absence of any evidence tending to show that possession or use of a "shotgun having a barrel of less than eighteen inches in length" at this time has some reasonable relationship to the preservation or efficiency of a well regulated militia, we cannot say that the Second Amendment guarantees the right to keep and bear such an instrument. . . .
>
> The Constitution as originally adopted granted to the Congress power—"To provide for calling forth the Militia to execute the Laws of the Union, suppress Insurrections and repel Invasions." . . . With obvious purpose to assure the continuation and render possible the effectiveness of [the Militia] the declaration and guarantee of the Second Amendment were made. It must be interpreted and applied with that end in view.

YES

Mark Udulutch

THE CONSTITUTIONAL IMPLICATIONS OF GUN CONTROL AND SEVERAL REALISTIC GUN CONTROL PROPOSALS

INTRODUCTION

The public is polarized on the issue of gun control. Anti-gun control activists believe that it is each and every American's individual right to bear arms. Various pro-gun control organizations disagree and propose different methods of gun control. For example, there are individuals who would ban all handguns; as well as those who take a less radical stand and who would simply increase the controls on firearms. Moderate gun control groups propose measures such as requiring an individual to successfully complete a firearms safety course before possession of a gun is allowed, or to wait for a mandatory period of time before taking possession of a gun.

Today, there are approximately 20,000 different gun control laws in existence, ranging from those enacted by municipalities and states, to those enacted by the federal government. Individuals opposed to gun control point to this fact, and assert that gun control is a failure. The truth is that, for the most part, these laws are ineffective because they lack scope, breadth and enforcement.[1]

SHOULD THERE BE GUN CONTROL?

In a democratic society, such as the United States, two things need consideration prior to the enactment of legislation for the purpose of solving a social problem. The first concern is whether there is a problem that can, in fact, be controlled through legislation. The second is whether the majority of Americans would support governmental intervention to provide a solution to that problem. Both of these questions must be answered affirmatively or further discussion of gun control legislation would be senseless.

Excerpted from Mark Udulutch, "The Constitutional Implications of Gun Control and Several Realistic Gun Control Proposals," *American Journal of Criminal Law,* vol. 17 (1989), pp. 19–54. Copyright © 1989 by *American Journal of Criminal Law.* Reprinted by permission. Some notes omitted.

Firearms are used to murder nearly 12,000 people annually;[2] another 1,750 persons suffer death by accident; and an estimated 200,000 people are injured. In addition, more than 16,000 people use firearms to take their own lives each year. Although they constitute only a third of all firearms, handguns are used in three-fourths of all firearm murders and one-half of all murders. Even in light of these statistics, the pro-gun advocates continue to herald the "virtues" of gun ownership.

Over the years, both sides of the gun control debate have used statistics in attempts to make their arguments. Statisticians, however, point out that the persuasiveness of a statistic lies in its ability to be factually verified. Here, the pro-gun control forces have had an advantage over the anti-gun control activists. They present the corpses and shattered limbs that result from the misuse of firearms as the evidence needed to successfully state their position. The pro-gun activists, however, argue that firearms actually prevent murders, rapes and burglaries. The problem with this argument is that it lacks credible statistical verification.

Returning to the central question, should additional legislative action be taken to regulate the nearly 70,000,000 handguns and 140,000,000 long guns now in the United States? The answer is yes. Firearms are certainly needed for national defense and law enforcement, but they are not needed by individual citizens to serve as the tools for social violence. Rational, workable federal legislation is the appropriate means to stop the misuse of firearms.

More aggressive gun control laws are needed to reduce the problem. However, legislative measures will work only to the extent they are supported by the majority of the people. While the public has not given its support to every form of increased gun control legislation, it has supported the less intrusive proposals.

Based on the analysis of public opinion polls from 1938 through 1972, one author wrote that "[t]he vast majority of Americans have favored some kind of action for the control of civilian firearms at least as long as modern polling has been in existence."[3] It should be noted that, depending upon how a question is phrased, public opinion polls on gun control generate different responses. For example, one Gallup Poll posed the question, "Would you favor or oppose a law which would require a person to obtain a police permit before he or she could buy a gun?" The first response given was 75% in favor of the law; that response has subsequently fluctuated from 68% to 78% in follow-up polls. In contrast, another poll asked, "Do you think that people like yourself have to be prepared to defend their homes against crime and violence, or can the police take care of that?" Some 52% of the people felt that they needed to be prepared. The difference in these questions was that the first dealt with other persons, while the second was concerned with the person responding directly to the question. . . .

SEVERAL REALISTIC GUN CONTROL PROPOSALS

When more than 30,000 people are killed annually by firearms and another 200,000 are injured, it is clear to most individuals that a serious problem exists.[4] Recognizing the problem is the first step toward a solution. Finding a solution is not easy, nor is it achieved quickly, but this should not obviate gun control.

Given American society and its attraction to firearms, legislation must not be so restrictive that, at its outset, it fails to enlist the cooperation of the American public. At this time, it would be unrealistic to ban all firearms from the private sector. Many pro-gun activists try to attack the pro-control position by arguing that one control will lead to another, and eventually guns will be outlawed all together. Although such a result is conceivable, a complete ban will never be successful unless it is supported by the people. Only public disinterest in firearms would truly result in eliminating them from the social environment.

Neither the approach of a total ban on firearms, as some gun control advocates propose, nor the do-nothing attitude of the anti-gun control activists, are realistic at this time. Yet firearms are a serious problem to the American society. Their destructive misuse cannot be allowed to continue. Some increases in regulations are definitely needed. These regulations will require a realistic compromise between the two extremes in the gun control debate.[5]

When constructing these controls, two goals must remain constant. First, and most importantly, it is necessary to decrease as much as possible the victimization of individuals through the misuse of firearms. Second, it is important to structure legislation in ways that accomplish the intended purposes while not being overly intrusive upon the individual. In essence, a utilitarian approach must be taken toward gun control. The benefits to society must be maximized, while the possible intrusions to individuals must be minimized.

Federal Legislation: the Only Realistic Answer

Even with 20,000 gun control laws already in existence, the serious problems due to firearm misuse continue. Obviously,

the controls that have been designed have not been sufficiently effective. There are three identifiable reasons for this problem: 1) the lack of uniform legislation; 2) the fact that most controls do not go far enough in their attempt to prevent the problems of firearm misuse; and, 3) the controls in place are not effectively enforced.

Sweeping federal legislation would go a long way toward resolving all three of these problems. Such legislation could offer a coherent, orderly means of addressing the gun problem, unlike the present hodgepodge of local, state and federal legislation.

One of the most significant problems resulting from the discrepancy in local, state and federal firearm laws is the transportation of firearms from one state to another. If every state had uniformly strict firearm control laws, interstate transport would not be a major problem. No longer would an individual like John Hinckley be able to purchase a firearm in a state with weak gun control laws, transport his weapon across state lines, and then use it to shoot the President of the United States. However, going to the legislatures of the fifty states to achieve uniformly strict firearm controls is not the most efficient course of action. The failure of even one state to adopt the uniform controls would severely weaken the entire chain of controls. Federal legislation would be far more effective; only one body of lawmakers would have to deal with the increased controls instead of fifty. Furthermore, once established, the controls could not be weakened by the efforts of one state legislature.

The Proposals

Having concluded that federal legislation is the best way to effectively control firearm possession and use, the next question is what kind of legislation? Some intelligently drafted controls are already in place,[6] but they have not proven sufficient. Controls that go further than present federal legislation in preventing the problems of firearm misuse and that are more rigorously enforced are needed.

1. *Licensing and Education*—A nationwide licensing program would be an effective first step. Such a program already exists for sellers, manufacturers and importers of firearms, but it does not extend to private citizens who buy and use the guns. Not every person who wants to own a firearm should be trusted with it.

To obtain a license, a person would have to meet three criteria. First, he or she could not belong to any of the classes of persons denied the privilege of possessing firearms. Section 922 of the Firearms Owners' Protection Act denies felons, fugitives from justice, drug addicts, illegal aliens, individuals dishonorably discharged from the military, individuals who have renounced their United States citizenship, and mental incompetents the privilege of owning guns. It would be wise to add to this list persons under eighteen years of age. A second criteria for obtaining a firearm license would be to pass a firearm safety course. Drivers are required to pass a drivers' training course, so why shouldn't a comparable test be administered to license potential gun owners? A firearm's safety course would reinforce student awareness of the danger involved in firearm use and misuse. A course of this nature could, at a minimum, be expected to decrease the number of accidental killings and injuries occurring from gun misuse.

The third criteria would require an extensive background check on a prospective licensee to make sure he or she did not belong to one of the classes of persons prohibited from owning firearms. This check would be made by the police department where the applicant resided. Additionally, this investigative program would be overseen by the Bureau of Alcohol, Tobacco and Firearms.

The cost of such a licensing program would not be insignificant, and, initially, some federal monies would be needed to organize it. Federal dollars, however, should not be used to keep the system running. Instead of being funded by general tax dollars, the licensing program should be funded by persons wanting to own firearms. These funds would be classified as special federal monies, to be used by the Bureau of Alcohol, Tobacco and Firearms to administer the licensing program and to subsidize local police forces for the costs involved in investigating applicants. Training programs would be conducted by federally regulated private businesses that charge for their services. Once a person acquired a firearm license, he or she would be allowed to possess a firearm within the limits imposed by other firearm controls. If after receiving a license to own a firearm the licensee fell into a disallowed class, the license would be revoked on a permanent basis.

2. *Firearm Registration*—With nearly 210,000,000 firearms already present in the United States, it is foolish to believe that a licensing program by itself will keep firearms out of the hands of people who should not have them. Another step toward keeping firearms from untrustworthy people is to require that all firearms be registered. Federal law already requires that "each manufacturer, importer and maker shall register each firearm that he manufactures, imports, or makes." However, because of the proposed licens-

ing requirements and the uncertainty of who currently owns what firearm, all firearms in the United States must be registered by their current owners. Each licensed firearm owner would pay for the costs involved in registering his or her own firearms.

Registration need not be a bothersome proposition to law abiding citizens. To keep a gun a citizen would only be expected to successfully complete the licensing process. Following the passage of legislation, all persons not licensed within a designated time, and still possessing a gun, would be required to sell the gun to a licensed owner. Failing to comply with this regulation would subject the person to harsh penalties. Suggested penalties include permanently losing the ability to become a licensed owner, a mandatory jail term, and forfeiture of a significant amount of money. The purpose of these penalties would be to make noncompliance with registration laws so risky that people would be forced to comply. Enforcement would take place in conjunction with normal police procedures. If during an investigation a person is found to be an unlicensed gun possessor, he or she would be prosecuted.

Realistically, not every individual now owning a firearm will comply with this firearm control. Some criminals will still have guns; this cannot be denied. However, with every gun removed from the hands of unqualified possessors, it is expected that the misuse of firearms will decrease.

3. *Mandatory Investigation of All Firearm Transferees*—A system whereby transferees are automatically investigated for fitness as a gun owner prior to any actual transfer of the weapon is needed to keep track of firearm ownership. Presently,

section 5812 of the National Firearms Act requires transferors to file applications for the transfer of their firearms with the Secretary of the Treasury. The transferor provides some information about the transferee in the application. In addition, section 922 of the Firearms Owners' Protection Act provides that it is a crime for anyone "to sell or otherwise dispose of any firearm . . . to any person knowing or having reasonable cause to believe that such a person" is a member of one of the groups of people not allowed to possess firearms. Unfortunately, neither of these requirements is sufficient since each fails to provide for actual investigation of the transferee.

Because the only lawful transferee of a firearm is one who possesses a valid firearm's license, the investigation required need not be extensive. The person would already have been investigated prior to obtaining his or her firearm's license. The transferee's history, dating from the time the license was received or from the time a firearm was last transferred to the transferee, is all that must be investigated.

None of the transfer costs would be assumed by the federal or local governments. They would instead be paid by the transferor. Unlike the original licensing investigation where the transferee paid the fee, the transferor would pay for the cost of the transfer investigation. In this way any possibility of violating the transferee's fifth amendment right against self-incrimination would be avoided. The failure of the transferor to comply with the transfer laws would subject him or her to the same penalties applicable to persons who fail to register firearms.

4. *A Waiting Period*—Intricately related to the formalities of a firearm transfer is a mandatory waiting period. Though the

idea of a waiting period is not new it is critical that it be established on the federal level. In 1988 Congress considered the "Brady Amendment," which required a one week waiting period before a transferee could possess a transferred handgun. During this time the police could conduct a thorough background check of the transferee. In the scheme presented here, the transfer investigation would take place during the waiting period.

Unfortunately, the "Brady Amendment" was defeated in Congress. Much of the blame for its defeat must be attributed to the National Rifle Association. The organization produced a mass mailing urging its members to contact their congressmen and to tell them to vote against the bill. The mailing contained substantial factual distortions; for example, that the Brady Amendment would devise "a system where firearm ownership is no longer . . . a guaranteed right but one controlled by a government bureaucrat who has dictatorial powers and you have no right of appeal on his decision." The letter went on to say that Congress could "call the bill whatever they want to, but it sets up a system that will eventually take away all your firearm rights and ban gun ownership in America." In reality the Brady Amendment had no intentions of banning guns, and, as discussed above, there exists no individual constitutional right to bear arms. All that this bill was attempting to do was to add a degree of sanity to the nation's handling of firearms.

A waiting period would not only allow time for the police to verify a prospective transferee's status, but it would also serve as a "cooling off" period. The otherwise reasonable person who, in the heat of the moment, wants to buy a gun to commit a crime will have to wait to get it. The expectation is that such a person will reconsider his or her plans while waiting.

Anti-gun control organizations are quick to point out that the majority of persons going through the legal channels to purchase a firearm are not in need of any "cooling off" period. Furthermore, they say that anyone who wants a gun badly enough can find a way around the law. These arguments are valid in many situations, but not in all. It is doubtful that a waiting period would stop a hardcore criminal in the quest for a gun. However, some individuals with criminal aspirations or designs will be thwarted. The inconvenience to prospective gun owners of waiting one, two or three weeks to obtain a firearm is minor when compared to the significance of the tragedies that could be avoided. A waiting period is needed.

5. Taxing Measure for Keeping Firearms Out of City Limits—It seems unlikely that most Americans would accept a ban on all firearms within the limits of their communities. This, together with the fact that most cases of firearm misuse occur in heavily populated areas, produces a serious dilemma. One of the principal reasons for owning a firearm within a city is for self-protection. Some people believe that if they have a firearm they will be able to ward off anyone wishing to do them harm. Although this reasoning is questionable, it has many adherents. The proposed solution is a combination tax burden-tax incentive scheme.

Those persons licensed to own guns and living in a city may still keep their guns at home, but will be subject to a federal tax for doing so. This tax should be progressive to avoid inflicting a disproportionate hardship on those least capable of paying. Even so, the tax would apply to everyone wishing to keep firearms at a private residence within city limits, and it must be relatively high in order to discourage people from exercising this privilege. Furthermore, the tax would double for every firearm over the first one kept at a private residence. All collected taxes would be used for increased law enforcement. Although the federal government would allow licensed individuals to keep their guns in their city residences, there is nothing that would prevent a community from banning firearm possession within its city limits.

Those persons licensed to possess a firearm who do not wish to keep them at their city residence may store their guns under lock and key at a gun club. The adoption of such proposals would no doubt encourage the growth of gun clubs. Guns stored at these clubs would not be subject to the federal taxes imposed on privately housed guns. Only club membership fees would have to be paid. This plan should create a migration of firearms from city residences. Gun clubs could be located either in the country or within city limits. Their main purpose would be to create a centralized secure place where firearms could be kept.

For enforcement purposes, guns would have to be returned nightly to the gun club. Exceptions would be made for hunters wishing to take their guns on hunting trips. To take their guns with them, the hunters would register removal with the club, which, in turn, would report those firearms not returned on time. To ensure that each gun club complies with the law, it would be subject to periodic, unannounced investigations by the Bureau of Alcohol, Tobacco and Firearms or the Internal Revenue Service. It would be presumed that those licensed gun owners not returning their guns to the gun clubs had opted to keep their guns at home, and would, therefore, be subject to the gun tax.

6. *Banning All Automatic and Military Style Semi-Automatic Weapons*—A semi-automatic weapon is one which requires a separate pull of the trigger for each shot. The weapons differ from automatic weapon[s] which fire more than one shot at the pull of the trigger. When addressing the need for increased controls on semi-automatic weapons, one must make a distinction between the types of semi-automatic weapons. There are two general categories of these weapons: the hunting style semi-automatic weapon and the military style semi-automatic weapon. The military style weapons are those semi-automatic weapons designed as assault weapons. They are designed and marketed with large capacity magazines, which allow them to fire many rounds without reloading. Senator Howard Metzenbaum has introduced legislation into Congress that would ban these weapons. Semi-automatic hunting weapons would remain unaffected by this legislation.

Unaltered, a military style semi-automatic weapon is quite formidable; however, its destructive potential can be increased even further by transforming it into a fully automatic weapon.[7] Such a conversion is generally not a difficult operation for a knowledgeable gunsmith.[8] As of 1985, it was estimated that 125,000 of the then existing 500,000 military style semi-automatic weapons had been converted to fully-automatic weapons. Actual statistics on the number of military style semi-automatic weapons in private hands do not exist because, unless the gun is technically considered an automatic weapon, the buyer need not be licensed. Even if owners of both automatic and military style semi-automatic weapons were licensed, the primary problem would still remain: namely, the possibility that the considerable firepower of these weapons could find its way into the hands of a disturbed individual.

There are numerous examples of semi-automatic and converted semi-automatics used in slayings. One such instance is the January 19, 1989, slaying of five school children in Stockton, California by a distraught gunman. The killer used an unconverted AKM-56S military style semi-automatic weapon. Also, in January of 1989, a member of the Los Angeles Crips Gang was indicted for possession of a converted M-11 with a silencer that had been used to commit murder. In December of 1988, six members of an Algona, Iowa family were killed by a Mini-14 semi-automatic rifle. Yet another incident took place in March of 1988, when nine people were killed in a crack house by an AR-15 semi-automatic rifle. In light of such occurrences, and the comparatively inconsequential benefits to society in allowing private citizens to possess these weapons, it is apparent that greater controls must be placed upon both automatic and military style semi-automatic weapons. These weapons were designed for one primary reason, to kill people quickly and in large numbers.

While Americans do not seem willing to accept a total ban on firearms, they might accept a ban on automatic and military style semi-automatic weapons. There will be some resistance to a ban on automatic and military style semi-automatic weapons, but its enforcement will be relatively easy compared to a ban on all firearms, or a ban just on handguns,

in that there are far fewer of these weapons in the market place.[9] The sale of new automatic weapons, to persons not having specific governmental authorization, was halted May 19, 1986.[10] In addition, all transfers of those weapons, lawfully possessed before that date, are now required to have specific governmental authorization.[11] The result of these measures is that the identity of a significant number of people owning automatic weapons is known. If needed, this information will help apprehend them. As for the military style semi-automatic and the converted military style semi-automatic weapons, no provisions have been made by the federal government to keep track of their whereabouts.

The average owner of a military style semi-automatic weapon, or an automatic weapon, is not a criminal, and substantial compliance with a ban on these weapons could be expected. This would be especially true if the federal government offered to buy these weapons. After a reasonable period of time given to comply, persons still in possession of automatic and military style semi-automatic weapons would be subject to harsh penalties. A ban on military style semi-automatic and automatic weapons is especially needed now, because these weapons have become the weapons of choice for the drug gangs in the United States. Congress made a good start when it required an additional mandatory ten year imprisonment for those individuals involved in a violent or drug trafficking crime in which an automatic weapon was used.[12] Nevertheless, the law, as applied to automatic weapons, is not yet broad enough, and it does not address the problem of military style semi-automatic weapons. The ten year mandatory penalty is sufficiently stern, but it should be extended to all persons in possession of an automatic or a military style semi-automatic weapon after the expiration of a buy back date. The potential for disaster that these weapons present is simply too great to allow them in the hands of the general public.

CONCLUSION

The need for strong, realistic gun control legislation becomes obvious whenever another life is taken or an injury inflicted as the result of the misuse of a firearm. This note has presented a number of proposals for increasing gun control nationwide. To be most effective, these proposals should be adopted together and they should be addressed by the federal government. The time to pass increased firearm controls is now. Too many lives have been lost because of firearm misuse.

NOTES

1. Kleck, *Policy Lessons from Recent Gun Control Research*, 49 LAW & CONTEMP. PROBS. 35, 50 (1986); *see also* TASK FORCE ON FIREARMS, NATIONAL COMMITTEE ON THE CAUSES AND PREVENTION OF VIOLENCE, FIREARMS AND VIOLENCE IN AMERICAN LIFE 87-95 (1969); J. WRIGHT, P. ROSSI & K. DALY, *supra* note 6, at 244. "Political jurisdictions with rather restrictive regulations often abut jurisdictions with barely any controls at all, [thus creating] an invitation to widespread law evasions." *Id.* Some pro-gun control advocates blame the National Rifle Association for the lack of unified legislation. The National Rifle Association is often referred to as the most effective lobby in Washington D.C. Note, *A Shot at Stricter Controls: Strict Liability for Gun Manufacturers*, 15 PAC L.J. 171, 192 (1983) (authored by Rose Safarian).

2. This figure was derived by taking the average number of murders committed with firearms from 1980 through 1987. . . . 11,403 persons on average are murdered by firearms each year. BUREAU OF THE CENSUS, U.S. DEP'T OF COMMERCE, NATIONAL DATA BOOK AND GUIDE TO SOURCES: STATISTICAL ABSTRACT OF THE UNITED STATES 1989, AT 168 (109th ed. 1989) (graph no. 281); BUREAU OF THE CENSUS, U.S. DEP'T OF COMMERCE, NATIONAL DATA BOOK AND GUIDE TO SOURCES: STATISTICAL ABSTRACT OF THE UNITED STATES 1986, at 171 (106th ed. 1986) (graph no. 290). . . .

Murder is "the 11th leading cause of death and the 6th leading cause of the loss of potential years of life before age 65." Sloan, Kellerman, Reay, Ferris, Koepsell, Rivara, Rice, Gray & Lo-Gerfo, *Handgun Regulations, Crime, Assaults, and Homicide: A Tale of Two Cities*, 319 NEW ENG. J. OF MED. 1256, 1256 (1988) [hereinafter Sloan & Kellerman].

3. Erskine, *The Polls: Gun Control*, 36 PUB. OPINION Q. 455 (1972); *see* Wright, *Public Opinion and Gun Control: A Comparison of Results from Two Recent National Surveys*, 455 ANNALS 24, 31 (1981).

The following are representative examples of gun control polls. First, a 1975 Gallup Poll found that 66% of all Americans living in cities of more than one million people favored a ban on handguns. Drinan, *Gun Control: The Good Outweighs the Evil*, in THE GREAT GUN CONTROL DEBATE 12 (1976) (Second Amendment Foundation Monograph Series). Second, an October 1987 Gallup Poll found that "60 percent [of the adult population surveyed] favored stricter laws on handgun sales," and 42% favored a ban on handgun possession. N.Y. Times, Oct. 25, 1987, § 4, at 5, col. 2. Lastly, a 1981 Gallup Poll showed that nine out of ten people favored a waiting period for the purchase of a handgun. N.Y. Times, Apr. 15, 1987, at A27, col. 3.

4. The mentality of anti-gun control organizations like the National Rifle Association is dangerously self-perpetuated. This is evidenced by a report commissioned by The Remington Arms Company. Columnist Jack Anderson commented in an article based on the Remington Arms Study that the zealous supporters of the National Rifle Association live "in a make-believe world of sacred rights, ancient skills and coonskins . . . like the inhabitants of Hitler's bunker in 1945, they talk only to themselves, reinforcing their own views." UNITED STATES CONFERENCE OF MAYORS, ORGANIZING FOR HANDGUN CONTROL 4 (1977).

5. One author contends that increased controls on firearms may have little effect on the overall rate of robberies and assaults but that the homicide rate at the minimum would be decreased. Cook, *The Effect of Gun Availability on Violent Crime Patterns*, 455 ANNALS 63, 78 (1981). A decrease in the homicide rate alone would be enough to justify increased gun control measures. *See generally 7 Deadly Days*, TIME, July 17, 1989, at 30.

6. *See, e.g.*, 18 U.S.C. § 922(d) (1988) (It is illegal to sell a firearm to a felon, a fugitive from justice, a drug addict, a mental incompetent, an illegal alien, one who has renounced his or her U.S. citizenship, one who was dishonorably dis-

charged from the military); 18 U.S.C. § 922(g) (1988) (It is illegal for a felon, drug addict, fugitive from justice, mental incompetent, illegal alien, one who was dishonorably discharged from the military, or one who has renounced his or her U.S. citizenship to possess or transport a firearm); 18 U.S.C. § 924(c)(1) (1988) (A mandatory sentence is imposed when a firearm is used in a crime of violence or a drug-trafficking crime).

7. Without federal or state authority to possess, make or transfer a machine gun, one violates the law in converting a semi-automatic weapon into a fully-automatic weapon, 27 C.F.R. § 179.105(a), (e) (1988).

8. Church, *The Other Arms Race*, TIME, Feb. 6, 1989, at 20, 22–23. Conversion kits are available today through some gun dealers, and until recently, through many gun magazines. *Machine Gun, supra* note 199, at 48. The buying and selling of conversion kits is of questionable legality since it is illegal for an unlicensed person to possess a fully automatic weapon. 18 U.S.C. § 922(o) (1988).

9. Currently the Bureau of Alcohol, Tobacco and Firearms estimates that there are between two and three million semi-automatic assault weapons in the United States today.

10. 18 U.S.C. § 922(o) (1988).

11. 18 U.S.C. § 922(o)(2)(A) (1988).

12. 18 U.S.C. § 924(c)(1) (1988).

NO

James D. Wright

SECOND THOUGHTS ABOUT GUN CONTROL

Gun control, it has been said, is the acid test of liberalism. All good liberals favor stricter gun controls. After all, doesn't the United States have the most heavily armed population on earth? Are we not the world's most violent people? Surely these facts must be causally connected. The apparently desperate need to "do something" about the vast quantity of firearms and firearms abuse is, to the good liberal, obvious.

At one time, it seemed evident to me, we needed to mount a campaign to resolve the crisis of handgun proliferation. Guns are employed in an enormous number of crimes in this country. In other countries with stricter gun laws, gun crime is rare. Many of the firearms involved in crime are cheap handguns, so-called Saturday Night Specials, for which no legitimate use or need exists. Many families buy these guns because they feel the need to protect themselves; eventually, they end up shooting one another. If there were fewer guns around, there would also be less crime and less violence. Most of the public also believes this, and has supported stricter gun control for as long as pollsters have been asking the question. Yet Congress has refused to act in a meaningful way, owing mainly to the all-powerful "gun lobby" headed by the National Rifle Association. Were the power of this lobby somehow effectively countered by the power of public opinion, stricter gun laws would follow quickly, and we would begin to achieve a safer and more civilized society.

When I first began research on the topic of private firearms, in the mid-1970s, I shared this conventional and widely held view of the issue. Indeed, much of it struck me as self-evidently true. My initial interest in the topic resulted from a life-long fascination with the bizarre: I certainly did not own a gun (I still don't), and neither, as far as I knew, did many of my friends. Still, readily available survey evidence showed that half the families in the United States did own one, and I wondered what unspeakable oddities or even pathologies an analysis of this half of the American population would reveal.

From James D. Wright, "Second Thoughts About Gun Control," *The Public Interest*, no. 91 (Spring 1988), pp. 23–39. Copyright © 1988 by National Affairs, Inc. Reprinted by permission of *The Public Interest* and the author.

My first scholarly paper on the topic, "The Ownership of the Means of Destruction," appeared in 1975. This demographic comparison between gun-owning and non-gun-owning households revealed no shocking information. Gun owners, it turned out, were largely small-town and rural Protestants of higher-than-average income. Fear of crime, interestingly enough, did not seem to be related to gun ownership. The general tone of my piece remained unmistakably "anti-gun," but the findings did not provide much new information to strengthen the "anti-gun" lobby's arguments. At about the same time, I prepared a more polemical version of the paper, which was eventually published in the *Nation*. The General Counsel of the National Rifle Association described the piece as "emotionally supercharged drum-beating masquerading as scholarly analysis." Clearly, I was on the right track; I had managed to offend the right people.

The *Nation* article was abridged and reprinted in the Sunday Chicago *Tribune*, a newspaper read by about two million people, many of whom saw fit to write me after the piece appeared. Almost all the letters I received were provocative; some were very favorable, but most were vitriolic attacks from gun nuts. I was accused of being "incredibly biased," "strange and contradictory," of telling "many outright 100% lies," of being "sophistic" and "intellectually dishonest," of being "unable to grasp truth," and of taking "thousands of words to say *nothing* constructive." I answered every letter I received. In a few cases, a long and profitable correspondence developed. The first wave of correspondence over the *Tribune* piece affirmed my assumption that many gun owners were crazy. Subsequent waves, however, convinced

me that many were indeed thoughtful, intelligent, often remarkably well-read people who were passionately concerned about their "right to keep and bear arms," but were willing, nonetheless, to listen to reason.

Two years later, in 1977, my colleague Peter Rossi and I received a grant from the National Institute of Justice to undertake a comprehensive, critical overview of the research literature on guns, crime, and violence in America. The results of this overview were published in 1981 in a three-volume government report and in 1983 as a commercial monograph, entitled *Under the Gun*. Subsequent to this work, we received another grant to gather original data on gun acquisition, ownership, and use from about 2,000 men doing felony time in ten state prisons all over the United States. We assembled this information in a government report and later in a monograph, *Armed and Considered Dangerous*. The felon survey marked the temporary end of my firearms research program, one that ran roughly from 1974 through 1986, when *Armed and Considered Dangerous* was finally published.

As I have already suggested, at the outset of the research program I had a strong feeling that the pro-gun-control forces had never marshalled their evidence in the most compelling way, that they were being seriously undercut by the more artful polemics of the National Rifle Association and related pro-gun groups. That the best available evidence, critically considered, would eventually prove favorable to the pro-control viewpoint was not in serious doubt—at least not to me, not in the beginning.

In the course of my research, however, I have come to question nearly every element of the conventional wisdom about guns, crime, and violence. Indeed, I am now of the opinion that a compelling case for "stricter gun control" *cannot be made*, at least not on empirical grounds. I have nothing but respect for the various pro-gun-control advocates with whom I have come into contact over the past years. They are, for the most part, sensitive, humane, and intelligent people, and their ultimate aim, to reduce death and violence in our society, is one that every civilized person must share. I have, however, come to be convinced that they are barking up the wrong tree.

WHAT IS "GUN CONTROL"?

Before I describe the intellectual odyssey that led to my change in thinking, it is critical to stress that "gun control" is an exceedingly nebulous concept. To say that one favors gun control, or opposes it, is to speak in ambiguities. In the present-day American political context, "stricter gun control" can mean anything from federal registration of firearms, to mandatory sentences for gun use in crime, to outright bans on the manufacture, sale, or possession of certain types of firearms. One can control the manufacturers of firearms, the wholesalers, the retailers, or the purchasers; one can control the firearms themselves, the ammunition they require, or the uses to which they are put. And one can likewise control their purchase, their carrying, or their mere possession. "Gun control" thus covers a wide range of specific interventions, and it would be useful indeed if the people who say they favor or oppose gun control were explicit about what, exactly, they are for and against.

In doing the research for *Under the Gun*, I learned that there are approximately 20,000 gun laws of various sorts already on the books in the United States. A few of these are federal laws (such as the Gun Control Act of 1968), but most are state and local regulations. It is a misstatement to say, as pro-gun-control advocates sometimes do, that the United States has "no meaningful gun control legislation." The problem is not that laws do not exist but that the regulations in force vary enormously from one place to the next, or, in some cases, that the regulations carried on the books are not or cannot be enforced.

Much of the gun legislation now in force, whether enacted by federal, state, or local statutes, falls into the category of reasonable social precaution, being neither more nor less stringent than measures taken to safeguard against abuses of other potentially life-threatening objects, such as automobiles. It seems reasonable, for example, that people should be required to obtain a permit to carry a concealed weapon, as they are virtually everywhere in the United States. It is likewise reasonable that people not be allowed to own automatic weapons without special permission, and that felons, drug addicts, and other sociopaths be prevented from legally acquiring guns. Both these restrictions are in force everywhere in the United States, because they are elements of federal law. About three-fourths of the American population lives in jurisdictions where the registration of firearms purchases is required. It is thus apparent that many states and localities also find this to be a useful precaution against something. And many jurisdictions also require "waiting periods" or "cooling off" periods between application and actual possession of a new firearms purchase. These too seem reasonable, since there are very few legitimate purposes to which a firearm might be put that would be thwarted if the user had to wait a few days, or even a few weeks, to get the gun.

Thus, when I state that "a compelling case for 'stricter gun control' cannot be made," I do not refer to the sorts of obvious and reasonable precautions discussed above, or to related precautionary measures. I refer, rather, to measures substantially more strict than "reasonable precaution," and more specifically, to measures that would deny or seriously restrict the right of the general population to own a firearm, or that would ban the sale or possession of certain kinds of firearms, such as handguns or even the small, cheap handguns known colloquially as "Saturday Night Specials."

EFFECTS OF GUN LAWS

One wonders, with some 20,000 firearms regulations now on the books, why the clamor continues for even more laws. The answer is obvious: none of the laws so far enacted has significantly reduced the rate of criminal violence. *Under the Gun* reviewed several dozen research studies that had attempted to measure the effects of gun laws in reducing crime; none of them showed any conclusive long-term benefits.

As it happens, both sides of the gun-control debate grant this point; they disagree, though as to why there is no apparent connection between gun-control laws and crime rates. The NRA maintains that gun laws don't work because they can't work. Widely ignored (especially by criminals) and unenforceable, gun-control laws go about the problem in the wrong way. For this reason, the NRA has long supported mandatory and severe sentences for the use of firearms in felonies, contending that we should punish firearms abusers once it is proven that an abuse has occurred, and leave legitimate users alone until they have actually done something illegal with their weapon.

The pro-control forces argue that gun laws don't work because there are too many of them, because they are indifferently enforced, and because the laws vary widely from one jurisdiction to the next. What we need, they would argue, are federal firearms regulations that are strictly enforced all across the nation. They would say that we have never given gun control a fair test, because we lack an aggressive *national* firearms policy.

This example illustrates an important point that I have learned and relearned throughout my career in applied social research: the policy consequences of a scientific finding are seldom obvious. On this particular point, the science is reasonably clear-cut: gun control laws do not reduce crime. But what is the implication? One possible implication is that we should stop trying to control crime by controlling guns. The other possible implication is that we need to get much more serious than we have been thus far about controlling guns, with much stricter, nationally-standardized gun-control policies. There is little or nothing in the scientific literature that would allow one to choose between these possibilities; either could well be correct.

GUNS, CRIMES, AND NUMBERS

What is the annual firearms toll in this country? Our review of the data sources revealed that some components of the toll, especially the annual fatality count, are well known, whereas other components are not. In recent years, the total number of homicides occurring in the United States has been right around 20,000. Of these, approximately 60 percent are committed with firearms. There are somewhat fewer than 30,000 suicides committed in an average recent year, of which about half involve a firearm. Deaths from firearms accidents have represented about 2 percent of the total accidental deaths in the nation for as long as data have been collected, and add about 2,000 deaths per year to the toll. Taken together, then, there are about 30,000 deaths from firearms in an average year; this amounts to some 1–2 percent of all deaths from any cause.

Both camps in the gun control war like to spew out exaggerated rhetoric. In the case of gun deaths, the anti-control forces shout that the total deaths due to firearms in a year are less than the deaths due to automobile accidents (about 50,000)—"but nobody wants to ban cars!" To counter, the pro-control people express the gun toll as a number of deaths per unit of time. The resulting figure is dramatic: on average, someone in the United States dies from a firearm every seventeen or eighteen minutes.

Death is not the whole story, of course. One must also include non-fatal but injurious firearms accidents, crimes other than homicide or suicide committed with guns, unsuccessful suicide attempts involving firearms, and so on. None of these things is known with much precision, and the lack of firm data is an invitation to exuberant formulations on both sides. Still, reasonable compromise values for the various components suggest a total incident count of fewer than a million per year—that is, incidents in which a firearm of some sort was involved in some way in some kind of violent or criminal incident (intentional or accidental, fatal or not). Pro-gun people have dismissed this estimate as much too high, and anti-gun people have dismissed it as much too low, so I figure it can't be too far off.

When we shift to the guns side of the "guns and crime" equation, the numbers jump by a few orders of magnitude, although here, too, some caution is needed. In the course of the twentieth century, so far as can be told, some 250 million total firearms (excluding military weapons) have been manufactured in or imported into the United States. Published guesses about the number of guns in private hands in this country run upwards to a billion—an absurd and inconceivably large estimate. Most of the published estimates are produced by advocates and thus are not to be trusted, most of all since both sides have vested interests in publishing the largest possible numbers: the pro-gun people, to show the vast number of people whose rights would be infringed by stricter gun controls; the anti-gun people, to show the obvious urgency of the situation.

It is not known for certain how many of the 250 million guns of the twentieth century remain in private hands; 150 million is a sensible guess. Survey evidence dating from at least 1959 routinely shows that about 50 percent of all American households possess at least one firearm, with the average number owned (among those owning at least one) being just over three. Whatever the exact number, it is obvious that there are lots and lots of guns out there—many tens of millions at the very least. . . .

The numbers do speak clearly to at least one point: if we are going to try to "control" guns as a means of controlling crime, then we are going to have to deal with the guns already in private hands; controls over new purchases alone will not suffice. Taking the highest plausible value for the number of gun incidents—1 million per year—and the lowest plausible value for the number of guns presently owned—say, 100 million—we see rather quickly that the guns now owned exceed the annual incident count by a factor of at least a hundred; in other words, the existing stock is adequate to supply all conceivable nefarious purposes for at least the next century.

These figures can be considered in another way. Suppose we did embark on a program of firearms confiscation, with the ultimate aim of achieving a "no guns" condition. We would have to confiscate at least a hundred guns to get just one gun that, in any typical year, would be involved in any kind of gun incident; several hundred to get just one that would otherwise be involved in a chargeable gun crime; and several thousand to get just one that would otherwise be used to bring about someone's death. Whatever else one might want to say about such a policy, it is not very efficient.

DEMAND CREATES ITS OWN SUPPLY

One of the favorite aphorisms of the pro-gun forces is that "if guns are outlawed, only outlaws will have guns." Sophisticated liberals laugh at this point, but they shouldn't. No matter what laws we enact, they will be obeyed only by the law-abiding—this follows by definition. If we were to outlaw, say, the ownership of handguns, millions of law-abiding handgun owners would no doubt turn theirs in. But why should we expect the average armed robber or street thug to do likewise? Why should we expect felons to comply with a gun law when they readily violate laws against robbery, assault, and murder?

For the average criminal, a firearm is an income-producing tool with a consequent value that is several times its initial cost. According to data published by Phillip Cook of Duke University, the average "take" in a robbery committed with a firearm is more than $150 (in 1976 dollars) and is three times the take for a robbery committed with any other weapon; the major reason for the difference is that criminals with guns rob more lucrative targets. Right now, one can acquire a handgun in any major American city in a matter of a few hours for roughly $100. Even if the street price of handguns tripled, a robber armed with a handgun could (on the average) recoup his entire capital outlay in the first two or three transactions.

As long as there are *any* handguns around (and even "ban handgun" advocates make an exception for police or military handguns), they will obviously be available to anyone *at some price*. Given Cook's data, the average street thug would come out well ahead even if he spent several hundred—perhaps even a few thousand—on a suitable weapon. At those prices, demand will always create its own supply: just as there will always be cocaine available to anyone willing to pay $200 a gram for it, so too will handguns always be available to anyone willing to pay a thousand dollars to obtain one.

The more militant "ban handgun" advocates urge what is easily recognized as the handgun equivalent of Prohibition. Why would we expect the outcome of "handgun prohibition" to differ from its 1920s predecessor? A black market in guns, run by organized crime, would almost certainly spring up to service the demand. It is, after all, no more difficult to manufacture a serviceable firearm in one's basement than to brew up a batch of home-made gin. Afghani tribesmen, using wood fires and metal-working equipment much inferior to what can be ordered from a Sears catalogue, hand-manufacture rifles that fire the Russian AK-47 cartridge. Do we ascribe less ability to the Mafia or the average do-it-yourselfer?

A recent poll of the U.S. adult population asked people to agree or disagree with this proposition: "Gun control laws affect only law-abiding citizens; criminals will always be able to find guns." Seventy-eight percent agreed. There is no reasonable doubt that the majority, in this case, is right.

CRIMES OF PASSION

Sophisticated advocates on both sides by now grant most of the preceding points. No one still expects "stricter gun control" to solve the problem of hard-core criminal violence, or even make a dent in it. Much of the argument has thus shifted toward violence perpetrated not for economic gain, or for any other good reason, but rather in the "heat of the moment"—the so-called "crimes of passion" that turn injurious or lethal not so much because anyone intended them to, but because, in a moment of rage, a firearm was at hand. Certainly, we could expect incidents of this sort to decline if we could somehow reduce the availability of firearms for the purpose. Or could we?

Crimes of passion certainly occur, but how often? Are "heat of the moment" homicides common or rare? The fact is, nobody knows. The assumption that they are very common, characteristic of the pro-control world view, is derived from the well-known fact that most homicides involve persons known to one another before the event—typically family members, friends, or other acquaintances. But ordinarily, the only people one would ever have any good reason to kill would be people known intimately to oneself. Contrary to the common assumption, prior acquaintance definitely does *not* rule out willful, murderous intent.

The "crime of passion" most often discussed is that of family members killing one another. One pertinent study, conducted in Kansas City, looked into every family homicide that occurred in a single year. In 85 percent of the cases examined, the police had previously (within the prior five years) been called to the family residence to break up a domestic quarrel; in half the cases, the police had been there five or more times. It would therefore be misleading to see these homicides as isolated and unfortunate outbursts occurring among normally placid and loving individuals. They are, rather, the culminating episodes of an extended history of violence and abuse among the parties.

Analysis of the family homicide data reveals an interesting pattern. When women kill men, they often use a gun. When men kill women, they usually do it in some more degrading or brutalizing way—such as strangulation or knifing. The reason for the difference seems obvious: although the world is full of potentially lethal objects, almost all of them are better suited to male than to female use. The gun is the single exception: all else held constant, it is equally deadly in anyone's hands. Firearms equalize the means of physical terror between men and women. In denying the wife of an abusive man the right to have a firearm, we may only be guaranteeing her husband the right to beat her at his pleasure. One argument against "stricter gun control" is thus that a woman should have as much right to kill her husband as a man has to kill his wife.

Some will gasp at this statement; no one, after all, has a "right" to kill anyone. But this, of course, is false: every jurisdiction in the United States recognizes justifiable homicides in at least some extenuating circumstances, and increasingly a persistent and long-standing pattern of physical abuse is acknowledged to be one of them. True, in the best of all possible worlds, we would simply do away with whatever gives rise to murderous rage. This is not, regrettably, the world in which we live. . . .

THE SATURDAY NIGHT SPECIAL

The notorious Saturday Night Special has received a great deal of attention. The term is used loosely: it can refer to a gun of low price, inferior quality, small caliber, short barrel length, or some combination of these. The attention is typically justified on two grounds: first, these guns have no legitimate sport or recreational use, and secondly, they are the firearms preferred by criminals. Thus, the argument goes, we could just ban them altogether; in doing so, we would directly reduce the number of guns available to criminals without restricting anyone's legitimate ownership rights.

The idea that the Saturday Night Special is the criminal's gun of choice turns out to be wrong. Our felon survey showed, overwhelmingly, that serious criminals both prefer to carry and actu-

ally do carry relatively large, big-bore, well-made handguns. Indeed, not more than about one in seven of these criminals' handguns would qualify as small and cheap. Most of the felons wanted to be and actually were at least as well armed as their most likely adversaries, the police. There may well be good reason to ban Saturday Night Specials, but the criminal interest in such weapons is not one of them. Most serious felons look on the Saturday Night Special with considerable contempt.

It is too early to tell how these data will be interpreted among "Ban Saturday Night Special" advocates. The most recent wrinkle I have encountered is that they should be banned not because they are preferred or used by criminals, but because, being cheap, they tend to be owned by unknowledgeable, inexperienced, or irresponsible people. One may assume that cheap handguns, like cheap commodities of all sorts, tend to be owned by poor people. The further implication—that poor gun owners are less knowledgeable, experienced, or responsible than more affluent owners—has, however, never been researched; it is also the sort of "elitist" argument that ordinarily arouses liberal indignation.

What about the other side of the argument—that these guns have no legitimate use? It is amazing how easily people who know little about guns render such judgments. When I commenced my own research, it occurred to me that I ought to find out what gun owners themselves had to say on some of these matters. So I picked up the latest issues of about a half-dozen gun magazines. It is remarkable how informative this simple exercise turned out to be.

One magazine that surfaced is called *Handgunning*, which is specifically for devotees of handgun sports. Every issue of the magazine is full of articles on the sporting and recreational uses of handguns of all kinds. I learned, for example, that people actually hunt game with handguns, which never would have occurred to me. In reading a few articles, the reason quickly became obvious: it is more sporting than hunting with shoulder weapons, and it requires much more skill, which makes a successful handgun hunt a much more satisfying accomplishment.

In my journey through this alien turf, I came upon what are called "trail guns" or "pack guns." These are handguns carried outdoors, in the woods or the wilds, for no particular reason except to have a gun available "just in case" one encounters unfriendly fauna, or gets lost and needs small game for food, or is injured and needs to signal for help. The more I read about trail guns, the more it seemed that people who spend a lot of time alone in the wilds, in isolated and out-of-the-way places, are probably being pretty sensible in carrying these weapons.

One discussion went on in some detail about the characteristics to look for in a trail gun. It ought to be small and light, of course, for the same reason that serious backpackers carry nylon rather than canvas tents. "Small and light" implies small caliber (a .22 or .25), a short barrel, and a stainless-steel frame (to afford greater protection from the elements). The article mentioned that some of the finest weapons of this sort were being manufactured in Europe, and at very reasonable prices. And suddenly it dawned on me: the small, low-caliber, short-barreled, imported, not-too-expensive guns the article was describing were what are otherwise known as Saturday Night Specials. And thus I came to learn that we cannot say that Saturday Night Specials have "no legitimate sport or recreational use."

It would be sophistic to claim that most Saturday Night Specials are purchased for use as trail guns; my point is only that some are. Most small, cheap handguns are probably purchased by persons of modest means to protect themselves against crime. It is arguable whether protection against crime is a "legitimate" or "illegitimate" use; the issues involved are too complex to treat fairly in this article. It is worth stressing, however, that poor, black, central-city residents are by far the most likely potential victims of crime; if self-protection justifies owning a gun, then a ban on small, cheap handguns would effectively deny the means of self-protection to those most evidently in need of it.

There is another argument against banning small, cheap handguns: a ban on Saturday Night Specials would leave heavy-duty handguns available as substitute weapons. It is convenient to suppose that in the absence of small, cheap handguns, most people would just give up and not use guns for whatever they had in mind. But certainly some of them, and perhaps many of them, would move up to bigger and better handguns instead. We would do well to remember that the most commonly owned handgun in America today is a .38 caliber double-action revolver, the so-called Police Special that functions as the service revolver for about 90 percent of American police. If we somehow got rid of all the junk handguns, how many thugs, assailants, and assassins would choose to use this gun, or other guns like it, instead? And what consequences might we then anticipate?

The handgun used by John Hinckley in his attack on President Reagan was a .22 caliber revolver, a Saturday Night Special. Some have supported banning the Saturday Night Special so as to thwart psychopaths in search of weapons. But would a psychopath intent on assassinating a President simply give up in the absence of a cheap handgun? Or would he, in that event, naturally pick up some other gun instead? Suppose he did pick up the most commonly owned handgun available in the United States, the .38 Special. Suppose further that he got off the same six rounds and inflicted the same wounds that he inflicted with the .22. A .38 slug entering Jim Brady's head where the .22 entered would, at the range in question, probably have killed him instantly. The Washington policeman would not have had a severed artery but would have been missing the larger part of his neck. The round deflected from its path to President Reagan's heart might have reached its target. One can readily imagine at least three deaths, including the President's, had Hinkley fired a more powerful weapon.

POSTSCRIPT

Should a National Gun Control Policy Be Established?

The United States has about 20,000 gun control laws, the vast majority of which are state or local ordinances. There is considerable variation, therefore, from place to place. There have been several federal statutes enacted to control firearms. The Federal Firearms Act of 1934 regulated possession of submachine guns, silencers, and several other weapons. In 1938, the National Firearms Act was passed, requiring the licensing of firearms manufacturers and dealers. As a result, all new weapons sold in the United States since 1938 have been registered and can be traced. The most important federal action was taken with the passage of the Gun Control Act of 1968. The Act prohibited the interstate retailing of all firearms. Its purpose was to prevent individuals like Lee Harvey Oswald from ordering guns by mail under phony names.

There has been renewed attention to the issue of gun control lately, partly as a result of rising drug-related violence and partly because of Robert Purdy's shooting spree at an elementary school in Stockton, California on January 17, 1989. Five children were killed and thirty injured. Purdy had a semiautomatic assault rifle, with which he sprayed the schoolyard, and a handgun, with which he killed himself. Following this incident, California banned the sale, manufacture, or unregistered possession of a wide variety of semiautomatic weapons. On the federal level, President Bush banned the importation of assault-style weapons. No restrictions were placed on the domestic manufacture of such weapons, which account for about three-quarters of those sold.

Public opinion polls suggest that a majority of the public wants more regulation. Ninety-one percent of adults surveyed in June, 1981, by the Gallup organization said they favored a law requiring a twenty-one-day waiting period before a gun could be purchased, during which time a check would be made to see if the prospective owner had a criminal record. Legislation to require a seven-day waiting period is currently pending before Congress. Many states do not require such background checks. While there is a prohibition against selling guns to minors, convicted felons, fugitives, drug addicts, and several other classes of persons, no prior check is required, and there is no way for dealers to know whether or not customers are legally qualified to own guns. In general, the Gallup poll found sixty-five percent favored stronger regulations. Yet, by a three to two ratio, those polled rejected an outright ban on the possession of handguns.

The meaning and history of the Second Amendment is discussed in Levinson, "The Embarrassing Second Amendment," 99 *Yale Law Journal* 637

(1989); Brown, "Guns, Cowboys, Philadelphia Mayors, and Civic Republicanism: On Sanford Levinson's 'The Embarrassing Second Amendment,' " 99 *Yale Law Journal* 661 (1989); Hardy, "Armed Citizens, Citizen Armies: Toward A Jurisprudence of the Second Amendment, 9 *Harvard Journal of Law & Public Policy* 559 (1986); and Stephen Halbrook, *That Every Man Be Armed* (University of New Mexico Press, 1984). Recent discussions of handgun regulation are contained in Franklin Zimring and Gordon Hawkins, *The Citizen's Guide to Gun Control* (Macmillan, 1987); James Wright and Peter Rossi, *Armed and Considered Dangerous* (Aldine De Gruyter, 1986); Don Kates, ed., *Firearms and Violence* (Pacific Institute for Public Policy Research, 1984); and Symposium, "Gun Control," *Law and Contemporary Problems,* v. 46 (1986).

ISSUE 16

DNA Profiling: Should It Be Used to Convict Criminals?

YES: James E. Starrs, from "The Dawning of DNA in the Legal World: A Red Sky in the Morning?" Statement before Subcommittee on the Constitution of the House Judiciary Committee, U.S. House of Representatives (March 15, 1989)

NO: Janet C. Hoeffel, from "The Dark Side of DNA Profiling: Unreliable Evidence Meets the Criminal Defendant," *Stanford Law Review* (vol. 24, 1990)

ISSUE SUMMARY

YES: Professor James Starrs claims that DNA tests are effective and reliable means for detecting perpetrators of violent crimes and should be available at trial.

NO: Attorney Janet Hoeffel denies that DNA tests are reliable and argues that admission at trial should be denied until standards are adopted and tests are conducted that show whether the test indeed is reliable.

In 1964 in Los Angeles a woman named Juanita Brooks was knocked to the ground and robbed while walking home from the supermarket. She didn't see her assailant but later testified that she saw a young woman with blond hair running from the scene. A man across the street, who looked up when he heard the victim's cries, saw a woman running and getting into a yellow automobile driven by a black man with a beard.

The police arrested two people who fit the description given by the witnesses. At the trial, the prosecutor was concerned about the circumstantial nature of his case and called a mathematician as an expert witness. The mathematician testified that the odds of any other couple in Los Angeles possessing all of the described characteristics were one in twelve million. The jury, apparently very impressed with this, convicted the defendants.

On appeal, the California Supreme Court reversed the conviction, finding both that the mathematical calculations were faulty and without foundation, and that the single statistic presented to the jury, without explanation of the calculations that were made, interfered with the defendants' constitutional right to a jury trial (*People v. Collins,* 438 P. 2d 33, 1968).

In the last three years, court testimony involving statistical probabilities has been increasing rapidly. The focus of this testimony has been on the analysis of evidence found at the scene of a crime, most often a violent crime. Laboratories analyze a sample of hair, skin, or some bodily fluid and compare the DNA[1] found in the sample with a DNA sample obtained from a person who has been arrested for a crime. As a result of such analyses, scientists have been testifying at trials that the odds of a false match occurring are anywhere from 1 in 500,000 to 1 in 5,000,000. Such testimony has been instrumental in many convictions by juries. In some cases, the lack of a match has led to the dropping of charges against an accused person.

We are living in an age of impressive technological achievements. Traditionally, however, the law has been reluctant to adapt very quickly to new technologies. Justice Oliver Wendell Holmes, for example, once wrote that "it cannot be helped, it is as it should be, that the law is behind the times." What Holmes meant was that one purpose of the law is to provide the public with a sense of order, predictability, and stability. Continually reacting to new technologies might undermine this function of the law.

In deciding whether a new technique is reliable enough to be accepted as evidence, courts use one of two standards. The traditional approach, first announced in *Frye v. United States,* 293 F. 1013 (D.C. Cir. 1923), requires that novel scientific evidence "have gained general acceptance in the particular field in which it belongs." In recent years, more courts have employed a different standard, which only requires the new technique to be relevant. The degree of reliability of the new method would then be considered by a jury in deciding what weight to give to the evidence. It is more likely that a judge would admit novel evidence using this standard than the *Frye* standard.

One question for you to consider as you read the following articles is whether DNA tests provide "proof" or merely probability that an event has occurred. One of the articles, by Professor Starrs, assumes that DNA tests are a sure thing, as reliable as fingerprints. Ms. Hoeffel, on the other hand, suggests that DNA tests may be more like a magician's trick, in which we are impressed with the outcome but do not see the means by which the trick was produced.

NOTES

1. DNA (deoxyribonucleic acid) is found in all human tissue. The basis of the tests described here is that the DNA sample can be arranged into a pattern, something like a supermarket bar code, and then compared with the pattern of other DNA samples.

YES

James E. Starrs

THE DAWNING OF DNA IN THE LEGAL WORLD: A RED SKY IN THE MORNING?

In truth, it is a second coming. At least in "forensics," that is. First there was fingerprinting to identify a suspect, without a shadow of a doubt, as having been present at a crime scene. And now the day of DNA (deoxyribonucleic acid) matching as an aid to law enforcement has dawned—in a heady and convincing fashion.

Crime scenes are being scoured for biological samples like hair, blood and semen on the fervent anticipation that the genetic building block (DNA) within them will provide a direct and conclusive genetic link to a particular suspect and to none other. Burglars, rapists and murderers are being caught and convicted in ever-increasing numbers in the all-enveloping gyre of DNA matching. Nationwide the public's pulse has been quickened by media-stimulated visions of the wondrous deeds that DNA matching has and will achieve for criminal justice. Lawyers and judges, emulating a mesmerized public, are paying hurried homage at the throne of this new prince in the realm of scientific technology. By all reports some twenty or so criminal cases have been concluded at the trial level in some seven states where DNA matching has been welcomed, with nary a word of judicial dissent anywhere.

Defense lawyers are willing to concede the legal admissibility of a DNA match that all but irrefutably fingers their clients as guilty, even of a hanging offense. Witness the defense tactics in the recently concluded capital murder trial of Timothy Spencer in Arlington, Virginia where, at a pre-trial hearing, the defense seemed to be off molly-gawking somewhere when the validity of DNA matching was under scrutiny.

Other defense attorneys, unable to ferret out an expert to oppose DNA matching, have perfunctorily toyed on cross examination with the prosecution's DNA experts in a feeble effort to demonstrate the flaws of DNA matching. The rape trial of Tommie Lee Andrews in Orlando, Florida was of that dispiriting order.

From U.S. House. Committee on the Judiciary. Subcommittee on the Constitution. *DNA Identification*. Hearing, March 15, 1989. Washington, D.C.: Government Printing Office, 1989.

Still other defense attorneys have, Henny-Penny-like, viewed DNA matching as bringing the sky to falling. In Las Vegas, it is reported that a suspect pleaded guilty to the rape of a policeman's mother after consultation with his attorney. The client was apparently goaded to throw in the adversarial towel upon learning that a court order would be sought to obtain a sample of his blood for DNA matching. No test had yet been performed; no DNA identification had yet been made and no blood had even been drawn but the accused, in terror of the dread portent of a DNA match, capitulated.

Whereas suspects and their attorneys have lacked conviction in the face of DNA matching, prosecutors have embraced it with "passionate intensity." In the capital murder trial of Timothy Spencer, the prosecution had the laboratory evidence of bodily secretions putting the accused within a population of only 13% of Virginians who could have been the contributor of the crime scene evidence. The state also had hair from the crime scene that matched that of Spencer in all microscopic characteristics. More, glass in a jacket, admittedly belonging to Spencer, was connected through its refractive index to the broken glass at the point of entry to the murder victim's home.

Add to this telling circumstantial evidence the incriminating statements Spencer made, without being coerced or cogged by the police, and his three prior burglary convictions, to which he himself testified, and the jury's decision to convict was well-nigh preordained. In light of this compelling evidence, the DNA matching that further established Spencer's presence at the murder scene was almost pleonastic, just a soupcon to fix with certainty the jury's decision to convict. . . .

DNA matching has not been borne into the legal world on an indifferent, slouching wind. On the contrary, its reception has been heralded, programmed and even pre-determined in the best corporate tradition. While the F.B.I. Laboratory at Quantico, Virginia has committed much of its massive resources to a crash research effort to assay the values of DNA matching for forensic purposes, three corporations have been quietly but effectively bridging the gap between the laboratory and the courtroom.

These three corporate entities, Lifecodes of Valhalla, New York, Cellmark of Germantown, Maryland and Cetus of San Francisco, all bear names redolent of an introductory course in biology, giving them a recognizable market presence. Each performs somewhat different functions and each is to a certain extent in competition with the other, particularly in the case of Lifecodes and Cellmark.

Cellmark, an offshoot of the British corporate giant, ICI Industries, lays claim to the multi-locus probe originated by Dr. Alec Jeffreys of the University of Leicester, England. Through the use of this probe, it is possible, according to the published reports of its inventor, to discern up to fifteen bands or individual markers in the DNA of a particular person or in that from a crime scene sample. These bands then can be compared to determine whether the crime scene sample originated from the same person from whom the known sample was obtained. The more the number of matching bands, the greater the statistical likelihood that the two DNA samples under study came from the same source.

It is this ability to pinpoint, with near perfect mathematical certainty, a particular sample to a particular person that led Dr. Jeffreys to affix the label DNA "fingerprint" to his multi-locus probe. This same certainty of individualization is what has caused defense attorneys to run scared when confronted with DNA evidence as well as that which has given prosecutors just cause to gloat with uninhibited glee at the distress of the defense.

Lifecodes, which prefers to be known as situated in Valhalla rather than Westchester County, New York, employs a single-locus probe in its DNA methodology. This probe sets its sights on a particular chromosome and a very specific site or locus on that chromosome. The band that is revealed when the probe binds to the assigned locus in a biological sample whose source is known can be compared to a crime scene sample whose source is unknown. A match between them puts the two samples within a pre-determined percentage of the population who have the identical banding pattern. All of this is familiar turf to biologists since the same Mendelian principles and the same establishment of population frequencies occurs in the every day genetic markers known as ABO blood grouping.

To narrow the percentages to a precious few so as to better fix a suspect either as guilty or not, it is imperative that the Lifecodes testing not cease with one probe. The more probes, the more discriminating the result and the more the probability that the right person is in custody for the crime. Heavily freighting the Lifecodes approach is a reliance on population frequencies, independently inherited genetic markers and the laws of Mendelian inheritance. If any one of these factors is misaligned or out of sync, then the accuracy of premising guilt or innocence on the single locus matching technique is sorely out of whack.

To an extent, Cetus complements the DNA work in legal matters performed by Lifecodes and Cellmark. In a manner of speaking, it picks up where they leave off. The aftermath of the rape trial and acquittal of Marine Corporal Lindsey Scott in Quantico, Virginia illustrates what Cetus has to offer the criminal justice system through its acting as a development hub for applications in other spoke-type laboratories.

Corporal Scott had put forward an alibi in support of his not guilty plea. The victim had contradicted Scott's assertion of absence from the crime scene. The DNA from the biological specimens from the victim and the crime scene could, in theory at least, tell which was tale and which was truth. But the comparison of the DNA from Scott's blood was thwarted by the inadequacy of the crime scene samples to meet the needs of sample size and lack of degradation required to conduct either a single or multi-locus probing of it at Cellmark.

Thus the bell sounded for the Cetus technology to perform its scientific wizardry through the good offices of Forensic Science Associates in Emeryville, California. The DNA fragments needed to be amplified (duplicated) by a process spearheaded by Cetus known as polymerase chain reaction (PCR). Single or even multi-locus probing could then follow on the heels of this amplification. Ruefully, the reverberations from California were a knell tolling the inability of PCR to produce anything more than the same inconclusive results as Cellmark had previously reported, according to a Washington Post news story.

While the scientific testing in the Scott case was demonstrably unrewarding for legal purposes, still the situation teaches a lesson well learned. DNA matching is no carminative preparation that will enable the criminal justice system in all cases to isolate the guilty from the innocent based upon biological samples obtained from a crime scene. It is rank hyperbole to intimate or state otherwise. So much depends upon the samples retrieved for testing and the effect of the ambient circumstances upon them.

Physical evidence from a crime scene, certainly of a biological nature, lacks the pristine qualities of controlled laboratory specimens. Suffice it to say, this is an inherent flaw, at present, in DNA matching for law enforcement purposes. Moreover, a DNA technology that is founded on the antiseptic testing of controlled laboratory samples cannot validly assert its utility in the market place of crime scene contaminated samples.

The reverse side of this coin gives promise of a more well-charted future for DNA matching in the legal world. The use of DNA matching in paternity contests should be pre-eminently reliable and assuredly dispositive, certainly if the Cellmark multi-locus probes are the method of choice. But, unfortunately, such an exhilarating conclusion depends on whether both parents are available for testing and whether there are any extraneous interferences. . . .

Women especially have just cause to acclaim the advent of DNA matching. For too many years the life of the lore in rape complaints has been that such grievances are easy to make and difficult to refute. Women who charge rape are thus put on the legal rack that at every turning accuses them of fabrication. Rape shield laws and changes in evidentiary rules requiring corroboration have acted as an effective anodyne for the discriminatory impact of such hidebound, gratuitous legal traditions. DNA matching can do even more to guarantee that the truth will be told in rape prosecutions. But, it is to be remembered, DNA matching in its most accredited form is non-partisan, letting the conclusions fall where they impartially may. It is, therefore, equally possible that a DNA matching may cement a victim's identification of a suspect as her assailant as it is that it will contravene her most positive declarations of a particular suspect's guilt. The pending Chavez prosecution in California is a case in troubled point.

Rigoberto Chavez was accused of a most brutal kidnapping and rape of a San Mateo County woman in 1987. At a preliminary hearing on the charges the victim without so much as a flicker of doubt identified Chavez as the culprit. But DNA matching of three semen samples recovered from the crime scene contradicted the victim's eye-witness identification.

The stage was then set, in the Chavez case, as it is already elsewhere, for a pitting of the direct evidence of an eyewitness against the circumstantial evidence of a scientific evaluation. Such a winner-take-all scuffle may be a first for DNA matching, but it is not at all a new phenomenon for science to be at odds with eyewitness assertions. As it happens, the classic illustration of such a clash of testimonial virtues occurred in the trials and tribulations of Adolph Beck, the case that was the corner-stone for the acceptance of fingerprinting in England almost a century ago. And so we have now come full circle. The lessons once learned in fingerprinting should not have to be relearned in the second coming of DNA matching, but apparently such is not to be the case.

Adolph Beck was twice confounded, once in 1896 by his conviction and sentence to seven years at hard labor for bilking numerous maiden ladies of their jewelry and again in 1904 by his conviction for a similar series of crimes. In both trials Beck's alleged victims trooped into court in droves and unquestioningly identified him as their swindler. Even two police officers queued up in further support of the victims' identifications. Beck protested his innocence, but to no avail.

Beck spent five years in prison for his 1896 convictions and he was about to be shunted off to another lengthy prison stint for his 1904 convictions when the terrible truth became known. Beck had been mistaken for William Thomas, alias John Smith, who was a Beck look-alike. Both men were in their middle fifties, of portly carriage, grey-haired, mustachioed and monocled. These resemblances apparently provided the stimulus for the victims to state their most convincing and conclusive misidentifications of Beck, misidentifications they all instantly recanted when William Thomas was paraded before them.

When fingerprinting, then a nascent law enforcement tool, was conducted on the persons and objects which had been purloined in the Thomas' "Murphy game" trickery, Beck was fully exonerated. There followed such a public outrage as England had hardly ever encountered in past instances of legal injustices. Science, stolid police work and old friend luck had put the quietus to claims of eyewitness certainty, but not until Beck had suffered much.

Like fingerprinting, its forensic progenitor, DNA matching is not error free. But if properly validated protocols are steadfastly followed and well trained personnel are at the helm, the chances of error are negligible. The results of DNA matching, therefore, should be given greater credence in the legal arena than the markedly error-prone testimony of eyewitnesses. The law needs no Adolph Beck redux to add to its embarrassments.

Regardless of the fragility of eyewitness identifications, in rape cases and others, DNA matching can give law enforcement, at the investigative level, a decided uplift in rape cases. Serial rapists, such as was shown at the penalty phase of the Timothy Spencer trial, can be demonstrated to be at their malevolent work through DNA matching of biological samples from the individual and disparate rape victims. Law enforcement needs to know whether one rapist is on the prowl or more than one. For sentencing purposes too, the issue is singularly relevant.

Traditional forms of blood grouping tests are also inadequate to the tasks of gang rape investigations. The mixed bodily fluids can be separated through their DNA content and identified to one rapist or to another, giving support to the victim's recollections or providing the necessary evidence where the victim was too traumatized to have a reliable memory of the events.

In many respects DNA matching in the legal order is tracking the path of its forebears among other scientific developments. What fingerprinting was to the justice system at the turn of the century, DNA matching is to the legal world in the 1980s.

Just as it is the law's pride to exhibit a briny irreverence in the face of scientific authority, so it is also the law's fame to embrace a scientific discovery of stature and proven merit.

Things did not fall apart when fingerprinting arrived on the legal scene a century ago. Nor will the center not hold with DNA matching having claimed its share of legal attention. Clearly there are scientific nodes yet to unwind in DNA technology and defense attorneys must be revivified in their adversarial tasks.

However, adversarial ardor, I have no doubt, can only have an annealing effect on the forensic legitimacy of DNA matching so as to dispel any portents of chaos in this second coming. It is only to criminals and others of that ilk that the dawning of DNA in the legal world should come as a warning.

NO

Janet C. Hoeffel

THE DARK SIDE OF DNA PROFILING: UNRELIABLE SCIENTIFIC EVIDENCE MEETS THE CRIMINAL DEFENDANT

Big Brother is knocking on our door only six years late. "It" is not quite as George Orwell envisioned, but do not let it fool you just because it comes masked in microscopic form and speaks the impenetrable language of the allegedly infallible scientist. DNA profiling technology[1] is making its entrance with the help of "Newspeak,"[2] which touts the technique as "the greatest boon to forensic medicine and law since fingerprinting"[3] and claims that "disputing the technology is like disputing the law of gravity."[4]

DNA profiling technology has limitless Orwellian possibilities, but the legal community is presently focused on the technology's ability to identify criminal suspects. Although it usually takes many years for the engines of justice to churn out a personal injury suit or a criminal appeal, in less than two years the combined efforts of commercial laboratories and prosecutors have steamrolled the so-called "DNA fingerprinting" technique through the courts.[5] The technique has been easy to sell. The current national obsession with crime-fighting and the apparent decrease in concern for individualized justice[6] create a receptive environment for a cutting-edge technology, dazzling in its promise of identifying criminals with "virtual" or "99 percent certainty." Courts lost all sense of balance and restraint in the face of this novel scientific evidence, embracing it with little scrutiny of its actual reliability and little concern for its impact on the rights of individuals.

. . . The courts and the public must be made aware of the full impact of the damage done and the precedent set as they allow prosecutors, commercial laboratories, and the media to push the currently unreliable and unproven DNA profiling evidence into court.

In the midst of all the cheers and exaggerations, this note presents the darker side of employing DNA profiling to identify criminals. . . .

Against the tide of unquestioning zeal for technological advances and warlike determination to sweep crime from the streets, this note urges restraint

From Janet C. Hoeffel, "The Dark Side of DNA Profiling: Unreliable Scientific Evidence Meets the Criminal Defendant," *Stanford Law Review,* vol. 42 (1990), pp. 465–538. Copyright © 1990 by the Board of Trustees of the Leland Stanford Junior University. Reprinted by permission of *Stanford Law Review* and Fred B. Rothman & Co. Some notes omitted.

on the acceptance of unproven novel scientific techniques that turn courtrooms into laboratories and defendants into guinea pigs.

I. OUT OF THE RESEARCH LAB AND INTO THE FORENSIC LAB: SCIENTIFIC CONCERNS . . .

C. Lack of Scientific Consensus as to Practice: The Castro Case

Despite the intentions of some members of the legal community to withhold the introduction of the novel forensic technique until it is proven reliable enough to withstand judicial scrutiny, the promise of DNA identification evidence in criminal cases has proven too tempting for law enforcement officials to resist. The technique has gained popularity at an exponential rate from its introduction in the United States in 1987 until now. It was initially hailed as "foolproof" and 99 percent positive; such exaggerations were based on the testimony of interested parties such as the scientists from those companies that sell their results at a profit and the prosecutors who use the results to gain convictions. Caught off-guard by the storm, and perhaps assuming that there was no way around the damning evidence, defense attorneys were unable to combat the evidence effectively or find scientists to testify against it.

The first case to make inroads into the infallibility mystique of DNA profiling was *People v. Castro*, a double murder case in the Bronx. Twenty-year-old Vilma Ponce and her two-year-old daughter were stabbed to death in their apartment on February 5, 1987. There were few leads until police arrested the building's superintendent, Joseph Castro, and found some dried blood in the grooves of his watch, which he said was his own. Prosecutors sent that specimen, samples of the victims' blood, and a sample of Castro's blood to Lifecodes for DNA typing. Lifecodes declared a match between the DNA in the blood on the watch and the DNA in Vilma Ponce's blood. If this case had followed the normal course of events in prior cases involving DNA evidence, Castro would have pleaded guilty right then, doubting his ability to fight the evidence in court.

This case did not, however, follow the usual course of events. Defense attorneys Barry Scheck and Peter Neufeld sought and located experts who agreed to testify against the admission of the DNA typing evidence. For twelve weeks, New York Supreme Court Acting Justice Gerald Sheindlin listened to experts from both sides. The defense experts were able to uncover such serious blunders committed by Lifecodes in performing the test that the prosecution's main expert witnesses recanted their position. In an unprecedented move, two expert witnesses for the defense and two for the prosecution, after huddling outside of court, issued a statement declaring, "The DNA data in this case are not scientifically reliable enough to support the assertion that the samples . . . do or do not match. If these data were submitted to a peer-reviewed journal in support of a conclusion, they would not be accepted. Further experimentation would be required." Ultimately, Justice Sheindlin ruled the evidence of the match inadmissible.

This important case appears to have increased the dialogue among those members of the scientific community engaged in related diagnostic research and interested in a critical review of the technique as applied to forensics. Scientists in diagnostic research do not declare matches involving samples of unknown origin, and thus there are currently no generally accepted standards in the scientific community for such matching. Scientists in diagnostic research are not testing contaminated samples. . . . Perhaps the most important difference is that, in the forensic process, an individual's future is linked directly to the accuracy of the result.

Recent literature reveals critical flaws in the application of the diagnostic technique to forensics which render it unreliable from a scientific standpoint. The main criticism is not that it will never be reliable, but that the lack of uniform standards and quality controls allows the ambiguities and problems in the technique to go unnoticed, thus resulting in the scientifically unreliable declaration of a match.

Specifically, before results of the DNA typing technique can be accepted as scientifically reliable in forensics, the following controls and standards must be developed: 1) controls to ensure the accurate interpretation of results; 2) standards for declaring matches; 3) standards for the choice and number of polymorphic sites studied; 4) standards for determining the probability of a coincidental match and for determining the relevant population studies; 5) standards for record keeping; and 6) standards for proficiency testing and licensing. This note will address each of these needs in turn.

1. Lack of controls to ensure accurate interpretation of results.

In the forensic laboratory, there are three problem areas which can lead to inaccurate results and thus errors in declaring matches between samples of DNA. One concerns the problems inherent in any scientific laboratory engaged in this type of research—namely, the problems of contamination and laboratory "slop." Second, specific to the forensic lab are the likely problems of contamination and degradation in the forensic sample. Finally, an inescapable problem for forensic DNA profiling specifically is the complexity of the results and potential examiner bias in interpreting those results. All three areas can cause the examiner to declare a false match and can remain undetected unless specific controls are employed. . . .

2. Lack of standards for declaring matches.

Even if interpretation of the banding pattern is eventually considered reliable, this does not solve the basic problem of the lack of objective criteria in the scientific community for declaring a match. For instance, Lifecodes's stated rule was to declare a match between two bands when they were within three standard deviations of each other. This is a much more liberal matching standard than used in most scientific studies which declare two standard deviations to be statistically significant. Furthermore, Lifecodes did not even adhere to this standard in *Castro*, when it used a new "averaging method" that was not scientifically sound and allowed it to declare a match outside three standard deviations.

Acceptable matching criteria for forensic purposes may elude scientists as long as patterns continue to be faint, blurry, and generally variable, and contamination and degradation of the samples cause the patterns to change. Furthermore, there is the possibility that two very different fragments on two separate samples or within the same sample will have the same length, a fact which substantially undermines the technique's reliability. This is one of the dangers of the whole scheme of distinguishing among individuals only by length of DNA fragments. Studies must be conducted to determine whether it is possible to construct an acceptable range of variation within which to declare a match.

Yet, a determination of a standard for declaring matches can never be truly objective. The question of where to set the threshold determination for declaring a match is ultimately a policy question. The dilemma that is raised can be illustrated as follows: If a sample matches another sample in ten out of twelve bands, it is probably more likely that the two extra bands were produced by slop than that two random individuals would share those ten bands in common. If the examiner adopts a high threshold for matches, she may exculpate a suspect whose DNA profile is a match. If the threshold is too low, she may declare a match between two different individuals and inculpate the innocent.

Thus, even if the scientific community defines matching standards, the standards will necessarily be political in nature. If the FBI is allowed to promulgate these standards, as is expected, then it is likely that the state's need to fight crime will take precedence over any desire to protect individual rights. A low threshold for declaring a match threatens the presumption of innocence we give to a criminal defendant and undermines a justice system predicated on the notion that it is better to let the guilty go free than to condemn one innocent person. . . .

4. Lack of standards for determining probability of a coincidental match and lack of relevant population studies.

The fact that no individual has a unique DNA profile *at a given locus* cannot be overstated. Only an individual's DNA taken as a whole is unique. Thus, the importance of DNA profiling lies in its ability to compare as many loci as possible between two samples, and if they appear to match, to calculate the probability that this match could be a coincidence. There are no standards in the scientific community for such calculations, since diagnostic research does not require this step. The methods used to determine the probability statistic are likely to remain hotly contested, since once the declaration of a match is in evidence, it is the statistical probability of a random match which the jury must consider to determine if the sample found at the scene is indeed the defendant's.

The probability determinations involved in this calculation are all very problematic as currently made. The most important criticism has been the choice of the relevant population when determining the probability of a coincidental match. For instance, the oft-quoted statistic that the chance that two individuals would have the same DNA profile is one in thirty billion is based on a study of fourteen British Caucasians. Based on such a small, homogeneous population, which could have a very different distribution of alleles than the population at large, the data generated simply cannot be translated into a reliable overall statistic for anyone in the population. . . .

5. Lack of recordkeeping standards.
The lack of recordkeeping standards is far from trivial. Validation and reproduc-

tion of the results by referring to accurate and complete records is crucial to the reliability of the technique. For instance, Lifecodes did not record which of its probes were contaminated, and it continued to use and sell such probes, which could produce false positives in a DNA typing test. . . .

6. Lack of proficiency testing and licensing standards.

"Forensic science, including DNA testing, is operating in a no-man's land where there are no accredited standards for the laboratories," according to forensic evidence expert Randolph Jonakait. Dr. Eric Lander echoes this sentiment: "At present, forensic science is virtually unregulated—with the paradoxical result that clinical laboratories must meet higher standards to be allowed to diagnose strep throat than forensic labs must meet to put a defendant on death row."

Critics have lamented the lack of proficiency in forensic labs in the past. In a three-year study funded by the Justice Department, forensic laboratories received identical dried blood stains; 71.2 percent of the 128 labs participating in the study either mistyped the sample or reported inconclusive results. This lack of proficiency in state laboratories is frightening, as most DNA typing will ultimately be performed by these same laboratories.

In 1987, the California Association of Crime Laboratories conducted the only proficiency testing to date of the three private laboratories engaged in DNA typing. Fifty samples were sent to each lab. Cetus and Cellmark mistakenly matched unrelated samples. They did not complete fifty tests without inculpating an innocent person—surely an unproficient result. Although Lifecodes called all fifty correctly, its researchers, rather than the technicians who usually perform it, completed the test. This type of testing is not nearly as rigorous as blind testing programs, where blind tests are interspersed among real cases. The test only required stating whether there was a match, and not how close the match was or where the bands were located, and so the laboratories had a fifty-fifty chance of getting it right.

The technique as currently practiced, without guidelines or standards, is complex and sophisticated, and it is doubtful that forensic crime labs will be able to perform the DNA typing test. Passing a battery of blind tests should be required before a crime laboratory is allowed a license to make determinations that affect an individual's freedom.

D. Proposal for Uniform Validation and Standards

Castro, as well as the March 1989 hearings before the House Judiciary Committee's Subcommittee on Civil and Constitutional Rights, convinced many interested parties that uniform standards are vital to ensure the reliability of DNA profiling in criminal cases. As a result of the hearings, the Subcommittee strongly recommended that the FBI take the lead in developing the following: 1) an independent system of proficiency testing and licensing; 2) guidelines and protocols in testing to serve as national advisory standards for forensic DNA profiling; 3) requirements that labs keep records and disclose scientific ambiguities in results; 4) uniform standards for declaring matches; and 5) continued research on population frequency data. In addition, the Subcommittee suggested that legislation may be necessary. . . .

II. OUT OF THE FORENSIC LAB AND INTO THE COURTROOM: LEGAL CONCERNS

The revelations by experts in *Castro* of DNA profiling's unreliability should serve to curb the zeal of prosecutors and judges who are pitting cutting-edge technology against the criminal defendant. The uncertainties of the technique should cause the legal community to pause and reevaluate the technique's reliability in the forensic arena. These uncertainties should provoke a probing examination of the admissibility standards for novel scientific evidence in the courtroom to understand why DNA profiling evidence was so quickly embraced as reliable in cases that preceded *Castro*.[7]

However, more recent cases are already attempting to portray *Castro* as a blip on the forensics screen, a mere "speed bump" on this technology's fast track to admissibility.[8] Even if the more glaring mistakes made by Lifecodes in *Castro* were not made in these cases, or if particular test results in subsequent cases were accurate, *Castro* uncovered a myriad of problems that demonstrate the unreliability of the technique as a whole. More importantly, . . . *Castro* teaches that the courts are not the proper forum for assessing the reliability of a forensic technique as sophisticated as DNA profiling.

Courts currently employ one of two tests to assess the admissibility of novel scientific evidence. The majority of jurisdictions follow the older, more stringent test promulgated in *Frye v. United States*,[9] described below. However, as the amount of scientific evidence in the courtroom proliferates,[10] a growing number of jurisdictions have abandoned the view that scientific evidence is distinct from other forms of evidence and have opted for a simpler relevancy standard. Thus far, despite the decisions of many courts to the contrary, DNA profiling, as currently employed in forensics, does not pass either test.

A. DNA Profiling Fails the Frye Test

1. Characteristics of the Frye test.
In *Frye*, the court excluded a form of lie detection evidence that was a precursor to the modern polygraph, stating:

> Just when a scientific principle or discovery crosses the line between the experimental and demonstrable stages is difficult to define. Somewhere in this twilight zone the evidential force of the principle must be recognized, and while courts will go a long way in admitting expert testimony deduced from a well-recognized scientific principle or discovery, the thing from which the deduction is made must be sufficiently established to have gained general acceptance in the particular field in which it belongs.[11]

Proponents of this "general acceptance" test have claimed that the test has the following advantages: 1) "those most qualified to assess the general validity of a scientific method will have the determinative voice";[12] 2) "a minimal reserve of experts [will exist] who can critically examine the validity of a scientific determination in a particular case";[13] 3) the test "may well promote a degree of uniformity in decision,"[14] since judges with differing opinions on a technique may find that there is consensus in the scientific community; and 4) the lag time produced between scientific advances and the acceptance of new techniques into the courtroom helps counter a "misleading aura of certainty which often envelops a new scientific process, obscuring its currently experimental nature."[15] . . .

2. Assessing DNA profiling under Frye: What it should look like.

Frye gives the scientific community, not the legal community, the last word on admissibility. What would a judicious assessment of the reliability of DNA typing under the Frye standard look like? First, the court must decide in which "particular field" the DNA profiling technique belongs. The obvious categorical choices for DNA typing are molecular biology, genetics, population genetics, statistics, and forensics.

The problem in cases thus far has been the inherent bias in having those scientists that market the technique act as the spokespersons for the "particular field." In many of the cases involving DNA typing before Castro, there were no expert witnesses for the defense, from which the court concluded there was general scientific acceptance;[16] the main expert witnesses for the prosecution were the scientists from the private laboratories who had vested interests in the success and profits of their companies.

Analyzing biological evidence and testifying about it in court has become an extremely lucrative business. Lifecodes representatives admitted that the ultimate objective of Lifecodes was not to do the testing, but to sell its probes, restriction enzymes, and training programs to crime laboratories in the U.S. Dr. Howard Cooke of the Medical Research Council in Edinburgh said that commercial pressures may be part of the reason private companies in the United States need to produce a result even when the evidence is of poor quality. Law Professor Barry Scheck, who represented Joseph Castro and is a member of the New York Governor's Commission on Forensic DNA Typing, testified before Congress in March, 1989:

> [I]t became a critical part of Lifecodes' marketing strategy to get into court first, before its competitors, so that its technology and reagents would gain an all-important competitive advantage—the judicial imprimatur of acceptability.
>
> Soon Cellmark, whose Directors had expressed reluctance to begin forensic testing on a commercial basis, started to take cases, if only to protect its market share.

The judiciary has unwittingly contributed to the making of an industry earning $40 million per year. . . .

The final issue the court must address is whether the relevant scientific community has accepted the technique. One measure of general scientific acceptance is publication of the technique in peer-reviewed scientific journals. Testimony in Castro demonstrated that reliance on this factor can be problematic. Lifecodes has published several articles, but those articles have not covered some of the more controversial aspects of the technique. For instance, a validation study Lifecodes published did not involve contaminated samples. Also, some of the techniques discussed in Lifecodes's articles have been refuted. For instance, the peer reviewer of Lifecodes's published article on allele frequencies testified in Castro that the findings in the article were unreliable. Furthermore, Lifecodes did not adhere in practice to its published procedures for computerized matching and for methods of determining allele frequencies in its database. Scientists understand publication as only the first step towards general scientific acceptance. Publishing provides the scientific community with an opportunity to reproduce the results. The more reproducible the results, the more reliable the technique employed. Wide publication by scientists in the related fields, and thus wide validation of results, avoids the pitfalls of self-validation by a small group.

Because the three private laboratories conceal much of their process from the public view with the shield of "trade secrets," their techniques cannot gain general acceptance in the scientific community. The scientists from these labs have not publicly revealed much of their protocols through publishing. On the individual case level, some defendants have not been allowed access to the laboratory documents. If during trial opposing experts have been allowed to review the protocols, the experts must sign agreements not to disclose them. Therefore, independent validation has not been possible. The private labs have also restricted access to their probes. The lack of universal availability of the probes in the scientific community means both the inability to reproduce results and the frustration of a shared attempt to build a large database of allele frequencies for particular probes. Clearly, scientific acceptance cannot occur with proprietary rights restricting access to the technology.

In addition, it is erroneous for courts to substitute the frequency of the use of a novel technique or its admission at trial for an analysis of its general acceptance. As an example of this reasoning, when the press reporting on *Castro* asked Lifecodes about the reliability of its test, a spokeswoman responded, "Our DNA technology already has been accepted in over 100 trials in this country and that's proof that it is considered valid and reliable technology."[17] This statement merely reveals that the courts may be going forward with the acceptance of this technique without the scientists. The appropriate scientific community has not been invited to scrutinize the results. Judges have been misled by mere use of a technique in the past.[18] Inferring the technique's general acceptance from the fact that some courts have admitted DNA evidence[19] only compounds ignorance about the technique, and it guts the *Frye* test entirely.

3. Assessing DNA profiling under Frye: What it looks like in Wesley and Castro.

Two cases in which courts have been confronted with DNA profiling evidence illustrate how courts have misunderstood or misapplied the *Frye* standard.

In *People v. Wesley*,[20] the court appeared enamored with the prospect of admitting into evidence a technique on the "cutting edge" of forensic science—one that will "constitute the single greatest advance in the 'search for truth,' and the goal of convicting the guilty and acquitting the innocent since the advent of cross-examination."[21]

The court placed the technique in the fields of molecular biology, genetics, chemistry, biology, biochemistry, and population genetics.[22] Misapplying the *Frye* test, the court stated that since the underlying principles and technology were uncontested by any of the expert witnesses,[23] *Frye* was satisfied despite the fact that an unbiased expert with personal knowledge of and experience with the forensic application was not present. The court eliminated the step of proving general acceptance of the forensic application, stating that defense arguments against the application of the technique in this case went to weight and not admissibility.[24] The court was satisfied that proper application of the technique to forensics may be possible because the technology exists to do so, but the mere possibility of proper application is not the same as having the proper application in place. Only after scientists have shown that they can reproduce results in the *forensic* technique should the courts move the focus of the analysis away from *Frye* admissibility questions to questions of weight, *i.e.*, whether the accepted steps were followed in an individual case.

The credentials of the prosecution's experts apparently overwhelmed the court. The experts were the best and the brightest that state money could buy, and their credentials obscured critical analysis of the substance of their testimony.[25] The court used glowing adjectives to describe the prosecution experts and believed that the experts' experience with the techniques as performed in diagnostics answered the question of the reliability of the technique as performed in forensics. Interestingly, the court disparaged the defense experts.[26]

The court relied heavily on statements by Dr. Roberts, which were later discredited in *Castro*. Dr. Roberts, of course, recanted his opinion on the reliability of Lifecodes's methods in *Castro*, where he joined in the statement by the defense experts. Dr. Roberts told the court in *Wesley* that it was impossible to get a false positive with Lifecodes's test; instead, the autoradiograph would be blank if any steps were performed improperly. This assertion was proven wrong in *Castro*, where the experts demonstrated that contamination could produce a false positive. . . .

B. DNA Profiling Fails the Relevancy Test

1. Characteristics of the relevancy test.

The Federal Rules of Evidence, adopted in 1975, although not explicitly overruling *Frye*, endorse a relevancy standard for all kinds of evidence. Rule 401 defines "relevant evidence"; Rule 402 states that relevant evidence is generally admissible; Rule 403 states that relevant evidence may be excluded on the grounds of prejudice, confusion or waste of time; and Rule 702 generally allows experts to testify on anything that will help the trier of fact. As applied to novel scientific evidence, these rules together provide a much lower threshold of admissibility than the *Frye* standard, since the evidence would only be subject to a relevancy-type balancing test of probative weight against prejudicial effect.

As courts abandon *Frye* and flock to the relevancy standard, their distaste for deferring to the scientific community the decision on the reliability of novel scientific evidence becomes apparent. In *United States v. Williams*,[27] the court explicitly rejected *Frye* and admitted spectrographic voice analysis, a technique that had received mixed reviews from the relevant scientific community. The court concluded that the reliability of scientific evidence cannot be determined "solely on a process of 'counting (scientific) noses,' "[28] and that "the courts cannot . . . surrender to scientists the responsibility for determining the reliability of that evidence."[29] . . .

2. Assessing DNA profiling under the relevancy test: What it should look like.

Probative value. The first part of the relevancy test is a measure of the probative value of the evidence proffered. Using the five *Williams* indicia, the DNA profiling technique as it currently is practiced is not reliable. Moreover, the indicia themselves are misguided and further manifest the courts' ignorance in or avoidance of what constitutes actual scientific reliability.

As for the first reliability indicia, the potential rate of error in the forensic DNA typing technique is unknown. The many complex steps involved in this test leave numerous possibilities for undetectable errors. . . .

Next, although the practitioners of DNA profiling maintain standards, if their internal standards are not accepted in the scientific community as reliable, DNA profiling fails to meet the second *Williams* criterion. Until the relevant scientific and forensic communities have agreed on uniform standards, the mere existence of standards within each laboratory is not very meaningful.

One part of the third factor, the care with which the technique was performed in the particular case, must be determined through case-by-case examination. One problem with this factor in DNA typing is that the prosecution's expert witness will simply describe an amazing number of steps which will appear to a jury to constitute due care. Hence, a second related problem is that the burden of proof will in essence be shifted onto the defendant to counter that assumption of care. Thus, the ability of the often indigent defendant to locate and hire an expert witness becomes paramount. Furthermore, the defense's witness has the extreme disadvantage of coming in after the test is done, and can only check the records the lab discloses and the autoradiographs, which may not readily reveal errors that led to a false match.

The second part of this third factor, whether the technique lends itself to abuse, was probably designed to monitor any subjective determinations made by the tester. For instance, the method of examiner questioning in polygraphy may lend itself to abuse. The possibilities for examiner bias in Lifecodes's method of DNA testing as exposed by *Castro* testimony makes it particularly suspect.

The fourth *Williams* factor, analogies to the reliability of other techniques, serves as an unfair substitution for the reliability of the technique at issue. For instance, although protein gel electrophoresis and DNA profiling are very different techniques, they both fall within the field of genetics and both analyze dried blood and semen with a great degree of specificity. Therefore, they are probably most "alike" in terms of analogies, yet the procedures involved are entirely different. Protein gel electrophoresis was initially accepted as reliable in the courts, but then was discredited and rejected by some courts.[30] Since it has not been completely rehabilitated as a reliable technique,[31] can one surmise that DNA profiling is also not reliable? The proponents of DNA profiling surely would answer no. Once protein gel electrophoresis is widely accepted, should it weigh in the balance then toward acceptance of DNA profiling, an entirely different technique? Surely not. If anything, perhaps the courts should analogize to the tortuous history of the admissibility of protein gel electrophoresis evidence and ask themselves if something is wrong with an admissibility standard that admits unreliable evidence.

Analogies may work relatively well in *legal* analysis, where precision is not as crucial as the creation of cohesive and logical categories of law which serve to aid people in ordering their actions. However, analogies are simply not a satisfactory mode of *scientific* analysis, which depends on the integrity of each individual result.

Applying the final *Williams* factor, there are no safeguards present in the DNA test itself. Although paternity testing and diagnostic research have built-in controls in comparing the DNA profiles of the parents to that of the child, forensic samples are of unknown origin and thus have countless numbers of possible alleles. Therefore, all of the controls for the forensic test must be imposed from the outside. . . .

III. OUT OF THE COURTROOM AND INTO THE COMMUNITY: PRIVACY CONCERNS . . .

B. The DNA Profile Database and Its Threat to the Privacy and Security of the Individual

. . . DNA profiling evidence is currently scientifically unreliable for application to forensics. Expert testimony in the *Castro* case highlighted the potential for error in declaring matches and cast doubt on the reliability of the outrageous statistical claims of the technique's proponents. Due to the novelty of the technique's application to forensics, testimony from unbiased expert witnesses who are familiar with the unique difficulties of the forensic technique is sorely lacking.

There is an urgent need for the scientific community to review the DNA profiling technique and designate uniform controls and standards to ensure accuracy in the declarations of matches. Judges, prosecutors, juries and the press have been too excited about the evidence to understand the significance of the

technical challenges in *Castro*. Only after the scientific community determines that forensic DNA profiling is a reproducible, reliable test, and only after those laboratories which plan to employ the test demonstrate proficiency, will the criminal defendant receive justice. We must not allow our enthusiasm for scientific and technological advances to overshadow our commitment to the Bill of Rights and to a fair and just society.

NOTES

1. Although DNA profiling is better known as DNA or genetic "fingerprinting," this note takes the view that equating the procedure with fingerprinting, a forensic technique considered so reliable that courts take judicial notice of its reliability, has contributed to the premature acceptance of DNA profiling as reliable in criminal prosecutions. *See* Dan L. Burk, *DNA Fingerprinting: Possibilities and Pitfalls of a New Technique*, 28 JURIMETRICS J. 455, 468–469, 469 n.65 (1988) (noting that "the name 'fingerprinting' may create unsubstantiated beliefs and expectations in the minds of judges and jurors," and recognizing that a similar problem occurred with the name "voiceprint" for sound spectrometry). In addition, the term "fingerprinting" suggests a relatively nonintrusive procedure, unlike DNA typing, which can result in lesser protection against unreasonable searches and seizures under the fourth amendment. This note may also refer to DNA profiling as DNA "typing," "testing," or "identification."

2. Newspeak is the medium through which George Orwell's "Big Brother" brainwashed individuals in *Nineteen Eighty-Four*. *See* G. ORWELL, *supra* note 2, at 246–56.

3. Jean L. Marx, *DNA Fingerprinting Takes the Witness Stand*, 240 Science 1616, 1616 (1988) (quoting Mac MacLeod of the State Attorney's office in Palatka, Florida).

4. Debra Cassens Moss, *DNA—The New Fingerprints*, A.B.A. J., May 1, 1988, at 66, 69–70 (paraphrasing David Housman, Professor of Biology, Massachusetts Institute of Technology).

5. Forensic DNA testing has been employed in hundreds of criminal cases nationwide. The data from these tests has been considered as evidence in over 80 criminal rape and murder trials in 27 states, leading to at least 64 convictions or guilty pleas. Marcia Barinaga, *DNA Fingerprinting: Pitfalls Come to Light*, 339 NATURE 89 (1989).

6. One powerful example of this phenomenon is the new federal sentencing guidelines which virtually eliminate judicial discretion in sentencing and have the effect of creating a class of strict liability crimes in the area of drug trafficking. Federal District Court Judge Schwarzer wept openly in court when he was forced by the guidelines to sentence to 10 years in prison a man who simply gave a ride to a drug-carrying acquaintance. *New Drug Law Is Backfiring, Judges Say,* San Francisco Chron., Sept. 25, 1989, at A1, col. 1.

7. *See, e.g.,* Andrews v. State, 533 So. 2d 841 (Fla. Dist. Ct. App. 1988); People v. Wesley, 533 N.Y.S.2d 643 (1988).

8. *See, e.g.,* Spencer v. Commonwealth, Nos. 890096, 890097 (Va. Sup. Ct. 1989) (WESTLAW, Database VA-CS); Cobey v. State, 45 CRIM. L. REP. (BNA) 2289 (July 26, 1989); Martin Berg, *Judge Rules DNA Test Admissible,* Daily J., Aug. 9, 1989, at 1, col. 5 (discussing People v. Axell, No. CR-23911 (Ventura County Super. Ct. 1989)); David Oltman, *Judge Allows DNA Tests in Alameda,* Daily J., Sept. 25, 1989, at 1, col. 5 (discussing People v. Barney, No. H-10291 (Alameda County Super. Ct. 1989)).

9. 293 F. 1013 (D.C. Cir. 1923).

10. A nationwide survey of judges and attorneys showed that almost half of them encounter scientific evidence in at least one-third of their trials. Edward J. Imwinkelried, *The Standard for Admitting Scientific Evidence: A Critique from the Perspective of Juror Psychology,* 28 VILL. L. REV. 554, 554 (1983). The growth of crime laboratories has been one of the major factors leading to the appearance of new techniques in the courtroom. In 1966, there were 110 crime labs in the United States; ten years later, there were 240. Richard Saferstein, *Criminalistics—A Look Back at the 1970s, A Look Ahead to the 1980s,* 24 J. FORENSIC SCI. 925, 925 (1979).

11. 293 F. at 1014.

12. United States v. Addison, 498 F.2d 741, 744 (D.C. Cir. 1974).

13. *Id.*

14. People v. Kelly, 17 Cal. 3d 24, 31, 549 P.2d 1240, 1244–45, 130 Cal. Rptr. 144, 148–49 (1976).

15. *Id.* at 32, 549 P.2d at 1245, 130 Cal. Rptr. at 149 (citing Huntington v. Crowley, 64 Cal. 2d 647, 656, 414 P.2d 382, 390, 51 Cal. Rptr. 254, 262 (1966)).

16. For instance, in *Spencer v. Commonwealth,* where the Virginia Supreme Court upheld the conviction and death sentence of Timothy Wilson Spencer based largely on DNA typing evidence, no defense experts testified in the pretrial hearings on the admissibility of the evidence and Spencer's defense attorneys were unable to counter testimony that the procedure was generally accepted in the scientific community. Alan Cooper, *DNA Case Is First Before a State High Court,* Nat'l. L.J., July 3, 1989, at 14 (discussing Spencer v. Commonwealth, Nos. 890096, 890097 (Va. Sup. Ct. 1989) (WESTLAW, Database VA-CS)). Likewise, no defense experts testified in Andrews v. State, 533 So. 2d 841, 847 (Fla. Dist. Ct. App. 1988). In *Cobey v. State,* the defense did not have experts and the court declared that "the trial judge did not err in finding that DNA fingerprinting was generally acceptable in the scientific community and in permitting its introduction into evidence, since there was no evidence to the contrary." 45 CRIM. L. REP. (BNA) 2289, 2289 (Md. Ct. Spec. App. July 26, 1989). However, expert testimony in *Castro* definitively showed that the scientific community was not unanimous.

17. Timothy Clifford, *Courtroom DNA Tests Hit Snag: Reliability Attacked in Bronx Case,* Newsday, May 24, 1989, at 3.

18. When protein gel electrophoresis, a technique for identifying genetic markers in bodily fluids, was first developed, courts readily admitted test results, some swayed by the fact that the technique had been used in many other cases. *See* State v. Washington, 229 Kan. 47, 52, 622 P.2d 986, 992 (1981) ("We are impressed by the testimony that the Multi-System analysis is reliable and generally accepted in the scientific field as illustrated by its present use in over 100 criminal laboratories in this country and that the FBI research laboratory uses the Multi-System analysis routinely and approves it."). Subsequently, however, after this widespread use, the reliability of the technique came under serious scrutiny and was rejected in several jurisdictions, causing a great deal of consternation among prosecutors.

19. *See, e.g.,* Andrews v. State, 533 So. 2d 841, 850 n.10 (Fla. Dist. Ct. App. 1988); Cobey v. State, 45 Crim. L. Rep. (BNA) 2289, 2289 (Md. Ct. Spec. App. July 26, 1989) (citing *Andrews* and widespread use by the FBI as support for general acceptance).

20. 533 N.Y.S.2d 643 (1988).

21. *Id.* at 644.

22. *Id.* at at 645, 659.

23. The defense experts included Dr. Neville Colman, Associate Professor of Pathology at Mt. Sinai School of Medicine, and Dr. Richard Borowsky, Associate Professor of Biology at New York University. Among the prosecution experts were Dr. Richard Roberts, Assistant Director of Research at Cold Spring Harbor Laboratory; Dr. Kenneth Kidd, molecular biologist and population geneticist at Yale University School of Medicine; Dr. Michael Baird, Director of Paternity and Forensic Evaluation for Lifecodes; and Dr. Sandra Nierzwicki-Bauer of Rensselaer Polytechnic Institute. *Id.* at 648, 651, 654, 655, 657.

24. *Id.* at 650.

25. One commentator explained that expert testimony has two components, the "message" component, which is the actual words verbalized by the expert, and the "paramessage" component, which encompass all elements that are not a part of the literal testimony, such as gestures of the expert, credentials, and prestige. The danger is that the triers of fact will be influenced by the paramessage when they do not understand the message. Steven M. Egesdal, *The* Frye *Doctrine and Relevancy Approach Controversy: An Empirical Evaluation,* 74 GEO. L.J. 1769, 1771, 1790 (1986) (student author).

26. For instance: "Dr. Colman's concern was with whether or not the laboratory procedures, methodology, and quality control used by Lifecodes were adequate to assure the accuracy and reliability of its testing results. He thought not! However, on every point raised by him he was overwhelmingly refuted—both by the facts and by the opinion of experts with superior qualifications and experience." People v. Wesley, 533 N.Y.S.2d 643, 651 (1988).

27. 583 F.2d 1194 (2d Cir. 1978), *cert. denied,* 439 U.S. 1117 (1979).

28. *Id.* at 1198.

29. *Id.*

30. The technique was used in thousands of cases in the late 1970s and was accepted by courts in several states. However, its reliability came under attack and the test was rejected in several states. *See* People v. Brown, 40 Cal. 3d 512, 709 P.2d 440, 220 Cal. Rptr. 637 (1985) (electrophoresis analysis of blood not reliable); People v. Young, 425 Mich. 470, 391 N.W.2d 270 (1986) (same); Randolph Jonakait, *Will Blood Tell? Genetic Markers in Criminal Cases,* 31 EMORY L.J. 833 (1982); Thompson & Ford, *supra* note 17, at 47.

31. Recently, proponents of the evidence have had some success reestablishing the admissibility of the technique.

POSTSCRIPT

DNA Profiling: Should It Be Used to Convict Criminals?

The law has been quicker to accept DNA tests than it has many other scientific technologies. Lie detectors are still generally not used in courts and other investigatory tools have also been found to be untrustworthy. But most judges have been sufficiently impressed by DNA tests to allow their use.

The acceptance of DNA in the trial context will have a variety of legal consequences. First, there will be questions about obtaining DNA samples. The FBI, which now has a laboratory doing DNA testing, has begun a DNA database that is similar to its fingerprint database. How the samples are obtained and who has access to them will have to be determined.

While it would be simple to apply the same rules to the DNA database as apply to the fingerprint database, the problem is that DNA is a lot more revealing than fingerprints. Fingerprints tell very little about a person other than what his or her fingerprints look like. A DNA "print," however, has information about one's genetic makeup, about whether one is a "carrier" of some genetic condition or is predisposed toward some disease. Fingerprints are useful in checking a criminal history and because of their limited use there is not much demand by employers or insurance companies for access to the FBI fingerprint database. Demand for access to the DNA database, however, can be expected to be enormous, and will raise significant questions about the right to privacy and the right to control information about oneself. As we learn more about which genes are responsible for personality traits and behaviors, legislators and courts will have to determine whether and how such information will be allowed to be used by employers, insurance companies, and government.

Recent articles on DNA testing are Burk, "DNA Fingerprinting: Possibilities and Pitfalls of a New Technique," 28 *Jurimetrics J.* 455 (1988); Note, "DNA Typing: A New Investigatory Tool," 1989 *Duke Law Journal* 474; and Note, "Trial by Certainty: Implications of Genetic 'DNA Fingerprints,' " 39 *Emory Law Journal* 309 (1989). *Schmerber v. California*, 384 U.S. 757 (1966), involved a forced taking of a blood sample. Shapiro, "Dangers of DNA: It Ain't Just Fingerprints," *New York Law Journal*, January 23, 1990, p. 1, outlines the dangers involved in a DNA database. A description of a case in which the reliability of DNA testing was challenged successfully is Parloff, "How Barry Scheck and Peter Neufeld Tripped Up the DNA Experts," *The American Lawyer*, December 1989, p. 50. This case is *People v. Castro*, 144 Misc. 2d 956; 546 N.Y.S. 2d 985 (1989).

ISSUE 17

Should the Insanity Defense Be Abolished?

YES: Jonathan Rowe, from "Why Liberals Should Hate the Insanity Defense," *Washington Monthly* (May 1984)

NO: Richard Bonnie, from *Statement Submitted to the Committee on the Judiciary,* U.S. Senate (August 2, 1982)

ISSUE SUMMARY

YES: Editor Jonathan Rowe examines the insanity defense as it is now administered and finds that it is most likely to be used by white middle- or upper-class defendants and that its application is unfair and leads to unjust results.
NO: Professor of law Richard Bonnie argues that the abolition of the insanity defense would be immoral and leave no alternative for those who are not responsible for their actions.

The verdict in the 1982 trial of John Hinckley, accused of shooting President Reagan, brought the insanity defense out of the pages of legal journals and onto the front pages of newspapers and popular magazines. What had been a subject of considerable scholarly and judicial debate during the last twenty years became a newsworthy topic as well. That an attempted assassination of a political figure has led to calls for abolishing the insanity defense is somewhat ironic, since the modern standard for the insanity defense originated in a similar incident 147 years ago.

In 1843, Daniel McNaughtan, suffering from delusions of persecution, fired a shot at a man he believed was Prime Minister Robert Peel. Actually, the victim was the prime minister's secretary and the bullet killed him. Englishmen were outraged, since three other attempted assassinations of political officials had recently taken place, and Queen Victoria was prompted to send her husband, Prince Albert, to the trial as an observer. When McNaughtan was found not guilty by reason of insanity, Victoria sent a letter to the House of Lords, complaining that McNaughtan and the other assassins were "perfectly conscious and aware of what they did." The Lords summoned fifteen judges who, after considering the matter, pronounced the McNaughtan rule (commonly referred to as the M'Naghten rule) as the most appropriate formulation of the insanity defense. This test requires that a jury must find that the defendant, when the act was committed, did not know the nature and quality of his act or that he could not tell right from wrong.

One of the problems with the insanity defense is in defining insanity. If one argues in favor of the defense, one should be able to define insanity with reasonable precision and in a way that can be applied consistently. The great difficulty in providing a definition is the basic argument against the insanity defense. The insanity defense issue has caused great controversy between lawyers and psychiatrists over the meaning of insanity and mental illness and over the ability of psychiatrists reliably to diagnose the problems of defendants.

A frequent objection to the M'Naghten rule was that there were persons who could distinguish between good and evil but still could not control their behavior. One response to this critique was the "irresistible impulse" test. Using this standard, a defendant would be relieved of responsibility for his or her actions even if he or she could distinguish right from wrong but, because of mental disease, could not avoid the action in question. A somewhat broader and more flexible version of the combined M'Naghten-irresistible impulse test was recommended by the American Law Institute in 1962. Under this formulation, people are not responsible for criminal conduct if they lack *substantial capacity* to appreciate the criminality of their conduct or to conform their conduct to the requirements of the law.

The most noteworthy and radical experiment with the reformulation of the insanity defense occurred in *Durham v. United States*, 214 F. 2d 862 (1954). The District of Columbia Court of Appeals ruled that an accused was not criminally responsible if his act was the product of mental disease or defect. The effect of this rule was to increase the amount of expert psychiatric testimony presented in court about whether mental disease was present and whether the act was a product of the disease. While welcomed by many since it allowed for a more complete psychiatric picture to be presented to the jury, the rule proved to be too vague and led to too much power being given to psychiatric experts. As a result, in *United States v. Brawner*, 471 F. 2d 969 (1972), the Durham experiment was abandoned.

Examination of the insanity defense opens up some extremely important issues of law. For example, what are the purposes of punishment? What assumptions does the law make about human nature, free will, and personal responsibility? What should be the role of the jury and what authority should be given medical and psychiatric experts in evaluating deviant behavior? How should we deal with the often competing goals of rehabilitation, retribution, and deterrence? These are among the questions raised in the following articles on the need for reforming or abolishing the insanity defense.

YES

Jonathan Rowe

WHY LIBERALS SHOULD HATE THE INSANITY DEFENSE

"It's the fallacy of your legal system," said Gary Trapnell, a bank robber who not long afterwards would hijack a TWA 707 flying from Los Angeles to New York. "Either the man falls under this antiquated psychiatric scheme of things, or he doesn't." Trapnell was talking about the insanity defense, which he had used with great acumen to avoid jail for his innumerable crimes over the years. "I have no right to be on the streets," he added.

The insanity defense has been much in the news of late. We read cases such as that of the Michigan ex-convict who pleaded insanity after seven killings, won an acquittal, but returned to the streets two months later when he was declared sane. In a month, he was charged with murdering his wife. Or take the 23-year-old Connecticut man who left the state hospital three months after an insanity acquittal for stabbing a man. The acquittee's mother pleaded to have him recommitted, but to no avail. Shortly thereafter, he repeatedly stabbed a man whose home he was burglarizing. Once again he was declared not guilty by reason of insanity.

It sounds like the warmup for a right-wing tirade against the coddlers of criminals. But the much publicized trials of John Hinckley and others have cast the issue in a somewhat different light. In a strange way, by jumbling liberal and conservative loyalties, these have made debate on the subject not only necessary, but possible as well. Take the "Twinkie Defense," which enabled former San Francisco City Supervisor Dan White to get off with a light eight-year sentence after shooting, with obvious deliberation, San Francisco Mayor George Moscone and his city administrator, Harvey Milk. As Milk was both liberal and openly homosexual, thousands who probably never before identified with the cause of law and order were outraged that this brutal act of (at least symbolic) homophobia should go lightly punished. John Hinckley, for his part, was the son of a wealthy upper-middle-class family, and not the sort of fellow who evoked sympathies usually reserved for the downtrodden. His trial prompted even *The Nation*, which rarely

From Jonathan Rowe, "Why Liberals Should Hate the Insanity Defense," *The Washington Monthly*, vol. 16, no. 4 (May 1984). Copyright © 1984 by The Washington Monthly Company, 1611 Connecticut Avenue, N.W., Washington, D.C. 20009; (202) 462-0128. Reprinted by permission of *The Washington Monthly*.

concedes the cops an inch, to suggest some mild reforms in the insanity defense.

In the wake of the Hinckley trial, a number of reforms have been suggested. *The Nation*, along with many others, advocates that we put the burden of proof upon the defendant. (In the Hinckley case, the prosecutors actually had to prove him sane, which is no mean feat.) Others have called for a tighter legal definition of insanity itself. Such changes might be helpful, but they amount to fiddling. The only way to resolve the injustices of the insanity defense is to do away with it entirely. This may sound cruel, but it is not. Nor is it a proposal to "lock 'em up and throw away the key." To the contrary, the injustices of this defense go much deeper than a few criminals getting off the hook. They go close to the core of our current practices regarding punishment and correction. Getting rid of the insanity defense would help to make us confront the need for humane reform in the way we sentence and confine those who break the law.

SUCH A DEAL

The insanity defense looms a good deal larger in our minds than it does in actual life. Somewhere between 1,000 and 2,000 criminals make use of it each year, or about 1 percent to 2 percent of felonies that go to trial (over 90 percent in many jurisdictions are plea-bargained before trial). The issue is important not because it arises frequently, but because it tends to arise in the most serious crimes: think of Son of Sam, for example, or the Hillside Strangler. Such people tend to be dangerous, and their trials attract so much publicity that they put our entire system of justice to a test. What single event of the last two years affected your view of the criminal justice system more than the Hinckley trial did?

It is hard to read about such trials without getting the impression that something is fundamentally wrong. Take the case of Robert H. Torsney, the New York City policeman who shot a 15-year-old black youth in the head from two feet away in November of 1978. In an article in the *Journal of Legal Medicine*, Abraham Halpern, director of psychiatry at the United Hospital, Port Chester, New York, tells the case in salient detail.

At first, Torsney's lawyer resisted any suggestion of psychological observation or treatment for his client. Such treatment for an officer who was only acting in the line of duty was "worse than putting him in the electric chair," the attorney said. As public indignation rose, however, and acquittal became more and more unlikely, the attorney decided that Torsney might have deep-seated psychological problems after all. At a hearing on Torsney's insanity defense, his paid psychiatrist explained the policeman's errant account of the incident, which was contradicted by other witnesses as an "involuntary retrospective falsification." Not a lie, mind you. The psychiatrist went on to explain that Torsney shot the kid because of an "organic psychomotor seizure" arising from a "mental defect."

The jury found Torsney not guilty by reason of insanity. After a year, however, the staff at the mental hospital recommended that he be released because they could find nothing wrong with him. When the lower court balked—such hasty releases are unseemly if nothing else—Torsney's attorney indignantly filed an appeal. "It can't be seriously argued," he wrote, "that the record in this case establishes that Mr. Torsney is either seriously mentally ill or presently dangerous. At most he may be said to have a personality flaw, which certainly does not distinguish him from the rest of society."

What really distinguished Torsney, it seemed, was that he had shot somebody and deserved to be punished. That such simple observations can become so obscured is largely the result of the wholesale invasion of psychiatry into the courtroom that has been underway since the 1950s. Back then, the stars of psychiatry and psychoactive drugs were shining bright. To many, we were on the threshold of a new age, in which psychiatrists could measure such things as responsibility and mental disease down to minute calibrations and effect cures with the precision of engineers. If only we could let these new wizards into the courtroom, to bring their expertise to bear upon the processes of justice.

The main opening came in 1954, when federal appeals Judge David Bazelon, of the Washington, D.C., District Court, declared the so-called "Durham Rule." Under the old "M'Naghten Rule," a criminal could be judged insane only if he or she didn't know right from wrong. This crimped the psychiatrists somewhat, since they tend to shrug their shoulders on questions of values. In the *Durham* case Judge Bazelon set them free, declaring that henceforth in the District of Columbia an accused was not criminally responsible "if his unlawful act was the product of mental disease or defect." Bazelon received a special award from the American Psychiatric Association, but not everyone was that enthused. The American Law Institute (ALI) produced a sort of compromise, declaring that a person wouldn't be responsible for a misdeed if he couldn't appreciate the wrongfulness of it or if he "lacked a substantial capacity . . . to conform his conduct to the requirements of the law." Though somewhat stiffer on paper, this ALI rule didn't vary from the Durham Rule in practice all that much. Adopted by a majority of the states, its various permutations have given the psychiatrists virtual free rein in the courtroom ever since.

The Hinckley trial demonstrated what the heavenly city of courtroom psychiatry has become. Three teams of psychiatrists—11 in all—picked over Hinckley's mind for hours in an exercise that 200 years from now will no doubt seem much the way that the heated debates over the medieval heresies seem to us today. The resulting trial dragged on for 52 excruciating days. One defense psychiatrist, Thomas C. Goldman, told the jury with a straight face that Hinckley saw actress Jody Foster as an "idealized mother who is all-giving and endowed with magical power," while President Reagan was an "all evil prohibitive figure who hates him, seeks to destroy him, and deny access to the idealized mother figure." No wonder he tried to shoot the man.

Or take the comments of Richard Delman, a psychiatrist who testified for the defense in the Dan White trial. As Lee Coleman, also a psychiatrist, tells it in his new book, *The Reign of Error,* Delman concluded on the basis of inkblot and other tests that it was White's deep concern for others that led him to sneak into San Francisco City Hall through a window rather than walk in through the front door. "He didn't want to embarrass the officer who was operating the metal detector [and would have discovered his gun]," Delman said.

On at least one occasion this kind of analysis has been more than even the defendant could take. Coleman cites the case of Inez Garcia, who was raped by two men in Soledad, California; afterwards, she went home, got a rifle, and shot one of her attackers. At her trial she sat listening to defense psychiatrist Jane Olden go on and on about her "reactive formations" and her self-image as a "saint-like idealized virgin." "If you trigger her negative feelings, which would be provoked by such an act as rape," Olden explained, "being a hysterical person who was striving always to express this sensuality and aggression, then you could indeed throw her into a state where she is emotionally relating to her own conflict."

Garcia stood up and yelled at the judge, "I killed the motherfucker because I was raped and I'd kill him again."

If you smell a fish in such psychologizing, it is with good reason. There is a cadre of so-called "forensic psychiatrists," who show up in these insanity trials again and again, plying their offensive or defensive specialties. Dr. Alan Stone of Harvard, former head of the American Psychiatric Association, describes the kind of trial that results as a "three-ring circus, in which lawyers are the ringmasters and the psychiatric witnesses are the clowns, and if they are carefully trained, then they will be trained clowns." Another Harvard psychiatrist, David Baer, was a defense witness in the Hinckley trial but does not regularly participate in these affairs, and he revealed some of the details to a reporter from *Harper's*. He spent, he said at least 20 to 25 hours rehearsing his testimony with the lawyers, who admonished him, among other things, not to "weaken your answers with all the quali-

fications you think you ought to make." They said, "Oh, don't mention the exploding bullets. My God, that's so damaging to the case," he recalls. Baer, who was paid $35,000 for his efforts, added that he was "determined never to tell a lie."

That may be. But what happens to most psychiatrists who resist the "training" of the defense lawyers? "If a man doesn't testify the right way, he is not rehired," said one defense attorney in a study published in the *Rutgers Law Journal*. (Section 6 of the "Principles of Medical Ethics" of the American Psychiatric Association, by the way, reads: "A physician should not dispose of his services under terms or conditions which tend to interfere with or impair the free and complete exercise of his medical judgment.")

DID YOU HEAR VOICES?

The theory behind our "adversary" system is that when you pit one group of experts like these against another the truth will somehow emerge. When the hired-gun psychiatrists do their act, however, the result is not information, but confusion. "None of them had the same conclusion," complained Nathalia Brown, a shop mechanic at the local electric utility and a Hinckley juror. "All of them said he had this illness, that illness, so how are we to know what illness he has? I felt on the brink of insanity myself going through this, you know."

This, of course, is precisely what defense lawyers seek. As far back as 1945, Julian Carroll, the New York attorney who handled poet Ezra Pound's famous insanity defense against treason charges, wrote a friend that insanity trials are a "farce" in which the "learned medicos for each side squarely contradict each other and completely befuddle the jury." What was true then is even more true today, and all it took was confusion and nagging doubts in the minds of the jurors to gain Hinckley's acquittal.

In the nation's prisons, fooling the shrinks is getting to be a science. Inkblot tests offer fertile ground for displays of psychosis, and inmates who have successfully pleaded insanity have instructed their cohorts on what to see— sexual acts, genitalia, and the like. Ken Bianchi, the Hillside Strangler, studied books on psychology and hypnosis before convincing a number of psychiatrists he had a dual personality, and only an especially alert one found him out. An experiment at Stanford University suggested that conning these psychiatrists may not be all that hard. Eight subjects, all without any record of mental illness, feigned hearing voices and thereby gained admission to 12 different mental hospitals. They did not falsify any details of their lives other than that they heard voices. Eleven of the 12 were diagnosed as "schizophrenic" while the 12th was diagnosed "manic depressive."

"I probably know more about psychiatry . . . than your average resident psychiatrist," boasted Gary Trapnell, who had some justification for his claim. "I can bullshit the hell out of one in ten minutes."

It's not that psychiatry has nothing to tell us, nor that many of its practitioners are not dedicated to helping others. The problem is the way this specialty is used in insanity trials: the endeavor itself is in many ways absurd. These psychiatrists are interviewing criminals who know that if they come off seeming a little bananas, they might get off the hook. The notion that something resembling

scientific data will always result from such subjective encounters is, well, a little bananas itself. On top of that, the courtroom psychiatrists are not purporting to inform us of a defendant's *present* mental state, though even that can be elusive enough. They are claiming to divine the defendant's mental state when he committed the crime, which probably was months before. "I can't even tell you what *I* was thinking about a week ago, or a year ago, let alone what someone else was thinking," says criminal psychologist Stanton Samenow, author of *Inside the Criminal Mind*, whose eight years working at St. Elizabeths hospital in Washington made him deeply skeptical of traditional attempts to understand and catalogue criminals according to Freudian concepts. Indeed, how would you begin to *prove* an assertion such as the one that John Hinckley tried to shoot Reagan because he saw the president as an "all evil prohibitive figure"? This is not evidence. It is vaporizing. Coleman testifies at criminal trials with delightful iconoclasm that psychiatrists such as himself have no more ability than anyone else to inform the jury as to what was going on in a criminal's mind at any given time.

POOR RELATIONS

But one should not conclude that the only thing wrong with the insanity defense is that it lets the felons free on the basis of recondite psychiatric excuses. The injustice goes much deeper. Some psychiatrists, for example, lend their courtroom aura and mantle of expertise to the prosecution. Jim Grigson, the so-called "Hanging Shrink" of Texas, will tell a jury after a 90-minute interview with a defendant that this individual "has complete disregard for another human being's life" and that "no treatment, no medicine, nothing is going to change this behavior." Psychiatric opinionizing can cut both ways.

There's the further problem that psychiatrists, the gatekeepers of this defense, have their greatest rapport with the problems of those closest to their own social status. A few years ago, Dr. Daniel Irving, a psychiatrist in Washington, demonstrated this attitude in an article Blain Harden wrote for *The Washington Post.* "I hate to say this," Irving confided, "but I don't like to work with poor people. . . . They are talking about stuff that doesn't interest me particularly. They are the kind of people who don't interest me." Over 95 percent of all psychiatric patients are white, and James Collins, a black psychiatrist who is chairman of the Howard University Medical School Department of Psychiatry, told Harden that "[the] biggest problem is that many psychiatrists cannot relate to poor people."

In fact, the insanity defense itself can be weighted heavily towards those who are well-off. This is not just because a Hinckley family can muster upwards of a million dollars to mount a prodigious legal and psychiatric defense. On a subtler level, someone from a "nice" upper-middle-class background who commits a heinous crime is more readily seen as off his rocker than is someone from a poorer background in which crime is closer to the norm (or is at least perceived to be). During the Hinckley trial the jury witnessed his family sitting behind him, the "perfect couple," as one observer said later. "Hinckley's father was sitting there with a pondering look on his face; his mother was wearing red, white, and blue outfits; and his sister was a former cheerleader and homecoming queen. Real Americans." Surely there must be something wrong with a young man who could enjoy such advantages and still go out and shoot a president. It was the sort of tableau that a black felon from, say, East St. Louis, might have some trouble assembling.

Such, considerations may help explain why Henry Steadman of the New York State Department of Mental Hygiene found that while whites account for only 31 percent of the prison population in his state, they were a full 65 percent of those found not guilty by reason of insanity. "Racial discrimination favoring whites in successful insanity defenses is strongly suggested by these figures," writes Abraham Halpern.

This in turn points to something even more fundamentally unjust about the insanity defense: the way it draws arbitrary and culture-bound distinctions between defendants with different kinds of life burdens and afflictions. A John Hinckley may well harbor anger against his parents and anguish at his unrequited love for actress Jody Foster. Such problems can be very real for those who go through them. But they are no *more* real, no *more* inclined to affect behavior, than are the problems of a teenager of lesser means, who may be ugly, or kept back in school two or three times, or whose parents may not love him and who may have been "passed around" among relatives and older siblings for as long as he can remember, or who may find doors closed to him because he is not blond and blue-eyed the way Hinckley is. If a Hinckley merits our compassion, then surely those with hard life circumstances do also. Under the insanity defense, we absolve Hinckley totally of responsibility, while we label his hypothetical counterpart a bad person and send him to jail.

So arbitrary is the line that the insanity defense invites us to draw that all sorts of prejudices and vagaries can enter, of which racial and class bias are just two. "The actual psychological state of the defendant may be a rather minor factor" in the decision even to use the insanity defense, writes C. R. Jeffrey in his book, *Criminal Responsibility and Mental Disease.* Rather, this decision is based on such factors as "the economic position of the defendant, the nature of the criminal charges, the medical facilities in the community," and the like.

BIG DIFFERENCE

This is not to say that you won't find any poor people or non-Caucasians in the maximum-security hospitals in which insanity acquittees are kept. You will, but it's important to understand how they got there. It probably wasn't through the kind of circus trial that John Hinckley could afford. Very likely, it was a plea bargain, in which a prosecutor decided it was better to put a dangerous person away, even if just for a short time, than to devote scarce resources to a trial that he or she might lose. One study, published in the *Rutgers Law Review,* found at least two jurisdictions in which the prosecutors actually raised the insanity defense more frequently than the defense attorney did. "Clearly the prosecutor saw the [insanity] defense as a means to lock defendants up without having their guilt proved beyond a reasonable doubt," the study concludes.

Given such realities, it should not be surprising that there is often not much difference between those who end up in maximum security mental hospitals and those who end up in their penal counterparts. "Lots of people could have ended up in either one or the other," says E. Fuller Torrey, a psychiatrist at St. Elizabeths mental hospital in Washington. Samenow goes further. On the basis of his own experience studying insanity acquittees at St. Elizabeths, he declares flatly that "neither [his colleague Dr. Samuel] Yochelson nor I found that any of the men we evaluated were insane unless one took tremendous liberties with that word."

That may be a bit of an exaggeration. But the similarities between criminals we call "insane," and those we call simply "criminals," cannot be dismissed. Take recidivism. There is evidence that criminals released from mental hospitals tend to repeat their crimes with about the same frequency as their counterparts released from prison. This point is crucial because the purpose of a criminal justice system is not just to punish offenders; it is to protect the rest of us from dangerous people as well. Through the insanity defense, we go to lengths that are often ridiculous to make a distinction that in many cases is without a difference.

Sometimes the experts are the last to see what needs to be done. Listen to Lawrence Coffey, one of the Hinckley jurors who was unhappy with the verdict for which he himself voted. "I think it [the law] should be changed," he told a Senate hearing, "in some way where the defendant gets mental help enough that where he's not harmful to himself and society, and then be punished for what he has done wrong." Maryland Copelin, also one of the jurors, agreed. "I think they [defendants] should get the help they need and also punishment for the act they did." In other words, Hinckley needed treatment, but he deserved punishment, too. Who could argue with that? Well, the law, for one. It said that Hinckley was either guilty or not guilty by reason of insanity. "We could not do any better than what we did," Copelin said, "on account of your forms," which gave the jury only these two options.

In short, the insanity defense cuts the deck the wrong way. I makes no provision for the vast middle ground in which offenders have problems but should bear responsibility too. Instead of persisting in making this artificial distinction between "normal" criminals (whatever that means) and "insane" ones, we should ask first a very simple question: did the individual commit the crime? That established in a trial, we should then, in a sentencing phase, take all relevant factors into account in deciding what combination of punishment and treatment is appropriate. "Either you did it or you didn't do it," says Samenow, who supports the abolition of the insanity defense. "I think we should try the criminal first, and then worry about treatment." In other words, don't expect the jury to make Talmudic distinctions on which even the experts cannot agree. Get the psychiatrists out of the courtroom, where they cause confusion, and put them into the sentencing and treatment process, where they may be able to help.

In this sentencing phase, which would take on a new importance, Hinckley's infatuation with Jody Foster, and Dan White's overindulgence in junk food, would be given due regard. So too would the incapacity of one who was totally deranged. The crucial difference from current practice is that the examination would be done by court-appointed psychiatrists (or other professionals) instead of by hired guns proffered by either side. Since psychiatrists are as human as the rest of us, this system would not be perfect. It would, however, be better than what we have today.

In almost all cases, some punishment would be in order. You don't have to believe that retribution is the whole purpose of the law to acknowledge that something very basic in us requires that when someone causes serious harm to someone else, he should pay. This approach would eliminate perhaps the most dangerous absurdity of the present insanity defense. When a criminal wins acquittal on this ground, the criminal justice system has no more claim on him. The only way he can be kept in confinement is if he is declared insane and committed to a mental institution through a totally separate procedure. (Some states require an automatic confinement for one or two months, ostensibly to "observe" the acquittee.) No Problem, you say. They've just been declared insane. The problem is, *that* insanity was at the time of the crime, which may have been a year or more before. By the time of the commitment hearing, the old problem may have miraculously cleared up. The commitment authorities are then faced with two bad options. Either they tell the truth and let a dangerous person out or they fill a bed in a crowded mental hospital with someone who will be there not for treatment, but only to kept off the streets. Eliminating the insanity defense would eliminate such charades.

Once punishment is completed, the question of danger to society would come to the fore. First offenders committing nonviolent crimes generally pose little such threat, and in most cases could be safely paroled. At the other extreme, violent repeat offenders would be locked up for a very long time. While reform is always possible, the sad fact is that most repeat offenders will keep on repeating until they reach a "burn-out" period sometime after they reach age 40. Since the recidivism rates cut across the categories we call "normal" and "insane" criminality, the insanity defense simply doesn't help us deal with reality in this regard.

Hot-blooded crimes, such as the Dan White shooting, should be seen for what they are. Such people generally don't pose a great threat because the circumstances of their crime are not likely to happen again. It costs between $10,000 and $20,000 a year to keep a prisoner in jail, and that money would be better spent on those for whom it's really needed. In other words, White's eight-year sentence was not necessarily wrong. The wrong was in the psychiatric speculation through which that result was justified. We can achieve justice in such cases through simpler and more honest means.

WHAT A TIME

But isn't the insanity defense necessary to protect the infirm? "People who are mentally ill deserve treatment," says Flora Rheta Schreiber, whose book *The Shoemaker* details the sad story of a troubled murderer. "They don't deserve to be locked up in prison."

Fair enough. The trouble is, virtually all criminals have mental problems. The difference between a bank robber and yourself is not in your shirt size or the shape of your hands. Is there any such thing as a "sane" rape or a "sane" axe murder? If anyone did such deeds with calm and rational deliberation, would that individual not be the most insane—and dangerous—of all? Samenow, more-over, says that for the vast majority of criminals, the kind of treatment that might be effective is pretty much the same. The secret scandal of the insanity defense is the way it justifies our atrocious penal system by purporting to show kindness for one group that is selected arbitrarily in the first place. We deny treatment to the many under the pretext of providing it for a few.

And a pretext it often is. Talk to someone who has visited a maximum-security hospital for the criminally insane. To be sure, there are good ones here and there. But in his book *Beating the Rap*, Henry Steadman describes a reality that is probably more common than not. Such hospitals in his state are "prisonlike," he writes, with "locked wards, security officers, and barbed wire fences. . . . There is a substantial level of patient-patient assault; homosexuality, both consenting and nonconsenting, is common, and guards are sometimes unnecessarily brutal . . . *It is simply doing time in a different setting."* (Emphasis added.) Barbara Weiner, who heads a special outpatient program for insanity acquittees in Chicago—one of the few programs of its kind in the country—told a Senate hearing that "few states have specialized programs for treating mentally ill offenders." (Those of means, of course, can often arrange a transfer to private facilities at which conditions are more genteel.)

So averse are American psychiatrists to helping people in life's lower stations that over half the staffs of this country's public mental hospitals are graduates of foreign medical schools, where standards may not be awfully high. In 11 states, including Illinois and Ohio, the figure is over 70 percent. Just try to imagine a psychiatrist from, say, India, trying to understand a felon from the South Bronx. Torrey cites a psychiatrist who left the Illinois state hospital system telling of a colleague in charge of prescribing drugs who did not know that .8 and .80 were the same number.

Much of the problem is that most of us prefer to keep a comfortable arm's length from such realities. The people who run our criminal justice system are no exception. After observing a year's worth of mental incompetency hearings in New York, Steadman observed that "of about 35 judges, 12 attorneys, six district attorneys, and 12 psychiatrists, not one had ever seen or been inside either of the two facilities to which incompetent defen-dants are committed." A former public defender in Washington, D.C., who had pleaded before the Supreme Court the case of an insanity-acquittee who was trying to get out of St. Elizabeths, told me he had never met the individual for whose release he was pleading.

Getting rid of the insanity defense would help to break the spell and make us confront the deficiencies in our correctional systems. No longer could we congratulate ourselves that we are being humane and just when we are being neither. If eliminating the defense would help get a few dangerous felons off the street, so much the better. But a great deal more is at stake.

NO

Richard Bonnie

THE NEED FOR THE INSANITY DEFENSE

The effect of most of the proposals now before you would be to abolish the insanity defense as it has existed for centuries in Anglo-American criminal law. I urge you to reject these sweeping proposals. The insanity defense should be retained, in modified form, because some defendants afflicted by severe mental disorder cannot justly be blamed for their criminal conduct and do not, therefore, deserve to be punished. The defense, in short, is essential to the moral integrity of the criminal law.

I realize that the figure of John Hinckley looms before us today. Doubts about the moral accuracy of the jurors' verdict in this sad case have now been turned on the insanity defense itself. I do not want to second guess the verdict in the Hinckley case, but I do urge you to keep the case in proper perspective.

The highly visible insanity claim, pitting the experts in courtroom battle, is the aberrational case. The plea is raised in no more than 2% of felony cases and the defense is rarely successful when the question is contested in a jury trial. Most psychiatric dispositions in the criminal process are arranged without fanfare, without disagreement among the experts, and without dissent by the prosecution. In short, the exhaustive media coverage of cases like Hinckley's gives the public a distorted picture of the relative insignificance of the insanity defense in the day-to-day administration of justice.

In another way, however, the public debate about the aberrant case is highly to be desired because the trial of insanity claims keeps the community in touch with the moral premises of the criminal law. The legitimacy of the institution of punishment rests on the moral belief that we are all capable of rational choice and therefore deserve to be punished if we choose to do wrong. By acknowledging the exception, we reaffirm the rule. I have no doubt that the Hinckley trial and verdict have exposed the fundamental moral postulates of the criminal law to vigorous debate in every living room in the Nation. Thus, in a sense, whether John Hinckley was or was not legally insane may be less important than the fact that the question was asked at all.

These are the reasons I do not favor abolition of the insanity defense. However, I do not discount or dismiss the possibility that the defense

From U.S. Senate. Committee on the Judiciary. *Insanity Defense.* Hearing, August 2, 1982. Washington, D.C.: Government Printing Office, 1982. (S521-18.6)

occasionally may be successfully invoked in questionable cases. There is, in fact, some evidence that insanity acquittals have increased in recent years. However, I am persuaded that the possibility of moral mistakes in the administration of the insanity defense can be adequately reduced by narrowing the defense and by placing the burden of proof on the defendant.

THE OPTIONS

You have basically three options before you.

The Existing (Model Penal Code) Law

One option is to leave the law as it now stands, by judicial ruling, in all of the federal courts (and, parenthetically, as it now stands in a majority of the states). Apart from technical variations, this means the test proposed by the American Law Institute in its Model Penal Code. Under this approach, a person whose perceptual capacities were sufficiently intact that he had the criminal "intent" required in the definition of the offense can nonetheless be found "not guilty by reason of insanity" if, by virtue of mental disease or defect, he lacked substantial capacity *either* to understand or appreciate the legal or moral significance of his actions, *or* to conform his conduct to the requirements of law. In other words, a person may be excused if his thinking was severely disordered—this is the so-called volitional prong of the defense.

Revival of M'Naghten

The second option is to retain the insanity defense as an independent exculpatory doctrine—independent, that is, of mens rea—but to restrict its scope by eliminating the volitional prong. This is the approach that I favor, for reasons I will outline below. Basically, this option is to restore the *M'Naghten* test—although I do not think you should be bound by the language used by the House of Lords in 1843—as the sole basis for exculpation or ground of insanity. Although this is now distinctly the minority position in this country—it is used in less than one third of the states—it is still the law in England.

Abolition: The Mens Rea Approach

The third option is the one I have characterized as abolition of the defense. Technically, this characterization is accurate because the essential substantive effect of the so-called "mens rea" approach (or "elements" approach) would be to eliminate any criterion of exculpation, based on mental disease, which is independent of the elements of particular crimes. To put it another way, the bills taking this approach would eliminate any separate exculpatory doctrine based on proof of mental disease; instead mentally ill (or retarded) defendants would be treated just like everyone else. A normal person cannot escape liability by proving that he did not know or appreciate the fact that his conduct was wrong, and—under the mens rea approach—neither could a psychotic person.

THE CASE AGAINST THE MENS REA APPROACH

Most of the bills now before you would adopt the mens rea option, the approach recently enacted in Montana and Idaho. As I have already noted, this change, abolishing the insanity defense, would constitute an abrupt and unfortunate departure from the Anglo-American legal tradition.

If the insanity defense were abolished, the law would not take adequate account of the incapacitating effects of severe mental illness. Some mentally ill defendants may be said to have "intended" to do what they did—that is, their technical guilt can be established—but they nonetheless may have been so severely disturbed that they were unable to appreciate the significance of their actions. These cases do not frequently arise, but when they do, a criminal conviction—signifying the societal judgment that the defendant *deserves* punishment—would offend the basic moral intuitions of the community. Judges and juries would then be forced either to return a verdict which they regard as morally obtuse or to acquit the defendant in defiance of the law. They should be spared such moral embarrassment.

Let me illustrate this point with a real case evaluated at our Institute's Forensic Clinic in 1975. Ms. Joy Baker, a thirty-one-year-old woman, admitted killing her aunt. She had no previous history of mental illness, although her mother was mentally ill and had spent all of Ms. Baker's early years in mental hospitals. Ms. Baker was raised by her grandparents and her aunt in a rural area of the state. After high school graduation Ms. Baker married and had two children. The marriage ended in divorce six years later and Ms. Baker remarried. This second marriage was stressful from the outset. Mr. Baker was a heavy drinker and abusive to his wife. He also was extremely jealous and repeatedly accused his wife of seeing other men.

The night before the shooting Mr. Baker took his wife on a ride in his truck. He kept a gun on the seat between them and stopped repeatedly. At each place he told listeners that his wife was an adultress. He insisted his wife throw her wedding ring from the car, which she did because she was afraid of her husband's anger. The Bakers didn't return home until three in the morning. At that time Ms. Baker woke her children and fed them, then stayed up while her husband slept because she was afraid "something terrible would happen."

During this time and for the three days prior to the day of the shooting Ms. Baker had become increasingly agitated and fearful. Her condition rapidly deteriorated and she began to lose contact with reality. She felt that her dogs were going to attack her and she also believed her children and the neighbors had been possessed by the devil.

On the morning of the shooting, Ms. Baker asked her husband not to leave and told him that something horrible was about to happen. When he left anyway she locked the doors. She ran frantically around the house holding the gun. She made her children sit on the sofa and read the Twenty-Third Psalm over and over. She was both afraid of what they might do and of what she might do but felt that reading the Bible would protect them. Shortly afterwards, Ms. Baker's aunt made an unexpected visit. Ms. Baker told her to go away but the aunt persisted and went to the back door. Ms. Baker was afraid of the dog which was out on the back porch and repeatedly urged her aunt to leave. At this time the aunt seemed to Ms. Baker to sneering at her.

When her aunt suddenly reached through the screening to unlock the door Ms. Baker said, "I had my aunt over there and this black dog over here, and both of them were bothering me. . . . And then I had that black dog in front of me and she turned around and I was trying to kick the dog and my aunt was coming in the door and I just—took my hands I just went like this—right through the screen. . . . I shot her."

Ms. Baker's aunt fell backward into the mud behind the porch. Although she was bleeding profusely from her chest, she did not die immediately. "Why, Joy?" she asked. "Because you're the devil, and you came to hurt me," Joy answered. Her aunt said, "Honey, no, I came to help you." At this point, Ms. Baker said, she saw that her aunt was hurting and became very confused. Then, according to her statement, "I took the gun and shot her again just to relieve the pain she was having because she said she was hurt." Her aunt died after the second shot.

All the psychiatrists who examined Ms. Baker concluded that she was acutely psychotic and out of touch with reality at the time she shot her aunt. The police who arrested her and others in the small rural community concluded that she must have been crazy because there was no other explanation for her conduct. After Ms. Baker was stabilized on anti-psychotic medication, she was permitted to leave the state to live with relatives in a neighboring state. Eventually the case against her was dismissed by the court, with the consent of the prosecution, after a preliminary hearing at which the examining psychiatrists testified. She was never indicted or brought to trial.

It seems clear, even to a layman, that Ms. Baker was so delusional and regressed at the time of the shooting that she did not understand or appreciate the wrongfulness of her conduct. It would be morally obtuse to condemn and punish her. Yet, Ms. Baker had the state of mind required for some form of criminal homi-cide. If there were no insanity defense, she could be acquitted only in defiance of the law.

Let me explain. The "states of mind" which are required for homicide and other criminal offenses refer to various aspects of conscious awareness. They do not have any qualitative dimension. There is good reason for this, of course. The exclusive focus on conscious perceptions and beliefs enhances predictability, precision and equality in the penal law. If the law tried to take into account degrees of psychological aberration in the definition of offenses, the result would be a debilitating individualization of the standards of criminal liability.

At the time of the first shot, it could be argued that Ms. Baker lacked the "state of mind" required for murder because she did not intend to shoot a "human being" but rather intended to shoot a person whom she believed to be possessed by the devil. At common law, this claim would probably be characterized as a mistake of fact. Since the mistake was, by definition, an unreasonable one—i.e., one that only a crazy person would make—she would most likely be guilty of some form of homicide (at least manslaughter) if ordinary mens rea principles were applied. Even under the modern criminal codes, . . ., she would be guilty of negligent homicide since an ordinary person in her situation would have been aware of the risk that her aunt was a human being. And she possibly could be found guilty of manslaughter since she was probably aware of the risk that her aunt was a human being even though she was so regressed that she disregarded the risk.

It might also be argued that Ms. Baker's first shot would have been justi-fied if her delusional beliefs had been true since she would have been defending herself against imminent annihilation at the hands of the devil. Again, however, the application of ordinary common-law principles of justification . . . would indicate that she was unreasonably mistaken as to the existence of justificatory facts (the necessity for killing to protect oneself) and her defense would fail, although the grade of the offense would probably be reduced to manslaughter on the basis of her "imperfect" justification.

At the time of the second shot, Ms. Baker was in somewhat better contact with reality. At a very superficial level she "knew" that she was shooting her aunt and did so for the non-delusional purpose of relieving her aunt's pain. But euthanasia is no justification for homicide. Thus, if we look only at her legally relevant "state of mind" at the time of the second shot, and we do not take into account her highly regressed and disorganized emotional condition, she is technically guilty of murder.

I believe that Joy Baker's case convincingly demonstrates why, in theoretical terms, the mens rea approach does not take sufficient account of the morally significant aberrations of mental functioning associated with severe mental disorder. I readily concede, however, that these technical points may make little practical difference in the courtroom. If the expert testimony in Joy Baker's case and others like it were admitted to disprove the existence of mens rea, juries may behave as many observers believe they do now—they may ignore the technical aspects of the law and decide, very bluntly, whether the defendant was too crazy to be convicted. However, I do not believe that rational criminal law reform is served by designing rules of law in the expectation that they will be ignored or nullified when they appear unjust in individual cases.

IMPROVING THE QUALITY OF EXPERT TESTIMONY

I have tried to show that perpetuation of the insanity defense is essential to the moral integrity of the criminal law. Yet an abstract commitment to the moral relevance of claims of psychological aberration may have to bend to the need for reliability in the administration of the law.

I fully recognize that the litigation of insanity claims is occasionally imperfect. The defense is sometimes difficult to administer reliably and fairly. In particular, I recognize that we cannot calibrate the severity of a person's mental disability, and it is sometimes hard to know whether the disability was profound enough to establish irresponsibility. Nor can we be confident that every fabricated claim will be recognized. Yet these concerns are not unlike those presented by traditional defenses such as mistake, duress and other excuses which no one is seeking to abolish. Indeed, problems in sorting valid from invalid defensive claims are best seen as part of the price of a humane and just penal law. Thus, to the extent that the abolitionists would eradicate the insanity defense in response to imperfections in its administration, I would reply that a decent respect for the moral integrity of the criminal law sometimes requires us to ask questions that can be answered only by approximation. Rather than abolishing the defense we should focus our attention on ways in which its administration can be improved.

Some of the abolitionist sentiment among lawyers seems to be responsive to doubts about the competence—and, unfortunately, the ethics—of expert witnesses. The cry for abolition is also raised by psychiatrists and psychologists who believe that the law forces experts to "take sides" and to offer opinions on issues outside their sphere of expertise. These are all legitimate concerns and I have no doubt that the current controversy about the insanity defense accurately reflects a rising level of mutual professional irritation about its administration. However, the correct solution is not to abolish the insanity defense but rather to clarify the roles and obligations of expert witnesses in the criminal process. Some assistance in this effort can be expected from the American Bar Association's Criminal Justice-Mental Health Standards now being drafted by interdisciplinary panels of experts in the field.

A properly trained expert can help the judge or jury to understand aberrations of the human mind. However, training in psychiatry or psychology does not, by itself, qualify a person to be an expert witness in criminal cases. Specialized training in forensic evaluation is necessary, and a major aim of such special training must be to assure that the expert is sensitive to the limits of his or her knowledge.

THE CASE FOR TIGHTENING THE DEFENSE

I do not favor abolition of the "cognitive" prong of the insanity defense. However, I do agree with those critics who believe the risks of fabrication and "moral mistakes" in administering the defense are greatest when the experts and the jury are asked to speculate whether the defendant had the capacity to "control" himself or whether he could have "resisted" the criminal impulse.

Few would dispute the moral predicate for the control test—that a person who "cannot help" doing what he did is not blameworthy. Unfortunately, however, there is no scientific basis for measuring a person's capacity for self-control or for calibrating the impairment of such capacity. There is, in short, no objective basis for distinguishing between offenders who were undeterrable and those who were merely undeterred, between the impulse that was irresistible and the impulse not resisted, or between substantial impairment of capacity and some lesser impairment. Whatever the precise terms of the volitional test, the question is unanswerable—or can be answered only by "moral guesses." To ask it at all, in my opinion, invites fabricated claims, undermines equal administration of the penal law, and compromises its deterrent effect. . . .

The sole test of legal insanity should be whether the defendant, as a result of mental disease, lacked "substantial capacity to appreciate the wrongfulness of his conduct." This language, drawn from the Model Penal Code, uses clinically meaningful terms to ask the same question posed by the House of Lords in M'Naghten 150 years ago. During the past ten years, I have not seen a single case at our Clinic involving a claim of irresponsibility that I personally thought was morally compelling which would not be comprehended by this formulation. Thus, I am convinced that this test is fully compatible with the ethical premises of the penal law, and that results reached by judges and juries in particular cases ordinarily would be congruent with the community's moral sense.

In sum, then, I believe that the insanity defense, as I have defined it, should be narrowed, not abandoned, and that the burden of persuasion may properly be shifted to the defendant. Like the mens rea proposal, this approach ade-quately responds to public concern about possible misuse of the insanity defense. Unlike the mens rea proposal, however, I believe this approach is compatible with the basic doctrines and principles of Anglo-American penal law.

POSTSCRIPT

Should the Insanity Defense Be Abolished?

The furor over the Hinckley case led to some changes in the federal insanity defense standard. As part of a major anti-crime bill passed in 1984, Congress has required the defendant to have the burden of proving that he or she was insane. In the Hinckley trial, the prosecution was required to prove beyond a reasonable doubt that Hinckley was sane. The defendant in such a case must now persuade a jury that, as a result of a severe mental disease or defect, he or she was unable to appreciate the nature and wrongfulness of the act.

In addition to raising questions about the diagnosis of mental illness, the insanity defense also requires consideration of treatment, of sentencing, and of institutionalization. Those advocating its retention argue not only that blameless people should not be punished, but also that such individuals need care and treatment for their problems. The fact that many mental institutions have failed to provide adequate treatment or are, by their nature, inappropriate places for some individuals who need help but not institutionalization, has been recognized recently in various lawsuits. As a result, the number of people in institutions has been declining. The ineffectiveness of prisons and mental institutions in reducing recidivism or promoting treatment should be considered in the debate over the insanity defense, since even those who wish to abolish the defense are willing to take the mental state of the defendant into account at the time of sentencing. There is, in addition, a possible relationship between the increase in the number of defendants invoking the insanity defense and the deinstitutionalization trend. The reason for this is that the insanity defense becomes more appealing as the expectation of a long stay in a mental institution decreases.

Recommended readings on the insanity defense include Smith and Meyer, *Law, Behavior, and Mental Health* (New York University Press, 1987); Eisner, "Returning the Not Guilty By Reason of Insanity to the Community: A New Scale to Determine Readiness," 17 *The Bulletin of the American Academy of Psychiatry and the Law* 401 (1989); Klofas and Yandrasits, " 'Guilty But Mentally Ill' and the Jury Trial: A Case Study," 24 *Criminal Law Bulletin* 424 (1988); Symposium, "The Insanity Defense," *The Annals*, v. 477 (January, 1985); Goldstein, *The Insanity Defense* (Yale University Press, 1967); Fingarette, *The Meaning of Criminal Insanity* (University of California Press, 1972); and Szasz, *Law, Liberty and Psychiatry* (Macmillan, 1963). Moran, *Knowing Right from Wrong: The Insanity Defense of Daniel McNaughtan* (Free Press, 1981), provides an interesting look at McNaughtan's trial and at the central figure in the history of the insanity defense. Other books about particular cases include Kaplan and Waltz, *The Trial of Jack Ruby* (Macmillan, 1965); Gaylin, *The Killing of Bonnie Garland* (Simon & Schuster, 1982); and Caplan, *The Insanity Defense and the Trial of John W. Hinckley, Jr.* (David Godine, 1983).

CONTRIBUTORS
TO THIS VOLUME

EDITOR

M. ETHAN KATSH is a graduate of Yale Law School, and is Professor of Legal Studies at the University of Massachusetts, Amherst. He has served as the chairman of the legal studies department, and as president of the American Legal Studies Association.

In addition to articles that have appeared in the *Wall Street Journal, TV Guide,* and *Saturday Review,* he is the coauthor of *Before the Law* (Houghton Mifflin, Second Edition), and has produced simulation games on plea bargaining and mediation. His work has been published in scholarly journals and has appeared in *Annual Editions: Criminal Justice,* published by The Dushkin Publishing Group. He is the author of *The Electronic Media and the Transformation of the Law* (Oxford University Press, 1989).

STAFF

Marguerite L. Egan   Program Manager
Brenda S. Filley   Production Manager
Whit Vye   Designer
Libra Ann Cusack   Typesetting Supervisor
Juliana Arbo   Typesetter
James Filley   Graphics
Diane Barker   Editorial Assistant
David Dean   Administrative Assistant

AUTHORS

STEPHEN ARONS is an attorney and professor of legal studies at the University of Massachusetts at Amherst. He has written widely on subjects of law and education and cultural freedom.

SARAH EVANS BARKER is a judge in Indiana's U.S. District Court (south district). She is on the board of directors of the New Hope of Indiana and a member of the Indianapolis Bar Association.

HARRY BLACKMUN has been an associate justice of the U.S. Supreme Court since his appointment by President Nixon in 1970. He wrote the court's majority decision in the landmark *Roe v. Wade* case.

RICHARD BONNIE is the director of the Institute of Law, Psychiatry, and Public Policy at the University of Virginia.

WILLIAM J. BRENNAN, JR., served as an associate justice of the U.S. Supreme Court from his appointment in 1956 by President Eisenhower until his retirement in July 1990 at the age of 84.

STEVEN BRILL is the founder and editor in chief of *The American Lawyer* magazine. He is the author of *The Teamsters* (Simon & Schuster, 1978) and the 1977 recipient of the John Hancock Award for excellence in business reporting.

ANDREA DWORKIN, the coauthor of the Indianapolis legislation defining pornography as a violation of women's civil rights, is an American nonfiction writer, essayist, novelist, and short story writer. She is best known for her controversial nonfiction works that examine the status of women in modern society.

KENNETH R. FEINBERG is a partner in the law firm of Kaye, Scholer, Fierman, Hays & Handler in Washington, D.C. He is the court-appointed Special Settlement Master in the Agent Orange Product Liability litigation and chairman of the Dalkon Shield Claimants' Trust.

OWEN M. FISS has been the Alexander M. Bickel Professor of Public Law at Yale University since 1984. He is an executive board member of the Lawyers Committee for Civil Rights Under Law and an editorial board member of Foundation Press.

MARC GALANTER is the Evjue-Bascom Professor of Law and South Asian Studies at the University of Wisconsin at Madison. He is the president of the Law and Society Association.

JANET C. HOEFFEL is a third-year student at Stanford Law School in California.

YALE KAMISAR is a lawyer and a professor of law at the University of Michigan Law School. He is the author of *Police Interrogation and*

Confessions: Essays in Law and Policy (University of Michigan Press, 1980).

ANTHONY KENNEDY has been an associate justice of the U.S. Supreme Court since his appointment by President Reagan in 1988.

KENNETH KIPNIS is a professor of philosophy at the University of Hawaii. He is the author of *Legal Ethics* (Prentice-Hall, 1986) and the editor, with Diana T. Meyers, of *Economic Justice: Private Rights and Public Responsibilities* (Rowman & Allenheld, 1985).

BAYLESS MANNING was formerly dean of the Stanford Law School.

THURGOOD MARSHALL, the first black member of the U.S. Supreme Court, has been an associate justice since his appointment by President Johnson in 1967.

JOHN B. MITCHELL is the Scholar-in-Residence in the School of Law at the University of Puget Sound.

ETHAN A. NADELMANN is an assistant professor of politics and public affairs in the Department of Politics and in the Woodrow Wilson School at Princeton University.

MICHAEL L. RADELET is an associate professor of sociology at the University of Florida. He is the editor of *Facing the Death Penalty:*

Essays on a Cruel and Unusual Punishment (Temple University Press, 1989).

WILLIAM H. REHNQUIST succeeded Warren E. Burger to become the sixteenth chief justice of the U.S. Supreme Court in 1986. He has been a justice in the Supreme Court since his appointment by President Nixon in 1971.

JONATHAN ROWE is a contributing editor of *The Washington Monthly*.

ANTONIN SCALIA has been serving as an associate justice of the U.S. Supreme Court since his appointment by President Reagan in 1986.

NICK SCHWEITZER is an assistant district attorney for Rock County, Wisconsin. He has been a member of the Wisconsin Bar Association since 1985.

JAMES E. STARRS is a professor of law and forensic sciences at George Washington University in Washington, D.C. He served as a consultant to Cellmark Diagnostics during their testimony before the United States Senate's Subcommittee on the Constitution of the Committee of the Judiciary.

The late **POTTER STEWART** was an associate justice of the U.S. Supreme Court from his appointment by President Eisenhower in 1958 to his retirement in 1981.

HARRY I. SUBIN is a professor of law in the School of Law at New York University. He is the author of *Criminal Justice in Metropolitan Court* (Da Capo, 1973).

MARK UDULUTCH is a law clerk to Judge William Moser of the Wisconsin Court of Appeals.

BYRON WHITE has been an associate justice of the U.S. Supreme Court since his appointment by President Kennedy in 1962.

MALCOLM RICHARD WILKEY has been the U.S. ambassador to Uruguay since 1985. He is a fellow of the American Bar Foundation and a member of the American Bar Association.

JAMES D. WRIGHT is a professor of human relations in the Department of Sociology at Tulane University. He is the author of 13 books, including *Address Unknown: The Tragedy of Homelessness in America* (Aldine de Gruyter, 1989).

INDEX